WIDOWS

WIDOWS

William R. Corson, Susan B. Trento,
and Joseph J. Trento

CROWN PUBLISHERS, INC.

New York

Copyright © 1989 by William R. Corson, Susan B. Trento, and Joseph J. Trento

Published by Crown Publishers, Inc., 225 Park Avenue South, New York, New York 10003

CROWN is a trademark of Crown Publishers, Inc.

Manufactured in the United States of America

Library of Congress Cataloging-in-Publication Data

Corson, William R.
Widows.
Includes index.
1. Espionage, Soviet—United States.   2. Soviet Union. Komitet gosudarstvennoi bezopasnosti.   3. United States. Central Intelligence Agency.   4. United States. Federal Bureau of Investigation.   5. Intelligence service—United States.   I. Trento, Susan B.   II. Trento, Joseph John.   III. Title.
UB271.R9C67   1989   327.1'2'0947   89-1145
ISBN 0-517-57235-4

10   9   8   7   6   5   4   3   2   1

First Edition

For Robert T. Crowley,
a member of the club, who has never forgotten the two key compo-
nents of intelligence are candor and integrity and who has lived by the
rule that national security is a goal not an alibi.

Contents

Acknowledgments

We wrote this book to try to show the citizens of the West just how difficult and demanding a task it is to protect ourselves from the Soviet intelligence services. Our point is that sometimes in doing this job we seem to forget what makes our system different from the Soviet system. That's when we get into trouble as a nation. That's when we become a threat to ourselves.

This book is reflective of the nature of counterintelligence. You never can get the whole truth, so you try to get enough bits and pieces of it to give you an approximation of what really happened. We claim no special patent on this truth.

We conducted more than five hundred interviews for this book. Many of our subjects asked that we not acknowledge their help publicly, and we respect that. They know who they are, and the authors are grateful. We are also grateful to those people who did help us for the record. Many of these people spent days with us in multiple interviews. Our thanks to Ilse Sigler, Ewa Shadrin, Richard Copaken, Leonard V. McCoy, William Branigan, Eugene

Peterson, Paul Garbler, George Kisevalter, Edward Paisley, Clarence Baier, Donald Burton, William Tidwell, Philip Waggener, John Novak, Bruce Solie, William Lander, Peter Kapusta, Noel E. Jones, Louis Martel, John Schaffstall, Donnel Drake, Carlos Zapata, James Wooten, Eleonore Orlov, George Orlov, Lt. Gen. Samuel V. Wilson, Mark Bowen, Col. Donald B. Grimes, Gen. C. J. Le Van, Stanley K. Jeffers, Carl Bernstein, Bob Woodward, John T. Funkhouser, Capt. Thomas and T. C. Dwyer, Jack and Peggy Leggat, Richard and Maria Odin, Ellie and Peter Sivess, Helen and Robert Kupperman, Jerry Edwards, Stanley and Janka Urynowicz, Darryl Du Bose, William E. Colby, Gen. Richard Stilwell, John Bross, Britt Snider, John Hall, Etta Jo Weisz, Nicolaine Weisz, Peter Stockton, Dale Young, Herb Kouts, Larry O'Donnell, Robert Maheu, Giselle Breuer Weisz, Suzanne Weisz, Sidney Diamond, Fred Duvall, Frank Steinert, Burton Weides, David S. Sullivan, Courtland J. Jones, Samuel Papich, Ambassador James E. Nolan, Jr., Cornelius G. Sullivan, Robert T. Crowley, Captain William and Mary Louise Howe, Patrick and Katherine Lenahan, Dale and Mary Paisley, Victor Marchetti, Gladys Fishel, Richard and Mary Jo Bennett, Norman and Barbara Wilson, Col. Gordon Thomas, Betty Myers, Leonard Masters, William Miller, Gen. Daniel Graham, Henry "Hank" Knoche, Clare Edward Petty, Paul O'Grady, William Brock, Ernest Meyers, Adm. Stansfield Turner, Adm. Thomas Moorer, William Mazzoco, Harold M. Kramer, Col. Guy Kent Troy, Raymond Wannall, Walter Sedoff, John C. Mertz, Philip A. Parker, Vincente Rosado, John Taylor, Capt. Rufus L. Taylor, Jr., Martha Mautner, Ambassador Robert T. Hennemeyer, Elisaeietta Ritchie, Col. H. A. Aplington, William G. Miller, William T. Bader, Senator Birch Bayh, Howard Leibengood, Dawn Mann, Michel Patu, Henry Shapiro, Egil Krogh, John Ehrlichman, Ken Ludden, David Thomas, Brig. Gen. Robert C. Richardson, Robin W. Winks, Laughlin A. Campbell, John Sherwood, Col. Roger G. Charles, A. D. Llewelyn, Thomas Kimmel, Col. George Connell, Fred I. Edwards, Frank Lyons, Capt. Albert Graham, Larry Patterson, J. Y. Smith, Alan Reed, Lothar Metcel, Bernard I. Weltman, Frank Sheraton, Lucy Breathett, John Picton, Douglas Wheeler, Thomas Hirschfeld, Thomas Koines, Col. Richard M. Johnson, Tom Sippel, Sam McDowell, Leonard M. Brenner, and E. Alex Costa.

We wish to express our thanks to Mary Lou Domres for her research help; to our unbelievably patient and dedicated transcriber, Linda Durdall; to Richard Sandza, who was ready with advice and assistance; to our agent, Jane Cushman; and to the terrific people at Crown Publishers, especially James O'Shea Wade, Jane von Mehren, and Katie Towson.

Widows is an extension of work that others have done. David Martin's breakthrough book, *Wilderness of Mirrors,* Henry Hurt's *Shadrin: The Spy Who Never Came Back,* and the excellent work of Seymour Hersh, Edward Jay Epstein, and John Barron. As Hurt said to us when we embarked on this project, "All our work ought to be a platform for the next writer to stand on." We have tried to push the frontier of intelligence reporting a little farther with this book. We only hope we have provided a platform that some future writers can stand on to discover more.

One final note: Both the CIA and the FBI refused to cooperate in this project. We expected that would be the CIA's attitude. However, the Bureau, after insisting for months that they would help, ended up stonewalling. After learning how the KITTY HAWK, Herrmann, and Sigler cases were handled by the Bureau, we now understand why. We also would like to extend a special note of thanks to Maryland State Medical Examiner Dr. Robert Smialek, who made available to us the suppressed documents and pictures used in the John Paisley identification.

The transliteration of Russian names from Cyrillic to English equivalents is not a precise science. We are grateful to Leonard V. McCoy for assisting us in establishing the versions of names used by those in the intelligence community for Shadrin/Artamonov and Vtorygin. In other cases we have spelled the names in the way the individuals concerned spelled them.

The words of the veteran FBI-CIA liaison man Sam Papich are a good reminder of what U.S. counterintelligence is really up against: "There is a weakness in the United States trying to assess Soviets, particularly Soviets in the intelligence field. So very, very few of us have any knowledge of the goddamned history, the language, the psychology. . . . I can give a Russian my concept or version of what freedom is, what justice is, and he is on another channel completely."

William Corson
Susan Trento
Joseph Trento
Washington, D.C.

WIDOWS

Prologue

Buried in the deepest recesses of our national intelligence archives is the sad truth about how the United States has stood up to the KGB since the outbreak of the Cold War. It takes more to make a successful intelligence service than flag-waving and brave talk about stemming the tide of Marxism. Without experience, competence, and good judgment, there is no hope of success. *Widows* gives you the opportunity to see if those characteristics are reflected by those charged with running our intelligence and counterintelligence services in three very important operations. The book also should provide American taxpayers, who have been footing the bill for effective U.S. intelligence and counterintelligence operations, with a better understanding of where their money has been going.

What we have tried to do is tell this story on a human scale—from the point of view of the spies themselves. Because to understand the state of counterintelligence in global terms, you must first know the soldiers and understand the history. We decided to tell this story as a personal one because to take a detached and antiseptic approach to the issue of counterintelligence might discourage your interest in what it is like to make and to carry out the decisions that could open up your country to Soviet penetration.

This book is about the human reality of spying. It is about the business of defending the secrets of the West from compromise. It is the story of a generation of intelligence and counterintelligence battles fought against the backdrop of the Cold War, detente, Vietnam, the aging leadership of the Soviet Union, and, today, the men running a troubled Soviet giant under the banner of *perestroika*.

It is a story of how two great nations try to cope with their own traditions and cultures in a world driven by economic and political pressures that neither nation has the power to control as they once did.

The Soviet Union has a long history of intelligence operations dating back to Peter the Great's personal survey of the West. Domestically, its citizens are raised to accept severe limits on personal freedom as part of the price of protecting the interests of the State. Its intelligence and counterintelligence operations are unified in the KGB, the offensive sword and defensive shield.

For the United States, which is an "open society," the very idea of a secret police, of a central government force using any means to make certain that the secrets of the state are protected, is repugnant. Though we have had national lapses in our history, the separation of the spying apparatus (the CIA) and the protection apparatus (the FBI) has been codified into our intelligence laws.

It is the very openness of American society and the separation between our protection service and our spy service that the Soviet KGB and GRU have exploited. This book will document just how complete the exploitation has been. These cases illustrate how the KGB used American bureaucratic infighting to further their own intelligence goals.

The dramatic differences between the Soviet and American approaches to counterintelligence also played a role in these debacles. The Soviet KGB is a patient institution. Its history reflects the institutional belief that seeds are planted and success is something that comes after years or decades of nurturing. At the CIA and FBI, ambition, internal politics, and national politics create an atmosphere that encourages short-term gain, not long-term operations. In the Washington, D.C., area, the Soviets have been running several cases for more than thirty years. A succession of FBI agents assigned to monitoring those cases have been rotated in and out of their assignments scores of times. J. Edgar Hoover demanded arrests from his counterintelligence men, when, in fact, it might have been far more fruitful simply to observe Soviet operations to see where they led. But in America, spending a career waiting and watching is neither glamorous nor profitable.

Counterintelligence remains one of the most undesirable jobs in the FBI. It has rarely been a career-booster in the Bureau. At the CIA the situation is not much better. A former high-level CI officer said that your colleagues treat you "like someone who farted at a tea party" when you have an internal CI success. Yet in the Soviet Union, where protection of the State is everything, there is no higher calling than that of a CI officer.

Counterintelligence is a complex business. It is a business driven by detail, by suspicion, and often by guesswork. Unlike a jigsaw or crossword puzzle, counterintelligence operations seldom result in a pretty picture or in answers in the next day's newspaper. As John Le Carré has pointed out, the Soviets are very good at taking operational details and using them "to turn the Circus inside out." That's precisely what was done to the CIA and FBI in the real cases that follow. If you come away from this book frustrated because there are no final answers, no last piece to the puzzle, you have shared in the plight of a counterintelligence officer. Yet that is only part of the CI officer's challenge. Add to that challenge the natural suspicion and long-standing jealousy between the Central Intelligence Agency and the Federal Bureau of Investigation. Remember that J. Edgar Hoover deliberately destroyed his own agent networks in Latin America to keep them out of the hands of the aborning CIA in the late 1940s.

Three men who came from totally different worlds found themselves as frontline soldiers in the intelligence war between the Soviet Union and the United States. According to the official American record, two of them committed suicide and one was kidnapped by the KGB. The United States says all the men were honorable and patriotic. John Paisley, the CIA executive who disappeared while sailing in Chesapeake Bay; Nicholas Shadrin, the dashing Soviet defector who became a double agent for the FBI, only to disappear into the Vienna night; Ralph Sigler, the Army warrant officer who ended an illustrious career as an American double agent by what the Army called self-inflicted electrocution. All American agents. All chapters from American intelligence lore that caused headlines and consternation at the highest levels of government, and all cases that have remained stunning mysteries. Three widows were left behind with their heartbreak and questions.

We have tried, with *Widows*, to show how each case is connected to the others. Through hundreds of on-the-record interviews with those responsible for the operations, the magnitude of the intelligence tragedy these cases represent is revealed.

Widows is the story of how wrong American intelligence has gone for a generation. The story begins with an account of the first high-level mole in the CIA. We outline the troubled life of a man who sat at the elbow of then CIA Director Allen Dulles, but whose actions were under the control of the KGB in Moscow. Until now, this story was kept so secret that it was purged from all but the most closely held files in the CIA. We move on to the Paisley case. Here we find a man who rose from poverty to the top rungs of the CIA. In Shadrin we examine how the KGB circumvented our counterintelligence capability. In Sigler we see how bureaucratic turf wars took a life.

What is the purpose of all this? It is not to embarrass good men who made mistakes, nor is it to denigrate our intelligence community; it has had many fine moments. The purpose is to provide a greater understanding, in human terms, of the cost of counterintelligence.

Spying is an economic shortcut. The Soviets have successfully used it to offset the shortcomings of an economy and a government incapable of creating the research needed to compete in the modern world since the time of Lenin. They have saved billions of dollars and made up for years of delay. An exaggeration? Hardly. In the case of Christopher Boyce and Andrew Daulton Lee in the mid-1970s, nearly five billion dollars in spy satellite research was compromised. Add the Walkers and the dozens of others who fill our national dishonor roll, and you understand why the Soviets, and even our allies, like the Israelis, try to steal our secrets.

For those who are breathing a sigh of relief at the good intentions of the new regime in Moscow and their talk of openness and reform, keep a few realities in mind. To succeed, the regime will have to deliver a consumer economy, something long promised. To do that, even fewer resources can be put into Soviet research and development. The Soviet military will need to garner a greater share of its technology from the West. It is the authors' view that they will rely more and more on espionage as a means of accomplishing this end. Our argument is bolstered by a lesson from recent history. In 1956, change at the top in the Soviet Union brought forth similar optimism in the West. But in the years that followed, instead of peace and understanding, America experienced the series of intelligence defeats chronicled in *Widows*.

For those who believe that our intelligence and counterintelligence shortcomings have all been remedied by the tough talk and generous money of the Reagan administration, consider this: The institutional memory is so lacking at the FBI that when Yuri Yurchenko came over for his brief "defection" in 1985, his allegations about SASHA, the spy, were then accepted and are still being pursued with great vigor. It would have been more beneficial to U.S. security if the young FBI agents conducting the SASHA probe had first been made aware of the fact that all these "recent" accusations had already been investigated *two decades* earlier. They weren't.

The First Death

I can't wait for 1984, Love Jim

MRS. LAVINIA THOMAS had been James Speyer Kronthal's house-keeper for many years. She enjoyed working for him. The daffodils in the small garden in front of the white brick town house in Georgetown welcomed her to work that cool spring morning. Usually Mr. Kronthal would be reading the *Washington Post* and finishing his juice when Mrs. Thomas arrived. It was April 1, 1953, at 8:30 A.M. and the paper was still on the front step.

Picking up the paper, Mrs. Thomas went inside. On the console table in the small foyer were several letters to be put out for the mailman and a note from Mr. Kronthal saying he had worked very late and wanted to sleep in. Mrs. Thomas shook her head and wondered about what really went on at her boss's State Department office.

When the telephone rang an hour later there was still no sign of her employer stirring. It was someone from Mr. Kronthal's office who wished to speak to him. Mrs. Thomas explained that he had worked late and did not want to be disturbed. The caller asked her to wake him, that it was important. Mrs. Thomas called to Mr. Kronthal. There was no response. The caller asked Mrs. Thomas to have Mr. Kronthal telephone his office as soon as possible, and hung up.

Later that morning, just as Mrs. Thomas was about to go up and knock hard on Mr. Kronthal's second-floor bedroom door, the front doorbell rang. The two men at the door identified themselves as colleagues of Mr. Kronthal from the Department of State. They moved past Mrs. Thomas into the foyer. One of them said that it was vitally important for Mr. Kronthal to come to a meeting, so they would go wake him. She reluctantly let them precede up the stairs.

They knocked hard on the door, but there was no answer. One of the men turned the doorknob. It was unlocked. Opening the door, they saw a man lying across the bed, fully dressed. James Speyer Kronthal was not sleeping. He was dead. Murdered? Later, all Mrs. Thomas could ask herself and her friends was how this could have happened to such a nice young man.

On paper, James Speyer Kronthal was a perfect recruit for the young, burgeoning intelligence service just beginning to emerge in the United States. He had graduated from two of America's aristocratic educational institutions—a B.A. from Yale in 1934 and an M.A. from Harvard in 1941. His linguistic abilities included fluency in German, French, and Italian. But it was his work during World War II in the Office of Strategic Services (OSS), the wartime forerunner of the CIA, that caught the eye of Allen Welsh Dulles. During the war, Dulles ran the OSS station in Bern, Switzerland, where Kronthal showed him his mettle.

Both men were born to the same upper class, and both shared a similar, nonisolationist attitude toward international politics. As the war ended and the OSS was disbanded, its membership drifted back to the traditional Old Money roles: completing their educations, joining law firms, and managing family investments.

Less than two years later, Americans learned hard lessons about their once-close ally, the Soviet Union. First came the loss of the atomic bomb secrets, then the Armed Forces Security Agency discovered VENONA. This breaking of the Soviets' code revealed that the war alliance was mere expediency and that the Soviets were not America's good friends; they were, in reality, its dedicated enemy. Most Americans soon regarded the Soviets as the new threat. Congress quickly passed, and President Harry Truman signed, the National Security Act of 1947, which chartered the CIA. The infant spy service comprised the cream of the OSS—mainly white Anglo-Saxon Protestant males from wealthy families with good educations and some experience in wartime espionage. On April 21, 1947, James Kronthal became chief of Bern Station, one of the first seven CIA overseas offices.[1]

On the opposing side, the Soviets had older, more established, very well organized and successful intelligence departments, known informally as "the organs." The postwar U.S. intelligence organizations were so weak that the Soviets virtually ignored them and concentrated instead on penetrating the British counterintelligence and intelligence services, MI5 and MI6, and the U.S. military forces deployed throughout Europe after the war. But the advent of the CIA offered the Soviets a rare opportunity to infiltrate a new service from top to bottom. The NKVD, the forerunner of the KGB, calculatingly decided not to miss this unique chance to learn from the start about each new employee of the Agency and, of course, attempt to recruit some.[2]

NKVD head Lavrenti Beria expected his resident agents in the United States to learn as much as possible about everyone being assigned overseas by the new CIA. He wanted each of the seven new stations' employees thoroughly evaluated for weaknesses—especially sex, money, or drugs. James Speyer Kronthal was no exception. Beria understood that the CIA was patterned after the OSS, and Bern proved to be one of the most important OSS stations. Counting on the predictability of the Americans, Beria gave the orders that all Bern personnel receive priority attention.

Beria had done very well in postwar Germany penetrating the young Bundesnachrichtendienst—the West German Federal Intelligence Service—known as the BND. That penetration would give the Soviets the information they needed on Kronthal to further their cause. By using old records from the OSS, the NKVD established that not only had Kronthal worked for Dulles in Bern, but also that Dulles and Kronthal were friends from the same social circles. That meant Kronthal had important connections. Establishing the true identities of those who worked for the OSS in Bern under Dulles helped the NKVD to determine whether these men were showing up under their true names elsewhere.

While the Soviets were busy trying to figure out whom to recruit in the CIA, President Harry Truman was trying to decide what to do with the new service. He looked upon the new CIA as a gatherer of information, not as a tool for fighting communist expansion in a direct way. Others wanted the CIA to be another OSS, only directed against the Soviets instead of the Nazis.

Operating under Soviet diplomatic cover in Washington, NKVD agents began to check into the backgrounds of the men who were being sent overseas by the CIA. They soon discovered something remarkable. The FBI was selected to perform the security checks on the new employees. The Soviet agents were astonished to learn that all these checks required was an inquiry at the various government agencies to find out if any unfavorable or derogatory information was known about an applicant. In addition, the Bureau would question neighbors, relatives, and classmates, seeking the same type of information. These "background investigations" were a far less rigorous test of loyalty than the NKVD employed for its agents and handlers.

While the FBI conducted its cursory check of Kronthal, the NKVD simultaneously performed a much more thorough one. The man whose resumé looked so good to the CIA and FBI was regarded in quite a different way by the Soviets. In Moscow Center, the KGB's headquarters, Kronthal's middle name—Speyer—set off alarm bells. NKVD headquarters cabled Washington to find out more about Kronthal's middle name. When word came back that Kronthal's presumptive namesake was James Joseph Speyer, of Speyer and Company, the interest in Kronthal became intense.

The banking house of Speyer had done business with the Tsar. During the 1930s it ranked with Morgan, Kuhn and Loeb in New York, and Lee, Higginson in Boston as one of the major banking firms in the country. The company was originally founded in Frankfurt am Main, Germany, in 1837, with the New York bank opening a year later.

The NKVD was able to learn that in 1913 when Leon Kronthal and his wife, Maude Mabel Ranger Kronthal, became parents, they decided to give their son a middle name after Leon's flamboyant business partner Joseph Speyer. Over the years Speyer treated young Kronthal like a member of his own family. Later this would bring heartbreak to Leon Kronthal, whose relationship with Joseph Speyer deteriorated as his son grew closer to Leon's business partner.

It is not hard to understand why Leon Kronthal and Joseph Speyer did not get along. They were exact opposites. Leon was a hardworking but dull man. Speyer, on the other hand, always dapper, was a womanizer and was the only Jewish member of several exclusive New York clubs. The young Kronthal's association with the Speyers was a great way for him to enter New York society.

Young Kronthal traveled on vacations with the Speyer family. He attended the Lincoln School in New York with Nelson Rockefeller and Michael Straight.[3] The NKVD found that at Yale, Kronthal did not take business courses as his father had urged him to, but majored, instead, in art history.

Yale was a heady experience for James Kronthal. He was young, reasonably attractive, and quite rich at a time when the Great Depression had swallowed up so many fortunes. He was elected to Phi Beta Kappa and was a member of the Yale rowing crew. His personality resembled that of James Speyer rather than that of his father. He found

Speyer's company more interesting too; upon graduation, James Kronthal ignored his father's differences with Speyer and joined Joseph Speyer & Co. Leon Kronthal "retired" from Speyer & Co. to found his own company in 1934.

The Soviet NKVD learned that Kronthal had been sent off to Germany by Speyer where he had used the Speyer family connections to sell artworks that the Nazis confiscated from Jews between 1933 and 1940. In addition to becoming the go-between for this financial service, he also became personally acquainted with Nazi leaders such as Goering, Himmler, and Goebbels.

It was during this period that Kronthal showed a sexual proclivity for young boys. He was entrapped by the Gestapo, and it took Goering's personal intervention to get him out of trouble. But the Germans kept very good records, and the Kronthal arrest record was carefully filed away.

The information on Kronthal later came into the hands of the NKVD through its penetration of General Gehlen's BND by Heinz Felfe. The moral of Kronthal's homosexual stumble is that knowledge of personal transgressions has a way of moving with a natural force from one intelligence service to another without regard to ideology or the sanctity of the sources. So when the NKVD took an interest in Kronthal, his history gave them a field day.

The NKVD kept digging. They learned that although Kronthal's work with Speyer & Co. had been financially rewarding, the emotional cost of profiting from other people's stolen wealth—people who were sent to death camps—had been enormous. Kronthal had decided to quit his job and return home to attend Harvard to get a graduate degree in art history. It was at Harvard that Kronthal became acquainted with a young Harvard Law School freshman named James Jesus Angleton. Years later, Angleton would rise to the highest ranks of the CIA as the man in charge of preventing its penetration by the Soviets—or any other country's service.

Both Angleton and Kronthal had similar personalities and both were deeply suspicious of the motives of those who pursued wealth without regard to political consequences. These suspicions arose because both men had been associated with families that did just that.

After Pearl Harbor, both Angleton and Kronthal answered the call to the colors. Kronthal ended up in the Signal Corps. In 1944, after some combat service, he was assigned to the OSS. It was here that he met the men who would later form the heart of the CIA.

Because of his experience in Germany before the war, Kronthal was very useful to Allen Dulles at the OSS station in Bern. From Dulles's viewpoint, James Kronthal was an ideal subordinate. Not only did he know all the "right" people, but he also possessed a considerable amount of the guilty knowledge associated with the activities of the station chief's older brother, future Secretary of State John Foster Dulles. Like Kronthal, the Dulles family had done business in Germany during the Weimar Republic and the early days of Hitler.

After the Germans were defeated, Kronthal proved how flexible a man he could be. On behalf of the OSS and its successors, he busied himself recovering the art that the Nazis had stolen during their ascendancy. Allen Dulles, fulfilling the paternal role that Joseph Speyer had once provided, largely left Kronthal on his own to handle these expensive and precious art treasures. Finding his personal life more freely fulfilled in the ruins of Europe, Kronthal simply did not want to go home and rejoin the banking business. His homosexuality would be too much of a burden to carry in that milieu.

Kronthal's appointment in 1947 as the head of the CIA's new Bern Station was the perfect solution to this unhappy young man's problem. Not only was Bern in charge of CIA operations in Switzerland, but also in much of the rest of Western Europe.

By now the NKVD had learned all they needed to know about James Speyer Kronthal. Moscow Center set two objectives: one was to blackmail him into becoming a Soviet agent, and the second was to make certain he was promoted up through the ranks of their new-found nemesis—the CIA.

The NKVD was not interested in the information Kronthal could provide from Bern in the short term. It was clear to Beria that Kronthal had the potential to go places in the CIA. The aim with Kronthal was to recruit him to become an "agent in place" at the highest levels of the CIA. Perhaps someday, if politics and luck came together, Kronthal might even head the American clandestine services.

Chinese boys were supplied to Kronthal in Switzerland. He was secretly filmed and then blackmailed. Moscow Center wanted him totally under its control. Although Moscow already had access to the information Kronthal was providing CIA headquarters from Bern, by forcing him to send regular "packets" of information to Moscow Center, the Soviets made sure that Kronthal committed treason. The NKVD had him firmly in its grasp, and there was no turning back. Kronthal had done the one thing that could ruin his life. The Soviets had him.

In May 1952, Kronthal's Bern tour ended. He returned to Washington and was assigned to help plan a reorganization of the CIA to meet future needs and growth. His earlier apprehensions about returning home were now compounded by his betrayal of America. He was not a willing double agent.

The pressures had aged Kronthal dramatically during his overseas tour. He was a man under great strain. On the surface, however, his perfect resumé was only enhanced by the addition of five apparently impeccable years in Bern. Kronthal was destined for greatness in the CIA. At Moscow Center, the NKVD believed victory was near.

In the United States, 1952 was an election year. The upcoming presidential election meant changes were coming to the CIA, and the NKVD was concerned. Walter Bedell Smith's declining health meant that he would probably step down as the head of the CIA. The NKVD pressured Kronthal to provide them with information on who was in line for the Director's job. It was critical to the Soviets. The exposure of their moles in 1951—Burgess and Maclean, Soviet agents in the British government—meant that the Americans would obviously cut off the British from sensitive intelligence. The Soviets had to get more men in the CIA. The CIA had now become their primary opponent.

The NKVD was not pleased with the information Kronthal provided. But the kind of information they wanted did not exist. Eisenhower had not given a hint what his intentions were for the CIA. General Smith wanted General Lucian Truscott to replace him at CIA. But Truscott turned down the job when Eisenhower offered it to him. Eisenhower then turned to Allen Dulles. For Kronthal, his old mentor becoming head of the service was a personal tragedy. He knew the NKVD would pressure him to wangle a top job from Dulles. It meant that Moscow Center now had a gold mine in Kronthal.

Kronthal's work on an internal reorganization of the CIA was almost finished. His Soviet handler told Kronthal, who was never very good at politics, to press for his appointment to head the clandestine services. Dulles so trusted Kronthal that he was prepared to give him any post he wanted. But the pressures caused by his fear of being exposed as a homosexual and a Soviet agent were beginning to tell. Kronthal became paralyzed by his fear of exposure. He could not bring himself to fight off other colleagues who were aggressively seeking the same position.

Then chaos struck the Soviet Union. On March 2, 1953, Stalin died —or may have been murdered. His death was not announced until three days later. Beria was fighting to maintain control over the intelligence organs. The pressures on Kronthal increased. Now, more than ever, Beria needed his agent in place. Beria moved to seize power too quickly. While he had the NKVD in his pocket, it was not a sufficient power base from which he could seize control of the Communist Party and the Politburo. Beria began to pull back and wage an internal war at home with the new leadership while pressuring his agents abroad to produce crucial intelligence.

On March 31, 1953, Dulles decided to find out for himself what position Kronthal wanted in the Agency. Dulles had to make the final top assignments in the CIA, so he invited his old friend over that evening for a working dinner. They lived only two blocks from each other.

What happened between the two men that night is lost to history. There is no evidence that Dulles ever discussed his last conversations with Kronthal that night with anyone else. What is known is that after dinner Kronthal walked to his Georgetown town house at 1662 32nd Street, N.W., sometime before midnight. At home, Kronthal wrote two letters. One letter was addressed to Allen Dulles and the other to Richard Helms. In addition, Kronthal left the brief note for his house-keeper, asking her not to disturb him.

At 9:30 A.M., when Kronthal failed to report to his office on the Mall, the CIA telephoned (under State Department cover) and asked Mrs. Thomas to wake him up. According to police reports, Mrs. Thomas called out but got no answer. She was hesitant to wake him because of his note. But within two hours, Gould Cassal and McGregor Gray arrived at the house from the CIA's Office of Security.

Over Mrs. Thomas's objections, the two men went to Kronthal's bedroom and found his fully clothed body lying on a daybed. His jacket was off, but he still had on a shirt and tie. An empty vial was on the floor. The two security men followed standard procedure and called the CIA's unofficial liaison in the Washington, D.C., Metropolitan Police Department.

Lt. Lawrence Hartnett had gotten such calls before. He was in charge of cleaning up messes like this one. His job was to cover up what the CIA wanted hidden when it came to Washington police matters. In return, Hartnett was given terrific local intelligence. His files on Washington-based politicians rivaled J. Edgar Hoover's in volume. He had enough details on the local power structure to remain on the force as long as he wanted.

Hartnett carried the ball. He told the press that investigators had found a handwritten letter to a male friend indicating that Kronthal was "mentally upset because of pressure connected with work." This letter, to Richard Helms, and another to Dulles were delivered to their addressees rather than held as evidence by the police. The death was quickly hushed up. An autopsy placed the time of death around midnight, but a chemical analysis failed to determine the cause of death or the contents of the vial found next to Kronthal's body. The cause of death was listed as "apparent suicide."

While the notes to Dulles and Helms were found unmailed in Kronthal's house, he did manage to mail one letter before he died. In a letter to his sister, Susan, Kronthal made a clean breast of his homo-sexual proclivities and made reference to the "tremendous difficulties" they posed. Susan, already aware of her brother's sexual persuasion, was not alarmed or fretful over these revelations. However, Kronthal's confession that he was not really in the Department of State but, as she had suspected, in the CIA, caused her great concern. The last sentence in James Kronthal's final testament to his sister was, "I can't wait till 1984. Love, Jim."

Susan became the first of a generation of relatives to be stonewalled and lied to by U.S. intelligence agencies over the details of a loved one's death or disappearance. Susan's futile attempts to find out more of the facts surrounding her brother's death led her to believe that the CIA was covering up or withholding information that she thought she had a right to know. But the facts surrounding his death were stamped "Secret" and withheld from her, just as they would be kept from the family members of other, future Cold War casualties.

Kronthal had become an embarrassment and a liability to both sides. He knew firsthand the cost of making a deal with the devil; it must have been clear to his sister that he had little hope or faith that his countrymen would have the wit or wisdom to do any better than he did.

For Beria, the loss of James Kronthal was a major failure. The opportunity to penetrate the CIA at its highest level had been squandered. At Moscow Center the damage report on the Kronthal case made it clear that the Center had pressed him too hard for basically useless or unobtainable political information.

Murder or suicide in the Kronthal case could not be determined. If the Soviets had concluded that he had been identified as a mole by the CIA, they would have killed him. The "organs" did not have any compunctions about arranging to kill any "asset" who had outlived his or her usefulness. They readily killed millions of Russians. A foreigner was not worth any hesitation. If the CIA had learned about Kronthal's "problems," it is possible that Dulles himself would have approved an "executive action," not just to eliminate the problem, but also to send a message to the Soviets that the Agency knew the man had been compromised and turned. Certainly the speed with which the Office of Security arrived at the Kronthal home adds some support to that alternative. More likely, however, is the possibility that Kronthal confessed to Dulles that night over dinner. The next day, when Kronthal did not show up at work, a concerned Dulles concluded that something was very wrong and dispatched the security men.

For the Soviets, only one thing mattered. Kronthal was lost and had to be replaced. With Stalin gone, the winds of change were sweeping the country, and the NKVD had to have information to survive. The only real external intelligence threat left was the CIA.

Long before Kronthal's compromise and recruitment, the NKVD had begun an arduous and methodical program to penetrate the CIA.

It was not a high-wire act like the Kronthal effort, but it did get the job done. The NKVD put together dossiers on thousands of Americans who had played a part in the joint war effort. Their World War II files on Americans were picked clean for potential recruitments. If an American showed an interest in the Soviet way of life or sympathy for the Soviet struggle, he became a candidate. He would be nurtured like a calf; he would be given help with his education and be guided toward a career in intelligence. It would be from this cadre that the CIA moles would be selected, trained, and sent on lifelong missions.

The file on Kronthal is buried deep in the archives of the CIA. It is a file on what is probably the first Soviet penetration of the infant intelligence service. It is a story known by only a handful of people who are alive today. The file of James Speyer Kronthal is a metaphor for what the Soviets have done to our intelligence services for a generation. James Kronthal was the first Soviet mole in the CIA. His previously untold story is the introduction to how the Soviets made a conscientious decision to penetrate the CIA and succeeded. His story would haunt CIA director after CIA director. The idea of penetration would never be far from Dulles's mind for the rest of his tenure. All the CIA directors that followed—John McCone, Admiral William Raborn, Richard M. Helms, James Schlesinger, William Colby, George Bush, Admiral Stansfield Turner, William Casey, and William Webster —would be held accountable for keeping the KGB out of the CIA.

Paisley: The Replacement?

❦

'Twas brillig, and the slithy toves
    Did gyre and gimble in the wabe;
All mimsy were the borogoves,
    And the mome raths outgrabe

'Beware the Jabberwock, my son!
    The jaws that bite, the claws that catch!
Beware the Jubjub bird, and shun
    The frumious Bandersnatch!'

He took his vorpal sword in hand;
    Long time the manxome foe he sought—
So rested he by the Tumtum tree,
    And stood awhile in thought.

Lewis Carroll, "Jabberwocky,"
from *Through the Looking-glass*

JOHN ARTHUR PAISLEY was the opposite of James Speyer Kronthal in every way. Paisley came from poverty, not wealth. His World War II service was not in the rarefied OSS but in the Merchant Marine. He did not go to Yale but to the University of Chicago. But he had two things that appealed to the CIA: a terrific capability for understanding technology and a deep interest in the Soviet Union.

The fact that there was no immediate and obvious explanation for his interest in or knowledge of the Soviet Union never seemed to bother those who gave him his first CIA job. Because the Kronthal incident was such a closely held secret in the CIA, the recruiters were not warned to look out for other possible "moles" (for replacements) or to alter the methodology of their background checks.

Those who actually worked with John Paisley remember a man who moved through the corridors of the CIA like a college professor. They

17

remember Paisley as a sharply intelligent but gentle man who had an extraordinary memory, a man to whom superiors turned in a crisis.

Politically, they remember a liberal who was outraged by injustice. Like most of the early CIA recruits, Paisley shared the passionate liberalism that dominated the men recruited in the late forties and early fifties. He found the CIA's secret-agent mystique and the "cowboy" behavior of some paramilitary operatives useless. As one of Paisley's CIA subordinates, Donald Burton, explains: "If I had to assess the way Paisley felt about covert stuff . . . [he felt] it was a lot of silly nonsense."[1]

Had the Office of Security really understood the background of one of the CIA's most highly cleared employees, perhaps things might have turned out differently. A few days before his disappearance, in September 1978, John Paisley was sent a set of forms to be completed before beginning another in his long history of routine background investigations. But this time, for only the second time since he officially entered the CIA in 1953, a polygraph examination was also scheduled. He never had the chance to fill out the forms before he disappeared. What follows is what they should have said.

John Arthur Paisley was born in Sand Springs, Oklahoma, on August 25, 1923.[2] He was the first son of John Joseph Paisley and Clara Stone Paisley. His parents were from two small Texas towns, but his father's family history could be traced back to Paisley, Scotland. Called "Jack" by his family and friends, Paisley was the middle child, born after his sister, Katherine, and before a sickly younger brother, Dale.

John Paisley's father, Joseph, had been raised in a Catholic orphanage and groomed to be a priest. Joseph Paisley devoted his life to something, but it was not Catholicism. Instead, he became a "boomer," a structural steel worker. He was so skilled with steel that as a young man he was hired to help build the Panama Canal. Upon returning to the United States, Joseph Paisley was baptized into Tom Mooney's labor movement in the San Francisco Bay area. He became a kind of priest, but in his new religion—the rights of the American worker. He was passionate about workers' rights, and immersed himself in the cause. He paid less and less attention to his wife, Clara, and the children. He was arrested for demanding such radical reforms as a six-day, ten-hour-a-day work week.

In 1925, Joseph Paisley's drinking and union arrests finally caused Clara to walk out. She could not reconcile her strict Southern Methodist background with her husband's behavior. With a very sick year-old infant who seemed unlikely to live, and a pair of young children to raise, she decided to end her marriage and return to Bellefonte, Arkansas, to live with her parents on their small farm. She thought she could use her hospital training as a nurse to start again, but Clara's hopes of being a nurse were dashed when she learned that most medicine in the area, including surgery, was practiced on the kitchen table.

For young Jack Paisley, life on the farm meant staying clear of his grandmother. He and his sister would hide under the porch steps, hoping to avoid the dour woman, who, at an advanced age, had not taken well to being suddenly saddled with three children. But for Katherine, John, and Dale, their maternal grandfather, Arthur Preston Stone, helped fill the void left by their father. Although he was quite strict with them, his affection and attention gave the children a substitute father.

The Paisley family spent four years on the little farm in Bellefonte. The center of Clara Paisley's life was not her lively daughter or her smart young son, Jack, but the very ill Dale. Doctors told her each year that the boy's kidney troubles would soon kill him. Clara Paisley and her parents decided that, for Dale's health, they would sell the farm and move the family to Phoenix, Arizona, in 1930 a small town of about 35,000. The move was traumatic for Arthur Preston Stone, but his granddaughter, Katherine Lenahan, still admires the courage he showed in providing for his grandchildren when they arrived in Phoenix: "He couldn't farm, naturally. He didn't have the ground. He bought this little house in an Okie cluster settlement and he raised a garden and he had a few chickens. We were outside the city limits. He couldn't find any work because he had been a farmer all his life. So he rigged up a lawn mower. He was a little bitty man. He rigged it up so that he turned it over and he had a platform [on it] that held his rakes and shovels. He'd go from door to door for yard work. He'd leave at four or five o'clock in the morning so he'd get to the residential areas where all the rich people were. . . . I can remember him coming home when the temperature was 110 or more."

That same summer, John Paisley's stern grandmother became gravely ill. The doctors told her husband that his wife needed certain foods and her fever should be brought under control by applications of ice in the 110-degree Phoenix weather. But such foods and especially ice were luxuries the family could not afford. Clara Paisley was working as a nurse and cook in a tuberculosis sanitarium at the time. She confided in one of the other cooks about her family's financial problems. Within a week of that conversation, deliveries of groceries and ice were made to the family's little house. Arthur Preston Stone, an intensely proud man and a Protestant, was shocked to learn the charity came from the Mormon Church. Katherine remembers that "to him the Mormons and the Catholics ranked right up there with the devil."

Refusing to accept charity, John Paisley's grandfather arrived early one morning at the Mormon Temple in downtown Phoenix with his little lawn mower and began to cut the grass—much to the astonishment of the large crew of full-time gardeners. Arthur Preston Stone could not be dissuaded by church officials. He and his family would not accept handouts, no matter how desperate they were. He continued to cut the grass every week.[3]

Young John Paisley missed his father desperately and gave him the unearned admiration and respect that only an absent father could attain in a young son's imagination. For the first few years after his parents separated, a handful of gifts would arrive from his father every Christmas. As time passed and Joseph Paisley slipped deeper into alcoholism, such tokens of affection came less frequently. Yet by the time John reached adolescence, his father, now only a distant memory, maintained a place in his life. Outraged at something one of his grandparents would do, Katherine remembers John "would always say, 'Well, if Dad knew about this.' Really we didn't even remember our father. . . . He was just a face."

According to Katherine and Dale, John was a hellion. His behavior did not sit well with either his mother or his grandmother. His practical jokes did not amuse them; both women were almost totally lacking in humor.

At age nine, John developed his lifelong fascination with electronics. While other kids played ball, young Paisley went to Vic's Radio Shop in downtown Phoenix and learned from Vic about the wonders of crystal sets and short-wave communication. It was while the Paisleys were living on Madison Street that Jack built his first crystal set. It was a device that enabled Paisley to escape from the restrictions and confinement of home, at least to a point.

One day Jack, Dale, and Katherine were all hunkered down, listening to Jack's crystal set, its alligator clip grounded to metal and faint, scratchy music emerging from the earphone. Looming over the whole scene was an outraged Arthur Stone, infuriated at the sight of his grandchildren listening to the sounds of dance music.

In school, John did well in math and loved to read. Katherine, struggling with algebra, was pulled through by her younger brother. Paisley was tremendously inquisitive. When they were washing the dishes or doing other household chores, he and his sister played vocabulary games that John organized to train and challenge his memory. By the time Paisley became a student at Phoenix Union High School, he excelled as a scholar. Despite a move during high school to North Phoenix, young Paisley's academic life prospered. While his scholarship was outstanding, his social life was not. He showed no active interest in girls in high school. His brother, Dale, believes it was because John was on the short side until his senior year. Then he shot up to five feet eleven inches.

Much to the dismay of his siblings, Paisley took up playing the accordion. Katherine and Dale recall that their brother was completely tone deaf. He studied the accordion not for the music, however, but for the challenge. John Paisley enjoyed conquering things that were difficult. All this was immortalized in a yearbook picture of Paisley surrounded by his friends, which carried the caption "No wine, no women and very little song."

In the window of Vic's Radio Shop was the most beautiful Hallicrafters shortwave radio set Jack Paisley had ever seen. He longed for that radio and described it in detail to his family. He would stop in front of the shop and just stare at it. But the Depression left the Paisleys barely enough for food let alone an expensive radio. That radio became John Paisley's dream.

One day near Christmas, young Paisley was heartbroken when he saw that the set had vanished from the window at Vic's. He never dreamed anyone would buy his set. A few days later, as the Paisley family settled down for Christmas, Dale and Katherine all grouped around John while he opened his present. It was the Hallicrafters. The family had foregone their own Christmas presents that year so that John could have his radio.

Despite the diversions of the Hallicrafters, life was restrictive for this restless set of teenagers in their grandparents' home. The kids were not allowed to attend movies, dance, or play cards. When their grandfather caught them playing a Monopoly game an aunt had sent the family, he was furious. He grabbed the game, took it to the kitchen, put it in the wood stove and burned it. What set him off was hearing the rolling of the dice.

Money was so scarce that there were no extra pairs of shoes for Dale and John. The boys had to make do with one pair each, and often went barefoot. Dale's wife, Mary, recalls, "Dale and John were barefoot for so many years when they were growing up in Phoenix that when they became adults they had this fetish about going barefoot. They just couldn't do it."[4]

For young Katherine Paisley, the late 1930s did not hold much promise for a great future: "All of us that were in our teens in the thirties were slightly pink [communist] because we had nothing to look forward to. We had no future, no education. . . . There were no programs to help us go to college. There were no jobs. We could look forward to getting our high school diploma and, if we were lucky, a twenty-five-cents-an-hour job that five or ten men with families were trying to take away from us. . . . If World War II hadn't come along, I am sure there would have been one hell of a revolution."[5]

At age sixteen, Katherine went to work for a crippled English lady who ran a French hand laundry. She labored hard after school, cleaning and pressing the fine linen of Phoenix's upper class. In school, Katherine was impressed by the writings of Karl Marx and his dreams of a workers' paradise. Her new employer encouraged those interests. The old Englishwoman had Communist Party cell meetings in her house. She would read Marx aloud to Katherine; the young, very impressionable Katherine was enthralled. She would learn from this woman about what America had done to the Indians, about what the Germans were doing to the Jews. Katherine even attended several of the cell meetings herself.

Jack Paisley teased his sister about her political views. Katherine says she quit the hand laundry and lost interest in the communist movement because of a combination of capitalism and hormones. The hormones increased her interest in boys, and the money of capitalism beckoned. She quit the hand laundry in favor of a job at a dime store that paid fifteen cents an hour more.

With the war looming, the Paisley children went their own ways. Katherine moved to Long Beach, California, to live with an aunt and uncle. Dale married his teenage sweetheart. And John left a few weeks after his graduation from high school in 1941 for the Maritime Service Training Station at Gallups Island in Boston. This Merchant Marine facility was turning out recruits to man the merchant fleet for the war effort. After a nine-month course, Paisley graduated from Gallups Island early in 1942 as a radio officer holding the commission of lieutenant junior grade. Now, for the first time, Paisley had a chance to explore the world he had heard about for so long on his radios.

Katherine does not remember Jack Paisley saying much about where he went on his Merchant Marine voyages. "He was a quiet kind of person anyway. He wasn't shy—just quiet. If he didn't want you to know something, you would never find it out from him," she recalls.[6]

His Merchant Marine jacket reveals that he got his radio operator's certificate on April 9, 1942. His first voyages were short ones, delivering war materials to ports along the Gulf Coast and in the Caribbean. Paisley spent time in Cuba, where he picked up a smattering of Spanish. Then the voyages took a more secretive turn. By 1943 Paisley was sailing ships like the *Seakay,* the *Fort Washington,* and the *Kenesaw Mountain,* helping resupply America's British and Soviet allies.

No one in Jack Paisley's family can explain his interest in the Russian language or why he decided to make the Soviet Union his life's work. The answer, however, appears in his Merchant Marine record. Working for steamship companies like the American Mail Line, the South Atlantic Steamship Company, and others, Paisley was first introduced to a world on which he would years later become one of the CIA's foremost experts—the Soviet Union. For security reasons, John Paisley's Merchant Marine records list only the first and last port of a voyage. Paisley made at least two trips to Murmansk during his Merchant Marine career. In making the Murmansk run, Paisley witnessed firsthand the titanic struggle of the Russian people for survival. It is curious that in his CIA employment application years later, he said he had never been to the Soviet Union. Maybe it was because it was no secret, within the intelligence community, that the Soviets began during the early 1940s to recruit for intelligence operations Americans who were sympathetic to the Soviet Union in the joint war effort.

During and after the war, while working for steamship companies based in New York, Paisley's insatiable desire to read and learn about the places he visited brought him to Columbia University, where several professors took an informal interest in him.[7] Though he was never officially a student, professors prepared reading lists for him, and he faithfully followed them during his long voyages. Sometimes a two-week voyage could take six weeks as the ships on which Paisley sailed zigzagged through the open sea to avoid German submarines.[8] His Pacific voyages were just as difficult.

What attracted Paisley to Columbia remains a mystery. What is known is that Columbia was then one of the American universities where more than a few on the faculty, largely for idealistic reasons, introduced young American men to the Soviet way of life. But Columbia was also a place where some members of the faculty conducted recruitment for U.S. intelligence agencies.

Paisley mastered the basics of the Russian language before World War II ended. The war had transformed this thin, young adolescent who was shy around women into a quiet and confident man. Like so many of his contemporaries, Paisley had seen a little too much for such a young man. John had worked hand in hand with Soviet seamen. He had now experienced the world he had listened to on his old Hallicrafters back in Phoenix, and the experience had forever separated the young man from his family in a way that would follow them all for the rest of their lives.

Paisley returned to Arizona in 1946 and worked as a radio operator for two months with the highway patrol in Phoenix. But the Merchant Marine paid better, so Paisley signed on with the Alaskan Steamship Company for a summer of cruising before enrolling at the University of Oregon in September 1946.[9]

Paisley's University of Oregon education was short-lived. In less than a year, Paisley was asked to leave for violating university rules. It seems Paisley, who had little luck with women in high school, had finally blossomed. In May 1947, university authorities caught him in his dormitory room with an attractive blonde. He was promptly expelled from the university.[10]

After his Oregon experience, Paisley postponed his academic career for a while and returned to sea for the Polaris Shipping Company in New York. He financed his expensive radio hobby with his winnings at poker. In the fall of 1948, Paisley landed a radio operations job with the new United Nations Secretariat in Lake Success, New York. Paisley spent that winter as a radio operator with the Bunche-Bernadotte peace mission in Palestine. His duties also brought him to Iraq, Egypt, Lebanon, Syria, and Jordan.[11] This experience was Paisley's first official exposure to what would be a long life of international intrigue.

Both the KGB and Israeli intelligence were operating and recruiting in the Middle East during this period. More worrisome is the fact that the KGB recruited a number of agents under "false flag." Their agents would pose as Israeli agents and recruit someone to work for the Zionist cause, when, in fact, the work was being done for Moscow Center and the KGB. The young CIA was still relying largely on the British for Middle East intelligence. When Paisley returned to the United States in 1948, he assisted in setting up the United Nations' first radio facilities in Lake Success, New York.[12] It was during this period that Paisley's friend, Jim Curran, introduced him to a striking brunette named Maryann McLeavy, who worked as a secretary and assistant in the Manhattan office of Thomas A. Yawkey, the owner of the Boston Red Sox. Maryann, born in Pittsburgh, also came from a broken home. She had attended some twenty schools before graduating from high school. Those who remember her from those days recall a young woman who would turn men's heads and who was great fun. Dale Paisley's wife, Mary, recalls seeing Maryann for the first time during a visit to Chicago, and being rather surprised by her looks. "She looked like Gene Tierney, the actress. She was strikingly attractive."[13] But beyond the multitude of schools and separated parents, John and Maryann had little in common. Maryann's family had enough money to live comfortably. She was largely raised by aunts or in boarding school. This environment produced a tough, confident, and self-assured young woman.

The man she fell in love with, and who fell in love with her, had a sense of what he wanted to do with his life. John Paisley continued his reading program and his UN job while courting Maryann. Paisley, deprived by the war and economic circumstances of a university education, taught himself to love literature and poetry. He used his mastery of poetry to great effect on women. Maryann and John were married on March 23, 1949.

To earn extra money, John Paisley continued to ship out as a radio operator. But he soon decided he needed to finish his education. He picked the University of Chicago in 1949 because, as he explained to his family, Chicago was one of the few places that took into account the life experience of a veteran and gave him credit for unconventional forms of studies. Using placement tests, the university gave him academic credit for what he knew.[14] Paisley entered a three-year program for a master's degree designed for students whose education had been interrupted by the war.

Financially, things were tough for the young couple. Paisley taught driving at the ABC Driving School and became a taxi driver for Checker during the school year. In the summers he shipped out with the Merchant Marine to earn money for school.[15] Maryann got a job with university chancellor Lawrence A. Kempton's office.[16] It was during this period that one of the first of many clouds came over their relationship.

Maryann did very well in Kempton's office. They wanted her to remain in the office and, in order to advance, take some additional education courses. To encourage her to do this, they offered John a full scholarship. Maryann was thrilled. This offer meant that John did not have to spend months away from her at sea to earn tuition money, or work two jobs during the school year. But John refused to fill out the forms for the scholarship. He insisted, instead, on once again shipping out with the Merchant Marine. Maryann believed it was just part of his attitude toward money, of which she said, "John had to have financial problems or he was not happy."[17]

Maryann found John's attitude toward money very disconcerting. In an effort to begin to save for their future—buying a house, having children—Maryann opened several small savings accounts. As soon as Paisley discovered them, he forced her to use the money for household expenses. Maryann is careful to point out that John was not a spendthrift, despite his interests in radios and, later, sailing.[18]

John's longtime friend and classmate at the University of Chicago offers other clues to his behavior. Leonard Masters met John when they were both studying international relations at the university. Both men had served in the Merchant Marine during the war, Paisley as a radio operator, Masters as an engineer. Eventually the Paisleys moved upstairs from Masters in the same apartment building on Chicago's South Side. Masters recalls that Paisley had a tough time financially, and that he had to lend him money. Masters says Paisley's politics were typical of a university "full of liberals, left idealistic, unrealistic individuals. John had known poverty. He had known what it was to work for a dollar, but he was never money-conscious. . . . He would go out and spend twenty dollars on a beer bust at the local bar and think nothing of it. Yet he owed the bookstore or somebody else money."[19]

Masters found Paisley's scholastic schedule bizarre. "He would work in the middle of the night. I could call him anytime during the day or night and I'd never know if he would be in bed or studying." But he always gave priority to his Merchant Marine jobs. "He used to take an incomplete in a course and take a job on a ship. . . . I think one time he missed an entire quarter."

Paisley shipped out during this period to a number of Soviet Bloc countries, including Yugoslavia. Masters says Paisley returned from one trip to Yugoslavia after the split between Tito and Moscow. "He told me he had run into some Russians on a Russian ship there." Masters is sure of one thing: that Paisley had a background and an interest in the Soviet Union well before he enrolled at the University of Chicago.

Paisley's Merchant Marine career should have sounded all sorts of alarm bells when he applied for work at the CIA. Many of the seamen's unions in Holland and Germany were controlled by the Comintern.[20] According to former CIA officer Robert T. Crowley, radio officers like Paisley were particularly important targets for GRU and KGB recruitment during the war years. The West Coast branch of the Seafarers International, then run by Harry Bridges, was thoroughly penetrated by the Soviets, according to Crowley.[21]

Masters took an interest in the Progressive Party at the university. "They were a red front kind of operation, and I knew people who got involved in that kind of thing. John never got involved in any of that. . . . I'd been through the war and I knew horseshit when I heard it. . . . John was also this way, but John never got excited about it. John had an even sort of temper about politics."

But for Leonard Masters, other aspects of Paisley's behavior are memorable. Masters recalls the visit of the American radical W. E. B. Du Bois to the University of Chicago campus. Du Bois was a civil-rights pioneer and Masters was surprised that Paisley, so devoted to civil rights, refused to go see him. Masters says, "He didn't want to be seen there, that was my feeling . . . that was the implication because he was interested in the subject and he asked me about it afterwards, but he himself did not want to go." According to Masters, this event took place several years before Paisley applied for a job at the CIA.

Masters says Paisley was picked to be president of the International Relations Club by faculty adviser Richard Innes. "John was like a lot of people who never aspire to positions of leadership but got them," Masters recalls. One day in 1953, Masters and Paisley traveled to

Washington together to look for work. Masters had several interviews lined up at various government agencies, but Paisley had only one. "I went to the CIA and he went to the CIA, but not at the same time. I assumed this was just a scouting expedition for a job. But, looking back on it, I think John was already recruited. He only went to the CIA, that was his one contact, and he got the job." Masters thinks that their faculty adviser at the university, Richard Innes, recruited him. "Looking back on it, all of his courses were focused on Russia. And we used to do a good bit of arguing back and forth because Russia was a controversial subject," Masters explains.

Back in Oregon, John Paisley's mother began getting visits from FBI agents asking questions about her well-traveled son. It was the first of a series of background investigations Jack would undergo. Complicating Paisley's security check was his sister Katherine's attendance at what she describes as some "rather pink meetings as a senior back in high school. But, hell, they [the Russians] were our allies back then." [22]

One summer, as John was finishing up at Chicago, he decided to take his wife to meet his mother in Oregon. By this time his mother had remarried, and John and Maryann stayed at his stepfather's farm in Lowell, Oregon. Throughout his entire life, John was very close to his mother and sent her money every month. Katherine recalls Maryann loving her first taste of rural life during her visit: "When she hit that farm, she went completely bananas." [23]

For the Paisleys, it was a time of spending the summer swimming in rivers and picking strawberries. That summer, Maryann discovered canning. She ended up canning so much that Paisley and his stepfather had to build a makeshift trailer for the couple to carry what she canned back home with them. [24]

In 1953, John Arthur Paisley joined the Central Intelligence Agency. He told his family he had accepted a job with the Department of State, but later confessed to his brother and sister that it was the CIA. Fearful that his mother would worry, he never told her and asked them to cooperate. It was several years before his mother figured out the truth.

William Tidwell hired Paisley for the CIA's new Electronics Branch, where his Merchant Marine communications expertise was badly needed by an agency that was booming. [25] Officially, Paisley was hired by the Directorate of Intelligence on December 16, 1953, as an Economics Intelligence Officer. The fact that he had no training in this area meant little, since his first year at the CIA was directed toward Soviet Bloc communications. John had not actually been awarded his master's degree, and would not get it until 1963, when he finally turned in his thesis on the Soviet electronics industry. [26]

With all the maturity Paisley had gained from his war experiences, he was still a neophyte when it came to intelligence, compared to the people who hired him. He passed the one and only polygraph exam he was given in his entire history with the CIA. On his employment forms he wrote that he had never traveled to the Soviet Bloc, even though he had been to the Soviet Union and to Yugoslavia.

Clarence "Bill" Baier, a longtime colleague of Paisley's at the CIA, said that he recalls Paisley "was open about his trips to the Soviet Union at work. I recall him telling me he had been over there during the war. I think it was generally known among the people who knew him very well." [27]

The CIA of the early 1950s was like NASA during the rush to the moon. It was the prime beneficiary of the fear being generated in the country by the Rosenberg case, the McCarthy attacks, the poisoned atmosphere of the Stalin era and the Korean War; all had done wonders for America's secret intelligence budget.

The Paisleys set up housekeeping on F Street in Washington. In those days the CIA was only a few blocks away, located in drab World War II "temporary" buildings on Constitution Avenue along a tract of land that is now the site of the Vietnam Veterans Memorial. In those rat-infested buildings, history was being made. Plans for foreign coups were being devised. And the CIA's future Chief of Counterintelligence, James Jesus Angleton, was having scores of meetings with the British Station Chief of MI6 in Washington, Kim Philby.

Paisley found himself in orientation class with Henry "Hank" Knoche in 1953. To Knoche, Paisley looked like an ascetic, the "sort of fellow who wouldn't eat more than a piece of celery and a hard-boiled egg. He was very, very slight." [28] Also in the same orientation class was Edwin Moore, who would be convicted of espionage twenty-five years later.

Soon the Paisleys moved to the suburbs in Arlington, Virginia, into a house on Buchanan Street. Maryann worked first as a temporary secretary in a local law firm, and then for the Superintendent of Schools in Arlington County. Inside the CIA, John Arthur Paisley excelled in the CIA's Electronics Branch. He had the unique ability to give the CIA a point of reference for where the Soviets stood in electronic capability. His colleagues recall that Paisley would seem to come up with answers from nowhere when others had studied the same data for months with no results. His competence in digesting all sources of classified data and turning it into usable information earned him a reputation as a real whiz in such matters. He quickly showed that he was a comer, and his fitness reports and evaluations reflected this approval. John Paisley demonstrated brilliant insights into, and knowledge of, the Soviet system, yet nowhere in his background was the academic training that would normally account for such a skill.

The Paisleys' friends were an eclectic group. At one of their first parties in Washington, they invited several neighbors who would become lifelong friends. Bernard Fensterwald, then a lawyer working for the Senate, attended the party. Gladys Fishel and her husband, Edwin, also came. After leaving an intelligence career of her own, Gladys became the Paisleys' family lawyer. She remembers the first time she met Fensterwald at the Paisley house. "He was the person John would have liked to have been, he told us at the party when we met the Paisleys. He had come to the party dressed as . . . a condom. You know, that really amused John and my husband, Edwin." Edwin Fishel was a colleague of John's when he was later on temporary assignment to the National Security Agency.[29]

At work, Paisley was making unprecedented breakthroughs in Soviet communications, but he had to travel quite extensively. For Maryann, John's absences on overseas missions were getting more and more difficult. According to John's sister, Katherine, Maryann told her that John was gone far too much. In 1956, Edward, the first of the couple's two children, was born. Two years later, their daughter, Diane, was born. In the 1950s and 1960s, Katherine remembers that during family emergencies, including a time when John might be needed to donate a kidney to his brother Dale, he could be reached on an emergency basis in Paris. "The bottom line was that Maryann basically raised their children, Edward and Diane, on her own," Katherine said.[30]

In 1955 Paisley was selected for a very special assignment. William Tidwell sent him to work at the National Security Agency because Tidwell wanted to show them that the CIA had employees who understood communications electronics just as well as they did. Tidwell said that Paisley did so well at NSA that "he was regarded as one of their guys." Paisley found himself at NSA when the electronic "take" from the Berlin Tunnel began to pour in. This was an electronic listening post William King Harvey and his staff had managed to establish by digging under the street from a warehouse in West Berlin into an intersection in East Berlin. Harvey and a top-notch CIA and British intelligence technical team had managed to tap into the land lines used by the Warsaw Pact nations for all military communications.

It was an unbelievable technical feat. But unfortunately, unknown to the CIA, the Soviets were aware of the tunnel from the start. George Blake, the British Soviet agent, had been part of the original planning meetings. It is now believed that the material from the famed tunnel was doctored from the beginning. Paisley prospered at NSA, trying to make sense of the data from the tunnel. He carpooled to work with his neighbor Edwin Fishel. He was promoted twice during his two years on loan to NSA.[31] For Paisley's branch, the tunnel did reveal a great deal about the state of Soviet military communications; that may have been its only real contribution to Western intelligence.

By the late 1950s, Paisley found himself immersed in the battle to prevent the Soviets, not from spying, but from simply *buying* Western technology. Working with the Department of Commerce's export control office, the CIA had to devise a way to prevent the Soviets from purchasing the technology they needed on the open market. Commercial technology transfer was a brand-new area for U.S. intelligence, and Paisley became one of its pioneers.[32]

According to his CIA travel vouchers, Paisley spent months in Eastern Europe, usually under State Department cover, trying to learn what Eastern Bloc diversions of Western technology were taking place. His colleagues explain that Paisley's expertise gave the CIA a good idea what was on the Soviets' shopping list. Using different names and passports, Paisley attended meetings all over Europe, participating in schemes to feed phony technology to the Soviets.

Paisley had two attributes on which the Agency grew to depend. He could grasp the mind-boggling technical details of a new age in computers and communications, and he had the ability to explain their effects on the Soviet Union to people without technical backgrounds.[33]

For all his solid work, he was proving to be less than solid as a family man. The forty-hour weeks turned to fifty- and sixty-hour weeks, with frequent trips overseas. The needs of the children, Edward and Diane, did not divert Paisley's attention from his work. He was caught up in the Cold War. By the time of the election of John F. Kennedy, Paisley had turned into what Maryann considered a compulsive worker—and with good reason. His devotion was beginning to pay off. While plenty of people in the CIA had Ivy League educations, few were advancing as fast as Paisley.

Paisley's talent and hard work finally brought him into the CIA's inner circle. He was elevated to what was then called the Office of Research and Reports with unusual dispatch. Because Paisley would need access to this country's most precious nuclear secrets, a special series of atomic-energy clearances were needed. Paisley was a pioneer in putting together a three-dimensional picture of the Soviet Union. Using the new technology of spy satellites, eavesdropping satellites, and listening posts, Paisley combined that electronic data with information from "agents in place" to give startling new pictures of Soviet society. Now he was going to be given the full view of the American side of the picture, and he was going to get it fast. No less than J. Edgar Hoover himself expedited Paisley's "Q" clearances with the Atomic Energy Commission.[34]

After 1961, Paisley had access to more and more codeword intelligence. He was now in the most rarefied atmosphere of the CIA, and professionally he seemed to be thriving in it. His colleagues believe he was scrupulously honest in drawing up his reports. Sometimes his information would be startling and disturbing. Paisley treated his analytical work as a nonpolitical exercise of the highest importance.

Paisley's sister would see him about once a year, when he visited his mother. Very often he would be by himself. Katherine says what was remarkable about her brother was that, for all his success at the CIA, he "would still look like an unmade bed when he came out to visit." What amazed his family was how this college-educated, high-ranking CIA official could come back to Oregon and blend in so easily with the locals. Katherine recalls that "he could sit down at the Barge Inn, for God's sake, and there's not a crummier dive. It's been around since 1886. Their slogan is 'Winos, Riffraff, and Dingbats of the Waterfront.' He would go in there with my husband and they would play shuffleboard or pool and fit right in with all of them. He was one of them." [35]

Katherine found her brother very outspoken for a CIA man. "One of his favorite soapboxes was what we were doing wrong in the Third World in giving them all this elaborate and expensive machinery that they didn't know how to use, instead of things like teams of oxen and chickens. He was very critical of that." [36]

Gladys Fishel also remembers the Paisleys, John and Maryann, as being politically liberal. But John did more than just talk about political philosophy. "One thing John did do was tutor disadvantaged children in the District of Columbia. He tutored them in math," Fishel said.

As part of his work, Paisley questioned defectors from the Soviet Union and other Eastern Bloc countries.[37] Paisley was frequently seen at Camp Peary, Ashford Farm, and safe houses in the suburban Washington area and in North Carolina, where the defectors were learning to adjust to their new country.[38] Paisley would question defectors, usually using the cover name William McClure.

Peter Sivess, a former major-league baseball player, ran the CIA's Ashford Farm. Here defectors were kept during the early part of their settlement into American life. Paisley loved visiting the Eastern Shore of Maryland, where he debriefed defectors in the farm's poorly furnished old mansion. Sivess used to get a great kick out of Paisley's informality, something not seen in most of his other CIA colleagues. At the farm, Paisley used his extensive knowledge of Soviet electronics to probe defectors. Among the better-known defectors Paisley questioned during his career were Nikolay Artamonov (Nicholas Shadrin), Anatolyi Golitsyn, and Yuri Nosenko.

Paisley's only passions were his work and his interest in amateur radio. While Paisley cared little about clothes, furniture, cars, or other middle-class trappings, his radio equipment was always the best available.

Hank Knoche, who later was Paisley's boss, recalls that Paisley never worried about his appearance. "For instance, when summer came he would get himself into a seersucker suit, and days would go by before it would occur to him that maybe it was time to change his suit. Not that he was unclean or anything."

According to Dale, John was cheap. "Jack refused to spend any money. . . . He didn't want to buy any furniture. He would never buy a new car." The family moved from Arlington to Tucker Avenue in McLean, Virginia, and eventually to the home Maryann Paisley still owns, a comfortable and roomy house on Van Fleet Drive in McLean. The house had a large porch that Paisley loved. Its interior seemed to be of little concern either to John or to Maryann during the years they lived there together. According to visitors to the Paisley home, the place was filled with old furniture, and some of the carpets were threadbare. Betty Myers, who became a friend of Maryann's in 1966, remembers the place as very informal. The two women met while taking university extension courses together.[39]

Betty Myers, who says she eventually became John Paisley's lover, remembers Paisley as "not a person to always tell you about how he felt about things unless you inquired."[40]

According to Betty Myers, Paisley never forgot the poverty from which he came. "There was some part of him that was accepting of himself. I once heard him remark . . . I think he and Maryann were with some friends and they were talking about middle-class values and John said, 'Don't knock it, I just got here.' "[41]

It was clear by the mid-sixties that Paisley was on the fast track at the CIA. Donald Burton, who followed Paisley into the Office of Strategic Research, said of his colleague: "He was a young, very effective analyst. He was getting ahead faster than other people. He was young for a branch chief. Most of the other branch chiefs were much older."

John Paisley had become a major player in the Office of Strategic Research. Using all the sources and information the CIA could muster from secret agents, satellites, open sources, and radio intercepts, this division forged the finished intelligence "product." By far the most important of these "products" were estimates of where the Soviet Union was going, based on its income and interests in terms of military spending.

According to Hank Knoche, it was Paisley who spearheaded the effort to develop new methods of using intelligence to determine how the Soviets were spending their military budgets. "He was one of the early leaders in an effort which was very difficult and had been forced on the Agency—to try and come up with methodologies, economic methodologies, to determine the level of investment the Soviets were making in their military machine."[42]

Knoche recalls Paisley as "almost Dickensian" in appearance. "He was one of the world's great characters, as far as I was concerned. He was a very quaint sort of man. He had a lot of different interests. But he was very reclusive in an odd sort of way. He was kind of remote. He was very scholarly in his approach to his job."

To both his superiors and his subordinates, Paisley behaved more as a friend than as an employee or a boss. Don Burton summed up his views of his onetime boss: "If you had to describe Paisley physically, he was a very unattractive guy. . . . He had incredibly poor posture. . . . He was an extremely dark-complected guy. He didn't have good features, but people liked him. Women liked him because he would talk with them. He could relate to them very well. But he was not a good manager. He was pretty scattered."

Paisley kept pushing for better and better intelligence—and by the late 1960s, the United States got it. The CIA's Soviet Russia Division had a series of agents in place at the highest levels of Soviet defense planning. Because the quality of the intelligence was so good and the sources so precarious, the material was very closely held within the CIA, according to Paisley's colleagues.

Such information is absolute power in the intelligence community. Those who are given access to this exclusive material have power, and those who don't have power spend a good deal of their days fretting about why they don't. Indiscriminate access kills agents. Two cases that directly affected Paisley's work during the 1960s were those of Penkovsky and Popov, two Soviet agents working for the United States in quite high positions in the Soviet government. Both men were discovered by the Soviets and eventually executed.

The reports officer who handled the "take" from Popov and Penkovsky, as well as other major assets, was a quiet and scholarly man named Leonard V. McCoy. McCoy, a tall, baldheaded man, takes life very seriously and feels that Paisley never quite took it seriously enough. It would be up to McCoy to rewrite and disguise some of the material our Soviet agents were sending back to protect their identities. But the problem he and any other reports officer faced was that because only a limited number of people had access to certain material, that alone could allow by deduction the location and access of a source. Paisley, by accessing not just McCoy's reports but also defectors and friends in the clandestine services, was fully capable of determining who the source was by deduction. Paisley's laid-back and unconventional manner, a personality described by McCoy and even by Paisley's admirers as "bizarre," raised suspicions about his motivations in some minds at the CIA.

Paisley was famous for demanding the original source of "humint," or human intelligence. Though the CIA prides itself on the safeguarding of secrets through compartmentalization, Paisley was smart enough and had enough experience to make a shambles of it. If the Soviet Bloc Division would not tell him who an agent in place was, Paisley could figure out a great deal just by considering the type of material to which the agent had to have access. Then, by going out to the National Security Agency, where he was considered one of the boys because of his tour there in the 1950s, Paisley could get the raw intercepts to look at. These intercepts were Soviet message traffic picked up by some electronic means—usually a satellite. They were the most closely held of NSA secrets. By using this material, Paisley could supplement his knowledge of what the Soviets were up to and, in some cases, where the United States had agents in the Soviet government.

According to Paisley's superiors, during the 1960s and 1970s it was these key sources that allowed the CIA to have the best information the United States had up to that point on the state of the Soviet strategic threat. They say that the bulk of that material came from one of Leonard McCoy's agents. Paisley downplayed McCoy's claims on these Soviet sources as exaggerated since McCoy had nothing to do with recruiting these agents or operating them in the field.

As Paisley became more and more caught up in his work, a frustrated Maryann turned to her friend, Betty Myers, to confide her unhappiness with John. Myers had gone through a divorce when she first met the Paisleys, and her low-key personality, combined with a sympathetic attitude, gave Maryann someone with whom she could share her troubles. Myers became a close friend of Maryann's. Maryann confided the most intimate difficulties she and John were having with their marriage.[43] Gladys Fishel, who handled Betty Myers's divorce, said Myers seemed always to be around the Paisleys, almost like a family member.

Paisley's career flourished at the CIA until January 1969, when Richard Nixon took office. For a generation the CIA had been regarded as an "independent" source of unbiased intelligence information. Paisley and his bosses in the Office of Strategic Research, Bruce Clarke and Edward Proctor, prided themselves on the fact that the CIA was not a policy-making arm of the government, but a provider of intelligence. As Paisley's colleague Don Burton explains, "The whole business of estimating was why the CIA was ever set up in the first place. Because Army, Navy, Air Force, and Department of State were all policy arms, truth and intelligence did not have to coincide. So when the CIA came on, theoretically, there was to be no policy to defend. 'The truth, ma'am, and nothing but the truth.' That was the CIA's self-image. That is the way we felt about ourselves and what we were doing.''

But Paisley found that as the military exaggerated their estimates of Soviet strength to garner more budget money from the administration and Congress, acrimony over the estimates increased. Defense contractors and right-wing groups began to make a political issue of the CIA's "low-balling" of Soviet spending. Conservatives saw the CIA as a liberal bastion. To make matters worse, military intelligence received orders requiring them to develop estimates to support the new administration's defense policy, regardless of what the facts showed. Beginning with Kissinger, the Office of Strategic Research received serious pressure to "adjust" findings to suit political expediency.

Paisley and Proctor, his boss at OSR, respected each other, but Proctor's personality was much more formal than Paisley's. Proctor was sometimes, and not always affectionately, called the "data doctor." Proctor served as the CIA's Deputy Director for Intelligence and later as Chief of Station in London. According to Knoche, Proctor and Paisley worked hand-in-glove. Gen. Samuel V. Wilson, who reached the heights of both the intelligence and military worlds in an almost storybook career, recalls Paisley as a little too informal for Proctor, who had a reputation for being very good at his work, but a stuffed shirt.[44] Wilson says Paisley had absolutely no pretensions. "I think he and Paisley got along only fair. Proctor had, in my view, a bit more of a brittle ego. . . . Proctor took himself a bit more seriously, or at least appeared to."

Hank Knoche recalls that, despite Paisley and Proctor's personality differences, "Their backgrounds and interests were very much the same. Earlier in the sixties, they had worked together developing the methodologies to determine the Soviet military budget." Knoche remembers both men trying to get information on the Soviet strategic missile program in the early 1960s, when the issue of the "missile gap" engulfed the country.

As the number-two man in the Office of Strategic Research, Paisley suddenly found himself in the middle of operations he had not even realized were taking place in the compartmentalized world of the CIA. Paisley was given supervisory control of clearing "feed" intelligence for a highly classified counterintelligence project called KITTY HAWK. The file itself had little information in it. It simply said that the Office of Strategic Research (OSR) was to provide naval and other intelligence material through OSR employee John Funkhouser to the FBI.

Funkhouser, who used to design ships, headed OSR's small unit on the Soviet Navy. He had been involved in the operation since 1966.

But Paisley, new to the case, was surprised to see the operation was being run for the CIA by Bruce Solie of the Office of Security. Within a few months, Paisley learned that Funkhouser was supplying naval material to the Soviets to support KITTY HAWK through a Soviet defector Paisley had debriefed in 1959 on communications, Nikolay Fedorovich Artamonov. Artamonov was now calling himself Nick Shadrin. Now, according to Paisley's colleagues in OSR, Paisley had to sign off on all material Funkhouser was to feed the Soviets through Artamonov.[45]

CHAPTER THREE

Paisley: The Plumbers

There was this bird that got a very late start on the passage south for the winter season. He got tired of flying and he rested on a telephone wire for the night. Well, the inevitable happened and the poor bird froze during the night and fell off the wire to the ground. Just as the bird woke up, a horse happened by and took a dump on the bird. The bird said, "Not only do I almost freeze to death, but now this happens to me." But the bird soon discovered that the horseshit was warming him up and he stuck his head out to look around. He let out a warble and a big cat came up to the bird and ate him. The morals of the story are: Just because someone shits on you, it doesn't mean they are your enemy—and if you're up to your neck in shit, don't sing about it.

John A. Paisley's favorite joke

PAISLEY AND MANY of his colleagues believed that Henry Kissinger was "cooking the books" by demanding that the CIA analysts work with political appointees to put together "intelligence memoranda." These National Intelligence [Security] Memoranda, or NISMs, were designed to carry as much weight as the Office of Strategic Research's estimates, but with Kissinger's stamp. They were devices to get the CIA to endorse White House policies—a hybrid combination that would supersede CIA estimates because they had the endorsement of both the CIA and the White House.

Kissinger was convinced that if the Soviets were painted as being too advanced in strategic missile construction, then the Senate would not approve a series of treaties that he was negotiating and promoting as the rewards of "detente" with the Soviets. Arms control had progressed greatly since the 1950s. But to move beyond what Kennedy accomplished with his Nuclear Test Ban Treaty in 1963 would take very bold moves. Kissinger seemed prepared to make those moves despite facts unearthed by some analysts at the CIA about the Soviets' true intentions.

By the end of 1969, Paisley was a "nervous wreck," according to Maryann. The battle between the Office of Strategic Research and Kissinger was raging. Paisley was in charge of putting together NISM-3. This memorandum on the state of Soviet air defenses included the Soviets' anti-ballistic-missile capability. In terms of the SALT I negotiations, NISM-3 was most important. According to Paisley's colleague Philip A. Waggener, the argument boiled down to a determination on whether or not the Soviet's new SAM V missile gave them an anti-ballistic-missile (ABM) capability.[1] Paisley had learned from a Soviet defector that the SAM V had such a capability. But, inside the CIA, a debate raged on the accuracy of this information. Suddenly, Paisley found himself having serious trouble getting his bosses to agree to include his discoveries about the Soviets' deployment of an anti-ballistic-missile system around major cities. They attempted to explain to him that because policy and intelligence were now being combined in the NISMs, other considerations had to be included. Paisley, according to his wife, actually resigned. But Paisley's CIA colleagues tell a different story. They say Paisley seemed more caught up in his personal troubles than in policy battles.

By late 1969, John Paisley's work left him with little time for Maryann, Edward, and Diane. His wife demanded that he reorder his priorities. Maryann says she threatened to leave him that year if he did not do something about his life.[2] Paisley went to his CIA superiors and was given what amounts to a year off—a year at the Imperial Defence College in London.[3]

To the CIA, Paisley's year at the Defence College was part of their grooming him for his eventual ascendancy to the top position in OSR. But to Maryann and the children, the London sabbatical was a great opportunity to get to know John again. There was little real work in the London assignment. Most at the CIA considered it a reward for Paisley's hard work and dedication. The Imperial Defence College curriculum included studies in strategic philosophy and detailed studies on the regions of the world. Here, colleagues from various Western military and intelligence services could exchange ideas. After Paisley disappeared, counterintelligence chief James Angleton speculated that this relaxed, academic atmosphere was the perfect place for the Soviets to try to plant an agent or make a recruitment. He argued that the Imperial Defence College was the sort of gathering place for Western intelligence experts that the Soviets would be "fools" not to penetrate.[4]

The course work at the Imperial Defence College was divided into three terms that were separated by short trips to various NATO installations, as well as longer overseas tours.[5]

The family rented a flat in London. Edward Paisley recalls spending much of the time sightseeing. But a disappointed Maryann said she soon learned that John was *more* distracted, not less. "He couldn't wind down," Maryann recalls. Paisley behaved very strangely that year. Even though he had secure facilities at the U.S. Embassy in London (which was located near the Paisleys' CIA-rented flat), Paisley opened a post office box fifty miles away at Greenham Common, the town that gave its name to a U.S.-run nuclear base in the English countryside. Paisley was not cleared for the base, yet he kept a box on the base's secure grounds. There was no real "official" reason for him to have the post office box.[6]

For a CIA man like Paisley to have a "secret" box, located very far away from where he was staying, when better and more secure facilities were available at the Embassy, is the kind of activity that strikes fear in the heart of any security officer. Following Paisley's disappearance in 1978, when a newspaper reporter learned of the box, the CIA's Office of Security made a major effort to investigate it. The very fact that they investigated indicates that Paisley's CIA superiors had not been notified of the box. One frightening conclusion some security officers made was that Paisley could have been using it for illicit purposes.[7]

What was Paisley doing in London? One possibility is that he had been asked by the CIA to personally recruit someone with whom he was acquainted while on assignment in London. Experts in counterintelligence suggest that Paisley was being contacted for this mission through some sort of "drop" at the nuclear base. But others are more skeptical, including Paisley's own colleagues, who say they have no explanation for his activities.

According to his son, Edward, Paisley was in good spirits in London. Edward does not recall ever going to Greenham Common with his father. He explained that the family did not have a car in London since their flat was not far from the American Embassy.[8]

For Maryann, the memories of London were not wonderful. Their marriage continued its downward spiral. She remembers his being called constantly to the American Embassy to work. On several occasions she heard him use false names over the telephone. She also recalls his going to the embassy to use its secure communication channels.[9]

During this period, Maryann would write to the Paisley family in Oregon that things were fine. Maryann Paisley took great pride in her family and did not want to worry John's mother.[10] But by the end of their stay in London, she had serious doubts that her marriage to John Paisley could continue. He was now working between seventy and seventy-five hours a week. Like other CIA families she had come to know, her family was "compartmentalized," kept separate from his real daily life—the Agency.[11]

John Paisley returned from London in January 1971, with a full beard. His marriage had deteriorated further, but his career was still soaring.[12]

Paisley's earlier unpleasant encounters with the Nixon White House receded as he and most of the Office of Strategic Research began to prepare for the marathon Strategic Arms Limitation Treaty (SALT I) negotiations. Paisley was providing briefings for Henry Kissinger.[13] Because of his high rank in the OSR, Paisley found himself being appointed to one troubleshooting team after another sent off to various points to do postmortems. These included Cyprus, India, Cambodia, and Geneva during the Nixon years. Paisley's professionalism never gave Kissinger or others he dealt with a hint of his personal disdain for the Nixon administration. Though his sister remembers him railing against Kissinger, Paisley found himself with increasing responsibilities as he played his part in putting together teams for the SALT I talks. The support work for such an arms limitation negotiation was tremendous. And it was Paisley's division that was charged with determining just how strong the Soviets were, and in what strategic areas. Those estimates would determine all U.S. negotiating positions with the Russians.

In spite of Paisley's earlier problems with Kissinger on the NISMs, it was Paisley who gave Kissinger one of his best pitches for selling SALT to political conservatives. Paisley and his CIA colleagues argued that the Soviets could no longer afford to support a huge defense buildup. Their Pentagon colleagues disagreed. The OSR's scientific division reported that the Soviet missiles, while being produced at ever-increasing rates, were heavier than ours, but were also amazingly inaccurate. They argued that because they were so inaccurate, it was necessary for the Russians to carry bigger warheads to destroy a target. Further, such information was being confirmed by FEDORA and TOP HAT, the code names of two Soviet agents who had been recruited by the FBI to work against the Soviet government. According to former CIA analyst David S. Sullivan, both agents reported that the Soviet ICBMs were inaccurate. This information, combined with Paisley's insistence that the Soviet economy could not support a massive nuclear buildup, created the foundation for America's negotiating positions. It was on these positions that Kissinger based his negotiations with the Soviets. In retrospect, they proved to be disastrous.

The image that Paisley and his colleagues painted of the Soviet

Union, based on their estimates, used methodologies that were "flawed," according to Phil Waggener. Waggener, who worked with Paisley, says there were "very basic problems" in some of Paisley's original methods of measuring the Soviet military economy. The net result was that for years the CIA advised U.S. policy-makers that the Soviets were less able to support a major strategic military buildup than they actually were.

Waggener and other OSR employees see nothing sinister in the errors. But other colleagues are not so charitable. David Sullivan said that, because of Paisley's estimates, the United States went into the SALT I negotiations convinced that the Soviets did not have the economic wherewithal to engage in a major secret buildup. "But, as history shows, that is precisely what they did," Sullivan asserts.

After John Paisley disappeared, his son, Edward, recalls seeing a document indicating that the Soviets approached John Paisley overseas. He believes it was during the SALT I talks. Edward says this document was later stolen from his mother's lawyer's office. According to Edward, the document said Paisley was approached and told to go ahead and take the bait by the CIA. Edward said that was the last reference to it.[14] Later on, he claimed, the document had disappeared.

Paisley's boss, Hank Knoche, says that if such an approach by the Soviets took place, he believes he would have been told about it: "I think maybe he would have mentioned something like that to me. Maybe not. Maybe not. If he reported that and had been told to keep to himself, then others would worry about it. He would play that security game. He was a bug on security. Reclusive. It's hard to put together his life outside the Langley building, isn't it? Strange."

What disturbs Paisley's former colleagues is that after establishing himself as tough and independent of Kissinger before going to England in 1970, Paisley came back as almost a different person. "He just didn't speak out, he seldom stuck his neck out," OSR colleague Clarence Baier recalls. The net result of the CIA information given to Kissinger was that the Soviets were allowed to build up their strategic weapons force to a level that erased the longtime U.S. advantage.

As Paisley became acquainted with Kissinger and his staff, he found himself being used more and more for White House chores. The CIA had known since the Johnson administration that the White House had been involved in domestic spying. After all, one of these operations had been established in the CIA's own basement offices: Operation CHAOS. President Johnson had been convinced the Communist Chinese and the KGB had infiltrated the antiwar movement. Over the years of CHAOS's existence, more than one hundred office-size filing cabinets were filled with personal information on Americans and so-called leads to subversive overseas contacts.[15] The Nixon administration used that same argument to intensify its own domestic spying effort.

In January of 1971, a White House aide to Henry Kissinger and the National Security Council Staff named David R. Young was given what seemed like a routine White House assignment by Egil "Bud" Krogh, Jr., to declassify documents.[16] Officially, Young was responsible for the classification and declassification of documents. His new position also required him to work with other government agencies, including the CIA, to determine the possible sources of unauthorized disclosure or "leaking" of classified documents and secret information. Joining Young as his assistants were George Gordon Liddy and E. Howard Hunt. Liddy, a lawyer, came to work for Young from an assignment at the Department of the Treasury on the recommendation of Bud Krogh during the early summer of 1971. Liddy had been working with Krogh on the international drug problem—an investigation to which Paisley was also assigned. Krogh was convinced Liddy's experience would give Young what he needed. One of Liddy's new responsibilities was to serve as liaison with the Department of Justice in connection with the project.

Hunt was recommended to Young by Charles Colson. Colson believed that Hunt's CIA background would be of great help on the project. Hunt's role was to deal with the CIA on an informal level while Young would be the formal contact to the top people at the CIA like Director Richard McGarrah Helms and his deputy, Gen. Vernon Walters.[17]

On the surface the declassification project Young was running seemed benign. Officially the White House said it was merely trying to speed up the normally lengthy declassification process. But below the surface, the Nixon administration officials had other motives. They were trying to get their hands on files that contained embarrassing information about previous, Democratic presidencies so they could release this material to the public. In June, when the Pentagon Papers appeared in the *New York Times,* Young and other White House officials expressed anger that only documents embarrassing to the Nixon administration seemed to be leaked. Colson and Young began a campaign to convince more senior White House staffers like Bob Haldeman and John Erlichman that a series of selective disclosures about Democratic administrations could strengthen Nixon's political position.[18]

According to former FBI officials such as William Branigan, the Nixon White House first approached J. Edgar Hoover for assistance in setting up the "Plumbers" to plug unofficial government leaks, but he flatly refused. At first Nixon wanted to conduct the Plumbers under the FBI's own black-bag operations. But Hoover did not buy allegations that the Pentagon Papers had been leaked to the Soviets and that, therefore, the Bureau should get involved in the investigation. Besides, Hoover had his own problems.[19]

The White House then turned to the CIA for assistance. When David Young requested that Richard Helms send someone from the CIA to help plug leaks, Helms did what he usually did in security matters, according to former Angleton staffer Clare Petty: he turned to Angleton for advice. Angleton suggested to Helms's staff that the Deputy Director of Strategic Research had experience in previous leak studies. Paisley's name was sent back to Young as someone who might be able to assist.[20]

Why Paisley?

One reason that Angleton may have wanted Paisley in Young's proximity was that Paisley may well have been working for Angleton all along. As Chief of Counterintelligence, Angleton was growing more and more disturbed with Henry Kissinger. Paisley may have been sent over by Angleton simply to report back to him on what was going on.

Angleton had reason to fear Kissinger. He knew that Young had been involved with Kissinger on discussions of how hundreds of pounds of enriched uranium were transferred illegally to Israel to seed their nuclear weapons program. It was no secret in the intelligence community that Angleton had played a major role in assisting in the transfer. Angleton had supervised the United States' intelligence relationship with Israel for its entire history. If the news of the illegal transfer was made public, Angleton stood to lose everything—including his role in running the CIA's "Israeli account."

On August 9, 1971, Paisley was personally requested by Young to conduct a crash investigation of security leaks to the press. He was asked to look at nineteen categories of leaked security information. The subsequent report sent out by Paisley under the signature of Director Helms so impressed the White House that Paisley was designated to handle CIA liaison with the Plumbers.[21]

Young's Plumbers unit was designed to paint as unpleasant a picture of the leakers as possible and to get this damaging information out in public. Soon Paisley found himself in the middle of this distasteful and paranoid world. Documents show that Young requested Paisley by name. Paisley's job was to provide fodder for Young's efforts from the repository of CIA secrets.

Soon Paisley was in the thick of efforts to discover everything embarrassing about Daniel Ellsberg, including the most intimate details of Ellsberg's sexual activities.[22] By August 18, 1971 the project to investigate Ellsberg and discredit the leakers of the Pentagon Papers took on new urgency. The White House code named the effort ODESSA.

All of these operations went on under an umbrella organization called the Task Force on Leaks. As John Paisley discovered, the Nixon leak task force was merely a team of second-story artists designed to uncover and then collect damaging and embarrassing evidence on "hostile" leakers. But domestic political "enemies" of Nixon and his administration soon became primary targets.

In one memorandum to Erlichman from Colson and Young is a reference to the CIA's performance in the project, saying the Agency had provided "little relevant material." It goes on to say that the "CIA has been understandably reluctant to involve itself in the domestic area, but responsive to the President's wishes, has done so. Overall performance to date is satisfactory." Donald Burton, who worked under Paisley at the CIA, said Paisley's being picked by the White House "does not surprise me. First a leak comes out and everyone says what are we going to do about those fucking leaks and how are we going to stop of all these leaks. This will come down right through the DCI and not the security side of things. . . . It happens in every administration. . . . So it will come down and hit the Chief [of OSR] and the Chief will then have to assign someone and it is going to be the deputy. So John's the deputy and it is a shit detail as far as John is concerned." [23]

What other operations did Paisley get involved in? There has been much speculation over what the Plumbers were really looking for in Lawrence F. O'Brien's office the night of the famous Watergate break-in. But perhaps the most important clues can be taken from Nixon's obsession with the Kennedys. Hanging over Nixon's head at the time was a $100,000 unreported campaign contribution to Nixon from Howard Hughes, accepted by his best friend, Bebe Rebozo. [24] Rebozo was under Justice Department investigation. In the 1960 campaign, a Howard Hughes loan to Nixon's brother, Donald, became a major issue. According to Robert Maheu, a former FBI and CIA man himself who managed Hughes's affairs for years, he had also delivered a $25,000 contribution to Robert Kennedy's 1968 campaign. [25] Maheu says the idea that O'Brien had any detailed knowledge of any further contributions to the Kennedys is absurd.

It may have been details tying Hughes to the Kennedys that the Plumbers were searching for that night. Maheu explains that by this time a group of Mormons hired by Hughes had taken over his affairs. But why wouldn't Nixon, considering his close relationship with Hughes in the past, simply ask him about the loans? According to Maheu, Hughes was not "operating on all cylinders by this time," and the "Mormon Mafia" around him largely cut him off from the outside world, even from the President of the United States.

Why, then, would Nixon believe that there was more to O'Brien and the Kennedy contributions than there actually was? Could Angleton, through Paisley, have planted that idea? Could the CIA actually tempt the Plumbers into an intemperate act over the promise of a memorandum showing a connection embarrassing to the Kennedys? Considering the fact that Young, Colson, Liddy, and Hunt left no stone unturned to find out damaging material about the Kennedys, having a trusted man like Paisley feed them this kind of a meal seems like a simple matter.

There are strong indications that some sort of Plumbers team was kept on even after the arrests that night at the Watergate. Top-level CIA sources suspect that it was the Plumbers who conducted an operation that ruined plans for the CIA's second mission by the Hughes-built ship, *Glomar Explorer,* to recover more of the wreckage of a Soviet submarine that sank in 1968. On June 5, 1974, two months before Richard Nixon resigned, the highly secure Hughes storage facility at 7020 Romaine Street in Hollywood, California, was burglarized. It was the third burglary of a Hughes facility in four months. According to Maheu, among the items taken, despite a security guard and impressive vaults, was a footlocker full of Hughes's records documenting his political contributions over the years, including the ones to the Kennedys. In that footlocker was also the memorandum detailing the *Glomar Explorer* arrangement. For then CIA Director William Colby, the burglary began the nightmare of trying to keep the *Glomar Explorer* operation secret from the Russians by keeping it out of the American media.[26] But to Maheu it was not the *Glomar* material that interested the burglars; it was the political material. Maheu believes it was the "Mormon Mafia" that tipped off the perpetrators in order to solidify their control of the Hughes empire. Maheu does not believe the break-in would have been possible without cooperation from inside the company. "I am familiar with 7020 Romaine. Hughes chose it for its total security. And some son of a bitch is going to show up in the wee hours and say to the guard, 'Take me to the vaults'?" Maheu asked.

Maheu also does not believe the documents in the trunk were for the exclusive use of the "Mormon Mafia." "This is funny. Here ends up top-secret information in the hands of a bunch of [Mormon] zombies that couldn't pass the lowest of security tests," Maheu said.

So who did burglarize Romaine?[27] Maheu believes that the "Mormon Mafia" that took control of the Hughes empire may have tipped off the Nixon White House about the footlocker in order to curry favor with the administration. Several FBI officials involved in the Watergate investigations believe Romaine Street may have been a last-ditch attempt to save the disintegrating Nixon administration. But perhaps the most logical suggestion comes from a former counterintelligence official of the FBI, who suggested that if Paisley had been working for the Soviets, using the break-in at Romaine to expose *Glomar* was the perfect way to keep the CIA from getting hold of several nuclear missiles the Agency had failed to retrieve on its first attempt.

For John Paisley's family, the first hint that Paisley might have been in the Plumbers came in 1973. Dale Paisley, then living in the San Francisco Bay area, recalls the incident vividly. "One time in late 1973 he came into the Bay area and called me up and asked me if I would drop him off at the Lawrence–Livermore Laboratory on the way back home. Well, a couple of days later, my son was telling me that a friend of his who was an Air Policeman said they had a raid down at Berkeley. [The friend said] in the background was a guy with a full white beard and he said he thought he was from the CIA or something. He described Jack to a T. . . . Well the next time I talked to Jack, I said, 'Hey, what's this I hear about that raid over in Berkeley that night?' And he said, 'How the hell did you hear about that?' That's all he said about it." [28] Confirming Dale's suspicions of Paisley's trip to Berkeley is a travel voucher dated December 3 through December 5, 1973, for "San Francisco and Berkeley, California." [29]

According to Paisley's sister, Katherine, "Mother was damn near psychic in a lot of ways about any of us if we were floating into some dangerous situation. And Mother was just paranoid over this Watergate thing that Jack was involved with, and I kept saying, 'Oh, Mother, no, he's not involved.' " While Paisley's mother had learned of her son's work for the CIA, she didn't believe him concerning his involvement with the Nixon administration. Katherine said Clara Paisley asked her son about his involvement with Ehrlichman, Dean, and Haldeman and he denied he had anything to do with them at the time. [30]

For Clarence "Bill" Baier, who worked with Paisley in the Office of Strategic Research, this was a period when John was absent "a great deal of time." Paisley never shared with his family his White House activities and the potential damage they could do to the CIA. He and Maryann grew farther and farther apart as he fell down the well of Watergate.

Of all of Paisley's mysterious behavior, none is more bizarre than his activities with "swinging clubs" in the Washington area. Paisley, who had a reputation as a sexual adventurer, was never known as a fool. For him to risk such indiscreet sexual activity could easily bring an end to his entire career. Yet, starting in 1972, John Arthur Paisley joined a series of sex clubs that would turn out to have the darkest of national security implications.

Given the fears today about AIDS, it is hard to imagine the Washington sex scene of the early 1970s. Even harder to fathom is why people with the highest forms of government clearances, like John

Paisley, would risk blackmail by engaging in such activity. In the beginning, the parties were simply colleagues from work swapping spouses at their various suburban homes—a dozen or so couples meeting in a member couple's house for a night of bed-hopping, drugs, and, in some cases, kinky sex. Usually the couples would chip in twenty dollars or more each to cover liquor and drugs, normally marijuana. But as the popularity of swinging grew, the parties among friends became more and more diverse as new swingers were recruited by word of mouth.

Eventually the sex clubs became more organized and were operated by a few people and run out of a wide range of bars. From "Capital Couples," which operated out of a former media hangout called The Class Reunion, to redneck watering holes in Prince Georges County, Maryland, the clubs flourished in the growing free-sex environment.

One party Paisley attended took place at the home of a couple Paisley met through his subordinate Donald Burton, who was a pioneer in the swinging scene. According to witnesses who asked not to be identified in order to protect their families, the setting was pretty typical. Paisley brought a dark-haired, attractive woman and not his wife, Maryann. The split-level, four-bedroom house in Falls Church, Virginia, seemed the picture of suburbia until one noticed couples having sex standing up against the kitchen stove, in the upstairs bedrooms, on the gold shag carpet in the living room, sitting on the upstairs stair railings, and even on the glass-and-wood coffee table.

Two participants in the sex parties recall an incident that they say demonstrated why they liked Paisley so much. Paisley had left a party. As he went outside, he saw that the house was surrounded by several police cars. Instead of taking off, Paisley calmly walked back into the house and told his host about the police and advised the guests to get rid of any marijuana in the house. It turned out to be a false alarm caused when a local youth next door was the subject of a high school prank.

Not all of Paisley's parties were in suburban homes. Paisley would, in later years, hold several sex parties on his sailboat *Brillig*. One female guest present said that "ten people trying to make love on a thirty-foot sailboat can get pretty intimate." Paisley loved to take nude photographs of his dates, and some of the parties were even videotaped. Paisley may also have hosted the least successful sex party conducted in the Washington area in the 1970s.

Today the Rush River Lodge is a peaceful country home near Washington, Virginia, about an hour south of the Washington, D.C., suburbs. In May 1972, Donald Burton and John Paisley formed the Rush River Lodge Corporation and bought the old lodge with the help of some other CIA friends in the hopes of turning it into a ski resort.[31]

The place never worked out as a ski resort, but Burton and Paisley staged several sex parties at the lodge. According to Burton, this was done without the knowledge of their "straight investors."

In the days when Paisley and Burton decided to throw their swingers' party, the lodge was extremely rustic. One guest describes the experience: "The whole idea of going to a swingers' party is to have comfortable sex in a relaxed and unobtrusive environment. . . ." The guest's wife finished the story: "Paisley and Burton decided it would be fun and very private to go down to their place. Well, there was nothing like it. A dozen people having sex with each other in every imaginable position for hours and then discovering that your weekend of passion doesn't include running water! The damn plumbing failed."

Most of the partygoers were middle-class, some were reporters, and most dropped out of the scene by 1980, when herpes came to wide public attention. Burton recalls bringing a clandestine CIA employee to one of the swinging parties. And some of Paisley's fellow guests were on the bizarre side. One high-level Nixon appointee enjoyed tying up women and beating them. A United States senator would walk around the parties nude and proclaim to every woman present that he was a senator.

Why was Paisley at the parties? Why in the world would he host some? As word got out about the parties and the fact that employees of the CIA, the FBI, the Pentagon, the NSA, Capitol Hill, and the administration were attending, the KGB resident in Washington wanted them penetrated. It was the perfect place for blackmail and recruitment. It was also the perfect place to make contact with other intelligence agents.

Paisley crossed paths at these parties with an attractive Czechoslovakian couple who would turn out to be high-level penetration agents from the Czech intelligence service. Karl Koecher was a tall and aloof man, and his wife, Hana, was a beautiful woman and Karl's opposite in personality. Worried intelligence officials now believe that Paisley may have worked in tandem with the Koechers.

The Koechers were placed in the United States as what counterintelligence agents call "sleepers"—agents who would work for years to build a solid reputation and a cover story before actually collecting intelligence. The Koechers left Czechoslovakia for New York in December 1965. They told U.S. immigration officials they were political defectors and had been forced to leave because of Karl's secret work for Radio Free Europe. In reality, Koecher had been a Czech intelligence agent since 1961.[32]

Trained in Prague in physics, Karl taught at Wagner College in New York between 1969 and 1973. Like Paisley, Koecher benefited from a connection to Columbia University. When Koecher took a two-year course offered by Columbia University's Russian Institute, he encountered Zbigniew Brzezinski. Prior to becoming well known as President Carter's National Security Adviser, Brzezinski had spent some time on the CIA's payroll.[33] Koecher hardly had to work at his role as a sleeper agent. The CIA was in such desperate need for language specialists that it did few background checks when he was recruited at Columbia for a job as a CIA translator in February 1973.

Koecher easily passed the CIA's vaunted Office of Security polygraph examination. He joined a long list of spies who had been "fluttered" and had fooled the operators completely. He went into the DDO, the covert side of the CIA, to translate cables from agents. His assignment to such a sensitive post is remarkable. It shows how lax security at the CIA had become. Koecher was given access to material from this country's most prized double agents, men hidden in the Kremlin bureaucracy.

Hana Koecher, an attractive blonde who was Karl's partner in espionage, remained in New York, working in the wholesale diamond business and assisting her husband in funneling out the secrets. The CIA put Karl to work in Rosslyn, Virginia, in a nondescript office building. Here, Koecher had access to important message traffic concerning Soviet Bloc agents and their CIA handlers. The name of this operation was the AE Screen Unit. Its job was to sift through material that was so sensitive that few people on the covert side of the CIA Operations Directorate could see it in its raw form. Koecher was given a top-secret clearance and access to some codeword intelligence. This practice was almost unheard of for defectors of any sort, according to the former deputy chief of CIA counterintelligence, Leonard V. McCoy.

The details of the sex parties and CIA involvement can be found in a lawsuit filed by the owners of one of the houses used for the parties. The neighbors grew tired of the traffic and noise in the usually quiet, posh, suburban Washington community of Fairfax Station, Virginia. The owners were a military officer and his wife, then stationed abroad. When word reached them that their home was being used for illicit purposes, they filed suit.

The owners had turned their sprawling, seven-bedroom house over to a Virginia realtor for management while they were out of the country. The owners and the realtor agreed before they left for their overseas tour that no singles would be considered for tenants. The owners then discovered that their house had ended up in the hands of a sex club known as the Virginia In-Place. Complaints over activities at the house caused the Fairfax County police to put the house under surveillance one weekend. It was during that weekend that several Paisley friends were identified as having attended a party. One car whose license plate was written down by the police belonged to Donald Burton. Burton was summoned for a deposition.[34]

Burton confirms he attended the parties and recalls bringing Paisley to some at a later period. But another Paisley friend went through his old calendars, which indicate he met Paisley in the swinging scene in 1972. In the major investigations that followed Paisley's disappearance, no references can be found anywhere to the parties or the Koechers. One reason is that Donald Burton says he never notified the CIA's Office of Security of the potential problem of his identity coming out in the court documents. To make matters worse, despite the FBI investigation into the Koechers, which led to their arrest and eventual trade for the Soviet dissident Anatoly Shcharansky on February 11, 1986, no one from the Bureau ever questioned Burton.

Burton is candid about why he did not reveal his attendance at the parties to the CIA's Office of Security: "They would have fired me if I told them." He said if someone *had* attempted to blackmail him, he was fully prepared to "run right down to Security and tell them."

That so many intelligence officials were involved in the sex clubs, had contact with the Koechers, and never were asked to reveal it in any investigation is a devastating comment on the current state of counterintelligence in the United States. Though evidence of Paisley's involvement was easily obtainable, investigators for the CIA's Office of Security, the FBI, and the Senate Intelligence Committee all failed to follow up leads on the swinging groups.

But, perhaps more significantly, Paisley also crossed paths with former *Washington Post* reporter Carl Bernstein at several parties. In the opinion of some people interviewed for this book, the fact that Paisley was serving as CIA liaison to the White House Plumbers at the time of his meeting Bernstein at sex parties raises many interesting questions. Could Bernstein's sexual activities, they ask, have made him vulnerable to pressure from a man like Paisley who may have wanted to get specific news stories slanted in a certain way? Bernstein denies even knowing Paisley. In a December 1979 telephone interview, Bernstein denied having attended any such parties. A few days later he called back to say, "I may have attended the parties, but I never met anyone named John Paisley."

Half a dozen Paisley intimates place Bernstein and Paisley at the same sex parties beginning as early as 1971. Donald Burton recalls: "Carl Bernstein, when I first met him, was going to the parties about 1971. I didn't know who he was. . . . One day he says to me or my wife Nancy he is on to something big. He said he is working on something and something is going to come out. You know all we knew was here was this guy with long hair and I saw him at two or four of these parties and then he disappeared."[35]

In a more recent interview, Bernstein confirmed that he attended swinging parties, but claimed he did not know Paisley and "Paisley wasn't Deep Throat." "I gotta tell you off the bat, I don't even know who the guy is," Bernstein said.[36]

But the behavior of his reporting partner on the Watergate affair, Bob Woodward, in the aftermath of Paisley's disappearance, raises questions. Woodward, by 1978, was an editor at the *Washington Post*. After Paisley disappeared, Woodward assigned two reporters to investigate Carl Bernstein. When asked if he was aware of the investigation into his activities, Bernstein said, "Oh that's crazy, Jesus . . . I think you got something very wrong there. I don't think there was such a thing." Bernstein said the question should be put to Woodward.

Woodward confirms that he and other *Post* editors authorized the investigation into Bernstein's activities. Woodward explained that two reporters came to him with "allegations about Carl and Paisley and he felt obliged to follow up."[37]

One of the reporters who did the follow-up, Timothy Robinson, enjoyed a reputation for being very careful. He was so concerned about the assignment at the time that he requested a meeting with the reporter from the *Wilmington News-Journal* who first broke the Paisley story to discuss what he said was an assignment Woodward had given him. Robinson was so nervous about meeting the reporter that it was arranged by a mutual source for the meeting to take place in the basement of the Federal Courthouse in Washington where the Watergate trials took place.[38]

"Deep Throat" was described, in Woodward and Bernstein's famed book *All the President's Men,* as Woodward's source in the Executive Branch. The authors say that it was the *Post*'s managing editor at that time, Howard Simmons, who dubbed Woodward's source "Deep Throat" because of the source's desire for secrecy and the pornographic movie in vogue at the time.

Was the fact that Bernstein was attending sex parties with the CIA's liaison with the White House Plumbers just a coincidence, or was that how the source really obtained his name? Both Bernstein and Woodward deny it.

Another bizarre connection of Paisley with the persona of "Deep Throat" is his possession of a *Washington Post* newspaper delivery agent's identification number in his own name. The number and ID turned out to be fraudulent. But why would a spy like Paisley need or even want such identification? If it was not to meet secretly with a reporter, one possibility might be that he simply wanted to have access to the *Washington Post* complex itself, on 15th Street in Washington. The newspaper's loading dock shares a common alley with the Soviet Embassy. Paisley would eventually move to an apartment two blocks from the embassy. Another possibility is that Paisley was using the newspaper's delivery system for dead drops and communication with agents to set up meetings.

Another point made in *All the President's Men* is that "if Deep Throat wanted a meeting—which was rare—there was a different procedure. Each morning, Woodward would check page 20 of his *New York Times,* delivered to his apartment house before 7:00 A.M. If a meeting was requested, the page number would be circled and the hands of a clock indicating the time of the rendezvous would appear in a lower corner of the page. Woodward did not know how Deep Throat got to his paper."

Woodward said flatly that Paisley was not Deep Throat. He then said: "You know, if Deep Throat were someone who was dead, we would name him." The problem is that there is no conclusive evidence that Paisley *is* dead.

What worries counterintelligence officials is not simply the aspect of Paisley meeting Bernstein or even giving him information. The haunting possibility that Paisley may have been working for Soviet intelligence and may have been under instruction to leak embarrassing material about the Nixon administration looms over the entire episode. It is also possible that Paisley may have been attending the parties to collect potentially damaging information on reporters like Bernstein or on other intelligence officials. Was Paisley collecting this information for David Young and the Plumbers—or for the KGB?

Paisley: Mole

❧

What do you think spies are: priests, saints and martyrs? They are a squalid profession of vain fools, traitors too, yes; pansies, sadists and drunkards, people who play cowboys and Indians to brighten their rotten lives.

John Le Carré,
The Spy Who Came in from the Cold

WHILE JOHN PAISLEY worked away at his Alice-in-Wonderland job with the Plumbers, the CIA itself was going through a series of investigations that shook its very foundations. James Jesus Angleton, the Yale-educated son of a National Cash Register executive and a Mexican-born mother, was about to be told that his services were no longer required.

Angleton cultivated an image as the CIA's mysterious chief of counterintelligence. He was no political novice. He would not make inflammatory charges without some clear evidence. A chain of events had forced Angleton to conclude that the Soviets must have penetrated the CIA. But to justify his office conducting an investigation, he had to believe it in his heart.

The CIA's vulnerability was obvious. The KGB and GRU were well run, and Angleton knew that penetration was their number-one assignment. Somewhere in the CIA, and perhaps elsewhere in the U.S. government, at least one mole was digging in, and this unbelievably bright and complicated man wanted him trapped.

Within the CIA, everyone realized how tough Angleton's job was. Hank Knoche recalls Angleton's outlook: "Angleton had a special view of the world . . . colored very much by the responsibilities he had as chief of the CI staff, [a position he had held] for years and years. You almost have to be 100 percent paranoid to do that job. You always have to fear the worst. You always have to assume the worst of your enemies. You always have to assume, without necessarily having the proof in your hands, that your own organization has been penetrated and that there's a mole around somewhere. And it creates this terrible distrustful attitude."

Angleton's power exceeded by far the responsibilities of his job at the CIA. Although he never had more than 120 people working for him, he became a feared and revered legend. CIA employees would point Angleton out in the hallway, only to discover years later that they had pointed to the wrong man. He cast a giant shadow across the entire CIA, and yet few people ever worked with him. His search for the mole was spurred on by the warnings of one defector. Angleton had become almost bewitched by the conspiracies woven by a Soviet defector named Anatolyi Golitsyn.

Golitsyn defected in Helsinki in late 1961. Characterized by those who had to deal with him as arrogant, nasty, and loaded with details of KGB operations around the world, Golitsyn was the only defector Angleton ever trusted. "With the single exception of Golitsyn, Angleton was inclined to assume that any defector or operational asset in place was controlled by the KGB," said Clare Edward Petty, who worked for Angleton.[1] But Angleton was so infatuated with this man that he lowered his carefully constructed guard, which had, in the past, always prevented him and his counterintelligence staff from being captivated by defectors.

Before and after Golitsyn, other defectors did not fare as well as he did. Michal Goleniewski—code name SNIPER—the highest-ranking Polish agent ever to defect to the West, had so worn out his welcome by the early 1970s that no one from the CIA even remained in touch with him. According to Petty, Angleton considered Goleniewski a provocation, a Soviet agent sent to the West with carefully prepared false information. He was not to be trusted. But from the time he defected in West Berlin in 1960 with his mistress, his information proved to be reliable. He had warned the West of a Soviet mole—a "midlevel agent," and his warnings were ignored. The mole was the infamous British agent George Blake, who turned out to have been working for the KGB.

In 1970 the British contacted Petty and told him that they needed to speak to Goleniewski about an investigation they were conducting into the loyalty of Sir Michael Hanley, a senior official in MI5. Petty explained that the CIA had broken off its relationship with Goleniewski, but the FBI in New York kept in contact with him. Months later the British called Petty to tell him how extraordinarily helpful Goleniewski had been. Then they dropped a bombshell. As an aside to Goleniewski's devastating accusations about Hanley, he charged that Nixon's National Security Adviser—Henry Kissinger—was a Soviet agent. Petty was told by the British that Goleniewski had an office mate who had previously run operations for the Soviets in East Germany during the last few years of World War II and after the war. This agent handler had run some very sensitive cases, and he had a safe. When the agent handler died, Goleniewski was commissioned by the UB (Polish intelligence) to open up his safe and read the contents and inventory them. It was during this inventory that Goleniewski ran across a case of two Soviet agents run by his deceased colleague. According to Petty, Goleniewski said both of them had cryptonyms, exact information as to when they had been recruited, and a case file of what they had done. Goleniewski identified one as Henry Kissinger. He said that Kissinger had been returned to the United States and had been contacted subsequent to his return to continue his work for the Soviets in the United States.

Goleniewski knew that Kissinger had been put to work on a CIA project at Harvard. Petty and his colleagues were reasonably certain that Goleniewski could have come up with most of his information from open sources, but not the part about Kissinger's CIA connections. That had been secret. In 1971, Angleton's staff reluctantly began an investigation of Kissinger. They had no choice, according to Petty: "Despite the fact that Goleniewski had been widely discredited as being mentally deranged or perhaps a Soviet agent, the specificity of his lead was comparable to that [which was] characteristic of his best work, and could in no way be ignored," Petty said.

The CI division began using all its sources to pull together a dossier on the flamboyant and egotistical National Security Adviser. In the opinion of the counterintelligence officials at the CIA, Kissinger treated them as bothersome meddlers when they requested that he follow normal security precautions in dealing with the Soviets.

Petty gave Angleton a memo on the charges. But instead of notifying the FBI and ordering an investigation, Angleton, according to Petty, "sat on it." Although the British had vouched for Goleniewski, some at the CIA thought the defector was mentally unstable, and that his insistence that he was related to the Tsar was symptomatic. Angleton told the British, through one of MI5's assistant directors, Peter Wright, that he and CIA Director Richard Helms were convinced Goleniewski was not a genuine defector.[2]

When alerted to the possibility of a domestic espionage case, the CIA is supposed to notify the FBI. Petty, believing that Angleton followed correct procedure, repeated the Goleniewski charges to a friend at the FBI whom he thought was already aware of the accusations. "At that point the Bureau came back with a real hot rocket at Angleton, and Angleton was furious at me for having mentioned it," Petty said.

Petty was surprised by Angleton's anger, since he knew that Kissinger's insistence on meeting with high-level Soviet officials, alone and one-on-one, upset Angleton. In a 1977 interview, Angleton made clear his opinion of Kissinger: "He refused CIA debriefings. He was really arrogant. We were worried that he would inadvertently say something. At first I thought it was arrogance. Later I began to suspect the worst."[3]

No follow-up investigation of Kissinger was done. Angleton discredited the Goleniewski report with the FBI. No one seemed willing to order an investigation into the President's National Security Adviser at a time when Kissinger seemed to be gaining Nixon's total confidence, at a time of delicate arms control negotiations with the Soviets, and at a time when this country was relying on flawed methodology to calculate the Soviets' strengths and weaknesses. While the United States' national security was lying on the operating table, it was the opinion of some informed observers that the surgeon was committing malpractice, but no one would stop the operation.

Leonard V. McCoy, who would eventually become the deputy to Angleton's successor and who himself ended up looking at Kissinger several years later, felt that Angleton was "more than obliged to look at the Kissinger charges."

But to Angleton, who spent years searching for moles in the CIA, Kissinger was just one of many who had been accused. In 1962, Anatolyi Golitsyn told James Angleton's staff that a Soviet penetration agent had done tremendous damage in Western Europe. He said this man was responsible for ruined operations and the death and imprisonment of several dozen Western agents. His code name was SASHA.

James Angleton's faith in Golitsyn's information was unshakable, regardless of how farfetched it seemed. For Angleton, the search for moles became the search for the Soviet agent in the CIA, SASHA. If SASHA was still alive and could be found, then the search would be over. Angleton was convinced that whoever worked with SASHA, whoever gave SASHA his jobs and provided him opportunities, was probably also working for the KGB.

In conjunction with top counterintelligence men such as William Lander, William Branigan, and Sam Papich, as well as CIA Office of Security investigator Bruce Solie, Angleton's team began their efforts carefully and methodically to zero in on SASHA. By the end of 1963 they had dismissed three potential SASHAS. By early 1964 they became convinced that SASHA was Igor Orlov, an agent who had worked in Munich and at Berlin Base in the 1950s.

For the young CIA, Berlin Base was the center of the espionage universe. It was a place where great careers were made and broken. "If you wanted to be a general, you had to be in the 82nd Airborne, and if you wanted to go to the top in the CIA, you had better have done some time at Berlin Base," Lt. Gen. Samuel V. Wilson said of the station. At its height, as many as a hundred CIA operatives worked at the base. It was run by William King Harvey, probably the most legendary figure in the CIA.

Berlin Base, in the 1950s, was where reputations were made, marriages were ruined, and the most bizarre of the CIA's old-boy networks was created. If you served at Berlin Base, you possessed the prerequisite background to do great things in the CIA. Unfortunately, for all the lore and history surrounding Berlin Base, most experts in counterintelligence believe it was a place that was thoroughly penetrated.

In 1925, Igor Orlov was born under a different name in Kiev. His father was a Red Army officer who served with distinction in the civil war and World War II. Orlov was a small but handsome man with piercing blue eyes and elegant European manners. He was a lady-killer. By the age of twenty, Orlov was an intelligence officer in the Russian Army. During World War II he parachuted into Germany as a Soviet NKVD agent. Terribly wounded in a jump in 1944, he remained at liberty in Germany by passing himself off as a Polish POW named Alexander Kopaskie. This kept him from being returned to the Soviet Union. He went to work in Germany with anti-Soviet emigré groups.

After the war, Igor Orlov was recruited to work as a contract employee for the CIA at Berlin Base. His bosses included men like Base Chief Bill Harvey, David E. Murphy, Theodore Shackley, Carl Nelson, Gus Hathaway, George Weisz, Paul Garbler, Richard Kovich, Hugh Montgomery, and Samuel Wilson. All in all, Orlov had at least a dozen handlers.[4] He also worked with David Murphy in Munich.

According to his German-born widow, Eleonore, Orlov was a very special kind of agent runner for the CIA. He would, using his own good looks and CIA funds, recruit the most attractive women in Munich and Berlin to entrap Soviet officers in the East, and then recruit them. He was running as many as fifty of these female agents at a time. In the late 1950s a number of the Soviets he recruited as agents ended up "blown" or exposed. The Soviets arrested them.[5]

In 1956 Orlov was transferred to Frankfurt, where he shared an office and a safe with Nicholas Kozlov, a more senior Soviet defector who had already lived in the United States. Both men were supervised by a former American Army officer named Lt. Col. Alexander Sogolov. Ironically, Sogolov, like Orlov, was nicknamed Sasha.

In 1959, Orlov left Frankfurt to go on a three-week mission to the International Youth Festival in Vienna, to meet several of his Soviet agents. When he returned, he opened the office safe that he shared with Kozlov and noticed that four pieces of mica he had placed in his compartments in the safe to enable him to detect tampering were gone. He found them on the floor.

Inside the safe were the names of more than three dozen agents whom Orlov was currently operating, as well as details of a score of other operations. Orlov asked Sogolov, his CIA boss, if he should file a report that reflected his opinion that Nicholas Kozlov had broken into the safe. But his boss, who frequently socialized with Kozlov, told him that would not be necessary.

Orlov kept in his safe a postcard that his maid had intercepted and given him; it had been sent to his wife by a man he'd never heard of. He thought his wife was having an affair, and he was insanely jealous. Orlov had actually held a gun to her head on several occasions, demanding that she reveal nonexistent liaisons with other men. Whoever broke into the safe gave Orlov's CIA handlers the postcard.

The postcard mentioned an earlier meeting and thanked Mrs. Orlov for a bottle of gin and some American cigarettes. Mrs. Orlov was accused of dealing in the black market. The CIA put her through a series of lie-detector tests and interrogations that lasted for almost a year. She lost her job as a translator for the CIA. In the end they could only prove that she had once traded a bottle of gin and American cigarettes for tickets to the opera.

Orlov was convinced that it was Kozlov who had broken into his safe and deliberately given the postcard to the CIA. He was so angry at his boss that he made him walk up the six floors to the apartment he and his wife shared, and apologize to her.[6] This did nothing for Igor's career. Compounding his anger toward Kozlov was his frustration at how much more money Kozlov appeared to have than he did. He concluded that Kozlov was padding overtime reports. He also became convinced that Kozlov was cheating on expenses. As proof, Orlov said he found that Kozlov, instead of giving his agents expensive Minox cameras, gave them cheap ones, but charged the CIA for the more expensive equipment and pocketed the difference.

Orlov, a meticulous agent, gathered evidence against Kozlov and presented it to their mutual boss, who refused to report it to his superiors. Instead, Sogolov told Orlov that the CIA had a new job for him in America, and that citizenship awaited Orlov's family. It was all a lie. As soon as the Orlov family set sail for their new lives in America, Sogolov reported that Orlov was a security risk and was responsible for several blown operations. He reported that Orlov was probably a KGB staff officer.

The Orlovs arrived in Washington, D.C., with very little money on January 15, 1961—President Kennedy's inauguration day. But when Orlov called his CIA contacts to find out about his new job, he was told there was no work for him. He called his friend from Berlin Base, Sam Wilson, who was then a colonel at the Pentagon. In the 1950s in Germany, Wilson had become very close to the Orlovs. He had even helped them come to the United States in 1957 so that Eleonore could give birth to her second son, George, there. Ironically, Wilson had also befriended Nicholas Kozlov and helped him settle in the United States as well. But this time Wilson would not take Orlov's calls.

The CIA offered Orlov a Berlitz course in English and a $2,500 settlement for all the years he had served the CIA, doing very dangerous work. He told them to go to hell. With George and Robert, their beloved sons, Igor and Eleonore lived hand to mouth, trying to make their way in a new and strange country. Orlov finally got a job as a *Washington Post* truckdriver, five hours a night, for sixty dollars a week. The family saved until they could afford to open a small picture-framing shop.

In 1962, when James Angleton was told by Golitsyn, the only defector he truly trusted, that a KGB plant had worked his way into Berlin Base and Munich in the 1950s, it raised a host of red flags in the CI chief's extraordinarily complex mind. Angleton's staff obtained all the files of contract agents in postwar Germany and turned them over to Bruce Solie, the trusted, high-level Office of Security official, who went through them. As a security man, Solie had an unusual reputation for giving people the benefit of the doubt. But when he learned that Igor Orlov's nickname was Sasha, and that his agents had been blown, the race was on.[7] Igor Orlov had worked with some of the future luminaries of the CIA at Berlin Base, and no one would be spared.

Angleton's choice for the mole in the CIA boiled down to three men. The most prominent of the three was David Murphy. Murphy, who began his career in the 1950s at Berlin Base, had been one of the CIA's golden boys. Murphy became head of the operation there in 1959, when Bill Harvey returned to the United States to mastermind the elimination of Fidel Castro.

On the surface, Murphy seemed the unlikeliest candidate for a Soviet agent. His ham-fisted attempts at recruiting Soviets caused the CIA public embarrassment from Tokyo to Vienna. He had made the local press in those countries by getting into brawls with the Soviets during two recruitment attempts. Leonard McCoy, a Soviet Division colleague of Murphy's, called him "accident-prone." But largely because of his Berlin Base background, Murphy's career prospered until Anatolyi Golitsyn told Angleton there was a Russian national who was a KGB agent working for Murphy in Munich and with others in Berlin Base. Angleton began to draw some conclusions. In the mid-1960s, Angleton used Murphy's ties to Igor Orlov to charge that Murphy, then head of the CIA's Soviet Division, was a mole.

According to former Angleton staffer Clare Petty, "there is every reason to believe Orlov was a Soviet agent." Petty recalls that Orlov was in fact a staff officer of the KGB. Petty said that in his search for the mole, Angleton concentrated mainly on agents Orlov was running for Murphy from Munich.[8]

Angleton made friends where he needed them. One friend he made was Sam Wilson. Of the dozen who worked with Orlov, the top U.S. Army man at Berlin Base, Sam Wilson, was the most important. Wilson worked with Orlov during the time of the National Labor Union, a Soviet emigré group that wanted to overthrow the Soviet communist regime. Like most of the others at Berlin Base, Wilson's career took off in the ensuing years. Angleton put together an exhaustive dossier on Igor Orlov. Then he let Wilson know through an intermediary that he had something vital to show him. At the time, Wilson was in Hollywood, where a film was being made about his World War II exploits. On his return, Wilson became an aide in Defense Secretary Robert McNamara's office. He remembers the day Igor Orlov's file arrived in his office: "The guy comes all the way from Langley down to the Pentagon, up to the suite of McNamara and [Roswell] Gilpatric. I threw whoever was in my office out and sat down and spent two hours going through the file. My hair was kind of going up on end, seeing this guy was a rat fink all the time." Instead of taking it as a warning, Wilson was grateful to Angleton for the favor: "He called me and told me. . . . It made me sad because I could see where things had gone wrong. . . . I am an optimist, even though I tend to have this suspicious streak. I tend to figure, 'Well, we can make this thing work if only we'll go a little further this way.' "[9]

Angleton was either taking Wilson into his confidence or giving him what former CIA official Robert Crowley calls a "barium meal" to see where Wilson went with the material and where it ended up.[10] Wilson could have been Angleton's mole as easily as Murphy or any one of the Orlov handlers. After all, it was Wilson who had befriended Orlov.

Yet, instead of accusing him, instead of destroying Wilson's career as he had destroyed Murphy's, Angleton shared his secret with Wilson. There is no evidence that any investigation was ever done of Wilson. In fact, just the opposite is true. For the next decade, Wilson moved with ease in and out of the CIA to higher and higher positions.

Why was the finger pointed at Murphy? Wilson says he does not know, but can only speculate: "Orlov was in West Berlin, Murphy was in West Berlin. I wasn't with him [Orlov] all the time. So during my time there I never knew of any contact between the two of them. Murphy, of course, was totally aware of my association with [Orlov], was aware of a couple of things that had blown—that I was trying to work with Igor Orlov."

The FBI was given the information on Orlov. They tracked him to the Old Town section of Alexandria, Virginia, within a few miles of both CIA and FBI headquarters. Angleton constantly pressed the Bureau to watch Orlov's picture-framing store and home to see if any CIA people under suspicion or Soviets visited the small shop. But a number of things made little sense to the FBI probe into Orlov. One was why the CIA was not looking at another Soviet defector who had served in Frankfurt with Orlov—Nicholas Kozlov.

There was clear evidence that agents had been "rolled up" [arrested or killed] in Berlin long after Igor Orlov was gone. Orlov had been transferred from Berlin to Frankfurt in October 1956. According to George Kisevalter, who worked at Berlin Base, more than twenty-six agents were "rolled up" by the Soviets between 1956 and 1959, after Orlov was gone. Kisevalter says the person responsible for that was a Berlin police official on the CIA payroll.[11]

It was a classic intelligence disaster. Kisevalter insists that Igor Orlov had nothing to do with the debacle. The incident, Kisevalter said, "shows how sloppy some of these recruitments were." Eventually the agent admitted that his office mate had full knowledge of what he was doing for the CIA. The office mate confessed, clearing Orlov in the incident.[12]

Despite the confession, Angleton continued to believe Golitsyn's version of events—that SASHA was the important Soviet agent operating at Berlin Base. In March 1965, Angleton's probe culminated in a raid on the Orlovs' house and shop by the FBI. For almost two months, Igor Orlov was brought down to the Washington Field Office of the FBI, in the Old Post Office Tower in downtown Washington, where he underwent continuous interrogation. Here, agents from the Soviet Section threatened "problems" for his mother, who was widowed and, he was told, living in Moscow. He had not been in touch with her since 1944 and was not even sure she was alive. Finally, Orlov broke down and panicked. The next afternoon, while at work loading his newspaper truck, he acted out of desperation—or so he told the FBI.

The *Washington Post* is across an alley from the rear of the old Soviet Embassy. Orlov saw a Russian official directing trash removal through a rear door. He quickly ran over to the man from the loading dock at the paper and began speaking to him in Russian. Orlov told him he needed help. The man invited him in. Orlov was taken into a small reception room with a large mirror on the wall. It was obvious to him he was being photographed through the glass. Orlov detailed his fears that his mother in the Soviet Union might be harmed and his problems with the FBI. Igor told the Soviets that his father was a hero of the Great Patriotic War, as was he. He said if he was arrested by the FBI, his wife and sons would have no one to take care of them. The Soviets offered the family asylum. Orlov made arrangements for the family to be picked up by the Russians the next afternoon.

The embassy official gave him an address to write to, and sent him on his way out the front of the embassy. Relieved, Orlov went home and told his wife of the arrangements he had made for her protection. When Eleonore protested, her husband told her, "How will you eat? You must do this for the boys." The next day she dropped Orlov off at the Old Post Office, where the FBI harshly interrogated him about his visit the previous day to the Soviet Embassy. An FBI surveillance team had watched him enter the building. After hours of merciless questioning, it became clear to FBI agent Courtland Jones and others in Soviet counterintelligence that it could not be proven that Orlov was a Soviet agent. But what finally convinced the FBI was a phone call from the Soviet Ambassador, asking the State Department if the United States had sent Orlov to the embassy as a provocation.

Mrs. Orlov picked up the boys from the Lutheran school they attended in Alexandria, but instead of taking them to meet the Russian, she took them home. To her great relief, her husband was released that sunny spring afternoon by the FBI. They told him he had been cleared.

But Angleton remained fixated on Orlov because of Golitsyn's warning as well as other information. He refused to allow the Bureau to close out the investigation into Orlov. It never dawned on Angleton to investigate Orlov's adversary Nicholas Kozlov, who could easily have been aware of Orlov's nickname—Sasha. By 1966, Nicholas Kozlov was entrenched in American intelligence, working for the Defense Intelligence Agency (DIA) in the Old Post Office Building, translating documents and advising on Soviet military strategy. He was the first Soviet ever to be given a security clearance in his work for the CIA.

Angleton pressed the FBI to pursue the Orlov case, even though the

Bureau considered the matter closed. They continued surveillance because Angleton was considered too powerful to buck. As a way of making amends for what they considered an extreme injustice to Orlov, Courtland Jones, Joseph Purvis, and a Who's Who in the FBI routinely had their pictures framed at Orlov's gallery. By the mid-1960s, much of Orlov's business came from the agents in the FBI's Washington Field Office.

By 1966, Angleton's mole hunt had built up a full head of steam. Adm. William F. Raborn, the Director of Central Intelligence, and his deputy Richard Helms gave Angleton a free hand. Angleton decided to set up a small unit for the express purpose of the mole hunt. Clare Edward Petty was selected to conduct the search. When he was recruited by Angleton into the Counterintelligence Division, Petty had just exposed several major KGB penetrations into the BND, the West German intelligence service. What he did for Angleton and the CIA between 1966 and June 1974 forever changed the course of CIA history.

Petty was a practical man who was as absorbed as Angleton in the work of CI staff. Almost immediately, Angleton designated Petty, along with three other CI staffers, to find out if there was a mole in the CIA and to discover who it was. Petty accepted the task knowing full well that it was one of those jobs that was very important to the CIA, but could be fatal to a career. It was unpleasant work. Petty knew that if his search was successful, his career would be over.

Petty and his small unit, never more than four people, conducted their main investigation with startling tenacity. The search for the mole began with a look at all the failed CIA cases, such as the Alger Hiss and Elizabeth Bently cases. Petty's team had access to the VENONA radio code decrypts. VENONA exposed massive Soviet espionage against the West back in a period when Moscow was supposed to be a friend. But the unit's most important resource of all was the defector case files. No one had ever taken the time to see what inconsistencies existed between the defectors' stories. Nobody had spent the years needed to weigh every defector's word. Petty examined the files of all defectors and sources. It was an immense task. Golitsyn's files alone filled a small secure room.

Petty worked in a netherworld. Seventy percent of the CI staff had never seen Angleton. Petty would get his specific instructions from Newton "Scotty" Miler, William Hood, Jean Evans, or James Ramsey Hunt, Angleton's top deputies. Over the years, Angleton, who traveled extensively, controlled Petty's operation by remote control. Petty would hear from the CI chief through Miler and Evans.

On rare occasions, Petty was allowed to see the master counterspy.

Petty's office looked out through a window across the second floor of the CIA headquarters building to Angleton's sanctum. If the shades were drawn in a certain way, Petty knew Angleton was in. He would walk across the hall to Angleton's secretary's office. Bertha, a woman whom some thought far too bright to be a secretary, would let Angleton know a subordinate was waiting. Adjoining her office was a vault to which only she and Angleton had access. That was where he kept the files that interested him most.

Angleton, not the DCI or anyone else in the CIA, would get a copy of every cable from every station in every classification. CI had its own set of ciphers because Angleton considered the CIA's communications compromised.

Angleton would barely acknowledge Petty's presence. Petty remembers it was always the same: "Angleton actually had direct contact with very few members of the CI staff. For those who had occasion to meet him on a one-on-one basis, whether at the insistence of the officer or Angleton, a visit could be a disconcerting experience. Normally, Angleton would be immersed behind a stack of cables reading a file of some sort. Or he could be engaged painstakingly in writing something in his most unusual minuscule hand. He might not acknowledge the presence of a visitor for some time, so that one began to wonder whether a quiet withdrawal was in order. Eventually, however, he would begin a conversation. He would often raise subjects which seemed to have no relationship at all to the matter at hand, and ramble on sometimes for an hour or two, sharing information which, on accession, the officer in question had no need to know." [13]

Petty found that Angleton, for all their differences in personality, had an incisive mind, and that he cared passionately about the CIA: "Aside from his various idiosyncrasies, Angleton undoubtedly understood counterintelligence better than any man alive. He understood thoroughly that counterintelligence rested upon institutional continuity of the CI staff, and on breadth of insight. He knew that an individual operating division could not possibly see the entire picture, and lived in an illusory counterintelligence world."

But Angleton's knowledge posed a threat, according to Petty: "The difficulty with this was, of course, that such continuity and centralization was in itself highly dangerous. It was no accident that counterintelligence organizations were high on the KGB target list."

As Petty went about his work, Golitsyn talked Angleton into showing him the personnel files of suspected CIA employees. Angleton actually showed the Soviet defector the backgrounds of CIA employees who spoke Russian, had Soviet relatives, had served in stations where others were suspected. It was an unheard-of breach of Agency security. Angleton even tried to persuade the FBI to do the same, but the Bureau refused. Angleton scared people. More important to the new leadership of the CIA, however, he tied the Agency up in knots. By 1973, to men like William Colby, Angleton's caution was paralyzing the Agency. He prevented the CIA from recruiting Soviet agents because they might end up being provocations or triples instead of sincere double agents. "Everything stood still. We had become an intelligence service that wasn't collecting any intelligence," Colby says.[14]

As Petty combed the defector files, he began to find disturbing things. The files of Peter Deriabin, a defector whose information led to the unmasking of two KGB penetrations of the West German service, the infamous PETER and PAUL, were especially revealing. When Deriabin defected to the Soviet Bloc Division, he made a list of the KGB officers in the Vienna Station in 1953. Number three on that list was Anatolyi Golitsyn, still eight years from defecting himself. He was working in Vienna under his own name. When Moscow Center learned of Deriabin's defection, Golitsyn and others at the Vienna Station were immediately recalled to Moscow, since they had been· exposed or "blown." The contents of the Deriabin debriefing reports were held on a need-to-know basis in the CIA. Only certain people in the Soviet Bloc Division and Angleton himself had access to the materials.

Petty, in sifting through the thousands of pages of transcripts of Golitsyn's debriefings, began to notice some inconsistencies in his story. It took Petty years to piece together the story, but when he did, the implications of what he found were shocking.

Golitsyn told the CIA that he had been accepted as a bright young KGB counterintelligence officer from the beginning. He claimed to have written a paper that actually reached Stalin, which concluded that the British intelligence system was on the wane and that the new and stronger enemy was the CIA. He bragged that this argument impressed the KGB's management, and that he was slated to come to Washington to head the KGB's section on CI penetration when Stalin died.

After Stalin's death, Golitsyn's duties changed. He became involved in the post-Beria purges. He was then assigned to operate Jewish KGB officers. The KGB made a major operation out of penetrating the Jewish community in Moscow as well as Israeli intelligence (the Mossad), and the Israeli Army. He explained that after the purges and his work with Jewish officers, he was scheduled to be reassigned to Vienna in the spring of 1958 under his own name. But then Petty found something very strange in Golitsyn's story. Golitsyn said that his assignment to Vienna was canceled because the KGB had actually acquired a copy of Deriabin's debriefing report that named Golitsyn as number three in the Vienna Station.

For Petty, the information that had been sitting in Golitsyn's files for more than thirteen years was startling. It meant that there was a major leak in either CI or the Soviet Division. In cardboard boxes in the Polish Branch offices, Petty then uncovered another major clue in his search. In those neglected boxes were the files of the United States' most important Polish defector, and probably the most important Eastern Bloc counterintelligence defector in history.

In March 1959, letters began arriving at the U.S. Embassy in Bern, Switzerland, that contained valuable intelligence information. The letters were signed by an agent code-named SNIPER. The letters contained some garbled information about KGB activities in Poland and England. Using a newspaper advertisement in a Frankfurt daily to acknowledge receipt of the letters, the CIA began a relationship with SNIPER that lasted for eighteen months. SNIPER turned out to be Michal Goleniewski, the Polish liaison between the KGB and Polish intelligence. Goleniewski was Angleton's old nemesis. Among the information Goleniewski was providing was how important Golitsyn was in the KGB.

According to Petty's report, it was SNIPER's bruised feelings about perceived mistreatment and lack of interest from the KGB that had caused him to write the letters originally. But once he had gotten the United States to bite, the KGB took a renewed interest in him. Because much of what he had sent to the West was garbled, the CIA asked him for corrected material and he began producing it. Petty says it was obvious the KGB was onto him. "They were using him for aggressive CI." Without his knowledge, the KGB was feeding SNIPER the material the CIA wanted.

But how did they get onto Goleniewski?

Only the Polish Branch of the Soviet Bloc Division of the CIA was made aware of SNIPER's letters. That meant that only four people had access to the SNIPER operation.

The answer to Petty's question came in the form of a blown operation. At the same time as the SNIPER operation, Pete Bagley was about to approach an employee of the UB—the Polish intelligence service. Bagley used a cover story; he claimed to be with the BND—West German intelligence. Bagley was going to try to recruit the Polish intelligence officer for the West. Using the most secure communications channel, a copy of Bagley's approach was sent to Angleton by the Eastern European Division. Two weeks prior to Bagley's meeting, a letter arrived at Polish intelligence headquarters from the KGB warning that the West Germans would approach a Polish UB man, and that they should take protective action. Bagley made the approach, and his contact turned him down.

Within a few weeks the Polish service suspended Goleniewski's travel privileges. But he said that what finally caused him to defect in 1960 in West Berlin was that he—as the KGB liaison—got a letter from the Russians saying, "There is a pig in your service, we want you to help us find him." Years later Petty would conclude that the Soviets had been fully onto SNIPER, but that they no longer had an interest in supporting the operation. Someone in the CIA was telling the Russians all they needed to know to wreck and manipulate CIA operations against Polish intelligence.

But if the Russians knew about SNIPER, why did they let him go? Petty wrote in his report to Angleton that they probably thought Goleniewski's defection would increase the validity of the information they had planted in SNIPER's letters—including the importance of Golitsyn. As Petty sifted through the Goleniewski material, he discovered that SNIPER's knowledge about many cases proved to be wrong. Petty concluded that much of his information had been fed to him by the KGB. This meant that Goleniewski's vouching for Golitsyn's story could have been done, unwittingly, under KGB direction.

Golitsyn defected a year after SNIPER. Golitsyn's last assignment at the KGB in Moscow Center had been to review NATO documents. It was the perfect place to give a "sent agent" an excuse to have a wide variety of intelligence information with which to tempt the West. Just before his defection, Golitsyn was sent to Helsinki, this time not under his real name. He used the name Klimov. He had been assigned to Helsinki with his wife and daughter. That action alone should have raised eyebrows in the Western services. It was hardly standard operating procedure for Moscow Center to allow families to go with agents in the field. In what turned out to be his audacious style, Golitsyn told the skeptical station chief in Finland, upon his defection, that "I have to be legitimate, otherwise they would have never let me out with my wife and daughter."

For Petty, the Golitsyn file began to read like a nightmare. The CIA's Soviet Bloc Division was supposed to handle his interrogation, but he was so difficult to deal with and so obnoxious that CIA management finally gave in to his request that he deal only with the CI Division and Angleton himself. This was contrary to all normal practice. Petty concluded that Golitsyn was a "sent agent" whose primary mission was to disrupt the Western services with disinformation. Petty realized that the disruption of the CIA was accomplished when Golitsyn dangled allegations of penetrations in front of Angleton.

Angleton's deputies—Jean Evans, Newton "Scotty" Miler, and William Hood—had begun a search in the Western services for a series of penetrations based on the vague information that Golitsyn had sold to Angleton. They became known as "the Golitsyn serials." Petty discovered that the scope of the investigations turned up some penetrations—but not the ones Golitsyn had pointed out. "He had thrown the Western services in an uproar and he had influenced the heart of our own service," Petty said in his report of Golitsyn's activities.

Golitsyn warned Angleton that the Russians would send a series of false defectors to try to discredit him. From Petty's point of view, if Golitsyn was successful in convincing Angleton of this, no future defectors would be accepted, whether they were legitimate or not. It was a strategy that worked.

After Golitsyn successfully damaged the CIA's relationship with other Western intelligence services and then discredited all future Soviet defectors, he started stirring up trouble between the FBI and the CIA. The FBI, still smarting from bad publicity over their handling of the Kennedy assassination, was desperate for intelligence on Lee Harvey Oswald's relations with the KGB while living in Russia. Hoover wanted the question answered once and for all: Did Oswald kill Kennedy for the KGB?

In June 1962, Yuri Nosenko, the dissolute son of the Soviet Union's former Minister of Shipbuilding, made contact with Pete Bagley for the first time.[15] Bagley was at the Nuclear Test Ban Treaty talks in Geneva. Nosenko told Bagley that he would like to work for the United States, but could never consider defecting as long as his wife and children were in Moscow. Nosenko gave Bagley valuable information in exchange for a small payment. Bagley was thrilled at what he thought was a great recruitment.

In reality, Nosenko was one of the Russian ruling elite's golden children. To escape war service, he had shot himself in the foot while at the Soviet Naval Academy, Frunze. He had succeeded more at womanizing and drinking than at his career in the KGB. His mother, whose husband's remains were ensconced in the Kremlin Wall in 1956, had to intervene on behalf of her son with other powerful wives to keep him from getting booted out of the KGB.

According to Petty, Nosenko soon paled in Bagley's eyes. Bagley was one of the few in the Soviet Bloc Division with a keen interest in CI, and since Angleton was the patron saint of CI in the Agency, Bagley came to worship Angleton professionally. When he returned from Geneva, according to Leonard McCoy, then a top reports officer in the Soviet Division, Bagley was ushered into Angleton's office.

What Petty discovered was that in a single weekend, Angleton had turned Bagley around by taking him into the inner sanctum of CI and showing him Golitsyn's predictions that agents would be sent to discredit him. "Golitsyn had predicted that a person such as Nosenko would arrive with the KGB mission of discrediting Golitsyn. Given that Nosenko was handled as a dispatched agent, the true effect was to consolidate the position of Golitsyn. On the question of whether Nosenko was in fact dispatched, all the lengthy analyses overlooked the point that, given convincing evidence of the presence of a well-placed mole, it is certain that a 'genuine' Nosenko, having returned to Moscow in 1962, would have never again been allowed to leave."

In December 1963, Bagley wrote a memo that Petty concluded was "one of the most bizarre pieces of paper I have ever seen." The memo said that the CIA had to look for the return of Nosenko as a "dispatched agent." The standard rule was that if you suspected someone was dispatched, you simply did not take him. This memo made Bagley look like a genius when Nosenko sent an emergency message in January 1964, just two months after the Kennedy assassination, that he was ready to come out.

Bagley, who spoke good German but only limited Russian, was accompanied to Geneva to debrief Nosenko by George Kisevalter, whose Russian was excellent. Kisevalter spoke Russian like the native he was. What was more, Kisevalter had been the CIA's premier case officer for a generation. But nothing prepared either man for the message they were about to receive from Nosenko.

On the afternoon of January 23, 1964, Yuri Nosenko arrived at a suburban Geneva apartment that the CIA used as a safe house. After discussing several minor operations, Nosenko got to the point. In Russian, he told Bagley and Kisevalter that he had been Lee Harvey Oswald's case officer when Oswald defected to the Soviet Union in 1959. Bagley was stunned. He turned to Kisevalter for verification of his understanding of what Nosenko had just said. Nosenko told the two CIA men he could give a complete accounting of Oswald's activities in the Soviet Union.

The Kennedy assassination wound was still wide open in the United States. Mourning was turning into widespread speculation that Oswald had not acted alone. The CIA and FBI could not account for Oswald's time in the Soviet Union. Now they were being given this gift?

Nosenko told Kisevalter and Bagley that it was time for him to come out. CIA headquarters told them to keep him in place, where he would be more valuable. But Nosenko told Bagley and Kisevalter that he was being recalled to Moscow and was fearful the Soviets had discovered that he had gone to work for U.S. intelligence. DCI Richard Helms had no choice. He approved preparations for the defection of Nosenko.

In the beginning, many agents were given access to Nosenko, including James Wooten and Elbert "Bert" Turner from the FBI, who wanted to know about Nosenko's claims that he was Lee Harvey Oswald's KGB case officer. Nosenko claimed that the KGB decided *not* to recruit Oswald because he was too unstable. Hoover had gotten similar information from FEDORA, Hoover's highly trusted source working for the KGB under United Nations cover. Hoover had refused to let the CIA check FEDORA's bona fides. Golitsyn claimed that both Bureau sources code-named FEDORA and TOP HAT were fakes. To aggravate Angleton and the CIA further, Hoover sent unverified FEDORA information directly to President Johnson about the assassination.

Without waiting for Nosenko's vetting, Hoover gave the Warren Commission Nosenko's version of Oswald's life in the Soviet Union. The CIA was furious. Bagley, convinced by Angleton and Golitsyn that Nosenko's recruitment was phony, concluded that Nosenko had been sent by the KGB. The CIA cut off the FBI's access to Nosenko. Nosenko was put in a specially built concrete blockhouse cell in the woods at Camp Peary, the CIA training base near Portsmouth, Virginia. A remarkable interrogation ensued. Camp Peary, nicknamed "Camp Wet-the-Bed," is normally reserved for basic training of CIA agents.

As Petty reviewed the history of the Nosenko case, all the signs pointed to Pete Bagley being the mole. "Pete was a good friend. But in the end you eliminate the possibilities," Petty recalled.

Petty took his report to James Ramsey Hunt, Angleton's number-two man, but hardly an expert on CI. Hunt read it and said to Petty that it was the best solution he had seen. But this was where Angleton's system broke down, because of the way he ran his office. Instead of getting Petty's entire report, Angleton was given a memo summarizing it by Hunt. The report went into Angleton's office, where it sat for several weeks.

Petty could not wait any longer for Angleton's reaction to his report. He had worked for years accumulating the material, and now wanted some recognition for his efforts. Curious, Petty went to see Angleton. They talked mostly about Nosenko. After several hours, Angleton finally turned around in his chair and, looking straight down at Petty, said, "Pete is not a Soviet agent."

Petty was stunned. "He had dismissed four years of work with that sentence. I spent two or three weeks just thinking about it. I asked myself, 'Where do I go from here?' Then I decided to flip the case over and not look at Nosenko but . . . directly at Golitsyn." So Petty went back through the Golitsyn material. He shut himself off in the file room, "reliving Golitsyn for months."

In the world of duplicity, Petty began to wonder about James Jesus Angleton's loyalty.[16] As Petty looked at Golitsyn again, he began to realize the magnitude of the disaster. Angleton had opened up agency personnel and case files to Golitsyn. He had even gone to the FBI and asked them to open up their files to Golitsyn. Perhaps most remarkably, Angleton had thrown the cardinal rule of defectors out the door. He had put three key Soviet defectors—Golitsyn, Peter Deriabin, and Nicholas Shadrin—together. Although Deriabin and Golitsyn met first by accident going into a Vienna, Virginia, barbershop, Golitsyn and Shadrin were brought together by the CIA and allowed to develop a very close friendship. The barriers between defectors and the secure information to which a sent agent needed access were virtually dismantled for Golitsyn by Angleton. The chaos that had overtaken the Western services through the accusations of STONE/Golitsyn were now spreading.

In late 1962, according to Petty's report, Golitsyn had gone to see Angleton's deputy, Raymond Rocca, and told him that he wanted the CIA to arrange to get him a job with British intelligence. Golitsyn had spoken to MI5 spycatcher Arthur Martin about Kim Philby, who was already under suspicion in London. He told Rocca that he had to be in England by January 25, 1963. Angleton made the arrangements. Golitsyn went to England and stayed with Martin. What shocked Petty was that Philby, who had already confessed his traitorous career, defected from Beirut to Moscow the same day Golitsyn arrived in London.[17] Petty learned that on the same day, the KGB resident from Washington also made a quick disappearance.[18]

For Petty, the search through Golitsyn's files, and other circumstantial evidence, brought him a new suspect. Petty pulled the early records of James Jesus Angleton. What he found shocked him. Harold "Kim" Philby, who had been recruited by the Soviets at Cambridge University in 1933, had been Angleton's counterespionage teacher. Angleton had first met Philby in London in 1943 when he was dispatched by the OSS as one of a score of Americans to be briefed on counterintelligence operations by the more experienced British.

In 1934, Philby married Litzi Friedman, a young Jewish girl and a communist. The wedding took place in Vienna, and among the guests was Teddy Kollek.[19] Later, during the war, Philby introduced Angleton to Kollek. Kollek worked with Angleton as part of the Jewish underground while Angleton ran OSS counterintelligence operations in Italy during the latter part of the war. In 1945, Philby, returning from assignment in Istanbul, stopped off to visit Angleton in Rome.

In 1949 the United States Armed Forces Security Agency, the forerunner of the National Security Agency, broke a Soviet code called VENONA.[20] The VENONA material revealed that our Soviet allies had been spying on both the United States and Great Britain at the highest levels since the 1930s. It also revealed that British intelligence was thoroughly penetrated by the KGB. But the most damaging losses had come from the U.S. atomic-weapons facility at Los Alamos and from the British Embassy in Washington.

Ironically, it was Kim Philby who, in 1949, was sent to Washington by the British SIS (MI6) as their chief of station for a two-year assignment. A main part of his job was to work with the FBI on tracking down names discovered in the VENONA intercepts. One of those names was STANLEY, which was also one of Philby's NKVD code names. But, unfortunately for Western intelligence, the connection was not made until long after Philby did his damage.[21]

As part of his investigation, Petty went into CIA security records going back to the 1949–51 period to determine how much official contact Angleton had had with Philby while the latter was in Washington. Petty concluded: "I went through all the security records showing Philby going in and coming out of the building and he was there constantly in Angleton's office. They were extremely close." Petty confirmed that Angleton and Philby ate lunch together at the old Harvey's Restaurant nearly every week, something that Philby claimed in his autobiography, *My Silent War*. Philby also claimed in his book that Angleton had no inkling of his involvement with the Soviets.

One reason Petty believes Philby and Angleton saw each other so often was so that Philby could bring Angleton up to date on the VENONA material. "At that time the CIA didn't have access to the material," according to Petty. Philby, as SIS station chief, in liaison with the Armed Forces Security Agency, did.

Making matters more curious is the fact that Angleton knew about the friendship between Guy Burgess and Donald Maclean. He was well aware that Burgess was under investigation. One of Maclean's jobs had been to brief the SIS on atomic weapons. He was also, as a Soviet agent, informing the Soviets about allied intentions during the Korean War. The FBI had Philby under surveillance as part of its investigation into Burgess. Burgess was a houseguest of Philby's in Washington at the time.

Another curious piece of circumstantial evidence against Angleton was the fact that until the time Kollek came to the United States as part of the new Israeli purchasing agency, Angleton had declined to advise the DCI to enter into a special relationship with Israel. Philby, Angleton, and Kollek socialized until the late hours on several occasions during this period. Two months after Philby left the United States, Angleton reversed himself and recommended not only that the CIA undertake a close relationship with Israeli intelligence, but also that Angleton himself be in charge of liaison with the Israelis.

After eight years of searching for the mole, Petty concluded that the most likely candidate was James Jesus Angleton, the master counterspy himself. Petty recalls a memo he ran across in his investigation in the aftermath of the Burgess and Maclean defections dated 1953. William King Harvey, the former FBI agent, who after being transferred by J. Edgar Hoover, quit the Bureau and went to work for the CIA, was the first to finger Philby. Petty says, "I think Harvey found it very difficult to believe that Angleton did not understand what Philby was up to."

Petty says that the then DCI, Gen. Walter Bedell Smith, asked each CIA employee who had extensive contacts with Burgess, Maclean, and Philby to write a memo detailing the relationship. "And Angleton wrote this and it was really a strange piece of paper. Talk about disjointed and long. But at any rate Harvey at some point had read the piece of paper and in his own hand writing on it was . . . 'What's the rest of the story. OSOD.' That meant Oh Shit Oh Damn."

Petty came to the end of his mole hunt in late 1973. William Colby had just taken over the CIA and his new Deputy Director for Operations, William Nelson, got the report. Nelson assigned a senior agency man, considered to be independent, to hear Petty's report. Petty spent a week closeted with this man and a tape recorder. He turned in two file drawers full of supporting material and thirty hours of tapes. The tapes, considered to be among the CIA's most important secrets, remain in the DCI's vault, unavailable to even the most highly cleared officials without the DCI's approval.

According to Peter Kapusta, a former SR counterintelligence case officer, reaction to Petty's effort came fast. Colby requested surveillance through New York authorities be placed on both Angleton and Golitsyn in 1973. In those days, Angleton was a frequent visitor to Golitsyn's farm in upstate New York.

Petty says that he is virtually certain that Angleton had no idea what direction his investigation took. Petty says the person who heard him out for the DCI told him that the evidence he put together was strong enough that Petty's conclusion about Angleton was ninety percent correct.

But to Petty "it almost didn't matter that Jim worked for them." Because whether he worked for them or not, his friendship with Philby and his absolute faith in Golitsyn all played into the KGB's hands. They had targeted CI. They had wanted to disrupt the CIA's relations with other services. They had succeeded.

Petty was asked to stay on another year to see what other leads he could track down. What worried him the most when he did leave was "you had to look for replacements, KGB replacements." Petty recommended that the DCI use his power of arbitrary dismissal on Angleton's deputies, Newton S. Miler, William Hood, and Raymond Rocca, on the assumption that they could be controlled agents.

Six months after Petty left the CIA, William Colby called James Angleton into his office in December 1974 and told him that he was no longer in charge of counterintelligence. Colby also dismissed Angleton's top aides. Colby says he should have fired Angleton earlier.

In September of 1975, James Angleton finally gave up his office space, got into his old Mercedes and drove home to Arlington under the cloud his subordinate had left behind.[22] Had the mole really resigned?

Sam Wilson does not think so. "No. Jim was an eccentric—an eccentric genius. He had the best interests of the United States at heart. He was sometimes grotesque in his reasoning process. He could think faster and more deeply than most human beings can. He reached the point, I think, that his hyper-suspiciousness simply became chronic and he may have reached the point of diminishing returns."

Wilson, who was back at the CIA in the 1970s as Colby's deputy for the Intelligence Community, recalls just what effect Angleton had on the CIA: "It was beginning to cause people to suspect each other. It was beginning to affect morale. . . . It was beginning to cause the haze of suspicion to hang in the atmosphere to the extent that it was a little sick. . . . He got locked in. You know, you got locked in. The whole system just kind of froze. He couldn't even get his diskettes out, you know."

By 1975, Angleton's replacements resumed attempts to recruit Soviets. According to then-DCI William Colby, the CI staff was instructed to recruit anyone and everyone they could. In setting up their new shop, the "rookie" counterintelligence team headed by George Kalaris and Leonard V. McCoy ran across some documents making reference to Petty's super-secret report on Angleton. The CI Division also learned that *Newsweek* reporter David Martin was writing a book about Bill Harvey and Angleton, and he had sensational new information about a secret report. The report was never made available to either McCoy or Kalaris.

But Angleton's successors did find a safe full of supporting documents for Ed Petty's original report on Angleton. McCoy assumed Petty's tapes had been destroyed. They weren't. That report was locked in a special file room; the only access was by permission of the DCI. The report could only be heard with an armed guard present, and no notes could be made.

In hopes of finding out what their predecessor in CI had been up to, McCoy and Kalaris dispatched Cleveland Cram, a CIA veteran, to see Petty at his home in a subdivision outside of Annapolis, Maryland. It became obvious to Petty fairly quickly that Cram's claim that he was doing a historical review was nonsense when he targeted in on questions that went to the heart of the allegations against Angleton. Petty said: "Goddammit, Cleve, what the hell is this all about?" Cram, not known for his ability to deceive, told Petty about his assignment. Petty explained that he had already spent years of his life on the report and it had been turned over to two of the highest officials in the CIA.

After his dismissal, Angleton, with his own network of contacts, spent many afternoons with reporters at the old Army Navy Club off Farragut Square in Washington, putting his own spin on events. Angleton would not talk about the mole investigation that concluded that he himself was a candidate. He denied it ever took place. When he was told by a reporter that Cram had been called back to look again at all the defectors that Angleton had been involved with, he said such an investigation of him by Cram never took place.

CHAPTER FIVE

Paisley: The Jabbermole?

❧

Beware the Family Jewels, my
son
The leaks that Spring, the tips from Smersh—
Taste not Nosenko's Plant, and
shun
The myriad Seymourhersh!
Golitzen to the Bagley man
Go find who serves another skipper;
Promotion lies with those who
can
Win one for the Double Dipper
But high in Langley's ranks he
stands,
The Jabbermole, untouched is
he
Kampiles' heel, a friend of
Stan's,
He snuckles in his glee.
'Board *Brillig* did the bearish
spies
Snatch Paisley's prints before
he blabbed;
All flimsy were the alibis
While the mole laughs, ungrabbed.

William Safire, in
the *New York Times*

IN AUGUST 1971, a young, bright Vietnam veteran joined the CIA. A Marine, decorated for valor in Vietnam, David S. Sullivan was recruited out of Columbia University. Equipped with battlefield experience and a new master's degree in international relations, Sullivan joined the Office of Strategic Research (OSR). But Sullivan was different. He was not one of OSR's traditional political liberals, nor was he a laid-back academic. If anything, his personality was a little jarring to some in OSR, a little too gung-ho. He became the only noncovert Agency employee recruited into the CIA's paramilitary reserve.

Having been a military officer, Sullivan knew something about using the system to advance his career. And that was just what he did. Sullivan understood that his job required him to have a complete mastery of the intelligence he used to write his reports. So instead of simply accepting what came into OSR and down to his level after being laundered by several layers of bureaucrats, Sullivan sought out the sources. He got to know the photo interpreters in the National Reconnaissance Office, where the spy satellites' pictures came streaming in every minute of the day. He made friends with the Soviet Division staff so he could get the word first on a new human source or a breakthrough contact.

In signals intelligence, perhaps the most important source on which OSR relied, Sullivan made certain he got the clearances to make the trip to Fort George Meade where the National Security Agency is located. It was here that Sullivan prospered; at NSA, by a process of elimination, he could figure out which messages were real and which were phonies. Back at CIA headquarters, Sullivan made it a point to befriend people in counterintelligence. They, too, might be helpful to him one day. In many ways, Sullivan was doing what John Paisley had done twenty years earlier to become so valuable to OSR.

When Sullivan selected the CIA for his career, he thought it was a glamour job. From the outside, the mysterious and exciting agency seemed the place from which the mentally and physically elite went forth to fight communism and protect the nation's security. He had no idea that, in reality, the CIA was in absolute turmoil. By the time Richard Nixon resigned in disgrace in 1975, the Agency had been turned into a highly politicized organization that was involved in illegal domestic operations and the overthrow of foreign governments such as the Allende regime in Chile, a "successful" operation that destroyed the CIA's credibility in Latin America for a generation.

Sullivan was a young man on the make. He saw Paisley from the vantage point of a subordinate looking up at a senior-level veteran. What he saw was a man who seemed the opposite of his division chief in the 1970s, Bruce Clarke. "He was just a total contrast to Bruce Clarke. Clarke used to be so American and CIA-like, you know. He was the epitome of management, of a WASP. Paisley was a bohemian."[1]

Sullivan developed a reputation for being a quick study, and began to write what ended up being more than a hundred classified papers on Soviet strategic strength. But as the months and then years went by, Sullivan began to detect something very strange in the Office of Strategic Research. "I began to get the feeling that they were 'cooking the books.' There was a tendency to underestimate the Soviets. It was almost a policy in OSR."[2] Sullivan's conservative politics conflicted with most of the liberals in OSR. Sullivan recalls: "I was naïve. At first I thought it was just a matter of suppressing my views. Then, by 1976, I began to believe the place might be penetrated."[3]

As a young analyst, Sullivan labored with more than three hundred others in the Office of Strategic Research. At the top of the office was John Paisley, who was juggling his leak-plugging activities with his regular duties as Deputy of OSR. Paisley's career was at its height. Not all of Paisley's White House work was connected to the Plumbers. Paisley found himself increasingly called upon to do the major damage assessments of crisis after crisis, like those in India and Cyprus, and a host of others. But it was during the 1973 Arab-Israeli War that senior policy-makers turned to Paisley. Paisley had a unique understanding of just how far the Soviets would extend themselves on behalf of Syria and Egypt. Paisley was sent to Israel to assist in the installation of a satellite communication system for the United Nations Peacekeeping Force that would patrol the war zone.[4] He became the senior CIA man responsible for writing the briefings for President Nixon. Former CIA Director William Colby said Paisley's job was "to prepare some of the summaries of intelligence for the rest of the community. To prepare some assessments for the President in various national security meetings."[5]

But at OSR, the battle with Henry Kissinger and the nightmare of the National Intelligence Memoranda continued. Normally, OSR's estimates would go into the Office of National Estimates, along with estimates from the military and other intelligence services. Here this coordinating body would hammer out the comprehensive "national intelligence estimates." Generally, this hammering out of the estimates was a huge and acrimonious battle that brought out the worst in the CIA, the DIA, the NSA, and other contributing organizations like the Army and the Air Force.

Kissinger's NISMs did not have to undergo such bureaucratic cleansing. Instead, the White House policy-makers were given access to the intelligence material and the analysts, and then, together, they wrote an NISM using the CIA statistics and information to support their cause, citing OSR as the authoritative source.

For Paisley, according to Don Burton, this was a tragedy. Burton said it meant Paisley was getting sucked up in the political process, not simply the information process. "We intelligence people, as part of our credo, don't want to drive things. We want someone else to make all those decisions. So now all of a sudden you're sucked into a thing where you are now becoming dirty. Paisley didn't want to get dirty," Burton said. But another colleague, Clarence Baier, remembers Paisley differently, as the kind of man who did not raise controversy. "Paisley was a very careful guy. He knew what the answer was supposed to be. I am not saying he was biased, but he was very careful to see the answer came out in the right way," Baier said.[6]

But the real end for Paisley was the firing of Richard Helms as CIA Director in 1972. Helms, more than anyone else, had protected OSR from the infringement of the Nixon White House. His personal charm had worked with Kissinger and Haig. But his steadfast refusal to allow the CIA to become involved in domestic law enforcement, and his later refusal not to accept responsibility for the Plumbers and cover for Nixon, caused his political demise. On November 20, 1972, Helms was summoned to Camp David and fired. Helms told the President that since the mandatory retirement age of sixty was coming up in March of 1973, that would be a good time for his departure. But by early February 1973 he was given the ambassadorship to Iran and was out of the CIA.

This inside man was replaced by an abrasive outsider named James Schlesinger. From the start, Schlesinger's temper tantrums and ego caused trouble at the CIA. Schlesinger began his reign by inviting only officers who had served less than twenty years to his welcoming speech. Five hundred young officers were told that intelligence careers were going to be kept to two decades, that intelligence was a young man's game.

Schlesinger cut out much of the heart of the CIA's management capability and got full backing from President Nixon for the effort. Schlesinger was so fearful for his own safety that he asked for and got additional bodyguards. The situation deteriorated to the point where a bodyguard sat in Schlesinger's outer office in the secure environs of the CIA's seventh floor. A closed-circuit TV camera was even aimed at Schlesinger's official portrait so that angry employees would not be tempted to deface it.[7]

According to Don Burton, Schlesinger infuriated Paisley. "He despised Schlesinger," Burton said, because Schlesinger attempted to tell OSR how to interpret intelligence. Schlesinger told Paisley that he did not like OSR's estimates and wanted them changed. Burton explains that at first the office was in shock, but Paisley and the rest of OSR had such little respect for Schlesinger that they ignored him. "So nobody changed it," Burton said. In less than six months, Schlesinger was gone and so was the pressure on OSR. But long neglected personal matters were closing in on Paisley.

If there is an opinion about John Paisley's character that is universal with his friends and associates, it is that he was a very gentle man. But for all of Paisley's idealistic views of the world, he paid little attention to Maryann and his children. Edward's adolescence was particularly difficult. He and his school friends in McLean, Virginia, were fast-paced, rebellious teenagers.

One factor that may have contributed to the final disintegration of John and Maryann's marriage was Maryann's own competitive nature. Maryann Paisley managed to get the new Director, William Colby, to give her permission to work at the CIA. Largely using her connections to John, she negotiated a one-year contract at the CIA, working in the Soviet Russia Division for Katherine Hart in 1973. When asked under oath about her CIA employment in a court case years later, Maryann said she worked in a vault at the CIA in the Soviet Russia Division.[8]

According to Leonard McCoy, Maryann had also worked for him in the SR [Soviet Russia] Division for one year in the late 1960s, compiling and editing intelligence reports from agents in the field.[9] McCoy, a quiet man, found himself embroiled in some of the Agency's major cases as a top reports officer. McCoy's office had the difficult and very sensitive task of keeping track of the CIA's agents inside the Soviet Bloc. McCoy openly says he did not like John Paisley, a man who had to rely heavily on the reports of Leonard McCoy and his colleagues. But he liked Maryann and said she was bright and competitive.[10]

Maryann's 1973 job was her last with the CIA, but it could not have been more delicate. Her assignment was to help reorganize the thousands of agent names—active and inactive—who had worked for the Soviet Division over the years. This work gave her access to the CIA's most important secrets. Colby steadfastly refused to reveal agents' true names when a congressional committee demanded the information in the aftermath of the Church Committee and Rockefeller Commission investigations into America's intelligence services. "We had no more important secret. I didn't want to know the names. There was no need for me to know," Colby said.[11]

But Maryann Paisley knew the names and the code names. She said she was required to take a polygraph for her new job. It was an extremely sensitive assignment that caused some friction with John.[12]

Norman Wilson, a retired Air Force colonel and a sailing friend of Paisley's, said that Maryann was "very proud of having changed some things about the machinery in the office and all that, which, according to John, she was able to get only by using his name and he was pretty irritated about it. He told us she was kind of running too much with it." Wilson said that "Maryann competed with him, and in talking to us, boasting about her accomplishments there . . . she was trying to compete with him." [13]

Paisley's own behavior during this period caught the attention of Clarence Baier, a colleague in OSR. "One time John took off for six weeks to go sailing. He called me and I was patched into his radio. He said he was sailing by himself in the Bahamas. I found that kind of a strange thing to do. But in many ways John was a loner—a poet." [14]

During the summer of 1973, a tragedy struck the Paisley family that had a profound effect on John Paisley's life. On August 19, 1973, young Edward Paisley—nicknamed Eddie—and a group of friends hopped into some cars and headed into Washington to go drinking. With Eddie was an old friend, Brian Patrick Demmler, who with Eddie and his friends bought six-packs of beer and began drinking heavily on their way into Washington. At midnight they piled into Eddie's 1966 Ford Galaxie and crossed Key Bridge from Georgetown onto the George Washington Parkway. The speed limit on the parkway is fifty miles an hour.

Eddie Paisley was followed onto the parkway by another car, with another group of friends. That car was equipped with a bright searchlight. The two cars began racing each other at higher and higher speeds. The car behind Eddie's shined the bright light on the Galaxie. At 12:10 A.M., Eddie Paisley lost control of his car while trying to make the turnoff for Route 123. Ironically, this is the parkway exit for CIA headquarters in nearby Langley. Young Paisley's car crashed into a tree. His best friend, Brian Demmler, was killed.[15]

Police estimated that Paisley hit the tree at somewhere between eighty and one hundred miles an hour. Brian's estate sued the Paisleys. More serious for Eddie was the fact that the accident took place on federal property. That meant he faced federal prosecution. In the end, Edward's lawyer negotiated a plea bargain to avoid a jail sentence. With John and Maryann present in the courtroom, Eddie confessed to the judge: "We went downtown and we drank a little too much and came back racing down the G.W. Parkway. We were playing tag on the G.W. Parkway and I hit a tree."[16] Eddie Paisley got parole and was treated as a juvenile. But for John Paisley, the family crisis that had been building so long came to this terrible and tragic conclusion.

Eddie's father felt enormous guilt about the accident. Some say that John Paisley never really shared his heartbreak over what Eddie had done. Others say John behaved as if he blamed himself.

John's boss, Hank Knoche, said, "John never let that interfere with his work, but you could tell it was a terrible, haunting thing to him."[17]

For one college friend, Leonard Masters, who kept in touch with John Paisley over the years, John and Eddie did not have a typical father-son relationship. John's problems with Eddie seemed to go very deep. "John never talked with a sense of pride about the boy," Masters said. Masters remembers John Paisley talking after the accident about how short and uncertain life could be, and how he wanted to take the time to get everything out of life that he could.

To Masters, the John Paisley he knew in college was very different from the one he was seeing at the end of his CIA career. Paisley had changed. "I knew that John was conning me so many times in the later years," Masters recalls. At first Masters says that he thought Paisley lied to him because "of his work . . . but you could tell it ran deeper than that."

Gladys Fishel, Paisley's lawyer, believes that it was the strain of Eddie Paisley's accident that finally pushed the marriage over the edge. To her, Maryann and John seemed close and appeared to be happy until the accident. Fishel said Paisley defended his son to Maryann. "But, you know, I think it must have made a wedge between them, and she told me that," Fishel said.

Maryann was threatening divorce, and Eddie had to face the world knowing he had taken another's life. John Paisley, under tremendous pressure both professionally and personally, could not look to the Office of Strategic Research for any stability.

According to David Sullivan, OSR in the early 1970s was a "sex pit." Sullivan said that senior officers were having affairs with assistants. "It was not the kind of place you wanted to be if you were trying to keep a marriage or family together." Sullivan said his memories of Paisley during this period "were of a man who was definitely one of the top guys in the CIA, but who was gone for large chunks of time." [18] Although Paisley seemed beloved by most of his colleagues in OSR, Sullivan did not share that feeling. "You would brief him on something and he would take it all in and not ask a question," he recalls.

Sullivan spent months researching the Soviets' compliance with the SALT I Treaty. Using the best materials available to him, he concluded that the Russians were cheating. But OSR did not rush to publish his findings. Sullivan became more and more incensed about what he considered OSR's stalling. "I just couldn't seem to get anyone to listen to me," Sullivan said.

In 1974, John Paisley suddenly retired from the CIA. It surprised many of his colleagues and friends who felt he was at the height of his mental powers at age fifty-one. No one really knows why Paisley retired. It coincided with the final convulsions of the Nixon administration, and he may have been concerned that his once-bright future at the CIA was spoiled by his links to Watergate. Or he may simply have been emotionally exhausted by his professional responsibilities and his personal problems. Some say he retired so that he could spend more time sailing. But others believe that Paisley never retired at all, that he retired in name only.

Sam Wilson says that he grew fairly close to John Paisley beginning in 1974, when Wilson became CIA Director Colby's Deputy Director for the Intelligence Community. Wilson says Colby valued Paisley's expertise, and the two men became very close "because Paisley could give you intelligence in a usable form." [19]

In the summer of 1974, Knoche helped organize a retirement party for Paisley aboard a Potomac riverboat with an open bar, good food,

Dale, Katherine, and John Paisley *(left to right)*.

Rush River Lodge, near Washington, Virginia. (JOSEPH TRENTO)

John Paisley receiving a medal honoring him for his service from CIA Director William Colby. (JOSEPH TRENTO)

John Paisley *(left)* and Norman Wilson at the August 1978 wedding of Wilson's daughter. (COURTESY OF BARBARA WILSON)

John Paisley in the fall of 1977. (COURTESY OF CARLY JANE DUNN)

John Paisley's first sailboat, *Quiescent*.

Brillig, with Norman Wilson on board, after Paisley disappeared.

Norman and Barbara Wilson.
(JOSEPH TRENTO)

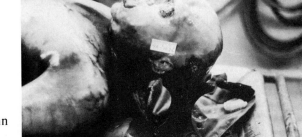

Body identified as that of John
Paisley by Dr. Russell Fisher.
(MARYLAND STATE MEDICAL
EXAMINER'S OFFICE PHOTO)

Igor and Eleanore Orlov in late 1940s. (COURTESY OF ELEANORE ORLOV)

and music. A crowd of OSR and other CIA employees came. Knoche got up and made a speech about what a great loss Paisley was to the CIA, but that at fifty-one, John had a lot to look forward to. Knoche talked about how a farewell for Paisley on the water was appropriate because of John's Merchant Marine and radio experience and his love of the sea. Then Knoche looked down at Paisley, who stood a head shorter, and said to his deputy: "John, you can consider this a retirement party if you want to, but I'd like to think of this as especially fitting for you. It's a Viking funeral."

"Paisley liked that," Knoche remembers.

Eddie was not the only child to give John Paisley problems. Paisley was also faced with problems that came up between his daughter Diane and Maryann. After his retirement, Paisley took Diane on a cross-country trip to visit her aunt and grandmother in Oregon and relatives in Phoenix. Paisley stopped off to see boyhood friends on the way. Paisley's sister, Katherine Lenahan, says one reason Paisley took Diane on the trip was that she and her mother were not getting along at the time. It is no wonder; all of the disciplining of the children fell on Maryann. Paisley's brother, Dale, explains that John's "theory was I don't see them day-to-day, so when I do see them, why should I spend all my time disciplining them?" [20]

During this period, John Paisley left two impressions on Katherine. One was that "he was a workaholic." Katherine continued, "I think even when he was in Washington, D.C., he was away from home fourteen, sixteen hours a day." The other was that her brother remained, as he was in his youth, a very private person. Katherine says, "He never discussed a great deal of his personal problems with us. A couple of times when he would be out, he'd ask me questions about a woman's response to a certain situation. I gathered he was trying to understand Maryann's reaction to something. . . . One time he asked me about infidelity and marriage."

The personal side of John Paisley's life changed drastically after his "retirement" from the CIA. The Paisleys agreed to give their marriage one last serious chance. John decided to buy a new sailboat. He wanted to sail down the Inland Waterway.

In 1974, Paisley called Richard Bennett in North Carolina to see if he had any leads on a used sailboat. Bennett is a grizzled old CIA man who left the Agency in 1969 because he thought his covert assignments were getting dull. Paisley told Bennett he was looking for a new, larger boat to replace his smaller one, the *Quiescent,* which he had sold two years earlier. Within a few weeks the Paisleys drove down for a visit, searching marinas while en route for a boat to buy. At a cocktail party at the Trail's End Marina, Paisley met a friend of Bennett's named Ike Ives. Paisley learned from Ives that he had a beautiful, thirty-one-foot

Columbia sloop for sale.[21] John immediately left the cocktail party with Ives to go look at the boat. Before the cocktail party ended, he bought it for $16,000. Paisley, who loved Lewis Carroll, named her *Brillig* from a line from "Jabberwocky." Dick Bennett remembers Paisley "being absolutely overjoyed at finding *Brillig*. It seemed exactly what he was looking for." Paisley's only concern was that *Brillig* wasn't a diesel, and gas would be expensive for her.

To the Bennetts, the Paisleys, for those few weeks that summer, seemed fun-loving and easygoing. The Bennetts detected no marital problems. Dick Bennett prides himself on only having friends who love to laugh, "and Jack Paisley was a funny man." The Bennetts recall that Paisley liked to drink and have fun, but he never appeared drunk. "I never saw Paisley the least bit tipsy. Never. Even at boat parties in the yard," Dick Bennett said.

Taking Maryann on a sailing trip turned out not to be the best avenue to save their marriage. Maryann, who never particularly enjoyed sailing, found herself roughing it at Trail's End. Mary Jo Bennett remembers: "She just tolerated it." Gladys Fishel agrees. She said that Maryann was never enthusiastic about living on *Brillig*, "but she did that because he was depressed." Fishel thinks the quarters may have been just too close for them on *Brillig*.

Paisley's retirement was sporadic at best. He frequently cut short sailing trips to go to Washington on what he said was CIA business. One reason Paisley was called back to the CIA was William E. Colby. "Colby loved him. He really was very fond of him," Sam Wilson remembers.[22] Wilson says Paisley agreed to come back in and do a few individual jobs for Colby at the request of John M. Clark, who was then Wilson's deputy. Wilson remembers that the first time he met Paisley, he was prepared to spend half an hour with him, but he was so enthralled with his abilities, he let the meeting go on for two hours. When he was done, Wilson found Paisley to be "erudite, sophisticated, cultured, witty." "Oh, what a sense of humor! He had it all together. Not greedy, not hungry, not ego-stricken . . . I liked him," Sam Wilson stated.

Wilson says Paisley enjoyed his new assignments. He "seized upon the new challenges with quiet alacrity. He didn't miss a beat—no pause, no hesitation—as though he'd gotten sort of reinfected."

At a retreat for top CIA officials in Warrenton, Virginia, Sam Wilson got a close look at Paisley. "I remember him as a very incisive reasoner. It wasn't so much inductive as deductive. I know because we worked problems together some. Sometimes he would circle a problem and then intuit an answer. I would wonder how he got that. Just a straight line right into the center of the problem. . . . He had a capacity to intuit that I have seen in some women, but I seldom see it in a man. I call it circular logic or a circular pattern of reasoning. You circle something like this, thinking about it, and all of a sudden inspiration hits you and wham-o, you've got it. I can't do it and don't trust it when I think I am doing it.''

Colby and Wilson liked Paisley not only for his professional abilities, but also for his personality. He was fun to be around. Wilson says that he was "a squirrel, a screwball. I love people who are screwballs. Once you'd get going and you'd get to laughing, then he would be sort of energized or stimulated to keep it going. . . . It's like a stand-up comic. The crowd had gotten with him and is driving him.'' Wilson says that "there was a little bit of a chameleon-like quality there, you know, he could show you different sides. There was a funny guy down inside there, and when he saw that you saw him, he'd give you more glimpses of him.''

According to Betty Myers, when John Paisley was on one of his Washington business trips in 1974 and Maryann was left with *Brillig,* Paisley and Myers had dinner. Betty had been getting letters from John and Maryann while they were cruising. But this dinner apparently marked the start of the intimate relationship between Maryann's close friend and her husband.

It was Bobbie Wilson's impression that Maryann's own actions may have encouraged the relationship between Betty Myers and John. "Betty told me one time that she was brought home by Maryann to try to psychoanalyze John or to act as kind of a free marriage counselor. Apparently a lot of drinking went on and Maryann would just get up and go to bed and leave Betty and John down in the living room. . . . I don't know when their relationship started but the inference was that Maryann dumped John on Betty.''

Hank Knoche remembers Paisley being "quite a ladies' man. . . . And yet every woman I ever talked to about him could not understand in the slightest what would make John Paisley the least bit attractive. But whatever it was, it must have been pretty good.'' [23]

Maryann ended the planned retirement on *Brillig* early and went home to McLean. The work, the sailing, the children were too much. By 1976, Maryann and John Paisley were no longer living together as husband and wife. Despite the separation, the couple were never really estranged. Paisley told more than one friend that it was Maryann who wanted to end the marriage, not him. According to one friend, when she brought up John's leaving Maryann, he interrupted her and said, "On the contrary, I did not leave Maryann.'' [24]

Gladys Fishel found it strange that Maryann and John "could live separately and maintain a close relationship.'' She said Maryann told her that some mornings John would still make her coffee and put it by her bedside, prompting Fishel to say, "How could you ever let someone like that go? . . . They had the benefits of marriage and none of the burdens." Maryann's pursuit of a new life in middle age reached a high point in February 1976, when she earned her BA from George Mason University.[25] But even with increasing evidence of Maryann's independence and John's absence from home, the Paisleys remained strangely close. "I'd describe them as some people who are separated but not estranged," Gladys Fishel said.

Between cruises south on *Brillig,* Paisley stayed in the homes of old friends. John Whitman, Bruce Clarke, and Norman Wilson provided shelter to Paisley from time to time. Sometimes Paisley returned home to McLean to spend a night.

When Leonard Masters visited Paisley just six months before his disappearance, Paisley was staying in the McLean house in a downstairs room. Masters recalls that Paisley "sort of wanted to give the impression that they were still together, that they were still a family unit, when the family unit had gone by the board." Masters thought the separation between Maryann and John a "very strange kind of split. I mean, I believe in good-natured splits, but this was sort of carrying it too far."

According to Betty Myers, by the fall of 1977 her relationship with Paisley was at its peak. Myers and Paisley had a few things in common. One was that they had both been born in Oklahoma. When she first met the Paisleys, Betty Myers was a "woman who had been taken care of all her life, who went out on her own." Eventually, Myers became a psychiatric social worker. She says she and John used to have long talks together, and she worried about what she calls Paisley's extreme depression. She persuaded him to go to a psychiatrist. Myers said, "I was worried about John. He had lost weight and just didn't look well, and I expressed my concern about him."

Professionally, Paisley undertook a series of outside activities for the CIA and the Defense Department. He was once again at the very center of disputes over the reliability of CIA estimates of real Soviet defense spending. In the mid-1970s, this political time bomb was about to explode. Armed with new evidence, conservatives were charging that only the faulty CIA estimates of Soviet strength had justified the United States' signing the SALT I agreement, thereby allowing the Soviets to catch up in strategic weapons.

The President's Foreign Intelligence Advisory Board (PFIAB), then chaired by Adm. George W. Anderson (ret.), wrote President Ford a letter in August 1975, proposing that an outside group of experts be given access to the same intelligence as the CIA analysts and be allowed to prepare a competing National Intelligence Estimate (NIE). This outside group would be called the B Team. The CIA and intelligence community estimates would be the A Team. The effort became known as the A Team/B Team Experiment.

CIA Director Colby understandably was not happy with the whole idea, but to be fair, he suggested that the PFIAB first examine closely a current CIA National Intelligence Estimate (NIE) and then make an evaluation. Colby intuitively knew that to allow critics to gain access to the estimates would politicize a process that had been almost apolitical and strictly empirical.

As Colby expected, PFIAB looked at the estimates and found them wanting. Anderson kept pressing for the experiment. On the same day, but for very different reasons, President Ford fired both his CIA Director, William Colby, and his Defense Secretary, James Schlesinger. With Colby out of the way, PFIAB's chairman finally won. Colby's replacement, George Bush, agreed to authorize the competition in June 1976.[26]

What Bush approved was revolutionary in American intelligence. For the first time, outsiders, many with an open anti-CIA bias, would be given free access to National Intelligence Estimates going back to 1959. Outsiders would now have access to all of America's classified knowledge about the Soviet military. The CIA had argued for years that since it set no policy, its research and information were not clouded by political bias. But critics and some conservatives believed the estimates created by men like Proctor, Clarke, and Paisley were tinged by their liberal views. Three B Teams were formed. One was assigned to examine Soviet objectives, and two looked at technical questions. The A and B Teams would be given an opportunity to go at each other in three formal sessions to argue their points.

The CIA had two major worries about the experiment. One was that conservatives on the B Teams would leak highly classified material to the press in order to support their case, and the other was that the CIA's reputation for impeccable strategic research would be forever damaged.

The experiment would require the use of reams of classified documents and thousands of hours of follow-up. The liaison between the CIA and the B Teams was a key appointment. This person would control the documents they saw and the information they got. The CIA chose John Paisley to be the CIA "coordinator" for the B Teams.[27] Hank Knoche, Paisley's old boss, who was Bush's top deputy, okayed the idea of the B Teams and lived to regret it. But the choice of Paisley as the "coordinator" was brilliant. Paisley, a man who had spent his entire career developing the very systems the B Teams were evaluating, was now the conduit for any information those teams received.

Paisley's appointment may well have been the CIA's effort at protecting its own interests. By December 1976 it was clear that the B Teams' Soviet Objectives Team's approach was thoroughly political. The B Teams were clearly going to be very critical of CIA estimates. The entire effort was supposed to be very secret.

David Sullivan, who by 1976 had become a respected member of the OSR staff, volunteered material for the A Team/B Team Experiment. He was assigned to the A Team. Sullivan was assigned to work in an office in Rosslyn, just across the Potomac River from Washington, to assist in the project. One of his jobs was to help get Paisley material for the B Teams. This assignment gave Sullivan a good idea what materials Paisley was giving and, more important, *not* giving the outside team. Sullivan said that Paisley had clearance to access "anything that he wanted."

Because Sullivan's views were more in line with conservative members of the B Teams, such as Harvard professor Richard E. Pipes and Air Force General Daniel Graham, he began to socialize with them. He wanted to tell them about his research that showed that the Soviets had cheated the United States during the SALT I negotiations.

What Sullivan wanted to share with Pipes was his discovery that the Soviets' SS-19 ICBM, never revealed to the United States prior to the SALT I agreement, gave the Soviets a much more powerful weapons system than the SS-11, which it was replacing. Prior to SALT I, the SS-11 constituted the bulk of the Soviet nuclear force. What angered Sullivan was a May 1972 telephone conversation of then Soviet chief Leonid Brezhnev picked up by electronic eavesdropping. In his report, Sullivan wrote about the incident that confirmed Soviet cheating.

GAMMA GUPPY was the code name of what was then an intercept operation U.S. intelligence ran on Moscow limousines. On May 26, 1972, at the height of the SALT I negotiations in Moscow, a conversation between Soviet General Secretary Leonid Brezhnev, Foreign Minister Andrei Gromyko, and Defense Minister Marshal Grechko at the SALT I Summit was picked up. Brezhnev began to talk about a "main missile" that the United States had been unaware of. Brezhnev had just agreed with Henry Kissinger to limit expansion of existing Soviet silos to fifteen percent. He was worried that the new "main missile," the SS-19, might not fit. Brezhnev said to Grechko, "Can we fit the new missile in?" Grechko went to his experts and called the General Secretary back to assure him that they could. The late Mr. Brezhnev's reaction when he heard the answer was to say, "Thank God."

Because the SS-19 was the Soviet Union's first truly accurate ICBM, Sullivan wrote in his still-classified report that Brezhnev lied to U.S. negotiators and told them that the Soviet Union had no intention of replacing the SS-11s with the new and more powerful SS-19s.

U.S. negotiators, anxious not to block an agreement, did not insist on getting a guarantee from the Soviets in writing that they would not replace the smaller missiles with more powerful and accurate ones. After ratification of SALT I, the Soviets replaced 360 of the smaller missiles with the SS-19.

Sullivan learned that the SS-19 had three to four times the throw-weight of the SS-11 it replaced. To make matters worse, the SS-19 was, because of its accuracy, more dangerous than even the super-heavy SS-18.

One reason the United States accepted the Russians' word was that we were absolutely convinced the Soviets were far behind us technologically. In addition to Paisley's reports saying that the Soviets could not afford a massive strategic arms buildup and that their missiles had serious technical flaws that affected accuracy and payload destructiveness, the FBI was weighing in with supporting information. The two top FBI Soviet sources, TOP HAT and FEDORA, were confirming to U.S. intelligence the inaccuracy of Soviet missiles. According to Sullivan, "This played right into the Soviet negotiating strategy at SALT."

Sullivan says that "both of these Soviet agents the FBI was running have now been judged to be phonies for [sent by] the KGB. But at the time, the FBI would not admit it. In the early 1980s they were reassessed under Webster, and it was determined these cases were bad." [28]

But before Sullivan could give Professor Pipes his material, he had to go through Paisley. He grew more and more frustrated. In Sullivan's view, Paisley was the liaison for the B Teams for one reason: "This guy was charged with spying on the B Teams and regulating all their access to CIA material."

Even in the heat generated between the A Teams and the B Teams, both sides knew that any press leaks could endanger national security. So when the lead story in the *New York Times* appeared on December 26, 1976, saying that the B Teams had changed the National Intelligence Estimate around by 180 degrees, there was anger, institutional embarrassment, and recrimination.

The CIA charged that PFIAB's insistence on the experiment caused important national security data to be compromised. Conservatives on the panel were accused of causing the leaks. The stories were written by David Binder, a veteran newsman known for his ties to conservative members of the intelligence community, including James Angleton. But it was no conservative who leaked the story to Binder.

According to David Binder, it was John Paisley who leaked to him details for the story, a story that he described as one of the "most important of my career." [29] Binder first met Paisley through Michael Yohn. Yohn worked for the United States mission to the Organization of American States and met Paisley when he answered a classified ad in 1972 to purchase Paisley's sailboat, the *Quiescent*. Yohn said that Binder called him and said he was doing a story about "morale" problems at the CIA and needed some help. Yohn gave him Paisley's telephone number. Yohn said that Binder later told him that Paisley had been very helpful.[30] Michael Yohn's former wife, Gretchen, said that Binder attended at least one party at their home and was a social friend.[31]

Maryann Paisley was very upset when she learned that her estranged husband had been named as the leaker of the B Teams story to Binder. She said, "When it first broke, John's name did not appear anywhere in the printed material and David Binder, who broke the story, telephoned our house. John was not there and he was up in arms over the security leak. And when he came home and I told him David Binder had called, he hit the ceiling. He said his name should have never surfaced."[32]

Seymour Weiss, a former U.S. ambassador who was also a member of the B Team, said that when Binder's story appeared in the *New York Times*, "We all got together and talked about it. I don't believe any member of the team leaked, but several of us thought it could have been Paisley."[33] Retired Air Force General John Vogt, also a B Team member, said that Paisley had "no policy-making or decision-making role on the team. It was true he did not get along with some members of the team." Vogt said that it was "certainly a possibility" that Paisley was working with the Soviets, although no one suspected that at the time.

But other B Team members pointed out that leaks about the B Teams could be helpful to the Soviets. After all, the B Teams were attacking CIA estimates for being too low. If it was determined the B Teams could not be trusted, then the CIA would be allowed to continue making estimates that were on the low side.

But Paisley's old boss, Hank Knoche, finds it hard to believe that Paisley was the source for a story that so badly damaged the Agency. "I think Binder is playing with mirrors here. The leaks as I recall them . . . the ones that gave us so much trouble and that we were so upset about, were leaks from the right-wingers. The hard right. The Danny Graham types . . . the ones that later became part of the Reagan . . . administration. And it was designed to show how mealymouthed— you know, pinkish—the CIA estimates had been. Well, I *know* that Paisley had great pride in the integrity of those estimates. Sure, hindsight might show them up or down to some extent. That's the nature of the beast. But the integrity of the process and the objectivity of those estimates is something that John was very, very fond of and that resonated deep within his soul. So the idea of leaking something that would reflect adversely on CIA doesn't make the slightest bit of sense to me."

One team member with whom Paisley clashed was Lt. Gen. Daniel Graham, the former head of the Defense Intelligence Agency. Graham and Paisley had a series of professional run-ins during their careers. Graham said of the leaks, "I know that one of the leaks came from Team A [the CIA team]." Graham describes Paisley as a "weepy liberal who was too soft on the Soviets." [34]

"He used to overestimate the Soviet threat," Fishel recalls Paisley saying of Graham.

The Binder-Yohn relationship would blossom in printed form again when Binder, in the aftermath of Paisley's mysterious end, was introduced to Paisley's girlfriend Betty Myers. The introduction would result in a magazine article for the short-lived revival of *Look* magazine. [35]

Paisley continued to be in demand after the B Team episode. At MITRE Corporation, a CIA contractor, Paisley worked with Clarence Baier, an old colleague from OSR, on how the Pentagon could develop a system of early-warning indicators to predict Soviet strategic behavior. In addition, he remained a consultant at the CIA. He was doing so much work for MITRE that he had to file a document indicating a potential conflict of interest over the MITRE and CIA work. [36]

After the B Team experiment, David Sullivan went back to his regular routine, except that now he noticed a major degradation in the quality of the intelligence he was getting. ROUGH is the code name for spy-satellite photography. Beginning in 1975, the Soviets began to disguise and camouflage their missile silos in a way that indicated they knew how our "Big Bird" satellites could take pictures at several angles to measure shadows. Sullivan understood that only someone who used the satellite photography for OSR purposes could have told the Soviets how to disguise their silos. By 1978, a new sophisticated surveillance satellite system called Keyhole-11, was also being tampered with. The photographs from the KH-11 satellite, which were code named TALENT, showed that the Russians knew how to hide things from the satellite. OSR's information on how many Soviet missiles were in their silos was no longer reliable.

But the biggest loss, from Sullivan's viewpoint, took place with the discovery that Geoffrey Arthur Prime was a Soviet spy inside GCHQ Cheltenham, the British government communications headquarters. Prime was a painfully shy Royal Air Force enlisted man who blossomed in the British equivalent of the NSA. He was on the career fast track and rose to the supervisory level in a unit that transcribed Soviet communications intercepts. GCHQ Cheltenham was responsible for all Moscow intercepts during the SALT I and II negotiations. Prime had been working for the KGB for his entire career at GCHQ Cheltenham. That meant the Soviets knew precisely what the Western intelligence services were concentrating on, and what they wanted.

By the time Jimmy Carter was elected, in November 1976, Sullivan was convinced something was drastically wrong.

George Bush had high hopes that Jimmy Carter would keep him on as DCI, at least until a placement was confirmed. Hank Knoche went with Bush to brief the President-elect. "We were invited down to Plains two or three days after the election. . . . We were to have a three-hour session with Carter and Mondale to brief them on the state of the world as we saw it. And I was going to describe some of the covert activities that we had under way. We had three hours down there with them that turned into eight. We were there well into the evening. A fascinating session. And when we arrived on the scene, George asked if he could see the two of them privately before we got into the briefing, and they were gone about ten or fifteen minutes. On their way back, Bush told me that what he had told them was that he wanted to resign effective Inauguration Day. . . . That was perfectly acceptable to them."

Carter selected former Kennedy speechwriter Theodore Sorenson to be the new CIA Director. But the appointment failed when Sorenson's liberal credentials made it clear he could not get Senate backing. On Inauguration Day, President Carter asked Hank Knoche, Bush's deputy, to serve as acting director until Admiral Stansfield Turner was named to the post.

Turner, a patrician-looking man, had first impressed Carter during their days at the Naval Academy. Turner finished first in their class; Carter was farther down the list. Turner had also played football. Eventually, Turner became the head of the Naval War College and used the position to invite the rich and the powerful to speak at the college. One person he invited was the then-little-known governor of Georgia, Jimmy Carter.

In the opinion of scores of CIA officers, Turner's temperament and personality would prove to be a disaster at CIA. He came to the Agency harboring deep suspicions. He did not know exactly what problems he was inheriting or who to trust or what the boys in the backrooms were up to. Turner certainly was no expert on intelligence. The CIA was a strange place that was culturally foreign to him. To protect himself, he brought with him a whole battery of Navy men and put them in positions throughout the Agency. When they started delving deep into operations, the CIA bureaucrats got nervous. According to Knoche, Turner "grew suspicious of anything connected with what he called the establishment of the old boys." After all, throughout the 1970s there had been one scandal after another at the Agency. Turner put aside the "old-boy network" and started promoting the "young turks." He sent out telegrams firing hundreds from the clandestine services. And when one intelligence disaster after another started taking place under his watch, he did not have the "old boys" around to help him clean it up.

Admiral Turner inherited Hank Knoche as his deputy. According to Sam Wilson, Turner soon discovered that Knoche was going around Turner, directly to NSC and White House officials. "On several occasions Turner would show up at the White House to find that Knoche had already been there." Sam Wilson says this was precisely the reason Turner set up a downtown office in the Executive Office Building. Knoche loved the CIA. He could not sit idly by and watch outsiders ruin what had taken years to build. It was not long after that that Knoche retired from the CIA.

Perhaps the problems Turner faced as DCI have clouded his memory, but the former DCI claims to have had nothing to do with Paisley. In fact, Paisley's address book featured both Turner's home and hideaway White House office numbers. Paisley was still a member of MEAP (Military and Economic Advisory Panel that reports to the DCI), and records show that Paisley briefed Turner during 1977 and 1978.

On July 15, 1977, a blond American woman walked across a bridge that spans the Moscow River at the Lenin Hills. She leaned over and started to move a rock on the ground. Suddenly another woman came up to her and, without saying a word, ripped open her blouse, revealing a radio receiver strapped to her chest. The thoroughly stunned blond woman was Martha Peterson, a CIA officer serving under cover as an official at the U.S. Embassy in Moscow. The radio receiver that her KGB adversary uncovered in such startling fashion was being used by Peterson to monitor KGB surveillance. Peterson was servicing what the trade calls a "dead drop"—a hollowed out rock that was used to conceal messages and equipment. The KGB later displayed its contents, which included gold coins, two cameras, poison pills, and a schedule for sending messages via a miniaturized burst transmitter (a device that sends a message directly to a satellite, making it virtually undetectable). The then-thirty-three-year-old Peterson was handling the most important "asset" or mole inside the Soviet government at that time, Aleksander Dmitrevich Ogorodnik.

According to Leonard McCoy, Ogorodnik was first recruited in Bogotá, Colombia, in 1973. He had fallen in love with a Colombian woman and needed money to support his love affair. This recruitment, one of several successful operations in Latin America in the mid-1970s, gave the United States a reliable and well-placed source in the

Soviet Foreign Ministry. Ogorodnik was eventually transferred back to Moscow to work at the Foreign Ministry, in the Global Affairs Section.

Ogorodnik was not a believer in American democracy, but he did believe in capitalism. He sold out the Soviet government for several large payments in gold. The CIA's Soviet Division gave Ogorodnik the code name TRIGON. For two years a wealth of material—much of it gossip involving key personalities in the Soviet Foreign Service— emerged from TRIGON. But the handling of this source was neither careful nor skillful. Use of standard tradecraft in Moscow, such as dead drops, was considered both dangerous and potentially embarrassing. The KGB is so overstaffed that putting full surveillance on *all* CIA people in Moscow is standard practice. The compromise of Martha Peterson was fairly predictable, considering the risks of working in the Soviet Union.

Once Peterson was arrested, the CIA considered TRIGON compromised. It was clear to McCoy that Peterson had been set up for her arrest at the drop site. What the CIA did not know was how long the KGB had been onto TRIGON, or how they had got onto TRIGON in the first place. Another thing the CIA had to know was if the KGB had forced TRIGON to start feeding back phony material, and if so, when. Almost immediately, Leonard McCoy, who had been a reports officer on so many similar cases, would now look at the TRIGON case as a counterintelligence officer. Since early 1975, McCoy had been the number-two man to George Kalaris, who had replaced James Angleton. Neither Kalaris nor McCoy had any real experience in counterintelligence when they took over from the renowned spymaster. And in the ensuing years, they did little to impress many counterintelligence veterans or the FBI. But, as discussed later in this book, the biggest body blow to Kalaris and McCoy was the bizarre management of the Nick Shadrin case.[37]

By 1977, when Martha Peterson was arrested, McCoy's reputation as a counterintelligence expert was suffering badly. McCoy says that CIA Director Adm. Stansfield Turner gave him only two weeks to find out how TRIGON was compromised. In an attempt to find out what had happened that caused the Peterson arrest and the subsequent execution by the KGB of TRIGON, McCoy found himself in a political mine field. For a brief time, McCoy suspected that Dr. Henry Kissinger may have played a role in the compromise of TRIGON. One piece of intelligence that came McCoy's way was a bizarre NSA intercept from the Soviet Embassy in Washington in April 1977. The cable was sent by Ambassador Anatoly Dobrynin to the Foreign Ministry in Moscow. It referred to advice Henry Kissinger had given Dobrynin on how to deal with the new Carter administration in the ongoing SALT II negotiations. For McCoy, the cable was a shocking document. The idea that a former Secretary of State and National Security Adviser would meet alone, as a private citizen, with the Soviet Ambassador to discuss negotiating techniques seemed almost beyond belief to McCoy.

The cable gave credence to an old file McCoy had inherited when he moved into CI—the file of the original investigation and supporting documents looking into Kissinger's loyalty that grew out of Michal Goleniewski's charges in 1969. What made matters worse was that Angleton's old office files also reflected long meetings Kissinger and Dobrynin had had alone during the Nixon years. Angleton noted that Kissinger had refused to be debriefed after those meetings. All McCoy knew was that Kissinger had displayed a questionable pattern of behavior. Now a key source in the Soviet Foreign Ministry had been lost, and it was a source that Kissinger was in a position to identify to the Soviets.

Paisley: The Investigator

—————————————— ❮ ——————————————

I think I knew him as well as I knew any human being, almost. But I am perfectly aware that there have been other circumstances where people have . . . been double agents and the person next to them didn't know. So I am aware there could have been a John Paisley that I didn't know. But it's hard for me to recognize that. Do you understand what I am saying?

Betty Myers

IN AUGUST 1977, a thoroughly frustrated David Sullivan came to Leonard McCoy. The two men had grown to know and respect each other over the years. Sullivan went to McCoy for advice on how to get his report on SALT I cheating published by OSR. The young analyst thought the number-two man in counterintelligence would certainly have the power to help him over what he considered more than just bureaucratic hurdles. "I had gotten nothing but resistance from the top brass in OSR, and I thought Leonard might be able to get it read to the right people," Sullivan said.[1] McCoy said he gave the paper to Rusty Williams, a top aide to DCI Stansfield Turner.

A week later, when Sullivan stopped by, McCoy told him that Williams had indeed made sure the report was seen by the "right" people.[2] The two men talked, as they often did, and Sullivan brought up a theory as to why no one was embracing his years of work on the

SALT I cheating study. He asked McCoy about the possibility of a mole in the U.S. government. Sullivan revealed to McCoy that in a right-wing book he had discovered in the CIA's library, he had run into a theory that Henry Kissinger was working for the Soviets. Sullivan told McCoy that in light of what he considered the U.S. giveaway at SALT I, and the obvious failure of America's satellites, human, and signals intelligence, he was deeply concerned about Kissinger. "I asked him, 'Am I crazy to think this about Kissinger?' He said, 'You are not crazy to think about it.' He [McCoy] said, 'Come back in a few days.' So I came back in a few days and he shared with me parts—only parts—of his damage assessment on TRIGON. What he shared with me was his punch line. His punch line said that [in McCoy's opinion] the only way to describe Kissinger's actions from what the evidence of this cable showed, if it was valid, was treason."[3]

McCoy said that he was trying to get Sullivan to help him with some specific information he wanted concerning the Soviet cable referring to Kissinger's luncheon advice to the Soviet Ambassador. "He let me see this cable that had him worried. McCoy wanted to make certain the cable was genuine before he forwarded his report on Kissinger. The key to the whole thing—was this last cable doctored up by the KGB to burn Kissinger, or was it a bona fide piece of information? That was his question. Then we went through the implication for either hypothesis, and both were very bad for Kissinger," Sullivan said. Sullivan recalls that McCoy told him that adding to the verification problem was the fact that Kissinger had refused to take a polygraph examination after his private meetings with the Soviets.

Now at the CIA, two men coming from totally different directions had reached the same conclusion. Sullivan turned McCoy's theory over in his mind and thought about McCoy's need to verify the cable before he could proceed. In January 1978, Sullivan went to see McCoy: "I got the idea if we really did have a piece of information like this we ought to check it out at NSA. So I went back to Leonard and said, 'Let's do it,' and he said, 'Fine.' "

The only way to confirm the authenticity of the cable was to go out to NSA, pull the transcripts of other cables sent from the Soviet Embassy, and compare the style, content, and timing. David Sullivan was "all source cleared" and had befriended the people at NSA who prepared the intercept transcripts. He suggested that he and McCoy get a car from the motor pool and go out to NSA together. At the last minute, McCoy said he was tied up, and he gave Sullivan a copy of the cable for him to work on at NSA.

"So I did a study all day, came back, wrote up a two-page memo, and gave him a copy and my chain of command a copy." Sullivan and the experts at NSA concluded that the cable was real, and not a Soviet disinformation effort. McCoy disagreed and now maintains that NSA could not have made a clear determination of the cable's authenticity. Sullivan handed the material back to McCoy. "He told me what we were doing was just between me and him, but I couldn't operate that way, so I told my entire chain of command in OSR," Sullivan said.

Based on Sullivan's efforts, McCoy finished his damage assessment on the TRIGON case. It included the damaging material about Henry Kissinger. A copy of the report was promptly sent to the White House, where it caused immediate concern. But Henry Kissinger still had a friend working in the Carter White House who protected his interests. William Hyland, Kissinger's longtime assistant, had stayed on to work with the Carter administration. When he learned of the report, he was furious.[4]

Sullivan said that "McCoy's report was hot stuff for a bureaucrat to be dabbling in." McCoy says that "because Admiral Turner gave me only two weeks to do the TRIGON damage assessment, the proper investigation was never done. It wasn't until after I left the CIA that I realized it was Karl Koecher that compromised TRIGON."

McCoy says that the haste of that investigation kept Koecher's connections to other CIA and intelligence officials from coming out, including those with John Paisley. Koecher and his beautiful wife and accomplice, Hana, had attended the same sex parties with Paisley in the 1970s. Koecher was inexplicably given a job as a translator in the Directorate of Operations "AE Screen Unit." According to McCoy, Koecher's bosses thought this was a misuse of his talents. Instead of just translating Koecher was allowed to evaluate all Soviet contacts by the CIA, including TRIGON, from the very beginning. Those CIA officials who put Koecher in this position were never called to account for their actions. The TRIGON material was so valuable, it was circulated to the White House on a regular basis. According to McCoy, Koecher, who had inexplicably been given a security clearance, was allowed to learn the most intimate details of TRIGON's life through the material he was given. McCoy said, "Koecher knew enough about TRIGON, including his shirt size, to make an almost immediate identification by passing it on to Moscow."

While McCoy was probably right to conclude that TRIGON had been compromised by Koecher, the FBI and the CIA Office of Security did less well with the Paisley connection. The CI office missed two important points about Koecher in their entirety. First, how did a Czech immigrant get such a high security clearance, considering that a score of better-known and better-connected defectors had been turned down routinely over a generation for such clearances? Second, how did Koecher get a contract from OSR, Paisley's former division, after he left the AE Screen Unit? Despite McCoy and Sullivan's efforts, no one connected Paisley to the TRIGON compromise.

McCoy's report also left out another significant bit of news. According to Washington lawyer John Carbo, the issue of TRIGON came up at a dinner party early in the Carter administration in January 1977. A National Security Council staff member was bragging to several Soviet diplomats at the party that the United States had a source right in the Soviet Foreign Ministry. According to Carbo, this conversation so alarmed Gen. Vernon Walters, who was also at the party, that he reported it to the CIA's Office of Security.

According to Sullivan and Clarence Baier, an OSR colleague, it was very unusual for senior analysts to be cleared for original source material, as Sullivan was. That same colleague was critical of Sullivan. Baier explained that Sullivan was so adamant in his positions that "we moved him over to S&T Intelligence (Science and Technology) because nobody could get any product out of him." Baier said this was probably where Sullivan got access to the material he needed to make a case that the Soviets had cheated on SALT I. He said, "I am very surprised he was able to go out to NSA and read diplomatic traffic." Baier cautioned that Sullivan became a zealot "over almost any issue he got into."

Phil Waggener, who was then the Deputy for Strategic Research, said that he blocked the publication of Sullivan's report because it was too political. "He wanted to turn us into a political organization with a point of view, and that wasn't our role." Waggener does credit Sullivan with uncovering new facts about the Soviets and SALT I. "But they could have found loopholes in a badly negotiated treaty, and he wrote that they had fooled and cheated us."[5]

Paisley sailed *Brillig* to the Florida Keys in late 1977, where he took scuba-diving lessons. On February 21, 1978, Paisley sent a postcard of a diver in the Florida Keys to his old CIA office. Betty Myers accompanied Paisley for portions of the voyage. She says John was particularly unhappy during this trip. On the voyage, Paisley visited Richard Scott, the former Director of Communications for the CIA and a fellow ham radio operator. After Myers left, Norman Wilson and his wife, Barbara, nicknamed Bobbie, joined Paisley. Paisley had met the Wilsons through Phil Waggener in 1971. The Wilsons had allowed Paisley to keep *Brillig* and an earlier sailboat, the *Quiescent,* berthed at their waterfront Maryland home. The Wilsons joined Paisley in Key West, but said his mood was so downbeat that they decided to leave him alone on *Brillig* and go off for a day. "He was obviously morose," Bobbie Wilson recalls. But the Wilsons and Betty Myers are the only ones who say Paisley was downbeat. Others, like Scott, describe his mood on that trip as very good.

By early 1978, Paisley had decided to go back to work full time. His cruise was interrupted by a job offer from the Washington accounting firm of Coopers & Lybrand and by awful news from Oregon about his mother, who was dying of cancer. Paisley arranged to leave *Brillig* with Richard Bennett. Bennett drove down to Beaufort, South Carolina, to meet Paisley and begin the nearly month-long trip to Washington with *Brillig*. Paisley flew back to Washington. To Bennett, Paisley was enthusiastic about his new job and seemed happy. There was no hint of depression. An old Paisley associate, Dr. K. Wayne Smith, had become the managing partner at Coopers & Lybrand and offered Paisley a job as his assistant at the firm. In 1976, Paisley had sent Smith a letter asking for a job. In the letter, which was handwritten, Paisley wrote that he was bored and low on funds, Smith said. Smith got the feeling at the time that "it was kind of a form letter" he had sent to a number of people. Then both men ran into each other at a MEAP meeting and got reacquainted. Smith brought John in as an executive assistant at a $36,000 salary—this was in addition to the more than $1,400 a month in retirement he was collecting from the CIA.

Paisley was one of 304 people working for Coopers in Washington. The fact that he could not balance his own checkbook seems to have had no bearing on his employment. Smith said he hired Paisley for his writing ability, not for his knowledge of accounting and finance. He said Paisley could boil huge amounts of facts down in a clear and concise way. Payments for Paisley's CIA contracts were to be funneled through Coopers & Lybrand.[6] But CIA documents on Paisley's employment at Coopers were backdated. The memo stating that Paisley's contract should be terminated on April 30, 1978, is dated July 26, 1978. It is clear that the Coopers position was needed as some sort of cover job for Paisley during that spring, quite possibly without the knowledge of Dr. Smith.

In April, Maryann Paisley flew to Oregon to spend time with her dying mother-in-law. Maryann never told John's mother about the breakup of the marriage. They passed the time making audio tapes of the family history. Maryann spent a month with her in-laws.[7] If anything, this personal tragedy Maryann shared with John seemed to bring them a little closer, according to friends and family.

Just before Paisley began work at Coopers, he flew out to Oregon to visit his family. This was the first time his sister would learn of his and Maryann's separation. Katherine wanted the rest of the family present because it was obvious that Clara Paisley was dying and some decisions had to be made. Dale's wife, Mary, remembers that "Dale and Jack were absolutely useless. They were a couple of basket cases. So we just forgot about them . . . and Kay [Katherine] and I went up to the funeral home to make the arrangements."[8]

Paisley's trip to see his dying mother was not an easy one. Katherine remembers that one night "mother was in very deep pain, I mean I wouldn't let a cat or dog suffer like that. I couldn't give her any more drugs. She wanted her pill bottle so she could take a pill when she needed it. I knew what she had in mind, and Jack said to me, 'So why don't you give her the bottle?' And I said, 'I can't. If you want to give it to her, you give it to her.' Well, he couldn't, either. But that was the hard part, because she was suffering so much and it really shook him."[9]

Paisley told his sister-in-law that he was trying to cut back on drinking and that was why he had made a decision to get rid of *Brillig* and get out of "the boating crowd because there was too much booze." Katherine said that her brother had been drinking very heavily in the two years prior to his disappearance. On an earlier trip to Oregon, Paisley had carried a bottle of rum with him, "and he kept it hidden from mother. He'd pour it in his coffee cup."

Beginning in May 1978, Paisley reported to Coopers, where he shared the assistance of Kay Fulford, Dr. Smith's secretary.[10] Fulford confirmed that Paisley charged some of his time at Coopers off to the CIA. What was Coopers doing for the CIA? Dr. Smith, who left the firm some years ago, says Paisley was finishing up commitments to the CIA. He said an arrangement was worked out whereby Paisley's contracts were transferred to Coopers & Lybrand, and the CIA would pay Coopers instead of Paisley. Smith said that Paisley was to phase out all CIA activity and commitments. "John wouldn't be doing any CIA work for Coopers." Adding to the mystery of Paisley's activities is that Dr. Smith ordered Kay Fulford to destroy all of Paisley's office files after Paisley disappeared. Smith said there was nothing of value or interest in the files.

Despite John and Maryann's separation, they continued a marital relationship, even during the time he was seeing Betty Myers. When Maryann confronted John about his affair with Myers, he told her he did not love Betty Myers. Maryann realized that the relationship with Myers might have started years before, when she and her family offered Myers comfort during her divorce. On May 1, 1978, Maryann Paisley told Betty Myers to stay out of her life—that she no longer wanted to see her.[11]

Betty Myers says that Maryann was very angry. "Well, we had been close friends. . . . We talked together once, and I think sometimes women are more angry with a woman friend when something like that happens for the loss of the friendship to the women rather than the fact of the man involved. And I really couldn't stay friends with her comfortably after John and I started seeing each other more."

Prior to taking the job at Coopers & Lybrand, Paisley had stayed with one CIA colleague after another when he was back in Washington on business and not sailing on *Brillig*. After his return from his last major sailing trip, in the spring of 1978, he stayed with Betty Myers in her Bethesda apartment for a short time while he looked for an apartment to rent. Of all of the places in the Washington area, John Paisley rented an apartment in the most interesting location. John chose an efficiency apartment at 1500 Massachusetts Avenue in Northwest Washington.

It is true that the apartment complex is just a few blocks from the Coopers & Lybrand offices, but Paisley, according to the staff at Coopers, spent very little time there. Most of the time he had to be reached at telephone numbers at CIA headquarters in Langley, Virginia. Paisley's shared secretary, Kay Fulford, did not see a great deal of him; their offices at 1800 M Street were on different floors. But when she could not find him, she called him at the CIA. Four years after his "retirement," Paisley still had an office at the CIA. When Paisley was not in his CIA office, Fulford left a message with an office mate in Langley.[12]

In addition to the fact that Paisley's move into town put him farther away from his CIA office, the building he moved to made his beloved ham radio gear almost useless. An eighth-floor, downtown apartment could not be the site for the elaborate and large antennae needed to send and pull in distant signals. There was no great economic incentive for Paisley to live downtown. While it was true that his rent at 1500 Massachusetts Avenue was only $220 a month, bigger, nicer and cheaper apartments were available in the Virginia suburbs, closer to the CIA. Why would a man give up the facilities for a lifelong hobby, live farther away from his real work, and pay more money for an apartment?

From the standpoint of United States national security, the answer is potentially very scary. The practical answer is a mustached Soviet named Vitaly S. Yurchenko. Yurchenko was in the United States as the KGB security man at the Soviet Embassy in Washington during this time period. In addition to running counterintelligence in the embassy, Yurchenko was in charge of security for the "nightcrawlers" — a dozen KGB operatives who lived in Paisley's building. These operatives would leave the apartment complex at night to troll nearby gay bars, looking for unhappy and lonely servicemen, clerks, and secretaries to compromise and blackmail for state secrets.

For security and counterintelligence reasons, Yurchenko had to visit 1500 Massachusetts Avenue on a regular basis in 1978, when Paisley lived there. But even stranger than a high-level CIA man living in an apartment building with known KGB agents were letters that were found addressed to "John Paisley, *Washington Post* Agent." One letter even contained money for newspapers that were delivered. John Paisley had no part-time job as a *Washington Post* agent. The newspaper's complex does, however, share an alley with the Soviet Embassy, on 16th Street in downtown Washington. Top counterintelligence officials say that chances are excellent Paisley used the newspaper as a cover to deliver messages to Yurchenko and his agents. The responses would come in code in the form of complaints about service and delivery.

The question is, was Paisley doing this under CIA orders? Or was it part of a pattern that includes the discrepancies in his early travel, the post office box in England, the leaks to the press, and the sex clubs involving Koecher? Paisley was once in charge of clearing the "feed" material for defector Nicholas Shadrin to give to the Soviets. In August 1985, when Yurchenko defected to the United States, he underwent an amateurish debriefing while staying in a house on the outskirts of Fredericksburg, Virginia.

There he told his CIA handlers that he was aware of how Nicholas Shadrin had disappeared in Vienna on December 20, 1975. The CIA took Yurchenko's comments on Shadrin at face value and immediately informed the FBI that the Shadrin case had been solved. The one possible, tenuous connection between Shadrin and Yurchenko took place in Washington, in 1978, through John Arthur Paisley. Despite the proximity of the two men, the CIA interrogators never asked Yurchenko about Paisley, even though they were well aware that Yurchenko had visited Paisley's apartment building during the time Paisley lived there. The net effect was to demonstrate one of the most feeble debriefings in defector history and to reveal the fact that the CIA did not have the institutional memory to ask Yurchenko about Paisley.

If Paisley was sent to 1500 Massachusetts Avenue to pose as a retired CIA man out in the cold, ready to sell out his country and make contact with Yurchenko or one of his agents, it was not done under the direction of the CIA's counterintelligence officers. Leonard McCoy denies he knew about any such operation involving Paisley. In fact, McCoy considered Paisley a man who was "coming unwound—apart at the seams" during his final days. "Paisley was like a big St. Bernard. He never broke anything big. He was always cautious and loyal," McCoy says. McCoy thinks it is possible that the interrogation team would have expected Yurchenko to volunteer whatever he knew about Paisley. That would make perfect sense if Yurchenko were for real. Yurchenko didn't volunteer information about Paisley before he decided to return to the Soviet Union.

McCoy says that if Paisley had been a Soviet agent, "it is possible that Paisley was being run not by Yurchenko at all, but by a different channel.'' McCoy points out that this is how the Soviets ran the infamous Walker family.

By early November 1985, it was too late to ask Yurchenko about Paisley. He had gone home, fed up, or so he said, with the CIA. The defector and possibly the man with answers about Paisley got away.

The facts remain that there is no evidence to show that Paisley was conducting operations on behalf of the United States government; in fact, the evidence is to the contrary. But if Paisley was acting in a counterintelligence function for American intelligence and had entered that dangerous game by making himself bait first at the sex parties with the Koechers and later by moving in with the KGB's nightcrawlers, then he could have been betrayed or found out—making the events that took place on the Chesapeake Bay the inevitable last act in a sad drama.

Maryann Paisley recalls John joking about living at 1500 Massachusetts Avenue. She says that in 1978 John joked about living so close to the National Rifle Association and the Soviet Embassy, two organizations for which he had little use.[13] Despite Maryann's estrangement from John, the two remained good friends. John's sister, Katherine, believes that they made better friends than husband and wife. In the late summer and early fall of 1978, Maryann would talk to John once a day on the phone. Though both were seeing other people, there was a closeness between them that seemed immune to their problems. According to a friend of the Paisleys, William Brock, Paisley and Maryann were ''attending some sort of marriage counseling together on a regular basis.''

Strangely, Paisley's own actions seem to indicate that he was a man running out of time by the summer of 1978. He called Leonard Masters and made a very strange request. He asked him about the possibility of his getting back into the Merchant Marine as a radio operator. ''I said there are vacation jobs and all kinds of opportunities. And he said, 'Well, there are certain parts of the world I can't go to.' '' Masters said he wrote Paisley just before his disappearance, telling him about jobs that had just opened up.

Masters was not the only one Paisley consulted about returning to his old profession of shipboard radio operator. Paisley's daughter, Diane, waitressed at a suburban Virginia restaurant called the Cedar Inn, where a radio club met once a week. She introduced her father to William Miller, a club member and longtime ham. Paisley began to attend the meetings and confide in Miller.

Miller, who had worked for companies that did intelligence work including supplying the CIA with top-secret burst transmitters, said that Paisley asked him to help him get his commercial radio licenses. Miller said that in 1977 he gave Paisley the proper handbooks to take with him to the Caribbean for his winter cruise on *Brillig*. Miller also got Paisley a new two-meter radio for *Brillig,* a radio that he says was never recovered after Paisley's disappearance.

Diane Paisley asked Miller to call her father via radio when he was cruising the Caribbean. "As a matter of fact, when he was down in the Caribbean, when he was on his tour, I used to communicate with him and pass word back to Diane. She'd monitor it at home. She couldn't get on [operate and transmit on the radio], of course. That's the reason she wanted to get her license. But whenever she wasn't working or at school, she would listen," Miller recalls.

Paisley confided in Miller that he had a varied career with the CIA, including a stint around 1975 that involved a defector. "He told me just a little bit about it," Miller said, "that he had been a companion for one of the defectors in North or South Carolina."[14] Paisley also made comments to Miller from time to time about the Watergate break-in that indicated to Miller "he knew more about it than your average guy on the street." But Miller said he had no reason to pry. "After all, I had security clearances at that point myself."

It was Diane, Miller explains, and her brother, Eddie, who pushed their parents into seeing a marriage counselor. "The kids talked them into going for counseling." Miller recalls that after the radio-club meeting Paisley would usually stay for an extra drink, but on some days "he'd say, 'I can't stay today. I have got to pick up Maryann. We're going to a marriage counselor.' "

Coinciding with the Paisleys' marriage counseling was the breakup of the Myers-Paisley relationship. According to Betty Myers, Paisley never told her they were breaking up. Myers's version of events is far different. She says that Paisley was depressed about her taking a job in Cumberland, Maryland and the couple being apart.

Myers says that Paisley spent most of his time at her Bethesda apartment during early 1978. One of the things Myers recalls is asking Paisley to get rid of a gun he had bought for protection aboard *Brillig* on his last cruise to the Caribbean. "I don't like guns and I asked him to take it away and get rid of it. And he said, 'Okay, I am going to sell it.' And he took it, and that was sometime during the last six weeks."

Though Paisley's other friends and members of his family remember him as never looking fitter than he did in the summer of 1978, Betty Myers and Norman Wilson say he looked poorly and was irritable. "But I talked to one of my psychologist friends and he said, 'Well, of course he's irritable; you're leaving and going.' He just said he thought it was just the ordinary thing, a couple having to spend some time apart when you really didn't want to do that."

Paisley was supportive of Myers's move to Cumberland without him: "I did go back after the interview and discuss it with John and how it would be for us to be separated, and he was reassuring and he said it would be all right—'there are trains and cars and buses, and you and I are both able to drive'—and he was just kind of reassuring on that point." But Myers says Paisley did get irritable with her. One example she gave of Paisley's irritability was an occasion when he read her a poem about the unfaithfulness of women.

Paisley genuinely liked Betty, but she seemed to want the stability of marriage. Paisley told friends that their relationship was now essentially over and marriage was the last thing on his mind. [15] But Betty saw things differently. Myers says that in the summer of 1978 she was worried about leaving Paisley, and he sensed that. "I expressed concern about it and he got very upset one evening just sensing that I was worried about it and he said—he told me not to cry—that he had only just begun to want to live."

There are conflicting stories of Paisley that summer. The Wilsons say that when they invited Paisley to their daughter's wedding on August 12, he did not know whether to bring Maryann or Betty. Bobbie Wilson said, " 'That's up to you, John, it doesn't matter to us.' So he came alone. All dressed up . . . I never saw him dressed up before, but he had on a white jacket and tie."

Norman Wilson noticed a remarkable difference in Paisley. The Wilsons had not seen Paisley since that trip to Florida on *Brillig* earlier in the year. The last time they had seen him, he was drinking too much and smoking too much. "His health was getting bad and he was uptight." But this time, to Norman Wilson, "he acted very different. He's always been very impersonal and kind of unapproachable and we never probed him personally, and it was all very casual but friendly for years and years. No confessions, no emotions, except at the wedding. He broke down and he was very emotional. He put his arms around my neck several times. He was just a different person almost."

Betty Myers found John morose and unhappy. On August 25, 1978, Myers gave John a fifty-fifth birthday party at his apartment. "He had this depression most of the time that I was close to him so I would only see flashes. I never really got to know him intimately when he was really feeling good. But after his birthday party, another lightness that I saw struck me. Someone had brought balloons and we blew up a few. . . . After everyone left, he sat down on the floor and blew up all the balloons, tied them, took them up in his arms, and opened the window onto Massachusetts Avenue and pushed them all out and they flew all over the park and that was a wonderful thing to see him do."

Shortly after the wedding, Paisley had called Norman Wilson to invite him to the party. Wilson was disturbed by his conversation with Paisley, who told Wilson he did not expect to exceed the speed limit. Wilson said he took it to mean John was living too hard and too fast and that he did not expect to live past fifty-five, not that he was depressed and contemplating suicide.

The last evening Betty and John spent together in her Bethesda apartment before her move to Cumberland was sad. The atmosphere was one of a place in transition, with moving boxes scattered all around. Paisley brought only a little half-bottle of wine to go with their dinner that evening. Betty found that strange, since John liked wine and liked to drink. Betty says John told her that his therapy group was critical of him for not being more supportive of her career move to Cumberland.

While Paisley was going to group therapy at the urging of Betty Myers, he was also going to marriage counseling sessions with Maryann at the urging of their daughter. And he still maintained a sexual relationship with Maryann as well as Betty Myers.[16] Myers says she was only aware of Paisley's platonic relationship with Maryann. "Well, she was an important person [to him]. I think they had been good friends and had some happy life together and I think, you know, he was a responsible man and I think he had some concerns about her welfare."

The last time Gladys Fishel got a call from John Paisley was in early September 1978. Paisley called Fishel to tell her that he had lost his wallet in the Dupont Circle section of Washington, a few blocks from his apartment. He told her he wanted to put a legal notice in the *Washington Post*. This seemed to Fishel a strange thing to do, and she told him just to notify the credit-card companies. But the call to Fishel was only the first in a series of strange events in that fall of 1978.

At the CIA that spring, David Sullivan was getting negative reactions to parts of his paper on SALT I deception. Sullivan says that Paul Warnke, negotiating the second SALT agreement in Geneva for Jimmy Carter, "cables back the comment that publication of my article would be very unhelpful to SALT II." In July 1978, Sullivan was attending a course in analytical methods for codeword-cleared agency employees. He met Richard Perle at the course, and since Perle was codeword-cleared as a top assistant to the late Senator Henry "Scoop" Jackson (D.-Wash.), he gave him a copy of his report on the SALT I cheating. Sullivan, thoroughly frustrated with a CIA he considered to be fully penetrated by the KGB, said he then began to give Perle OSR material at luncheons and at meetings at Perle's home.

In late July 1978, Paisley stopped by to see an old adversary at the CIA. Despite Paisley's "retirement," he still maintained his codeword clearances and his VNE (Visit, No Escort) building pass that gave him almost limitless access at the Langley headquarters. So when Paisley dropped in to see Leonard McCoy, McCoy found himself more annoyed than surprised. McCoy noticed the badge on Paisley's shirt pocket and considered challenging the presence of a retiree on the second-floor inner sanctum of CI. But he didn't. Much to McCoy's surprise, Paisley mentioned he was looking into problems with leaks of secrets from Capitol Hill to the KGB. McCoy listened to Paisley politely and felt uncomfortable when he left. "It was kind of spooky and, I must admit, rather vague, but being busy, I just wondered what it was all about."

Paisley gave McCoy the impression that he was doing a leak study for MITRE, a major CIA contractor. But Clarence Baier, Paisley's colleague at both the CIA and MITRE, said Paisley's work for MITRE in 1978 was limited to studying early-warning indicators of Soviet strategy for the Pentagon. McCoy, to his regret, discovered just a few weeks later what Paisley's visit was all about.

One thing is clear: Paisley was not doing security investigations for Coopers & Lybrand, MITRE, or the Office of Strategic Research. William Tidwell, who had originally hired Paisley at the CIA and who later brought him into MITRE as a consultant, confirms that Paisley's responsibilities had nothing to do with security matters. Paisley's telephone book indicates that he did have contact with then-DCI Stansfield Turner's office in 1978, but Turner denies ever meeting John Paisley. What may have prompted Paisley's visit to McCoy were OSR staff member David Sullivan's leaks to Capitol Hill. But if Paisley was not working for Turner, then for whom was he snooping around McCoy's office? The KGB?

In late July, Sullivan was notified that his five-year polygraph exam, already two years overdue, was going to be administered. Sullivan says that he was called into the Office of Security and faced the best polygraph examiner the Agency had. Realizing he would be questioned about them anyway, Sullivan, before his polygraph, detailed his contacts with McCoy, the trip to NSA, and finally what he had given and told to Richard Perle. Sullivan was given three polygraph exams and says he passed them all.

Then McCoy was visited by a representative of the Office of Security. He was informed that he had violated an unwritten rule called "need to know." By sharing part of the Kissinger study with Sullivan, he had violated compartmentalization. In fact, Sullivan was fully cleared for everything that McCoy showed him about a case that had been closed by the death of the agent involved. Finally, McCoy was summoned to a meeting with Deputy CIA Director Frank Carlucci and DCI Stansfield Turner. He was assured that Carlucci had been thoroughly briefed by the Inspector General and told there were no grounds for disciplining him. McCoy thought he would simply be reprimanded by Turner.

Turner opened the meeting by saying to McCoy, as if he were a child: "I think you know you have done the wrong thing." McCoy, who considered Turner a pompous amateur, responded by saying, "I don't realize that at all." McCoy was amazed that Carlucci, who knew the story, did not say a word. McCoy recalls that "he simply sat there in a passive manner." Admiral Turner dropped Leonard McCoy one civil service grade and effectively ended his CIA career.[17]

In August 1978, David Sullivan was more angry about security charges being filed against him than afraid. He realized that he had not shown a single document to anyone who did not have all the proper clearances. In a meeting with CIA security chief Robert Gambino, Sullivan said he believed the Agency was penetrated with KGB agents. Gambino shot back that Sullivan was the leaker. Then Sullivan, his Irish temper flaring, looked at Gambino and said, "We have lost spy satellite capability, human intelligence, and signals intelligence. Do you think all of this is by accident?" Gambino did not respond.[18] Sullivan then said, "I think there is something rotten in Denmark in this Agency. Too much shit has gone wrong. There should not be this much resistance to my work. My work ought to be applauded."

Sullivan told Gambino, "You have got moles here." And he was very specific. "I gave Gambino a list of ten names," Sullivan says. "I will not tell you who is on that list, but on August 25, 1978, I told them that I believed that John Arthur Paisley, the former Deputy Director of Strategic Research, was working for the KGB."[19] While Paisley was blowing up balloons and celebrating his fifty-fifth birthday, a former employee was accusing him of treason.

For Sullivan, the allegation against Paisley was very serious. "I knew he was clearing stuff on his authority. . . . I guess, in the end, I never trusted him. . . . I never liked him. There was just something that wasn't right. He seemed like some kind of burned-out old fart who had a beard and looked like a queer. I am convinced he was the mole."

Sullivan's accusation could not be ignored by Gambino. Gambino took Sullivan's list and had subordinates make cursory reviews of the names. One disturbing item popped up in regard to Paisley: he had not been polygraphed since 1953. Gambino also learned that Paisley still had virtually unlimited access to codeword intelligence. None of this was normal, but there was nothing unusual about a once-senior official falling through the bureaucratic cracks of security. Gambino did not consider Sullivan a very reliable source. After all, he had no direct evidence that Paisley was a mole. But then, Angleton had no direct information about those he had charged with working for the KGB. All of CI is supposition and guesswork. All of it is the working up of a few facts into a plausible theory.

Leonard McCoy went on to an assignment in West Germany with

his new wife and, in retirement, to teach CI at the Agency from time to time. Before McCoy left for his new post in Germany, he sent the TRIGON damage assessment on to the FBI. The report stated his opinion that Kissinger's role required further investigation. No one from the Bureau ever contacted him about the report. There is no evidence that the FBI ever followed up on the years of work the CIA put into the Kissinger case.

Paisley: The Bay

And as in uffish thought he stood,
    The Jabberwock, with eyes of flame,
Came whiffling through the tulgey wood,
    And burbled as it came!

One, two! One, two! And through and through
    The vorpal blade went snicker-snack!
He left it dead, and with its head
    He went galumphing back.

'And hast thou slain the Jabberwock?
    Come to my arms, my beamish boy!
O frabjous day! Callooh! Callay!'
    He chortled in his joy.

'Twas brillig, and the slithy toves
    Did gyre and gimble in the wabe;
All mimsy were the borogoves,
    And the mome raths outgrabe.

          —Lewis Carroll, "Jabberwocky,"
          from *Through the Looking-glass*

10:00 A.M., Thursday, September 21, 1978

The pressures of the early-morning deadlines were beginning to sub-side in the *Washington Star* newsroom when the first of the calls came in. A man who had a foreign accent, but one that could not be easily placed, told the woman who answered the city-desk telephone that a "CIA man would be attacked." The accent was neither North Ameri-can nor Caribbean. It could not be pinpointed as coming from any-where else. There were several calls that day. In one of them, the man identified himself as Ghawzi Ullah of the Moslem War Council.

The FBI and CIA shared an informant in the newsroom of the *Washington Star*. Whenever anything of possible interest came up, the in-formant called the Washington Field Office of the FBI and told his agent handler. He made fewer but similar calls to the CIA. Today was no exception. The informant told the FBI about the strange phone calls; then he called the CIA and told them. He was not paid—at least not in money. Instead, the FBI would help him with stories. The relationship had served him well. He never knew what they did with what he gave them.[1] All he knew was that the newspaper got many crank calls and he figured that his information might as well do somebody some good.[2] Besides, the ever-pragmatic reporter counted on the help from his friends in the FBI.

7:00 P.M., Thursday, September 21, 1978

John and Maryann Paisley met for an early dinner. Although they were still technically separated, the children's problems and counseling had kept their relationship friendly. Maryann's anger over the Betty Myers affair had not subsided. But her anger was directed more at her former friend than at her estranged husband. The dinners had become almost routine. Paisley had told friends conflicting stories about his marriage. He told Don Burton he did not want to be married. He told others that it was Maryann who had thrown him out, and he would like to go back. What is clear is that Paisley continued to maintain a very close relationship with Maryann.[3]

8:30 P.M., Thursday, September 21, 1978

When the FBI officially notified the CIA about the phone call to the *Star,* the CIA duty officer reacted routinely. A call threatening a CIA official was handled by the book. He called FBI headquarters and passed on the information already provided to them by a source at the *Washington Star.* The caller, who identified himself as Ghawzi Ullah, said that unless his demands were met in seventy-two hours, the Moslem War Council would execute three CIA agents in the United States who were foreigners.

11:00 A.M., Friday, September 22, 1978

Because of the mole allegation, the security file on John Arthur Paisley was reviewed for possible reinvestigation. Copies of the detailed security forms were sent to Paisley. For the first time since 1967, he would be required to undergo a full security investigation. This was an odd procedure for a man who had "retired" in 1974. But a look at Paisley's security file showed that in 1978 his access to codeword intelligence was more extensive than ever. He continued to have access to ROUGH (spy-satellite photography), signals and human intelligence. On Friday morning a new personal history form was mailed to

Paisley so that the long, full-field investigation process could get under way.

2:00 P.M., Friday, September 22, 1978

John Paisley called Maryann at the Washington Home for Incurables where she worked. He arranged to have dinner with her on Sunday night, when he returned from sailing. John said they would talk again on Sunday to make the final dinner arrangements.[4]

7:00 P.M., Friday, September 22, 1978

Paisley called Betty Myers. She told him he had sent the wrong clothes by Greyhound bus up to her earlier in the week for an evening event at the hospital where she had taken a job. He told her that he was going to attempt to sell *Brillig* over the weekend. Weeks before, when Betty was looking in Cumberland for a place to live, John had suggested that he sell *Brillig* and that they buy a house together with the proceeds. Betty told him she was not sure she wanted a house in Cumberland.

3:00 P.M., Saturday, September 23, 1978

As John Paisley loaded the rental car in the basement of 1500 Massachusetts Avenue, he probably hoped this early-fall weekend would provide some decent wind for sailing *Brillig*. Betty had borrowed his car to use for moving, so John had rented a car. The 1978-model rental still had a new-car smell to it. It is not known if among the items John Paisley packed for the weekend was a paper bag containing tapes Maryann had made of his mother's recollections. They were his only link to home. Paisley climbed into the rental car and pulled out of the parking garage for the drive down to Lusby, Maryland, where he kept *Brillig* at Norman Wilson's dock.

At age fifty-five, Paisley was not an impressive-looking man. Although he stood five feet eleven inches, his posture was so bad that he appeared much shorter. He was thin, quiet, and almost catlike in his movements. He smoked too much. To see this plain-looking fellow with a beard drive by on Route 4, one would think he was just another bureaucrat heading down to the Chesapeake Bay for the weekend. When he finally reached the little non-town of Lusby, he made the turn from Olivet Road and headed to 81 Joy Road. Paisley always chuckled when he saw the Wilsons' road sign as he drove down the sandy driveway to Norman Wilson's empty and never-quite-finished cottage.

7:00 P.M., Saturday, September 23, 1978

John Arthur Paisley sipped a daiquiri and read James Clavell's latest novel, *Shogun,* in the Wilsons' living room. The Wilsons were at their Falls Church, Virginia, home entertaining friends who were visiting from Japan. Paisley was well into the book when Gordon Thomas walked in the door with his grown son, Richard. Thomas, a retired Army Intelligence officer who had gone into the yacht brokerage business, had heard Paisley was in the market to sell *Brillig.* Thomas, Wilson, Paisley, and many others in Lusby had spent time in the intelligence world. Lusby had become known as "Spooks' Cove." [5] Thomas was also a friend of Norman Wilson.

Thomas had met Paisley before, and thought him an odd man but a genius. Thomas had also met Maryann and thought "she was more odd than John was. . . . John is, to my mind, typical of a real professional spook. . . . They have a spook personality. . . . They're very secretive and they're very introspective . . . and they don't necessarily make sense, but they're as smart as [a] whip because they are playing a role more than they are playing reality."

While Thomas and Paisley talked, Thomas's son inspected *Brillig.* He had to step over a set of diver's weights to get into *Brillig*'s cabin. While Richard Thomas was deciding that *Brillig* was "a great boat," the elder Thomas and Paisley negotiated. Thomas offered $15,000. Paisley said he wanted $17,000. Paisley mentioned that his only interest in selling *Brillig* was that his children only had a few years left in school, and he wanted to buy a bigger sailboat to live aboard. He indicated to Thomas that he would not be needing *Brillig* for the next few years. Thomas told Paisley that he would be happy to charter it for Paisley, if he did not want to sell it.[6]

Chartering interested Paisley. Gordon Thomas explained that the boat would need some cleaning up and minor repairs. The Thomases said good-bye, adding that they would talk again next week. Paisley went right back to reading *Shogun.* Thomas felt as though Paisley was not really there during their conversation: "He seemed so distracted, like his mind was someplace else."[7]

10:00 A.M., Sunday, September 24, 1978

In 1972, Michael Yohn had bought his first sailboat from John Paisley —*Quiescent.* Though Yohn was far too tall to fit comfortably in her cabin, he grew very attached to the boat. Yohn and his wife at the time, Gretchen, had a love for the Chesapeake Bay. Yohn met Paisley through friends when Paisley decided to sell *Quiescent.* Now both men kept their boats together at Norman Wilson's pier, the larger *Brillig* bobbing next to her predecessor in the tree-lined, very private cove.

Yohn found sailing the perfect way to relax after taking on the world's problems as a political adviser to the Department of State's mission to the Organization of American States.[8] While the *Quiescent,* for which he had paid $6,000, looked like a toy next to Paisley's sloop *Brillig,* it gave Yohn what he wanted. Yohn doubted that he would ever have Paisley's deeply felt devotion to the water.[9] Two years before, the Yohns, who had gotten to know the Wilsons through Paisley, bought some of Wilson's property to build their own home on the water.[10] Yohn never considered himself a close friend of Paisley. Both he and Gretchen said they had grown close to the Wilsons.

Paisley and Norman Wilson had much in common. In his more than twenty years at the CIA, John Paisley became the foremost expert on the strategic strength of the Soviet Union. During much of that time, Air Force Colonel Norman Wilson was picking the targets for B-52s inside Vietnam and Cambodia. But the targeting officer and the spy did not meet until 1972, after Paisley returned from his year-long course at the Imperial Defence College in London. Paisley met Wilson through Phil Waggener, who had been Wilson's deputy at NORAD.

Wilson and Paisley shared a whimsical, almost bizarre sense of humor. Wilson took great pleasure in recommending that first-time visitors take a walk down a path through the woods on his property for the "view." What they came upon, looming in the woods, was Diana—a full-size, plastic replica of a dinosaur. Wilson had rescued it when the Sinclair Oil Company decided a lumbering beast was no symbol to use to peddle high-octane gasoline.

That morning the Yohns brought a friend sailing. He was John Elsbree, who worked for the U.S. Public Health Service. The Yohns and Elsbree saw Paisley at the Wilsons' cottage. They chatted with Paisley for a few minutes on a bluff overlooking the cove at Lusby where *Brillig* and *Quiescent* were berthed. Yohn wanted to know why Paisley had a new car. He presumed Paisley had purchased it, since it had a ham radio antennae on it. Paisley told him his own car was in the shop and he had put a portable radio in the rental car. Yohn told Paisley he was going to go down to *Brillig* to retrieve his windbreaker, which he had left on the boat while sailing with Paisley in August. Paisley seemed surprised, according to Gretchen Yohn, and rushed down to the dock after Michael. Paisley was carrying a briefcase. As Yohn was getting off *Brillig* and Paisley was coming on, Paisley knocked his own leather briefcase into the water. As Paisley quickly reached to retrieve it, he explained that he had been working on a report for six months and he wanted to finish it today. Gretchen Yohn felt Paisley's rushing down to *Brillig* in such an odd manner was really inconsistent with his usual laid-back demeanor.[11]

Elsbree, on the few occasions he had met Paisley, had thought him a very nervous fellow.[12] Yohn remembers Paisley being in a good mood and really up for a sail. Paisley and Yohn both agreed to monitor the same radio channels. Paisley carefully set *Brillig*'s radios for 146.04 and 146.52. Both of them decided to sail to the eastern side of the Bay in their respective boats. *Quiescent* left Wilson's dock first. About ten minutes later, Paisley cast off *Brillig*.

Yohn remembers that Paisley was wearing loose khaki pants, a sport shirt, and some sort of shoes.

From across the small cove, Mrs. Caroline Niland waved at Paisley as he sailed *Brillig* out toward the Bay. Paisley waved back. As *Quiescent* and *Brillig* made the journey away from Lusby, Yohn and Paisley chatted over the radio. Paisley spoke to another Lusby radio ham, George Schellhas, over his radio at about 11:00 A.M. The two men discussed Paisley's selling *Brillig* and buying a new boat.

At the mouth of the Patuxent River, Yohn radioed Paisley that there was not much wind and he was going in. Paisley agreed that the wind was not good, but he encouraged Yohn to stay out anyway. Wind conditions did not make for exciting sailing on the Chesapeake Bay that day.

Yohn shared Paisley's passion for amateur radio. But, as with sailing, his attraction to amateur radio did not match Paisley's. On this windless Sunday, the two men periodically resumed their conversation across the radio waves. But Yohn recalls growing bored with the lack of wind. Finally the pull of the Washington Redskins–New York Jets football game on television was too much. Yohn radioed Paisley that he would see him later. Paisley radioed back, asking playfully if Yohn was a "football fan or a sailor." The *Quiescent* arrived back at Wilson's dock at 1:45 P.M. Yohn had missed most of the first quarter of the Redskins game.

At halftime, around 3:15 P.M., Yohn decided to raise Paisley on a new little handheld radio he had purchased, to test its range. He continued to call Paisley at random moments. Paisley responded at about 4:30 P.M. that he had found some wind and made a pretty good day of it. He asked Yohn to tell Wilson when he arrived that he would be getting in late. Paisley indicated that he was having a good time. Two other ham radio operators recall talking to Paisley that afternoon. Paisley tried to raise Lusby radio ham George Schellhas again, but Schellhas ignored the call. He was watching the football game and did not want to be bothered. Schellhas always found Paisley a little strange. "He was out of left field—a little bit weirdo."[13]

5:15 P.M., Sunday, September 24, 1978

Ray Westcott and his wife liked to take family drives because one of their daughters who had serious health problems and had to use a wheelchair enjoyed them. That Sunday afternoon, Ray, his wife, and the four children left their Brandywine, Maryland, home and drove toward the Bay. The Calvert Cliffs nuclear plant is near Solomons Island, Maryland. Ray, then a scientist for NASA's Goddard Space Flight Center, pulled the family car into a parking lot that offered a view of the Chesapeake Bay and the nuclear facility. There were coin-operated telescopes to enhance the view.

After Ray dropped his coin into a telescope, he watched a pretty white sailboat that appeared to be being towed by a barge. It was an optical illusion. The boat was really sailing behind the barge. Then, suddenly, something very strange happened. The Sunday-afternoon calm was quickly erased when a car pulled into the small parking lot. To Ray, the car seemed to park out of the way so as not to be seen by the security guard posted at the entrance. Two men and a woman, all dressed in business clothes, jumped out of the sedan. One of the men removed from the trunk what looked like a case that held electronic equipment. Ray did not like what he saw. It seemed too secretive— too strange. He grabbed his daughter's wheelchair and hurriedly got the family in the car and on the road as quickly as possible. As he drove toward his home, he felt chilled by the entire experience.[14]

5:30 P.M., Sunday, September 24, 1978

Surprised she had not yet heard from John about their dinner date, Maryann called his apartment. There was no answer.

8:00 P.M., Sunday, September 24, 1978

When the Wilsons arrived at Lusby, Yohn told Wilson that Paisley wanted to talk to him. Yohn, again using his new radio, called out Paisley's call letters, K4BM. Wilson remembers the conversation being relaxed. Paisley said he was still doing paperwork and would remain anchored, out by Hooper's Light, a little longer. Wilson said he would leave the lights on the dock turned on, since it would be dark when Paisley brought *Brillig* in. Paisley thanked him, and Wilson said he would have a brass band waiting for him.

Wilson remembers a mellow Paisley: "He told me he was off of Hooper's Light and it was very pretty and peaceful out there. He'd talked to Mike, but he told Mike that he wanted me to call him [on Mike Yohn's radio] when I got in, which I did. I guess in retrospect he was sort of saying good-bye without giving any clues." The men signed off of Yohn's new portable radio. The Yohn family returned to their home in Bethesda.

8:15 P.M., Sunday, September 24, 1978

Wilson prepared to make good on his promise, and rigged up a tape recorder with a John Philip Sousa march to surprise Paisley with when he docked. But the evening went by without any sign of Paisley. Because Wilson had no radio of his own, he could not try to contact him.

It had been several hours since Bobbie Wilson watched Norman rig up a speaker on the dock to play "Stars and Stripes Forever" to herald Paisley's expected arrival. Bobbie was beginning to worry. Norman pointed out that John was a "big boy" and the weather was fine.

Witnesses saw *Brillig* and her trailing dinghy anchored near Second Island in the Hooper's Island group. The boat had one man aboard. She was there all night, and on the morning of the twenty-fifth, she sailed away.[15]

4:00 A.M., Monday, September 25, 1978

Norm Wilson awakened and realized that Paisley had not brought *Brillig* back in. He turned off the dock lights.[16]

9:00 A.M., Monday, September 25, 1978

On this cool, crisp autumn morning, Robert McKay was enjoying the morning crab fishing on his boat, *Miss Judy,* two miles off his hometown of Ridge, Maryland, when he saw *Brillig* coming toward him. *Brillig,* under full sail, was dangerously close when she passed by. Apparently no one was on board. McKay guessed *Brillig* was doing about seven knots. "It looked so pretty, like it was in a race," McKay recalls.[17]

For the next forty-five minutes, McKay kept an eye on *Brillig.* As the wind changed direction, he noticed that she was heading into shore and decided to follow. He watched the boat go aground. He pulled up as close as he could and yelled across to *Brillig*—shouting to find out if anyone was on board. When he received no response, he notified the Coast Guard on his radio.[18]

10:00 A.M., Monday, September 25, 1978

Braced for the cool fall morning, a woman dressed in a black coat was pulled forward toward Scotland Beach by a little black dog on a leash. Her view was toward Point Lookin. The weather was crystal clear. The weekend had been beautiful on the Bay. The powerboaters, the fishermen, and the sailors all tried to stretch another few days out of the dwindling summer season. And so far this Monday promised more of the same lovely weather. When the woman saw *Brillig* with the sails fully set, but with no one at the helm, she had to look twice.

Brillig was in full sail coming from the direction of Point Lookout when she ran aground. Her deep keel trapped her five tons in the mud of the Chesapeake Bay. *Brillig*'s mainsail was fluttering in the breeze. She was aground directly in front of the Hayes Beach Hotel in the tiny town of Ridge, Maryland.

The woman thought it was strange, but she headed home and did not give the incident much thought.[19] Others had seen *Brillig* go aground, as well. An abandoned boat under full sail is not a common sight on the Chesapeake.

10:25 A.M., Monday, September 25, 1978

The Coast Guard, responding to Robert McKay's radio call, notified the Maryland Park Service. They reached Gerald J. Sword, a ranger at the Point Lookout State Park, and asked him to conduct a search for a sailboat that had apparently washed ashore two miles north of Scotland Beach.

10:30 A.M., Monday, September 25, 1978

At the downtown Washington offices of Coopers & Lybrand it was turning into a bad day for Paisley's boss, Dr. K. Wayne Smith.[20] Smith and his boss were anxiously waiting for Paisley to show up for a meeting to go over key budget figures for the firm. Embarrassed and irritated that Paisley was late, Smith asked Kay Fulford to track Paisley down.

Like many other women, Fulford was fond of the easygoing, bearded man who had come to work at Coopers the previous spring. She had had Paisley as a guest in her home. She realized it was unlike John to leave the office high and dry without some notice. She tried all the numbers she had for him, including his apartment a few blocks away at 1500 Massachusetts Avenue, but no one answered. Fulford then decided to call the building manager, Mary Truxton Cummings, and ask her to let William Richbourg from Coopers into Paisley's apartment to see if he was all right.

10:45 A.M., Monday, September 25, 1978

Norman Wilson was surprised to see that John Paisley and *Brillig* had still not come in. Wilson was not worried: "I thought he was out with Betty or one of his girlfriends and had spent the night out there. But that's the first time he had ever done that."

Although Paisley usually called in—using a fellow ham to then phone a message to Wilson—there was nothing unusual about his staying on *Brillig*. Paisley did not pay much attention to traditional comforts. It used to amaze Bobbie Wilson that Paisley thought nothing of opening a cold can of ravioli and eating the contents out of the can with his free hand as he sailed. To Paisley, that was dinner.

10:55 A.M., Monday, September 25, 1978

Ranger Sword arrived on the scene and saw *Brillig* within six feet of the water's edge. He saw no tracks leading from *Brillig* up to the beach. Sword called out to see if anyone was aboard. When he got no response, he climbed aboard *Brillig* and descended into the cabin. He shouted out again. He still got no response. What he saw made him uncomfortable. The cabin seemed to be unusually messy; clothing was scattered about, and a stack of papers with a pencil was on the table.

Sword looked down at the top paper. Shocked by what he saw, he moved the pencil out of the way. The first page contained information relating to the strategic missiles of the Soviet Bloc. On the other side of the table, Sword noticed an open leather briefcase containing letters and personal papers. The top piece of paper in the briefcase was a letter addressed to "John A. Paisley, Washington Post Agent #1401, P.O. Box 9355, 1500 Massachusetts Avenue #847, Washington, D.C." One letter to Paisley complained about deliveries of the *Post* not being made regularly and that payment was enclosed for what had been received.

Sword noted the sophisticated radios on *Brillig*. He climbed out of the cabin, left the boat, went to his car, and drove to Mrs. Edith Dean's house to call the Coast Guard.

11:00 A.M., Monday, September 25, 1978

Richbourg and Cummings entered John Paisley's apartment. Outside the door were Sunday and Monday's *Washington Post*. Paisley's scuba gear was in the apartment. Paisley was not in the small apartment. Richbourg took Paisley's Rolodex in hopes of finding someone who might know his whereabouts.[21]

11:20 A.M., Monday, September 25, 1978

Ranger Sword gave the Coast Guard a full report of what he had seen. Concerned that the boat, with obviously classified documents and expensive equipment on board, was left unguarded, he proposed that he report back to *Brillig* immediately. He was somewhat puzzled when the Coast Guard told him to wait fifteen minutes before going back to *Brillig*.[22]

The Coast Guard sailors who arrived in a boat and boarded *Brillig* before Sword could return noticed some things that Sword had not. Although no one was aboard, the self-steering gear was engaged. But why was she under full sail? Any sailor would know the boat would go in circles. *Brillig* was now twenty-four miles from Hooper's Light, where Paisley had last reported her.

The coastguardsmen observed that the table in the galley was broken. On the floor were the remnants of a meal—pickle loaf. It looked as if someone had been interrupted in the middle of eating. The boat was messy, but it contained a fortune in sophisticated radio gear. High-speed key sets and other expensive ham gear made the cabin different from those of other boats they had seen. Then there was a group of small electronic boxes and antennae that the coastguardsmen found in a suitcase. They had no idea what these were. They found the boat's registration papers, which indicated that the owner was John Arthur Paisley. Two of the radios had been left on.

There were no liquor bottles, but there were cigarette butts in several ashtrays, and papers were scattered about—lots of papers. In a wallet they found, there were some business cards for an accounting firm, two strange, color-coded government building passes, a driver's license, and a MasterCard. Apparently, Paisley had lied to Gladys Fishel earlier about his wallet being stolen. Then they found something useful. According to the letters in the briefcase and the name on all the identification their owner worked for the *Washington Post*. One coastguardsman wondered how a truckdriver delivering newspapers could afford such an expensive boat.

Whatever the fate of the missing master of the vessel, *Brillig* had to be refloated and towed to safety. The boat was valuable, and it was a navigation hazard. As the men prepared to set up the tow, they speculated that the boat's owner might have gotten drunk and gone for a midnight swim. One of them wondered if he had gone swimming with a girlfriend. His shipmate thought the water had been too cold the day before. But the speculation came from experience. People get drunk on boats and do stupid things. One ruled out piracy because the valuable radio equipment seemed to be undisturbed.

It seemed strange to the two men that the radios were turned on. And there was an uncashed check in the briefcase as well as cash in the wallet. The tan pants with the wallet in them were found hanging on the collapsed table. The table seemed almost torn from its hinges.[23] Under the table were a pair of deck shoes and a metal cigarette lighter. A brightly colored shirt was found lying on the aft deck. The Coast Guard vessel radioed back that a man was probably overboard.

St. Inigoes Station immediately put out the word for an air-sea rescue effort. The search area was to cover the water between the Patuxent and Potomac rivers.

When Sword finally drove back to the scene after waiting as instructed, the two coastguardsmen were already aboard *Brillig*. A large Coast Guard vessel was close by in the bay, waiting to assist. Sword noticed that sightseers had gathered on the beach, and wondered if any of them had disturbed *Brillig* before the Coast Guard had arrived.

One of the coastguardsmen told Sword a wallet had been found in the tan pants. He added that he hoped this was not a suicide case. Sword noticed a portable typewriter he had not seen on the boat the first time. The coastguardsmen then lowered the sail and began to tow the boat free. By the time Sword left the area, he realized that what he had seen that morning was not routine. He wondered who was the missing master of *Brillig*.

The men guided *Brillig* expertly back to St. Inigoes. The man in charge of the little Coast Guard station there, Chief Petty Officer James Maxton, had already notified the Maryland Natural Resources Police that another sailor had been parted from his boat. They in turn notified the Maryland State Police, who took no immediate action.[24] The Natural Resource Police treated the case as a possible drowning.

For Maxton, the pending arrival of *Brillig* was just another case of a careless boater. The Coast Guard station at St. Inigoes had its hands full with careless boaters, lost fishermen, and breakdowns. Maxton did not have enough people on hand for this sort of thing. Now he had to notify this guy's family and babysit an expensive boat until the whole matter could be resolved. When *Brillig* came in, Maxton decided he had better have a look himself.

Maxton thought *Brillig* was really a pretty boat. First he noticed the radio gear. He had never seen so much on a boat. The radio equipment was so advanced, he could only recognize a few pieces. It seemed to him to be wildly sophisticated for a sailor. He noted the broken table, the pickle loaf on the floor. Neither Maxton nor his colleagues ever stopped to consider that they might be tromping through a potential crime scene.

The chief petty officer had the kind of mind that notices detail. There were things about *Brillig* that did not seem right. The radio gear was neat and orderly. The radios looked pristine, with cabling just right. Yet the rest of the cabin was in disarray. The contradictions in the condition of *Brillig*'s cabin bothered Maxton.[25] Then, behind the collapsed table was the battered briefcase.

Chief Maxton began the process of trying to identify someone to notify of Paisley's disappearance. He decided the best place to start was the *Washington Post*, to ask them about an employee named John

A. Paisley. Some time passed before the *Post*'s circulation manager, Joseph Haraburda, reported back that he had no *Post* agents by the name of John Paisley. In fact, the *Post* ID number belonged to a longtime *Post* employee named Archie Alston.[26]

Maxton returned to *Brillig,* read the other papers on board, and then realized why no one at the *Washington Post* knew who Paisley was. The report in the briefcase dealt with the military strength of the Soviet Union. The papers mentioned the CIA again and again. They were covered with pencil markings, as if they were being edited. Under some of the papers were a checkbook and register and a phone directory—an old-fashioned flat metal box with a sliding lever that pops up at the correct letter of the alphabet. In the phone directory, Maxton saw hundreds of telephone numbers. Some had the Oxford prefix that Maxton knew was the Pentagon. Then there were many more with a 351 prefix. Maxton did not realize that exchange was reserved for the Central Intelligence Agency. In the back were various extension numbers. There was no way for Maxton to know these telephone numbers were classified. They were part of the "red line," the highly classified phone system at the CIA. There were also less-classified "gray line" numbers.

Then there were the Coopers & Lybrand business cards.

Maxton realized that what he had now was more than a routine boating accident. It was clear from the papers that this fellow Paisley had some government connection. Maxton left everything as he found it and posted an armed guard on *Brillig.* He then contacted his headquarters at Portsmouth, Virginia, to tell them about the briefcase and the report and the radio equipment. In preparation for possible boating accidents that could affect any of its 30,000 employees, consultants, and retirees, the CIA had an arrangement with all major police and emergency services as to how the Agency should be contacted if one of its people was involved in an incident. A Lieutenant Murray at Portsmouth went to the book to determine whom to call at the CIA.

Lieutenant Murray called the CIA's Office of Security to tell them the news. After Murray had passed on the information about the CIA papers aboard the empty *Brillig* and the radio equipment, he told the duty officer that on the night of "Mr. Paisley's disappearance, a Soviet vessel was proceeding up Chesapeake Bay, and on the same night there was an unusual amount of communications traffic from the Soviet summer residence on the eastern shore of Chesapeake Bay."[27]

The Coast Guard, using Paisley's phone directory that was found in his briefcase, succeeded in reaching Diane Paisley.

Noon, Monday, September 25, 1978

Norman Wilson received a call from his old deputy at Colorado Springs, Phil Waggener. In 1977, Waggener had risen to Paisley's old job as the number-two man in the CIA's Office of Strategic Research. Wilson was stunned by the call. When he hung up, he told Bobbie that *Brillig* had run aground about twenty-five miles to the south, at Point Lookin, with no one aboard. Waggener, who liked Paisley very much, seemed very upset. He had been called by his boss, who had in turn been called by the Office of Security after the call came from the Coast Guard.

Wilson quickly tried to reach Betty Myers before Maryann called her. But he did not have her new telephone number. Betty Myers found a series of messages waiting for her at the hospital where she worked, and knew something had probably happened to John.[28] The call from Norman Wilson was not really a surprise. "I was shocked, and I wasn't shocked. I guess I thought he was dead. Maryann didn't think so, but I thought he was dead from the time they told me about finding the boat. But I tried to hope with everybody else."

By the time Richbourg returned to Coopers & Lybrand with Paisley's Rolodex, Phil Waggener had called K. Wayne Smith to tell him that *Brillig* had been found aground and abandoned in the Chesapeake Bay. For Smith it was shocking news. His anger at Paisley's tardiness turned to apprehension.

Smith considered Paisley a good man. He had last seen Paisley the previous Wednesday, before he had to go to a firm meeting in New York. Paisley seemed in good spirits. Smith was puzzled. Paisley had been in good health; he had just passed a physical exam as a condition of employment.

3:00 P.M., Monday, September 25, 1978

By the time Phil Waggener called Paisley's estranged wife, Maryann, it was afternoon. Waggener told her that John was missing and that the Coast Guard had recovered *Brillig*. Waggener said that the Coast Guard had advised him that classified documents were found on board. He informed Maryann that the material had to be recovered—including anything at John's apartment.

Later that evening, Maryann called Waggener and said she had to see *Brillig*. Waggener says that in his opinion Maryann suspected foul play from the start.[29] Waggener picked up Maryann and left the Paisleys' McLean residence for the long ride to St. Inigoes.

Midnight, Monday, September 25, 1978

Waggener and Maryann Paisley met Norman Wilson at the St. Inigoes Coast Guard Station. Maxton allowed only Wilson and Maryann access to *Brillig*. He denied entry to Waggener because he had not been forewarned that a CIA official was going to be present, and it was impossible to verify his identification at the late hour.

Still, no formal police investigation team had been dispatched by the Maryland State Police to go over *Brillig*. Wilson and Mrs. Paisley went out to *Brillig* with Maxton and began to search the boat. Maxton pointed out a suitcase full of sophisticated attachments for the radio gear, and the report mentioning the CIA that he found in Paisley's briefcase.

Waggener said that, strictly speaking, the material was not classified. But it was not classified because it had not as yet been turned in. In the report, Paisley was making recommendations on how to use a new generation of spy satellites to collect data on the Soviet strategic missile program.

Waggener told Maxton the CIA's security people would be out to look at the draft report and the notes. The Coast Guard agreed to release *Brillig* to Mrs. Paisley, and she arranged for Norman Wilson and her son, Edward, to sail her back to Wilson's dock over the upcoming weekend.

To Maxton, Mrs. Paisley's behavior was very strange. "She was more concerned about getting *Brillig* back than worrying about what happened to her husband. Her attitude really bothered me."[30]

Wilson confirms Maxton's observations that finding Paisley did not seem to be Maryann's first priority. Waggener remembers her being convinced that foul play had taken place, but that she believed she "could sense John in a spiritual way and that he was alive."

9:00 A.M., Tuesday, September 26, 1978

The rebuff the Coast Guard gave Phil Waggener the night before would not be repeated. Armed with credentials supplied by CIA lawyers, Joseph Mirabile and Frank Rucco from the CIA's Office of Security drove to St. Inigoes Coast Guard Station.[31]

It was CIA security head Robert W. Gambino's job to protect the Agency from penetration. His number-one concern was to keep the Soviets out of the CIA. Gambino became very active in the Paisley investigation; David Sullivan's sixty-day-old allegations were now coming back to haunt him.

Gambino already knew from Waggener that no "classified" documents had been found aboard *Brillig*.

In a report to Gambino, the security men described their visit to St.

Inigoes to see the papers, *Brillig*, and Maxton. Aboard *Brillig*, they noted a standard marine transceiver that was found in the "on" position by the Coast Guard. Also a Kenwood transceiver, which Gambino later speculated may have been what Paisley used to communicate with Wilson that Sunday afternoon, and a Gladding Islander receiver. In a suitcase in *Brillig*'s cabin was an Atlas 210X transceiver, with a high-speed and regular CW key, as well as other hardware.[32]

The two security men adjourned to Maxton's office, where the contents of Paisley's briefcase were laid out on the desk. The papers were not classified, and revealed that Paisley had been the "coordinator" of a controversial operation called the A Team/B Team Experiment. What the CIA men found was a history of the exercise as well as related documents and notes.[33]

They also ran across the draft of a Paisley article for Sid Graybeal, then the director of Strategic Research, which set out ways that competitive analysis, like the A Team/B Team Experiment, could be incorporated in the National Intelligence Estimates of the CIA. Even though these studies were based on the most classified of CIA sources, Gambino felt that the papers presented no security threat. But Paisley's draft report on the expanded role of spy satellites was another matter.

Although no major secrets were found aboard *Brillig*, Gambino had to face the fact that a man with access to nearly every secret the CIA had was missing. With that in mind, he ordered the Office of Security to continue to monitor the Paisley case carefully. Because the Soviets would have a natural interest in Paisley, he decided the CIA had to let the FBI in on "the general circumstances of this incident." Fearful that Paisley may have had other classified documents, Gambino ordered his people to contact Mrs. Paisley to gain access to John's apartment to see what could be found there.

9:00 A.M., Wednesday, September 27, 1978

At Maryann Paisley's request, Philip Waggener notified the *Washington Post* that retired CIA analyst John A. Paisley had disappeared while sailing on the Chesapeake Bay on September 24. For the first time, Paisley's disappearance became public. The story was treated like a minor police matter by the *Post*.

Maryann and Edward visited the apartment at 1500 Massachusetts Avenue. They were shocked to find that the place looked like someone else had been there first. To Edward, the most puzzling item missing was a paper bag containing cassette recordings that his mother had made of his grandmother the previous spring. The only other things they could find missing were a tape recorder and some coffee cups from a set John had bought for the apartment.[34]

9:00 A.M., Thursday, September 28, 1978

When Robert Gambino's two-page memo to the FBI was hand-delivered to the Washington Field Office on Thursday morning, the FBI went into action. The FBI is nothing if not devoted to procedure. J. Edgar Hoover drummed one tradition into the Bureau—write it down. Every contact, every telephone call, every minor act an agent takes part in, is put down on paper. That is the FBI way.

No agents went rushing out to examine *Brillig* at St. Inigoes. No one even contacted the local police. In fact, the Maryland State Police had not entered into the investigation. And no one turned the case over to the FBI's Soviet Section, because a high-powered CIA man was missing. No, what the special agent who got the memo did was to look for paperwork indicating threats against CIA employees. He was engaged in a classic piece of protecting his rear. His reasoning was good. When one of the FBI's finest veteran agents overlooked a file the FBI had on Lee Harvey Oswald, his fast-track career was derailed forever. This agent was not about to let that happen to him.

A week had passed since the threats to "a CIA man" had come into the city desk of the *Washington Star*. The FBI agent found the "Ghawzi Ullah" memos. The FBI had written the threats off as crank calls.[35]

As part of the case, the Bureau sent an agent to investigate Coast Guard comments about a Soviet ship making its way up the Bay the night Paisley disappeared. In addition, the agent was asked to check out the increased radio communication the Coast Guard had reported out of the Soviet summer compound at Pioneer Point on the Chesapeake Bay. What the Bureau found was not a Soviet ship in the bay, but a Polish ship. The *Franciszek Zubrzycki* had sailed from Wilmington, Delaware, via the Chesapeake and Delaware Canal, to Baltimore. The next day it had departed for Rotterdam. The FBI concluded that the boat had not been in close proximity to *Brillig*. The FBI also pointed out that at all times while the vessel was in U.S. waters, a U.S. pilot was aboard.

Perhaps the strangest FBI assertion was the claim that the Bureau never monitors Soviet radio traffic at the Pioneer Point compound. It concluded, therefore, that the increase in radio traffic detected by the Coast Guard "may have been boat traffic, which is in their realm of responsibility."[36]

An interesting aspect of the FBI's lack of interest in the Paisley case is that a fellow ham radio operator and friend of Paisley's was an FBI agent who was on duty in the Washington Field Office when word of Ullah's threats came in on September 21. That agent, Ken Rupach, later confirmed that he was aware of the threats.[37] The FBI seems to have gone out of its way to downplay the Soviet-related aspect of the Paisley case. Based on information Gambino received from the Bureau, he wrote a memo that the FBI had determined that no particular significance should be attached to the Coast Guard's concerns.

1:00 P.M., Thursday, September 28, 1978

The FBI notified Gambino that it was initiating a kidnapping investigation. He immediately notified key CIA officials. He ordered staff members to brief Dale Peterson in the Public Affairs Office. That afternoon he received a call from Maxton saying the Coast Guard was calling off its active search for Paisley.

Still missing was Paisley's VNE (Visit, No-escort) badge. This badge gave Paisley access to most of the compartments in the compartmentalized world of the CIA by means of various color codes on the badge.

After obtaining keys and permission from Maryann Paisley, Mirabile and Rucco headed to Paisley's building. The eighth-floor apartment was modest. The building had seen better days. The tenants ranged from bureaucrats wanting to be close to work to diplomats who called it home. Its downtown location was very convenient and quite interesting, just six blocks up 16th Street from the White House. But the neighborhood was still a little rough.

For Paisley's immediate neighbors on the eighth floor—eight KGB agents—the building's location was ideal, just two blocks from the Soviet Embassy. And these were not your average, run-of-the-mill KGB agents. They were, after all, the KGB's sexual entrapment artists. In the language of intelligence operatives, they were called "nightcrawlers." Their assignment was to entrap lonely government bureaucrats who handled information of interest to the Soviets.[38]

Paisley's building, 1500 Massachusetts Avenue, N.W., in addition to being close to the KGB resident's office on the third floor of the old Victorian mansion that was then the Soviet Embassy, was a quick walk to a number of gay bars and strip joints in one of Washington's seedier sections. In 1978 the massive redevelopment of downtown Washington had not yet encroached on the hangouts where the Soviet "nightcrawlers" usually hit pay dirt.

Did the FBI have 1500 Massachusetts Avenue under photographic surveillance? Despite the Bureau's public image of being everywhere, the fact remains that the FBI's counterintelligence efforts are hopelessly outmanned by Soviet KGB operatives working under diplomatic and commercial cover. The FBI just does not have the money to keep a constant eye on all of the Soviets. While the Soviets' big new Tunlaw Road compound north of Georgetown, the old embassy, and the military attaché's office on Belmont Road get special treatment, other Soviet facilities are largely ignored.[39]

John Paisley had never reported to the Office of Security that he was living in proximity to so many Soviets. In fact, CIA security rules were so lax they did not require such reporting—even though Paisley was still doing work at the highest levels of the Agency.

That afternoon the two CIA men did not have the slightest idea who Paisley's neighbors were. Their only interest was to make certain no classified files were in Paisley's apartment. After searching the small apartment they removed four linear feet of documents. A great deal of the material consisted of personal papers ranging from old bills and income tax returns to a photograph of a beautiful woman—naked and reclining aboard *Brillig*. All the material was carted back to the Paisley home, not far from CIA Headquarters in suburban Virginia.

In front of Mrs. Paisley, the two men, along with Phil Waggener, rummaged through the documents looking for classified material. Some materials with limited classification stamps on them were taken into custody by the CIA men. Happily for Security, both Paisley's VNE badge for CIA Headquarters and his Pentagon building pass were recovered.

In the pile of papers, Waggener spotted a short note on a yellow legal pad in Paisley's handwriting. Written in large block letters was a name followed by a question mark: "Shevchenko?" The note obviously referred to Arkady Shevchenko, a Soviet United Nations official who had secretly defected to the United States.

Oddly, in his own report on the Paisley case, Gambino simply reported the note. No follow-up investigation on the matter was indicated. Phil Waggener decided to put the note into a CIA burn bag and destroy it. It did not matter. The significance of the Shevchenko note would become apparent in less than two weeks.

Paisley: Death on the Bay?

———————————— ❡ ————————————

I must go down to the seas again, to the lonely sea and the sky,
And all I ask is a tall ship and a star to steer her by,
And the wheel's kick and the wind's song and the white sail's shaking,
And a gray mist on the sea's face and a gray dawn breaking.
I must go down to the seas again, for the call of the running tide
Is a wild call and a clear call that may not be denied.

John Masefield, "Sea Fever"

10:00 A.M., Friday, September 29, 1978

There were two more calls from the man identifying himself as "Ghawzi Ullah." The *Washington Star* informant took the calls. It was the second call that compelled him to notify the FBI.

Ullah, in a voice that sounded "white" to the informant, said that CIA agent John Paisley had been seized by the Moslem War Council's commando units in the Chesapeake Bay area.[1] Ullah told him they found Paisley valuable because he could identify "Zionist agents in other countries."

That weekend the caller to the *Star* seemed to know more about John Paisley, including his work in Palestine, than did anyone in the FBI. After enormous bureaucratic battles between the two agencies and Capitol Hill, it was not until February 5, 1979—more than five

130

months after Paisley's disappearance—that the CIA very reluctantly turned over sanitized versions of Paisley's personnel and other files as well as the Inspector General's report on the case. Gambino took pains to note to the FBI that "transmittal of this material constitutes the first instance wherein complete and unsanitized copies of security and personnel files have been furnished to another agency."[2]

Five days after Paisley's disappearance, the FBI was operating blind. If the FBI believed it was a legitimate kidnapping, it behaved very strangely. Local law enforcement in Maryland was never notified, and nobody from the FBI bothered to visit *Brillig* to look at the potential crime scene.

A CIA memo dated September 29 said the caller claimed his group had kidnapped a CIA employee named "John Taysle." The memo added that the Office of Security indices of past and present CIA employees were searched, and the closest name was John Paisley. The memo continues that "while this memo was being typed," an agent in the FBI's Washington Field Office called to advise the CIA that Ghawzi Ullah had again called the *Washington Star* and stated that his organization had "kidnapped Mr. Paisley and that they grabbed him at Chesapeake Bay. The caller further noted that Paisley had been valuable in identifying Zionist agents in other countries."

The CIA memo said Ullah demanded, in addition to one million dollars, that all Moslem prisoners be released, and that Henry Kissinger be delivered to them. According to the memo, the caller said that he would call again with more details. The caller concluded the conversation by saying "this is no joke—not a game and the fate of Islam hangs in the balance."

The memo says that it was the FBI's conclusion that the caller may have read the short account of Paisley's disappearance in the *Washington Post*. But that does not explain how Paisley's connections to the Middle East, where he spent time in Iraq, Iran, and Israel, were known by "Ullah."[3] And no one in the FBI or CIA gave any indication that perhaps it might have been Paisley himself who had made the calls. After all, they had started several days before he took *Brillig* out that weekend.

11:00 A.M., Saturday, September 30, 1978

Norman Wilson felt very sorry for Edward Paisley. The young man had not had an easy time. In recent years he had been involved in a fatal car accident, he had witnessed the disintegration of his parents' marriage, and now his father was gone.

There was surprisingly little conversation among Edward Paisley,

Norman Wilson, and Michael Yohn as Bobbie Wilson drove them down to St. Inigoes to sail *Brillig* back.

The big former Air Force colonel watched Edward sign the receipts that gave him custody of *Brillig*. Yohn, Wilson, and Eddie Paisley prepared to cast off from the pier at St. Inigoes. The trip back up to Solomons Island would take a couple of hours. Young Paisley's head was filled with questions about his father.

No one at the FBI notified the Paisley family that a kidnapping investigation had been opened. No one called the family to tell them about the "Ghawzi Ullah" threats.

Michael Yohn listened to the University of Maryland football game on the radio as they sailed back to Lusby.[4] Earlier in the week, Phil Waggener had phoned him to tell him that Paisley was missing. Eddie Paisley finished the voyage believing that Norman Wilson knew more about what had happened to his father than he was letting on.

Sunday Afternoon, October 1, 1978

The cloudy and threatening sky and the coolness of the water kept many pleasure boats from venturing out on the Chesapeake Bay that day. But work boats like the *Miss Channel Queen* were used to braving the weather. The *Miss Channel Queen* was cruising two miles southeast of the Patuxent River and three miles off the western shore of the Chesapeake Bay when the three fishermen aboard spotted a green and bloated object floating in the water. It took only a moment for one of the professional fishermen to figure out what it was.[5]

The *Miss Channel Queen* radioed the Coast Guard station at Taylor's Island, and a cutter was dispatched to the scene. Using a wire basket, the cutter hoisted the object aboard. A "floater" usually bears very little resemblance to a living human being. The Bay is particularly unkind to a defenseless human body. This body had ballooned in size and was hairless. A small bullet hole was oozing brain matter behind the top of the left ear. The body looked as if it had on white gloves; in fact, the skin on the hands was sliding off. Obviously the Bay's famed crabs had nibbled away at the corpse until the process of decomposition had set in enough to create the gases that floated the body to the surface. And this body had plenty to keep it down—two nineteen-pound diver's weight belts were wrapped around the corpse.

It was raining when the Coast Guard boat arrived at the Navy's recreational center on Solomons Island. John Murphy, a young Maryland State Police corporal, was sent to investigate. The county coroner, Dr. George Weems, arrived with a local fishing buddy and marina owner Harry Lee Langley, Sr. Langley had seen Paisley around his marina from time to time, and knew *Brillig*.

What these men found was not a pleasant sight. The body was dressed in light blue dungarees, blue socks, a white T-shirt, and a wristwatch called a Chalet, with a black face and green numerals and hands. There were no shoes on the body. Wrapped around the lower chest and abdomen were two diver's belts. The set around the chest had long, thin weights on a black belt with a silver-colored "S" at the buckle. The other set were wider weights and were on a red belt. The body was hairless, and very bloated. One fisherman who had been the first to see it said it was so "grotesque as to be almost not human." Coroner Weems and Corporal Murphy noted the "numerous markings around the neck."[6]

"The body was in bad shape but recognizable," Weems said later. He explained that the neck "looked like it had been irritated, like a kind of squeeze, or there had been a rope around the neck. You get that type of lesion on your neck from hanging. . . . I thought there was foul play."

According to Langley, when he was looking at the body, one of the police officials told him not to say anything. "They told me this fellow worked—had worked—for the CIA and not to say anything about this to anyone. It was all supposed to be all government, all secret."[7]

Weems never mentioned the mark around the neck in his written report on the body to then State Medical Examiner Dr. Russell Fisher. Later, Weems said that he would bet his reputation as a coroner for twenty years that the circle around the body's neck was made before the person was killed.[8] Dr. Weems arranged for the Beall Funeral Home to take the body to Baltimore for forensic examination.

Sunday Night, October 1, 1978

For Robert Gambino, the weekend was no escape from the pressures of the Paisley case.

The last three years had not been kind to the Office of Security. Espionage by a TRW Systems, Inc. employee named Christopher Boyce and his drug-dealing friend, Andrew Daulton Lee, had cost the American taxpayers billions in spy-satellite technology sold to the Soviets for thousands of dollars. A low-level, fired CIA employee named William Kampiles had sold the Russians the manual they needed to confirm Boyce and Lee's information. What the public never learned about the case was that a high official in the CIA's Counterintelligence Division had withheld details of Kampiles's sale of the Keyhole-11 (or KH-11) spy-satellite manual to the Soviets for several weeks while that CIA official underwent hospitalization. This delay gave the Soviets the chance to confirm that the material they had been buying from Boyce and Lee matched what Kampiles had given them. A billion-dollar satellite system was compromised. The United States had been counting on this very sophisticated satellite to verify President Carter's cherished Strategic Arms Limitation Treaty (SALT II).

But the great disaster for the Office of Security had taken place in Vienna in December 1975, when a handsome Soviet defector, who had come to the United States with his lover in 1959, disappeared in Vienna without a trace. Nicholas Shadrin had been a U.S. double agent since the early summer of 1966. Because top CIA officials felt the Agency had been penetrated by a Soviet mole, only the Office of Security was entrusted with the full details of the Shadrin operation. And a high-ranking Office of Security official was sent to protect Shadrin in Vienna. When his disappearance broke in the newspapers during the summer of 1977, the Office of Security's reputation was badly damaged. John Paisley had been in charge of approving the material that Shadrin fed to the Russians during the ten years before Shadrin disappeared.

So when Robert Gambino's phone rang late Sunday night, he had every reason to believe more trouble was ahead. He learned that the wire services were reporting in small stories that an unidentified body had been found floating in the Chesapeake Bay. Gambino was frustrated to learn his deputies were getting no cooperation from the Maryland State Police or the Coast Guard.

That Sunday evening was the first time the Maryland State Police actively entered the case.

Monday Morning, October 2, 1978

Paul Terrance O'Grady looks a bit like Jack Lemmon and practices law in Falls Church, Virginia. O'Grady was on an approved list of lawyers that CIA employees could use for routine personal business. He came to Maryann Paisley's attention through a real-estate deal in which her husband and other CIA officials invested. O'Grady was an unlikely fellow to pick to take on the CIA. But when Maryann Paisley came to him, she was beginning to believe that the Agency for which she and her husband had worked was not being forthcoming.

O'Grady called Gambino and told him that Mrs. Paisley had not been kept informed of the progress of the investigation by the CIA, the FBI, or the Maryland authorities. A patient Gambino explained that the FBI was an independent agency and that the CIA's only concern was for classified documents Paisley may have had. Gambino called the FBI and informed them that Mrs. Paisley had hired a lawyer.

10:00 A.M., Monday, October 2, 1978

Maryland State Police Corporal John Murphy began his investigation of the Paisley case with a phone call to the Director of Security for the CIA. Murphy told Gambino that the body probably could not be officially identified without extensive tests because of the amount of damage done by the water.

Murphy decided to interview Norman Wilson.

Before the body was found floating in the Bay, Norm Wilson had an intuitive flash about what he thought had happened to John Paisley. He told his wife, Bobbie, what he thought: "That he had hung over the side with one hand and shot himself with his left hand and then just dropped in the water with his belts on . . . I described that scenario before they found the body with the bullet in the left side."

When Murphy arrived at the Wilsons' cottage, Norm told him that he had seen Paisley's diving weights on *Brillig*. Corporal Murphy walked down to the pier and boarded *Brillig*. Wilson explained that he had already "cleaned up the boat." Murphy's visit marked the first time that a police official had been aboard the boat, more than a week after the Coast Guard had recovered it.

Wilson advised Murphy that he had seen no sign of an altercation aboard *Brillig,* but that he had found a 9mm bullet under the table, which he then turned over to Murphy.[9] Wilson told Murphy that Paisley had owned either a 9mm or .32-caliber gun that he had purchased when he went sailing in the Florida Keys. Wilson said Paisley bought the gun for protection from pirates. Wilson informed Murphy that it was strange the gun was not on board, because Paisley always left it aboard *Brillig.*[10]

As Murphy was leaving, Wilson stated that Paisley had been extremely depressed up until about a week before his disappearance. He thought it could have been a result of the separation from his wife Maryann, but that he just was not sure. Wilson told Murphy that Paisley had borrowed $2,500 from him to pay taxes, and that Paisley had paid it back within a month.

11:00 P.M., Monday, October 2, 1978

The grim building in downtown Baltimore that serves as headquarters for the Maryland State Medical Examiner was deserted when Dr. Stephen Adams began the unpleasant task of trying to determine how the John Doe recovered from the Bay had died. Looking down at the corpse on the table, Adams saw a five-foot-seven-inch, 144-pound white male. The corpse's brownish gray tongue was sticking out from its bloated face. The single gunshot wound above and behind the left ear had caused the skull to fracture much like a plate-glass window hit by a baseball. The jacket and slug were found separately in the head. As Adams removed the slug from the skull, he noted that the brain had turned to liquid.

Maryland state troopers Frank Rawson and T. C. Cooke witnessed the macabre scene. Dr. Adams arrived at several important conclusions. The first was that the gunshot wound had killed the person. There was no food in the stomach. There was not enough blood left in the body to successfully determine blood type. Skin slippage on the hands was so bad that successful fingerprint identification might be nearly impossible. The body had a complete lower plate and partial upper plate, making a dental confirmation difficult.[11] The only serious medical condition Adams discovered was the presence of six gallstones. The other key systems seemed to be normal.

Adams's boss, Dr. Russell Fisher, who has since died, did not like loose ends. Although Adams had no conclusive evidence that the body he examined was John Arthur Paisley, Fisher made a decision to reconcile the abandoned *Brillig* and the recovered corpse as one incident. Cause of death was listed as a gunshot wound to the head. Fisher and Adams made no determination as to whether Paisley had killed himself or been murdered. Adams removed the hands from the corpse and turned them over to the Maryland State Police for fingerprint identification, who in turn delivered them to the FBI.

The marks around the body's neck that so alarmed Dr. George Weems, Corporal John Murphy, and Harry Lee Langley were ignored by Fisher in his report. Remarkably, without any confirmation of the fingerprints, Fisher included a sheet in the report dated October 1, 1978, identifying the corpse as John Arthur Paisley. The fact that no one from his office had looked at the corpse until October 2, 1978, did not seem to bother Dr. Fisher. Fisher wrote that identification of the corpse as Paisley's came from fingerprints the FBI had on file for Paisley.[12]

After Midnight, October 3, 1978

Gambino reached Corporal John Murphy of the state police. Murphy told him the body recovered was in terrible shape and not identifiable through simply exterior examination. Murphy told Gambino the only possible way of confirming that the body recovered was Paisley's was through fingerprint and dental examination.

10:00 A.M., Wednesday, October 4, 1978

The only stories about John Paisley in the press so far had been very minor, routine police items. But when a small newspaper in Wilmington, Delaware, ran a detailed account of who Paisley was and that CIA officials were concerned that Paisley might have been a KGB target because of the important information he had access to, the story was picked up and carried in newspapers around the world.[13] The private matter of John Paisley's disappearance was no longer private.

The CIA was caught totally by surprise not only by the story, but by the public reaction to it. Dale Peterson, a naval officer who was a spokesman working for Herbert Hetu, one of the many non-CIA people Admiral Stansfield Turner brought into the Agency, called the story nonsense and described Paisley as a "low-level analyst." With that statement began the most severe erosion of the Agency's credibility since the public hearings held by the Church Committee in 1975.

As papers in the Washington area began to investigate the story, the Wilmington paper kept pressing two issues: the problems with the identification of the body, and what Paisley really did at the CIA. The CIA press office, largely through Peterson, continued to issue incorrect information about Paisley to the point where it became relatively easy to contradict the Agency's version by facts gathered by the newspaper reporters. An open war erupted between much of the press and the CIA. Hetu's office put out statement after statement of misinformation concerning Paisley that began to seriously undermine Admiral Turner's credibility. The statements also upset Paisley's CIA colleagues, according to Phil Waggener. Turner, highly unpopular in the Agency because of his firing of thousands of veteran employees and his remote personal style, found himself isolated on the Paisley matter. Instead of experienced Agency executives coming forward to advise him on the subject, Turner and his inexperienced staff were allowed to twist in the wind before the news media.

9:00 A.M., Thursday, October 5, 1978

The chill that Ray Westcott and his family felt that Sunday when the three strange people jumped from their car at the Calvert Cliffs nuclear plant overlook took on new meaning when Westcott heard on his way to work at NASA's Goddard facility in Greenbelt, Maryland, the news about Paisley and his boat. Westcott told a friend at work that he might have witnessed something important. Westcott was called by the CIA's Office of Security that same day. That afternoon, two men who used the names Donald Hoffman and Ron Inners came to see him at Goddard and asked him to repeat his story of the events of that afternoon.[14]

Noon, Thursday, October 5, 1978

Newport, Oregon: Katherine Lenahan is a strong woman. But many family problems, in addition to her mother's long and painful battle with cancer, were beginning to take their toll on her. Hearing about the bizarre disappearance of her brother from Maryann was too much. From the start, she did not believe the body recovered from the Chesapeake Bay was that of her brother. Katherine had several reasons for believing the body was not John's. One was that the body had no shoes. John always wore shoes. He had an aversion to not wearing shoes, one that he had developed during the poverty of their childhood, when the family could not afford them.

All Katherine could think about was keeping the story from her dying mother. The cancer that was sapping Clara Paisley's strength had grown into a huge tumor in her hipbone. Katherine instructed the extended-care facility where Clara Paisley had spent her last few months not to let her have access to any televisions, radios, or newspapers. But somehow Clara—slipping in and out of reality because of her painkillers—heard that one of her sons had died. She was sure it was Dale, since he had had one major illness after another since birth. Clara would not be reassured until Dale called her to let her know he was alive and well. It never crossed her mind that John was the one who had died.

Clara Paisley adored her elder son, John, and he her. Katherine could not accept the notion that Jack would kill himself while his mother was still living. It made no sense. For Katherine Lenahan, 1978 was a nightmare. Her opinion of the Maryland State Police's efforts to investigate her brother's disappearance was not flattering: "When all hell broke loose, they took the first floater that popped up and slapped the weights on it. If I ever want to commit a murder, I would go to Maryland to do it." [15]

1:00 P.M., Friday, October 6, 1978

Robert Gambino was now faced with a full-blown scandal. He had not told anyone outside the CIA about the mole allegation. Senator William Roth (R.-Del.), an important member of the Senate Intelligence Committee, charged with oversight of the CIA, demanded an investigation into the disappearance of John Paisley. Roth was, of course, reacting to the stories in his hometown newspaper. The small lies the Office of Public Affairs had put out about Paisley's background were coming back to haunt them. What had begun as the death of a retiree was turning into a political nightmare for the CIA.

To complicate matters, Fisher's claims of an identification being made of Paisley had not convinced the Maryland State Police. Gambino made the hour-and-a-half trip to Maryland State Police headquarters in Pikesville to meet the investigating officers. They asked most of the questions and were clearly not convinced the CIA was being forthcoming about Paisley. The officers were disappointed to learn that the CIA had no fingerprint card for Paisley, but only a fingerprint classification card, which was useless for identification purposes. Gambino told the officers that all fingerprint cards of new employees were turned over to the FBI.[16]

The FBI had already told the Maryland State Police that they, too, had no fingerprint cards for Paisley. In 1972, Paisley's prints were destroyed with six million others as part of an FBI housecleaning. To Corporal Murphy it was inconceivable that there were no fingerprints available in Agency files of a CIA official as high-ranking as Paisley.

10:00 A.M., Saturday, October 7, 1978

The last hope that the Paisley case would quietly go away was swept away with a single telephone call from the office of the head of FBI intelligence, William O. Cregar, to Gambino. The FBI's Washington Field Office was reporting to headquarters that Paisley had lived in a building that was home to at least eight top-level KGB agents.[17] In a subsequent phone call, Gambino told the state police that Paisley had voluntarily retired in 1974 and his monthly annuity was $1,440 a month. In addition, Paisley received up to $24,500 in annual consultant's fees. None of this included his part-time work for the MITRE Corporation or his full-time job at Coopers & Lybrand. Money, contrary to what Wilson had told the police about Paisley, did not seem to be a problem.

7:00 P.M., Saturday, October 7, 1978

Leonard Parkinson, Eugene Leggett, and other Paisley colleagues and friends from the CIA had hurriedly put together a memorial service at the McLean Community Center. Parkinson's wife, Judy, played violin, someone else played guitar. The Beatles song "Let It Be" filled the room and sent a not-so-subtle message to the men and women who largely occupied a secret world.

Bill Miller, Paisley's ham radio buddy, was amazed by the fact that some people had flown in from overseas CIA assignments just to attend the memorial service. For Gladys Fishel, who is used to Washington society and power, the turnout was impressive. But what was more impressive to her was the fact that she learned some new things about Paisley: "They said at the memorial service he wrote poetry and I never knew that." The Fishels had only been called the night before for the quickly arranged service. "Every seat in the McLean Community Center was taken," Mrs. Fishel remembers.

The people who spoke at the service, like Parkinson, sat on the stage. Gladys Fishel recalls that "there were no clergy at the service and there was beautiful music."

Betty Myers went to the service and sat with the Wilsons. Myers was already upset because the family would not let her retrieve her belongings from John's apartment. Instead, they just wanted her key returned. Betty wondered what had happened to the heavy gold neck chain she had given John. It was the only piece of jewelry she had ever seen him wear.

Myers thought the nonreligious memorial service reflected Paisley: "John had a terrible time with religion. He really was a nonbeliever in a sad way. It would have been helpful to him if he could relate to some kind of spiritual life. . . . He didn't." Betty Myers felt the tension between Maryann and herself at the service. They even disagreed on the very circumstances of John's death. Maryann believed the body that had been recovered was not her husband's. Betty thought that Maryann was looking for a dramatic outcome and was merely playing the role of the grieving CIA wife.

For Norman Wilson, the memories of the evening included the recital of John Masefield's poem "Sea Fever," which was one of Paisley's favorites, and the fact that Betty Myers brought John Paisley's psychiatrist with her to the memorial service. This psychiatrist had angered Maryann when he gave Blaine Harden of the *Washington Post* a detailed interview about his treatment of Paisley. Charges were filed against him over the interview as a breach of doctor-patient confidence. His presence at the memorial service could only have been an affront to Maryann Paisley, because he, along with Betty Myers, advanced the suicide theory, which Maryann did not believe.

For Wilson it was all very uncomfortable: "Betty was on one side of us all the time and followed us out to the door and hung around us, and Maryann was over on the other side and wouldn't come anywhere near as long as the other one was there. We were sort of in the middle."

As Clarence Baier listened to the strains of "Let It Be" on the guitar, he wondered if anyone there really understood what had happened to Paisley. He kept wondering how the Agency could claim that they had no fingerprints for Paisley.

Week of October 9, 1978

Interviews with family members indicated that the Maryland State Medical Examiner, Dr. Russell Fisher, discouraged anyone from the family from identifying the body. When Paisley's distraught daughter, Diane, entered the medical examiner's building to find Dr. Fisher, she could not help but see the words written in raised letters across the

entrance to the reception desk: "Wherever the art of medicine is practiced, there is also a love of humanity." But Dr. Fisher must not have
read those words recently. When Diane demanded to see her father's
autopsy pictures, Fisher refused her request by having his receptionist
turn her away.[18] Later, Fisher said the corpse was in no condition for
family members to examine it: "In this case it was out of the question.
The face was totally distorted. The hair on the head and the beard
were gone. The gases in the body made him look like a balloon."[19]

Fisher had another, more serious problem. He had been unable to
get any fingerprints off the hands. The skin simply peeled away until
there was nothing to fingerprint. His only hope of fulfilling the positive
identification he had already publicly announced was to pray that the
Maryland State Police could successfully take fingerprints by putting
a chemical solvent onto the hands to dry them enough for ridges to
reappear on the fingers.[20] The fingerprints would then be given to the
FBI for identification.[21] "I couldn't print the hands," Fisher said, "the
skin slipped off in mass. They were too soft and decomposed to make
dermal prints."[22]

To make matters worse, Fisher could not locate any copies of Paisley's fingerprints. Both the CIA and the FBI had already notified the
Maryland State Police that they had no fingerprints. When a reporter
asked him what he had relied on to make the identification of Paisley,
Fisher said, "The FBI read the prints. I have to rely on them." But
Fisher could not explain how a fingerprint match could be made when
no prints could be taken from the cadaver he called John Paisley.

Although the FBI, the CIA, and the Maryland State Police could not
find fingerprints for Paisley, the Wilmington paper's reporters located
a set. When the reporting team showed Dr. Fisher a fingerprint card
for the real John Paisley, made when he entered the Merchant Marine
in 1942, that they had obtained in one day from the Coast Guard
records room in Washington, Fisher expressed surprise. When the
reporters pointed out to him that the real John Paisley, according to
his Merchant Marine files, was five feet eleven inches tall and weighed
170 pounds, and that the body that Dr. Adams autopsied was five feet
seven inches and weighed 144 pounds, Fisher pulled out the Paisley
report and, in front of the reporters, scratched out the height and
weight recorded by Dr. Adams and replaced it with the numbers supplied by the reporters. Fisher further certified the event by attaching a
special notice to the Paisley file of the change, reflecting the date of
the reporters' visit.[23]

No family member or friend of Paisley's was ever permitted to see
the body before it was picked up by the CIA-approved Colonial Funeral Home in Arlington, Virginia, several days after the autopsy.
Maryann Paisley got the impression from Dr. Fisher and the Maryland

State Police that Norman Wilson had identified the body. Wilson got the impression that others in the family had identified the body. By the time the Paisley family found out that no one who knew John firsthand had identified it, the corpse had been turned over to the Colonial Funeral Home.[24] It took more than ten days from the time Fisher identified the corpse as Paisley's, until the time it was cremated. This delay means that while family members and the media were already questioning Fisher's identification, the body was still intact.

6:30 P.M., Monday, October 9, 1978

For Robert Gambino, the dinner hour must have been a nightmare. As big as life on NBC news was Arkady Shevchenko, the highest-ranking diplomat ever to defect to the United States from the Soviet Union. Shevchenko was supposed to be under FBI protection. But NBC reporter James Polk's story did not just publicly expose a high-ranking defector. Polk also exposed a first-rate scandal. Shevchenko had been lured to the Iron Gate Inn by Judy Chavez, a prostitute, who had been paid more than $40,000, plus gifts and a car, for her services on behalf of Shevchenko by the CIA in the six months he had used her.[25]

Suddenly, John Paisley's handwritten note about Shevchenko that Phil Waggener had stuck in a CIA burn bag was beginning to loom large. James Polk said his source for the story, Fred Fielding, had ties to the Nixon White House and Watergate. Considering Paisley's ties to Watergate, it is possible that Paisley destroyed the defector's credibility by indirectly leaking the information to Polk's source. After all, it would not have been the first story Paisley leaked. There are, however, no indications that Paisley ever had official ties to the defector. But the Chavez story was a public-relations disaster for Shevchenko, the FBI, and the CIA.[26]

3:30 P.M., Tuesday, October 10, 1978

Troopers First Class Ron Inners and D. E. Hoffman made their second trip to see Dr. K. Wayne Smith at Coopers & Lybrand. Smith gave them a copy of Paisley's company life-insurance application and the Rolodex that Smith had retrieved from Paisley's apartment, as well as some other minor papers.

Friday, October 13, 1978

The remains identified as those of John Arthur Paisley were delivered to the Cedar Hill Cemetery and Crematory in Washington, D.C., where they were cremated. Melva Richardson, manager of Cedar Hill, said Colonial Funeral Home was charged $75 for the cremation.

Maryann Paisley signed a document, identifying the corpse as Paisley's, as required by Maryland law. Mrs. Paisley would later say she never saw the corpse.[27] Betty Myers was distressed when she learned that "John's remains were not promptly picked up. . . . I heard for a long time nothing happened with them."

Despite claims by Fisher that he had successfully identified Paisley through the FBI fingerprint match on October 1, 1978, it was not until four months later that the FBI completed its tests and sent the medical examiner a form letter saying the prints matched. Fisher's successor as Maryland Medical Examiner, Dr. Robert Smialek, after reviewing the entire Paisley autopsy file, found no independent corroboration that the body was John Paisley.

Late Afternoon, Monday, October 30, 1978

Katherine Lenahan sent her mother some flowers in her brother John's name. The family had decided not to tell their dying mother that the police were now saying Jack killed himself. That afternoon, when Katherine came by Clara's bedside, her mother said, nodding to the flowers, "Look what Jack sent me." For John Paisley's sister there was no more difficult moment. John Paisley's mother would die on November 24, 1978—two months after her son went for his last sail on *Brillig*.

By late October, people who knew Paisley were beginning to talk. Betty Myers was described in the *Washington Post*, much to the chagrin of Maryann, as the "woman closest to John A. Paisley for the last two years." Myers gave reporter Blaine Harden a statement to the effect that Paisley had sold a 9mm handgun he had bought while sailing in the Florida Keys. Her statement could not have come at a worse time for Admiral Turner's inept public-relations machine, which was still reeling from the *Wilmington News-Journal* stories.

The stories, as Turner's public-relations man, Herbert E. Hetu, wrote Turner in a memo, "never stop."[28] To add to Turner's problems, Maryann Paisley was now getting angry. She had begun to talk to the Wilmington paper and others. Hetu and Turner himself became preoccupied with the media stories.[29]

For Maryann Paisley, the loyalty she had once felt to the CIA was beginning to wear thin. She was angry that her estranged husband had been described by Dale Peterson, an Agency spokesman, as a "low-level employee." She was angry that the CIA denied officially that

Paisley had contact with defectors. She remembered John's telling her how he would go out to the Eastern Shore of Maryland, to the CIA's "farm," and meet dozens of defectors. Paisley would never use his own name on these trips.[30]

Maryann Paisley was fed up with the Maryland State Police as well, and had come to distrust Norman Wilson. Although she brought Wilson a bottle of Scotch to thank him for his troubles following John's disappearance, Maryann always believed that Wilson was "not telling everything he knew."[31] She knew that John never left the helm of any sailboat without first lashing down the wheel. Yet the wheel of *Brillig* was on self-steering when the boat was found. Wilson had testified that the table was held by pins and that they were always coming loose. But that awful night when Maryann went to see *Brillig* at the Coast Guard station, the screws holding the table had been pulled out of the wood. She was convinced there had been a struggle on *Brillig* and that John probably had been murdered.[32]

In the opinion of Maryann Paisley, the mild-mannered Falls Church attorney, Paul Terrance O'Grady, whom she originally hired to work with the CIA when John first turned up missing, was not sufficiently aggressive toward the CIA. She abruptly pulled the business from him and hired her old neighbor, Bernard "Bud" Fensterwald, Jr., a controversial man who had a reputation as a fighter and a Kennedy assassination buff.[33] The Paisleys first got to know Fensterwald when they were neighbors on Buchanan Street in Arlington in 1961, and he was a young lawyer just starting out. Fensterwald had represented Martin Luther King, Jr.'s, assassin, James Earl Ray. But the most curious client Fensterwald represented was Watergate "Plumber" James W. McCord. McCord had once been a mid-level employee in the CIA's Office of Security.[34]

Maryann considered herself abandoned by the CIA. She could never believe that John would use a gun to take his own life. She knew her husband to be a very, very gentle man who was not aggressive. Hopelessly frustrated, on January 16, 1979, Mrs. Paisley wrote a scathing letter to CIA Director Turner. The letter was a devastating attack from a CIA wife, who herself had worked in the Agency:

> I find writing this letter a difficult but necessary task. Throughout my twenty years as a CIA wife, I have felt that I could depend upon the Agency to help me anytime that my husband was not available. As a matter of fact, when the Maryland State Police refused to tell me whether the body fished out of the Chesapeake Bay had a beard, my first call was to the Watch office for help. From that moment on, the attitude toward me has been a betrayal of my husband's devotion and unquestioned loyalty to the Agency.[35]

She continued, ". . . nor have I told anything that I have gleaned of John's CIA activities over the years which, as you know, were certainly not confined to the overt side." Mrs. Paisley said in the letter that the height and weight discrepancies in the body recovered and those of Paisley had caused her and her children to believe it was not her husband's.

Maryann charged that the CIA and FBI's claims that Paisley's fingerprints were not available were something she did not believe. Then she went to the heart of her letter:

As you know the Maryland State Police returned a great deal of evidence in this case after the body had been cremated. They quite casually handed me a telephone book [i.e., the flat metal directory] with a red tape on the cover. I don't know, even today, where they got it. If I had seen it earlier, I would have automatically turned it in with his badges. That book, as you must know, raised a great many more questions than I had before. It was essential that my lawyer look into the implications of the red line names listed in this book. The few red line [highly classified] numbers were people I would recognize from my brief years in the DDO. Noticeably absent were names of DDO personnel who worked closely with my husband, but not with me. I think I have a right to know why. You have known John long enough to realize that he would not keep a book of this nature out of a safe without an implicit reason.

The questions Maryann raised about her husband's actions were serious. Why did he have red-line numbers on *Brillig* with him that afternoon? Why did Paisley not call her to cancel their dinner date? Why did Paisley not call the Wilsons to let them know he would be out for the night?

Had Maryann known about the mole accusation, as Turner presumably knew, she might have been even more surprised at the lack of interest by the DCI. Turner responded to Maryann in a February 2, 1979, letter saying he "regretted any cloud over Paisley's honorable career," but that the CIA had no investigative powers and "must defer to the Maryland State Police." The response understandably infuriated Mrs. Paisley.[36]

The newspapers and Maryann Paisley were not alone in crying "cover-up." The Senate Intelligence Committee was frustrated by the FBI's superficial report on the Paisley case, and angry at the Maryland State Police effort. The police concluded that Paisley had killed himself based largely on statements made by Betty Myers and Norman Wilson. Although the physical evidence defies that conclusion, the police determined that Paisley had wrapped two nineteen-pound weight belts around himself, jumped from *Brillig,* and shot himself in the head in midair.

Contradicting that theory is the fact that there was no sign of brain tissue on *Brillig.* Paisley was wearing tan slacks when he left to sail that morning. Not noted for being a neat dresser, it is unlikely he would change into a pair of very stylish blue jeans with zippered pockets like the ones found on the corpse just to shoot himself. The police conceded their theory had problems. But they cited as evidence the fact that shortly before he disappeared, Paisley had bought an unneeded diving belt, and therefore had intended to do himself in and dispose of his own body in a mysterious way.

Were the state police reacting to political pressure to close the Paisley case as a suicide? That was the rumor for years following the case. The recently released Maryland State Police investigative reports indicate why those rumors had some substance. One of the key reasons the police cited for concluding that Paisley had killed himself was his purchase of an extra diving belt from a skin-diving shop on Wisconsin Avenue in Washington, D.C. The police cite as the source of that information Dr. K. Wayne Smith. They say they interviewed Smith at 3:30 P.M. on October 10, 1978, at Coopers & Lybrand, and reported: "While at the firm, Dr. Smith advised that he had information that Paisley bought some scuba gear at National Diving Center located at 4932 Wisconsin Avenue, N.W. Washington, D.C. 20016. With this information the investigators went to the diving center."

But Dr. Smith strongly denies that he ever gave the police any such information. "That's not true. I have no idea where he bought his diving supplies. I could not be the source because I don't know." [37] Yet it is largely on the purchase of the additional diving belt that the Maryland State Police pushed the suicide theory.

On October 16, 1978, the police convened a meeting with Dr. Russell Fisher and went over the new weight-belt "evidence." Based on that evidence and Fisher's prodding, they concluded that "John Paisley died as a result of taking his own life sometime on or about 9-24-78." [38] In reality, there is no independent evidence that Paisley bought the belt. The National Diving Center provided a cash receipt that the police said was a record of Paisley's purchase. But Paisley made most of his equipment purchases using a bank charge card. Betty Myers was also cited as a source for the weight-belt information. But all she told the police was that Paisley's regulator valve had blown out and he had gone to the diving shop to replace it. Yet there is no indication on the cash receipt provided to the state police that a regulator valve was purchased. Perhaps the most mysterious aspect of the receipt is that the date had been altered. It was changed from 8/9/78 to 9/8/78. [39]

Just as likely a scenario as the state police theory would be that Paisley was meeting with his Soviet control agent. His control agent was given instructions to kill Paisley because the Soviets had ascertained that Paisley was now being fingered as the mole. Paisley knew very well what his fate would be if his true activities were revealed. The lost wallet, the phone calls to a *Washington Star* reporter used for leaks by the Agency, and the discussions of Paisley's resuming a Merchant Marine career, all should have been investigated by the police. They were not. The possibility that Paisley indeed had no way out except to murder his control and manage his own escape makes as much sense as the suicide theory.

When Maryann began her fight with the CIA to try to force them to tell her what John had really been doing, strange things began to happen to her. After her January 1979 letter to Stansfield Turner, Maryann's neighbors on Van Fleet Drive told her they heard a strange sound coming from her house. One of them, Jean Bergaust, told Maryann it was "like a sound barrier." [40]

William Miller, her husband's friend from the radio club and a man who had installed the most sophisticated of radio systems in some of the world's most difficult areas, concluded that the "sound barrier" was in actuality a warning alarm to let whoever was monitoring the house electronically know when someone was about to enter or leave the premises. Miller found that they [the CIA] had put a tap on Mrs. Paisley's telephone and, he believes, planted listening devices elsewhere in the house. "Not only on the phone, but they had a sensor mounted on the chimney. There was one woman in the neighborhood, a young woman that went out jogging every morning early, you know, just at daylight. The first time she heard it, it scared the hell out of her. And they lived on a corner. . . . That gal used to jog down there around the corner and that thing would beep all the way around the corner," Miller said.

On a cold Saturday night in mid-January 1980, Maryann came home late to find that John's radio gear and scuba equipment had been tampered with. Maryann said that because her husband's scuba and radio gear were kept in rooms she normally did not use much, she did not discover the break-in until Saturday night. However, she believed that it had taken place sometime Friday while she was at work. She stated that she noticed it when she returned home from dinner with neighbors after an evening at the theater. "I found John's scuba tanks placed so you would trip over them, when both my son and I know they had been put away in a workshop near the laundry room. I kept all the radio gear in boxes, put away. I had recently had it itemized and appraised for possible sale. I found one Atlas radio on the workbench with a white belt lying on top of it." [41]

Later her lawyer, Bud Fensterwald, would claim "it was an obvious attempt by the CIA to scare her." But the CIA denied Fensterwald's charges. Maryann Paisley said at the time that "there was no question I was supposed to see that the house had been broken into." She said that nothing had been taken and she "had the feeling" she had been followed the entire week.

Around this same time, Bud Fensterwald, another lawyer, Mrs. Paisley, and *Washington Post* reporter Tim Robinson were having lunch in a downtown Washington restaurant. Fensterwald said, "The couple sitting at the next table was closely monitoring our conversation. Later I saw the man from this couple waiting in front of my office building." Robinson confirmed the incident and said, "Someone was definitely following us and seemed to want us to know it." Neighbors of Mrs. Paisley said that they saw a silver Camaro in front of her home, stopping for periods up to half an hour, going away, and then returning and stopping again.

Maryann's problems did not end with the CIA. Two life-insurance companies that had policies on Paisley at first refused to pay because, like Maryann, they did not accept the fact that he was dead. Both the Mutual Life Insurance Company of New York and Mutual of Omaha held separate $100,000 policies on Paisley and resisted paying for months. Eventually, both companies made a settlement with Mrs. Paisley. But another company, The Travelers Insurance Company, did not. Mrs. Paisley filed suit against The Travelers. Her lawyer, Bud Fensterwald, successfully used the suit to get a parade of witnesses to tell what they knew about Paisley under oath.[42]

In late April 1980, Mrs. Paisley received a letter from Senator Birch Bayh of Indiana, saying that the Senate Intelligence Committee had found no evidence that Paisley had been disloyal to his country. Bayh also told Mrs. Paisley that because of the highly classified work John did for the CIA, the report could not be made public. According to one of the Senate investigators, "the only reason it was classified at all was because of a few personnel records the CIA insisted we protect. . . . But there was nothing in the report [that was really classified]." But Intelligence Committee Counsel Michael Epstein, who spearheaded the investigation, spoke more frankly: "Chances are we will never understand the outcome of the case. It is a mystery. We never really had the resources to . . . investigate it."[43]

Despite the report, Maryann's suspicions about the case continued. She contacted William Miller, the radio friend of John's, whom he had met the year before he died, to get help on reports that a burst transmitter was aboard *Brillig*. A burst transmitter is a small device that can deliver an encoded message in a fraction of a second to a communications satellite passing overhead. The Soviets started using them with great success in the late 1960s to communicate with their agents. Maryann learned from Miller that a burst transmitter was small enough to conceal in any of Paisley's radios.[44] The fact that Miller helped Paisley obtain a new portable radio, inside of which a burst transmitter would fit, and the fact that the radio was never recovered, left Miller with plenty of questions concerning Paisley's use for the radio.

The little material Maryann did receive from the CIA about her husband was curiously misleading. While the CIA claimed publicly that John had never traveled to the Eastern Bloc, copies of travel orders showing that Paisley went to Eastern Europe were included in the information she got by virtue of an expensive lawsuit against the CIA. More curious is that key trips Paisley made to Iran and Iraq, for example, were omitted. What was interesting about the trip to Iraq was that John had been issued a sidearm by the CIA.[45]

For Paisley's friends, there is no simple answer to his end. Some, like Norman Wilson, Leonard Parkinson, and Betty Myers, insist Paisley committed suicide. But many others, like Clarence Baier, Gladys Fishel, and Sam Wilson, are not so sure. Gladys Fishel believes that Paisley "might have been an agent on the other side. . . . It is hard to believe that someone would go to that extent to . . . burn their bridges that thoroughly."

Betty Myers found it odd that the tape recordings Maryann made of John's mother before she died were missing. She says the Paisleys asked her about the tapes. "Maryann called me when I was living here and asked me where the tapes were and I said, 'I haven't the faintest idea. Maybe at the bottom of the Bay with the gun and everything else,' because I could have imagined him in that kind of state being angry and hurt and throwing a lot of things over like that."

There is no memorial to John Paisley except a small bench that Betty Myers had installed on the Wilsons' property at Lusby. Even that has raised controversy. Barbara Wilson said it was put in without her permission and she would prefer to see it gone.[46]

Clues about John Paisley's mysterious disappearance were left all around: the information he sought about jobs overseas with the Merchant Marine; the lost wallet; the possible warning about a new security investigation from someone inside the CIA; the bizarre telephone threats against a CIA man just before his disappearance; the calls being placed to a newspaper that had benefited by CIA tips before, and the fact that they involved a professional leaker for the Agency; the proposed sale or charter of *Brillig;* the mysterious people on the cliffs; and the missing tapes of his mother.

The only thing that is certain is that the CIA, with the FBI's assistance, botched the investigation of the Paisley case. The Senate Intelligence Committee certified Paisley as a patriot when it was never told about the discrepancies in his background or that he had been accused a month before he disappeared of being a Soviet mole in the CIA.

But in the Paisley matter a bigger issue looms like a shadow over all of U.S. security: the possibility that someone may have tipped him to the mole allegations and the security investigation. What else could have prompted him to set all these events in motion? To someone in counterintelligence, the conclusion has to be that Paisley was working with someone inside the CIA.

Perhaps the most startling aspect of the Paisley case lies in the mysterious postcards.

After John's disappearance and Clara Paisley's death, Kay and Pat Lenahan tried to put some of the misery of 1978 out of their lives by visiting relatives in Arizona in early January 1979. Several weeks after they returned home, a postcard arrived with a Valparaiso, Chile, postmark. It said, "How is everybody, how's the family? Hope to see you." It was signed "Sandy." It did not refer to anyone's trip.

Kay Lenahan asked her husband, Pat, "Who the devil is Sandy? And he said he did not know." Kay said, "We first thought it was somebody Pat ran into in a bar and started yapping with . . . because he will talk to anyone." The Lenahans tried to remember if they had ever met a Sandy, but finally they decided they had not. The only Sandy they could remember was a close friend of John's who had disappeared on a flight to Sri Lanka. Neither the plane nor the bodies were ever found. Paisley had been scheduled to be on that flight in 1970, but had canceled his reservations at the last minute.

The cards kept coming about once a month. Katherine reluctantly began to believe there might be some connection between John and the cards. One night when she was talking to Maryann on the telephone, Maryann said she believed that if John was still alive, he would manage to get word to someone in the family. Katherine mentioned the postcards. Katherine said she told Maryann, "Well, maybe he is sending me postcards. . . . I am getting some weird postcards." John Paisley loved to send postcards.

Maryann asked Katherine to send her the cards, including one that quoted a poem about sailors. The poem was a favorite of John's, although the handwriting was nothing like her brother's. Another postcard quoted a line about a sunset. Because she didn't initially see the possible significance of them, Kay had kept only two of the five or six cards that came. She sent them to Maryann, who turned them over to Bud Fensterwald. Later, Maryann told Kay Lenahan that the postcards had been stolen from Fensterwald's office. After their phone conversation, no more postcards ever came.

CHAPTER NINE

Shadrin: The Escape

RUSSIAN AND POLE GET ASYLUM

STOCKHOLM, Sweden, June 25, 1959 (Reuters) A Soviet naval captain and a 22-year-old Polish woman medical student who escaped to Sweden this month in a launch from the Polish Baltic port of Gdynia have been granted political asylum in Sweden, the Aliens Commission announced today.[1]

THAT WAS HOW the story of Nick Shadrin began. In the sixteen years he was in the West, the man who used to call himself Nikolay Fedorovich Artamonov captured the hearts and imagination of much of official Washington. At Christmas, 1975, when he disappeared in Vienna, he became a legend. At first, only official Washington knew the secret. The disappearance was kept quiet for over a year. Then the public was told the Soviets had kidnapped him. In 1981, a book said this man was a double agent for the FBI.[2]

In 1985 a pair of FBI agents walked up the driveway of Ewa Shadrin's split-level brick house in McLean, Virginia. She had known in her heart that one day this moment would come. For ten years she had hoped some miracle would occur. She had spent a fortune waging a personal war with her government, trying to find out what had happened to her husband. For the first year and a half after her husband's disappearance, Mrs. Shadrin and her lawyer, Richard Copaken, had pried out bits and pieces of the truth. Then the FBI and CIA simply cut them off. Now, seven years later, the message the FBI agents carried that day was from Soviet defector Vitaly Sergeyevich Yurchenko. The agents told Mrs. Shadrin her husband, Nick, was dead. She could take comfort, however, in the fact that he did not suffer.[3]

For Ewa Shadrin, the long ordeal was finally over. Officially, the man she fell in love with one winter in Poland almost thirty years ago, the man who took her to the West in a small boat on an awful night, was gone forever. The defector's story had to be true. The FBI assured her that they had confirmed Yurchenko's story through other sources. And Yurchenko, after all, had been validated by CIA Director William Casey, personally.

Then, suddenly, after three months Yurchenko redefected to Russia. But before he left, he said CIA officials had "forced" him to tell the story of Shadrin being kidnapped by the KGB and killed, by accident, as he was being driven across the Iron Curtain from Vienna. Once again, Ewa Shadrin was adrift in a sea of lies, most of them from the government of the country to which she had come for refuge.

In March 1958, Captain Nikolay Fedorovich Artamonov got a new assignment in the Soviet Navy. He left his wife Elena and ten-year-old son Sergei Nikolay behind. The sacrifice seemed minor. After all, Artamonov's wife was the daughter of Sergei Gorshkov—the admiral of the Soviet fleet. His future success was virtually guaranteed.

By 1958 Admiral Gorshkov was on his way to turning his navy into a world-class fighting force. First he had to sell off an assortment of aging vessels and persuade the Kremlin to provide the huge amounts of funds necessary to build a modern navy. So he turned to his son-in-law for help.

Artamonov was given command of a two-destroyer squadron and assigned to help carry out the sale and transfer of the ships to the Indonesian Navy as part of a military assistance pact that the Soviet Union had negotiated with Indonesia's President Sukarno. The two destroyers were actually a pair of aged Soviet corvette-class vessels that had initially been built in the mid-1920s by the Weimar Republic and that were subsequently claimed by the Soviets as part of the spoils of World War II. Besides the two corvettes under Artamonov's command, there was also a diesel-powered submarine of pre–World War II vintage, and assorted yard and auxiliary vessels. Together these vessels constituted a flotilla command.

The squadron limped its way from the Soviet Baltic Fleet headquarters in Leningrad to a maintenance stop at the auxiliary Soviet naval station at Kaliningrad. Before crossing the tranquil Gulf of Danzig to the Polish naval base at Gdynia, the ships needed additional repairs. The voyage was uneventful.

Upon Artamonov's arrival in Poland, he quickly realized that teaching the Indonesian officers about running a navy was more of a challenge than he had ever anticipated. It was obvious to Artamonov that the Indonesians were not terribly interested in learning how to operate the ships. To make matters worse, all Soviets—officers and enlisted men—were not welcome in Gdynia in 1958, or many other places in Poland. Time passed very slowly, and Artamonov was not known for being a patient young man.

Jadwiga Gora was flabbergasted when her shy and normally obedient twenty-one-year-old daughter announced that she was dating a Soviet naval captain assigned to Gdynia to train Indonesians. Gora could only imagine how her husband, Zygmunt, a Polish merchant marine captain, would react to his daughter's actions. She was grateful he was away on a voyage to China.

Ewa Gora could not bring herself to tell her mother that Artamonov was a married man. All she knew was that she was very much in love with a naval captain she had met through friends at an October 1958 dinner dance.[4] The dance was hosted by the Poles for the Indonesian naval contingent and their "fraternal brothers" in the Soviet Navy. The introduction of Nikolay and Ewa was made by Polish Navy Commander Janusz Kunde, the husband of one of Ewa's closest friends. Ewa believed that Kunde was in charge of liaison with the Soviet Navy in connection with the turnover of the Soviet ships to the Indonesians.[5] Kunde did, in fact, have that assignment, but it was in addition to his major role as the resident director in Gdynia of its *Sluzba Bezpieczenstwa* (SB) detachment, the Polish version of the KGB.

The dinner dance was one of those social occasions expected to promote goodwill among the three navies. Artamonov was so frustrated with the Indonesians that he had a hard time thinking of them as sailors and officers, let alone a navy. Photographs taken at the party show a smiling, dashing, debonair Captain Artamonov, his navigator, Lieutenant Commander Yakovlev, and some dour Indonesians observing the scene. Ewa is looking up at Artamonov, obviously taken with the Soviet naval officer.

Ewa's infatuation was understandable. Artamonov had movie-star good looks. He had full, dark hair that framed his face in a widow's peak, a deep and resonant voice, and a commanding presence. Officially he was six foot two, although Ewa says he was taller than that. He was, by all descriptions, a powerful figure. He was the type of man who could win over almost anyone with his charm and intelligence. When he entered a room, women noticed. Ewa, unlike Artamonov, was genuinely shy.

As the ranking military man at the party, Artamonov was the only guest who could afford to let himself go and enjoy the dancing and conversation. Ewa clearly got his attention. She remembers that Artamonov stayed "just for a short time. He was there for just two dances and he asked me to dance twice."[6] Later Ewa's friends reported back to her that Artamonov liked her very much, but at first she did not express much interest in him.

The relationship blossomed when Ewa's friends told her that Artamonov had canceled a hunting trip when he heard that Ewa was going to be at a birthday party that December. Her affection for "Nick" is still reflected in her eyes thirty years later, when she talks about him walking her home from the party.

Artamonov had little to do with the actual training of the Indonesians, and that left him with plenty of free time, something that is universally dangerous for any nation's sailors on dry land. As a consequence, Artamonov and Ewa spent more and more of their time together. Ewa, who had never had such male attention in her brief and sheltered life, found herself falling in love with the Russian.

The relationship did not seem to suffer from a two-week leave Artamonov took over Christmas to go back to the Soviet Union. Nikolay had told Ewa that his marriage had gone badly and the child he left behind was his wife's from a previous marriage.[7]

When Artamonov returned, he tried to win the friendship of Ewa's mother, but she flatly refused to see him when he called on Ewa at the house. Every time he knocked on her front door, the same thing would happen. Her brother, Roman, would open the door and "receive" Artamonov. What finally broke the ice between Artamonov and Ewa's mother was when he pulled out all the stops to try to cheer Ewa up when she had a severe case of flu. Nick literally besieged her with flowers, candy, fruit—all hand-delivered by officers from Artamonov's command. Under normal circumstances, only an admiral—or an admiral's son-in-law—would have that kind of clout. Clearly, Artamonov had exceptional latitude. Ewa said that there seemed to be no limit to his resources for entertaining, getting limousines and drivers, or being allowed to mix with the local population. After displaying how willing he was to spoil her daughter, Mrs. Gora finally accepted Artamonov. Ewa never questioned Artamonov's special privileges: "He seemed to be able to do almost anything he wanted to. . . . I thought it [was] because his admiral liked him."

What is puzzling is that under normal circumstances this relationship would have never been allowed to happen. Although the Polish Navy personnel had to be deferential to their "colleagues" in the Soviet Navy, there was no love lost between the Soviets and the local Polish citizens. Petty officers and crew members of the Soviet Navy group, who were prohibited from fraternizing with the Poles, went on "liberty" in carefully controlled groups in Gdynia. They went to events such as a soccer game without speaking to, and pretending not to notice, the local female Polish population. For a Soviet sailor to make an attempt at fraternization was to invite disciplinary action.[8]

Although Artamonov enjoyed unusual freedom of latitude in the way he spent his "off duty" time, he was in clear violation of Communist Party official regulations, which specifically prohibited fraternization with the local Poles. It is hard to imagine that those in the GRU (Soviet military intelligence) assigned to watch Artamonov and his shipmates did not notice his relationship with Ewa. On their dates, for example, Artamonov used an official limousine provided by the Polish Navy and driven by a Polish driver named Konstantine, who probably was working for Polish military intelligence, which reported to the GRU. The limousine's "trip tickets" would be routinely checked by Artamonov's superiors.

There was so little for Artamonov to do, either officially with the Indonesian naval contingent, or unofficially in the rather hostile environment of downtown Gdynia, that his relationship with Ewa occupied a great deal of his attention. Nick became so attached to Ewa that he had a special telephone line installed from his "sea cabin" on his ship to Ewa's bedroom.[9] The special line bypassed the ship's switchboard as well as the one in Gdynia. U.S. intelligence officials say there is an excellent chance that this line was tapped by the GRU, the KGB, or the Polish intelligence service. Ewa would pick up the phone in her bedroom and talk to Nick for hours.

It was not long before Artamonov proposed marriage. Ewa remembers the first proposal: "It was in March. He thought maybe we should get permission to marry, and we would go to the Soviet Union. And I said, 'I could never come to the Soviet Union. . . . No, no, no . . . I'll never live in the Soviet Union.' "[10] Although Ewa was young and naïve, she was old enough to realize that despite her affection for the handsome naval captain, life for a Pole in the Soviet Union would be intolerable.

Artamonov realized that the Russians' heavy-handed enforcement of the "socialist relationship" by the Soviet Union in putting down recent riots in Poland did not make people wearing Russian uniforms very popular. When Artamonov went out, he wore civilian clothes. "I was very nervous when he wore his uniform because the Poles really did not like the Russians," Ewa said.

According to Ewa, Artamonov threw a shipboard party for Easter in 1959, even sending launches out for the guests. Her father was back in port, and the old merchant captain was less than convinced that Ewa was being truthful when she described her friendship with Artamonov as fraternal. After attending the party, her father saw through the charade. He was so fearful his daughter would end up in the Soviet Union, and out of reach, Ewa said that he suddenly sailed off on another voyage to China. Ewa's father feared that if she moved to the Soviet Union she would never really be accepted, and the political situation was such that he would never see her again. Even today, Ewa insists that if Nick had not been a Soviet naval officer, but just an ordinary Soviet citizen who tried to take her away, her father would have "killed him."

On May 19, Artamonov's birthday, as they were riding in the rear seat of the limousine provided by the Polish Navy on their way to dinner in Sopot, Artamonov made his second marriage proposal. This time, however, the offer was to flee Gdynia and seek asylum in the West. "I was shocked," Ewa recalls. "I never thought, because he had such a high position and such a bright future, that Nick would consider anything like that. But he said he just couldn't be happy doing all those things without me. . . . I agreed to go with him. But if I would say no, he would never go. He told me to give him twenty-four hours' notice and he would prepare the boat."

From the beginning, Ewa never had any serious hopes about their relationship. The odds were too much against them. Now Artamonov told her that he was willing to toss a seemingly limitless future away so they could both go to the West and start a new life together. It seemed amazing to her that this man who had so much power and prestige would do that for her. She understood the risks; if they were caught escaping, there would be severe penalties for both of them. She said that Nick refused to discuss any details of how they would escape. He told her he wanted an answer in one day. She thought about leaving the comfort of the relatively easy life she had in Poland. Then she balanced that against what he would give up. There seemed to be no comparison. He agreed to wait until she got her diploma from dental school; this was sufficient to overcome her reservations.

With Ewa's acquiescence, Artamonov put into motion his plan for their escape. In his position as the captain of the ship, Artamonov inspected the launch and the equipment he would need on the voyage from Gdynia to Sweden, the proposed destination. Artamonov's behavior and actions were consistent with his rank, and thus did not arouse suspicion. Nor did they seem important enough for the ship's crew to remember what he had done before the time when he and Ewa presumably set out on a night-fishing interlude. Enlisted personnel in the Soviet Navy are thoroughly schooled in "boot camp" to see nothing, hear nothing, and say nothing about what their officers do, or fail to do.

Besides the physical preparation of the twenty-two-foot-launch used in their "great escape," he had to plot the course from the Gdynia anchorage area to the intended landfall on Öland Island, located directly off the southeast coast of Sweden. It involved a voyage of approximately 115 nautical miles. The launch was capable of making seven to nine knots in the open sea.[11]

Artamonov checked the scheduled Polish ship movements along the intended route and reviewed information about the anticipated movements of other nations' vessels through the Baltic on the night of their voyage. It was planned for Saturday, June 6. One reason a weekend was picked was the social reality that the following day, a Sunday, was one on which a "holiday routine" would prevail at the Gdynia base. Although it was a day off for the Poles to attend church, it was a day given over to nursing hangovers for the Russians assigned to the Indonesian turnover operation. Even the KGB slowed down on Sundays.

Captain Artamonov made every calculation imaginable to ensure the success of his voyage. Nothing was left to chance. But at the last minute, just as everything seemed ready, something happened that could destroy his plan. It was a party for the commanding officer of the Polish naval base on Saturday night, June 6, 1959—the date set for the couple's escape. The party complicated matters. Both Ewa and Artamonov had to attend. Their absence would have set off alarm bells for the Soviet and Polish security personnel. Artamonov postponed their adventure one day. He told Ewa on Saturday afternoon that they would depart on their "fishing trip" on Sunday evening. This notification was the first time Ewa knew the specifics of his plans. He also informed her that they had to attend the birthday party as if it were nothing more than another night out together.

Ewa displayed some signs of cold feet. Her calls for a delay were out of the question. They had already lost twenty-four hours, and Artamonov was scheduled to return to Moscow to report on the Indonesian turnover operation to a so-called Military Assistance Group in the Kremlin. This bureaucratic command performance could not be finessed. If Artamonov had to go to Moscow, the window for departure would be closed, possibly forever. There was no assurance how long these meetings would last, or that Artamonov would not be transferred to the Assistance Group by some naval official, or sent to school for a new command. He overcame Ewa's fears by his excitement about the escape and his confident persistence.

The twenty-four-hour delay threatened the escape in a more serious way; the weather and sea conditions began to deteriorate, something Artamonov hadn't allowed for. The weather expected for late Sunday evening was marginal at best, but Artamonov was confident he could make the passage in spite of the hazards. His confidence was not ill-placed, and, as later events proved, the results of the voyage became an important part of the reason the CIA and the U.S. Navy believed Artamonov was a real sailor rather than a dispatched agent posing as a defector.

The first leg of the voyage went as planned. A young Soviet Navy petty officer, Ilya Aleksandrovich Popov, picked up Ewa and Captain Artamonov at a landing near the anchorage for what he assumed was a night of fishing. It had happened before, and Popov had no reason to be suspicious. Artamonov told him to set a course in the direction of the tip of the Hel Peninsula, and he and Ewa went below. The time of departure was approximately 8:00 P.M. The weather on this leg of the voyage was fair. The estimated arrival of darkness was 9:45 that night.

Fifteen minutes later, Popov could see the intended "fishing site and the eastern tip of the Hel Peninsula, which was illuminated by marker buoys and navigational aids. As the launch approached the tip of the Hel Peninsula, at about 11:00 P.M., Artamonov came up to the bridge and told Popov to go below and get something to eat from the picnic basket that had been placed aboard the launch on the captain's orders.

With Artamonov at the helm, the little launch plunged ahead on the planned initial course of 320 degrees into the rough Baltic. This course enabled Artamonov to steer toward a Swedish navigational light. But the weather worsened, as predicted, and it took all of Artamonov's seamanship to keep the launch on course.

Huge waves nearly swallowed the little craft. Fortunately, the launch's length-to-beam ratio enabled it to ride up and down the waves rather than cut through the chop of the stormy seas, and possibly founder or broach. It was a roller-coaster ride. Ewa remembers it as one of the longest nights of her life.

The voyage was supposed to last only seventeen hours. By now Popov, after having waited below for hours, must have thought they had been blown off course in the storm. Artamonov, the consummate actor, reinforced that view when he called Popov back up to help identify the coastal lights. Artamonov directed the little launch up the more peaceful waters of the Kalmar Sound, which separates Öland Island from the Swedish mainland. They proceeded north until Artamonov spied the Swedish fishing village of Farjestaden and ordered Popov to bring the launch alongside a wharflike pier that jutted out into the water.[12] To Artamonov, the wharf looked like the kind used for a motor vehicle ferry landing. It was now nearly twenty-four hours since they had left to go "fishing."

Artamonov, Ewa, and Popov were exhausted. To the west on the mainland, Artamonov could see the twinkling lights of Kalmar as the shadows lengthened over the Kalmar Sound. After they had tied up the launch, a few of the Farjestaden villagers came to the wharf to see the strangers who had come to their little village seemingly out of nowhere. Artamonov broke out a bottle of cognac and poured drinks for the welcoming committee.

Meanwhile, back at Gdynia, Artamonov's absence had not set off any alarms. The storm that had affected Artamonov's passage to Farjestaden had also kept Gdynia closed for most of the day on Monday, June 8. It was assumed that Artamonov had sought safe harbor someplace along the lee of the Hel Peninsula the night before and would return, if not later on Monday, then the following day. This assumption gave Artamonov back the time, without detection or alarm, built into his plan before the twenty-four-hour delay. It was an auspicious beginning as they proceeded to undertake the more difficult psychological phases of their odyssey.

The Farjestaden villagers were most hospitable. One or two of them spoke some Russian, but not enough to carry on much of a conversation. But Artamonov's cognac and charm bridged the communication gap. In spite of the language barrier, the villagers fed and entertained their visitors. Artamonov, Ewa, and Popov spent the night in the local jail. It was clean and dry, and was the place a villager was lodged for the night when he'd had too much to drink, rather than let him go home and cause trouble.

The next morning, the "Finnish ferry" that normally used the dock made the first trip of the day to Farjestaden.[13] The captain and owner of the ferry, a Finn who spoke Russian, invited Captain Artamonov and his party to cross over with him to the Swedish mainland on his return trip. The Finn allayed Artamonov's concerns about the delay the channel crossing would entail. He assured the Russian captain that he would call his friend in the Swedish Navy who was in Stockholm, and that his friend would come to Kalmar and help him.

The Finn was true to his word, but instead of his friend, the Swedish naval authorities sent Commander Sven G. T. Rydström, a very experienced staff and line officer with extensive experience in intelligence matters. Interestingly, Ewa was not even an afterthought in these early communications, as Artamonov's presence became known to the Swedes. Rydström, who was fluent in Russian, arrived in Kalmar on Tuesday evening and immediately took charge. Artamonov told him it was his and Ewa's plan to ask for political asylum. This intention raised serious complications for Rydström and, more important, for the Swedish government. He thought it would be a good idea to postpone setting off the international turmoil that Artamonov's request for asylum would produce. So Artamonov, Ewa, and Popov had the hospitality of the Kalmar jail on Tuesday night.

The following morning, Wednesday, June 10, Commander Rydström called his superiors in Stockholm and briefed them on this potentially volatile political situation. Rydström was told to "stand fast" in Kalmar, and that the Soviet Embassy would be notified about their two errant sailors, with no mention of their ranks or name. Late in the afternoon, Commander Rydström turned Popov over to two minor Soviet functionaries who had been sent to retrieve the two errant sailors. Much to the Soviets' surprise, Artamonov sent them packing. His behavior was consistent with that of a haughty, if not arrogant, Soviet military officer in his dealings with underlings assigned to one of its foreign embassies.

With a thoroughly chastened Popov in tow, the Soviets drove the 250-plus miles back to Stockholm, a journey that took approximately seven hours, owing to repairs being made to the coastal road to Kalmar. Before they left, the Soviet officials did not notify their embassy what they had encountered in Kalmar. The embassy did not yet know that Captain Nikolay Fedorovich Artamonov had refused to come along with them. If these minor functionaries who were sent to Kalmar had, in fact, been KGB, it would have been a different story. However, for the time being, it appeared to be nothing more than a case of some Soviet sailors straying into Swedish waters.

Several days later, the Swedes moved Artamonov and Ewa to Stockholm, where the couple formally announced their intention to defect and to ask the Swedish government for political asylum. The Swedish naval and foreign ministry officials who heard their declarations realized the gravity of the situation and notified the Soviet and Polish embassies in Stockholm.

By the end of the week, Moscow knew of the escape. A blistering telex from Moscow to the KGB resident in Gdynia announced that Artamonov and Ewa were seeking political asylum in Sweden. KGB security personnel conducted an after-the-fact search to determine what had happened, and if there were any accomplices to Artamonov's act of treason. It was a typical KGB "investigation." Lacking any real suspects, owing to the coherence of the cover story and the apparent ignorance of Soviet Navy personnel in Gdynia, the KGB was left with only Ewa's mother to interrogate. Her father was still on his voyage to China. Fortunately, Ewa's mother knew nothing.

Similarly, aboard Artamonov's ship, his sea cabin was in perfect order. All of his official "pocket litter"—his party membership card, internal travel passport, naval identification documents, pay book, and money—were in plain sight and his uniforms were hung neatly in his wall locker. Nothing appeared to be missing, save one of Artamonov's civilian suits. The KGB was baffled. It was further confused after an inventory of the ship's classified materials disclosed that there were no missing documents. The only theory left for the KGB was that

Artamonov had defected out of an uncontrollable infatuation with Ewa.[14] It was better than no theory at all, but it did little to satisfy the KGB in Moscow Center.

When KGB Chairman Aleksandr Nikolayevich Shelepin informed Admiral Gorshkov that his son-in-law had apparently "stolen" a Soviet Navy boat and defected to the West in the company of a young Polish woman, the admiral expressed his personal dismay. Shelepin, known widely among KGB professionals as Khrushchev's "boot licker," had built his career in the KGB upon this kind of case. But neither he nor the KGB security division were able to connect Artamonov's defection back to Admiral Gorshkov in any way.

In Stockholm, the Soviet Embassy made a determined effort to see Artamonov to convince him that all would be forgiven if he came away with them without any delay. Both Artamonov and Ewa refused their request. It became obvious to the Swedes that this couple was not the sort of run-of-the-mill defectors they had encountered in the past. To avoid a messy confrontation with the KGB, the Swedes moved the pair to a safe house in the Stockholm suburbs while their request for political asylum was under consideration by the Swedish government's Aliens Commission. In those days and times, it was not unheard of for the KGB either to kidnap or to murder a Soviet citizen who had fled and sought political asylum. And because Artamonov was a ranking Soviet naval officer, the threat of a KGB "wet operation" directed against both him and Ewa was considered quite real.

During this period, Swedish naval authorities carried out a "soft interrogation" of Artamonov concerning the Soviet Navy's submarine capabilities, especially their operations in Swedish waters. Commander Rydström and a driver from the Swedish Naval Intelligence Directorate would bring Artamonov and Ewa to the headquarters of the Swedish Navy.[15] From all accounts, it was an amicable relationship. The couple was assured by Commander Rydström, who had become their "case officer" and friend, that the Swedish government would honor their request for asylum and that they would be welcome to stay in Sweden.

All of this attention was heady wine to the ego of Artamonov, but left Ewa with little more to do than look at magazines and wait for the "serious" business to be concluded. She was in some respects a hostage to Artamonov's status, lacking the notoriety he possessed. She also was considered a likely target if the KGB wanted to try to murder or kidnap them, and consequently there was little chance for her to see the sights of Stockholm or do some shopping.

Back in Moscow, the Artamonov defection was a "non-event," as far as the general public was concerned. No mention of it appeared in the Soviet press. Among the Communist Party's *nomenklatura* hierarchy, the Artamonov incident was a matter of salacious gossip in its Moscow "village." Admiral Gorshkov weathered the gossip with his customary dignity and reticence. The Soviet Navy "family" closed ranks behind Admiral Gorshkov and his family by keeping its collective mouth shut.

In Poland, things went less well for Ewa's father. He would only be allowed to make two more trips as a merchant sea captain. The KGB ordered him to report to the Soviet Embassy in Warsaw for months of interrogation. His career was over at the age of fifty-three because of his daughter's defection to the West.

In Stockholm, the debriefing of Artamonov proceeded at a leisurely pace. The Swedish Navy was looking at Artamonov as a potential, long-range intelligence asset, but they were not prepared to offer him a job. Commander Rydström tried to plumb Artamonov's attitudes to ascertain his real intentions. When Artamonov discreetly revealed his interest in moving on to another country, Rydström advised Artamonov to stay away from the Americans. According to Ewa, it was Rydström's view that the Americans would only exploit them and then cast them aside. In reality, there were only two Western countries that might have a serious interest in Artamonov, the United States and England. But Ewa had strong opinions about not going to England because of the way her father had been treated by the English during World War II.[16]

Captain Artamonov had made his decision, and it was not to stay in Sweden. One morning, when Artamonov and Ewa were getting ready for their daily visit to Swedish Naval Headquarters, he asked Ewa to take a taxi and go to the United States Embassy and make their interest in going to the United States known to someone who "spoke Russian." It was not a particularly explicit order, but it would most definitely get the attention of the CIA station in Stockholm.

Later that morning, Ewa took the brief taxi ride from Swedish Naval Headquarters to the U.S. Embassy at 101 Strandvagen to seek out a Russian-speaker to whom she could relay their desire to go to the United States. There was some risk involved in this attempt to contact the Americans, but Ewa was brave and did, in fact, do as Artamonov had requested.

Disembarking from the taxi, which had entered the circular driveway in front of the U.S. Embassy, Ewa was a bit taken aback by the building's appearance. It was early 1950s modern Swedish architecture, bright with a great deal of glass and stark, straight lines. It was the first modern building Ewa had ever seen up close. Entering the U.S. Embassy's L-shaped reception area, the first American Ewa saw was a Marine security guard, Cpl. Karl Larson, resplendent in dress blues, standing in a modified parade-rest position behind a pedestal-type lectern that contained a telephone.

Looking down at the diminutive Ewa from his six-foot-plus height, Corporal Larson said in Swedish, "Good morning. How can I help you?" When this produced no reaction other than an anxious look from Ewa, Larson asked, "Do you speak English?" Still no answer. In response, however, Ewa uttered a few words in Russian. Larson did not understand what she was trying to say, but he did realize that she was speaking Russian. With nods between Larson and Ewa, the point was communicated for her to wait there just a moment.

Corporal Larson called Lt. Col. Anthony Caputo, the assistant naval attaché, and told him that he thought he might have a Russian at the desk. He advised Colonel Caputo that she was dark and did not look like a Scandinavian.[17]

Caputo, a twenty-eight-year veteran of the Marine Corps, was multilingual. Fortunately, one of his languages was Russian, which he had learned at the Navy's language school and from a tour in Moscow on a partially "spooky" assignment. Colonel Caputo told Corporal Larson to "stand fast" and that he would be there in a moment. Colonel Caputo's office was on the second floor of the embassy, along with the other U.S. military attachés' offices. He walked down the single flight of stairs and caught the eye of Larson as he approached the lectern from Ewa's blind side. Ewa was standing off to the right, looking as if she were about to run away.

Colonel Caputo was courtly in his appearance and demeanor. He was in civilian clothes and did not identify himself by his rank or title as he asked Ewa how he might be able to assist her. He quickly put Ewa at ease and escorted her into the anteroom off the entrance foyer. Relieved that she had located someone who spoke Russian, Ewa blurted out her story, never considering for a moment that she had gone well beyond just finding someone who could speak Russian. Colonel Caputo let Ewa tell the entire story of the couple's escape from Gdynia and the turbulent sea voyage to Sweden.

Ewa's revelations did not come as a complete surprise to the colonel; he had been apprised by his contacts in the Swedish Naval Intelligence Directorate about Artamonov and Ewa's defection and the results of their debriefing. Although Artamonov was of interest to U.S. Naval Intelligence, Colonel Caputo realized that the couple's defection fell under the CIA's general jurisdiction and was a matter of greater concern to the Agency than to his office. Washington had already been notified of the little information Caputo had about Artamonov.

Colonel Caputo told Ewa that if it was the couple's decision to seek further asylum in the United States, it was his responsibility to turn her over to the head of the CIA in the U.S. Embassy. After providing

Ewa with a cup of coffee, he called the embassy's second secretary, Paul Garbler, with the message that there was a potential defector in the reception anteroom.

In most U.S. embassies, there is little love lost between the military attachés and the CIA's "spies" who pretend to be diplomats. Colonel Caputo's attitude about the CIA station in Stockholm was no exception to the general rule.[18] No matter the basis of Colonel Caputo's attitude, Second Secretary Paul Garbler did come as requested and talked with Ewa. At this stage, Colonel Caputo excused himself from the proceedings and returned to his office on the second floor.

According to Garbler, Ewa's appearance at the embassy could not have come at a more inopportune time for him personally. At the time, Garbler was literally waiting for the packers and movers to come to his house in preparation for his return to the United States for duty with the "Department of State."[19]

To Ewa, Garbler seemed a huge man, bigger even than Artamonov. Garbler was the picture of a diplomat, with polished good looks and manners to match. Just a few years later he would be called a Soviet agent by James Angleton and his career in the CIA ruined. Although he would be cleared of the charges, the years he lost could not be replaced.[20]

Because he was leaving as chief of station, Garbler turned Ewa and what later became known as the Artamonov "case" over to his designated replacement, Edward G. Goloway.[21] Goloway, almost as big as Garbler, could see at once how nervous Ewa was. But she was gaining confidence with each successive conversation, first with Caputo, then with Garbler, and finally with Goloway. The generous solicitousness and courtesy she was being shown relaxed her. Goloway suggested to Ewa that once she and Artamonov had been granted political asylum by the Swedes, they come to the embassy and let Goloway take it from there. Ewa's visit to the U.S. Embassy made the CIA's job much easier in getting Artamonov to America.

In the CIA's parlance, Artamonov was a really "hot" case. Defectors, especially ranking Soviet officers, whether in the military or in the intelligence organs, were "career makers" for those in the CIA who aspired to promotions. Colonel Caputo did not share his CIA colleagues' view about the urgency of the Artamonov situation. There were procedures and safeguards in dealing with defectors, just as there were in dealing with prisoners of war, the most important of these being an orderly approach to interrogation so that the information obtained could be checked thoroughly.[22]

Because Artamonov was a "hot prospect" for the handful of specialists interested in the growing Soviet Navy, Garbler and Goloway prevailed on Lt. Col. Caputo to provide them with the "raw take" from the Swedish Navy's debriefing of Artamonov. They enlisted some "gentle persuasion" on the part of the U.S. Ambassador, James C. Bonbright, who suggested that the naval attaché's office "cooperate" with the CIA station and its chief on this matter.

This was done, and the unevaluated Artamonov information was sent back to CIA Headquarters as a "hot flash" from the field. In this case, Artamonov was identified as a "NIP," an individual with national intelligence potential.[23] The "hot flash" went to Leonard V. McCoy, a reports officer in the CIA in charge of a broad range of Soviet subjects. McCoy says that he had tremendous fears that the Swedes might send Artamonov and Ewa back to the Soviet Union to avoid political problems.

Instead of allowing the Artamonov defection to run its normal course, McCoy short-circuited the process. Without informing his boss, Soviet Division head Jack Maury, McCoy, who at that time was a relatively low-level CIA employee, set off a remarkable series of events. McCoy, who insists "the Soviets have never sent an intelligence officer to penetrate the CIA," said he took the action because "I was at the end of my rope. I really thought there was nothing more we could do to get this guy here."[24]

A tall and serious young man in 1959, McCoy decided to go over his boss's head to one of the most powerful men in the CIA. Without an appointment, McCoy went to see the closest man to CIA Director Allen Dulles: James Jesus Angleton. McCoy wanted to convince Angleton of the danger of losing this important naval source back to the Soviets, and to get Angleton to put pressure on the Swedish government to guarantee he would come to the United States.

McCoy approached the office of James Angleton with more than a little trepidation. He was a lowly reports officer. Angleton was the head of counterintelligence. McCoy told Angleton's secretary that he needed to speak to her boss about an urgent matter. She asked him to wait and informed Angleton. A few minutes later, McCoy was told he could go in to see Angleton. Actually, McCoy's boldness was bureaucratically shrewd. Angleton, according to McCoy, had no use for Jack Maury. McCoy was giving Angleton a classic way to undermine Maury on a major defection case.

McCoy explained to Angleton, with unaccustomed enthusiasm and urgency, that a real Soviet naval officer had defected to Sweden. McCoy expressed some fear that the Russians would get him back while the Swedish Aliens Commission took its time making a decision on his fate.

In the Sweden of the 1950s, the determination of formal political asylum was made by the Aliens Commission, a governmental body that was very conventional and slow in extending asylum to defectors.

The Swedes had never turned anyone away who sought sanctuary in their country, nor had they given in to either Soviet or Nazi demands for the return of one of their fleeing "subjects," but they were not about to be hurried, or so their past performance indicated. Despite this obvious contradiction in McCoy's argument, Angleton listened.

Angleton must have been a little amused and surprised by McCoy's presumption. After McCoy made his arguments, Angleton told him he was going to call Dulles, and to wait outside. McCoy was called back in and told that Dulles would tell Olof Palme, at that time an assistant to Tage Erlander, the prime minister of Sweden, that Artamonov was coming to America.[25]

For McCoy this was a great victory: "Here was an opportunity for quite an intelligence coup of extremely great importance to the United States. What we had on the Soviet Navy to that point from one earlier defector was very, very trivial. Now here was an officer who we could ask a heck of a lot of questions." The handful of people in the CIA interested in the Soviet Navy were starved for intelligence. One of their few sources of information was from an earlier defector who knew very little. McCoy described him as so useless that he "didn't seem to know the difference between a ship and a house. . . . He described his submarine as if he were in a building on land . . . that it had hallways instead of companionways."

Dulles cabled Olof Palme. The message requested that the Aliens Commission be pressured to speed up the granting of formal political asylum to Artamonov and Ewa.[26] By sending this message, Dulles raised a red flag in many sectors. The cable revealed that Palme had a "special relationship" with the CIA, which meant that he possibly was or had been on the Agency's payroll.[27] The cable, which was intercepted by the Soviets, allowed them to discover this relationship. The KGB finally had discovered who was sniffing around their traitor.

Leonard McCoy's plea for Angleton's intervention to get Artamonov to the United States was successful. In addition to McCoy's risking his young career on the acceptance of Artamonov, he brought Angleton, the powerful chief of counterintelligence, aboard the Artamonov bandwagon. Further, he had gotten Dulles to commit himself. This ensured that Artamonov would come to the United States if he could get through the hurdles of a background check and debriefing. His defection now had attracted the direct interest of the DCI.

Ewa believes that it was her own and Nikolay's decision to come to America. Leonard McCoy says flatly, referring to his visit to Angleton and the subsequent call from Dulles to Palme, that "they had no choice. It was out of their hands. They could have made a great fuss and refused to come to the United States. I don't know what the Swedes would have said. They might have said, 'We have to get rid of you and we will turn you back to the Soviet Embassy down the street.' ''

No matter what may have been Palme's motivations or actions, the Aliens Commission did in fact hasten the granting of political asylum to Artamonov and Ewa. Once that status was conferred, they were free to approach the U.S. Embassy in Stockholm and request a visa for travel to the United States.

Under instructions from CIA Headquarters, the station processed their request for a visa and moved them to a CIA safe house. It was the first in a long line of such facilities the couple would see over the next several months. There they were asked rather routine questions and were made to feel comfortable and welcome.[28]

Orders from CIA Headquarters were promptly forthcoming. Dulles directed that Artamonov and Ewa be taken by a "black flight" from Sweden to Frankfurt for operational debriefings by the defector-handling facility known as the Westport Station. The next phase of the adventure was about to begin.

Shadrin: Westport

❦

One evening we sat around having a couple of glasses of vodka,
and I said, "Nick, if you had to do all over again, would you?" And
he just looked at me and shook his head.

Captain Thomas Dwyer

AT 2130 HOURS on August 1, 1959, a modified DC-3 with International
Red Cross markings, loaded with "humanitarian medical supplies"
touched down with hardly a bounce at the Frankfurt am Main airport.
After completing its short roll, the aircraft taxied off the main north-
south runway and fell in behind an airport jeep. The procession of jeep
and aircraft went past the line of commercial hangars marked with the
names Lufthansa, Pan Am, BEA, and stopped in front of an unmarked
hangar that stood off alone at the south end of the field.

As the DC-3's cabin door was opened, the CIA's ground crew,
composed of "good Germans," ones who had been declared to be de-
Nazified and certified to be anticommunist in their current political
orientations, rolled a mobile stairway into place and placed chocks
against the plane's wheels. Standing on the tarmac were three men.
There were two Mercedes sedans waiting with drivers in each car.

After the DC-3 killed its engines, the only sounds that could be heard were those of traffic from the Autobahn about a half-mile away and the hum of the idling Mercedes. The night was quiet and there was no apparent observation of the plane's arrival by anyone other than the CIA personnel involved.

Anxiously looking out from the door of the aircraft, the CIA "babysitter" from the Stockholm Station whose job it was to turn the "humanitarian medical supplies"—Captain Artamonov and his companion, Ewa Gora—over to the CIA base in Frankfurt, was relieved to see the burly, rumpled chief of base standing on the tarmac. The arrival of Artamonov and Ewa was of sufficient importance that George Carroll, the chief of base in Frankfurt, was there to meet them. The greetings and introductions all around were not unlike those at thousands of similar VIP arrivals at overseas air bases where the CIA maintained an aviation presence. Usually the base or station duty officer would handle the arrival of a VIP, but in this case, Artamonov and Ewa were to be given special treatment because of Dulles's interest in the case.

This meant that CIA Headquarters had to be notified that the arrival had been handled by the most expeditious means, and that updates from the debriefing and interrogations would be handled similarly.

From this moment on, Carroll knew that CIA Headquarters would be looking over his shoulder at each step. He also knew that any mistakes made by his base personnel would reach the Director's ears, or those of East German intelligence, before a report on it reached his desk. In the summer of 1959, the Frankfurt chief of base was completing a long tour in Germany and he was weary. He and the rest of the U.S. intelligence forces in Germany had been defeated all too often by the East Germans.[1]

George Carroll was a rather dour individual who had seen it all before in World War II, and during the so-called Cold War.[2] He realized that the presence of Artamonov and Ewa could mean real trouble in the tranquil backwater of Frankfurt Base.[3]

Carroll knew that East German intelligence—the SSD—and the KGB knew about every facet of Frankfurt Base's "Westport" defector operation.[4] He knew they would not act against Artamonov and Ewa unless some unknown, highly unusual circumstance precipitated such action.[5] His opinion was based not on the usual sources of intelligence available to and supposedly developed by the CIA, but on information bought from the snitches he had developed and cultivated in the apolitical underworld of black marketeers and assorted criminals.

In his report to Dulles, Carroll indicated that Artamonov and Ewa seemed content with the arrangements. He anticipated no problems in their handling while in Frankfurt. As Stockholm had indicated, Artamonov was a cool but arrogant character, and Ewa was overwhelmed by the whole situation, as if it were a combination of a schoolgirl sorority initiation and a visit to a house of horrors. His confidence that there would be no real problems in this operation was based in large measure on the fact that there was so little real intelligence work to be done at Frankfurt Base, that Artamonov and Ewa would get more attention than they probably deserved. Also, it was Carroll's view that the SSD and the KGB would be more interested in tracking the progress of the debriefing and handling of Artamonov and Ewa than in any attempt to seize or kill them while they were in Frankfurt.

Three days later, in his office located on the unmarked top floor in the prewar, former I. G. Farben corporate headquarters building, Carroll reviewed the "take" from the first of the couple's debriefing sessions.[6] Cross-checking this information with what the Swedes had given Stockholm Station, he was uneasy, but inclined to reserve any judgment about Artamonov and Ewa until the interrogation teams had completed their work.

The new Berlin base chief, David E. Murphy, had cooperated by sending his top counterintelligence case control officer, George Kisevalter, to help out.[7] Kisevalter was one of the more popular men in the CIA. Nicknamed "Teddy Bear" and born in Kiev, he had been involved in one big agent operation after another. The only reason he was free to question Artamonov was that the subject of the biggest case he had ever worked, Major Popov, had been called back on leave to Moscow.[8]

Carroll had the highest regard for Kisevalter and, as a consequence, asked him to find out what he could. Using a different name, Kisevalter visited the mansion in which Ewa and Artamonov were staying. He already assumed that Artamonov had been properly vetted. "I could care less about his bona fides, that wasn't my job," Kisevalter said.[9] His job was to see what Artamonov knew about Soviet intelligence operations.

From the start, Kisevalter was given incorrect information at Westport about Artamonov. He was told that Artamonov had pursued Ewa in secret, thus explaining why a Soviet was allowed to socialize with a Pole. Previously, Artamonov had convinced his Westport handlers that he had the rank in Poland to prevent his Soviet intelligence watchdogs from interfering in his personal life.

For three to four hours each day for three consecutive days, Kisevalter grilled Artamonov about command structure, intelligence organization, and personalities. After two days, Kisevalter determined that Artamonov's knowledge was good, but limited. Captain Artamonov knew what Kisevalter expected from a line military officer of his rank, but "he didn't know all the ins and outs a senior military intelligence officer would [know]."

"Artamonov told me as much as he knew and didn't hold back anything," Kisevalter felt. The two men discussed "intelligence points," how the Soviets controlled their intelligence operations from centralized command organizations in countries on Western borders. Each point faced a neighboring country. The Soviets used a unique command structure, which, for example, controlled operations against West Germany from East Germany, rather than from Moscow.

Although the polygraph is not foolproof, in the hands of a skilled operator it is a useful tool. It can indicate appropriate areas for additional interrogation by determining which questions elicit emotional responses to "yes" or "no" answers. Thus the polygraph can be used to identify potential areas of deception from the person examined. Paul Bellin, who was considered one of the most talented polygraph operators in the Agency, was selected to conduct the examinations of Artamonov and Ewa. Artamonov was the latest in a long line of defectors he had "fluttered."

Besides being an expert polygraph examiner, Bellin was a Soviet defector himself, and had a sincere appreciation and understanding of what Artamonov and Ewa were going through. Also, owing to personal experience in the Soviet intelligence services, he was extremely sensitive to the techniques used by Soviet defectors to "con" their interrogators.

Results from the first polygraph examinations of Artamonov and Ewa worried Carroll and Bellin. They revealed areas of possible deception that called into serious question much of the basic personal data provided by Artamonov and Ewa to Swedish naval intelligence and the CIA station in Stockholm. Routinely, because initial polygraph examinations of defectors were frequently found to be inadequate, Carroll told Bellin to reexamine the young couple. These facts were forwarded to Director Dulles. So far, nothing had been revealed by the first polygraph examination to prove conclusively that Artamonov and Ewa were lying to Bellin and the interrogation teams.

Artamonov was growing testy over the polygraphs. He told his handlers he considered the process silly. The second polygraph examinations proved even more inconclusive. The original areas of suspected deception that should have been resolved by the second examination remained in question, and in some instances it appeared that Artamonov and Ewa were trying to be more evasive in their responses. Again, these facts and conclusions were reported to Dulles. A decision was made to give a third and final polygraph examination to Artamonov. It, too, revealed areas of deception.

Coinciding with the polygraph examinations, other members of the Westport staff interrogated Artamonov and Ewa in separate interviews. Here Artamonov demonstrated his true mettle. The interviews were less question-and-answer interrogations than "tutorials" conducted by Artamonov on the subject of the Soviet Navy. He was a smash hit. He confirmed the Westport staff's opinions on matters ranging from the subordination of Polish intelligence to the KGB, and to the supply situation of the Warsaw Pact forces. In short, Artamonov was a provocative if not almost inexhaustible source of information about all Soviet matters. The interrogators were impressed.

Ewa, who lacked the knowledge and confident style of Artamonov, was also a welcome source of information about Polish matters, especially the dissatisfaction of the Polish people with their plight under Soviet occupation and rule. Ewa was disingenuous and guileless in the hands of her interrogators. All of this was good for Artamonov and Ewa, but still there remained the question of their failed polygraph examinations.

Paul Bellin was convinced Artamonov was a fraud. But the political situation at Westport prevented him from broadcasting his opinions. He confided to his old friend Peter Kapusta, a CI officer in the CIA's Soviet Division, that Artamonov was not "real," and gave him the details of the polygraph exams. Long after Artamonov became Nick Shadrin, Kapusta and Bellin tried to shake the CIA's acceptance of Shadrin. But by that time, too many careers had already become hostages to the "authenticity" of Artamonov. There was no going back. To his dying day, Bellin fretted over the Artamonov case.[10]

At the time, few analysts raised any questions about the "old news" aspects of the Artamonov revelations: that Artamonov was only telling the CIA what it already knew, assumed to be true or had been told by "friendly intelligence services." In resolving the all-important issue of whether to accept or reject his bona fides, only the quality of the information, and not its exclusivity, was considered.

What Artamonov was giving his interrogators was basic information about the Soviet Navy; it was not exceptionally revealing, but was far better than anything previously collected. It was decided that Artamonov's polygraph troubles would simply be ignored. His truthfulness would be determined by the reliability of the information he had given on the Soviet Navy, and not by the tests. Artamonov would not be put through a counterintelligence interrogation or the normal vetting procedures.[11]

The Westport Station gave a guarded endorsement of Artamonov, pointing to the intelligence information he had already provided. The weakness of the polygraphs was partially attributed to the difficulties inherent in the examination of Soviet officials who had, quite literally, been indoctrinated by the communists since birth. As a general rule, Soviet defectors who had been raised under the communist system were evasive in their responses, or revealed areas of deception during their polygraph examinations, when they were asked "lifestyle" questions.[12]

During the period when the couple's fate was being discussed in messages between Washington, Berlin, and Frankfurt, Ewa recalls that Artamonov was extremely moody. He considered the delays foolish, and his "Imperial Russian" demeanor was beginning to be evident in his behavior. He and Ewa spent their free time walking in the beautiful grounds of the safe-house estate and talking about their future. At night he took long walks on the grounds and was quite taciturn in his conversations with Ewa. He told her that he was beginning to hate the CIA. "They are no different from the KGB," he advised Ewa.[13]

Finally the orders came to send Artamonov and Ewa to the United States for further interrogation and debriefing at CIA Headquarters by the Soviet Bloc Division staff. Once Artamonov and Ewa were told that they would be leaving shortly for the United States, Artamonov's spirits brightened considerably, but he was less forthcoming in the interrogations, which continued after the notification.

Artamonov and Ewa's departure from the Frankfurt am Main airport at midday on August 21, 1959, went off without a hitch. The U.S. Air Force C-54, which had been configured for VIPs, was a comfortable aircraft for the ocean crossing. Their arrival at Andrews Air Force Base, outside Washington, in the predawn dark of August 22, 1959, was not unlike their welcome at Frankfurt some three weeks earlier.

The CIA handlers, led by Walter Onoshko of the Soviet Division, were happy to see Artamonov and Ewa. It had been a long time since the Russian-speaking officers in the Soviet Division had a real, live Soviet military officer to debrief and interrogate. From the first moments on the tarmac at Andrews, Onoshko warmed to both Artamonov and Ewa. His feelings were reciprocated by the young couple. According to Ewa, Onoshko was Artamonov's favorite American, official or otherwise.[14]

Artamonov and Ewa were taken to the top-of-the-line CIA safe house in Leesburg, Virginia. The accommodations were not as grand as the mansion in Frankfurt, but for a pair of weary travelers they were just fine. The hospitality was genuine. Unlike the support personnel in Frankfurt, who had seen defectors come and go to the point that it was a boring routine, the CIA personnel at the Virginia safe house were not jaded. To them, Artamonov and Ewa were a pair of intelligence "celebrities" rather than just another burdensome administrative chore. The reports of Artamonov and Ewa's romantic involvement, which had preceded their arrival, also added to their hosts' curiosity and readiness to accept them as a hero and heroine.

Onoshko, who was old enough to be Artamonov's father, was more like a solicitous den mother than a case officer in his treatment of the defectors. From the outset, Onoshko blurred the distinction between his actual job and his feelings about them as individuals. Artamonov and Ewa were defectors and refugees, but above all, until they had been thoroughly debriefed and exploited, they were at best only potential intelligence assets, and at worst communist agents.

It took several days for the couple to settle into a routine. A basic wardrobe and other necessities were purchased for them. The CIA's Office of Security kept a close eye on the safe house, and there were no reports from the FBI or the local police to indicate that the presence of Artamonov and Ewa had provoked any Soviet or Eastern Bloc intelligence interest.

Once the settling in was completed, Onoshko headed up the initial debriefings at the safe house. He was very solicitous of Artamonov and Ewa's well-being and made sure that the interrogations and debriefings were carried out in a nonthreatening, almost conversational mode. Artamonov and Ewa were tutored in English between debriefings. There was no need to be hostile, since it appeared that the couple was making a serious effort to be cooperative and helpful. The negative aspect to Onoshko's protective behavior, however, was to elevate Artamonov to the role of a colleague, rather than to allow the interrogators a free hand in finding out what he knew or was trying to withhold. There was very little talk about Artamonov and Ewa's bona fides, which seemed to be tacitly accepted. The interrogations became even more conversational in tone and approach.

During these months, Artamonov was made available to other intelligence agencies, including the Office of Naval Intelligence (ONI) for extensive questioning. Thomas Dwyer, the only ONI man who was given access to Artamonov from the beginning of his stay in America, was his main contact. Dwyer, a tall and easygoing Naval Intelligence officer, also became Artamonov's friend. Although at first they had to work through an interpreter, the two men grew very close. Artamonov was quickly mastering English. And Dwyer, like so many others, "just assumed that they brought him to America and at some point established that he was legitimate. I was never disabused of that idea, although we all realized the possibility that Nick could be a double, and we should conduct ourselves accordingly."[15]

It was also during this period that the Navy gave Artamonov their own test of his bona fides. The former assistant naval attaché in Moscow escorted Artamonov to Newport, Rhode Island, where he was taken on board a destroyer and allowed to con the ship and run an antisubmarine-warfare exercise against a U.S. nuclear submarine. Artamonov performed well for three hours. Observers said his greatest troubles came from having to use a translator to convey orders. The Navy was impressed enough with his effort to take a very serious interest in the defector.[16]

But within the CIA's Soviet Division, opinion was divided about the intelligence value of "Onoshko's Russian." One group asserted that Artamonov was argumentative, evasive, and ill-informed about subjects he should have known, given his background and political training in the Communist Party. Others contended that Artamonov was being pressured to affirm or take positions on information that was outside his scope and experience. This latter group was interested in finding out as much as possible about Soviet maritime activities and capabilities, a subject that had only limited interest to most of the Soviet analysts in the CIA.

Artamonov's technical expertise disappointed many of his CIA debriefers. But perhaps the biggest event that worked against him at the time was the fact that the very ship he knew the most about was removed from the Soviet fleet within six months of his arrival. This incident made much of Artamonov's information useless.

For Peter Kapusta, the questioning CI officer in the Soviet Division, it was a red flag. Kapusta had a longer memory than did his colleagues who valued and authenticated Artamonov because of his knowledge of the Soviet Navy. The fact that most of this information was now obsolete was a disturbing development. Kapusta let his colleague at Westport, Paul Bellin, know about the sudden decision by the Soviet Navy to dispose of Artamonov's entire class of vessel. He also informed Leonard McCoy and other CIA officials of the questions this development raised about Artamonov's pedigree. But he was dismissed as being overly suspicious. As Leonard McCoy put it, "What Nick offered did not have a lot of appeal elsewhere in the CIA." Only Onoshko, Leonard McCoy, John T. Funkhouser, and a handful of other Soviet naval specialists relished Artamonov's presence. Now Ewa and Nick were turned over to the Domestic Contact Division for resettlement.

Part of this transition involved the shedding of their past and the establishment of new identities for Captain Nikolay Fedorovich Artamonov and Ewa Gora. At the time, Ewa was told the new names were only temporary, to get them on the Social Security rolls and to further hide them from the Soviet intelligence services. It was only a mild deception. The names became permanent—and the Soviets had shown no real interest, either diplomatically or physically, in either Artamonov or Ewa since their defection. The names chosen, ostensibly by Onoshko, were Nicholas George Shadrin and Ewa Blanka.

According to a Sunday-supplement magazine article that appeared several years after Shadrin's disappearance, the name Shadrin was taken from the protagonist in Pushkin's story "The Captain's Daughter."[17] The truth is more prosaic. The protagonist in Pushkin's story is named Alexei Ivanich Shvabrin, and although the name sounds a bit like "Shadrin," this is not how "stiff names" are assigned to defectors by the CIA. Sometimes the names chosen are contractions of the defector's name, or one formed by its first two syllables. In the case of Shadrin, his new name was selected in accordance with the CIA's "Manhattan telephone book" rule—the name chosen is not in the phone book.

The CIA turned Nick Shadrin and Ewa over to the careful ministrations of Peter Sivess, who was in charge of its "Ashford Farm," located on Maryland's Eastern Shore.[18] This operation was part of the Alien Branch's Overt Contact Division. As such, it was part of the settlement procedure for defectors. Peter Sivess and his wife, Ellie, both liked Nick Shadrin very much. "Nick was larger than life," Sivess said. Ellie remembers Nick being baffled by CIA security rules. Pete spoke fluent Russian and was also a consummate outdoorsman. He introduced Shadrin to the pleasures of goose-hunting and fishing on the Eastern Shore of Maryland. But one aspect about Nick's hunting bothered Pete: "He was quite a hunter, but he never approached an animal while it was still moving. He wanted to shoot it first. I would go up and break its neck . . . but he would shoot it."[19]

In the early days "there was talk of approaching Ewa's father by the CIA," Sivess explained. According to George Kisevalter, Eastern Bloc merchant marine captains, like Ewa's father, are frequently used by the Soviets for intelligence gathering. "They can operate with freedom in ports where Soviet and Bloc military just couldn't get in," Kisevalter said.

Most defectors were given extremely short shrift during the early 1960s. They were squeezed quickly to elicit whatever operational information they possessed, and then brushed aside. Very, very few defectors were picked up by the CIA as "contract employees." Frequently they were enrolled in the local Berlitz program, taught conversational English, and then told to "get a job." But this kind of solution was ruled out in the case of Shadrin and Ewa.

By early 1960, the CIA was looking for a way to rid itself of the administrative burden of Nick Shadrin and Ewa Blanka without totally abandoning them. Although Ewa had her Polish certification in dentistry, she still needed some additional training in both dentistry and English before she could be certified to practice in the United States. No similar option was available for Shadrin. Regardless of the amount of time he spent in the States or the additional degrees he earned, he would never be the captain of a ship.

Nick Shadrin worried about his future if he was dropped by the CIA without either citizenship or a decent job. With regard to Shadrin's citizenship, the haunting warnings of Commander Rydström back in Sweden, that the Americans would squeeze him dry and then cast him aside, proved true as far as the CIA was concerned. The CIA could easily have supplied citizenship for the couple, but found it was not necessary.[20]

For the first time Shadrin expressed openly the idea that he might have made a mistake and perhaps he ought to consider going home. He confided in Peter Sivess that he was very unhappy in the United States. He told him that there was no challenge to what he was doing, and he was fearful that he would never get the protection of U.S. citizenship if the CIA lost interest in him. Sivess immediately notified the CIA of his worries about Nick. He had seen enough of defector disillusionment to recognize the signs. And, in Shadrin's case, these were magnified by his "Imperial Russian" personality.

Tom Dwyer confirms Shadrin's mood during this period. "He could have those periods of dark depression in the early days. I'd go out there to see him, and he would be sitting on a stump out in the back of the safe house and his head would be down and he would be in a terribly glum mood. I usually could get him cheered up a little bit to talk, and we got him a project: he built a twenty-four-foot motorboat. And I remember the ONI said, 'I hope the son of a bitch doesn't take it to Cuba.' " [ONI means William Abbott, the director of counterintelligence for the Office of Naval Intelligence.]

Shadrin's depression evaporated as soon as the Navy began to take a real interest in him. Word had spread of Shadrin's successful exercise in Rhode Island. U.S. Naval Intelligence was starved for information and opinions on the Soviet Navy. They began to seek him out for information on the basic structure and organization and personalities of the Soviet Navy. Shadrin became a much hotter intelligence prospect for the United States Navy than for the CIA. For example, although Naval Intelligence was very curious about the Soviet Navy's officer-selection process, much of this information was of little or no interest to the CIA.

William R. Corson, then on duty with Naval Intelligence, was assigned to debrief Nick Shadrin about the radar on his ship that was being turned over to the Indonesians.[21] Corson, working for then Captain Rufus L. Taylor, the assistant director of Naval Intelligence, was driven to a CIA safe house in Deal, Maryland, to interrogate Shadrin.[22]

The old mansion was located at the end of a long driveway guarded by Doberman pinschers and CIA security personnel. Dark and foreboding, it looked like something out of a Charles Addams cartoon. Shadrin was a little uneasy at the outset of the interrogation because there had been no attempt to introduce Corson, other than to indicate that he wanted to talk about "your ship." To Corson it was clear that Shadrin was as advertised—intelligent, cool, and quick to shift the line of interrogation if it placed him at a disadvantage. He found Shadrin "personable to a fault. It wasn't so much that he made a conscious effort to please, a common failing of defectors who are particularly insecure, but rather it was an expression of his personal self-confidence."

The interrogation went rather smoothly. Shadrin was forthcoming in most instances. However, when the line of questioning became quite specific, he was unable to answer the precise questions which were posed. These questions were ones he should have been able to answer on the performance characteristics of his own ship's radar. It was only discovered much later, after the ships were turned over to the Indonesian Navy and finally reached Djakarta, that the radar on Shadrin's ship wasn't operational. It had been sold to the Indonesians as well-maintained radar, but in reality it was a nonfunctional copy. As Shadrin himself later confirmed in his dissertation for his Ph.D. from George Washington University, the Soviets' "fire sale" of naval vessels and military equipment to the Indonesians was at best a billion-dollar rip-off.[23] Looking back, Shadrin probably wondered why Naval Intelligence wanted to know about his nonfunctional radar, but at the time he evidenced no direct curiosity.

Nick Shadrin displayed reasonable restraint during the interrogation. He declined to rise to the bait when questioned about the projections of a Soviet blue-water navy. Instead, he turned on his anticommunist frequency and played the theme of the "professional" military man who had become disillusioned by the "lies" of the party apparatchiks.[24]

After the interrogation was completed, Shadrin relaxed and became more conversational. Together the two men moved out onto the house's front porch to wait for the Navy car. It was a pleasant and clear day. Corson smiled up at the six-foot-two Shadrin and asked him why he had really defected. Nick laughed and said, "Did you look at my personal things?" When Corson indicated he hadn't, Shadrin went back inside and returned with a photograph. It was a picture of two women standing in front of a building. They looked as if they belonged in a railroad yard, working on the track. Nick asked, "Have you ever been to Leningrad?" Corson said he was only asking questions, not answering them. Pointing to the picture of the two unattractive women, one older than the other, he laughed and said, "Can you

imagine living in Leningrad . . . where the housing is still very scarce
. . . in a one-bedroom apartment with these two women?'' Shadrin
never identified the two women as his mother-in-law and wife, but
insinuated that was who they were.

Later, Corson learned that a photo mission had been assigned to
check on the bona fides of the address Shadrin had provided in Leningrad. Based on Shadrin's descriptions, the erroneous assumption
was made that he had lived in the apartment with his family. In reality,
the apartment in question was simply Shadrin's "shore cabin," which
he used as a place to stay overnight when it was not feasible to stay
aboard his ship.

At the time, 1959, U.S. intelligence did not know that Nick Shadrin's actual family quarters were in Kaliningrad, in a spacious apartment that had been occupied during World War II by a German
brigadier general. Kaliningrad, unlike Leningrad, did not suffer any
significant damage when the German forces launched their blitzkrieg
assault against the Soviets in June 1941.

By the spring of 1960, the Navy was impressed enough with Shadrin
that it offered him a contract as a consultant to the Office of Naval
Intelligence. Ewa was enrolled in her dentistry program, and it appeared that Nick would finally be rid of the CIA.

Among the last assignments Nick and Ewa had for the CIA before
joining ONI came as a surprise to the couple in May 1960. Almost out
of the blue, a CIA officer named Daniel "Bucky" Awanto sought out
Nick and Ewa and said that they had to get married. Why they should
marry, and why at this time, was not answered by Awanto. Nick and
Ewa were not opposed to the idea. However, as they and the CIA
knew, Shadrin was still married to the wife he had left behind in the
Soviet Union.

This giant matrimonial obstacle was waved aside by the CIA official,
who said "we can take care of that." The absurdity of this remark
made no impression on Nick and Ewa, who accepted without question
that the CIA did indeed have the power to dissolve a marriage. In
response, Shadrin and Ewa accompanied Awanto to Raleigh, North
Carolina, where, on May 31, 1960, Nicholas G. Shadrin of Arlington,
Virginia, and Blanka E. Pawlovska (a name made up for the occasion)
of Washington, D.C., were joined in matrimony by James A. Rowland,
a justice of the peace.

Their marriage license (number 536) filed in the Office of Register of
Deeds, Wake County, State of North Carolina, indicates that Shadrin
was thirty-two years of age, the son of F. E. Shadrin and Nina Shadrin,
both deceased. Ewa, twenty-two years of age, was the daughter of
Zigmunt and Yadwiga Pawlovska, both living and residents of Gdynia,
Poland. Legal impediments to the marriage notwithstanding, it did take

place. The "administrative" marriage of Nick and Ewa Shadrin was later followed by a Catholic wedding in Baltimore, Maryland, to satisfy Ewa's mother. (They would tell her about the marriage when they thought it would be safe to do so.)

A very happy Nick Shadrin started his consultancy at the Office of Naval Intelligence on June 1, 1960. Nick felt he was finally doing useful work. Tom Dwyer said of his new colleague, "He absolutely thought the people at the CIA were a bunch of nuts from the very beginning. . . . He was very happy to be coming to ONI."

Shadrin:
The Trusted Adviser

It always amazed me. He knew more important people than I did. I don't see how he had the access.

Pete Sivess

THE OLD NAVAL OBSERVATORY stands in a parklike setting toward the top of one of Washington's most attractive areas. Driving up the section of Massachusetts Avenue known as Embassy Row, a visitor passes mansion after mansion with pristine lawns, foreign flags, and occasional statues to unremembered heroes. Every morning, Nick Shadrin left his small, two-story Colonial home in the nice, all-American suburb of Arlington, Virginia, and made this drive to the Observatory—to the heart of security for the U.S. Navy. At the time of Shadrin's employment with the Office of Naval Intelligence, the quarters of the Chief of Naval Operations were located in a large, white Victorian house on the Naval Observatory grounds. Today these quarters are the official residence of the Vice-President.[1]

Nick Shadrin's boyishly attractive friend, Tom Dwyer, had pressed for a consultancy for Shadrin at ONI, but it took Captain Rufus Tay-

lor's considerable clout to push it through.[2] To Taylor, Shadrin represented an in-house expert on the Soviet Navy who would be at his
elbow with advice. For too long the impatient Taylor had suffered
through meaningless speculation on the Soviet Navy. Now he had at
his fingertips a real Soviet naval officer. He came to believe that Shadrin, if properly handled, could be extremely helpful to ONI.

An old hand in the bureaucratic wars of the intelligence community,
Taylor knew that Shadrin's contract as a special consultant had to be
sold to the security people, not just forced down their throats. The
biggest opposition came from William Abbott, the civilian head of
counterintelligence at ONI. Abbott was convinced that bringing a defector into the core of ONI was bad policy.

When Dwyer first brought up the idea of hiring Shadrin, "Abbott
was arguing that we should keep him at long arm's length," Dwyer
remembers. Eventually, Taylor overcame Abbott's objections and
sold Shadrin as such a unique intelligence asset that ONI had no choice
but to put him on the payroll. The affable Russian had broken through
to the highest levels of the Navy. He was now part of the team.[3]

Shadrin's colleagues at the Naval Observatory took their cue from
the way Taylor treated Shadrin. Jerry Edwards, a former naval aviator
and ONI analyst who worked across the hall from Shadrin, remembers
Taylor coming into the translation section where Shadrin worked, pull-
ing up a chair, putting his feet on the desk, and having long, involved
conversations with Shadrin about a multitude of intelligence questions.
Edwards was surprised that Taylor discussed the most classified matters with Shadrin. He said nothing at the time, out of deference to the
fact that Taylor was in a position to make need-to-know determina-
tions about intelligence.[4] As Edwards noted, "I was told carefully by
Admiral Taylor's aide, 'Remember, discuss nothing with Shadrin except what you might find in the *New York Times.*' That was the phrase
he used." But to Edwards, it was clear that Taylor himself was exempt
from the rule.

Shadrin thrived in his role as an ONI "special consultant." He was
a helpful, hard worker and well liked by his colleagues, at least in
those early days. He translated and explained the significance of the
suddenly increased supply of Soviet naval documents coming into
U.S. hands.

Shortly after Shadrin went to work for ONI, as part of one of his
"special assignments" he made a presentation about the Soviet Navy
and the Soviet government's hostile intentions to an interagency group
of bureaucrats, analysts, and congressional staffers. His spiel was cap-
tivating to many who heard it, because it confirmed some of their
suspicions and opinions about the Soviets' true intentions. In May of
1960, the U-2 affair and Khrushchev's hardened attitude had given the

anticommunists in the United States government a new lease on life. Also, the country was in the middle of a heated presidential election in which national security loomed large.

Even with Shadrin's broken English, his booming voice, anticommunist message, and charismatic personality put him in demand in Washington. Taylor was asked to supply him as a witness before the House Un-American Activities Committee—one of the last vestiges in Congress of the McCarthy era. Taylor believed it was politic to approve the appearance. But others, including Leonard McCoy and Tom Dwyer, thought it was far too dangerous and risky to parade Nick Shadrin, a Soviet naval officer who had defected, before the public and the press. Surely the Soviets would then know where to find him. But the CIA hierarchy had the final decision, and Shadrin agreed to testify. Dwyer said that he "thought it was stupid. Absolutely stupid, but we were not consulted. This was arranged between the House Un-American Activities staff and the CIA."[5]

HUAC was chaired by Representative Francis E. Walter, a Democrat from Pennsylvania, who had a longstanding reputation as a red-baiter who was quick to accuse those with whom he disagreed. But he was not very effective in the task of uncovering subversive activities or "closet" communists, or in changing the body of laws that dealt with the crimes of conspiracy and espionage. Walter and his committee staff, like many in the communist-bashing days, lacked the sophistication and patience to deal with the real Soviet espionage threats.

In preparation for the public hearings that would make the case that the Russians posed a formidable military and espionage threat to the United States, Shadrin was interviewed by the HUAC staff. His attitude and charm captivated them. His flamboyant statements were eagerly received by the committee. He was the perfect witness. He would say exactly what the chairman wanted to hear, without any prompting or directing.

Preparations for the public hearing enabled Shadrin to widely expand his sphere of influence. His contacts outside the circle of CIA and ONI personnel grew to those in the Congress who were sympathetic to his cause. The arrangements for the hearings also gave Shadrin a perfect excuse to be away from his job at the Naval Observatory. These absences and the upcoming hearings added lustre to his mystery and status in the eyes of his colleagues.

In laying the groundwork for the hearings, the HUAC staffers tried to compile a short biography of Shadrin. Despite dozens of inconsistencies, the most public of government organizations certified Shadrin's self-declarations as fact; what were considered "minor" inconsistencies in the witness's background were overlooked. The HUAC staffers' jobs were to make their committee members look good, not to seriously evaluate the communist threat. In the opinion of the authors of this book, their actions did more to harm the country than to help it.

On the morning of September 14, 1960, Chairman Walter gaveled the committee to order and said the hearing was "conducted in response to the duties imposed upon us by the Congress of the United States to make a continuing study of Communist activities."[6]

Walter gave the familiar litany of Shadrin leaving a promising naval career in Russia in exchange for freedom in America. In doing this he once again gave Shadrin's accepted biography. Thus the bare bones of the Nick Shadrin "legend" were given the imprimatur of the United States Congress. Like much that went on before HUAC, not much of it was accurate. In subsequent telling and retelling by himself and others, Shadrin's "legend" took on a life of its own.[7] For example, Chairman Walter said, "Articles concerning him have appeared in the Soviet Ministry of Defense newspaper *Red Star* and the newspaper *Soviet Navy*, in which he has been cited for such things as outstanding performance and leadership . . . his destroyer having been chosen as one of two Soviet destroyers to pay an official visit to Copenhagen." In reality, the trip to Copenhagen was little more than a "day sail," and the "articles" did little more than mention Shadrin's name as "one of those in attendance." A few stories fell into the category of "Sailor of the Week," but were singularly lacking in any specifics. No serious effort was made by HUAC staffers to really check out his self-proclaimed biography. It was accepted as fact because he was a communist who had seen the light and left the Soviet Union.

In an amateurish disguise, Shadrin read a statement to the committee that fell on receptive ears. In it he said:

> Monday, Khrushchev arrives in the United States. He says he is going to talk about disarmament. I feel obliged to point out, from the information available to me as a Soviet officer and Communist Party member, that Soviet military strategy is inconsistent with Khrushchev's pronouncements on disarmament. Since February 1955, Soviet strategy has been based on the doctrine of surprise attack in nuclear warfare. This doctrine was established in a Soviet military publication which is known only to officers of flag rank and above. Several times over the past four years it has been said again and again. It has never been changed. I believe that the Soviet dictatorship would undertake a surprise attack if she felt that she could win in one stroke. Make no mistake—they are power seekers, not political idealists.[8]

This bombshell played well in the media. It produced a *New York Times* headline that proclaimed, SOVIET DEFECTOR IN U.S. WARNS

MOSCOW HAS NUCLEAR-RAID PLAN.[9] But Shadrin's more revealing testimony went unnoticed:

> The question arose—where is my place, what am I to do?
>
> Should I pursue the "brilliant" career promised me as a naval officer?
>
> Should I keep on saying things which I myself do not believe to be true, things which I know are absolute lies?
>
> Should I keep on spreading ideologies which I do not share, which I detest?
>
> Should I keep on helping the Kremlin to accumulate more and more power, to deceive my people, to dominate my people, and help the Kremlin to perpetrate crimes on an international scale?
>
> But I was an officer; wouldn't I be betraying my own people by running away from them?
>
> No. I shall never betray my people and I shall never forsake them—I was, I am, and I shall always remain a Russian, a Russian—but not a Soviet Russian, not a toy in the hands of Khrushchev and the company in the Kremlin.[10]

Chairman Walter took note that one of the secretaries from the Russian Embassy was present throughout the entire hearing. He added, "I hope that from his appearance he will have learned that, in this free society of ours, witnesses are not told what to say and they may select any topic they choose to talk about."[11] The "secretary" was Vladimir L. Bykov, a second secretary at the Soviet Embassy who was also the number-three man in the KGB/GRU station. Bykov was there to be seen and to take notes. If Chairman Walter had looked toward the rear of the hearing room (which was half-filled), he would have noticed three men and a woman who also were present "throughout the entire hearing." They were Rear Admiral Yashin, the senior Soviet naval attaché; Capt. Alexander R. Astafiev, Soviet naval attaché; Comdr. Lev A. Vtorygin, assistant naval attaché, who had been a friend of Shadrin's in the Soviet Union; and Admiral Yashin's daughter, the very attractive Tanya. One can only surmise what went through Admiral Yashin's mind as he listened to Shadrin's testimony.

The Soviets reacted promptly to Shadrin's appearance before HUAC. It was reported on Monday, September 19, 1960 (the day of Khrushchev's arrival in the United States), in the Kaliningrad newspaper, that "Nikolay Fedorovich Artamonov is accused of betraying the motherland while carrying out a special assignment on a ship in the Polish port of Gdynia and of fleeing to Sweden, where he sought polit-

ical asylum which was granted; that is, of committing a crime as stip-
ulated by Article 1 of the law on criminal responsibility for state
crimes."[12] A further terse, two-line announcement was made in
Pravda on September 23, 1960, which said, "Nikolay Fedorovich Artamonov has been found guilty in absentia by a special People's Court
of the crime of treason against the State. Under the laws for state
crimes he has been sentenced to death." Justice is swift in the Soviet
Union.

Following Shadrin's testimony, he became a full-fledged "star" in
the Washington society of vocal anticommunists. ONI was pleased,
the CIA was pleased, and Shadrin's presence was sought with increased frequency in the interagency "task forces" that were organized to deal with the Soviet "threat." Shadrin was an artful and
charming speaker. Audiences around the country, from Rotary Clubs
to the Naval War College, clamored to hear his views. In almost every
case these audiences, the CIA, ONI, Congress, and the FBI were
convinced of his stated motive for defection—that at the age of thirty-
two he had discovered that the Soviet leaders were telling their people
lies.

Had U.S. tax dollars been put to work more effectively, the individuals entrusted with national security would have discovered that there
were some problems with Shadrin's personal history. Unfortunately,
even a cursory examination of Shadrin's background does not make
sense. In Shadrin's resumé he said he was born on May 19, 1928, in
Leningrad, USSR.[13] This date conflicted with the birthday he gave the
Swedes, which was 1926. Yet on his and Ewa's application for a visa,
which was filled out in Stockholm in 1959, the date was listed as 1928.
This discrepancy might have been a typographical error that Shadrin
failed to correct, or it might have been done intentionally to make the
search for his lineage more difficult. Regardless, it made his claim to
be the "youngest" Soviet naval captain more meaningful.

In his 1981 book about Shadrin, Henry Hurt describes Shadrin's
early dramatic and heroic actions by saying:

> He was an exceptional student, and in 1941 he was enrolled at a
> special secondary naval school on Vasil'evskii Island. He began to
> dream of becoming a naval officer and never gave serious considera-
> tion to anything else. It was considered an honor to attend the prelim-
> inary school, and during this period Nikolai first learned something
> about real war.
>
> When the Germans were attacking Leningrad, Nikolai and his fel-
> low students stood on the rooftops of the school buildings and fired
> small weapons at the attacking German planes. Not only were the
> weapons ineffective, but for the rest of his life Nikolai's legs would

bear small scars from the shrapnel he and his classmates caught as their weapons misfired and ricocheted off the buildings.[14]

According to Captain Albert Graham, U.S. Navy (ret.), currently a member of the U.S. Intermediate Nuclear Facility Inspection Team in the Soviet Union, "There never was a special secondary naval school on Vasil'evskii Island, during, before, or after the siege of Leningrad."[15] Similarly, in response to the siege of Leningrad, which began shortly after the Germans invaded Russia in June 1941, The Executive Committee of the Leningrad Soviet ordered the evacuation of children up to the age of fourteen from the city.[16] Also, the Executive Committee ordered the closing of schools other than a few technical institutes and trade schools, which were kept open to help provide specific training for the war effort. Although it is possible that Shadrin was not evacuated from Leningrad, owing, perhaps, to his physical size, the idea of a special secondary naval school operating during the siege of Leningrad is not supported by any credible evidence.

An explanation for his claimed stay in Leningrad during the siege may be the disputed date of his birth. If he was born in 1926, he would have been older than fourteen. Complicating this point, however, is Shadrin's congressional testimony, which says: "Early in World War II, I felt the strong national pride of all Soviets, at times mixed with bitterness for our suffering. In spite of the hard times caused by the blockade of Leningrad and *our evacuation from the city* (emphasis added), I never once doubted the policies of Stalin and our government."[17]

Shadrin's educational claims are also dubious. In response to HUAC Counsel Nittle's question, "What elementary schooling did you have, and when did it commence?" Shadrin replied, "I had seven years of school in Leningrad from 1934 to 1941. Then I entered a special naval school where I completed my intermediate education. From 1945 to 1949, I studied at the Frunze Higher Naval School, and from the fall of 1955 to the fall of 1956, I attended special courses for destroyer commanders."[18]

Embellishing this question and answer, Shadrin said in his prepared statement, "Since my graduation from the seven-year school in 1941, my life has been closely connected with the Soviet Navy. During World War II, from 1941 to 1945, I attended a Special Secondary Naval School, and from 1945 to 1949, I studied in the Higher Naval School. After receiving my commission I served as a naval officer for ten years—starting as a watch officer, then advancing to the rank of commander of a combat unit, and finally reached the rank of commander of a destroyer."[19]

By 1965, Shadrin had "refined" his educational background for his resumé to show the following:

1945: Graduated from Special Naval High School. Awarded All-Union High School Diploma. Received naval education preparatory to entrance in Naval Academy.

1945–49: Attended Naval Academy, graduated near top of class (fifty-seventh out of class of 550) with rank of lieutenant, junior grade, with "right to select fleet and privileges in assignment."

1949–51: Duty with operating (DD) forces as Head of Mine-Torpedo Department (rank: lieutenant).

1951–52: Assistant commanding officer in charge of Combat Information Center, Coordination of Fire Control, Organization, ASW.

1952–54: Executive officer (rank: lieutenant commander).

1954–55: Advanced studies at school equivalent to Naval War College.

1955–59: Commanding officer of destroyer. In 1957, simultaneously commanding officer of tactical group of destroyers (2 DDs). Last year and one-half involved in training of foreign personnel (rank: commander).[20]

The inflation and padding of a resumé in preparation for public testimony is not unprecedented. Many congressional witnesses and job-seekers put the best possible spin on their background and experience. However, individuals with personal knowledge of the Soviet educational system and navy found Shadrin's self-inflating claims beyond belief. Peter Sivess, who had experience with the Soviet Navy both during and after World War II, as well as with other defectors, did not believe Shadrin's advertised educational accomplishments. Neither did Frank Steinert, a fellow defector and colleague who caught Shadrin in many contradictory statements about his background over the years. Steinert, who did attend Frunze, the Soviet military academy in Moscow, categorically stated his belief that Shadrin never attended the naval academy in Leningrad as he had claimed. "I attended Frunze [the main school in Moscow]. I questioned him about his attendance there. He could not answer obvious questions. . . . It was clear to me he never graduated from Frunze," Steinert said.[21]

Confirming Steinert's view is that Jim Wooten, an FBI agent at that time, showed Soviet defector Yuri Nosenko, also a former Frunze student, thousands of pictures including many of Shadrin, and Nosenko had no memory of the tall, young student at Frunze.

The important aspect of this deception is that "legends," no matter how artfully designed, like false documents, cannot stand up to careful scrutiny. In this case, it seems that Shadrin's "legend" was not carefully checked, or that the United States lacked the capability to do it.

The next phase of Shadrin's background that was accepted as true involved his family. The hearing transcript shows:

MR. NITTLE: Are your parents living?

CAPTAIN ARTAMONOV: No; they have died.

MR. NITTLE: When did your father die?

CAPTAIN ARTAMONOV: In 1958.

MR. NITTLE: When did your mother die?

CAPTAIN ARTAMONOV: In 1956.[22]

And according to the Shadrin book by Henry Hurt, "His parents were well educated—his mother, the former Aleksandra Grigoryeva, a teacher and his father, Fedor, a mechanical engineer."[23]

When Shadrin made these assertions in the course of his odyssey from Sweden to Germany to the United States, they were readily accepted by intelligence personnel who should have known better. However, because Shadrin was wanted by CIA careerists, he was accepted, quite literally, without question. This acceptance effectively foreclosed any interest in a search of his lineage bona fides. Shadrin had a mother and father who were both dead, and no brothers or sisters. It was a very convenient aspect of Shadrin's "legend" to explain how leaving the Soviet Union was somewhat easier for him than for other defectors.

The truth, however, is much different. It emerges from Shadrin's attendance at the Nakhimov School in Leningrad. Admittance there, and to the other Nakhimov schools in 1944 and into the early 1950s was reserved for children whose fathers were killed or died during military service in World War II—the "Great Patriotic War of the Motherland." Evidence shows that Shadrin was a war orphan, and his father did not die in 1958 as Nick had told Ewa and others.

Beginning in 1944, the Soviet cruiser *Aurora* was anchored in Leningrad and used as the dormitory for the "Nakhimovite," the fledgling members of the Soviet Navy. Today the *Aurora* is still anchored in Leningrad. It is no longer used as a dormitory for the Nakhimov naval cadets, who are now housed in buildings across the Neva River that look out on the *Aurora* at its ceremonial anchorage. The *Aurora* is maintained by the Soviet government as a symbol and shrine for Russians to visit, much in the way Americans view the USS *Constitution* in Baltimore Harbor. Aboard the ship, on the bulkhead along the companionway leading to the ship's mess, is a series of plaques with the names of naval cadets and their fathers. On one of the plaques for the entering class of 1944 are the names of one Nikolay F. Artamonov and his father, Col. Fyodor V. Artamonov (1906–1944).[24]

The genealogy of the Artamonov family is a study in itself.[25] Shadrin's branch of the family tree is military- and intelligence-oriented. Perhaps the most noteworthy was his great-uncle, Col. Viktor Alexeivich Artamonov, who was the Tsar's military attaché in Belgrade, the man who funded the assassination of Archduke Ferdinand, which in turn led to the start of World War I. Other family members were involved with British intelligence and the operations of Felix Dzerzhinsky's Cheka after the Bolshevik Revolution in 1917. Thus, Shadrin's genealogical "tickets" were more than acceptable to the communists, as was the fact that his father worked as an unskilled laborer in a sawmill from 1919 to 1925, before joining the Red Army. Shadrin's father had come up from the political ranks of the Komsomol and had full membership in the Communist Party of the Soviet Union in 1930.

The identity of Shadrin's mother is also perplexing. According to Hurt's 1981 book about Shadrin, her name was Aleksandra Grigoryeva. On his marriage license application, Shadrin listed his mother's name as "Nina." Ewa remembers a further reference to "Tina" or possibly "Tanya." His visa application and the information from the Swedes makes reference to Elena. All in all, there is considerable confusion surrounding his mother's actual name. However, on one point about both his mother and father there is no dispute. In the sixteen years he was with Ewa, he made only brief references to his family and their background. This lack of familial pride is quite inconsistent with the sense of family that animates most Russians.

In spite of the Soviet death sentence, Nick and Ewa lived a very public and busy life. The CIA provided Shadrin with a lump-sum payment for "services rendered" from the date of his defection. With the tax-free money from the CIA in hand, the Shadrins made a down payment on a modest bungalow located at 5432 North 23rd Street, Arlington, Virginia. Ewa, after encountering difficulties at the Georgetown University Dental School, was attending the predominantly black Howard University Dental School to complete the courses she needed for accreditation to practice dentistry in the United States. Nick had his consultancy with ONI and his lectures around the country.

By 1962, James Angleton's hand had reached into Shadrin's life. The only defector Angleton ever trusted, Anatolyi Golitsyn, was abusing Angleton's staff, threatening to write letters to President Kennedy, and driving his handlers to distraction. Since Shadrin was a model defector and had been represented to Angleton as the most well-adjusted defector the CIA had, Angleton decided, against all previous policy, to bring them together.

It was a great success for Shadrin and Golitsyn, but for Ewa it was a nightmare. In her opinion, Golitsyn was abusive and sometimes terrifying. Many evenings, Nick would insist that Ewa leave her studies and go with him to visit the Golitsyns. Golitsyn's wife, a large and gregarious Russian, "would sit at the piano and play and sing those Russian songs and with Nick it was wonderful because Nick was singing and she was giving him [a] copy of those Russian songs," Ewa recalls.[26] One of the songs that Nick most cherished was a copy of "Moscow Nights." Shadrin spent weeks perfecting the song and playing it on his guitar. "Nick enjoyed their company very, very much. She was very pleasant. He [Golitsyn] was always unpleasant, and I remember Nick insisted one evening that I go with him. And I went and Golitsyn opened the door and he saw me and his face dropped and it was so obvious when he saw me that he was so unhappy," Ewa remembers.

One of Ewa's most bitter memories about Golitsyn is of his harsh comments to her about endangering Nick by her phone calls home to Poland. "Nick must have told him I was calling home. But it was so normal. We went always to Baltimore when we called (a hundred-mile round trip from where the Shadrins lived). We were afraid of the phones. . . . Nick was worried about the Soviets tapping the phones. We went to the post office, and we waited for three or four hours for connections. It was really very inconvenient. It was like a whole-night affair. He would go with me to Baltimore and talk to my mother and father," Ewa recalls.

Because Golitsyn was too afraid to go, in 1963, Mrs. Golitsyn attended the visiting Bolshoi Ballet with Ewa. According to Ewa, Golitsyn was "very much afraid of everything. He was just paranoid. Once he and Nick went to a restaurant on Connecticut Avenue and Nick says the way he walked was just looking behind his shoulder all the time. Just looking behind. He was so afraid."

After Golitsyn left the United States for England in 1964, Shadrin missed him terribly. "He would blame me for him leaving because I did not make more of an effort to be friendly," Ewa explains. The last communication between Golitsyn and Shadrin was in late 1964, when Golitsyn called Shadrin from Canada and the two men spoke for over an hour.[27] According to Peter Sivess, in 1964 Nick also asked to meet Yuri Nosenko, who had recently defected to the United States from the Soviet Union, but the CIA denied his request.

In 1961, Shadrin, under pressure from Ewa, decided he should further his American education to gain greater acceptance in Kennedy administration circles, in which advanced academic training carried great weight. He agreed that his circle of potential contacts would expand with his credentials. He entered the Graduate Engineering School of George Washington University.

At George Washington, Shadrin came into contact with a wide mix of U.S. military officers who, through its evening program, were also trying to enhance their credentials. In those days, the night school at George Washington looked like "CIA South" or "Pentagon East"; many officers wearing their uniforms, complete with name tags, came directly to the school from work. Officers from both agencies struggled to survive in the bureaucratic wars of survival of the fittest. Vietnam was still a few years off, and what one did in World War II or the bizarre campaigns of the Cold War made little difference in the promotion boards and panels.

Shadrin fit right in. He was a professional, and could grouse with fellow professionals about the politicians and their civilian appointees and how they fouled up the military. These contacts also provided him with some interesting biographical material about some of his classmates who would later move up in the military and the CIA as the Vietnam War generated a new cycle of rapid promotions.[28]

Shadrin's performance at George Washington was nonpareil. His papers submitted in courses such as operations research, linear programming, and the theory of games were top-drawer. Shadrin's academic prowess amazed some of the faculty members who maintained a relationship with the CIA, and raised the question that the Agency might have lost something of value when they gave him up to ONI. The interesting feature about the curriculum Shadrin completed to receive the degree of M.E.A. (Master of Engineering Administration) was that he took no examinations along the way. Rather, the requirements of the various courses were all met by the submission of "research" papers suggested by the individual professors.[29]

Ewa Shadrin urged Nick to undertake and complete his postgraduate education because "it was so easy for him. . . . Nick didn't have to study. . . . Why shouldn't he do it." Tom Koines, a thirty-year-plus veteran of ONI and a Shadrin colleague while he was at the Naval Observatory, remembers, "Nick had written it in Russian and brought it to me for translation into English."[30] Koines, who was one of the Navy's preeminent Russian linguists, was glad to help Shadrin as he had other emigrés and defectors who were struggling to master English as part of their efforts to gain a U.S. education.

The ease with which Shadrin completed the master's program at George Washington, and the additional contacts it provided, prompted Ewa to suggest that he continue his work at the university. Thus, in September 1964, Shadrin shifted over to George Washington University's College of Arts and Sciences graduate program in International

Affairs. Part of this Ph.D. curriculum required a reading knowledge of two foreign languages. Because Shadrin claimed Russian as his native language, he took and passed an examination in English in October 1964. His second language was Polish, and he passed that reading examination in September 1968.

Ewa completed her training in dentistry and was certified to practice in the United States. Outwardly, Nick and Ewa were a thriving, industrious couple who had come to America with nothing more than their brains and energy, and had done well. Ewa emerged as an independent career woman. Nick was known as a popular, generous, gregarious, and outgoing Soviet naval expert. His work performance at ONI commended him to many persons. Naval officers such as Tom Dwyer and William Howe counted Nick as a trusted, competent colleague.

Mary Louise Howe, the wife of Navy Captain William Howe, was something of a guardian to both Nick and Ewa, but especially Nick. A well-connected Alabaman, she introduced the couple to Washington society and was very outspoken in her support of the Shadrins.[31] She also knew which strings to pull and which numbers to call to make things happen in the Congress. In the second session of the Eighty-eighth Congress, Senator James Eastland, Mrs. Howe's neighbor, introduced Bill S.2789 to give citizenship to Nick Shadrin.[32]

For the first time, Shadrin was no longer at the CIA's mercy. The delicate status of legal alien is one that can be very useful to the Agency. Shadrin now had the full rights and privileges of an American citizen. From Shadrin's point of view, his naturalization was all to the good, because it made him independent of the CIA, an agency that, according to Tom Dwyer, he had grown to despise.

By early 1965, Shadrin's influence was at its peak in ONI. His star quality had not diminished since the congressional hearing in 1960.[33] To the contrary, his prophecies about the Soviet Navy and its buildup came true. He looked like a genius. Also, the aftershocks of the Cuban Missile Crisis were such that many people involved with national security matters, both inside and outside of the White House, became convinced that the Soviet "threat," a threat similar to the one Shadrin had been preaching about for years, was real and imminent.

According to his colleagues, Shadrin's point of view on the capacity of the Soviet Navy to wage war and his belief that the commanders of the Soviet Navy were the voices of reason in the Kremlin's corridors of power found an audience at ONI. Shadrin's presentation also implied that the Soviet naval buildup was much further along than was commonly supposed, and would continue unabated no matter who might make it to the top of the Politburo.

By the spring of 1965, Shadrin's assignment to the Naval Observatory was drawing to a close. Admiral Taylor did not want to lose

Shadrin's expertise. The contract signed in 1960 was due to expire June 30, 1965. In an attempt to buy some time and still retain control over Shadrin, Taylor arranged for a six-month extension of his contract and provided him with a short consultancy to the Naval Scientific and Technical Intelligence Center.[34]

But events beyond Shadrin's control would forever change his future and mission. The Taylor era was coming to an end at ONI, and Shadrin, though liked, was not part of the plans of the men poised to take over ONI. Taylor was promoted in June 1966 to vice admiral and appointed Deputy Director of the Defense Intelligence Agency.

In Moscow, the winds of change were also blowing through the Kremlin's corridors of power and producing a chilly draft in the KGB's Moscow Center. Brezhnev had ousted Khrushchev in 1964, largely through the support of the Soviet military, who wanted to get on with rearming the motherland. The Soviet Navy had fared better, quietly and without fanfare, than its sister services in the battle of the Soviet defense budget during the Khrushchev era, but they were strongly in Brezhnev's corner both during and after the ouster of Khrushchev.

By mid-1966 the Soviet Army and Air Force demanded from Brezhnev, as part of their payoff, a concerted effort by the KGB and the GRU to come up with the technical and scientific information they needed to modernize their forces. There was pressure to get rid of Vladimir Yefimovich Semichastny, the chairman of the KGB and a holdover from the Khrushchev regime. He ran the KGB the way Mayor Daley ran Chicago.

Within the confines of the "Moscow village," the games of power played by the members of its *nomenklatura,* their families, and their mentors in the Central Committee and the Politburo is a deadly serious business. By mid-1966, Semichastny was in deep trouble. He was on his way out, and those who had prospered under him and Khrushchev were trying to find a way to maintain their power. Many believed that Perepiltysn, Semichastny's sycophantic deputy, would take over as KGB Chairman. But they had not counted upon the singleminded quest for power that drove Yuri Andropov.

The remnants of the Khrushchev regime feared losing power and position. They knew all too well they would be forced to give up their perks such as shopping rights in *nomenklatura* stores, dachas outside of Moscow, and all the thousand and one things that made life livable in Moscow. One mother who worried not so much about her personal fate but her daughter's, son-in-law's, and grandchild's future was Yekaterina Alekseevna Furtseva. She and her husband, Nikolai Pavlovich Firyubin, would do whatever they could to protect their children.[35] And what they could do was tremendous.

Yekaterina and Nikolai were truly charter members of the Soviet Union's powerful first families. Their daughter's name was Svetlana. She was married to Igor, the son of Frol Romanovich Kozlov. [36] The couple had a two-year-old daughter named Marina, born in 1964. Furtseva, Ambassador Firyubin, and the elder Kozlov had made it up through the ranks in the Soviet system. They held positions of importance, but their power and authority would not be automatically conveyed to their children. Furtseva was a political realist. She had virtually slept her way to the top. In 1960 she was appointed Ministress of Cultural Affairs after having been Nikita Khrushchev's lover. As age and new faces were closing in on her, she wanted to assure her comfort and also her daughter and granddaughter's future. Her son-in-law in the KGB had little of his late father's style and less of his luck.

Like many children of the *nomenklatura,* Igor Kozlov had drifted into the KGB, and by early 1966 his career had faltered badly. He was a major in the Inspectorate Division of the First Directorate (Foreign Intelligence Operations), with little chance of being promoted to the rank of lieutenant colonel. Many are chosen to enter the KGB, but lieutenant colonel is the make-or-break rank. If a major makes it, he has moved into the KGB's inner circle of power, and is able to claim major perks in his own right. Major Kozlov's career had stalled in early 1966, not long after his powerful father's death on January 30, 1965. Major Kozlov was known, albeit only fleetingly, to the CIA, owing to a tentative overture he had made to the Agency in Pakistan in the early 1960s. At the time, Kozlov thought he was going to be sent to America until he learned that a colleague, Oleg Sokolov, had gotten the assignment instead.

By early March 1966, Yekaterina Furtseva had to act. She had avoided having a frank discussion with her son-in-law since his marriage to her daughter, but she was running out of time. One intelligence officer's version of what Furtseva told her son-in-law was passed on to a prominent Soviet journalist who used to socialize with the family. According to the Soviet source, Yekaterina Furtseva asked her son-in-law to take a walk with her on the snow-covered road in front of their dacha. Her suspicion was that Semichastny had had her house bugged a long time ago. She told Igor that there was a good chance the dacha and all the family position could be lost with the coming changes. She explained that the Chairman of the KGB was more than a weak fool—he had failed on a very important mission. The military was crying out for Western technology. Kozlov only nodded. She stopped in the snow and began to tell Kozlov a series of secrets that were far more important than anything he had heard in his undistinguished career.

Furtseva told Kozlov that the husband of Admiral Gorshkov's

daughter, Captain Nikolay Fedorovich Artamonov, was an influential man in the United States and had access to key U.S. naval secrets. Kozlov instantly knew that this information could make his KGB career. If he could recruit Artamonov, it would make his archrival in the KGB, Oleg Sokolov, look like a fool. Now he had an opportunity to get his career moving again.

But that was not the only secret Yekaterina Furtseva told her son-in-law that snowy day. She described how she had kept Semichastny from recruiting Lee Harvey Oswald in Minsk years earlier. She told Kozlov how the Americans had not believed the defector, Yuri Nosenko, when he brought them that message. But they would believe him. Now Igor Kozlov had been given a real gift by his mother-in-law. She had presented him with an opportunity to rescue a faltering KGB career with a tremendous intelligence coup.

As the couple approached the dacha they saw Victor Louis, Furtseva's nearest neighbor, get out of his Mercedes. Furtseva greeted him effusively. Louis wondered what she was so cheerful about.[37]

Shadrin: KITTY HAWK

―――――――――――――――― ❧ ――――――――――――――――

I wasn't particularly fond of Nick. Nick was oily. Nick was a glad-
hander. Nick told KGB kind of dirty jokes, you know. If you run into
a Soviet at a cocktail party and he starts pouring dirty jokes in your
ear, chances are he is KGB.

Lt. Gen. Samuel V. Wilson

THE CHASE AFTER the Soviet mole, the illusive SASHA, continued
throughout the 1960s. The CIA's James Angleton would not rest until
he caught SASHA. And validating the threat of penetration was Angleton's favorite defector, Anatolyi Golitsyn. But by mid-1966, Courtland
Jones, the head of counterintelligence in the FBI's Washington Field
Office, was getting very tired of the chase. His investigation of the
picture framer Igor Orlov, at Angleton's behest, had proven to be
fruitless.[1] With the exception of getting some nice pictures framed,
Court Jones had no use for the continued surveillance. He and many
of his colleagues at the FBI were weary of what they saw as a wild-
goose chase. Even if Igor Orlov *had* been SASHA, what harm could the
man do now? He was driving a truck and making picture frames.

William Lander, William Branigan, and others at FBI headquarters
agreed with Jones and wanted the Orlov probe shut down. They were

short of staff and could put their agents to better work handling more promising cases. But by May 1966, relations between Angleton's counterintelligence shop and the FBI were not good. The CIA's top intermediary, Sam Papich, even with his best efforts, could not close the widening rift between the FBI and CIA.[2] Angleton believed Golitsyn. The Bureau's CI men concluded that Angleton had been snookered.

Courtland Jones's best CI man, Elbert "Bert" Turner, had enjoyed access to Yuri Nosenko along with his partner, James Wooten, when Nosenko first defected from the Soviet Union in 1964. But Angleton cut the FBI off from Nosenko. He was embittered about J. Edgar Hoover's leaking to the White House and Congress, without CIA permission, Nosenko's message about the Russians not being involved in Lee Harvey Oswald's assassination of President Kennedy. Nosenko had stated flatly to the CIA and FBI that he had been ordered to review the Oswald case, and that the decision was made not to recruit him because he was too unstable. This denial of access to Nosenko was a particularly bitter pill for Bert Turner to swallow. He, of all agents, wanted the answers to the KGB's involvement in Lee Harvey Oswald's life in Russia. After all, the Oswald case had effectively prevented Turner from rising to the top echelons of the FBI.[3]

But the FBI's credibility on defectors and agents was not the best. Angleton had made it clear that he believed Hoover's most beloved Soviet agents-in-place—TOP HAT and FEDORA—sometimes referred to as SCOTCH and BOURBON, were counterfeit. Angleton was now telling the FBI that Nosenko did not look any better. The FBI wanted desperately to clear its name on the Kennedy assassination, and Nosenko was their best hope. Without access, they could do nothing. And now Angleton was saying Nosenko was a phony. The Bureau was back to holding the Kennedy assassination bag. All the top FBI and CIA people connected to these operations acknowledge that relations were, as William Lander put it, "at a very low ebb."[4]

Within the CIA itself, the situation was not much better. Largely owing to Angleton's conviction that Soviet Division chief David E. Murphy was recruited as a Soviet agent at Berlin Base, Angleton had isolated the Soviet Division. This freeze on the Soviet Division made the CIA unable to recruit new Soviet agents. Any new cases that did come in were sent to other divisions. Angleton's mole hunt was in high gear. The Soviets had succeeded in disrupting America's counterintelligence capability.

Adding to all this confusion was a change at the top of the CIA in June 1966. Admiral William Raborn was stepping down, and Richard McGarrah Helms, the smooth career CIA man, was preparing to take over as the Director of Central Intelligence. Helms's personal life was undergoing some changes as well. His long marriage to Julia Bretzman

Helms was over. Julia Helms was six years older than her estranged husband, and a sculptress of some repute.

At eight-thirty in the morning on Saturday, June 18, 1966, the phone rang at the Helmses' Georgetown residence. Mrs. Helms answered the telephone. In response to Mrs. Helms's request, the caller identified himself as Major Igor Kozlov. In an obvious attempt to impress Mrs. Helms, the major asked how her leg was doing since she hurt it when she fell while attempting to hang a picture. Mrs. Helms, as smooth as her estranged husband, was not taken in.[5] She had been married to a "spook" too long to respond to that line. However, she did say that Richard Helms was not there, but he could be reached at the Congressional Country Club.

The KGB's intelligence was good enough to know about a minor accident in the home of the future head of the CIA, but not quite sophisticated enough to know that Richard Helms had only recently moved out pending his divorce.

Igor did call Richard Helms at the Congressional Country Club and quickly identified himself as a major in the KGB.[6] Igor Romanovich Kozlov, then in his late thirties, told Helms that he wanted to work for American intelligence. He explained that several years earlier he had talked to a CIA officer in Pakistan—an agent by the name of Gardner Rugg Hathaway. Kozlov referred to him as "Gus," his nickname. Helms knew Hathaway; he was considered to be a very bright light in the clandestine services. Helms was intrigued: first the knowledge of his estranged wife's injury, and now a "friendship" with Hathaway. Kozlov gave Helms more details of his own background that could be checked out.

Few men are more careful than Richard Helms. Helms had not risen to the top of the CIA by being totally trusting. In two hours, Igor advised Helms, he would call him back. After that, he would be out of touch. This kind of "call back" contact is always hazardous. It could be a provocation or an attempt to create an embarrassment. Helms knew that the White House was on the verge of sending his nomination for DCI to the Senate for confirmation. He could not afford an embarrassment.

When confronted with any security question, Helms knew just what to do. He called James Angleton at his home in Arlington. Naturally, the chief of CI was immediately skeptical of Igor and warned Helms that under no circumstances could they risk the Soviet Division getting wind of such a sensitive case while its management was under suspicion. Instead, Angleton suggested that Bruce Solie from the CIA's Office of Security work with William Branigan and his colleagues at the FBI on the case. Solie and the Bureau got along well. Helms wrote down Solie's telephone number. When Igor called back, Helms arranged a meeting between Igor and Solie for 1:00 P.M. that Saturday, a few miles from the Soviet Embassy in Northwest Washington.

Bruce Solie is a very serious and taciturn man of medium height. His colleagues only heard his flat Wisconsin voice when it was absolutely necessary. Now Solie, who had little in common with the Ivy League insiders at the CIA, began to play on his strength. Solie worked strictly "by the book" and was well aware that the CIA could not legally run Igor while he was in the United States. He immediately called Bill Branigan, the head of Soviet counterintelligence at the FBI, and told him about the 1:00 P.M. meeting.

Branigan, who looks like the classic Irish cop, had a reputation for writing the best memoranda in the FBI. He also was a man under siege. J. Edgar Hoover's preoccupation with subversion from within the United States by anti–Vietnam War protesters, student radicals, and black activists had left Branigan with precious few agents to work against the Soviet and Eastern Bloc "diplomats" and "commercial representatives" who were in fact Russian spies.

The notorious Washington summer had already made the city very uncomfortable. On weekends, many local residents try to escape the heat and humidity. And Court Jones was no exception. He and his family were packing their bags to go to their summer retreat at Kitty Hawk, North Carolina, when his phone rang at ten-thirty that morning. It was Bill Branigan. In his firm voice, Branigan described Igor's contact and the upcoming one-o'clock meeting. Branigan asked Jones for a code name for their new Soviet contact.[7] Jones, a tall and thoughtful man, hesitated for a second and then said, "Well, my wife and I are going to Kitty Hawk. Why don't we call the case KITTY HAWK?"[8]

Branigan agreed. They decided that Solie would go to the first meeting with KITTY HAWK alone. Court Jones immediately assigned Bert Turner, his most experienced CI agent, to work with Solie and eventually to become KITTY HAWK's case officer in the United States.[9] It did not take long before KITTY HAWK was shortened to KH around the Bureau.

At precisely 1:00 P.M., KITTY HAWK arrived at the CIA safe house not too far from the Soviet Embassy that Solie had arranged for the meeting. At their first meeting, Solie was impressed "by his unusually good command of English." It was obvious that this young man was a cut above the typical KGB agent. His manners and refinement indicated that he came from a very high social standing in Moscow. "He was a very intelligent individual," Solie recalls.[10] KITTY HAWK, Igor Kozlov, explained to Solie that he was on a temporary embassy inspection mission that would last only sixty-five to seventy days. Normally he was assigned to "KR" or Kontra Razvyebka—KGB counterintelligence.

KH emphasized that he was willing to work with the CIA, but under no circumstances with the FBI. Court Jones later explained Igor's reluctance to deal with the Bureau as a fear on the part of most KGB officers of the Bureau's power to arrest them. A more likely reason was that the KGB's target was not the FBI, but the CIA. The FBI really had nothing to offer the KGB in the way of information. Any operation with the FBI would be merely a counterintelligence game.

KH tantalized Solie by explaining that although he was only in the United States on a temporary basis, if things worked out well for him, he would be returned to the KGB station in the Soviet Embassy in Washington as head of CI and security in a few years. KH then made an offer every CIA agent dreams he will hear someday. Igor Kozlov proposed becoming a CIA agent in the KGB—a U.S. agent-in-place. With the CIA's help, KH argued he would have no trouble reaching his KGB career goals, which, in turn, would put him in a better position to assist the CIA. KITTY HAWK expressed no desire to defect to the United States.

If the CIA was interested in his proposition, KITTY HAWK needed its assistance on his main assignment that summer. While he was in Washington, he had to recruit a former Soviet naval officer who had defected seven years earlier, a man named Captain Nikolay Fedorovich Artamonov. Igor proposed that the CIA assist him in the recruitment of Nick Shadrin.[11]

Coolly and calmly, Solie asked KH why the CIA should help him recruit Artamonov. Then the sauve Kozlov plucked the string closest to Solie's heart. He told Solie that he would assist the CIA in its mole investigations. Because he was responsible for finding ways to penetrate the CIA, he was aware of who the "sent agents" were. KH played his trump card and knew it would hold. Solie, who now had spent several years on the SASHA investigation of Igor Orlov, tried to get Kozlov to offer some details. KITTY HAWK refused to say any more until he first got an answer to his proposal. Kozlov did mention, however, that he would feel more comfortable dealing with his CIA contact that he had met in Pakistan a few years earlier; perhaps the Agency could arrange for a meeting. Solie, ever the correct professional, made no promises. Before leaving, the two men made arrangements for another contact within a few days.

The minute Solie got back to the CIA, he wrote down in longhand on a yellow legal pad his notes of the meeting. Always the security officer, he jotted down every aspect of their conversation that gave him cause for concern. Then he reported back to both Angleton and Branigan. Angleton, of course, did not trust KITTY HAWK from the start and expressed his view that Kozlov had probably been sent by the KGB. But as any CI professional knows, the case had to be played out.[12]

Angleton asked an old friend and one of the few that he trusted in the Soviet Division, Peter Kapusta, a CI officer, to get the details of Igor Kozlov's first contact in Pakistan. In the meantime he had to figure out how to get Gus Hathaway, a Soviet Division staffer, back to the United States without telling the division chief, David Murphy, what was happening. Angleton's answer was to make Hathaway, then serving in Brazil, the subject of a summons by the DCI.

Gus Hathaway was a specialist in trying to recruit and penetrate the KGB. He had earned his reputation as a headstrong field man at Berlin Base under William King Harvey. After service in Eastern Europe, he was sent to Pakistan, where he first encountered Igor Kozlov. When the Kennedy administration began to concentrate on problems in the Western Hemisphere, including massive political activity in Brazil and Chile, Hathaway found himself in Latin America.[13]

As Angleton and his staff studied the Kozlov approach, they asked, Why Shadrin? What did the KGB want with a Soviet naval captain who was of such little use to the CIA that they had farmed him out after a year to the Navy? Angleton, preoccupied with his own investigations, never questioned the CIA background check on Shadrin and, more important, relied on the trust Golitsyn placed in Shadrin during their brief friendship.[14] The consensus in CI was the KGB wanted to show that no defector was unreachable. But to Angleton, the real point was that Nick Shadrin was simply bait for information the CIA wanted from Kozlov about the KGB. He would be run, after all, by the FBI. Angleton had no reason to object. Nick Shadrin would be an FBI case.[15]

But there was a problem with Shadrin, a big problem. Since Shadrin had become a naturalized citizen the year before, the FBI had no leverage, legitimate or otherwise, over him to pressure him into becoming a "counterspy" for the Bureau. What if he did not want to cooperate? In plain words, Shadrin could tell the FBI to forget it, and that would be the end of the operation. Furthermore, Nick was "between jobs." He was expecting to be plucked from a temporary assignment in the Defense Intelligence Agency's translation unit by Rufus Taylor any day now.

At the FBI, Bert Turner enlisted the aid of his slightly younger partner, Jim Wooten. Turner would handle KITTY HAWK and Wooten would handle Shadrin. But first the FBI agents needed to find out all they could about KH, Major Igor Romanovich Kozlov. Immigration records showed that he had traveled into the United States on a temporary-duty visa under diplomatic cover. He had come into the country with a man named Vladimir P. Zaystev. As far as the CIA and the

FBI were concerned, all that KITTY HAWK told them proved true. It was not until almost a year later that the FBI discovered that Kozlov's traveling companion was one of the most aggressive, tough, and feared KGB operatives ever sent to the West.[16] But because the FBI misidentified Zaystev at the time, KITTY HAWK did not get as close a look by the Bureau as he should have.[17]

The recruitment of Shadrin needed to be handled as delicately as possible by the Bureau. The FBI approached the Director of DIA, General Joseph Carroll, and his deputy, Admiral Rufus Taylor. Both men agreed to arrange a meeting between Shadrin and Bert Turner.

For Taylor, Shadrin's recruitment meant cutting him off from Navy and DIA secrets. Taylor gave orders that Shadrin was to be permanently assigned to the small DIA translation unit where he was currently working. After all, it was a perfect location, two floors above the FBI's Washington Field Office in the Old Post Office Tower in downtown Washington. If his new assignment worked out, he would be at the FBI's doorstep. Just down the hallway was a larger translation unit, run by the CIA.

"[A] colonel friend of Shadrin's was approached to help talk Nick into cooperating. The poor fellow was very sick with cancer," William Lander said.[18] "He buttered up Nick quite a bit. He told Shadrin it would enhance his position to cooperate with the FBI." Next, Bert Turner approached Shadrin and advised him that the translation unit where he worked was under Soviet observation. Playing to Nick's enormous ego, Turner said, "You are the only one important enough in the unit for the Soviets to risk doing that for."[19] Then Turner asked Shadrin what would he do if a KGB agent approached him for recruitment. Shadrin replied that if approached, "I would punch him right in the fucking ass."[20]

Turner "convinced" Shadrin that it would be better if he heard the Soviet out before knocking him out. Thus the FBI "recruited" for the KGB a former Soviet naval captain. At that point, the only information the FBI really had on Nicholas G. Shadrin was contained in the memo sent to J. Edgar Hoover by Admiral Taylor six years earlier, which indicated that he had become a special consultant to ONI.

Despite a series of warnings from his good friend Tom Dwyer that he should avoid being "dangled" by the CIA before the Soviets, Nick Shadrin became an FBI double agent. Shadrin knew the KGB had control of him. He knew that his failure to follow orders would jeopardize his wife and son in Kaliningrad. Thus, for reasons that the CIA and FBI never understood, Shadrin had no choice but to cooperate fully in the KITTY HAWK operation. The recruitment ended any hope Shadrin had of getting close to Rufus Taylor or the naval hierarchy again. Subsequent to Shadrin's recruitment, Admiral Taylor issued orders to segregate Shadrin from any contact with DIA secrets. Issuance of these orders marked a change in Admiral Taylor's dealings with Shadrin. He was still friendly the few times they met during the three months Taylor was at DIA, but the days of the long strategic conversations were over. Admiral Taylor had been around long enough not to be curious about what the FBI was doing. It was their "case."

The next meeting with KITTY HAWK was scheduled within a week of the first. Gus Hathaway, looking as patrician as KH remembered the Danville, Virginia, native, greeted the taller Kozlov with a warm handshake. Hathaway explained to KITTY HAWK that while he could act as a contact overseas, another "CIA" man—Bert Turner (of the FBI)—was better qualified to work with him here.

At a meeting at a Hot Shoppes restaurant in suburban Virginia, Solie introduced KH to Bert Turner as his new "CIA" case officer. Solie again pressed KH for details on CIA penetrations. Before responding, KH asked Solie if Shadrin had agreed to the recruitment. Solie told him that Shadrin would not run away if he was approached. Kozlov then got right down to business and began to give Solie and Turner the details on the KGB penetrations into the CIA. One case was still active, KH told Turner. Then the magic word came out of KITTY HAWK's mouth—SASHA. Kozlov verified what Golitsyn had said years before about SASHA, except Kozlov went much further. He identified SASHA without reservation as Igor Orlov, the picture framer. He said Orlov was using his little framing gallery for dead drops and recruitment.

Satisfied that they had caught KH in a ploy, Solie and Turner said that Igor Orlov had been cleared a year earlier, after years of surveillance and a seven-week interrogation. Without hesitating, KITTY HAWK came right back with stinging information. "Then you know he visited the Soviet Embassy through the back door in April 1965," Kozlov said. With that sentence, KITTY HAWK's credibility increased tremendously. As a further test, Solie and Turner reminded KH that if Orlov had gone to the embassy, the FBI would have his picture, and since they had no such picture, it could not have happened. KITTY HAWK, in his most confident voice, told Solie and Turner to "look again, you did take his picture."

Then Kozlov dropped a bombshell. Like Santa Claus, he had a present in his bag for everyone. He confirmed to Turner that he knew he had a concern about the Kennedy assassination. Turner, far too professional, never rose to the bait. Kozlov explained that he had personal access to information that could conclusively prove that Nosenko was assigned the Oswald case by the KGB, and that because Oswald proved so unstable, any attempt at recruiting him was forbidden.

KITTY HAWK was right about Igor Orlov's photograph. Back at the FBI's Washington Field Office, they found it. The agent on duty across the street from the Soviet Embassy that day was having a bout with diarrhea, and he did not properly log the film in on the automatic camera. The FBI had the picture of Igor Orlov leaving the Soviet Embassy, but it had been misfiled.[21]

In a 1980 analysis of the KITTY HAWK case, the FBI concluded that the mole information and the prospect of having a high-level U.S. agent in the KGB caused the FBI and CIA counterintelligence divisions to suspend their critical faculties. Solie's handwritten list of potential red flags in the KITTY HAWK approach ran to nearly two pages. According to a former FBI official, "After that meeting, all that was forgotten. The case had a life of its own. All the Bureau could see was a high-level KGB guy in place."

For Turner, Wooten, and Solie, there was no time for analysis. KITTY HAWK and the FBI only had five weeks left before his TDY (temporary duty) assignment would end. Those red flags that Solie and Turner had expressed at the start of the operation faded into a distant memory with the rush and the pressures to get as much out of KITTY HAWK as possible.

Within a few days of Bert Turner and Nick Shadrin's conversation, a puzzled Shadrin was approached outside the old Irving's Sporting Goods Store in downtown Washington. Just a few blocks from the Department of Justice and around the corner from Ford's Theatre, the site was across the street from the construction site for the new FBI headquarters in what was then a very unattractive part of downtown Washington.

There was no way for Shadrin to know what the Soviets had in mind. When they met, Igor Kozlov was friendly and professional. As instructed by the FBI, Shadrin went into the story that Turner had coached him on. He told Kozlov that his defection had been a terrible mistake. His marriage to the Polish woman was a failure, and he missed his wife and son. He wanted to make amends for the wrongs he had done to the Soviet Union.

Kozlov told Shadrin that a pardon for his crime of treason might be arranged if Shadrin could prove his loyalty to the State. But Kozlov warned that getting a death penalty reversed was very difficult. He said Shadrin would have to write a formal appeal that Kozlov would deliver through appropriate channels. The document would get the KGB's endorsement only after Shadrin had proved himself.

As coached by Wooten and Turner, Shadrin explained to Kozlov that he worked for the CIA as a contract consultant and had access to classified naval material. He could be of great service to his homeland. Kozlov agreed that the KGB was in great need of such material, but a more pressing item on the KGB's agenda was information on other defectors and emigrés with whom Shadrin worked. As instructed, Shadrin immediately gave up the names of his co-workers and Reggie Kicklighter, his office supervisor. He was careful not to volunteer any more than Turner had advised. Shadrin had no real way of knowing whether Kozlov was KGB or whether the FBI was putting him through some sort of test.

Kozlov outlined Shadrin's general assignment. Shadrin would remain in place, passing on as much material as he could get from the CIA, and reporting on the activities of certain emigrés and defectors in whom Moscow Center was interested. At the right time—perhaps several years from now, Kozlov said—the KGB would try to get his legal troubles cleared up so that he could come home. Shadrin was appropriately grateful and told Kozlov he would begin to gather the documents. A simple signal system for future meetings was arranged. They agreed to meet in a supermarket not far from Shadrin's suburban Virginia home.

Shadrin walked back down E Street to 10th Street, to avoid the porn shops and strip joints on 9th Street. He crossed Pennsylvania Avenue and rode the rickety elevator back up to the DIA's offices on the seventh floor in the Old Post Office Building.[22] He had only been in his new job for a few months, but already he hated the translation unit, both the work and the people. Shadrin had given up a brilliant naval career when he defected to the West. Although he knew there might be setbacks, he'd never dreamed that seven years later he would wind up working as a double agent for the FBI against the KGB. Shadrin now faced the prospect of working for years with defectors and emigrés who raised his bile every time he spoke to them, according to Ewa.

The second meeting with KITTY HAWK convinced Shadrin that Kozlov was KGB and not some sort of trick. CI head Bill Branigan did not like the meeting site. The grocery store where Shadrin was "accidentally" to encounter KITTY HAWK was right across the street from the Cardinal House, a large, high-rise apartment complex in suburban Virginia, not far from Shadrin's home. Branigan knew a number of KGB agents lived in those apartments, and he worried for Shadrin's safety. But Wooten and Turner convinced him that Shadrin would be all right.

Major Kozlov had Shadrin's first specific assignments. He wanted the addresses of Yuri Nosenko and Anatolyi Golitsyn. Truthfully, Shadrin told KITTY HAWK he did not have access to either one, but would attempt to get them. Kozlov divulged that the KGB had a sighting of Nosenko in the Maryland suburbs. KITTY HAWK also encouraged Shadrin to get acquainted with an older Soviet defector who worked on his floor, named Nicholas Kozlov.[23] KITTY HAWK explained that the KGB wanted to recruit Kozlov, and Shadrin should do whatever he could to facilitate that.

Shadrin had five meetings with KITTY HAWK before his TDY ended, while Turner, Solie, and Hathaway attended a total of six meetings with Kozlov/KITTY HAWK. Before leaving, KITTY HAWK warned Shadrin that he was being handed off to a very tough character named Oleg Sokolov, who was a KGB specialist in emigré and defector recruitment. Kozlov cautioned that Sokolov tended to be brazen in his approach and did not accept failure in any of his operations.

Just before he returned to Moscow in October 1966, KITTY HAWK met with Turner for the last time. KH was much more frank about Sokolov. "You have got to get him thrown out of the United States in the next six months." Turner, taken aback, asked why. KITTY HAWK explained that Sokolov was his key competition for the CI and security job in the Soviet Embassy. If Sokolov could be thrown out of the United States for cause, there was an excellent chance that KH would be reassigned here as everyone hoped.[24]

At their last meeting together, KITTY HAWK handed Shadrin a thick envelope. In it were two letters—one from his wife and one from his son. There also were pictures of both of them. His son was as tall as he, and looked like Nick when he first became a naval officer. Shadrin read the letters, studied the pictures, and then, as the rules were set down, returned them to Igor Kozlov. KH reiterated that Moscow Center wanted a full report on the activities and translation work of several emigrés he worked with, and he also instructed Shadrin on the specific kinds of classified naval documents the KGB expected from the operation. At the end of their conversation, KITTY HAWK offered Shadrin a word of encouragement. He told Shadrin that the KGB had bigger things in mind for him.

That same afternoon, Jim Wooten debriefed Shadrin in Courtland Jones's huge office. Shadrin told Wooten that KITTY HAWK had tried to force letters on him, and pictures from his family, but he refused to take them. Shadrin explained that KH was demanding classified military documents of a very specific nature. Wooten assured Shadrin that that phase of the operation was being arranged.

Peter Sivess's call surprised Shadrin.[25] It was not about fishing or hunting. Sivess and his wife, Ellie, were among the few true friends Shadrin had in the CIA. The Shadrins had lived in a series of safe houses when they first arrived; it was Sivess who really assisted Nick and Ewa in adjusting to American life. Nick still loved to visit Pete at

Ashford Farm and to go goose hunting or fishing with him on Maryland's Eastern Shore. He also helped Pete with odd jobs around his home from time to time.

But this call was different. It was business. Sivess had called to arrange a meeting between Shadrin and his new CIA contact, John T. Funkhouser. Shadrin knew Funkhouser from their debriefings years earlier. It seemed odd that Pete Sivess would be asked to set up a meeting with someone Shadrin already knew. But those were their instructions. Sivess was told to pick Nick up and drop him off at a park along the Washington waterfront called Hains Point. There, Shadrin would be reintroduced to Funkhouser, one of the CIA's old naval specialists. Sivess would wait in his car after delivering Shadrin to Funkhouser's sedan.

Funkhouser, a frail, sickly man, had been a designer with the old Navy Bureau of Ships. Shadrin's appearance in 1959 dramatically enhanced Funkhouser's knowledge of the Soviet Navy. Now Funkhouser had been tapped to supply the information Shadrin needed to feed back to the KGB in support of the KITTY HAWK operation.

For nine years, Shadrin fed the Russians thousands of pages of real secrets. Funkhouser, Wooten, and Shadrin would meet and then adjourn to various FBI safe houses to rehearse questions that Nick's Soviet handlers might ask about the material. One fear was that Shadrin did not have a security clearance. What would he say if the Soviets asked him how he had acquired certain documents? The answer they worked out for that was partly true. Shadrin would tell the KGB that he had cultivated high-level officials who shared classified information with him. In addition to the documents he passed to Oleg Sokolov, Shadrin would prepare memos for the KGB on U.S. intelligence plans for dealing with the Soviet Navy.

Throughout the time Shadrin was working as an FBI double agent, he still received many speaking invitations and made many new contacts from these appearances. In addition, in order to tell the KGB he had important sources for his classified information, he began to seriously court Washington's social elite and as many high-ranking government officials as possible. One of these contacts was Robert Kupperman, then chief scientist for the Weapons Evaluation Group. After Shadrin made a speech to this group in 1965, he and the rotund expert on weapons and terrorism became close friends. As Kupperman's career advanced, so did Shadrin's in the eyes of the KGB.

But other, more experienced professionals did not fall for Shadrin's charm. Igor Orlov's onetime American mentor, Lt. Gen. Samuel Wilson, got acquainted with Shadrin during this period and was not as impressed with him as were some of his intelligence colleagues. Wilson, who would later serve as U.S. defense attaché in Moscow, got enough of a queasy feeling from Shadrin that he "never sought Nick out socially. The only times I ever went to lunch with Nick . . . [were] when he was asking for it," Wilson remembers. During Shadrin's doubling operation, Wilson recalls one particularly uncomfortable incident: "I went over to the Old Post Office Building to see someone there . . . and there was Nick and he jumps up and gives me a big embrace in front of everybody. Hell, I don't know Nick that well. . . . He was not one of my close friends. He would have people think that he was." [26]

According to his FBI handlers, Shadrin constantly pressed for better-quality material. Jim Wooten told a panel reviewing the Shadrin operation, "Virtually everything he passed was dug up by Funkhouser and cleared by the Agency. We in the FBI didn't have the expertise or the access to this stuff. Some of it was disinformation that would not be possible to easily verify as disinformation. The important thing to keep in mind [is] that KH needed Nick, and that Nick's safety was vital to KH. Because if something happened to Nick, KH would be exposed." [27]

To protect KITTY HAWK, Shadrin was given top-flight secrets to pass on to the Russians. As Wooten told investigators later: "If they had any suspicions of Nick, the Soviets would go to the person that recruited him and decide whether he was part of that suspicion. If Igor was legitimate and they suspected Nick, then Igor would also come under suspicion."

Funkhouser and Shadrin became luncheon regulars, usually having a bag lunch while discussing the KITTY HAWK operation in a car or on a park bench every Wednesday. For the first several years of the doubling operation, Funkhouser was employed in the CIA's Office of Strategic Research. Here he cleared the real and altered intelligence that Nick gave to the Soviets with John Arthur Paisley, his boss. [28] After Funkhouser retired, he still serviced the Shadrin operation, now as a consultant to the CIA. John Paisley was in charge of all consultant contracts for the Office of Strategic Research as part of his duties. [29]

The FBI helped Nick prepare his appeal of his Soviet death sentence, and he passed it back to the Russians. As the operation continued, Shadrin pressed harder and harder for better material for the Soviets. The normal clearance procedures for classified documents were not observed in the Shadrin case. On a number of occasions, Shadrin told his FBI handlers, "I can't make it with this information, it's too phony for them to buy it as real." [30] Complicating matters is the possibility that Paisley was in a position not only to approve quality materials for the Russians, but also to warn them of faulty documents.

Peter Kapusta, a CI specialist for the CIA's Soviet Russia Division, said he had a formal complaint from a senior analyst in the Strategic

Research Division that secrets for the KITTY HAWK operation were given to Shadrin in "amounts that stagger the mind." Kapusta, who had been told about Shadrin's polygraph failures years before, said, "The CIA and FBI gave Shadrin a legitimate, legal way of meeting with the Soviets on a regular basis. They gave the Soviets access through Shadrin to the U.S. secrets they needed to build their navy. And they gave him amounts of material that could not be reduced to photography." [31]

To the FBI, the result of the Shadrin operation was merely to put additional pressure on an already severely understaffed and overburdened FBI Counterintelligence Division. J. Edgar Hoover, more interested in domestic intelligence, refused to give the CI staff the additional personnel that it needed. According to William Branigan, at one point during the Shadrin/KITTY HAWK operation, he had less than twenty agents assigned to his division. In addition to supporting Shadrin, KITTY HAWK had renewed the FBI's investigation of SASHA, the picture-framer Igor Orlov. As Bert Turner pursued this latest lead, Court Jones could only shake his head in disbelief.

James Angleton's views on Shadrin changed during the KITTY HAWK operation. According to Wooten, when Shadrin verified that he and Yuri Nosenko had attended the same military academy together, and verified Nosenko's claim that he had shot himself in the foot to avoid active military service, red flags went up in Angleton's mind. "Anyone supporting Nosenko in Angleton's eyes had to be not just a plant, but part of a KGB conspiracy," Wooten said. Angleton was also fascinated with a change in Golitsyn's attitude toward Shadrin, in which Golitsyn concluded that Shadrin had been a "sent agent" all along. The FBI's reaction to this development reflected the Bureau's feeling that anything Golitsyn said was probably opinion and not fact.

The CIA counterintelligence staff's research on KITTY HAWK's bona fides also disturbed Angleton. Angleton concluded that Igor Kozlov's tradecraft was better than that of 90 percent of our own agents. KITTY HAWK seemed to anticipate the CIA's questions too well, and he had ready answers for them. But what made Kozlov suspect in Angleton's mind was that he had too much information across too many watertight compartments in the KGB. [32] Angleton pointed out that there was no reason for KITTY HAWK to know anything about Yuri Nosenko or the Oswald case. His job was CI, not recruitment. Angleton cited this evidence as proof that KITTY HAWK was a phony, a provocation. Angleton would later tell Mrs. Shadrin's lawyer, Richard Copaken, that "I took the extreme step of keeping Igor's identity unknown to the Soviet Division because I wanted to send a message to the Soviets that I was really taking Igor seriously and was taken in by him, by virtue of the fact that I kept his identity from the SB division." [33]

Shadrin's fellow workers at the DIA translation unit on the seventh floor of the Old Post Office Tower have mixed emotions about their old colleague. Shadrin's two closest associates in the unit were Richard Oden and Frank Steinert. To save money, they carpooled together for years. Oden was a Polish MiG-17 pilot who in 1964 flew his wife and two sons to the West, hidden in a Polish Air Force plane. A lieutenant colonel in the East German army, Frank Steinert left his wife and son behind and literally crossed over the Berlin Wall that he had helped build.

Richard Oden, who is an extraordinarily deft man with his hands, resented the fact that Nick took credit for many of the favors he did for the Shadrins. For example, when the Shadrins bought their new home in McLean in early 1969, the couple decided to build Ewa's dental offices on the bottom floor of the house. Both Ewa and others credited Nick with the construction. In fact, it was Oden, according to other friends, who masterminded the job. The offices are still in use by Ewa and her patients.

Although Steinert and Shadrin were very close, the East German defector would become enraged when he discovered that Nick was using Steinert's research to cultivate powerful new friends, without giving any credit to him. Steinert was an expert on Soviet military tactics, and he felt Shadrin was stealing his work to further Shadrin's own influence and reputation around town. "There were many inconsistencies about Nick," Steinert said. Oden said that Nick "always had to play the role of a bigshot." Both men freely admit that although they often disagreed with Shadrin, they also enjoyed his company. His nickname in the office was "the Admiral," a term that was used to his face when colleagues felt frustration or anger toward him. They often found Shadrin to be two-faced, talking behind their backs and treating them as inferiors.

But the troubles between Nick and his colleagues were nothing compared to the hardships Nick caused his nemesis, Reggie Kicklighter. A career bureaucrat whose job was to play "mother hen" to the assorted defectors and emigrés, Kicklighter "was hated by Shadrin," according to Richard Oden and others.[34] Kicklighter was the by-the-book paymaster, tax man, and long arm of Uncle Sam in the unit. According to John Novak, a retired DIA officer who worked as a supervisor in the unit, Shadrin hated Kicklighter because of his very tough editing of the reports and translations Nick wrote as part of his job.[35] But regardless of the unit's feelings toward Kicklighter, many credit him with lobbying to get them a contract that included some semblance of standardized pay and fringe benefits after years as stepchildren in the government. Shadrin's most bizarre behavior in the unit came when colleagues caught him going through their desks and looking through their work. The FBI knew that Shadrin was reporting back to the Soviets on people in the unit. After he disappeared, Oden, Steinert, and other colleagues were not happy to see their names and job descriptions, which were supposed to be kept secret, appearing in the Soviet press.[36]

Shadrin's life as a defector was easy compared to the emotional and psychological burdens involved in becoming a double agent. At the very least, it produces personality changes and strains upon the double's relationships with associates, acquaintances, friends, and, of course, spouse.

The persons who knew and liked Shadrin before he became a double tended to explain or rationalize his changed behavior in terms of his dissatisfaction with his job in the translation unit and other personal problems. Friends revealed that he found his work "degrading," and that he resented Ewa's success as a practicing dentist and the fact that Ewa did not want to have children. Tom Dwyer and Ewa credited many of Shadrin's problems to his frustration over not being granted a security clearance so he could leave the government for a better job.

At home he became less and less pleasant. Richard Oden's wife, Maria, became close friends with Nick and Ewa. She said that the couple's relationship deteriorated because of Nick's temper.[37] Another couple close to the Shadrins were Stanley and Janka Urynowicz. They had met in a supermarket, when Shadrin overheard Stanley speaking Polish to Janka. The couple watched Shadrin change over the years. Janka recalls that "Nick had quite a temper . . . I was present when everything was all right and all of a sudden boom, boom, boom. And he was just screaming at Ewa saying, 'Get out, leave me alone.' . . . She would snap back, and he would pick up the sugar bowl and throw it and she the milk pitcher and on and on."[38]

Shadrin's friends lost patience with him when he refused to take part in "American" pastimes and activities, and made fun of them if they did. In fact, he resented American institutions and argued that the Russian way of life was far superior. Shadrin and Richard Oden got into a heated argument about baseball. Shadrin made fun of Oden's devotion to a game he considered "stupid."[39]

Both Bert Turner and Jim Wooten tried to keep Shadrin on an even emotional keel, but it was not an easy task. Arguments between Shadrin and his colleagues at the translation section were often vitriolic and close to violent. According to Eugene Peterson, the fear of penetration of the unit by the KGB caused the FBI to worry about Shadrin's outbursts.

But at work Shadrin still could break new ground. One officer in charge of the translation section at the Old Post Office was Bernard I.

"Buzz" Weltman.[40] He and Shadrin had long conversations on subjects as diverse as Russian literature, philosophy, and the relative merits of over-and-under shotguns versus those with side-by-side barrels. Weltman was indeed a welcome temporary port in the emotional storm Shadrin faced as a double agent.

The Weltmans and the Shadrins socialized together, sometimes attending holiday parties with each other at the homes of other defectors and emigrés who were not part of the Post Office operation. Weltman indicated that he had no idea that Shadrin was serving as a double agent while he was at the Post Office, but he was not particularly surprised when that fact emerged in the wake of his disappearance. He noted only two anomalies in Shadrin's performance during the years they worked together.

The first involved some very fuzzy photographs that had been taken by an Allied intelligence service of a covered shipyard. The classification had been cut off the photos and they had been given to Weltman to see if he or any of his employees could identify what was being built in the way. The pictures were not very clear, but without hesitation Shadrin said, after giving them a cursory look, that they showed the new Soviet giant *Typhoon*-class "boomer," or ballistic missile submarine, more than two football fields long.

At the time, conventional wisdom was that there was no such submarine of that huge size, either in conception or under construction by the Soviets. One defector who had passed through Westport on his way to Israel had said it was a submarine, a very large submarine, but his statement was discounted even though the defector had worked on the boat and was a shipwright by trade. Several years later the *Typhoon*-class submarine joined the Soviet fleet on a shakedown cruise, and the United States was left with the question, "Where did that come from?"

Another anomaly involved a rather complicated treatise that had come into U.S. hands, ostensibly written by Admiral Gorshkov. Weltman gave it to Shadrin and asked him to make a "sight translation" of the document. By the close of business that day, Shadrin had dictated a sight translation of the document. One might say it was all in a good day's work. However, as Weltman noted, others elsewhere in the intelligence community, not in the Post Office translation section, who were cleared and who were Russian linguists themselves, had been working on the document for several weeks, and their versions were clearly inferior to that prepared by Shadrin. Shadrin's was so good that the only logical explanation for this linguistic tour de force was that he had prior knowledge of the document and its contents.

Shadrin pursued his doctorate during the double operation. He got extra help from colleagues in the office. Frank Steinert pulled together translated source material for him, and secretaries in the FBI's Washington Field Office helped type the seven-hundred-page paper.[41]

A careful reading of Shadrin's dissertation produces some interesting observations. It is a blueprint of Soviet maritime intentions not found anywhere else in the literature on this subject, and some of the information Shadrin wrote did not come into the hands of U.S. intelligence agencies until well after Shadrin had completed the work.[42]

For those who have struggled with the problems of graduate training at night school, Ewa's assertion that "Nick didn't seem to spend much time on schoolwork, and he sort of whipped it out without much effort," is not much comfort. The Ph.D. program at George Washington is no snap, and many highly motivated, well-educated persons who have attempted it have failed to make the grade. Trying to hold a full-time job, maintain some semblance of family life, and study the kind of curriculum pursued by Shadrin in his "spare time" is difficult to say the least. And in Shadrin's case he had to contend with the demands of his "second job" as a double agent. But DIA colleague Frank Steinert believes Nick got some help from what he calls "CIA connections. . . . They had ways of making sure he got the degree," Steinert asserts. Others in the translation unit contend that Shadrin merely plagiarized some of the Soviet documents they were translating.

By early to mid-1971 the KITTY HAWK operation was losing its luster. According to Branigan, the biggest disappointment was that KITTY HAWK's reappearance in Washington never happened. Branigan's deputy, Eugene Peterson, blamed it on the State Department refusing the FBI's request to throw KGB agent Oleg Sokolov out of the country. To the FBI, the KITTY HAWK operation, after five years, had produced nothing of value.

Bert Turner attempted to keep track of KITTY HAWK in Moscow through Bruce Solie. The Bureau had no control of the KITTY HAWK operation overseas, or input into it, but Solie passed on whatever he knew about Kozlov's activities. Sightings of KITTY HAWK were infrequent, however. Once, contact was made in Sofia, Bulgaria, by a CIA agent.

Shadrin's relationship with the KGB included occasional meetings, but the KGB did not like operating face-to-face in Washington. Generally, Shadrin would drop his material via brush contacts and dead drops arranged via an effective but confusing system of secret writing.[43] The KGB seemed satisfied with the information provided by Shadrin, however, the FBI was getting much less than it hoped for from the operation.

After KITTY HAWK returned to Moscow, it was reported that he had won his promotion to lieutenant colonel and a coveted assignment in the KGB's Second Directorate, where he had been assigned to a cover job at the International Atomic Energy Agency to escort Soviet delegations traveling around the world. With this news came the hope that the FBI would get another shot at KITTY HAWK.

Then Angleton's shop developed a piece of electrifying news that reinvigorated everyone's attitudes toward the KITTY HAWK operation. An Israeli intelligence source in Moscow reported back that Lt. Col. Igor Romanovich Kozlov had married for the second time. His new wife was the daughter of one of the most powerful couples in the Soviet Union, Yekaterina Alekseevna Furtseva and her husband, Nikolai Pavlovich Firyubin. The source further reported that Kozlov's father, Frol, who had died in 1965, had been a powerful figure himself. The KGB was fully aware of how much more attractive KITTY HAWK/ Kozlov would be to the Americans if news of this high-level connection came via an "independent" intelligence service.

When word of the discovery reached Bruce Solie, the normally reserved security man immediately called Sam Papich and Branigan. Solie announced that there was important news of KITTY HAWK. For Papich, Branigan, Solie, Wooten, and Bert Turner, the name Furtseva was not new. They had heard it from Yuri Nosenko in 1964, before Angleton had cut off the FBI from access to the defector. Nosenko explained that the main reason Lee Harvey Oswald was not recruited by the KGB was that one of the most important women in the Soviet Union, reputed to be a lover of Khrushchev himself, had blocked the weak head of the KGB, Vladimir Yefimovich Semichastny, from recruiting the unstable Oswald when he lived in Minsk. In the mid-1960s the CIA had confirmed Furtseva's power and influence in the Soviet Union to the FBI. Nothing was passed on to the Bureau, however, about Semichastny's troubles, and that the remnants of the Khrushchev era were in decline.

For the Bureau, this new confirmation of KITTY HAWK's information meant that they could finally clear the books on Oswald's involvement in the Kennedy assassination. KITTY HAWK's relationship with Furtseva proved that Nosenko had been right about Oswald's role. Now it was clear to the FBI and the CIA where Igor Kozlov was getting his information. He had sources better than the KGB. Angleton's arguments against KITTY HAWK, based on Kozlov's apparently unlikely access to a wide range of secrets, were explained away by his relationship with his mother-in-law.

For Solie, it was further justification for his report clearing Yuri Nosenko. Angleton, despite all of his suspicions, realized that there was no way a potential source at that level could be ignored. Now the KITTY HAWK operation had to be kept going, and had to be supported with the best material the United States could supply. Even Angleton realized that, whatever his doubts about the case, not to play KITTY HAWK out would be a squandered opportunity. Never had the United States had the potential for a better-placed Soviet official as an American agent. The men in counterintelligence for the FBI—Branigan, Peterson, Jones, Turner, and Wooten—believed they were on the verge of developing the greatest source in the history of the Cold War.

CHAPTER THIRTEEN

Shadrin: Tightrope

❧

Somewhere it should occur to you the orchestra is not playing your
tune. Nice tune, but it isn't the one you wrote. It doesn't seem to
have occurred to anyone on this case.

James E. Nolan, Jr.

THE FBI'S FRUSTRATION with the State Department's failure to cooperate in removing Oleg Sokolov from the Soviet Embassy grew more
intense when KITTY HAWK's true identity was established.[1] To the
FBI, Shadrin seemed to be a gutsy double agent, and they wanted to
exploit that trait. For an untrained "spook," this former Soviet naval
officer impressed the FBI's CI men with his quick adjustments to the
convoluted assortment of tradecraft that Sokolov made him go
through.[2]

Branigan, Wooten, and Turner decided that Shadrin should attempt
to draw out KITTY HAWK/Kozlov. They instructed him to demand a
meeting outside the country, to get an explanation from the KGB on
the status of his pardon and of his future as an agent. If the meeting
was arranged, Shadrin could also request a new case officer, circumstances permitting.

Shadrin had his own reasons for wanting Oleg Sokolov replaced. In spite of his nearly perfect English, Sokolov was in every sense a KGB career man. In addition to demanding all the personal details about Shadrin's fellow workers in the translation unit, Sokolov also ordered Shadrin to befriend several KGB targets. Sokolov's pressure on Nick to learn everything he could about Nicholas Kozlov, the World War II–era Soviet defector and office mate of SASHA/Igor Orlov, was obvious to his friend Richard Oden, who said, "Nick was preoccupied with Kozlov . . . Nick was hounded to find out about Kozlov."

Shadrin's Kozlov assignment threatened peace at home because of an incident involving Julik, the German shepherd that Golitsyn had given the couple. As Ewa recalls the incident, "Kozlov was my patient and Nick was working with Richard Oden outside—I think they were making a duck house—and Kozlov immediately entered the backyard and Julik ran up to him and bit him. And I know Nick was very unhappy because he went to the hospital, and Kozlov needed eight stitches. And Kozlov is telling Nick to report this to the police. And Nick really didn't want to report it and Kozlov says, 'Well, they told me at the hospital you have to do it.' I was very upset. I said, 'If he wants to call, let him call.' And we had all kinds of problems."[3]

In June 1971, Sokolov met Nick on the Skyline Drive, a scenic road through the Blue Ridge Mountains, about seventy miles west of Washington. Sokolov told Shadrin that Nick had to go to Canada in September for a face-to-face meeting with a very important man. Shadrin was pleased. He created the possibility of another meeting with KITTY HAWK and the opportunity to attempt to get rid of Sokolov as his case officer. For five years Shadrin had been an FBI double agent and had passed thousands of documents to the Soviets. In return, he had delivered nothing to the Bureau. To the FBI, KITTY HAWK was a phantom.

To James E. Nolan, Jr., who was a top FBI official during this time, KITTY HAWK was a bad operation from the time Igor Kozlov returned to Moscow and left Shadrin's case to surrogate handlers. "If you look at this thing from the external perspective, you would say KITTY had achieved the miraculous. You had four hundred Soviets assigned to the United States in one form or the other. They couldn't find Shadrin. Here comes [a] whiz kid from Moscow and in the course of one hundred days he finds him, he recruits him, and he sets up an operation. He'd just done the high-wire act blindfolded on one foot. So he [KITTY HAWK] should have . . . risen in the system like a rocket. . . . But he's not moving up like a rocket, and he was never available. Visible, but never available," Nolan said.

According to Nolan, the desire for KITTY HAWK to be real became almost quixotic within the Bureau's counterintelligence section. The push for the Canadian meeting was typical of the case: "The Soviets

didn't start the meeting in Montreal and they didn't
later in Vienna. We did. . . . There's no Soviet follo
wasn't any Soviet initiation," Nolan explained. Nola
gan never got the message. "Somewhere it should o
orchestra is not playing your tune. Nice tune, but it
wrote. It doesn't seem to have occurred to anyone or

Only in Canada can the FBI, by treaty, operate
afoul of the CIA or the American legal system. Gen
the Royal Canadian Mounted Police (RCMP) to assi
of operations. Shadrin had some expectation that KI
surface for the early-September 1971 meeting in Montr
and Wooten assisted Shadrin in putting together their
the meeting, mostly dealing with the plan to oust Soko

While the Bureau was salivating at the prospect of a
in the KITTY HAWK operation, James Angleton had bec
in a darker activity that would have grave and lasting impact
and CIA relations for years. Once again, Golitsyn, this time ope
as a guest of the RCMP in Canada, advised Angleton that the Canadi
service was penetrated. Angleton's CI staff concluded that the mole
was James Leslie Bennett, the longtime head of RCMP security.

Angleton decided that the Shadrin meeting would be an excellent
opportunity to test Bennett. The RCMP was placing fixed-point photographic surveillance on Shadrin and his meeting with the KGB, and
agreed to withhold the details of the operation from Bennett. Instead,
it was arranged for someone on Angleton's staff to phone Bennett
shortly before Shadrin's meeting and tip him off that there would be
no surveillance on Shadrin. If the KGB behaved without caution, the
RCMP investigators could safely conclude that Bennett had told them
there was no surveillance, since under normal circumstances the Soviets were very cautious. For "security" reasons, Angleton never
notified Branigan what was going on.

Shadrin told Ewa that he had business in Canada, and that she
should join him and they would have a short vacation together. While
Ewa stayed at the hotel and watched an old movie on television, Nick
went for his meeting with the KGB. William Lander said the meeting
was with a high-level KGB man who had never before appeared inside
the United States. As Wooten described the meeting, "It was an assessment situation. He was really being sized up by a person superior
to anyone he was dealing with in Washington. We don't know how
high a level. The conclusion was this fellow had never been to the
United States." According to Wooten, "Both men walked for an hour
[or] so, that's all they did."

The FBI insisted on surveillance on Shadrin because, in their view,
there was a real possibility that the Soviets might try to kidnap him.[5]

here agents would actually follow Shadrin to
_k, was ruled out as being too risky. If Soviet
detected the U.S. surveillance, it would destroy
AWK operation. The sad fact was that even in Can-
were so effective at countersurveillance that they
etect the RCMP's efforts. The FBI had had a terrible
earlier with sloppy tradecraft, when America had lost
t agent, Colonel Popov, because the KGB had de-
llance. They would not make the same mistake again.
eration against Bennett, using Shadrin as bait, was
nned. Since the KGB did not provide their usual high
ty for the meeting, Angleton concluded Bennett was
Soviets.[6] When the FBI found out they had been
s between the two agencies reached an all-time low.
put through a severe interrogation that lasted for days.
ed a year later. According to Leonard V. McCoy, he person-
arried a formal withdrawal of Angleton's allegation against Ben-
t and an apology from the CIA to the RCMP in Ottawa in 1975.[7]

Not long after the Montreal meeting, Shadrin was contacted by a
"new" case officer from the Soviet Embassy named Oleg Kozlov.
Oleg Kozlov, who was not related to Igor Kozlov/KITTY HAWK, was
new to Shadrin, but not new to the FBI. He had been in Washington
since 1970 and was even tougher than Shadrin's former handler, Oleg
Sokolov. A head shorter than Shadrin, Kozlov looked more like an
aging California surfer than a tough KGB agent. Curiously, Shadrin
got along better with Kozlov than he had with Sokolov.

Oleg Kozlov had a well-earned reputation for being a brazen recruiter of vulnerable, elderly defectors and emigrés. He was mean,
ruthless, and relentless. To do his recruiting, he used the time-honored
KGB method: blackmail. In the FBI's files is the case of Alexander
Malyj, a post–World War II Soviet defector. Malyj was alone in the
United States, old, and in poor health. But Kozlov would not leave
the old man alone. The FBI finally entered the case and began to run
the old man against Kozlov. That was when Kozlov turned up the
pressure. He had the old man's brother write him letters from Russia,
with the KGB's gun to his head, urging his expatriate brother to cooperate with the KGB for the good of the family. The FBI backed off
the case because of the emotional strain it was having on Malyj. Not
long after that experience, the hapless emigré died.

Shadrin was told by his new KGB handler that he could expect a
very important assignment, that in the coming weeks a very special
"package" would arrive for him in parts. The first delivery came at a
dead drop in a Safeway supermarket parking lot not far from Shadrin's
home. Shadrin went to the back of the lot and pulled a paper bag from

behind a pile of discarded boxes. It was the first delivery of several that would eventually add up to a burst transmitter. The Russians sent the pieces into the United States by diplomatic pouch.

The Bureau had never yet obtained one of these devices, but knew all too well why the Soviets used them.[8] The burst transmitter was the means of communication with a Soviet illegal agent. Though it seems redundant, the term "illegal agent" refers to a Soviet or Eastern Bloc agent who has entered the country illegally, under a false identity, and lives covertly in the United States. An illegal could be an emigré, usually "laundered" by a stay in a Western European country first, or a trained Soviet agent dropped off by submarine, or someone who crossed via the relatively open borders of Mexico and Canada and established a life based on a false story or "legend."

The original purpose of the illegal agent was to give the Soviets a spy presence should diplomatic relations be broken off and the "legal" spies—those under diplomatic cover—were sent home. For the FBI, the search for an illegal is the ultimate goal in counterintelligence. When Shadrin reported back that Moscow Center was sending the burst transmitter, Wooten, Turner, and Branigan were ecstatic. Not only would the FBI now have access to its own burst transmitter, but they also knew the capture of an illegal would not be far behind. The KITTY HAWK operation was now back in full gear, with a real chance for the Bureau finally to get paid for their years of investment in the case.

To James Nolan, the notion that his colleagues in the FBI had any chance of catching an illegal seemed preposterous: "With two hundred KGB officers working around this town, suddenly this case is so important the Soviets are going to service it with an illegal in Washington, D.C.? It almost boggles the mind." Deputy FBI Counterintelligence Chief Eugene Peterson said, "That's what they [the Soviets] always threw out at you. They'd always dangle something . . . an illegal, the burst transmitter . . . and, of course, we slobbered and drooled because it was a burst transmitter."

Meanwhile, in January 1972, the FBI got more tantalizing news. To help celebrate the new spirit of detente, KITTY HAWK's now legendary mother-in-law was coming for a visit to Washington. It was hoped that KITTY HAWK would accompany her. Sadly, accompanying Furtseva was her daughter—KITTY HAWK's wife—but not Igor Kozlov. The Nixon administration and particularly Henry Kissinger got a taste of just how tough a character Furtseva was. At a reception at the Soviet Embassy, she told the National Security Adviser, "I have heard you had great success with Hollywood stars. Is that true?" Soviet Minister Counselor Yuri Vorontsov, acting as interpreter, conveyed the question to Kissinger in English. Furtseva then eyed Kissinger up and down and gave him a frank appraisal of his looks. "I thought you were taller . . . yes, much taller," she said. As Kissinger flushed, she raised a glass of water to his glass of vodka, and proposed a toast to the success of President Nixon's proposed Moscow visit. After Kissinger left the embassy, without replying to her taunts or the toast, she recited an old Russian proverb: "Out of conflict the truth is born." [9]

Back in Moscow, Furtseva was a busy woman. According to a source in the CIA station at the time, Furtseva found herself attracted to General Sam Wilson, the defense attaché there. Wilson, who cut a dashing figure, was a married man and a devoted husband. At one reception, where KITTY HAWK was present, Furtseva would not leave Wilson alone. Over the next few days the World War II hero was besieged with phone calls and even flowers from her. Wilson had described her to people in the embassy as having seen her best days. Wilson would not comment for the record on what his colleagues said about Furtseva's pursuit of him.

The FBI's disappointment over KITTY HAWK's absence during his relatives' Washington visit was once again overcome when Shadrin got word that he was being summoned to Europe for another high-level meeting, this time in Vienna. He was told he would have to be gone overnight for purposes of training. Shadrin told Ewa that he was meeting with a Russian man who had worked for the U.S. government for twenty-five years. He and Ewa planned a European vacation. After a two-day stopover in Madrid and attendance at the 1972 Olympic Games in Munich, at which the tragic terrorist attack against the Israeli Olympic team took place, Shadrin arrived in Vienna. [10]

Although the CIA was notified of Shadrin's trip to Vienna, there was no request for any CIA support, and none was given. The FBI reasoned, largely based on the Montreal trip a year earlier, that Shadrin could pull off the operation without any help from, or interference by, the CIA. If the Soviets were going to kidnap or kill Shadrin, they would have done it in Canada.

While Ewa went shopping, Nick spent one night away from the Hotel Bristol at a Soviet villa twenty miles west of Vienna. [11] According to FBI and CIA sources, Shadrin's contact with the KGB in Vienna was as smooth as silk. Shadrin reported climbing into a KGB car in front of the Votivkirche, where the officer in charge of the meeting, Vladimir Aleksandrovich Kryuchkov, the Deputy Director of the First Directorate, greeted him. He was patted on the back for his good work, received training on his new code, and got instructions for putting together the pieces of his burst transmitter. When Shadrin returned to the Hotel Bristol, Ewa remembers he was in exceptionally good spirits. They then went on to enjoy a stay in Greece before returning to the United States.

But that account is not the whole story. A missing piece has come to light through the bizarre tale of another FBI double agent, as subsequently related by his wife.

After Ilse Sigler's husband returned from a similar meeting in the summer of 1974 with the KGB in Vienna, she discovered that he had brought back a very frightening souvenir. While cleaning a closet in her El Paso, Texas, home, Ilse Sigler opened her husband's black plastic briefcase. In it she found a large manila envelope with several glossy black-and-white photographs inside. One showed her husband shaking hands with General Secretary Leonid Brezhnev and receiving some sort of award. When she confronted him about the picture, he told her in a rage that if she ever mentioned those pictures to anyone, their lives would be in danger.

When former FBI counterintelligence chief Eugene Peterson was asked if he was aware of the Sigler picture with Brezhnev, he thought for a moment and said, "That wasn't Sigler, that was another asset . . . it was Shadrin." [12] Other FBI officials confirmed that Brezhnev routinely met with Soviet KGB recruits and pinned medals on them. The KGB put them on "black flights" to Moscow for the awards presentation and photograph with Chairman Brezhnev.

From an intelligence officer's point of view, on either side, this type of recognition is the ultimate reward for a life in the shadows and the back alleys. Shadrin was given his photograph with General Secretary Brezhnev, and, according to the FBI, was made a lieutenant colonel in the KGB. Upon his return from Vienna, Shadrin dutifully turned his ceremonial photograph with Brezhnev over to the FBI. Sam Wilson called the pictures "a touch of genius on the Soviets' part."

After an evaluation, FBI technicians reported that Shadrin's burst transmitter was not what they had hoped for. It was an older, much larger model, and was more cumbersome than expected. It was serviceable, but it held no secrets. Wooten instructed Shadrin to take the device home and keep it hidden in his attic, just in case the elusive illegal ever made contact. If and when this occurred, he would expect Shadrin to be able to turn over the device to him on a moment's notice. While newer, state-of-the-art models of the device were very small, the one Shadrin was given was about the size of an old table radio.

To operate the burst transmitter, the agent must punch out a coded message, usually a short series of numbers, on a paper tape much like those used in old telex machines, only smaller. The message is then loaded into the device, the aerial is extended, and the agent waits for a particular satellite to come overhead. When the satellite reaches the correct position, the agent presses a button, and instantly the message is reduced to a single burst of coded material relayed up to the satellite. It is then bounced back to Moscow Center for decoding and action.

Some transmitters have a built-in nonsense message that automatically goes out before the code groups. According to Bill Branigan, the burst transmitter Shadrin got was so big and so heavy that it would be difficult if not impossible to use it in an inconspicuous fashion.

Like so many Soviet agents before him, Shadrin would sit for hours at the big desk in his corner office in his McLean home and listen via shortwave radio for coded notification of his next meeting. Family friends say that the study was Nick's refuge. The bookcase on the wall next to his old wooden desk was lined with scores of old volumes in Russian. One of the volumes was hollowed out. Here he kept his code book, a card that listed when Soviet communications satellites would be overhead, a key list of call signs of the frequencies the KGB told him to monitor, and other material the Soviets had given him.

Ewa recalls Nick staying up late at night, listening with great intensity to the shortwave radio the Soviets had ordered him to buy.[13] The signal he was listening for was one being sent from Cuba by an operator dubbed "Michelangelo" because his Morse code transmissions were so clear and precise. From the Cuban station, Michelangelo was sending information to KGB agents in the United States and Canada. The transmissions monitored by Shadrin and anyone else with a shortwave radio indicated that the KGB had many agents throughout the United States and Canada who were listening for instructions. Michelangelo was a "dispatcher" for these agents. He would send out instructions forwarded by Moscow Center, much the way a taxi dispatcher sends out instructions to cabdrivers. The FBI had no problem with Shadrin's Morse code; as a navy man, he was highly skilled.

The KGB told Shadrin to expect a telephone call from the long-awaited illegal. Weeks went by, but no call came. Then one evening it happened. Ewa Shadrin recalls it vividly. She picked up the phone and the caller hung up on her. This happened several times. Ewa went down the hall of their Colonial house to Nick's corner study. "He was working in his study. I said, 'It is strange. Somebody calls and whenever I pick up the phone, they hang up on me. Maybe next time you can pick up the phone.' And next time Nick comes and picks it up and I am in the kitchen, and he is in his study. He talks to somebody—I just forget if it was in Russian or in English—but a very strange and very tense conversation. Just a few words . . . I started talking to Nick when he finished . . . and he tells me with very strange expression on his face that he has to go and he will be back shortly. I said, 'Where are you going?' And he said, 'Well, some Russian people, they're on Lorcum Lane and they are having some car trouble,' and they are calling him." Ewa was worried. The telephone call frightened her. She asked him not to go out. "I said, 'No. You are not going. You cannot go. It doesn't make sense' . . . and Nick became very upset and he started calling Jim Wooten, who was not at home, and later Funkhouser."

According to Wooten, Shadrin had trouble understanding the message. "Nick thought at first it was a canned advertisement until she [the illegal] mentioned the permanent signal site [Cuba], at which time it wasn't. [Then] . . . Nick made her repeat some of the stuff," Wooten recalls. The call, from the wife of the illegal, was a commercial sales pitch for a portrait studio. The pitch for a photograph session was a code telling Shadrin the illegal was calling to set up a meeting. In the call, Shadrin could not remember what he was instructed to bring to the meeting, but was convinced it was the cumbersome burst transmitter. Facing objections from Ewa, he tried to call Funkhouser and Wooten, but could not get either one of them. He later told Wooten he never made the meeting.

The woman who tried to call Nick Shadrin was the wife of Ludek Zemenek, a Czech-born man who became a Soviet illegal. Zemenek's name was changed to Rudolph Herrmann, an identification stolen by the KGB from a dead German prisoner.[14] Herrmann, his son Paul, and his wife were all KGB agents. Herrmann was the illegal resident for the entire country. That meant that if war broke out or diplomatic relations forced the legals to go home, Herrmann would be in charge of all Soviet agents in the United States.

Herrmann and his wife, who were later caught by the FBI, confirmed to writer John Barron for his book *The KGB Today* that among the assignments he carried out was to confirm the location of defectors in the Washington, D.C., area, including Yuri Nosenko. Herrmann told the FBI he found Nosenko in 1969, some four years prior to the call to Shadrin. According to Shadrin's FBI handlers, these were precisely the same activities Nick had been engaged in for Sokolov, at approximately the same time.

Even though the illegal contact was never made and the equipment given to Shadrin was dated, the CIA continued to supply a steady stream of secrets for Nick to give the KGB, and the FBI decided to keep the operation going. All of the FBI officials connected to the case confirm that Shadrin never brought back anything in return. But no one wanted to risk losing KITTY HAWK.

One secret Shadrin may have given to the Soviets was not one that John Funkhouser got for him. In the early 1970s the CIA engaged in the most massive technological endeavor since the advent of spy satellites. The decision to try to recover a Soviet submarine that had sunk near Hawaii was supposed to be one of the most closely held secrets in the government at that time.[15] After the Soviet submarine sank in 1968, the Navy suggested the operation to the 40 Committee, which at the time was the approving body for covert operations. But this project was too big and too expensive for just the Navy, so the other intelligence agencies were brought into the act. The need for secrecy dictated that the CIA become a major partner in the operation.

As with the U-2 operation, the CIA turned to private industry to come up with the plans and means for the attempted submarine recovery. Their scheme called for the Hughes Tool Company, along with one of its subsidiaries, the Summa Corporation, to design a recovery ship that could be operated as part of the Glomar Marine Corporation's fleet. Shadrin's old friend Tom Dwyer played a key role in the operation.[16] It was through the Navy's amazing SOSUS system that the submarine's 1968 sinking was actually recorded on audio tape and its location pinpointed. The unusual ship that was built for the recovery operation, the *Glomar Explorer,* was deliberately publicized, as part of its cover story, as a deep-sea mining ship.

By the spring of 1974 the go-ahead was given for the *Glomar Explorer* to try to lift the Soviet diesel submarine—with, it was hoped, its nuclear missiles, code books, and operational systems intact—from the seabed 750 miles west of Hawaii. The recovery operation was only partially successful. The *Explorer* locked on to the sunken sub and was bringing it to the surface, when, at a depth of about five thousand feet, the submarine broke into several large sections when the giant claw lifting it failed. About a third of the submarine was recovered, as well as two nuclear-tipped torpedoes.

For the United States, a bigger problem than the malfunctioning recovery ship was that of U.S. relations with the Soviets. The Soviets had informally asked the United States to help in locating the lost submarine when it first disappeared, and the U.S. government had responded by saying it had no useful information. Kissinger and others in the administration, in the midst of writing a seabed mining treaty, were fearful that the Soviets would learn of the recovery and would be furious if anything less than a formal Soviet funeral service was provided for the sailors, should they be recovered in the operation.

The bodies of six Russian sailors were in the portion of the hull that was recovered. One of them was the sub's nuclear weapons officer, and a diary that belonged to him was also retrieved.

Because time was short, the only source on Soviet sea burial rites to which the Navy had access was Nick Shadrin. It is not known whether he actually conducted the funeral or whether he was just consulted by the Navy. A film exists of the funeral service, but the CIA has consistently refused to release it. General Sam Wilson, who served in Moscow during much of this period, said the Navy's efforts paid off and "the Soviets were, in a very particular and peculiar way, very gratified that we had the funeral services."[17]

Richard Oden remembers Shadrin complaining about the huge

amounts of money spent on the still-secret operation: "Nick said [to the Navy and CIA], 'Listen, fellows, you are wasting a lot of energy and resources because in that period of time the Soviets had at least two new generations of submarines on line.' "[18] Oden's statement could mean that Shadrin, like John Paisley, may have been in a position to warn the Soviets about the Glomar operations—code-named DESKTOP and JENNIFER—that caused them to become public before any attempt was made to recover the remaining portions of the submarine, including its nuclear missiles. It was because of that exposure, according to DCI William Colby, that a second attempt to recover the missiles, more valuable than the submarine itself, was not made.[19]

The early 1970s kept Nick Shadrin very busy. Besides the Glomar operation, the Soviet "blue water" navy made its massive debut with its first Pacific exercises. Shadrin was called out to Pearl Harbor to advise on the exercises. But once back at the translation unit, Shadrin's life settled into a routine again. His role as a double agent seemed to diminish as KITTY HAWK became more and more a memory. An angry FBI discovered through a State Department cable that the CIA had, in fact, sighted KITTY HAWK at an International Atomic Energy Agency reception in Moscow, but had failed to pass on the information.[20] According to Wooten, it was obvious KH was not traveling outside the Soviet Union as had been hoped.

By 1974, Shadrin's moods were dark and depressed. His second job as a U.S. intelligence agent was losing its luster and excitement as Moscow Center seemed to be in no hurry to deal with the operation. Richard Oden says that Shadrin was more melancholy than he had ever seen him.

Nick loved children, and spent a great deal of time with the Odens' boys. Frank Steinert, who was close to Shadrin, recalls a sad moment with the big Russian. Ewa had refused to have children, and Nick had told his friends he desired a family. One day, Steinert was sadly talking about the son he had left behind in East Germany, and "Nick said, 'Yeah, we have the same problem.' He had left one son behind. And he was telling us, you could see it, he was close to crying, you know."[21] Jim Wooten once asked Shadrin about why he and Ewa had not started a family, and Shadrin told his friend that "it takes two to tango."

The Shadrins' closest friends understand why Ewa did not know that her husband was a spy. Janka Urynowicz recalls Ewa's reaction to odd letters Nick would receive, frequent unexplained meetings, and the hours he would disappear into his office, monitoring his radio. Janka said Ewa was not the kind of wife who would "question Nick about every little thing. Why? Because she didn't like to be questioned either." Her husband, Stanley, a tall, youthful-looking man, who is a patent judge by profession, said that any time Ewa said anything to Nick that might sound probing, "he would become immediately defensive and cut her off."

The Urynowiczes, along with many of the Shadrins' other friends, wondered how the Shadrins seemed to be able to afford so many expensive trips and other luxuries. They had bought a second home on the water in nearby Solomons Island, Maryland.[22] Nick had a twenty-eight-foot, twin-screw power boat that he used for fishing on weekends. Tom Dwyer said the boat was almost too big to tow. Nick was proud of his boat and kept it in "spit and polish," just like a big Navy ship. He named it *Ewa*. "He loved the best of everything, from gin to fishing tackle," Pete Sivess said.

"Nick liked to spend, you know. Nothing was ever [too] expensive for Nick. He always had to have the best. He wanted to show he could afford it," Maria Oden remembers.

"They were living ahead of their income from what I could tell. Nick spent eighty to ninety dollars a week on lunch," Stanley Urynowicz said. "Nick once told me that 'I am not concerned about saving money because if I disappear or die, Ewa has the means to survive. She has her profession.' "[23]

The Urynowiczes also said that Nick was never afraid that the Soviets would harm him, even though he was under a death sentence. He would joke that they had forgotten about him by this time. According to Ewa, the Shadrins would, on occasion, visit friends aboard Polish merchant vessels in Baltimore Harbor and often stay for dinner. Jim Wooten said he was not aware that Nick and Ewa had spent time on Eastern Bloc vessels visiting the United States.

As the 1970s went on, Shadrin's temper got shorter and shorter at home; his sleepless nights increased in frequency. Stanley Urynowicz recalls what it was like to go fishing with Nick overnight: "I would wake up at night and hear Nick pacing around on the bow of the boat. Then he'd come back to bed and everything would be quiet and I'd fall back to sleep again. . . . And something would wake me and Nick was out again. . . . It was sad. He was very hyper. Of course, in retrospect, I know why."

Janka Urynowicz recalls Ewa's unhappiness in 1974: "Poor Ewa would say, 'I just can't take this anymore.' I would ask what was wrong, and she said, 'I have had enough of this unhappiness. No matter what—I don't do it right.' "

By 1974, Shadrin was relying more and more on Valium to get a semblance of rest. Because of Ewa's dental practice, it was easily available to him. He had been a defector for fifteen years, and it was beginning to show. Health problems in September 1974, which included surgery, also slowed Shadrin down.

People on the outside who came into contact with Shadrin found him overpowering, charming, and brilliant. The CIA used him as an example of the well-adjusted defector. His academic pursuits were nearly flawless. But in his last years in the United States, signs of his true feelings were beginning to emerge clearly. Pete Sivess recalls that Shadrin was frustrated with the American system: "He was very critical about what we did here. He thought we had too much freedom here. He believed we had to have discipline. He wanted to take the First Amendment and throw it down the drain."[24]

Stanley Urynowicz does not recall that Shadrin liked a great deal about the United States: "He didn't put our system in any superior light at all. . . . He thought the Soviet system was workable . . . and that with the right people it could work better than what we have here."

But by December 1974, revolutionary changes at the CIA would renew the KITTY HAWK operation, at least as far as the Agency was concerned. James Jesus Angleton was fired from his job as Chief of Counterintelligence by Colby, and his top aides resigned as well. Colby, tired of Angleton, appointed George T. Kalaris to head CI. For the first time in years, the CIA was openly recruiting Soviet agents again. Things were also changing at the FBI. Courtland Jones, who had been Jim Wooten's genial boss, retired along with Wooten's experienced partner, Bert Turner. Jim Wooten, who had, according to Eugene Peterson, "fallen in love with his agent," was now fully in charge of the KITTY HAWK operation for the FBI. For the first time since the RCMP incident, FBI relations with the CIA were warming up. George Kalaris seemed willing to work with the FBI and eager to get a new approach to KITTY HAWK going.[25]

Wooten decided that it was time to stoke the KITTY HAWK fire again. In February 1975, Nick announced to Ewa that they were going skiing in St. Moritz. Since the FBI thought Nick had lost all communication with the Soviets, Wooten instructed him to reestablish contact with the KGB in Vienna. William Lander recalls how: "If you lose contact completely and you have no means of getting back in touch with us, they told him to do this. You either call this number or write a letter to the visa section of the Soviet Embassy in Vienna."[26] Nick was instructed to mail a letter to a special Vienna address, but from within Austria to re-contact the Soviets. That was the sole purpose of the trip. But, according to Mrs. Shadrin, Nick wrote to a "Herr Rudiger Lehman" at an East Berlin address prior to their vacation. This would suggest that Nick had never lost contact with the Soviets.

When the Shadrins left for Switzerland, Nick still felt terrible from his earlier illness, and his mood matched. The German-run hotel in St. Moritz—the Schweizerhof—infuriated Shadrin when the maître d' seated him and Ewa at an inferior table in the dining room. Ewa decided to stay clear of Nick and his temper. While Ewa skied, Shadrin drove across the border to Austria to mail a letter to re-contact the Soviets. He was gone the entire day. Ewa said that when Nick returned, his mood was improved dramatically.[27]

That spring, the Shadrin case came full circle. Leonard V. McCoy, who as a young reports officer had walked into Angleton's office and enlisted his aid in getting Shadrin to America, now found himself involved with the defector again. McCoy had been selected as one of two deputies to Kalaris. It soon became clear that McCoy was the more equal of the two.

To James Nolan, the renewal of the Shadrin/KITTY HAWK operation was a disaster. In his opinion, having McCoy at the apex was even worse: "I have to be very honest. I don't like McCoy. I don't have any respect for his judgment. He doesn't know beans about counterintelligence, and in my view, he doesn't know a hell of a lot about the Soviets." McCoy has just as critical a view of Nolan, saying, "He didn't like any of our operations."

Neil Sullivan, who replaced Court Jones, recalls that the first discussions of a 1975 meeting between Shadrin and the KGB began not long after he took over in January 1975. Others place the time a little later. But it was clear that both the Bureau and the CIA were pushing to reestablish contact with the long-elusive KITTY HAWK. The first thing that Leonard McCoy did when he received what he described as the very thin KITTY HAWK file was to begin to cut Bruce Solie out of the operation.[28] Solie said, "I was in the matter until 1975, when they gradually learned of the matter and took it over." Solie said that Kalaris and McCoy "were both neophytes in the business."[29]

Ironically, both Solie and McCoy had taken courageous stands for Yuri Nosenko's bona fides that Angleton had strongly opposed. McCoy, outraged by Nosenko's confinement, walked into DCI Richard Helms's office, without an appointment, and spoke of the unjust imprisonment of Nosenko. Solie was responsible for writing the report clearing the defector.

While Jim Wooten was grateful that the CIA was interested in pushing KITTY HAWK again, he had fears that in their enthusiasm they might try to contact him in Moscow—a very dangerous proposition. By early 1975, Wooten suspected that they had done just that. "It was new people taking over. It was hard for us to assess that was the case, or they had, in fact, had contact with him. My own feeling is that they did."[30]

Wooten was right. Contact was made on a Moscow subway train, and KH passed a vague message into the coat pocket of a CIA man, holding out the possibility that he might be able to travel outside the country to a meeting.³¹ Once again the KGB had the FBI and CIA's attention. Why the high interest in KH continued is an important question. Igor Kozlov's powerful mother-in-law had died nearly a year before of a massive coronary. Furtseva's death came on the heels of a scandal. She had wanted so much to keep her dacha, that to make sure she never lost the perk, she appropriated government funds and workers to build a "private" one for herself. Her enemies finally caught up with her. Igor Kozlov would no longer have his important source of KGB influence and, more important, gossip.

In 1975, just as the cherry blossoms were blooming in the nation's capital, Kalaris, McCoy, Branigan, and a woman named Cynthia Hausmann, who Branigan thought looked like a spinster, gathered in Neil Sullivan's office at the FBI's Washington Field Office. The Soviets had given Shadrin a choice of Berlin, Helsinki, or Vienna for the upcoming meeting. The CIA recommended Vienna as the safest place. Then, with some drama, Kalaris announced that there was an expectation that KITTY HAWK would be present at the meeting.

Branigan had to restrain himself from rolling his eyes. He had heard the promises of KITTY HAWK before. But in order to keep the "new" relationship "friendly," Branigan asked his CIA colleagues how KITTY HAWK would be approached if he came. McCoy explained that Shadrin would set up a meeting with KH and pass the information on to his handler, Cynthia Hausmann, who would in turn contact Gus Hathaway. Hathaway was to be dispatched to Vienna to see his old contact, Igor Kozlov. After the meeting, most of the group left. Cynthia remained behind with Wooten to meet Shadrin for the first time.

Planning for the meeting continued for several months. The Shadrins took a trip to Spain early that fall, and Nick called Vienna to confirm the meeting with the Russians. In November the same group met again to finalize the details of the meeting now scheduled for December 18, 1975, in Vienna. Nick told Ewa that after his business in Vienna, they would head for Switzerland and a Christmas of skiing.

As the meeting drew near, the smooth relationship between the CIA's counterintelligence staff and the FBI began to unravel. Neil Sullivan was shocked to learn from Wooten that Hausmann had been identified by Philip Agee, the "renegade" CIA agent, in a new book receiving wide attention, which had been published earlier that summer.³² "He told me she had already been burned. That she had already been identified as an American intelligence agent. I said, 'That's the person they are sending over? Somebody isn't thinking very carefully.' "

Wooten says categorically that he did not know Hausmann had been blown by Agee. Sullivan said he did not object to Hausmann because he trusted Wooten, and Wooten said to him, "We are working closely with the CIA. Everything is fine." Sullivan said Wooten told him he had faith in Shadrin: "I thought the whole operation was paste [a police term for fake]. I didn't know who the hell was really controlling the Shadrin operation. Supposedly it's Jim Wooten in the Washington Field Office. But to me, after the thing developed, it seems like everybody and his uncle had control over the operation," Sullivan continued.

Two weeks before their departure for Vienna, Nick asked Ewa to take a walk in the December cold. Nick believed the house had been bugged by the FBI and the CIA. Ewa says that on the walk, Nick told her that his frustrated professional life would change drastically if the Vienna meetings went well. He told her that he would get a security clearance so he could reach his full potential. Later that evening, Ewa Shadrin remembers Jim Wooten bringing a tall and very cool woman by. She was introduced to Mrs. Shadrin as Ann Martin. Ewa was told that Ms. Martin would be joining them for the Vienna portion of the trip. Ann Martin was the cover name Cynthia Hausmann used for the Vienna mission.

A few days after the final plans for the Vienna meeting were ironed out by Bill Branigan and the CIA, Branigan's deputy, Eugene Peterson, received a disturbing phone call from Jim Wooten. Wooten told Peterson that "Bruce Solie had been cut out of the operation."[33] Instead of sending Solie, who had first met and assessed KITTY HAWK in 1966 in Washington the CIA counterintelligence people had decided to send KH's old friend Gus Hathaway. Hathaway, who had first met KITTY HAWK/Igor Kozlov while both men were on temporary duty in Pakistan, was a serious security problem, as far as Wooten and Peterson were concerned. "The Soviets probably were aware of the Hathaway/KITTY HAWK relationship. They certainly knew who Gus was. He had been up against the KGB for years. To have him meet KH in Vienna was just too dangerous. It could endanger Shadrin as well."

Coincidentally, while Wooten was informing Peterson of the Hathaway problem, Branigan was having a final meeting with McCoy and Kalaris firming up final plans. When he emerged from the meeting, Peterson broke the news to Branigan. Branigan's famous temper flared at his old friend Peterson. "Jesus, we made an agreement, I don't need these kinds of problems," Branigan remembers telling Peterson. When Peterson explained the security risk to Branigan, he shook his head and instructed Peterson to call McCoy, and tell him in no uncertain terms that Hathaway was not acceptable. Peterson explained the rationale he used with McCoy: "We were afraid that if the Soviets saw Gus and KH there, they would put two and two together. It was a matter of security. McCoy had no choice but to listen."

The CIA's rationale for sending Hathaway was unknown to the Bureau. Hathaway and another agent had had brush contacts with

KITTY HAWK over the previous two years. This information was never passed on to the FBI, a violation of the operating agreement between the two agencies. As far as McCoy and Kalaris were concerned, Hathaway was a more experienced field agent than Solie, who had spent the better part of his career in the United States. In the blowup over Solie and Hathaway, the Bureau and the CIA let the issue of Cynthia Hausmann being blown in Agee's book go by. If Shadrin and KITTY HAWK were believed to be real, then the FBI and CIA could have scarcely found a better way to endanger both men.

The next issue was surveillance. Cynthia explained that the station in Vienna had already planned fixed-point surveillance for the operation. Branigan, fearful of countersurveillance, asked the Agency to call it off. Branigan said no effort was made to explain to him that the U.S. Consulate overlooked the steps of the Votivkirche, a huge cathedral not far from the University of Vienna, where Shadrin was supposed to meet with the KGB. It was a perfect spot for safe, fixed-point photographic surveillance. Eugene Peterson says the Bureau was relying on the CIA's judgment: "What the hell. Vienna is a place on the Danube, and the guy wrote waltzes there. That's about all we know about Vienna." Branigan is more emphatic: "You had to be stupid not to look out that window. . . . Anybody knows that. All we ever knew [was] that we didn't want anybody out there on the street pussyfooting around."

In KH's message it was suggested that the Vienna meeting with Shadrin might best be accomplished in the Vienna Woods, on the outskirts of the city. Wooten explained that Nick had been studying a map of the area, should the meeting take place there. Sullivan said he told Wooten that the lack of surveillance bothered him: "You don't just send a double agent out to meet a guy in the woods and forget about him."

Sullivan saw Shadrin a few days before the trip, and recalls that he was in a very self-confident mood, a mood that was inexplicable to Sullivan: "For him to go back to Vienna with so little protection and coverage, he should have been scared out of his wits. He should have said, 'I don't want to do it. I don't want to go.' But he was happy to go," Sullivan said.

The Shadrins spent the last days prior to the trip attending Christmas parties and seeing old friends. The Dwyers were visiting from Hawaii, and when it was time to say good-bye at National Airport, Nick seemed in black spirits to Tom and his wife, T.C.: "I had never seen him, except in the earliest days, seem so dejected. . . . I don't know what Nick was apprehensive about, but he must have known something," Dwyer said.

At the office, Shadrin kept a map of Vienna in his desk that he would study. After he disappeared, Frank Steinert found the map; details of the Vienna Woods had been cut from it.

In his last days in the United States, Shadrin's behavior began to change drastically. At work, he dictated for hours into a tape recorder with the door closed. He missed the annual Christmas party, but he made certain that he delivered several bottles of Russian vodka at a smaller get-together before he left. He handed the vodka to a woman who worked in the office, with whom he had been fighting in the previous weeks. He kissed her good-bye and wished her and her son a happy new year. To her, his behavior seemed very strange.

A few days before he left, Nick gave one of his expensive rifles to Frank Steinert. "I had the feeling when he didn't come back . . . that this was his good-bye to me," Steinert said.

For Maria and Richard Oden, the good-bye was especially emotional. Nick tried to give Richard his pistol—an expensive Magnum. Maria Oden kissed Nick good-bye. Then Nick said to Maria, " 'I hope I see you again.' " And Maria asked, "Nikolay, what are you talking about? You are coming back." She said he had no tears in his eyes, but his voice was very heavy. Pete and Ellie Sivess also found Nick very nervous and uneasy before he left.

Darryl Du Bose, a neighbor of the Shadrins, remembers that Nick walked over to his house around five o'clock on the evening before the Shadrins were leaving for Vienna. "I was home by myself, and . . . Nick came over. He lived right across the street. And he had with him a little dog chewy-squeaky toy. I had a young shepherd puppy—maybe a year old—but Nick liked him very much. . . . Nick gave him the toy and made fun of him and kicked him back and forth, and the dog loved it. He was very hyper. . . . I remember he lit a cigarette up and he held it like a Russian, you know, the back of his hand, and he only took a couple of puffs or something, then he put it out. And he lit [his] pipe and he couldn't keep it lit, naturally. A pipe's hard to keep lit if you're not paying attention. So I asked him, 'Do you want to go downstairs and get a drink?' And he says, 'Yeah,' and he went down to the recreation room and he used to drink nothing but wine and so I said, 'Do you want some wine?' He said, 'Beer,' 'cause he knew that I drank beer. He lit another cigarette, took a couple of puffs, and put it down, and we talked about him leaving early the next day going to Vienna. . . . I asked Nick, 'That's right there next to Czechoslovakia, isn't it?' Oh, he was going to take Ewa skiing. And I let it go. A few minutes later my wife came home . . . and he hugged her. Now, we were always friendly, but not that friendly. . . . It was out of the ordinary for Nick." A few minutes later, Ewa joined Nick and said her farewells. She explained that she still had packing to do for the trip before they left in the morning for Vienna.

CHAPTER FOURTEEN

Shadrin: Going Home

The first thing that leaps to mind when you say "Shadrin" is ama-
teurism.

Lt. Gen. Samuel V. Wilson

Who knows, maybe Nick was sent from Poland . . . from Russia
to meet some Polish girl and came with her and had a mission to live
[with] her for twenty years . . . and it was time to go home.

Maria Oden

VIENNA IS A CITY of political and moral accommodations. On the
surface it is refined, culturally rich, historic, and pleasant. But it is
here that the spy games are played out. If there were a scorekeeper,
the East would be far ahead. When the games end in violence, the
Austrian National Police can make embarrassments disappear with the
grace and dispatch inherent in a people used to serving royalty, who
now serve two competing ideologies that could swallow them in an
afternoon. Here, truth is sacrificed to survival.

Bruce Solie was the first arrival from the CIA. He had beaten a
snowstorm that engulfed much of Europe by coming a couple of days
early, on Tuesday, December 15, 1975. He was uncomfortable with
the assignment. He knew the only reason he was there was that the
FBI had insisted. For a year, Solie had been progressively cut out of
the KITTY HAWK operation. Had it not been for the confidence and

235

friendship of Jim Wooten and others at the Bureau, he could easily have known nothing about this trip. His relationship with the CIA's new counterintelligence staff was not good. Solie's instincts told him that McCoy and Kalaris were holding details back from him and the Bureau.[1] On the flight over, Solie had seethed about the treatment they had given him since they took over CI operations.

In many ways, Solie had been underestimated throughout his career. Despite his tight-lipped personality, his plain Midwestern looks, and his personal sense of fairness, he seemed to be always in the midst of controversy. Solie was loyal to his friends and not judgmental. He dealt in facts and had a personality much more like an FBI agent than the more cerebral CIA operative.

Solie never intended to get caught up in the political crossfire between DCI William Colby and Angleton. But that was what happened. In retrospect, it is clear that Solie's spirited defense of Soviet defector Yuri Nosenko was used to help push Angleton out. Angleton, who remained adamant that Nosenko was a provocateur, believed Solie had gotten too close to Nosenko to be objective.[2] After all, Solie had been the best man at Nosenko's wedding, and had helped him resettle into American life. How ironic it was that Solie, a man credited with helping end the career of James Angleton, was at such odds with those who profited from Angleton's removal.

Solie realized that he would have had nothing to do with the KITTY HAWK operation, had it not been for Angleton in the first place. When the call came to Richard Helms that fateful spring Saturday morning in 1966 from "Igor," it was Angleton who recommended that Bruce Solie meet with him. Now Solie was looking at just a few more years until retirement. He had nurtured KITTY HAWK for a decade and still had not made up his mind about the authenticity of the case. Never neglecting the investigation, before Solie left Washington for Vienna, he dropped off a picture to be framed with Igor Orlov at his Old Town Alexandria, Virginia, store. Because so much of the bureaucratic memory was gone by 1975, only Solie survived from the original "Igor" operation to make the trip to Vienna.

As Solie surveyed Vienna, the late-afternoon traffic slowed his cab ride as he headed across the Danube canal and into the old city. Solie felt a nagging discomfort that something just wasn't right about this mission. But he never strayed from his assignment. His job was simply to be there should KITTY HAWK, Igor Kozlov, at long last show up in Vienna. As he looked out the taxi window at the Kursalon on his left, Solie noticed snowflakes. It reminded him of Wisconsin winters. He did not like being away from home at Christmastime. He looked at his watch and moved it up six hours as his cab headed toward the Imperial

Hotel. He thought to himself that he had to buy some Christmas presents if he got a little spare time.

The Washington-to-London leg of the Shadrins' trip to Vienna was uneventful. Unlike most other major European cities, there are few direct and convenient ways to reach Vienna. So the traditional dinnertime takeoff from the United States, with an early-morning landing in Vienna, simply was not possible. Adding to the Shadrins' problems was an early snowstorm that blanketed most of Europe and a good part of Austria. The snowstorm and a delay at London's Heathrow Airport turned what should have been a nine-hour trip into a twenty-hour ordeal.

It was 2:00 P.M. by the time the Shadrins' plane touched down at Vienna Airport. At precisely that same moment, a short, stocky, baldheaded man was sitting on another jetliner, waiting to take off from Vienna on his way back to the United States for the holidays. This man had never met Shadrin, but he knew almost everything about Nikolay Fedorovich Artamonov. The two men had a great deal in common. They shared the darker side of Vienna.

Just as Nick and Ewa were arriving in Vienna, the CIA station chief, a Hungarian-born Jew named George Weisz, was leaving town. Weisz was much like Shadrin. He was proud, incandescently bright, and would not hesitate to use others to get ahead. Weisz was one of the CIA's originals. He had served Bill Harvey in Berlin Base in the 1950s.[3] He never advertised his Eastern European Jewish background to his Ivy League WASP colleagues at the CIA. Instead, many thought George was German, and that was fine with him. Most of his subordinates in the CIA's Vienna Station did not like him. Some respected him. George was making his second trip to the United States since he had taken over the station from Hugh Montgomery, just six weeks before. He was a political survivor, a careerist.

Weisz smelled trouble over the Shadrin operation. Just as the key chapter in the KITTY HAWK saga was about to unfold, Weisz went home on leave. Nothing was more out of character for this spy. He was known as a man who never missed out on the action. He had volunteered for Vietnam. Weisz was not the kind of man to leave his station when a major operation was going down.

The CIA is supposed to be compartmentalized. Employees are assumed to know just enough to do their work. But George Weisz made it his job always to know much more. After a terrible time in Vietnam, Weisz was sent back to Berlin as chief of base in 1971. But in 1971, Berlin was far different from the Berlin of the 1950s. Sam Wilson saw firsthand how close a hold Weisz had on operations in his territory.

Wilson had business in Berlin at one point, and had scheduled an important meeting with an agent there. While Weisz was cordial, Wilson found that he lorded over the twenty or so people in the station: "I was involved in something of an operational nature in Berlin, which some of George's people were helping me on, and while I am right in the middle of this damn thing, George, who knows generally where I am, but doesn't know the details, came sauntering through, and the fella gives me the fish-eye, and he comes by the table and keeps on going. I later challenged him and he says, 'Well, I was just doing a little countersurveillance.' " What Weisz did caused a number of people to question his loyalty and his professional judgment.[4]

Weisz was a political survivor, and he had the book on Artamonov. Weisz's friends in the CIA had concluded that Artamonov was a sent agent from the beginning.[5] Weisz did not like being associated with failure. And he did not trust the new CI staff. When he got the details of the plan the rookies in CI had cooked up with the FBI, Weisz decided to leave town. The last thing he needed on December 18, 1975, was another trip home. He had gone back and forth to the States monthly since leaving as head of the Foreign Intelligence staff and being assigned to Vienna in late September. And home was not a particularly happy place for George Weisz in 1975. He had a troubled marriage and would have preferred to spend more time with a young secretary at the U.S. Embassy in Vienna, with whom he was having an affair.[6]

Weisz's deep understanding of political survival and treachery, which he had gained as an agent in Berlin during the most trying of times, told him to get on that airplane for New York. He had seen agents rolled up and killed. He knew that the penalty for accepting a phony defector would be paid in the field and not by bureaucrats at headquarters. To Weisz, the idea that men he considered amateurs like McCoy and Kalaris had been put in charge of CI was too much. He would not take the blame for their mistakes.

Nothing that happened in the three weeks since Weisz had learned about the operation had eased his mind. The message traffic indicating that a major double operation would be conducted in Vienna began arriving in the station about a week after Thanksgiving. The station was put on full alert for the operation. All leaves for the weekend before Christmas were canceled, Weisz informed his staff.

According to reliable CIA sources Weisz also told another government's spy service about Shadrin's mission. Weisz worked not only for the CIA, but also for Mossad—Israeli Intelligence. Vienna was a key operations point for Mossad. Here agents would be sent East and Soviet Jews debriefed upon exiting into the West. Mossad advised

Weisz to leave Vienna during the upcoming Shadrin operation and take home leave.

For all the talk of Vienna as a spy mecca, the CIA had less than fifteen people in the Vienna Station in 1975. The top men on George Weisz's staff were all seasoned professionals. After a tour in Moscow, Robert T. Dumaine, under official cover as an embassy political officer, had arrived in Vienna two years earlier, in August 1973. He had been put in charge of the Soviet Section of the station. Since he had spent a career up against the KGB, the suave Dumaine understood his role.

The other senior man in the station was Charles T. "Chuck" Malton. Malton was a Harvard man who was better known for his exceptionally attractive wife and daughter than for his abilities as a spy. The utility man in the station was a red-haired, friendly man named Stanley K. Jeffers. Jeffers, his wife, Jan, and two children looked like the picture-book American foreign-service family overseas. Jeffers was in charge of logistics. His job was the practical side of the CIA. He had been an intelligence agent long enough to have seen that mistakes can cost lives. Jeffers hated Weisz. His nickname for the new station chief was "Napoleon."

When the station was informed that the Votivkirche was the meeting place, it made life immensely easier. At that time, the American visa section was in a building directly overlooking the Votivkirche, which faced a large square park along Ring Schotten. The visa section's location would make surveillance of Shadrin's initial contact with the KGB much easier. Malton, Dumaine, and Weisz decided there would be no moving surveillance. Not in Vienna. According to Jeffers, the Soviets would probably run up to twenty agents in a countersurveillance for the meeting. Soviet countersurveillance was automatic, "like the sun coming up," Jeffers said.[7] If any of the Soviets picked up CIA activity, the prized American double agent would be uncovered and, probably shortly thereafter, killed. But fixed-point surveillance would be no problem. And to the men and women in Vienna Station, it was necessary.

So many Army and FBI operations were run in Vienna by people who had no idea of the dangers and the Soviets' ten-to-one numerical superiority that some protection—both real and bureaucratic—was necessary. Based on what Shadrin told the CIA and FBI about his 1972 Vienna trip, a week prior to the operation, a fixed-point surveillance was planned. There was some grumbling from some in the station about Christmas leave being postponed, but leaves for all personnel were canceled, and they had their instructions.

The grumbling was soon to turn to concern and anger. On December

17, at 9:30 A.M., Cynthia Hausmann arrived at the American Embassy. After telling the Marine guard that her name was Miss Martin and she had an appointment with the "Peripheral Reports Section," she was ushered up to the embassy's fourth floor, into George Weisz's office at the back of the building. Weisz had known Cynthia when she used student cover as a field officer in Munich in the late 1950s. Jeffers had also served in Munich with her.

Weisz kept an impersonal office. A few old maps hung on the wall, but a big cleared desk and a large couch and chair dominated the room. He gestured Cynthia to sit down in the large easy chair near his desk. After twenty minutes of getting reacquainted, Weisz, impeccably dressed, escorted Ms. Hausmann to the "bubble," a specially designed secure room adjoining his office in the embassy. The bubble was directly over the Ambassador's third-floor office.

Assembled in the room were Dumaine, Malton, Weisz, and Hausmann. It was during this meeting that Cynthia presented shocking news. She told her colleagues that the FBI had insisted on no surveillance of Shadrin at all—in any form, including fixed-point. Weisz immediately said that it would be foolish not to use the visa section, with its windows looking down on the meeting site. Hausmann was emphatic. The FBI said *no* surveillance. No one in the station was in a position or a mood to challenge her. Officially, she was simply carrying out the FBI's orders. And Shadrin was their operation.

As Weisz's plane took off the next, snowy afternoon, he had taken himself out of political harm's way.

The ride from the Vienna airport to the old city begins in a very unpromising fashion. The outskirts of the city look no better than those of more industrialized cities, such as Milan or Frankfurt. It is only when a visitor turns off onto the inner Ring Road that the trees and the architecturally interesting buildings combine with the old diversion canal from the Danube to create the charm that is Vienna.

Nick Shadrin felt renewed in Vienna. For Ewa, the trip was a lovely surprise. After all, it was an afterthought; Nick had some business here. Ewa had fallen in love with the city during their trip to Vienna in 1972, when Nick was here earlier on business. To Ewa it was old Europe at its best. The taxi made the half-hour trip in from the Flughafen just ahead of rush-hour traffic. As the cab pulled into the first district across the Aspern Bridge, the Shadrins once again saw the old city. Stadt Park was covered in snow. A few blocks farther down, the Imperial Hotel was looming on the left in all its palatial glory. It was hard to believe that the hotel had once been the palace of one family. Now it was pampering on a smaller scale many well-heeled guests. The Imperial, along with the Sacher and the Bristol, were the best hotels in Vienna. But when the Shadrins passed by the Imperial, there was no way for them to know that a CIA security man was waiting inside, just in case their visit was successful.

The Shadrins were staying in the Bristol Hotel, a quarter of a mile farther up the Kartner Ring. The old hotel was only a fifty-pace walk to the Opera House and offered excellent service. What Shadrin's handlers at the FBI did not know was that the KGB had at least four people on the Bristol's staff supplying the local KGB resident with information on various guests.[8] Anyone coming to see Shadrin would be identified, and the information would eventually make its way back to Moscow Center for processing.

Christmas was only a week away, and the town was full of shoppers trying to get in and out of stores before they closed. Shopkeepers in Vienna keep shorter hours than anyplace else in Europe. With the snow and the holiday decorations, the picturesque city was a delight for Ewa to visit. Although Nick was Russian and Ewa was Polish, the Austrians evoked none of the intense discomfort for them that the Germans did. Shadrin, like most Russians who had lived through the war and lost relatives, had little regard for Germans. But the Austrians had a softness, a reasonableness that Nick liked. To Ewa, Nick seemed optimistic and happy on the ride to the hotel. He smiled when he saw the Bristol and the uniformed doorman with his top hat assisting taxi drivers with luggage. It was a city used to dealing with power. As the staff welcomed the couple, Shadrin demonstrated the confidence of a returning guest.[9]

Vienna, Ewa remembers, always seemed to cheer Nick after the long flight. He was comfortable in Vienna. After registering in the modest reception area, Ewa and Nick, with a bellman, crossed the lobby to the main elevator and took it to the third floor. Unlike most European hotels, the Bristol's hallways are brightly lit. The bellman led them off the elevator, passed the open staircase to the right, then turned right into the main hallway and right again into a dead-end hallway leading to their room, number 361. Room 361 was the last room on the Opera side of the Bristol, a corner room with a nice view. The window looked out on the imposing Opera House and down Kartner Street. From it, Ewa could watch the formally dressed couples go to the opera.

After washing away the grime of the trip, the Shadrins went downstairs for a snack and a drink. Nick seemed nervous about his 5:00 P.M. appointment. He had told Ewa that he was meeting with a Soviet man who had a long history of working for the United States. He said this was the same man he had met with on other trips. Nick advised Ewa that he would not be back in time for dinner. Ewa was not concerned that her husband—a Soviet defector—was meeting with another Soviet under mysterious circumstances overseas. She assumed it was just part of his job. After all, Nick worked for the Defense Department.

So when Nick walked out of the Bristol and the doorman hailed him a cab, Ewa Shadrin thought her husband was acting on instructions from his government. She went for a walk to enjoy the city's Christmas decorations.

Nick Shadrin's meeting place, an old cathedral called the Votivkirche, faces a beautiful square named after Sigmund Freud. The Votivkirche is several miles from the Bristol and really not on the usual tourist agenda, especially in a snowstorm.

The taxi ride to the Votivkirche took ten minutes through the evening traffic. Shadrin had been there several times before, as far back as 1958, when he stayed at the less luxurious Hotel Nagler. Shadrin crossed the street from the park where the cab dropped him, and walked to the low steps of the dark, immense Gothic-style cathedral. The snow had stopped earlier and the air seemed almost comfortable. Shadrin put his back to the bronze doors of the cathedral and looked out on the street from the little elevation the steps gave him. He watched vendors selling freshly cut Christmas trees in the park across the street. To the right were the buildings of the University; to the left, office and apartment buildings stretching for blocks around the far end of the park. The windows in the American Consulate building were dark.

About eight minutes after Shadrin arrived, a dark four-door sedan pulled up. The passenger in the front seat pushed his door ajar so that the light inside the car went on. He then lit a cigarette. Shadrin recognized Oleg Kozlov, his old Soviet handler from Washington. Shadrin walked down the steps and cautiously got into the back seat of the car. The sedan eased away from the curb and pulled out into the traffic of Vienna. Driving was Mikhail Ivanovich Kuryshev. Shadrin knew them both well. They did not call Shadrin by any of his adopted American names. He was addressed as Colonel—his new KGB rank—Artamonov, the name he had left behind sixteen years ago. The greetings in the car were warm and full of congratulations upon his promotion.[10]

If Nick behaved as instructed by Jim Wooten, he then asked the Soviets questions about his wife Elena and his now-twenty-four-year-old son. If the meeting went like earlier ones, the KGB men took turns assuring their prize agent that all was well with young Artamonov and his mother.

It is at this point that what Shadrin told Cynthia Hausmann later that evening differs greatly from what the Vienna police and other Western and Soviet intelligence sources say happened. What follows is based on still-classified Austrian Interior Ministry files and more

Nikolay Fedorovich Artamonov, as he was then, dancing with Ewa Gora in Gdynia, Poland, in 1958. (COURTESY OF MRS. EWA SHADRIN)

Nick and Ewa at party shortly befor
leaving Poland.

(COURTESY OF MRS. EWA SHADRI

Nick and Ewa at their church wed
in Baltimore. (COURTESY OF MRS. EWA SHAI

a Shadrin, her brother, and Nick Shadrin
the living room of their home in McLean,
rginia. The mounted head of a buck behind
ck was one of his hunting trophies.

(COURTESY OF MRS. EWA SHADRIN)

Nick and Ewa on vacation in
South America.

(COURTESY OF MRS. EWA SHADRIN)

ick Shadrin in disguise testify-
g before House Un-American
ctivities Committee in 1960.

(ASSOCIATED PRESS PHOTO)

Yekaterina Furtseva, the previously unknown key to the KITTY HAWK operation.

Oleg Sokolov.

Above: The Restaurant Winter, where Nick Shadrin had his final meal in the West. (JOSEPH TRENTO)

Left: The Hotel Bristol in Vienna. The Shadrins' room was located just above the *t* in the sign. (JOSEPH TRENTO)

it: A panoramic view of the s of the Votivkirche as seen the U.S. Consulate's offices in arby building. Today the view is ructed by a new building built e years after Shadrin vanished. (PHOTO BY RICHARD D. COPAKEN)

Ewa Shadrin with Nick Shadrin's gun and the shortwave radio he used during the KITTY HAWK operation. (COURTESY OF MRS. EWA SHADRIN)

The attic in Nick Shadrin's house where he kept the KGB's burst transmitter hidden. (JOSEPH TRENTO)

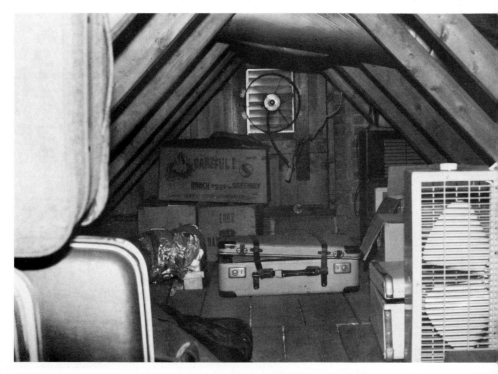

Ewa Shadrin, in Marseilles, France, holding an FBI surveillance photograph of Nick Shadrin meeting with a high-level KGB contact in Canada.

(PHOTO BY RICHARD D. COPAKEN)

Richard Copaken, Mrs. Shadrin's determined lawyer.

(COURTESY OF DEBORAH COPAKEN)

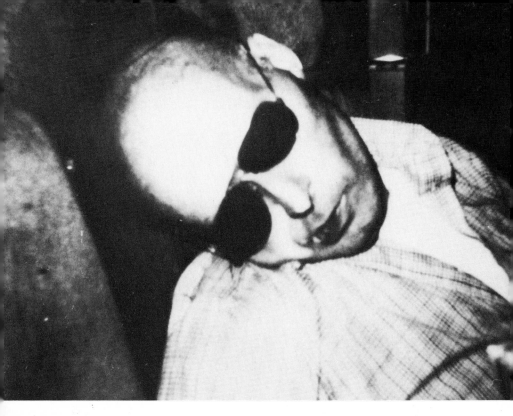

George Weisz as found dead in his car.
(MARYLAND STATE POLICE PHOTO)

George Weisz.
(COURTESY OF MRS. ETTA JO

than twelve years of additional material gathered not only from Western intelligence services like the Israeli Mossad, but also by Soviet sources on which the Austrian authorities rely. It is a shockingly different version of events from what has been previously reported in American and Soviet publications.

As Shadrin and his handlers drove around the near suburbs, they told him, as he had been told earlier, his long operation was over. It was time for him to go home. Ewa was financially prepared to be independent of him. The Soviets did not like loose ends. Shadrin knew his handlers were already aware that he never managed to make as much money in his work as she did in her dental practice.

Kuryshev informed Shadrin that for political reasons in the Soviet Union, the highly successful operation with Igor Kozlov had to be terminated. Kuryshev, as Shadrin later reported, excused himself from going to dinner. But, according to the Vienna authorities, he left not because he was afraid he might be recognized, as the FBI and CIA later speculated, but because arrangements had to be completed to get Shadrin to Russia. As always, Shadrin brought some more secrets with him to Vienna, and these had to be sent to Moscow Center. Kuryshev bid him a quick farewell and pulled the sedan over. Oleg Kozlov took the wheel. Oleg told Nick he was taking him to the best carp restaurant in Vienna.

A little before six-thirty, Ewa returned from her walk to her room at the Bristol. The phone rang. The woman to whom she had been introduced ten days earlier as Ann Martin was on the line. Miss Martin told Mrs. Shadrin that she was just a short distance away, at the Imperial Hotel, and that she would like to wait in the Shadrins' room for Nick to return from his business meeting. Though Mrs. Shadrin found Miss Martin anything but good company, she readily agreed. Half an hour later, she let the woman who called herself Ann Martin into her room.[11]

Cynthia Hausmann had phoned Ewa from the Imperial Hotel after seeing Bruce Solie. While Hausmann was staying at a CIA safe house, Solie found himself in residence at one of the fanciest and most expensive hotels in Vienna. Although Solie did not like the new crowd in CI, Hausmann made him especially uncomfortable. It was made clear to him that his job was merely to be available to talk to Igor Kozlov if he showed up. Nothing more. When Hausmann left to go see Ewa, Solie continued to sit in his hotel room, waiting for KITTY HAWK.[12]

Although Cynthia Hausmann and Ewa Shadrin spent the next three hours together, Hausmann would not warm up to Ewa. A tall, angular woman, Hausmann had been working for the CIA for years as a counterintelligence officer.[13] She had been assigned under Department of the Army cover to the U.S. Embassy in Mexico City in 1966.

In the opinion of Sam Wilson, Bruce Solie, and a score of top intelligence officials, Hausmann's activities on the evening of December 18 violated basic tradecraft for an intelligence officer. First, instead of calling from a safe telephone, she called Ewa from a hotel whose housekeeping staff, like the Bristol's, was not above making a few extra dollars selling information about guests.[14] Since Ann Martin's real identity was already known, her call to Mrs. Shadrin and her presence at the Bristol shortly thereafter immediately tied her to Shadrin's trip. If Shadrin was the brave double agent that the CIA and FBI claimed, Cynthia Hausmann's inexplicable actions that night would have put him and the operation in grave danger.

In the opinion of many intelligence professionals, the simple action of going to the Imperial to see Solie, and the more outrageous action of going to the Bristol to meet Nick and spending hours waiting with Ewa, could have compromised Solie and endangered KITTY HAWK as well as Shadrin.

After Ewa had managed to drag a little information out of Cynthia Hausmann, such as that she was not married and lived with her cat in the Georgetown section of Washington, she tried for more. Hausmann told Ewa that she had studied in Germany as a young woman. What she didn't tell Ewa was that she had operated one of the most difficult and unusual cases ever run in Germany. It is a case still secret to this day, and it helped make her reputation in the CIA.

It had taken more than half an hour for Oleg and Nick to reach the suburbs of Vienna. Nick had caught a glimpse of one street sign, and it seemed to him that they were out of town on the way to the airport. But they had not taken the Autobahn to get there. The car turned off onto a wooded driveway. A hundred meters in front of them was a restaurant right on a canal. Oleg explained to Nick that Nikita Khrushchev had been fond of the carp here. After going up a few steps and past the bar, the men were seated in the nearly empty restaurant at a table in the back.[15]

A round of Russian vodka was ordered, along with carp dinners for Nick and Oleg. After the first drink, Nick was toasted on his promotion to colonel and congratulated that his mission to America was over. Nick asked Oleg how he was going to get home. The KGB man's answer shocked Shadrin; he told him that a special escort had been brought to Vienna to accompany him home.

Nick pressed. He wanted to know who it was.

In Russian, Oleg Kozlov said, "Your son, of course."

The reason that Nick's son was brought to town was that the Soviets feared that Artamonov had been gone so long that possibly, out of apprehension, or love for Ewa, Nick might change his mind. The son was there to make certain he did not. For Nick, the first few years away from his wife and son had been the hardest. After 1966, with the appearance of Igor Kozlov, came the first news of his wife and son.[16] It was more than clear that his family was never treated like other defectors' families. On the contrary, their housing and lifestyle improved with his years of service. Ironically, after Shadrin officially agreed to become a Soviet agent, the treatment of Ewa's family also improved.[17] But to see the young man, who was even taller and better looking than Nick himself, would clearly remind Nick of home and the years they had missed together.

Years later, when the Carter administration undertook a President's Foreign Intelligence Advisory Board investigation of the Shadrin case, a former investigator for the Church Committee, Burton V. Weides, was permitted to go through all the cable traffic on the case.[18] To Weides's surprise, the cable traffic indicated that a young man fitting the description of Shadrin's son was indeed in Vienna at that time. Weides said the thrust of the cable was that "the young man's arrival was a surprise." Weides was instructed not to include any mention of the cable in his final-draft report to President Carter.

Oleg told Nick that he would have time off when he got home, and then he must think about what he wanted to do in the future. Of course there would be no more overseas assignments, to protect him from American retribution. All in all, it was a momentous evening for Nick.[19] As they ate and drank, Oleg Kozlov expertly debriefed Nick, fishing to see if the KGB's prize agent had in any way been turned against the motherland.

Kozlov asked Nick about his last contacts with top U.S. arms experts. He wanted to know what recruitment prospects Nick saw among them. In turn, Nick inquired about Igor Kozlov's situation. Oleg hesitated. He explained that the scandal over his mother-in-law's dacha had subsided after her death, and that Igor's KGB role seemed to guarantee no retribution against the family. Besides, Andropov and Igor's father-in-law were the best of friends. After all, they shared the blood of Hungary and Czechoslovakia on their hands.

Oleg Kozlov instructed Nick to rent a car and familiarize himself with the streets of Vienna. Nick explained that he had purchased a good map of the city in Washington and had studied it. Kozlov expressed concern that surveillance from the local CIA station might cause problems when they met again on Saturday. Nick understood his anxiety. They agreed to a 7:00 P.M. meeting time, again on the steps of the Votivkirche, two days later.[20]

Nick and Kozlov drank to the end of one of the most successful missions in KGB history. Artamonov had behaved with great courage and resourcefulness for Mother Russia. His personal sacrifices had been immense. Oleg then explained the cover story for Nick's disappearance from Vienna. The Soviets, Kozlov said, would simply deny any knowledge. It would be implied that Nick had attempted to come home, but that the CIA had somehow stopped him. Kozlov advised that Shadrin would have to live a quiet life in the Soviet Union, but that his operational experience in America would be invaluable to the training of future agents. Passing an envelope to Nick, Kozlov advised him that if something went wrong Saturday night, Nick might need this money until the KGB could get to him. In the envelope was $1,000 in cash.

Kozlov said that if the Americans were on to Nick, there was more than an even chance that they would attempt to kill him before he could make the meeting. Shadrin laughed and replied that he did not think that was even a remote problem. He took the envelope and put it in his inside coat pocket. Kozlov dropped Shadrin at the Stuben Ring, where he got a taxi to return to the Bristol.

At 10:00 P.M., just as Cynthia Hausmann's continued presence was making Ewa almost intolerably uneasy, Nick walked in the room. At six foot two, he was only two inches taller than Hausmann. He told Hausmann that the meeting had gone very well. He said nothing specific that Ewa remembers, except that he raved about a fish restaurant he went to outside of town. He remarked that the restaurant was nothing very fancy, but after three double vodkas with his Soviet companion, the carp tasted exceptional. Mrs. Shadrin recalls that at this point Hausmann pulled out a pad and pen and motioned for Nick to go into the bathroom. No explanation was given to Ewa. It was all very strange. Ewa could hear their conversation for fifteen minutes coming from the bathroom.

Nick admired Jim Wooten, but his male chauvinistic, "Imperial Russian" personality made him regard being debriefed by a woman as demeaning and merely another manifestation of a flawed and inept American intelligence system. Shadrin did not tell Hausmann much except that in addition to his promotion to full colonel in the KGB, his request for a pardon had been considered and granted for his "unauthorized leave" in 1959.[21] Then, unexpectedly, he told Hausmann that the Russians wanted to meet him again on Saturday evening. He thought there was a possibility that KITTY HAWK might be at the Saturday meeting.[22]

After Nick and Cynthia emerged from the bathroom, Nick helped her with her coat. She pulled a street map of Vienna out of her purse and gave Shadrin instructions on how to meet her at a safe house where she was staying. She told him that she wanted to meet him on Sunday, the day after the second meeting. The Shadrins, scheduled to go on to Zurs, Austria, later on Sunday for a week of skiing, set the meeting with Hausmann for Sunday afternoon. Nick was given the telephone number at the house where she was staying. As she said good night and turned toward the main hallway, Nick told Ewa that he had withheld some information from Hausmann. He confided in Ewa that he would wait until he returned to Washington to tell Jim Wooten what the Russian had told him that night.

Ewa thought Nick's delight at the success of his meeting meant that he was finally going to get his security clearance, and his miserable job in the Defense Intelligence Agency would be over. She had no clue that anything was amiss.

On Friday, December 19, after breakfast, around 11:00 A.M., Nick stopped off at the front desk of the Bristol and asked the concierge to obtain a pair of tickets for a performance of a Strauss operetta that evening, and he also bought a single ticket for Ewa for Saturday night's performance of *The Gypsy Baron*. Ewa joined Nick and they left the Bristol and walked around the corner to the Hotel Sacher, behind the Vienna Opera House. Here they purchased several Sachertorte to be sent as gifts back to friends in the United States. The expensive cakes were a combination of chocolate and apricot and came packed in small wooden boxes.[23]

After buying cakes and shopping for clothes, the Shadrins went out for an early dinner and attended the operetta. It was during the performance that Ewa noticed that Nick seemed uninterested in Strauss and was fidgeting. They left the Opera House and returned to the bar at the Bristol. Nick ordered Martel cognac and Ewa had coffee. Nick, acting almost impish, pulled an envelope out of his blazer pocket. The envelope, he said, contained a thousand dollars. He explained that it was money the U.S. government had given him for the Soviet, but that the Soviet had refused the funds. He told Ewa that he would try to give it to him again during Saturday's meeting.[24]

Nick ordered a second cognac and Ewa drank another cup of coffee. Although their discussion turned to music and their skiing vacation, she sensed that something was not right. When they got back to their room, Nick took a Valium to help him rest. He explained to Ewa that he was taking the tranquilizer to make certain he got as much rest as possible for Saturday's meeting.

After rising late on Saturday morning, Nick went out to buy a new shirt and tie. Ewa said this was part of the Russian custom of buying something for New Year's. When they got back, a rental car was waiting for them in front of the hotel. Nick said he wanted to take Ewa to the fish restaurant where he and the Soviet had eaten on Thursday evening, but since he could not remember the name, they would have to search for it. This behavior seemed odd because at the time there were only two such restaurants on the Danube canal, and the concierge could have told him where to go. But Nick never asked. They drove around Vienna, but the search was futile.

The Vienna police speculated that Shadrin was driving around the Vienna Woods, trying to get acquainted with that part of town, and was merely using the restaurant as an excuse. Nick did tell Ewa that Premier Khrushchev had been a customer in the restaurant. Because of the nature of their relationship, she never thought to question his not asking for directions. Finally the couple gave up and returned to the Bristol. It was after 3:00 P.M. and the main dining room was closed. Instead of feasting on carp, the Shadrins ate pickled herring and drank vodka at the Bristol bar. The police report shows that Shadrin put only twenty-two miles on the rental car before coming back that afternoon.[25]

Ewa noticed that Nick became more and more tense as the time for the meeting grew closer. He told her the meeting site would again be the Votivkirche. He showered and dressed for the evening. He wore a new Pierre Cardin blue blazer and a gray turtleneck sweater.[26] He took the cash he had gotten two nights before with him and gave Ewa a piece of paper with Cynthia Hausmann's local telephone number on it. On the back of the paper was the notation in Shadrin's handwriting, "Ann stays with Grimm." He reminded Ewa to call these numbers if he did not return. To lighten the mood, he told her that if he finished early he would meet her outside the Opera House and they would go for a late dinner. At about 6:20 P.M. he left for his 7:00 P.M. meeting with the Russians. Ewa Shadrin would never see her husband again.

The doorman at the Bristol remembered Nick patting his jacket pockets as if he had forgotten something.[27] Nick had forgotten his reading glasses. The doorman nodded at Nick, a cab pulled up in front of the hotel, and the doorman opened the cab door for him. There is no way of knowing if Shadrin felt elation that his mission was nearly over, or sorrow over what he had done to Ewa and, to a lesser extent, scores of others.

This time the taxi ride to the Votivkirche took only seven minutes. Nick climbed from the cab, paid the driver, walked to the top step, and waited. He again patted his pockets. Now he realized that he had forgotten his hypertension pills. A cab stopped in front of the Votivkirche. The passenger in the back seat waved and slid over. Nick walked toward the cab. Oleg Kozlov greeted Nick and instructed the driver to go to the West Bahnhof train station. The station restaurant provided quick service, but barely edible food by European standards. Nick was handed keys to a small car parked in the station lot, and an address near the Vienna Woods. He was told that he would spend the night at the safe house and that on Sunday afternoon he was to drive himself out to the Restaurant Winter, the same carp restaurant on the Danube canal, where arrangements would be made for his trip home.

For security reasons, there would be no more KGB contacts until Shadrin appeared in the parking lot of the Restaurant Winter.[28]

At 6:45 P.M., Ewa left for the performance of *The Gypsy Baron*. The performance lasted until 9:34 P.M. When Ewa came out of the Vienna Opera House, there was no sign of Nick. She really had not expected him to be there. In 1972, Nick had been gone for the entire night, and she had the feeling that his meeting would run late.

Back in the room, Ewa relaxed and read her program. Although hungry, she did not eat. She was hoping that Nick still might make it back in time for dinner. By 11:00 P.M. she gave up the idea of dinner and decided to get ready for bed. By 12:30 A.M. all the inconsistencies in Nick's behavior, combined with the odd visit from Cynthia Hausmann, began to churn inside Ewa. Worry was now overcoming her confidence in Nick's ability to handle any situation. She kept telling herself that he had done this sort of thing before. She thought back to that night on the Baltic when her lover, Captain Nikolay Artamonov, had engineered a fishing trip in a small boat that concluded with their defection to the West in Sweden. He had done dangerous things before. He would get through this.

It took Nick nearly an hour to find the KGB safe house. The apartment building was in one of the wealthier suburbs of Vienna. As instructed, he used the key to open the automatic garage door and park the car in the building. It was nearly 9:30 P.M. When he reached the second-floor entrance, he fumbled with the lock and let himself in. The plainly furnished entry hall offered a view of a small bedroom. Shadrin had to walk around the corner before he saw at a kitchen table a handsome young man dressed in a white shirt and tie, standing up to greet his father.[29]

Cynthia Hausmann gave little thought to the Shadrin meeting that evening. She met her old acquaintance from Munich, Stan Jeffers, and he drove her from the embassy to his home in the late afternoon for a night of dinner and drinks with him and his wife. "It was just a normal Saturday-night get-together for a friend from out of town," Jeffers said. Everyone had a fair amount to drink, but Jeffers insists that he was not too drunk to drive. He says they spent a pleasant evening recalling their Munich days and trading terrible stories about George Weisz, a man neither of them liked. According to Jeffers, at a little before midnight Cynthia said her good-byes and he drove her to the safe house he had arranged for her as part of his job. It was only a fifteen-minute drive. He estimates that she was in the safe house by 12:15 A.M., perhaps 12:20 at the latest.

At 1:35 A.M., Ewa's inner reserves began to collapse. She dreaded calling Cynthia Hausmann, but she had to know what was going on. She picked up the old-fashioned telephone, requested an outside line, and dialed the night number Nick had left on the piece of paper. After letting the phone ring more than a dozen times, she hung up, having never felt more alone in her life. At 1:55 A.M., she repeated the process. This time Hausmann answered the phone. The first greeting Hausmann gave Ewa was a question: "Have you tried to call this number before?" Ewa said she had tried before, but there was no answer. Hausmann explained that she had just returned from dinner with friends.

Where Hausmann was for the missing hour to forty-five minutes is still under dispute. Hausmann told investigators that Mrs. Shadrin had the time wrong, but Jeffers recalls the time precisely. Leonard V. McCoy, Cynthia's boss, said Jeffers got her home late because he had had too much to drink "and poor Cynthia was trapped." Jeffers categorically denies this. McCoy insists that "that time discrepancy is not in any way Cynthia's fault . . . she was absolutely a prisoner at his house."[30]

Upset, Ewa advised Hausmann that Nick had not yet returned, and she was very worried. Hausmann reassured her that it was not yet too late. She reminded Ewa that Nick had returned late on Thursday. However, Hausmann's words were not comforting when she told Ewa to bolt her room door and make certain to open it for no one except Nick.

At around 5:00 A.M., Hausmann notified Charles Malton that Shadrin was missing.[31] Malton told her that "she had to notify Langley immediately." She said no, she would wait. Hausmann explained that Shadrin sometimes got drunk with the Russians and may have simply made a late night of it. After a night of tears, Ewa called Hausmann at 5:30 A.M. to tell her that Nick had still not returned. With great confidence, according to Mrs. Shadrin, Hausmann told her that there was nothing to worry about, that she would cable Washington. Again, Hausmann warned Ewa to keep the door bolted and let in only Nick.

As Ewa had done throughout the night, she listened impatiently for Nick in the hallway, but none of the footsteps reached room 361. It was now past 7:00 A.M. Already the bells at the Augustinerkirche had sounded, but they held no joy for Ewa. The joy the city had brought her had evaporated. Finally there was a knock at the door. Ewa was sure it was Nick.

She composed herself before opening the door. But her last hope of the night was gone when she saw Cynthia Hausmann standing there, towering over her. Still the voice of confidence, Hausmann said that while she expected Nick back "anytime," she had asked officials at the American Embassy to check with the police and hospitals to make certain there had been no accident.

Trying to be helpful, Ewa suggested that they get in touch with the

Russian man Nick had said he would be meeting with. She told Hausmann that, according to Nick, this man had been working for the United States for a quarter of a century.

Coolly, Cynthia Hausmann informed Ewa that they had no way of getting in touch with the man Nick was meeting with. Ewa blurted out something to the effect of, "How can you not know who Nick was meeting with, if he worked for the U.S. government?" For the first time, in the cold light of that awful morning, as she watched people walking by outside the window, past the Opera House on their way to church, Ewa Shadrin began to understand that Nick had not told her everything.

Ewa watched Hausmann make phone calls while they waited for Nick. As each minute passed, Ewa became a little more convinced that he was gone forever. Ewa answered the phone again and again, but on the other end a voice always asked for "Ms. Martin." She would hand her the phone. At 10:00 A.M. Sunday, when Malton learned from Hausmann that there was still no sign of Shadrin, he cabled the CIA on closed channels. Nearly half a day had gone by before Washington was told that their prize agent was missing. Meanwhile, Bruce Solie, one of the CIA's top security men, sat in his room and waited for word about KITTY HAWK. He was not even told that Nick Shadrin was gone.

As Ewa Shadrin's despair grew and Cynthia Hausmann waited in room 361, a hotel maid was dusting in front of the elevator around the corner from the room. When the doors opened, Nick Shadrin smiled at her and asked if Room 361 was occupied. The maid said it was, and it had not been cleaned. She went about her business, and the man left.[32]

Shadrin left the Bristol, climbed into a car, and drove on to Mahlerstrasse and back to the Ring Road for the ride out to the Winter Canal. This time Shadrin drove on the Autobahn and exited at Neualbein. After a false start, he found the entrance to the Restaurant Winter parking lot. As instructed, he parked the car under a large oak tree and waited. The parking lot was deserted.[33]

When Nick saw Oleg Alekseyevich Kozlov and Mikhail Kuryshev, he stepped out of the car and locked it. Shadrin got in the back seat of their sedan, promptly handed Kozlov the keys to the car and the safe house, and thanked them for the reunion. Kuryshev handed Shadrin an official KGB passport and identification cards in the name of Nikolay Fedorovich Artamonov. He also gave Shadrin specific instructions on his cruise down the Danube to Bulgaria. The drive to the barge pier took less than fifteen minutes. The Danube was not yet frozen, and Shadrin boarded the barge for its slow sail on the Danube, making an early-winter voyage toward Hungary.[34]

With each passing minute, Ewa was growing to hate Cynthia Hausmann. Finally, at dinnertime, Hausmann disclosed that she herself could not continue to stay where she was staying, because if Nick had been kidnapped by the Soviets, there was a chance that he could have given up that information. She said she would stay with the Jefferses, where she had had dinner the previous evening.

Hausmann finally notified Bruce Solie that Shadrin had disappeared. "I was pretty angry," Solie said. "I guess you could say I was set up." [35]

On Monday the torture continued. Hausmann did not join Ewa until late in the afternoon. She had no positive news to report. Ewa, now at the end of her emotional tether, no longer could control herself in front of Hausmann. She recalls what she considered Hausmann's one clumsy attempt to comfort her after Nick disappeared. She said to Ewa, "Don't worry, you will get used to it." Ewa was shocked out of her tears. This seemingly cold and remote woman could not muster enough human warmth, in Ewa's view, to show any real concern.

In the opinion of many intelligence officers interviewed for this book, Hausmann was operationally unsuited to work with a man of Shadrin's particular temperament, and worse yet, she had been blown. In the end, the assignment of Hausmann to this case was contrary to her own professional well-being and would shadow the remaining years of her career. Someone handling an agent like Shadrin in the precarious environment of Vienna needs to be able to project warmth and confidence in order to control the agent effectively.

On Tuesday morning, Cynthia Hausmann instructed Ewa by phone to go to the Pan Am ticket office and book passage for herself on the next flight to Washington. She was to connect through Frankfurt. Ewa hung up the phone, shaking her head. She remembered when she and Nick had been brought to Westport, the defector reception center in Frankfurt. She recalled the big old house with mixed emotions. Although their every need was met and they were waited on constantly, Nick was in a constant state of agitation because of the polygraph examinations that he kept having trouble with. Why Frankfurt, why conjure up more of the sadness? Would Hausmann never stop?

It did Ewa good to get out to go pick up her ticket. But when she returned to the hotel, she found Hausmann there waiting for her. After asking several questions about Nick, saying the information was for the embassy, Hausmann asked Ewa for Nick's passport. Reluctantly, Ewa turned over the passport. All Ewa could think of was how hard it had been for Nick to get that passport and United States citizenship. She remembered Nick warning her that after their defection, the U.S. government would use the threat of statelessness like an iron fist over them.

Now all she had of her Nick were his new, unworn shirt and tie, his clothes from home, his reading glasses, and his hypertension medicine. Hausmann advised Ewa that a government official had been dispatched to Vienna to escort her home, since it seemed there was no possibility that Nick was still in Vienna. She left Ewa alone to pack, and returned at 12:30 P.M. with a car driven by Stan Jeffers. They drove up the Ring to the Imperial Hotel, where they picked up Bruce Solie. Solie climbed into the front seat for the ride to the airport. Ewa remembers Hausmann telling her during the drive to pretend she did not know Bruce until they cleared customs in Frankfurt.

To Ewa, Solie seemed incompetent, bland, and without feeling. He was the quintessential government bureaucrat—the type that she remembered Nick describing with contempt. Of course, she had no way of knowing that Bruce had been kept in the dark for almost a full day after Nick disappeared, and felt the same way about Cynthia Hausmann that Ewa did. Ewa and Bruce spent the night at a hotel near the airport in Frankfurt. Although they dined together, there was little conversation. The next morning they flew to London, where they changed planes for a flight to Dulles International Airport, in the suburbs of Washington.

It was a gray Christmas Eve when the big mobile lounge brought Bruce Solie and Ewa Shadrin to airport customs. Amid the joy of visitors arriving to spend Christmas with their friends and families, this grim couple disembarked and passed quietly through the required checkpoints to a car waiting for them in front. Ahead for Ewa would be con men, lies, huge legal expenses, the discovery that her husband was a double agent, and the nightmare of never knowing what had really happened to him. That Christmas, for her, was the first of many of not being sure if Nick Shadrin was alive or dead.

Shadrin Epilogue: The Theory of the Admirals' Plot

I don't think Shadrin—even if he was recruited the day before he got on the boat to go to Sweden—could have done half the damage by what he collected than we did to ourselves [by] how we used him.

James E. Nolan, Jr.

THE FOLLOWING THEORY, supported largely by a series of intercepts by Western intelligence agencies in Europe, is one explanation of how Captain Nikolay Fedorovich Artamonov came to America. It is not as romantic a story as that of two, wide-eyed young lovers meeting on a quay along the Baltic Sea. According to this theory, the Nick Shadrin story began much earlier than that. Based on analysis of the intercepts, the Shadrin story started without even the knowledge, awareness, or personal participation of the forceful and handsome young Captain Artamonov.

In 1956, these Western European intelligence organizations only shared a limited amount of material with the United States' still very young and very inexperienced Central Intelligence Agency. But, according to these sources, the story of Captain Artamonov began that year, when they began to pick up bizarre message traffic from a meeting of Soviet admirals. The pattern of the traffic indicated that the admirals, speaking in coded messages, were attempting to keep the topic of their conversation secret from the rest of the Soviet government. At first, when evaluating the strange communications, the Western intelligence organizations suspected some sort of military coup. But since the message traffic revealed nothing threatening to the West, the specialists turned their electronic ears to more pressing matters. The bizarre message traffic was sorted and placed in a file called "The Admirals' Plot."

According to a later analysis of this message traffic, the scenario of how Artamonov came to defect to the West began in the minds of several Soviet Navy admirals who had a plan to make the Soviet Union one of the greatest sea powers in the world. Part of the plan was audacious. The admirals decided to send a Soviet Navy man to America to help carry out their strategy for a Soviet blue-water navy. His role was to pose as a defector and try to take up the extremely complex role of an "agent of influence."

The electronic evidence indicates that the plan originated at a meeting at Soviet Baltic Fleet headquarters near Leningrad in November 1956, following the British and French disaster at Suez, when, with the Israelis, those countries invaded Egypt after Nasser nationalized the Suez Canal. The meeting was called by Adm. N. G. Kuznetsov. It was attended by Rear Adm. Boris Dmitriyevich Yashin, Vice Adm. Vasily Danilovich Yakovlev, and Adm. Vasily Maximovich Grishanov.[1] At the time, their leader, Adm. Sergei Gorshkov, was in bed, seriously ill. The purpose of the meeting was, even by Soviet standards, conspiratorial. It involved settling upon a plan to ensure the development of a great Soviet Navy.

Suez opened a window of opportunity for the Soviet Navy to play an important role in the expansion of Soviet influence in the Middle and Far East. But first there was one large, very critical problem that needed to be addressed—namely, a navy worth the title. To create such a navy, Admirals Kuznetsov, Yashin, Yakovlev, and Grishanov had to execute a carefully conceived "plot" in the corridors of Kremlin power. This "plot" of the Soviet admirals, not unlike power grabs in the U.S. military, was designed to gain acceptance among key members of the political and military hierarchy of the necessity and desirability for a blue-water Soviet Navy. To this end, the admirals knew that the simple logic of this idea would be insufficient to carry the day in the Politburo and the Main Military Council.

The history of the Soviet Navy, and its Tsarist predecessor, is long on tradition and short on substance or performance.[2] Prior to World War II it was largely a ceremonial force used to provide coastal security at Soviet ports. Its officer corps was generally politically neutral

—or seemingly neutral, a condition that spared them most of the wrath and the purges of the military ordered by Joseph Stalin in the late 1930s. Unlike the Red Army and, to a lesser degree, the Red Air Force, the Soviet Navy came out of World War II with not much in the way of a military reputation. This rankled many of the Soviet admirals, who were eager to be in the forefront of the task of spreading Soviet influence beyond the littoral land mass of the USSR and the Eastern Bloc states brought under Soviet control at the end of the war.

The year 1956 was much like 1988 for the Soviets and their putative leader. Calling for reform and blasting the past, there was the overpowering presence of First Secretary Nikita Sergeyevich Khrushchev. At the Twentieth Party Congress, in February 1956, Khrushchev delivered a major speech that denounced the excesses of Stalin, and conveniently did not hold the Communist Party and its *apparat* responsible for those excesses. The new open leadership still would not tolerate independence. The Poznań riots in Poland were effectively ended in the brief period of seventy-two hours by Polish forces operating in conjunction with Soviet KGB security forces. More significantly, the Red Army was employed in a totally ruthless fashion to put down the Hungarian uprising. This latter operation, carried out in concert with KGB units under the direction of then USSR Ambassador to Hungary, Yuri Andropov, clearly established Khrushchev as Stalin's successor. But Khrushchev was dependent upon the continued support of the Red Army and the KGB.[3]

In contrast to the Soviets' effective crushing of the Hungarian revolution and Khrushchev's consolidation of power during 1956 was the British and French military and diplomatic debacle at Suez. This climactic event changed the balance of power in the Middle East and created a window of opportunity for the Soviet Union that has bedeviled the West, especially the United States, to the present day.[4]

The admirals took their proposal to the new head of the Soviet Navy, Admiral Sergei G. Gorshkov. They had reason to be optimistic. Admiral Gorshkov was reported to have said, in emphasizing the peacetime role of navies, "It is a political force at sea which continues to have paramount importance as an instrument of policy of great powers."[5] He agreed that the Soviets had a chance to build a navy rivaling that of the United States, and that the British-French debacle at Suez had opened the political door to sell it at home. This decision would have an enormous impact on Gorshkov's personal life.

The meeting in Leningrad in November 1956 and the later backing of Admiral Gorshkov set in motion the search for a strategy to gain acceptance and support within the Kremlin for a blue-water navy, and for a Soviet naval officer who could be "sent" to the West to take up the complex role of an "agent of influence" to promote that strategy overseas. Such an agent would be necessary to understand America's defense against a growing Soviet Navy and to learn as much as possible about the U.S. Navy and its ships and weapon systems. The admirals understood all too well that their country lacked the technical capability to incorporate the latest available technology into their fleet. The sent agent could assist them with that. But, more important, if handled properly, he could learn what the leaders of the American Navy were planning that would help the Soviets determine what kind of navy to build. Having an agent at the elbow of one's enemy was, for the admirals, a shortcut to success.

In early 1958, Western intelligence services picked up reports that there was a search under way in the Soviet Union for a Soviet naval officer, or one from the GRU, to undertake a special mission in the West. The NATO allies could not agree on the meaning of the recruitment and could not get enough corroborating intelligence to determine the purpose of the mission. As time passed, the phantom agent never appeared again on Western intelligence "radars," and the earlier reports were filed away as spurious. One reason senior intelligence experts so easily discounted the reports was that exaggerations about the expansion of the Soviet Navy had been heard before. Earlier warnings had circulated of a massive increase in the size of the Soviet Navy. This most recent allegation was filed away with the earlier ones.

The decision to "send" an agent is one of the most complex in the business of intelligence and counterintelligence. It is never taken lightly because of the danger of exposure and the necessity to select extremely talented personnel to carry out such a difficult mission. No intelligence service has an excess of people who are capable of being sent to another country to take up one or more of the varied roles of "sleeper," "provocateur," or "agent of influence."

The Russians are the admitted masters in the technique of sending an agent into another country to take up one of these roles. The term used to describe this activity is "the trust." To the Soviets it means the dispatching of an agent into the enemy's camp with the mission of gaining the trust of the persons who are in charge. The Russians have developed and cultivated the trust techniques over several centuries. But the refinement of the use of the trust tactic generally coincided with the emergence of the Revolution's protector, Felix Dzerzhinsky. Dzerzhinsky established, in December 1917, the All-Russian Extraordinary Commission for Combating Counter-Revolution and Sabotage, known as the Cheka, the forerunner of the KGB.[6]

One fact that the Soviets understand and exploit is that the West will bend over backwards to accept those who have fled communism.[7] This does not mean that there have not been genuine defectors from the Soviet Union. But by sending agents to nations with "open door" policies, the Soviets can use the existing communities of emigrés as sources for intelligence. Emigrés are often hired as translators, and some gain acceptance at the periphery of the intelligence community. This acceptance puts the sent agents closer to their targets. If the Soviets send an agent with rarer skills or access to secrets, he is placed under greater scrutiny. But if he can get past the counterintelligence experts, the potential for success is enormous. That was the bet the admirals were making.

The admirals knew all too well the West's inability to conduct effective screening and related counterintelligence activities. The Soviet Union's KGB and GRU had exploited for years this essential element in their efforts to send agents into Western camps. But this time the admirals had to keep their plan secret from the KGB. They feared that the KGB leadership would recognize the plan for what it was—a power play. Instead the admirals had to use whatever resources they could acquire from military intelligence. They wanted one of their own men to become the sent agent.

The success of the sent-agent mission depended upon getting U.S. intelligence officials to stake their reputations on the bona fides of the sent agent, who would be posing as a defector. Once that commitment was secured, the admirals knew that, as with bureaucrats everywhere, these officials' careers would be in jeopardy if they changed their minds about that defector's legitimacy.

The admirals wanted their agent to be much more than a spy. He was to be a salesman. Armed with information, he was to confirm just how small the Soviet Navy really was. He was to sell the idea that, while the Soviet Navy was growing, it was not threatening U.S. interests. His role was to buy time for the Soviets to build their navy. He was to learn all he could about the new U.S. ballistic missile-launching submarine capability, a technology that baffled the Soviets, but one they viewed as necessary to their national survival. But the agent's most important task was to learn about key personalities of the naval establishment in America and to influence them as instructed.

Based on the intelligence available to the Soviet admirals about the United States and the gullibility of its officials, they had confidence in their strategy. However, its successful execution depended on finding the right person. To make their plan work, the admirals needed a credible "salesman." According to officials from other Allied intelligence organizations, four, or possibly five, Soviet naval officers were interviewed and considered by the admirals who acted as a "selection board" for the assignment.

There is much more involved in the selection of a sent agent than a simple call to the KGB's "central casting" department, or to its "charm school," located at Bykovo, outside Moscow, which trains potential illegals.[8] The kind of man the Soviet admirals were looking for had to have several key characteristics. First, the individual had to be credible as a naval officer. There could be some "legendary" enhancement of the individual's naval career, but the basic facts of his naval background had to stand up to examination. This meant that he had to have the capability to command a ship. In addition, in terms of rank, the individual had to be high enough up the promotion ladder to be credible, but not too high, because of the difficulty in creating the "legend" used to justify the individual's decision to defect. The agent's decision to defect had to seem credible to the U.S. Navy, the Pentagon, and the CIA.

Two of the five potential candidates had to be eliminated because they could not stand up to basic scrutiny. This left three on the Soviet admirals' "short list": Nikolay F. Artamonov, Lev A. Vtorygin, and Yuri A. Yakovlev.[9] Each of these men met the criteria the admirals had set for the sent-agent assignment, but Artamonov's demeanor and self-confidence won the day. The admirals picked Artamonov to be the Soviet Navy's sent agent.

Artamonov had some basic characteristics that sold him to the admirals. He had the capacity to manipulate others without any real regard for their feelings. He could betray a trust and feel no remorse or empathy for the victims. He would be trained to tell the most cold-hearted lies. He was self-sufficient, a characteristic which was vital for an agent who must overcome the depression caused by loneliness.

To make Artamonov acceptable to the West, a legend that could stand up to scrutiny had to be prepared. The Soviets had been creating such legends for more than seven decades.[10] The KGB is quite aware that a sent agent cannot masquerade as a brain surgeon for the obvious reason that he may be called upon to operate on someone. Rather, the deception must be within the competence of the person selected.

How long could the sent agent stay out in the cold? In the Shadrin case, the cabal of admirals, operating under the aegis of the GRU, planned on a three-to-five-year mission.[11]

Artamonov had already passed several tests with flying colors.[12] The first occurred in 1956, long before the admirals knew Artamonov would be their man. Artamonov was one of the young naval officers aboard the Soviet cruiser *Ordzhonikidze*, which docked at Portsmouth, carrying Khrushchev and Bulganin to an April 1956 visit to England. The *Ordzhonikidze* was the symbol of the Soviets' new Navy, and was faster than similar Western ships. The year before, in a Soviet port, the British had attempted to determine the reason for the ship's speed. But attempts to send in a miniature submarine failed. In Portsmouth, MI6 decided to use a diver to inspect the screws of the ship to see if their design had something to do with its unexpected speed. Unfortunately for the diver, Comdr. Lionel "Buster" Crabb, the mission ended with his headless body emerging from the bay. For the British, it turned into a full-blown embarrassment.[13] But for Artamonov, it was a chance to see the other side at work. The West "had almost nothing on the Soviet Navy at that time," Leonard V. McCoy, then a Soviet reports officer for the CIA, confirms. The *Ordzhonikidze* incident convinced the admirals that the West was so hungry for naval intelligence that acceptance of a sent agent would be possible.

To turn a Soviet naval officer into a sent agent takes very special training. Artamonov was not sent to the KGB's Bykovo school, which trains Soviet illegals. Nor was he sent to one of its specialized schools that train assassins and assassin controllers as well as terrorists and terrorist controllers. Nor was he sent to the GRU's Diplomatic Military Academy. Artamonov received a specially tailored "tutorial" that prepared him for a specific mission.

Artamonov's mission was far too important to leave to training in standard tradecraft, nor could the admirals risk discovery by the KGB. Artamonov, as his performance in the United States later proved, was an extremely quick study. His background, experience, and prior formal training as a naval officer enabled him to grasp easily the details of the Soviet blue-water navy envisioned by the admirals. Their dreams and plans were planted in his mind. It would be this information that the Americans would find most valuable, and it would prove Artamonov's worth over years of inquisitions. If he was to get something from the Americans, he had to give something in return, and the admirals would give him all he needed to impress them. For those who knew Artamonov after he came to the United States, his grasp of these issues was almost uncanny. During the five years he was "under contract" as a consultant to the Office of Naval Intelligence, Artamonov displayed an almost prescient knowledge about a Soviet Navy that was yet to be built.[14] As his predictions came to pass, Artamonov's reputation soared to an almost unbelievable degree in the minds of senior U.S. naval officers, thus justifying the extraordinary training he was put through prior to his leaving the Soviet Union.

Artamonov was also a very apt pupil in the study of personalities. This phase of his training was extremely important because it gave him access to everything known to the KGB and GRU about the senior U.S. officials he was targeted to influence.[15] Correspondingly, he reviewed the personnel files of key individuals in the Soviet Navy, with special emphasis on the "comers" who had been identified by the admirals as its leaders of the future. These personnel, who were destined for the fast track in the GRU, had to be identified for Artamonov. The point being, of course, that, according to his legend, Artamonov was himself one of these fast-track personnel, so he had to know his own peers. This information would enhance his reputation as a "genius" with many U.S. naval officials when he accurately predicted, time and again, who would emerge as the Soviet Navy's new leaders.

When this phase of Artamonov's tutorial was completed, the admirals were still not certain that he was the right man for the assignment. He had mastered all the information he had been furnished or required to study, but the question about his emotional stability in a prolonged sent-agent environment was still a matter of concern. Artamonov's motivation was not at issue; he was eager to embark on the mission, and confident of his ability to sell the admirals' message to the United States. But first Artamonov had to be tested. He must be sent on a mission to the West, more or less as a dress rehearsal in the field, to test his acting ability and see how he "played" outside the Soviet Navy.

A simple two-week assignment was created, under his true name, but a different identity. Artamonov would assume the identity of a nuclear engineer, an older civilian, traveling to Vienna to the International Atomic Energy Agency, the IAEA. If Artamonov passed his test there, he could be readied for the next phase of training. The key point of this test was to see if Shadrin could fool the rather large KGB contingent in Vienna.

The IAEA is one of the most penetrated international organizations in the world. It would be a good test to see how Artamonov behaved in a civilian setting, with people scrutinizing him closely. On March 18, 1958, Artamonov was sent to Vienna. His acting fooled everyone —including the KGB. Artamonov registered at the Hotel Nagler under an International Atomic Energy Commission passport issued to Nikolay Fedorovich Artamonov. He was posing as a man a decade older than he was. His passport, phony birthdate, and real name all went into the strict Austrian immigration service records. Eighteen years later the United States would learn that the passport Artamonov had used back then in Vienna was not a real IAEA passport.[16]

Not long after Shadrin's return from Vienna, he left on his voyage to Poland and then, later, Sweden. But once in the United States, how did Artamonov stay in touch with the Soviets? How did he get his orders? The answer is interesting. It involves a man who was the Soviet assistant naval attaché in Washington when Shadrin worked at ONI—a man who was on the admirals' short list for the sent-agent assignment.

Because Shadrin was *the* authority on Soviet naval matters when he worked at ONI, he was consistently consulted by the more action-oriented members and by Admiral Taylor, who believed that the evaluation of intelligence should be done on a timely basis rather than turned into a scholarly exercise that never produced a conclusion.

However, for Shadrin to continue to succeed in the role of an intelligence expediter and be an integral part of the intelligence-evaluation process, he had to come up with inside information that gave meaning beyond the facts shown in the acquired documents and "agent" reports.

In 1961, Nick reported to the CIA that he had spotted his former colleague in the Soviet Navy, Lev Vtorygin, on a street in Washington. That sighting set off some alarm bells in CIA counterintelligence. Was Vtorygin, the best shot in the Soviet Navy, here to assassinate Shadrin?[17] Or had Shadrin reported the meeting to cover up being seen with Vtorygin? The answers lie in the method of communications the admirals used to provide Shadrin with the materials he needed, and to receive his reports and information.

The location of Shadrin's ONI employment and the lack of surveillance on his movements held the key to the admirals' access to their agent of influence. The rear-gate entrance to the Naval Observatory, the one used by Shadrin and others in ONI, can be reached from Wisconsin Avenue, N.W., via Observatory Road. Shadrin would alternate parking on either Observatory Road or Wisconsin Avenue. Two short blocks from the intersection of Observatory and Wisconsin, on Tunlaw Street, are the Soviet Embassy's living quarters for married diplomats and their children, as well as a separate building for support personnel. In addition, an elementary school for the children of the diplomats and support personnel is maintained in the Tunlaw facility. Besides embassy personnel who oversee the operations of this school, its teachers are U.S. citizens who are bilingual, contract employees.

The location of these facilities and the working hours of all concerned provided Shadrin with an almost foolproof means of communication with his old colleague Commander Vtorygin, and his boss, Admiral Yashin. Both men would have a great interest in what Shadrin was doing at ONI. Commander Vtorygin did not live in the Tunlaw facility. Rather, he lived in an apartment building at 2800 Wisconsin Avenue, four blocks from Observatory Road. Similarly, Commander Vtorygin's place of business was the Soviet naval attaché's office, located at 2552 Belmont Road, several miles away in the opposite direction.

Every morning, Commander Vtorygin's wife, Eugenia, would walk their daughter, ten-year-old Elena, to the school at the Tunlaw Street facility. On the way up Wisconsin Avenue she made a dead drop at Shadrin's car. This possibility that she serviced this drop for Shadrin is enhanced because in the four and a half years Shadrin worked at the Naval Observatory, security was more relaxed after the transfer of some highly sensitive materials up the street to the Naval Security Headquarters at Massachusetts and Nebraska Avenues. Coincidentally, not long before Shadrin left ONI, Commander Vtorygin was given orders to leave Washington in late August 1965, to take over a major desk office in the naval section of the GRU.

According to this theory, Shadrin was under the admirals' control until 1965–66, when, under normal circumstances, he would have been brought home to the Soviet Union. But during this period his secret mission was discovered by Yekaterina Furtseva and used for the benefit of her son-in-law, the infamous KITTY HAWK. Shadrin suddenly found himself in the employ of the KGB and stuck in America for another nine years. There is no hard evidence to support the theory of the admirals, but there is plenty of circumstantial evidence.

Robert Kupperman, Nick Shadrin's old friend, was also a good friend of the station chief in Vienna, George Weisz, who left town before Shadrin's December 1975 disappearance. In November 1982, George Weisz died under mysterious circumstances. His body was found in the garage of his isolated farmhouse, sitting in his daughter's Honda, wearing sunglasses, with a week-old copy of the *New York Times* lying across the steering wheel. The death was ruled a suicide by the Maryland State Police. But the body examined by the Maryland Medical Examiner's Office, the same office that had handled the Paisley identification four years earlier, was certified to have its gallbladder intact. George Weisz had had his gallbladder removed in Germany in 1976. Sometime before George Weisz died, he confided to Kupperman that he believed Nick Shadrin had been working for the Soviets from the beginning.[18] Shortly before his death, Weisz promised to tell the story of Nick Shadrin to his daughter, Nikki.[19]

After Shadrin's disappearance, Richard Copaken, the lawyer who fought long and hard in Ewa Shadrin's struggle to discover what had happened to her husband, became involved with East German lawyer Wolfgang Vogel. Copaken hoped that through Vogel he could offer to trade a Soviet spy held by the Americans for Nick Shadrin, who he thought was being held by the Soviets. Vogel had a long history as a go-between for these types of transactions. Copaken soon decided that then Secretary of State Henry Kissinger had no real interest in making any deals to get Shadrin back. Copaken believes to this day that Kissinger wanted to avoid doing anything that would endanger detente between the United States and the Soviet Union.[20] The contacts with Vogel, which were supposed to be kept secret, were leaked by Kissinger's staff, effectively ending Copaken's negotiations. Copaken thought for years that it was simply a matter of detente winning out over the humane treatment of a spy and his heartbroken wife.

In the spring of 1988, at the National Press Building, the East Ger-

mans held a reception. Francis J. Meehan, the U.S. Ambassador to
East Germany, who, in 1975, was the deputy chief of mission at the
Vienna embassy when Shadrin disappeared, ran into Copaken at the
event. Meehan, like other government officials, had quit talking to
Copaken about the Shadrin case years before. Meehan greeted Copaken. In their conversation, Copaken asked Meehan if he still kept in
touch with Wolfgang Vogel. Meehan said he had seen Vogel recently
in connection with the February 11, 1986, swap of Czech spies Hana
and Karl Koecher for Soviet dissident Anatoly Shcharansky. Copaken
asked him if Vogel had mentioned anything about Nick Shadrin. To
Copaken's shock, Meehan said matter-of-factly, "You know what
Wolfgang has always thought about this?" Copaken shook his head.
Meehan went on, "He thinks he [Shadrin] may have been dispatched
and went home."[21]

Jim Wooten, the FBI agent who was Nick's case officer, and who ad-
mittedly grew too close to Shadrin, wanted to tell his story. But when
he submitted a manuscript to the FBI, they asked him to destroy it.

Peter Sivess believes in his heart that his hunting and fishing companion Nick Shadrin is not dead. "In my book he is still alive," Sivess
insists.

According to John Novak, Shadrin's former supervisor at the DIA's
translation unit, there was an official sighting of Shadrin in Moscow in
1980. Sources at DIA confirm Novak's assertion and say there have
been other sightings.

In June 1988, United States intelligence sources learned details of
events that took place in Moscow on May 17, 1988, at the funeral of
Sergei Georgievich Gorshkov, admiral of the Soviet Fleet, member
of the Central Committee of the CPSU, and deputy of the Supreme
Soviet of the USSR.

Prior to the funeral, Admiral Gorshkov lay in state at the Red Banner Hall of the Central Palace. This public viewing of Admiral Gorshkov's corpse produced a string of people who came to pay their
respects. The honor guard by the coffin was manned by senior officials
of the Soviet military and the CPSU. It was an impressive sight.

Admiral Gorshkov's actual funeral ceremony was held at the Novodevichy Cemetery in Moscow.[22] This cemetery is for the *nomenklatura* and their families. Although the Kremlin Wall is the symbolic
burial place, the Novodevichy is the Forest Lawn of good communists.
The grave of Khrushchev is only three away from Admiral Gorshkov's. Mme. Furtseva, her husband, and Frol Kozlov, KITTY HAWK's
father, are also interred at Novodevichy.

At the service (funeral services are referred to by the Russians as
"meetings") high-ranking members of the staff of the United Armed

Forces of the Government, members of the Warsaw Pact countries, and the military attachés of the embassies of the socialist countries in the USSR gave their personal eulogies to Gorshkov. Off to the side of the gravesite stood four persons away from the group of mourners. They were Admiral Gorshkov's family.

In a black dress and veil, almost purdah-like in its covering, stood a quietly sobbing Mme. Gorshkov. Next to her, with her arm around her mother, was Gorshkov's daughter, Mme. Artamonov. And next to Gorshkov's daughter stood her husband, Nikolay Fedorovich Artamonov, in full uniform. Next to Artamonov stood his son, a dead ringer for the young Soviet naval officer who left Gdynia three decades ago on a strange odyssey in the U.S.A.

CHAPTER SIXTEEN

Sigler: The Search for GRAPHIC IMAGE

In the beginning I was so innocent.

Ilse Sigler

RALPH SIGLER was like a million other immigrants who came to the United States as a boy and put a life together for himself and his family. He had made a good career in the Army. He had a solid life at Fort Bliss, in El Paso, Texas. On the surface he seemed an unlikely hero. But in 1966, Sigler found himself becoming part of intelligence history. Bureaucrats in Washington made him an objective. This small man would serve as the bait for a deadly game with the Soviet Union.

When you stand in the summer heat of El Paso, Texas—in front of Sigler's brick house with white trim, on Kenworthy Street—you wonder how high were the odds against history reaching into this middle-class neighborhood for this man. But that is precisely what happened.

In 1966, Ralph Joseph Sigler was on his way to being classified as a "national intelligence asset." The selection process was meant to be just as rigorous as that for an astronaut. But instead of selecting Ralph for his talent or technical expertise, he was selected because he had a mother behind the Iron Curtain, a European wife, and a reputation as a tough guy. The judges for this contest were the FBI and Army Intelligence. The grand prize was the chance to become a double agent for the U.S. government.

First the FBI list was narrowed to thirty-five names. Then John Schaffstall of the Army and Jack Radigan of the FBI flew to El Paso, Texas, to meet with a local Army Intelligence man named Carlos Zapata to make the final selection.[1] The file on Ralph Sigler told quite a story. Sigler had come up the hard way. Although he could be tough as nails, he had been an enlisted man with a good record and a predictable future. The Army and the FBI were not looking for James Bond. They were looking for a man who would have the peculiar kind of courage and nerve to walk into the Soviet Embassy in Mexico City and allow himself to be dangled like a worm at the end of a fisherman's hook, waiting for the KGB or GRU to bite.

Ralph Sigler was a candidate to be the bait. He was a small man, about five feet six inches tall; he weighed 145 pounds. He had hazel eyes, short brown hair, a tiger's-head tattoo on his left forearm, and he wore glasses. He was a Catholic. Sigler spoke Czech and German; he understood Russian and some other Slavic languages. What attracted the FBI and the Army to Sigler was that in addition to his having the right "profile," Ralph was a quick-witted, aggressive, and self-confident man. He had a keen memory and an ability to recall details, all very necessary for the life the two agencies had planned for him.

Sigler was not above correcting someone who was wrong, and he believed that the "old customs" were the best. That meant he could talk to the Soviets in a language they understood. The "search committee" discovered that he earned about $860 a month from the Army. He lived in a suburban neighborhood not far from Fort Bliss. His wife, Ilse, worked in a dress store. They had one child, an attractive and energetic young daughter named Karin. Ralph had trouble holding hard liquor, so he drank beer.

What made Ralph interesting to Army Intelligence and the FBI was his Eastern European background. His mother was still living in Czechoslovakia. Ralph was born Rudolph Ciglar on May 24, 1928, in Hertnik, Czechoslovakia. When Ralph was six years old, his father, along with several of his uncles, went to the United States to seek their fortunes. While in the United States, Ralph's father learned that his mother was having an affair with another man. When Ralph was eight years old, his father returned to Czechoslovakia and took Ralph and his older sister, Anne, back to America with him. The mother was left behind.

The family arrived by ship in New York on September 1, 1936, full of hope and excitement, only to be dashed by the realities of the Depression and worsening political news from home.

Ralph grew up in poverty. His father, Alex, worked in the coal mines of eastern Pennsylvania when he could get the work. If mining was not available, his father worked for two dollars a day as a meat cutter and sausage maker. Alex Sigler bought a small house and gradually traded up to a small farm, where he raised pigs in addition to his other jobs. The elder Sigler believed in hard labor and brought Ralph up that way.

Ralph would pick up garbage from nearby hospitals and hotels to use as feed for the farm animals. He would then go to school, and start back to work as soon as he got home from school. It was not a storybook childhood. His sister, Anne, was more pampered. She was sent to a private Catholic school and even attended college.[2]

Alex always pressured Ralph to finish his work. "I made him hardworking, no question about it," Alex Sigler told the *El Paso Times*. On Ralph's employment records, he listed his home address as his place of employment and his father as his supervisor. Ralph never had time for ball games or dates. Once he asked his father if he could have five dollars for a date, but his father turned him down.[3]

Ralph grew tired of the authority and began to threaten to run away from home. He did not get along with his father's many "housekeepers," who were really girlfriends. One of them even had him arrested and incarcerated in a reform school during the summer of 1944, when he was sixteen years old.[4]

At age seventeen, to escape his unhappy home life and what he perceived as a dead-end future in Pennsylvania, Ralph and a friend dropped out of high school and enlisted in the U.S. Army on March 19, 1946. After basic training, young Sigler found himself stationed in the rubble of postwar Berlin. In late October of 1946, Ralph took the train to Czechoslovakia to find his mother and to visit his birthplace. When he arrived, instead of receiving a loving welcome, he found his mother living with a Russian soldier. Heartbroken that his search for his mother had ended with a confirmation of his father's worst assertions about her, he left after only one day. Years later he would tell his wife, Ilse, "I want nothing to do with my mother."

Three years later, Sigler was honorably discharged as a corporal on August 26, 1949, and returned home to Pennsylvania. His father had been in an automobile accident and needed Ralph's attention. Eight months later, on May 5, 1950, Ralph reenlisted in the Army and was on his way back to Europe.

In 1951, at age twenty-three, Ralph was stationed near Stuttgart, Germany. The city was just beginning to recover from the World War II bombings. Ilse Margarete Oehler was one year older than Ralph. She was born in Stuttgart on May 30, 1927. She, too, came from a poor family. Because Ilse spoke no English, she felt uncomfortable around American soldiers like Ralph. She was a very pretty, twenty-four-year-old reddish blonde. She was slender and had bright blue eyes. A girlfriend of hers worked in a nightclub frequented by American servicemen. One night she insisted Ilse go with her to the club. When Ralph walked in, he noticed Ilse sitting on a bar stool. He walked over to talk to her. She was amazed that he spoke fluent German. He asked her for a date. She said, "Yes. You can meet me here tomorrow night." The next night, Ralph arrived on time, but Ilse stood him up. Ilse's girlfriend told her Ralph had waited for two hours. The next time he saw her at the nightclub, he asked her, "Where were you?" She made an excuse and they made another date. But again Ilse stood him up.

Two days later the doorbell downstairs at Ilse's apartment rang. She was living on the fifth floor and would have to push a button to let in a visitor. She looked out of the window, and there was a taxi driver. He shouted, "Ilse?"

She said, "Yes."

"I have somebody in the car for you."

It was Ralph, and she said, "How did you find me?"

"It was easy," Ralph replied, "your friend told me where you lived."

So Ilse said, "Okay. You did it. Come on up." [5]

Ilse was working as a salesclerk during the day and helping her friend at the nightclub part-time in the evenings. As Ralph became more interested in Ilse, he also became jealous of the other men around Ilse at the club and tried to persuade her to stop.

When Ralph was transferred from Stuttgart to Coblenz, he lived in the French barracks. He tried to persuade Ilse to leave Stuttgart and join him. At first, Ilse traveled back and forth on the train to visit him, but eventually she relented and rented a place in Coblenz to be with Ralph. Though initially unable to marry, Ralph and Ilse enjoyed these two years together. Ilse remembers this time as among their happiest. In 1952, Ralph started the Army paperwork for permission to marry Ilse, but it took more than two years to get it approved. When Ralph made sergeant, he started the paperwork for Ilse's immigration, and on February 4, 1955, they were married in Stuttgart in two services, a German one and then an American one. Two months later, Ralph left for the United States to wait the required three months before Ilse could join him.

When Ilse left Germany for America aboard the USS *Randall,* she was told that the Army would notify Ralph, and he would be waiting for her in New York. On July 1, 1955, Ilse saw the Statue of Liberty and the skyscrapers of New York, but not Ralph. The Army had never told him Ilse was on her way. Ralph had left the Army and was working for his sister's husband, Edward Ancas, in the family coal business in West Wyoming, Pennsylvania. In New York, a GI took Ralph's telephone number from Ilse and placed the call to him. Ralph arrived about four hours later, picked Ilse up, and they left for Pennsylvania. She was excited and a little nervous. She was a stranger in a new country, and for the first time she was going to meet Ralph's family.

Ilse and Ralph's father, Alex, liked each other from the start. Alex enjoyed a good time. He liked to dance. He appreciated women's company. But he was also a hard worker. Ilse respected that. But Ilse was uncomfortable in coal-mining country. Having been an independent woman in Germany and having worked in dress stores, she had a sense of style and had accumulated a wardrobe of fine clothes. Her European sophistication and her taste, which some in Pennsylvania saw as "flashy," were foreign to the small community. She resented the constant questions from her sister-in-law about where she got a dress or how much she must have spent for it. Money problems and the dead-end prospects of West Wyoming caused Ralph to turn once again to the Army, which was offering bonuses for reenlistment.[6]

After six weeks of training at Fort Benning, Georgia, Ralph was assigned to Fort Gordon in Augusta. On September 28, 1955, Ralph received his citizenship and his name was legally changed from Rudolph Ciglar to Ralph Sigler.

Ilse landed a job in a local dime store, but she quickly learned that a Southern dime store was much different from a European department store. It was in Augusta that Ilse first experienced racial prejudice against blacks. Separate bathrooms and drinking fountains for blacks and whites were common.

From Fort Gordon, Ralph was transferred to Panama in early 1957. They spent a little over three years in the Canal Zone. Ilse first applied for her citizenship there. It was also in Panama that the Siglers' daughter, Karin, was born on July 4, 1958. Life was good for the Siglers in Panama. Ilse hired a maid to clean the house and take care of Karin while she worked at the base PX. Ilse saved enough money from her job to buy Ralph a Rolex watch for his birthday.

In hopes of getting reassigned to Germany, Ralph went back to Augusta to reenlist. In March 1960, the Siglers rented a duplex about four miles from Fort Gordon. This time Ilse did not work because she had Karin. But when Ralph's assignment came up, he did not get Germany; he got Fort Bliss, in El Paso, Texas.

Ilse was devastated. Ralph had leave coming, so he said, "Let's go to Washington. Fly up to Washington and go up to the Pentagon. I'm going to ask if they will give me an assignment to Germany." The good news was that Ralph's gamble with the Pentagon bureaucracy paid off, and Ralph got an assignment to Germany. The bad news was the family was on its way to West Berlin in the middle of the 1961 Berlin Wall crisis.

The young family was in Berlin for a year before being transferred to Bittberg for two more years. It was in Bittberg that Ilse realized that Ralph was getting involved in top-secret work on missiles at the local air base. Ralph's sister, Anne, kept writing to Ilse, telling her to visit Ralph's mother, who was still in Czechoslovakia. Unlike Ralph, Anne had stayed in touch with their mother. She thought Ilse could go because she was still a noncitizen and could travel anywhere. But Ralph would not allow such a visit. Ralph told her that if she went he would lose all his clearances. "I want nothing to do with her," he said.

So Ilse said, "Let's send her a postcard."

"*No*. I cannot do that," Ralph insisted.

But Ilse did it anyway. She got a friend to mail the postcard for her. It was just a friendly note saying, "Hello from Ilse, your daughter-in-law."

Ralph's mother, who didn't speak German, got someone to respond to the card for her. But that was their only communication. Ilse never had a chance to meet her mother-in-law and Karin's grandmother.

In 1965, Ralph and Ilse were transferred back to the States and again assigned to Fort Bliss, in El Paso, Texas. Ilse had never experienced anything like El Paso, especially such extremes in weather. But Ralph had finally made it to Texas, a place he had tried to run off to twenty-one years earlier, to seek his fortune. The Siglers rented a house on Fairfax Avenue in northeast El Paso, near the Northgate Shopping Center. Ilse found a job as a salesclerk in town, and Ralph worked as an electronics repairman at Fort Bliss.

By this time, without the Siglers' knowledge, the FBI was combing through their backgrounds. Ralph was under consideration for a very important job. He was the prime candidate to be the first Army double agent used in a program to penetrate the KGB's increasingly aggressive operations from Mexico against the United States.

From 1964 on, the FBI grew increasingly concerned about the large expansion of Soviet personnel at their embassy in Mexico City, and the accompanying buildup of the Soviets' Mexican operational capability. What did the Soviets want to accomplish, once they had all this capability in place? The Bureau decided it would try dangling an agent in front of the Russians in Mexico, to see if they would bite. If it worked and an American double was successful in penetrating the

Russian operations in Mexico, the FBI could get a clearer picture of GRU and KGB operations on the American doorstep. "We were going to dangle people, pick out people we thought that we could control, and dangle them and see what the Russians did with them," says former FBI counterintelligence head Eugene Peterson.[7]

The FBI's initial objective was to test the Soviets' performance out of Mexico. What would be their operational capability? Would they send official people into this country to handle their new agent, or would they commit an illegal? Another bonus to the FBI's plan was that their agent would confuse the Soviets. Since the Bureau knew there were real American military traitors (called "walk-ins") going into Soviet embassies all over the world, the Russians would have a hard time determining whether this agent was genuine or fake.

The first question the FBI asked itself was who would be appealing to the Soviets in Mexico. "Is it going to be some civilian professor out of Johns Hopkins, a neurosurgeon? No. It's going to be somebody in the military. An E-5, E-6," Eugene Peterson explains. The locations considered for finding a serviceman and basing the operation included the very secretive Army facility at White Sands, New Mexico, the Army's Fort Bliss, which was closest to the Mexican border, the Atomic Energy Commission's Sandia National Laboratory, and various Air Force installations. But only the Army would go along with the FBI scheme. "Well, they [the FBI] wanted something on the border, and the sexiest place . . . had to be [Fort] Bliss," Peterson says.

At Army Intelligence headquarters, then in Baltimore, a team, headed by Army Warrant Officer John Schaffstall, was anxious to begin operating double agents. When offered the opportunity by the FBI, they eagerly accepted. The next hurdle to overcome was that of who would control the operation. FBI Director J. Edgar Hoover insisted on complete control by the Bureau. The Army wanted a joint operation. "The hangup was . . . terminology. Hoover would not accept 'joint,' the word 'joint,' so we had to waltz around the pole and find a word that he could understand that . . . would connote that the Bureau was in control. The Bureau ran it. The Army supported us. So that's what they always called it. [It] was an FBI double-agent operation supported by military intelligence," Peterson says.

Once approval was granted, the search was on to find the perfect agent. Jack Radigan, a very competent agent in the FBI's Washington Field Office, traveled all over the country and screened many men.[8] Schaffstall's office assigned a local Army Intelligence officer, Carlos Zapata, to search through the files at Fort Bliss. Zapata was looking for men who were tough and resourceful, had technical backgrounds, knew Russian, were capable of selling their cover stories to the Soviets

—and would actually enjoy living the complex and dangerous life of a double agent. As useful as double agents can be, they are sometimes liked, but seldom trusted, by their handlers. Once in place, they become suspect because they always provoke the question, "Is he still ours?"

When Zapata had the list of prospective spies narrowed down to thirty-five, Schaffstall, Army Major Al Daub, and Jack Radigan, the FBI recruitment agent, went to El Paso to make the final selection. John Schaffstall liked Ralph Sigler because he was gutsy. He was not afraid to step over the line. And Ralph had other attributes that set him apart from many of the others. "He just fitted the profile. He was from that part of the world. And he had a relative. And he just fit the mold all the way across," remembers Colonel Donald B. Grimes, the former head of Army counterintelligence.[9]

Once the Army and the FBI agreed that Ralph Sigler was their man, they began internal security checks and clearances that would continue for the next ten years. Ralph's family and friends were all screened, analyzed, and reviewed. After Sigler had successfully passed the vetting process, he was approached by Zapata at Fort Bliss. Ralph showed an immediate interest in pursuing a career in intelligence. And why not? He was thirty-eight years old. He had been in the Army off and on for twenty years. He was a sergeant working as an electronics repairman at Fort Bliss—hardly an exciting and challenging life. He thought he would be doing something good for his country. And to be picked for such a sensitive assignment was very flattering. It would be prestigious and exhilarating.

Carlos brought Ralph to a hotel room to meet John Schaffstall and the others. John told Ralph that he was under consideration for a very sensitive mission for the U.S. government. They talked to Ralph for several hours and then returned to Washington to evaluate their data and confer with their superiors at Army and FBI headquarters.

During the late 1960s, J. Edgar Hoover was more concerned about the threat from within—from student radicals, black activists, and antiwar demonstrators—than about a communist threat outside the country. FBI Headquarters in Washington did not have enough men or money to assign an agent experienced in counterintelligence to handle Ralph. So the FBI field office assigned a local El Paso agent, Francis "Joe" Prasek, to the case. Most agents in El Paso wanted to stay there as short a time as possible. "If it were an island, it would be called 'Devil's,' " says Eugene Peterson. Sometimes the agents were sent to El Paso because they had done something wrong somewhere else. "Well, that was at one time one of the disciplinary places —El Paso, Kansas City, and Butte." But when Joe Prasek got to El Paso, he liked it.

Special Agent Joe Prasek was a nice-looking man—about six feet tall, slender, with dark, curly hair, a clear, medium complexion darkened by the El Paso sun, and blue-gray eyes. He dressed nicely, liked horses, and knew a great deal about cars. Also of Czech heritage, Prasek liked Ralph from the start. Both men spoke Czech and they had common interests.[10]

To most Americans at that time, FBI agents were heroes. Ralph thought working with the FBI would give him the kind of status he could never acquire in the Army. He thought the FBI was in charge of everything when it came to counterintelligence, and he was working with the best. In Washington, the FBI, not having any organizational slot to put the new Sigler operation in, assigned it to a unit that handled illegals and Soviets outside of the United States.

Since the FBI had assigned a local El Paso man to handle the case, the Army felt that it, too, should have someone there on a full-time basis. Army Intelligence assigned its man to look after the Army's interests in the operation on a continuing basis. Carlos Zapata, a man of medium build, about five feet eight inches tall, with a square face and salt-and-pepper hair, is of Mexican American heritage. At the time, Zapata's job with Army Intelligence was to keep the commander at Fort Bliss apprised of any information learned by Army Intelligence that would affect the fort. He did not stay very busy. Servicing an Army double agent would be a new and primary responsibility for Zapata.[11]

On December 9, 1966, Washington gave final approval to the operation, and John Schaffstall returned to El Paso. Schaffstall, Carlos Zapata, and Joe Prasek advised Ralph that he had been selected to be a double agent. At a local hotel, the Army administered its first polygraph test, which Ralph passed with no problems. Army Intelligence regulations would require him to take a routine polygraph exam about once a year in his new role. In the early years, the polygraph exams confirmed his veracity to the complete satisfaction of his handlers.

Operationally, Carlos Zapata was Ralph's control officer or handler, Joe Prasek was his Bureau project officer, and John Schaffstall was his Army project officer. The Army assigned the code name GRAPHIC IMAGE to Sigler. Ralph liked these men from the start. He trusted them. Carlos was assigned to provide support for Ralph, to answer any of his questions, to make arrangements for his leave and his travel, and to handle any other day-to-day tasks that needed to be done, or problems that arose. John Schaffstall, a gentle and soft-spoken man, who worried about every detail of the operation, was in charge for the Army. Over the years, John ran nine or ten other agents, but Ralph was always his best, the most important agent John ever had. Ralph would also prove to be his last.

Carlos, John, and Joe were Ralph's new best friends. Carlos and John made arrangements for Ralph to be promoted to warrant officer. They also asked to visit his wife at the Siglers' Fairfax Avenue house. Ralph came home and told Ilse that there were two men coming over to the house to visit that night, that he was now working for them in military intelligence. Ilse did not understand exactly what he meant. She thought Ralph was working on criminal investigations, not counterintelligence. Ralph told her not to ask any questions and just to listen to them. She said, "Fine."

Around nine o'clock on a December evening in 1966, Zapata and Schaffstall rang the doorbell. They had brought with them some paperwork for Ilse to sign, and explained to her that Ralph was going to be a courier. He would be gone two or three days at a time, delivering sensitive materials that could not be sent through the mail or by other means. They asked her to sign some papers, but gave her no opportunity to read them. To please her husband, Ilse signed the papers without knowing what they said.

After the two men left, Ilse began to question Ralph. "What is that, anyhow—Army courier?" "Oh, just mind your own business. That's strictly for the Army. It has to do with Army security," Ralph replied. "How come I have to sign papers for the Army?" Ilse asked. "Well, that is the way it works. [That was] . . . a paper from the government that . . . [says you agree to] do nothing against the government." Then, very firmly, Ralph said, "I think I am doing something good for my country. All I'm asking you is to stay out. Don't ask me any questions. Don't be nosy. Don't tell your friends anything. All I want is for you to stay out!"

At their next meeting, in a motel room in El Paso, John Schaffstall outlined to Ralph what the Army wanted him to do. He was to make contact with the Soviets in Mexico. Ralph was excited by the proposition and thought he could handle it. The Army and FBI knew already he was a confident, fearless, and very gutsy man. But they also knew dozens of questions would race through his mind, and one by one, John walked him through the answers. The first thing Ralph wanted to know was how he could get to meet the Soviets. How would this happen? And how should he act? He indicated that he did not like the Soviets. Would they find him convincing, even if his dislike of them showed through? His questions centered on the operational side of the plans. He never expressed concern for his own safety. John explained that Ralph's first contact with the Russians would be as a walk-in to the Soviet Embassy in Mexico City.

As the time of the first mission grew nearer, John Schaffstall grew increasingly nervous. "I think it was more nerve-racking for us than it was for him," Schaffstall remembers. He was not as concerned about Ralph's safety as he was about his performance. If push came to shove, Schaffstall thought he could get Ralph out of the Soviet Embassy alive, but what he did not know was whether Ralph was the man of steel he was supposed to be, or whether he would crumble under the pressure. The only way to find out was to send him in.

CHAPTER SEVENTEEN

Sigler:
The Operation

Most of the people in this world are in the shades of gray. . . . And if you come at these things with "it's good" or "it's bad," "bona fide" or "he isn't bona fide," "he's honest" or "he's in the hands of the enemy"—you can't run counterintelligence. You can't run anything. I don't think you can run a hot dog stand.

James E. Noland, Jr.

THE RUSSIANS KNEW that the CIA station was right across the street from their embassy in Mexico City and that the Agency photographed everyone entering and leaving. So they were very suspicious of anyone who just walked in the front door. But they also had certain quotas to fill for contacts and information. When Ralph Sigler walked in, the resident for the KGB was trying to figure out just how he was going to explain to Moscow Center why his quotas were coming up short.

Upset that Ralph had just walked in the front door, but happy to have him, the Soviets told him that they had to get him out of the embassy so that he would not get into any trouble. They took him to the back of the embassy, put him in the back of a car, underneath the back seat with a rug on top of him, and whisked him off to another location.[1]

Ralph knew his lines and performed admirably. He told the Soviets that he was stuck in the Army and wanted to get out. He needed money to start his own business, to make a break from the military. He told the Russians he was too smart for the Army. He was only a sergeant and he should have been promoted. He said the Army did not recognize his talents. He complained constantly about the things he wanted to do, and how the Army did not pay him enough money to do them.

During the mid-1960s the Soviets believed that Americans would do anything for money, that they were capitalistic to their very souls. They seldom trusted or even encountered anyone who contacted them for purely ideological reasons. In the years to come, they were proven right. The high point in their years of accepting walk-ins was Andrew Doulton Lee, a Southern California drug dealer, and Christopher Boyce, the son of a former FBI agent and an employee at a CIA defense contractor. In April 1975, Lee walked into the Soviet Embassy in Mexico City and turned over to the KGB the first of billions of dollars' worth of spy-satellite secrets that his partner, Boyce, had supplied him. One wonders what the CIA did with all the photographs it took of walk-in traffic into that embassy.[2]

The Russians accepted Ralph immediately. They gave him a shopping list of general items they were interested in receiving, for which they would pay him handsomely. They asked for nothing specific. The requests were things like, "We want information on your guidance systems," or "We want anything to do with electronics or anything to do with missiles." In the early years they never pressed him for substantive material. "They're garbage eaters. They'll take anything you can give them. We could have given them anything and they'd take it. And they'd tell Ralph, 'This is good,' " John Schaffstall remembers. "I mean, their philosophy is 'Get everything you can and we'll sort it out later.' So if it was classified, they wanted it. If it was unclassified, they'd take it. But they were never happy about it. And they would say sometimes, 'You have to get better things, Ralph.' But they wouldn't say what would be better."[3]

Throughout the late 1960s, the Army was in charge of providing all of the information Ralph was to pass to the Soviets. Their mission, called "cover and deception," was to plant deceptive information. But as far as the Army knows, Ralph never gave the Soviets disinformation. It was always undoctored classified material. Like Shadrin and KITTY HAWK, which began about the same time as GRAPHIC IMAGE, the Army's agent was too important to risk the operation with phony information. Unlike the KITTY HAWK operation, the Army used much more formal clearance procedures. Most documents were cleared through an Army clearance committee set up for just that purpose. On several occasions, the information selected for Ralph to give the Russians was so sensitive that a higher board, made up of members from the entire intelligence community, needed to approve the materials. The Army had to defend its recommendation by explaining why it thought releasing the documents to the Soviets would not harm U.S. security. In some instances it knew from other reports that the Russians already had the information, although it was still classified. According to John Schaffstall, Sigler's handler, the committees would still be very reluctant to approve passing certain materials to the Soviets. Usually Noel E. Jones, Schaffstall and Zapata's boss at Army Intelligence, would lobby the committee for clearances of the material.

Sigler passed to the KGB classified documents on the fabrication and design of ceramic battle armor that the Army was considering for its future tanks. Years later, through CIA sources, the Army discovered that the Soviets had built tanks with the ceramic armor; the tanks collapsed and the armor failed.[4] Even if the Soviets were convinced Ralph was feeding them secrets from failed U.S. projects it didn't deter them. In fact by 1987, after years of failure, the Soviets had succeeded in developing successful ceramic battle armor.

The Soviets tested another piece of equipment that Ralph passed them: a multi-tiered rocket launcher that could roll into launch position toward targets automatically. The Army had tried to develop such a device, but when it proved unworkable, the material was given to Sigler to sell to the Soviets.[5] According to John Schaffstall, "Everything looked good about it until they fired it and it fell over backwards. They could not figure out how to keep it upright." After the Russians spent tens of millions in research, the project was abandoned. To enhance Ralph's credibility, he would later pass documents showing that the earlier designs he had given the Soviets were defective.

After Ralph delivered documents to the Soviets, the usual payment was $3,000. It was not a tremendous sum, but his visits were frequent, usually monthly, and the payments were steady. Over the years he collected more than $400,000. The Russians must have figured that, to a man making less than a thousand dollars a month from the Army, the payments looked pretty good. But Ralph was not in it for the money. According to Schaffstall, Ralph did it for the thrill and the challenge of being a spy. "He liked the danger," Colonel Grimes said. Sigler loved the exhilarating feeling of completing an operation, and worked hard to present colorful, exciting debriefings to the men he considered close friends—John, Carlos, and Joe.

Ralph used every excuse in the book as to why he needed more money from the Soviets. He told them it cost him a great deal of money to send his daughter to school. He told them she was having problems and that there were costs associated with that. And he told them his wife loved clothes and the house needed fixing. But to the Army, Ralph never indicated any interest in spending the money the Russians gave him. Finally the Army had to pressure Ralph into spending some of the money so that the Russians would not become suspicious. "But, see, we tried to get him to spend this money. He was a pretty stingy guy," John Schaffstall recalls.[6] At Schaffstall's urging, Ralph reluctantly used some of the KGB money for modest home-improvement projects. He took up the sod at his new house and replaced it with white gravel, a covering more practical in the El Paso sun than grass. And if Ralph got an exceptionally large payment, $5,000 or $6,000, he was told to tell the Soviets his daughter needed a new car.

Before each operation, John, Carlos, Joe, and Ralph would meet, usually in a hotel room in El Paso, to go over the documents and give Ralph his instructions and airline ticket. When Ralph returned, John Schaffstall was very careful not to meet him to debrief him until a day or two afterwards, just in case the Soviets were watching him. Usually, John would stay at a room at the La Quinta Hotel in El Paso. Zapata would pick Joe Prasek up at different places around town, and bring him to the hotel, and Ralph would come over. Or sometimes Ralph was told to meet Carlos Zapata someplace in town and drive out with him. The debriefings always took place in El Paso. Schaffstall did not want Ralph compromised. If the KGB followed him after one of their meetings and spotted Army and FBI men with Ralph, it could put him in real danger. Sigler's Army handlers feared that if Ralph did anything out of the ordinary, it would spook the Russians.[7]

After an operation, one of the first things Ralph did was to turn over to the Army the money the Russians gave him. John and Carlos would count the money, and Joe would photograph it for the Bureau. The FBI would then use the serial numbers to determine what bank the money went through, and where the Soviets might be picking up American money.[8] Usually, John would begin the debriefings by asking Ralph, "Well, just tell us what happened. Take us through it step by step." And Ralph would begin to tell them about his latest trip to Mexico. He was instructed to provide detailed descriptions of the men he met, especially their personalities. Then they would ask him questions. These sessions lasted about two or three hours.[9]

In the beginning, Ralph always brought the Russians documents or copies of documents. He never passed microfilm or other, more exotic forms of communication. Later the Soviets trained him in photography and more sophisticated espionage tradecraft. Sometimes Ralph would bring the KGB one document at a time, and sometimes he would bring them several manuals. It all depended on how much the Army could get cleared before a mission.

The Army kept up internal security checks on Ralph to make certain that he was not turned by the Soviets. Sometimes the Army would give him documents with instructions that they had *not* been cleared, to see if he would hand them over anyway. The Army would not risk using its own men to watch Ralph when he met with the Soviets. It would not try a moving surveillance. But it did put men at checkpoints, locations that Ralph would have to walk past when he was in Mexico. The FBI followed him in places closer to the border, such as Juarez. "Technically . . . we weren't supposed to, but there was an agreement. We could go twenty-five miles [into Mexico]. They [the CIA] could come twenty-five miles [into the United States]. But it was supposed to be a liaison-type thing. It was kind of like a wink [and a nod]," Eugene Peterson explains.

The Army was afraid to use the CIA in Mexico because the Agency used local people, some of whom Army CI suspected might be working for the KGB. Very few countersurveillance checks were ever run on Ralph by the Russians. When he went to his drop sites, they used all the safe signals and other techniques commonly employed for these operations. But in contrast to the way things were done in the Shadrin case, the Soviets' instructions were not complicated. "It was easy for him," John Schaffstall says. "The Soviets told him, 'You go here and just keep walking and we'll meet you,' and that's what they did. 'If you get to a telephone pole, put an X on it. If you see a little X [already on the pole], don't come.' " [10]

Ralph's own personal notes give a unique look at the procedures he would follow for a meeting with the KGB:

> *Cathedral 16 Sept.*
> *Park. Boldly, walk*
> *around . . . 2000 or*
> *2300 at*
> *Bar Chionoco*
> *if not*
> *eat breakfast*
> *at 1000.*
> *1800 (11 Sept) walk to*
> *Mexicana airline*
> *(16 Sept) or*
> *2400—Hilton Bar*
> *10 Sept*
> *Sport shirt in trousers*
> *O.K. no meeting yet*
> *Shirt out of trousers*
> *had meeting. Is finished.*
> *Carrying camera:*
> *Had meeting, but will have another.*

Ralph would draw a map of these locations.

Once, the Russians pressured Ralph for more detailed information. They said, "We don't like what you've given us. It's not good enough." Ralph apologized and explained that was all he could get his hands on at the time. But as the time for his next meeting with the Soviets grew nearer, he became very concerned. The Army had not cleared anything at all for him to take. Knowing of the Russians' displeasure over the past materials, Ralph did not want to go empty-handed. On this visit he gave the Soviets materials that had not been cleared first by the Army, a manual he took from Fort Bliss. At the debriefing, he told John Schaffstall about it. He said, "I didn't have anything this time to give them, and I needed something. And I used that as a crutch so I could go through with what I'm supposed to do." He was sorry, but he felt he had no choice.[11] The Army took no action against Sigler. He was now their most valuable double agent.

In July 1967, Ralph and Ilse built a new house, on Kenworthy Avenue in El Paso. Ilse liked the builder's European open design as opposed to the more traditional Colonial and Spanish architecture of the other homes in the area. She had the builder enlarge the windows and install high ceilings to admit more light and to set off her large pieces of German furniture. And at least once a year, Carlos and John would come for their visit. They guaranteed Ilse that if anything ever happened to Ralph, the government would take care of her and Karin. They assured her that Ralph was not meeting with other women on his excursions, and that he was being well protected by the Army. And they always complimented Ralph on his work and told him what a great job he was doing.

On the instructions of the Soviets, and after the FBI and the Army approved the purchase, Ralph bought a 35mm Olympus camera and a copying stand for documents with some of the money the Soviets gave him. The Russians also told him to purchase a good shortwave radio, and gave him two frequencies to monitor. They kept in touch with Ralph through coded Morse code messages transmitted to the shortwave radio via "Michelangelo" in Cuba. This "dispatcher" was the same one Nick Shadrin listened to every night. The Bureau successfully identified Michelangelo, even though he had moved from country to country. But his "fist," or keying style, was unmistakable.[12]

These messages were usually fairly general, nothing really definite, such as, "This month, if we get in touch with you, you should do this." They would also send him postcards. According to John Schaffstall, the Soviets told Sigler the messages were being transmitted to him by a satellite aimed directly at his house, especially for him. In reality, they were being transmitted from Cuba.[13]

The Soviets also gave Sigler code pads (pads that were made to be used only once). He used them to decipher the shortwave Morse code messages. The pads looked like little rolls of paper. "It looked like a roll of caps when you were a kid. . . . And they gave him a roll of codes that he would use. And he would just peel it off the roll. It was like caps. He would peel it off and then use that code. And that would tell him where to meet, when to meet. And they would substitute numbers for letters. Things like that. But it was all Morse code," Schaffstall explains.

Ilse knew the routine: "The messages came once a month and I still have the book where they are marked. He used to go [to meet with the Russians] after the messages came in. He first put [on] his little tape recorder. He wrote all the foreign alphabet down [Morse code messages], and had the message on the tape [to play back] and then he wrote it all slowly again to make sure he got it all. Then, sometimes, if it was something urgent, he used to go on the phone and call Joe. Joe was the one who had [understood] the messages if he [Sigler] didn't get a letter or get it right."

Each number sent by Morse code over the shortwave radio represented specific instructions. Ralph wrote down a grid of numbers and letters and then outlined the code:

1 Don't want to see me
2 No Drop
5 Stop everything destroy
  everything, wait 6 months
7 Go ahead—as planned
9 Danger, Go to Austria
0 No message

And as in the Shadrin case and others, the Russians always promised Sigler more sophisticated equipment. They promised him a burst transmitter. "But they were always going to give him something much better that they had as far as the tradecraft goes," John Schaffstall says. But, he goes on, as far as the Army knew, Ralph "never got it. They come up with that shortwave radio instead of the burst transmitter."

Sigler was not very good at Morse code, so the Army sent him to training school at White Sands to brush up for his messages from the Soviets. The Bureau was so concerned that he might miss one of the messages that they made arrangements to listen in and record the messages to compare them with Sigler's translation of them.[14] After Ralph transcribed the messages, he would call Joe Prasek to compare notes. This procedure also served as a check on Sigler, too. "He wasn't too good at the Morse code. No. But it was also a check to see if Ralph was telling us everything that he heard on the radio," Schaffstall admits. But the Army never listened to the transmissions or knew about the tapes of the transmissions Ralph kept at his house.[15]

In 1967 and 1968, Ralph met with the Russians twelve to fourteen times a year, or approximately once a month. He always met them somewhere in Mexico, either in Mexico City or Chihuahua or the surrounding countryside. The bullfight arena in Chihuahua was one of his drop sites. At the Army's instruction, he often tried to coax the Soviets into meeting him in the United States, but they refused. The closest he could get them was just across the border, in Juarez, and even that was a struggle.

But the FBI is not so sure the Russians did not operate along the border in the States. "We knew they had a capability out of Mexico [to do surveillance]. And we had to assume that they came to the border periodically because they would come up to pick up cars for the embassy—military guys. But we really never knew what the hell they did because they'd come in and get the car and we didn't have any resources to [follow them]," Eugene Peterson explains.

Throughout the week, Ralph served as a typical sergeant in electronics at Fort Bliss. No one who worked with him on the base knew of his secret, after-hours life. Usually only the base commander knew in general about Ralph's work with Army Intelligence. Carlos Zapata was in charge of briefing him. But no one, not even his wife and family in those early years, knew that on weekends, Ralph was one of the Army's most successful double agents. "He was the biggest thing that they ever had. I mean it was that way for years. And he was classified [by the Army] as a national asset," Schaffstall confirms.

Throughout the operation, Ralph's Soviet contacts grew higher and higher in rank. The Russians always told Ralph he was working with the GRU, and he always dealt with military people. But in reality it was the KGB. "In fact, the first one that he had was GRU and the KGB took it away from them," Schaffstall says. Once Ralph's Soviet contact got drunk at one of their meetings in a Mexican border town. "And Ralph laid it on his replacement about how the guy acted. . . . But anyway, the next Soviet that met him was fairly high-ranking . . . somebody from Moscow," Colonel Grimes remembers.[16]

During the early days, Ralph would go to a drop site in Mexico to pass his documents or retrieve a message, and the next month he would have a personal meeting. One of Ralph's Soviet control officers used the name "Major Alexander." He always traveled with a chauffeur. They would go on picnics in the Mexican countryside and try to get Ralph drunk. The sight of two Soviets and Sigler getting drunk while having a picnic must have puzzled Mexican passersby. The KGB men would spread out the tablecloth and feed him all sorts of drinks. Ralph always said he thought the chauffeur was more important than the person actually doing the talking. He said Alexander always looked at the driver whenever he said anything.[17]

Ralph was instructed never to act afraid of the Soviets. "Show yourself as an individual," John Schaffstall told him, "and he would." On one trip to Chihuahua, Ralph was in his prime. He was meeting with his Soviet contact, Major Alexander, in a motel room.

The Soviet said, "Didn't you get a motel room?"

"No," Ralph replied, "I thought you'd arrange for it."

"No, I didn't," said Major Alexander.

"Well, I don't know where I'm going to stay. I don't know this town."

"Well, that's up to you."

Ralph ended it by telling the Russian, "Good. I'm staying here with you."

Major Alexander and the chauffeur did not know what to do. "Oh, I don't think we can do that."

Ralph said, "Yes, you can. If you don't do that, then I'm not talking to you anymore."

When it came time for bed, Ralph said, "Here. I'm going to put everything I own on the nightstand here. I want you to do the same." Ralph walked over, emptied his pockets, and put his wallet on the table. But Alexander did not budge.

"You don't trust me?" Ralph asked.

"Well, it's my wallet. I don't know . . . I trust you with my wallet, but there are things that are in it that I don't want you to have," a flustered Alexander responded.

Ralph walked toward the bed and said, "Well, I'll tell you what. You can look through everything I have. I'm going to sleep." And he went to bed. Before he went to sleep, Ralph joked, "I don't want to catch you going through my wallet, now." But Major Alexander and the chauffeur had nowhere to sleep. There was only one bed in the room, and Ralph had taken it. They were up all night, afraid to go to sleep.[18]

Like Nick Shadrin, Ralph was told that if for some reason he lost contact with the Soviets, he was to contact a man in Vienna, Austria. Today, Mrs. Sigler still has the name and address of the man in Vienna, written in Ralph's handwriting:

Herr Karl Rypar
Leber Strasse 112–114 [sic]
Post Fach 116 [sic]
Austria 1114 VA Wienne [sic]

Army counterintelligence at Fort Meade was organized into two major groups: operations and investigations. Col. Donald Grimes was in charge.[19] Grimes is a big man who, at well over six feet and more than two hundred pounds, has the look of an old-fashioned Army colonel. He is bald and has blue eyes, big ears, and an oval face.

Grimes's operational CI command included fourteen men divided into five color-coded teams, usually with two or three men on a team. The color designated the area of the world in which Soviet operations were being targeted. The Gold Team, in charge of the GRAPHIC IMAGE operation, was targeted at the Soviets in Mexico. The team chief was John Schaffstall. At the time, this same group was also trying to penetrate Communist Chinese intelligence operating in Asia. No small task for two to three men.[20] Lieut. Col. Noel Jones was deputy to Grimes in charge of counterintelligence operations in the mid-1970s. Known as a slick operator, Jones is heavyset, of medium height, with a round face. It was a small, close-knit group that Colonel Grimes supervised closely. It was called the Army Intelligence Special Operations Detachment (SOD). At Fort Meade, the Special Operations Detachment worked in a plain-looking, narrow room lined with cubicles for the case officers.

In the spring of 1968, the Siglers got some long-awaited rewards. On March 20, 1968, Ilse Sigler finally became an American citizen. Ralph's long-promised promotion to warrant officer was handled through a series of bureaucratic shortcuts. On May 6, Ralph was honorably discharged from the Army, in what had to be one of the shortest retirements on record. On May 7 he was appointed a reserve warrant officer, his bonus for being a successful double agent.

The Army knew that the Soviets would get suspicious if Ralph did not receive his share of normal assignments and rotations overseas. By 1968, Sigler was due to be transferred. GRAPHIC IMAGE's performance in Mexico was so outstanding that the Army wanted to attempt to run him in Europe. When Ralph told John and Carlos about his upcoming routine overseas assignment, they already knew about it. The decision was made to send him once again to Germany. Ilse was thrilled to be going home. She made arrangements with a realtor to rent the house. John Schaffstall temporarily turned the operation over to his headquarters, United States Army Intelligence at Fort Holabird, in Baltimore, where Bill Sole and Bob Arnold would now be receiving the reports of Ralph's clandestine activities in Europe.

Sigler was officially attached to an Army command unit at Nuremberg, Germany, in late 1968. The family was assigned an apartment in the city. To Ilse it seemed as if Ralph was more or less on his own. Then came time for Ralph to go on his first assignment. That night, Ilse watched from a window as men in civilian clothes pulled up in a

Mercedes and picked Ralph up. When he came back home, she asked him where he had gone. To Switzerland, he said. She pressed him— was this part of his courier assignment? And then, for the first time, Ralph told Ilse that he was more than just a courier, he was really an agent. She did not quite understand. "Does this mean you are a spy?" she asked.

Ralph hedged, answering vaguely, "Sort of."

Ilse was incredulous. She began to ask Ralph about the details. "How are you going to get your connections? You don't know anything about it."

Ralph assured her that the Army would handle all of the details. Ilse said she was flabbergasted. She asked Ralph whom he was really working for: "Do you work for the Czechs?" The Czechs were assuming more control from the KGB over intelligence matters in Eastern Europe.

But Ralph put an end to her questions. "No. Now listen," he said, "I'm working. I'm a secret agent."

Ralph was not telling Ilse anything the Army did not want him to. The reason he was telling her all of this now was that the Army wanted to use the whole family, not just Ralph, to give legitimacy to the operation. Instead of Ralph going alone for weekend meetings with the Russians as he had done in Mexico when they lived in El Paso, in Europe the entire family—Ralph, Ilse, and Karin—would have to travel together on the weekend trips. Sometimes even Ilse's brother in Stuttgart would accompany them.[21]

While Ralph was in Germany, the Army sent him to Oberammergau to study Russian. Regensburg was one of the cities to which Ralph used to travel to meet with his contacts. On one Sunday he drove his family to the train station in Regensburg, left them there for two hours, and then returned and took them home. Another time, when he was away in Switzerland, he did not come home the night Ilse expected him. This was the first time she really began to worry for his safety. But she did not know what to do.

When she went to the commissary the next day, the man working there asked, "Where's Ralph?" She said, "Oh, he's visiting my relatives." She did not realize that Ralph would need a pass to go to Stuttgart and back. That night an Army captain called. "Is Ralph there?" "No, he's not here." Then a major called. "Is Ralph there?" "No. Of course he's not here." The phone kept ringing until Ilse finally told her brother, who was visiting from Stuttgart, to answer the phone in German and tell whoever was there that they had the wrong number. The Army reported Ralph for being AWOL.[22]

When Ralph got back, he was furious at Ilse. He was in trouble, but he could not tell his Army superiors where he had been or what he was doing. Ilse had been worried about him, and when he got home, she was puzzled about why he was so angry. She wanted to know where he had been. Was he all right? He wanted to know what the hell she was doing, telling the Army he had gone to Stuttgart. He told her he could not make his contact on time, so he had had to wait and couldn't make his train connection, and it made him late. "You should have told them to go to the base commander," he told her.

She said, "I forgot."

The Army eventually took these events off his record, but shortly thereafter the Siglers were transferred to Stuttgart. From Stuttgart it would be easier for Ralph to travel.[23]

Ilse had finally returned to live in her hometown of Stuttgart. They had a house on a hill in the woods. It was beautiful, and she was very happy. From there, Ralph traveled to Switzerland several times, and to Garmisch and other cities. He told Ilse that his project officer was a retired colonel, and that he also had a civilian boss from the CIA. One evening Ralph came home and said that the colonel and the CIA agent wanted to take them out to dinner. They wanted to talk to Ilse. He told her to go out and buy a new dress and to look very nice. For her this was a treat.

Ralph and Ilse drove to a small restaurant in a town just outside of Stuttgart, where the colonel and the CIA agent were waiting for them. Ralph introduced Ilse to them by their first names. They thanked Ilse for being helpful and loyal, and praised Ralph for the work he was doing for his country. They told Ilse that if anything should go wrong, the family would get benefits from the government; there was a trust fund for them. And they told her she should not worry about Ralph. He was very well protected.

During 1969 the family traveled frequently. But on one trip to Switzerland, Ilse became frustrated and tired of the game. When they got to Zurich, they went to an old and inexpensive hotel. There were men hanging around on the streets, the stairs to their floor were very narrow, and there were what Ilse described as "crazy-looking guys" in the hotel. The room was small and the bathroom was downstairs. Ilse put her foot down. "I will not go with Karin to places like this! Karin at least has to have her own bathroom."

They looked for a better hotel. While driving around the city, Ralph said, "I have to go and look for a street." He detoured to a nice street with small shops, and then, despite the traffic, he made a stop by a mailbox. Then another car stopped. A tall, attractive man who looked foreign but spoke perfect English walked up to the car and asked directions to a particular street. Ralph said he did not know where it was.

Ilse knew it was not natural. She said, "He's not a Swiss. He looks more like an American. Is this the way you make your connections?"

Ralph snapped back, "Just mind your own business."

When the Siglers finally checked into a hotel, Ralph, as always, left the room to make several telephone calls from a pay phone to names and numbers he kept with him in little notebooks. He never made the phone calls from his room. When he returned, they got something to eat in the hotel dining room and then he told Ilse he had to go. He picked up a little black suitcase and left. Two or three hours later, around three or four o'clock on a Saturday afternoon, he came back to the room. He seemed nervous and a little frightened. He handed Ilse an envelope and told her that there was money in the envelope. Stunned, Ilse asked him, "They give you money?"

He said, "It's not mine. I have to turn it in." He told her that she should carry the money in her purse.

She asked him, "How much money is it?"

He said, "Three thousand dollars."

Kidding him, Ilse responded, "Oh boy, am I going to have a good time."

But Ralph did not laugh. Any time Ilse would joke about keeping the money and making up some sort of story for the Army about the money having been stolen, Ralph would get angry at her.

Then, in July of 1970, Ralph got orders for Vietnam. At first Ilse was concerned, but Ralph explained that the Army was just using these orders as a procedure to get him back to the United States, and his orders would be changed in Washington. He said they would have to stop in Washington for a few days and see John Schaffstall. Ilse packed their belongings and they left for Washington. After they checked into a hotel in Washington, Ralph told Ilse to take Karin out for a while. She knew this meant that he needed to meet with John. After two or three days in Washington, they returned to El Paso and moved back into their home on Kenworthy Avenue.

Not long after the people who were renting the house moved out and the Siglers' furniture arrived, Carlos Zapata, along with a security officer, dropped by to welcome the family back home and to ask questions about their life in Germany. Ilse's relationship with Ralph's colleagues was always very formal. She called Carlos "Mr. Zapata." Zapata noticed some of the new furniture she had bought in Germany and commented on how much nicer her home looked than his, only a few blocks away.

Ralph had to show Zapata the receipts for the furniture to prove he had not used any of the money the Russians had given him in Europe.[24] A couple of weeks later, John Schaffstall and Carlos came again to the house to assure Ilse that everything was fine and that if there were ever any problems, the government would take care of them. The original men—John Schaffstall, Carlos Zapata, and Joe Prasek—were now back in charge of the operation.

At first the operation seemed to follow the earlier pattern. During the end of 1970 and throughout 1971, about once a month Ralph would leave on Friday, go to Mexico to meet with the Russians, and return on Sunday evening. He told Ilse never to go to Mexico while he was there. And John and Carlos would come for their yearly visit and tell Ilse what a great service Ralph was providing for his country and the President.

The Russians started pressuring Ralph to get a better job. Once they suggested that Ralph try to get a job with one of the defense contractors in California. John Schaffstall told Ralph that it would be no problem. The Army would handle everything, from finding Ralph the job to buying and selling the houses. Carlos seemed upset by the prospect that Ralph might leave El Paso. But the Russians did not pursue the issue. Then, in 1972, the operation changed dramatically. Colonel Grimes noticed the change. "Well into the operations, I just began to have questions. Was he playing straight with us? . . . This was just before he went to Korea."

When Ralph came home from one of his Mexican weekends, in May 1972, he seemed troubled. Ilse was watching television when he came into the room, very upset, and sat on the floor with his notes of the meeting. He explained that when he had arrived at the airport, a couple of the civilians he had worked with at Fort Bliss were there. They came up to him and asked him where he had been. Caught off guard, he quickly told them he had been to visit his father in Pennsylvania. That was always his cover story. They insisted that he go out for a drink with them. Ralph did not know what to do. He realized that it was against procedure for him to meet anybody when he returned from a mission, but he had no excuse ready for why he could not have a drink with his friends. When he got home he was in a panic. He knew he had to call Carlos right away and explain what had happened. But something else, much more important, was bothering him, something far more disturbing than breaking Army regulations.

Ilse asked him, "What is wrong?" She knew he was very anxious.

Ralph sent Karin to play with her friends down the street, then told Ilse, "This time they sent me somewhere and I had to do something I didn't like."

Confused, Ilse asked, "What did they make you do?"

Ralph explained that this time he had had to tell the Russians about his mother in Czechoslovakia, and that he would bring them more information if they would take care of his mother. The FBI had decided it would strengthen Ralph's case to the Soviets if his mother was now brought into the picture. Ralph had been instructed to tell the Soviets he wanted to help her.

Ilse could not believe what she was hearing. "How can you do that?" she asked him.

"Well, that was my assignment," Ralph replied. "Now we just have each other. We cannot talk to anybody about it and we have just each other." His trust in American intelligence was wearing thin.

Throughout the next few years, the Russians kept in regular contact with Ralph's mother. They sent a female agent to visit her in Czechoslovakia to give her money. They gave Ralph letters from her, thanking him for the money. Sometimes the mother would address the letters to Ralph's sister in Pennsylvania. One note said:

> Mrs. Maria Healey [a Soviet KGB agent using an American name] brought me 3600 koruns [sic] and one hundred $100 dollars. My dear son please don't worry [or "be at peace"] I will not write to you again, but I am asking you to send me a photograph of your daughter or a letter when Mrs. Maria comes again. Best regards—From your mother.

As far as the Army was concerned, they did not object to the mother being used. Ralph had never indicated any affection for his mother, whom he had not seen in thirty-six years. "Well, he didn't seem to give a damn about her one way or the other," Colonel Grimes remembers.[25] As far as they knew, Ralph did not even know where she lived. Using the mother "would have been Ralph's idea or the Bureau's. Not ours. Because we (the Army) didn't think the mother was that important to the whole case," John Schaffstall explains. "Ralph didn't care for his mother at all. He had no feelings of motherly love or anything or a son's love for his mother. It didn't bother him."[26]

Nick Shadrin had been told by the FBI to show concern to the KGB for a wife and son in the Soviet Union, a wife and son from whom his FBI handler, James Wooten, insisted Shadrin was emotionally divorced. The top people in Bureau counterintelligence during this period openly confirm that letting the KGB believe their agents were susceptible through family members under KGB control was a widely used FBI technique. But as both the Sigler and Shadrin cases show, it is a technique full of incalculable, unresolvable risks.[27]

Ilse knew how much using his mother disturbed Ralph. She knew her marriage was now under great strain, and she was frightened. She tried to comfort Ralph by telling him, "Why don't you get out of there? You have been in the Army for more than twenty years now. You can get out at any time." But Ralph shook his head and said, "No. I cannot

292   W I D O W S

get out. The FBI would never let me get out. I am in too deep now. There is nothing I can do. I guess I am stuck with it." For the first time he mentioned Joe Prasek to Ilse. He explained that Joe was his FBI control officer, who had deliberately avoided meeting Ilse for security reasons. He did not tell his wife Joe's last name.[28] And for the first time it was clear to Ilse that the FBI was controlling Ralph and the operation, and not the Army.

It was at about this same time that John Schaffstall noticed what in his opinion was a significant change in Joe Prasek's attitude and mannerisms. During the debriefings, Prasek appeared to lose interest. Schaffstall said, "He took the money and he wouldn't count it and things like that. And we'd have to do that to make sure it was counted right."[29] Schaffstall complained about Prasek to Noel Jones, Schaffstall's boss at Fort Meade, but nothing was ever done about it, as far as Schaffstall knew.

Eugene Peterson of the FBI explains why: "They may say they complained, but they never complained to anybody where it could do any good." Peterson said that there were "undercurrents" of rumors indicating that the men in the field—Carlos, Joe, and John—were at odds. But by the time their operational plans bubbled to the top of the bureaucracy, "there was never any indication that they were not other than buddy-buddy down there."[30]

Prasek worked with Graham Van Note in the El Paso FBI office. Noel Jones says it was his understanding that Prasek "did not have the initiative in this case, all his orders came from Van Note."[31]

Army Intelligence and the FBI were always competing for control of the operation. Eugene Peterson insists that the FBI was always in total control. "He's [Ralph] an Army guy. They had responsibility for his personal security and they had responsibility for selecting the material to feed, and they would supply it. So they did that . . . and if they disagreed we would resolve it at headquarters one way or the other. . . . So who was in control? Sure. It was us." But John Schaffstall disagrees. "I was really the controlling agent," he says.

When Schaffstall was in El Paso, he felt he was in charge. But he knew that when he left town, Joe Prasek took over. Carlos Zapata would do what he was told by Schaffstall, but when Schaffstall was not around, Prasek filled the void and gave Zapata his orders regarding Sigler. "He followed everything I told him to do. . . . He wouldn't do anything on his own," Schaffstall said of Zapata. But he never told Carlos to be careful what he said to Joe Prasek. "I doubt we would tell him, because Prasek was still a handler for the Bureau. But . . . we didn't say, 'Go tell Prasek this.' We would just say, 'Do this,' and he would tell Prasek. I'm sure he [Zapata] would tell him anything he [Prasek] wanted [to know]," John admitted. By this time the working cooperation between the Army and FBI handlers of Sigler was deteriorating. This would have grave consequences for Sigler.[32]

For security reasons, Joe Prasek was not supposed to go to Ralph's house or be seen meeting with Ralph. "[Those were] the instructions that we [the Army] had put out. *Nobody* meets with Ralph except Carlos. And the reason . . . is Carlos is Army and Ralph is Army and to protect Ralph," John Schaffstall explains.[33]

Schaffstall complained because Prasek was meeting with Ralph and not telling the Army that he was doing so. Eugene Peterson of the FBI said, "I remember there was some concern evidenced at one time that Prasek was spending too much time with the guy. Well, in theory, he was never supposed to have any unilateral meetings that had any operational connotations. So, if he was meeting . . . to say, 'Are you okay? How's everything with Ilse?' . . . there was no reason for the other guy to be there. Only if it impacts on the operation. So we would say, 'Jesus, Don [Grimes], you're nitpicking. You're making a mountain out of a molehill.' "

John Schaffstall knew the FBI was really making the decisions, but he worked hard to maintain some control. "I mean if they [the FBI] want to do it, we would have to step back and say, 'Okay, we'll do it, but *we'll* [the Army] do it.' "[34] The battle of the two bureaucracies was enormous. "They [the FBI] really did not want us [the Army] around," Schaffstall says. The Bureau wanted the Army basically to take care of Ralph and provide the material he gave to the Russians, and leave the rest to them. The FBI cared mainly about the information Ralph brought back on the Russians he was meeting with, and how they operated. "Right. They wanted everything. And they said that they should get it first. They really wanted Prasek to do all the debriefings and not us," Schaffstall remembers. "They were supposed to get all the goods. They wanted the money. They wanted everything. And we said no."[35] But as the operation wore on, this would change.

According to Schaffstall, when it came time for Ralph's next tour of duty, the Army decided "to keep him on ice. . . . This time we said, 'Yeah, let's not get him involved. Where can we send him where we can control him ourselves and he won't have any contact with them [the KGB]?' " The Army picked an isolated area at one of the missile sites in Korea where they knew the Soviets were not operating. "That's the only place we had records that said that the Soviets weren't operating. And that's where we sent him. . . . That was the only place that we knew of that the Soviets did not have a mole located."[36] The FBI had no choice but to go along. It would look suspicious to the Soviets if Ralph did not follow his normal rotation of duty.

Ralph spent a little more than one year in Korea, from July 1972 to September 1973. Schaffstall went to visit him once while he was there.

He said Ralph was bored and was anxious to get home and back into the operation. Ralph made one close friend in Korea, Capt. Bruce McCain. On one particularly slow day, Ralph got drunk and confided in McCain that he was a double agent. Just talking about the operation excited Ralph. He told McCain that he would see if he could get him into the field.

According to Donnel Drake, who was a key member of the Army's SOD Blue Team, which targeted the Far East, Ralph "attempted to lure the Soviets to a meeting in South Korea. We wanted to see how they would operate there. But they didn't show up for the meeting. Ralph did have one debriefing in Tokyo." [37] On November 1, 1972, Ralph took seven days of leave and went to Japan. [38]

When Ralph finally returned from his overseas tour at the end of the summer of 1973, Ilse picked him up at the airport. While he was kissing her, he said, "I hear you've got good eyes." He got into the car and asked her, "Did you see anybody?" He would always tell her, "You've got your eyes everywhere."

But this time she had not seen anyone. She said sarcastically, "No, I didn't see any of your buddies."

Within a week after Ralph's return from Korea, Zapata and Schaffstall came by the house for one of their now routine meetings. Officially Ralph's code name, GRAPHIC IMAGE, was changed to LANDWARD HO. But Schaffstall still used GRAPHIC IMAGE. John and Carlos went through their usual litany of praise for the great job Ralph was doing, telling Ilse that if anything should happen, the government would take care of her, and that her husband was really helping his country.

Ralph renewed his contacts with the KGB by sending a coded postcard to an address in Vienna. With that one simple card, Sigler was back in the middle of the spy game.

Sigler: LANDWARD HO

When he was a double agent, he told me, "I'm doing something good
for my country." He trusted them, right. My opinion is they used
him until they cannot use him anymore. . . . You know, the big people get the big ceremony—the big ones, they get all the treatment
and the little ones, they use them. They get kicked out, and they
throw them away. . . . I feel like this.

Ilse Sigler

TO REESTABLISH CONTACT with the Soviets, Ralph had to go to Mexico
City and walk through Chapultepec park until the Soviets approached
him for a prearranged meeting. The operation was back in full gear.
The Soviets told Ralph to pick a place out in the desert to secure a
burst transmitter. Officially, the Army never knew if the Russians ever
gave Ralph the transmitter. They did know, however, that Ralph had
been told earlier to buy the shortwave radio.[1] But Colonel Grimes had
his suspicions. One of Ralph's operational notes indicates that he did
receive one. The note says:

German Passports
Direct Flight to
Finland
Bulgaria

Ostreich [sic]
Will provide signalling device
Will give telephone number
to notify them of change
in readiness status. Not Practice
Future = will provide signalling device for satellite
explained in detail   CTD

Ralph needed a burst transmitter for one reason: in the opinion of his handlers at the Army and FBI, the KGB was going to put him in touch with an illegal.

It was after Ralph's return from Korea that Ilse noticed that she was being followed when she went to the swimming pool or shopping or to work. Sometimes military officers watched her. She thought one of the generals at Fort Bliss who did not know what her husband was doing was the one who had her followed. When she came home one night, she told Ralph. He became angry and told her she should not pay any attention to things like that. But he told John Schaffstall and Carlos Zapata about his wife's concerns. Schaffstall advised him that the Army had tried to determine whether or not Ilse was being followed, but could not turn up any evidence of it. They concluded that at best Ilse just had an overactive imagination. Schaffstall says, "She was always saying somebody was following her. And we would put on countersurveillance and never find anybody. And she would never say that she saw us [Army people] walking around. It was always somebody either at the airport or someplace that she saw them following her. A black guy, one time . . . but we couldn't find anybody." [2]

About once a year, Ralph had to go to Washington. On one visit he got a medal from CIA Director William E. Colby for his good work. Showing Ilse the medal, he told her he could not show it to anyone else. He hid it in a separate box from the one in which he kept his regular memorabilia.

About a year after Ralph's return from Korea, the operation took another unusual turn. Ralph came home one day and told Ilse that they had to go to Europe for his biggest assignment. Unknown to his wife, the Russians had asked Ralph to meet them in Vienna instead of Mexico. During the summer of 1974, Ralph was to spend several days with them. Ilse was told to plan a vacation for the family in Stuttgart.

To Ilse, everything about the Vienna trip was odd. Before they left, she noticed Ralph taking the metal trim off his suitcase and then replacing it. When they left the house, they did not drive straight to the airport, but took side streets through the Army base. Security at the airport seemed tighter than usual to her.

When they arrived at Dulles International Airport to change planes from American Airlines to Lufthansa, Ilse noticed that Ralph was not wearing the Rolex watch she had given him in Panama; he was wearing a cheaper watch, and he told her he had traded watches with Zapata. She said angrily, "Boy, that time we were so poor and I give you this for your birthday and you traded this to Carlos." But on the flight to Germany, in a seat in front of the Siglers, a Spanish-looking man lifted his arm above his head and rested it on the headrest. He was wearing Ralph's Rolex. Excited, Ilse exclaimed, "He's got your watch!"

Ralph replied, "Mind your own business, you're getting too sharp."

Ilse thought they must have hidden something in the watches.

Ilse noticed that a black-haired, short, "Polish-looking" woman seemed to be keeping an eye on the Siglers throughout the entire seven-hour flight, never getting up to stretch or to go to the bathroom. But when they got to Frankfurt, the woman was not there. Then, when they changed to a commuter plane in Frankfurt to go to Stuttgart, the woman reappeared. Although the black-haired woman had changed clothes, Ilse recognized her. She went to her husband and told him about the woman. His response was, "Yeah, we have been watched on both sides."

After a brief visit with Ilse's brother in Stuttgart, the Siglers rented a car and set off for Nuremberg to meet with an Army captain to go over the final details of the operation in Vienna. Ilse remembers that outside of Nuremberg they stopped at a base and Ralph met with a man in the bar of the officers' club. Then Ralph told Ilse he had to go meet with the captain, who was married to a German and who lived in a beautiful house outside of Nuremberg. The Siglers spent the night at the house, and Ralph and the captain took long walks together in the woods.

The Siglers left for Nuremberg the next day. When they arrived, the transient quarters for U.S. military personnel and dependents were full, so they stayed in a hotel. Ralph told Ilse that she and Karin should stay in Nuremberg and go shopping for a couple of days, then take the train back to Stuttgart, where he would meet them. He said, "If anything goes wrong, if I don't come back, you should contact the captain," and he gave Ilse the Army officer's telephone number. The next morning Ralph said, "I have to go back to Stuttgart for a meeting." He left Ilse and Karin behind and returned to Stuttgart. From Stuttgart, Ralph took the night express to Zurich and then to Vienna. He had to be in Vienna in the morning. He told Ilse that he would be gone for two to five days, and he would call when he got back.

When Ralph arrived in Vienna, he checked into the Hotel Fuchs. According to Louis Martel, a colleague of Schaffstall's in Army Intelligence, "Ralph had problems on that trip. He met the KGB at the wrong place. He said he waited for them at the Tivoli Theatre for an hour in the rain." But, like Nick Shadrin, Ralph was supposed to meet the Soviets on the steps of the Votivkirche. This time there was fixed-point surveillance on the meeting, with one lone CIA agent keeping an eye on Ralph.

After getting soaked in the rain, Ralph was picked up and driven by the KGB to a cement plant outside of Vienna, on Breitenfurterstrasse. Then he was told he would have to go farther. This unscheduled travel worried U.S. intelligence, but they had no choice but to wait and trust Ralph to handle the mission. The KGB took Ralph by car to a safe house inside Czechoslovakia. Ralph wrote that his KGB handler was about fifty years old, was six feet two inches tall, weighed 210 pounds, and had brown hair and no identifying marks. His handler told him he was chief of the American Section and was "personally acquainted with Schlesinger" (James Schlesinger, who was briefly the CIA director). The driver was about the same height, but a little heavier. He was around thirty-five years old and had light brown hair and "sort of a high-pitched voice." The "gopher" was fifty years old, six feet two inches tall, had black hair, weighed 180 pounds, and spoke German with no accent. They made Ralph wear sunglasses and read the paper during the drive. There was no talking in the car. The drive took around thirty minutes from the outskirts of Vienna to a "rundown villa." [3]

According to Ralph's notes, on July 18 and 19, from 8:30 A.M. to 3:30 P.M., he "practiced coding and photography . . . megs [messages] will be sent [to Sigler] for shorter period, at 6 wpm" (a slow speed, since he was not adept at Morse code). He wrote, "I think all was taped." Ralph always kept an eye on his driver and the "gopher" who accompanied him. He noted that they would "sit in a chair facing the wall," and would come and go throughout the day. Louis Martel said that Ralph's KGB handlers took turns posing for pictures with Ralph, their prize agent.

The KGB praised Ralph's work. Then, to Ralph's shock, they escorted an old woman into the room. Ralph suddenly realized it was his mother. They embraced, and she handed Ralph a small package of lace. Later that afternoon, like Nick Shadrin, Ralph was flown on a small KGB jet to Moscow. The most powerful man in the Soviet Union, Leonid Brezhnev, personally made Ralph a colonel in the KGB. It was a replay of the Shadrin episode. He gave Ralph a medal, and the moment was captured by a KGB photographer. Ralph had gone about as far as any double agent could hope to go. In Moscow, he was also given a new code for the messages he received over the radio. [4]

Alone with Karin in Nuremberg, Ilse was upset and scared. She now understood that her husband was more than a courier, even more than a spy. He was a double agent working for both the Americans and the Russians. She took Karin to the downstairs lounge in the hotel to exchange some American Express traveler's checks for German marks. The bartender was drunk and tried to give her less than the fair exchange rate. While she was arguing with the bartender, she noticed a black man standing in the lounge. When they rode around Nuremberg shopping, he followed them in a little white car. She would change trams and go into shops to try to evade his surveillance so that he would not follow them back to the hotel. Another man came and sat at their table every morning for breakfast. He was very polite and they always talked about innocuous topics. When she and Karin took the train back to Stuttgart, Ilse noticed a couple watching them. Understandably, she felt she was under unusual surveillance. But by whom?

When they got to the hotel in Stuttgart, she could finally relax. She called her brother and father, and the family got together and had a good time reminiscing. Ilse and Karin arrived on Friday, and Ralph returned the next day. But he didn't seem to be himself. He seemed upset and nervous. They were supposed to stay in Germany two more weeks, but Ralph said he was taking Karin back to El Paso with him, and told Ilse she should stay on by herself those last two weeks. Ilse knew he had learned something on that trip to Vienna that upset him. She thought he had learned that one of the other American intelligence agents was a KGB mole.

Ralph and Karin returned to El Paso on July 23, 1974. He was debriefed by John Schaffstall, Joe Prasek, and Carlos Zapata on July 25. He returned eighty dollars in unused operational funds to Carlos, and was paid $247.80 for the six days' leave.[5]

Now alone in Stuttgart, Ilse enjoyed visiting the places she used to frequent as a young girl. But it seemed as though every place she went, she was followed. When she went to pick up a lampshade, a man came up behind her at the counter. He had something in his hand. She moved quickly, and he ran down the back stairs. She thought he had a knife and was going to kill her. When she stopped to get a cup of coffee, a woman came in, sat at another table, and watched her. By the time she got home to El Paso, on July 29, she was a nervous wreck and very, very angry. Ralph had to go out that evening for another debriefing. When he returned, she waited until Karin went to bed and then confronted Ralph. It was the first time she remembers really shouting at him.

"Now I want to know, why was that guy after me? Lucky I took my bag and he runs down the stairs. He had something in his hand. *What the devil is going on?*"

"Don't ask me any questions!" Ralph shouted back. He explained that he was meeting with the Russians, and something very important had come up. "Stay out of my work!" he shouted. Hurt and upset, Ilse snapped, "Fine, I stay out." And for a while she did not ask any more questions.[6]

John Schaffstall insists that Ralph and his family always traveled alone, and that no one from Army Intelligence followed or surveilled them. Of course, he can only speak for the Army, not for the Bureau or for the CIA or the Russians. He says Ilse "could dream up a lot of things. . . . Ralph even said she was paranoid."[7]

After the 1974 trip, none of the men—Carlos, John, or Joe—came by the house again. Carlos used to call on the phone when he wanted to talk to Ralph about procedures. He would always say, "Good evening ma'am, this is Carlos Zapata. May I speak to your husband, please?" He would say, "How are you?" but he never came to the house again.

In the early days of the operation, the money the Russians gave Ralph was turned over to the Army, and photographs were taken of it and given to the FBI. But around this time, the FBI started keeping the money and giving the photographs of it to the Army. The Army did not object, because Army regulations stated that a profit could not be made on an operation, and the money had to be turned over to the U.S. Treasury. But under FBI regulations, the money could be used for operations. John Schaffstall does not know, however, why the FBI continued to give them pictures of the money, "because we couldn't do anything about it. If we wanted to trace money, we'd have to go to the Bureau to trace it."[8]

Ralph complained to Ilse that there were problems with the money. "He one time said the FBI was cheating him on the money, and that's when I said, 'How can you trust them? They are not honest people,'" Ilse remembers. Ralph began to keep extra copies of his reports, which accounted for the money. "He kept everything written down," she says. Ilse knew Ralph did not keep any of the money the Russians gave him. They always budgeted their money and lived a modest life-style for a two-income family. John Schaffstall agrees: "We never had any reason to doubt Ralph on the money."

Then, one day when Ilse was housecleaning, she started to polish the silver-colored handles on a small black suitcase she found on the floor of the closet in the spare room. The handles clicked open, so she decided to take a look. Inside the suitcase was an envelope. She opened the envelope and saw several eight-by-ten glossy photographs. One was a picture of William E. Colby, the CIA Director, presenting an award to her husband. Then she looked at the other pictures. At first glance, one of the pictures looked like a photograph an insurance company might take of their top salesmen: a black man; an Oriental; a short, wiry man with glasses; a tall, distinguished man with a widow's peak; another man. All of them were wearing suits.

The short man with the glasses was Ilse's husband, a lowly U.S. Army warrant officer. Next to Ralph stood the all-powerful leader of the Soviet Union, Leonid Brezhnev, with his unmistakable bushy eyebrows. Also in the envelope were pictures of Ralph with George Bush when he was CIA Director, and also of Ralph and Yuri Andropov, when he was head of the KGB. Ilse was horrified. She hurriedly stuffed the pictures back in the envelope, put the suitcase away, and waited anxiously for Ralph to come home. She had many questions to ask him.

That night, Ilse said to Ralph, "I opened your little suitcase there. What is that you got in there?"

"Did you look in?"

"Yes. How far does that stuff go?"

Calmly and slowly, Ralph said, "I want to tell you that you are *never* to mention those pictures. You may be killed. I don't want you to *ever* mention those pictures to me again."

Defiant, Ilse shot back, "Then you shouldn't keep them in the closet. Karin comes to listen to records with her teenage friends. Anybody can go in that suitcase and open it."

"You just stay out," Ralph demanded. "I told you to just stay out!"

Ilse believes that her husband had a meeting with the FBI to show them the pictures. The Army said they did not know about the pictures until Ilse gave them to them in April 1976. But there is evidence that the FBI was aware such photographs were taken of agents when they went overseas.[9] Mrs. Sigler has since tried to get the pictures back under the Freedom of Information Act, but the Army has classified them secret.

One day when Ralph came home, he wrote down a license plate number. He knew he was being followed. Ilse did not know if the Army did not trust him anymore, or if Ralph had found out something. But on November 17, 1975, Ralph was temporarily transferred from Fort Bliss to the White Sands Missile Range, just outside of El Paso in New Mexico. His temporary duty was through April 9, 1976.[10] John Schaffstall said, "We put Ralph out there for Morse code training. . . . He was having trouble with the messages the Russians were sending him."[11]

Just before Christmas 1975, Ilse knew there was something bothering Ralph deeply about his work. One afternoon, when Ralph was watching television, the phone rang. It was Lewis Beasley, a neighbor who worked with Ralph. A few minutes later, Beasley rang the doorbell. He and Ralph talked a few minutes. Then Ralph came back into the house and sat on the living room floor, just in front of the Christmas tree surrounded by presents, mainly for Karin. He refused to go with Ilse to her store's Christmas party. He was too upset. Ralph told Ilse, "I cannot trust my surroundings. No one. That guy from Greece, that CIA agent, and then the one from France. The only one I can trust is the Mexican right now," by which he meant Zapata.

Ilse asked him, "How can you trust the Mexican?"

"He is pretty trustworthy," Ralph replied.

Colonel Grimes understands Ralph's feelings. "Well, you've got to remember that Ralph, he was in this business a long time. Too long, perhaps. And you get to where you can't trust anybody. You get to where the only person he can trust is his handlers . . . and Ralph did not have any friends." [12]

In the opinion of John Schaffstall, Joe Prasek apparently continued to lose interest in the case in the last year or so. When they would debrief Ralph at the hotel, according to Schaffstall, Prasek would say jokingly, " 'We'll write a book, Ralph, we'll write a book.' . . . He'd [Prasek] call him [Ralph] 'the little shithead.' He always was like he was joking, and I never could figure out why he acted like he didn't take too many things seriously. And that always worried me because I couldn't figure out if this was an act on his part or what. And it sort of said to me, 'Jesus, this guy is really not all together.' . . . Perhaps it's because . . . he knew what the hell was going on." It was Schaffstall's opinion that Prasek's attitude might compromise the operation. He was concerned because Prasek lived in El Paso and Schaffstall was in Washington most of the time. He did not know what Prasek might tell Ralph to do when he was not around. [13]

In Schaffstall's opinion, Ralph did not care too much for Prasek's or the Bureau's handling of the operation. But Sigler liked Joe as a person. And he liked Carlos. [14] "Carlos was his buddy. 'Carlos, let's have a beer together.' . . . Things like that," Schaffstall said.

But the minute Schaffstall left El Paso, the operation was under Joe Prasek's control. Prasek complained to FBI Headquarters that the Army would not let Carlos Zapata run the operation with him. In Schaffstall's opinion, Prasek would have liked to cut him out of the operation altogether. Schaffstall said he thought Prasek cultivated the Army staff. He and Carlos Zapata regularly visited the brass at Fort Bliss. [15] Zapata had an office at Fort Bliss, and according to Schaffstall, Prasek got him a desk at the FBI. "He really was impressed that he had the desk and he was treated like one of the boys," Schaffstall said. "Well, I think they were trying to con Zapata." [16]

The FBI knew there were problems with Prasek. According to William Branigan and Eugene Peterson, Prasek's superiors at FBI Headquarters, Graham Van Note told Headquarters that "something was amiss." But no action was taken to correct or investigate the situation.

On the cover of Ralph's January 1976 pocket diary, where it lists the entire year, he circled April 24 and May 8. On the first and second pages are two maps of streets in Mexico. On one location on Avenida del Churubusco was the notation "between tree and wall (7th tree) April 23 or 2 weeks later." Ralph then made the following notes. The numbered items are written in pencil and were probably written in preparation for his upcoming meeting with the Soviets, and the final quote is in ink, probably written after the meeting as a reminder of what actually happened:

1. Too elegant in dress
2. Rent a Car
3. Domestic problems
4. Justification—
   for visit (woman)?
5. New Car to get rid of excess funds
6. Check out other routes of transport
   Phoenix—Albq.
7. San Francisco
   Phone Operation
   "detail"
8. Telegram via phone
   "Talked about my father—in relation to my mother
money etc
Told him sister too"

Looking at Ralph's notes for the first time, John Schaffstall said he didn't know what they meant. He found it strange that Ralph would have them, because the second item on the list—renting a car, apparently in Mexico—"was against Army Intelligence rules. It was just too dangerous for our agents to drive alone down there."

On January 13, Ralph met with Joe Prasek, Carlos Zapata, John Schaffstall, and another FBI agent named Murphy at the La Quinta in room 133 from 6:30 P.M. until 11:15 P.M. for the debriefing. He repeated the process on Saturday, January 17, with only Prasek and Zapata, and "signed receipts." Examining the notes, Schaffstall said, "I just don't understand this. There would be no reason for another meeting, another debriefing like this." Besides, if Ralph needed to sign receipts, he should have met Zapata at Fort Bliss.

According to both Noel Jones and Louis Martel, both from the Special Operations Detachment at Fort Meade, there had been a serious problem with the FBI giving orders to Army Intelligence agents without clearing it with the Army first. "They ran roughshod over our agents. It would not surprise me if they did that with GRAPHIC IMAGE," Jones said.

One day about this same time in January 1976, Ralph came home and asked Ilse to sign a blank piece of paper using a strange name.

"For what?" Ilse asked.

Ralph said, "To change our names."

Ilse asked Karin if she had ever signed anything for Daddy. She said she had, and that Ralph had instructed her to write a couple of different names.[17]

That same month, Ralph got a call one night and left the house.[18] A half hour later he came home and took three Canadian identification cards out of an envelope. He handed her two of the cards, and kept one. She said, "Why the cards? It is getting too ridiculous now. Are you going to make an Ethel Rosenberg out of us?"

Ralph replied, "It is getting pretty edgy. We're probably being shipped out."

Ilse begged him again to get out of this job.

"I'm out in July anyhow," Ralph explained. "I'll stick for those couple of months." In July 1976, Ralph would have thirty years in the Army and was planning to retire. (John Schaffstall maintains to this day that while Ralph did plan to retire from the Army he intended to continue being a double agent.[19])

Ilse asked, "What are these for?"

Ralph told her that the cards were issued under assumed names, "in case we have to leave the country." On the cards, Ilse and Karin's names were Elizabeth Marie Engler and Karin Anna Engler, from Ottowa, and Ralph's name was Howard Louis Rindler, from Toronto.

Before Ralph left for his next meeting with the Soviets in Mexico, he told Ilse, "If there is trouble, you will be contacted by Carlos." Throughout the entire operation, Ilse was under strict instructions never to contact Zapata. If anything should ever go wrong, Carlos would contact her. The night Ralph was supposed to come home, it was growing later and later. Ilse was very worried. A colonel called because Ralph was supposed to be back for duty. Ilse told him Ralph was on special assignment and he was supposed to get back that night. Ralph arrived in El Paso at nine o'clock and was picked up by the FBI and debriefed for two hours before he came home.

According to John Schaffstall, it was the Russians who gave Ralph the Canadian ID cards, at a January meeting in Mexico City. Ralph gave the cards to Joe Prasek during the debriefing so that the FBI could check out the names and numbers on the cards with their counterparts in Canada, the Royal Canadian Mounted Police. Schaffstall believed that the Russians gave Ralph the cards because he was always pretending to worry "what is going to happen to me if I get caught." The Soviets gave him the cards and told him to use them if he needed to leave the country quickly. The Soviets had given some of Schaffstall's other agents identity documents, but he had never seen them give anyone Canadian identification cards before. When he asked Prasek about the cards later, Prasek would avoid the question. "Well, we'd ask him, where are the ID cards? And he'd say, 'Don't worry about them.' " [20] (As will be seen later, the cards ultimately ended up in Sigler's possession.)

Starting in late 1975, Ralph was picked up every morning by two men, a colonel and a warrant officer, and driven to work. He told Ilse they were in a car pool, but Ilse watched when they came to pick him up. They would park and look up and down the streets. Sometimes his friend and colleague, Lewis Beasley, would take him to work. When Ilse asked him, "Why you riding always with Beasley? What does he do? Is he in with them too?" Ralph got mad.

"Mind your own business," he snapped. "We want to save gas." Ralph was very edgy. Ilse knew something was terribly wrong.

For weeks in 1976 Ralph sat at his dining room table, typing up his handwritten notes. Against all rules and regulations, he kept notes of the operation. Sometimes he would take the notes with him to work and type them during the day at White Sands. One Sunday, Ralph and Ilse were watching the Sunday-morning interview shows. Former CIA Director William Colby was discussing his testimony before the Senate Committee investigating the intelligence community. Colby had refused to release the names of intelligence assets to members of the committee. Ilse said to her husband, "Now they're going to trace your name, too."

Ralph joked, "Oh, I have so many names, they'll never trace me." Then, very seriously, he said, "And if they do, I have everything written in memos. Joe and me, oh, we could write a book about what they are doing."

At one of Ralph's last meetings with the Russians in Mexico, they gave him $4,700. The Army wanted to give Ralph a bonus of some type, and had been discussing giving him enough money out of his KGB earnings to build a fireplace in his house. But Ralph said the wear and tear on his car from driving back and forth to White Sands was tremendous and he needed a new car. One night around midnight, Ralph got a call from Zapata, who told him to buy a new car. The Army told him to use a $2,500 bonus for the down payment. But Ralph did not want car payments. He told Ilse to take from her savings account the difference between the cost of the new car, the trade-in, and the $2,500 the Army gave him. On Saturday, March 20, 1976, Ralph bought a brand-new, bright red Pontiac Trans Am. He actually planned to give the car to his daughter, Karin. [21]

Ralph loved his daughter, who was now an attractive, seventeen-year-old blonde, getting ready for her high school graduation. Schaffstall recalls that Ralph "was pretty upset," when he learned that his daughter was having typical adolescent problems.[22] He asked the Army to help him. "Ralph . . . called us right away. 'Do something.' And we said, 'Gee, Ralph, I don't know what we can do with your daughter,' " Schaffstall remembers. "But he was really concerned about the daughter and I'm glad that she evidently turned out fine." [23]

In the mid-1970s the Army implemented a new policy requiring polygraph examinations of intelligence personnel as directed by their superiors. The request for authorization for a routine polygraph for Ralph Sigler was dated September 22, 1975. It stated:

> This polygraph examination pertains to an Offensive Counterintelligence Operation conducted under the provisions of AR 381-47 (S) and involves meeting with a Source targeted against the Soviet Union. It must be conducted in such a manner as to insure maximum operational security. The use of government quarters or other government facilities as a meeting site would jeopardize the security of the operation and of the individuals involved. Travel is necessary at this time to permit essential operational test of Source.

Two days later, on September 24, 1975, in one of the routine debriefings with Ralph involving Carlos Zapata, Joe Prasek, and John Schaffstall, Schaffstall told Ralph about the lie-detector test. Ralph said, "If I have to, I'll take it." But for numerous reasons the polygraph test was postponed until March 1976.[24]

It had been five years, before Ralph's Korean tour, since his last polygraph test, on August 12, 1971.[25] John Schaffstall expected to schedule the test for April 1976, when Ralph's TDY to White Sands ended. But in February, Ralph said that because of his work load, it would be better for him to take the test in mid-March. Knowing that the test needed to be administered away from El Paso, John asked Ralph where he would like to go for the test. Ralph suggested San Francisco. John agreed. He thought that Ralph could use a short vacation. And besides, Ralph had at times expressed a desire to see San Francisco. Schaffstall also wanted a place where he could talk to Ralph alone about his plans after retirement. Since the Russians were still interested in Ralph, the Army intended to run the operation for as long as it could. The military was making arrangements for Ralph to go to work for a defense contractor after his "official" retirement, and they planned to continue the operation.[26] Noel Jones, who supervised the operation from Fort Meade, insists that the Army was planning to turn the operation completely over to the FBI once Ralph retired from Army service. Jones said it would have been impossible for the Army to run Ralph after he left the service, "not to mention illegal."

On March 1, 1976, Ralph told Schaffstall that he would be available for his polygraph examination from March 23 through March 27. But what Schaffstall did not know was that Ralph had not picked San Francisco as the location for his polygraph so that he could relax, eat crabs, and enjoy the dramatic scenery, but because he was scheduled to meet with the Soviets there. "Well, then, if he met with them [the Soviets], it was on the instructions of Prasek," Schaffstall says. Ralph made a reference to the San Francisco "operation" in his January 1976 pocket diary.

Noel Jones says flatly, "We in the Army did not know there were any scheduled meetings in San Francisco with the Russians." Louis Martel, who would eventually run Army CI operations in San Francisco, said, "If Ralph had a meeting with the Soviets in San Francisco, the FBI had to know about it, because they cover the Soviets there like glue." Jones says it is possible that Ralph *thought* he was meeting with KGB agents, when, in fact, they may have been FBI agents posing as Soviets in an effort to "test" Sigler before he became a full-time FBI operative upon his retirement.

Ralph listened to both frequencies on his shortwave radio on March 4, but "nothing could be heard." On March 12 he went to the allergy clinic. He was in perfect health, except for his hay fever and other allergies. He wrote in his pocket diary on March 15, "San Francisco? must know to go next week," and met with Carlos and Joe the following evening at the Ramada Inn in room 334 and "discussed trip and job."

On March 16, 1976, Ralph's paperwork for his leave was filed for five days, March 23 through March 27, 1976, even though he was not supposed to meet John Schaffstall until March 25.[27] On March 18, Ralph received his message over his shortwave radio. In his pocket diary he wrote "radio tonight."[28]

According to John Schaffstall and Colonel Grimes, over the years the FBI never gave the Army any of its information about the operation, but the Army had to give the FBI a copy of all of its reports. When Grimes would ask his FBI counterpart, Eugene Peterson, for a copy of their reports, Peterson would refuse. "Well, you know, I can't release that, but what is it you want to know?" Grimes remembers the Bureau saying. Peterson confirms, "We probably didn't give them copies in those days because . . . it was not a joint operation."

According to John Schaffstall, Joe Prasek always acted as if the FBI were the "ultimate" intelligence organization. "Joe was a little bit pushy and it was *his* agent all the time. . . . 'My agent.' . . . And with the Czech background, and he's talking, 'We're Czechs. We stick together,' and blah, blah, blah. . . . It's possible that Ralph would say, 'Well, Joe has asked me not to do this, so I won't tell them.' "

Ralph's pocket diary says that he flew to San Francisco on Tuesday, March 23, and took a taxi from the airport ($13.80) to the Travelers Lodge at Fisherman's Wharf. Later that day he went to the Vagabond Hotel at Van Ness and Filbert streets, where the Army had made a reservation at his request. He stayed in room 442. Schaffstall was surprised when he learned where Ralph was staying; the Vagabond is not in one of San Francisco's better areas. Later a complete set of blueprints of the Vagabond was found in Sigler's house.[29] What Ralph did at the Vagabond Hotel is still unknown to the Army.

At 8:06 A.M. on Thursday, March 25, 1976, Ralph met John Schaffstall at the breakfast lounge of the Bay Street Ramada Inn. During their conversation, Ralph seemed calm and did not appear at all apprehensive about the upcoming polygraph tests. After breakfast they went upstairs to room 377, which had been rented for the specific purpose of conducting the tests. Schaffstall introduced Ralph to Odell Lester King, a polygraph examiner with Army Intelligence from Fort Meade.[30] Schaffstall wished headquarters had sent another operator. He did not feel that King was one of their best.[31] John Schaffstall explained that "if you get a bad operator, you've got trouble. . . . The polygraph is easy to screw up. I never was a fan of it."[32] Other agent handlers, including Louis Martel, agreed with Schaffstall's assessment of King.

In addition to his opinions of King's skills, his demeanor concerned Schaffstall: "He'd wear a suit, but his tie might not be too firm and when he smoked, everything, ashes all over him."[33]

Schaffstall left King and Ralph alone in the room to conduct the test. As a matter of formality, King explained to Ralph that he was neither a suspect nor an accused, and that it was a voluntary polygraph examination. King discussed with Ralph the questions he was going to ask him, and asked Ralph if any of them bothered him. Before King came to San Francisco, members of the Gold Team had assisted him in preparing the questions. He also had Ralph sign the routine consent forms for the examination, which waived his right to an attorney. As a matter of practice, King asked Ralph whether he had eaten, how much sleep he had gotten, and whether he had used drugs or alcohol on the day prior to the test. Ralph said he was fine, so King attached the polygraph wires to Ralph's body as he sat in one of the motel chairs. From 9:00 A.M. to 11:30 A.M., King sat at a table behind Ralph, so he could not see him, and asked a series of questions:

Is today March 25, 1976?
Are you in the U.S. Army?
Do you have a license to operate a motor vehicle?
Have you ever illegally disposed of PX items?

Are you now in the state of California?
Have you ever illegally disposed of commissary items?
Is this the month of March, 1976?

Ralph's reactions to the polygraph were perfectly normal. After the morning session, Schaffstall and Ralph met for lunch. Ralph said he was not hungry, so they walked to the Cannery coffee shop on Fisherman's Wharf and had coffee. Schaffstall asked him how it was going. Ralph said, "Fine." They talked about Ralph's retirement, his new job prospects, and his new car for about an hour. On their walk back to the motel, Ralph gave Schaffstall a copy of his government employment record. Schaffstall indicated that after Ralph's retirement, the FBI could probably get him employment with a defense contractor or in some government position. Ralph then returned to the motel room for further testing.[34]

Nothing abnormal was indicated on the examination until King asked Ralph a couple of very general questions, such as "Did you tell the Soviets anything that you haven't told us?" Then the needles on the polygraph went off the scale. "He blipped on that one," Schaffstall remembers. When King told Ralph that his answers were indicating an emotional response, Ralph agreed and said he felt guilty about something, but he didn't know what it was. At about three o'clock that afternoon, King asked Schaffstall to come to the room. Both King and Ralph told Schaffstall that there was a problem. King explained that Ralph's responses indicated deception in response to questions regarding disclosure of unauthorized information to Soviet intelligence agents. Shocked, Schaffstall asked Ralph what was provoking the difficulties. Ralph said he did not know, and repeated that he felt guilty about something, but didn't know what. Ralph assured Schaffstall that he had never revealed his association with Army Intelligence to the Soviets. But Sigler never told the Army about his San Francisco meeting with the Soviets.

King left Schaffstall and Sigler alone. They talked for about half an hour about what might be causing the polygraph to indicate deception. Ralph was told to think that night about what might be causing his reaction, and they would meet the next morning for breakfast. Nervous and upset, Ralph left to return to his hotel room. The minute Ralph left, Schaffstall picked up the phone and called his boss, Noel Jones, at Army Intelligence at Fort Meade.[35]

Since Jones and Schaffstall were not talking over a secure phone, Schaffstall simply said, "We're having a problem with GRAPHIC IMAGE." Jones knew immediately what Schaffstall meant.[36] "I'm coming right out," he said. He was pretty upset. "See if you can find out what his problem was," Schaffstall remembers Jones saying.[37] When

Jones told his superior, Colonel Grimes, that they had a problem, shock waves began to roll throughout Army Intelligence. One of their most valuable and trusted agents was failing a lie-detector test. It could be a career-breaker for all of them.

The next morning, March 26, Ralph checked out of the Vagabond Hotel. He met Schaffstall for breakfast at 8:30 A.M. at the Ramada Inn. Ralph seemed to be in good spirits, but still was at a loss to explain his previous reactions. Ralph said that as soon as he heard a question starting "Did you . . ." he experienced a "tight feeling" across his chest. Again Schaffstall left King and Ralph alone in room 377 to continue the polygraph examination. Ralph made some minor admissions that did not specifically address the problem areas from the previous day, and told King that he had taken one Dilantin tablet that morning to help him relax. He said he used this drug when he was going to meet the Russians because it helped him remain calm. Then King started the test.[38]

Again, when it came to questions about the operation, Ralph showed deception on his answers. He then admitted to King that he may have told his father about his work with Army Intelligence, and also mentioned an incident in 1967 when he told a co-worker that he was involved in an intelligence operation. He volunteered that many people he had worked with in Europe from 1968 to 1970 knew that he was involved in something related to intelligence, but he said he had not divulged his intelligence activities to any unauthorized person in Europe other than one. He admitted that his wife had known about the operation since the beginning, but said his daughter knew nothing about it.[39]

At 11:45, John Schaffstall came to meet Ralph for lunch, but Ralph said he had to go to his room at the Vagabond Hotel to pick up his bags, since he had checked out of the room that morning. He told Schaffstall that he had checked out because he had thought he would be through with the test by the end of the day. It took most of the lunch hour for Schaffstall to drive Ralph to the hotel, for Ralph to collect his personal belongings, and for them to return to the Ramada Inn. When they got back to the motel, Ralph said he was not hungry, so they went straight to the room. Since Ralph did not have a place to stay, Schaffstall told him he could sleep in room 377 that night. In addition to his luggage, Ralph was carrying three beers that remained in a six-pack container. Schaffstall left King and Ralph to continue the testing.

Odell King noticed the beer cans. Ralph told him he had consumed beer over the lunch hour, and that those beers were left over from the night before. King explained that the consumption of more than one beer might interfere with his suitability for testing. Defiantly, Ralph finished a can of beer and popped open a second.[40] Ralph's behavior was no surprise to John Schaffstall. "That would be Ralph. He would do that because Odell said it wasn't good for him to drink them. . . . That was Ralph. I wouldn't think it was unusual for Ralph to do that to Odell."[41]

Schaffstall said King should have stopped testing Ralph at this point, and made certain he stayed off substances that would skew any future tests.[42] But King continued testing Ralph. At 2:30 P.M., John called to check on their progress. King told Schaffstall to come to the room. As he walked into the suite, Ralph began drinking the last beer. King advised Schaffstall in front of Ralph that there were still problems. He said the problem seemed to arise in connection with questions relating to Ralph's unauthorized disclosure of his association with U.S. Army Intelligence, and also in connection with possible unauthorized disclosure of information.

Schaffstall suggested that they take a break so that King could prepare some new questions. King told Ralph that when he got back, they were going into some new areas on the polygraph exam. Schaffstall took Ralph to the bar during the break, and Ralph had a draft beer. He told Schaffstall, "I can't figure out why I'm failing." He said he had this guilty feeling, and whenever he heard certain questions, he had a tightening in his chest.[43] After a few minutes, Ralph returned to the room by himself to continue the exam.

Ralph told King that over the break he had two more beers. In spite of this, King continued the testing. By 4:30 P.M., King decided that Ralph was not suitable for further testing. Schaffstall arrived about the same time, and King told him that Ralph was still having problems. Schaffstall spent the next two and half hours with Ralph, trying to figure out what was wrong.[44] "Well, I walked him [Ralph] all over San Francisco and talked to him. 'Do you remember anything that could be causing it?' But he said no."[45] Ralph told Schaffstall that he felt "guilty" when King asked about the Soviets, but he did not know why. He confided that he needed the operation for his ego, and valued greatly his companionship with Carlos and Joe. He told Schaffstall he would be willing to take truth drugs or undergo hypnosis to clear up this matter—that he would do anything the Army wanted to continue the operation. Schaffstall reassured Ralph that the Army did not intend to charge or court-martial him for any mistakes he might have made. He told Ralph to relax that evening, and the polygraphs would continue the next morning.[46]

Schaffstall left Ralph in the room at the Ramada Inn and went to the motel's lounge to brief Noel Jones and Odell King. Jones had just flown in from Fort Meade. They decided that Jones would meet with Ralph to see if he could determine what was causing the problems.[47]

Schaffstall brought Jones up to the room to meet Ralph. Jones had met Ralph briefly on two previous occasions. Schaffstall introduced Jones and left. The next thirty minutes were very difficult for Ralph. He expressed surprise to see Jones, and told him that the Army must really be worried if he'd flown all the way out just to talk to him. Jones replied that they were very concerned and they needed to resolve these problems. Unlike Schaffstall, Jones was firm with Ralph, not friendly. Ralph reassured him that the operation was secure, and that the Army should not be worried about his problems with the polygraph examination.[48]

Unconvinced and somewhat irritated, Jones stopped Ralph and told him that he had come more to talk than to listen. Jones, with a no-nonsense demeanor, told Ralph that if he had any additional information to offer beyond what he had already provided, he should give it to Schaffstall and King. Very emphatically, Jones reminded Ralph that the Army had chosen him and placed its faith in his integrity, that the Army had always been good to Ralph through promotions and in other ways, and that the Army had always treated him fairly and truthfully. Ralph knew that Jones was deeply disappointed, suspicious, and upset. He agreed that Army Intelligence had been "extremely good" to him and had fully accepted him as a partner. He anxiously tried to assure Jones that there were no serious problems. He became agitated and asked if the operation was "over." Jones told Ralph to consider the operation "suspended" until the matters at hand were resolved.

Ralph became very thoughtful. Twice he started to speak and then stopped himself. Finally he said, "I have nothing to tell you now." Throughout the meeting, Jones felt that Ralph was seriously considering making a major revelation to him, but then he would stop. Ralph repeatedly reassured Jones that he and Carlos Zapata and Joe Prasek were okay, that the operation was secure. Eventually, Jones told Ralph to "sleep on it." He admonished Ralph to think very carefully about what might be causing him to indicate deception in the polygraphs, and then left.[49]

That Friday night, Ralph called Ilse. He wanted her to pick him up at the airport the next day. Ralph also took two more tablets to help him relax. He needed them. He was going to his meeting with the Russians, a meeting the Army knew nothing about. According to the notes in Sigler's diary, the Soviets had told him to dress elegantly. He had to "interview" a Russian agent in a hotel in San Francisco and ask him how it was going with the KGB. At the meeting, Ralph was asked about his marital status and domestic situation. He told both of the KGB men that he enjoyed working for the Soviets in addition to the money he was getting. When he asked one of the KGB men, whom he called "Vladie," about being in the KGB, Vladie replied that it was a job, "same as your FBI, or intelligence." [50]

When Ralph got back to the Ramada Inn on Friday night, he could not sleep. At 7:45 A.M. on Saturday, March 27, Schaffstall and Ralph met for coffee. Ralph seemed relaxed, but not his usual jovial self. King started the polygraph examination at 8:00 A.M. Without telling John, Ralph gave King a list of admissions he had prepared the preceding evening in the hopes of clearing up the exam. Ralph told King that he had taken two Dilantin tablets the night before, and he had only slept two hours.

> Is today Saturday?
> Are you now in the state of California?
> Did you arrive in San Francisco by airplane?
> Other than what you mentioned, have you ever illegally disposed of PX items?
> Do you own an automobile?
> Other than what you mentioned, have you ever illegally disposed of commissary items?
> Other than what you mentioned, have you ever dealt on the black market?

Again, when the questions left the administrative and inconsequential areas and started into the operation—Did anything happen with the Soviets that you have not told us about?—the indicators on the polygraph showed deception. When Schaffstall returned to the room to get Ralph for lunch, King told him that Ralph was still having problems.[51] Since Ralph had already made plans to fly home to El Paso that afternoon, Schaffstall and King agreed to suspend any further testing. "I'm a polygraph operator and . . . I did recommend that they stop. In San Francisco I stopped it after so many [polygraph tests]. I said, 'You're not going to get any more. This guy, he's going to flag out on everything if you keep trying to do this,' " John Schaffstall said.[52]

King told Ralph that he would like to meet with him again to discuss these matters further. In the meantime, he said Ralph should spend some time thinking about these particular areas. Packing his equipment into a suitcase, King informed Ralph, "I feel sure that we will meet again in the near future."[53]

After King left, Schaffstall told Ralph they needed more time to resolve the problems and asked Ralph whether he would be willing to come to Washington and try to work them out. Ralph responded that he wanted very much to clear up these difficulties because the operation was very important to him. Schaffstall was concerned, but reassured by Ralph's willingness to cooperate. He told Ralph that what was bothering him could be anything: "If you can't remember anything that happened that would cause you to react this way, don't worry about it now, because we can clear it up later. . . . This first initial thing doesn't necessarily mean that we have any suspicions that you've done anything wrong." He advised Ralph to take a few days off to relax, and told him they would handle all of his travel arrangements. It would probably be a week before they would have him up to the Fort Meade area. He also told Ralph that if he thought of anything that might be causing him to react to the polygraph, Ralph should tell him and not Carlos or Joe.[54]

Schaffstall watched as Ralph caught a taxi in front of the Ramada Inn for the airport. It was obvious that Ralph was withholding something, and the Army intended to find out what it was.

CHAPTER NINETEEN

Sigler: The Last Assignment

You're going to get caught. I don't care how good you are, if you
stay too long, you'll get caught.

John Schaffstall

RALPH CALLED ILSE and told her his plane from San Francisco was
delayed and he would be getting home late. When Ilse pulled up at the
El Paso Airport, she noticed Ralph was talking on the telephone. In
his hand was a Continental Airlines bag. As Ralph got in the car, Ilse
said, "What do you have in the bag?"

Ralph explained all the passengers on the flight had been given a
bottle of champagne from Continental Airlines. Ralph was in a bad
mood. He said to Ilse, "Let's drink that champagne." When they got
home, Ilse noticed he was very quiet. Ilse was not feeling well. She
was suffering from high blood pressure. "All that [was] because I
know there was something not working the right way again," Ilse
explains.

On Monday morning, members of the Gold Team, John Schaffstall,
and Louis Martel met at Fort Meade with Noel Jones and Odell King

315

to discuss Ralph's reactions to the polygraph exam. A more thorough review was made of Ralph's background material. Later that same day in El Paso, Ralph went into Fort Bliss and picked up the forms for his retirement physical.[1]

At the end of March, he made a list in his pocket diary of anything he could think of that might be causing him problems on the polygraph exam:

>money
>gold coin [There is a box drawn around this entry.]
>• slip of tongue.?
>• *manual.*
>• talked of classified items.
>• (cannot remember details
>guilty feeling, waiting
>for radio contact
>ashamed of not being
>able to hold liquor
>afraid?
>Why the trace?

Each item on the list represented an indiscretion or incident that was either admitted to by Ralph in San Francisco, or of which the Army was already aware. The notation "money," according to Schaffstall, represented the money that the KGB was sending Ralph's mother. The "gold coin" notation went back to an incident in which the Soviets gave Ralph some gold coins and he did not tell Schaffstall, "out of fear we would take them away. All we would do is check them out and return them." The notation "manual" referred to the time Ralph slipped a classified manual out of Fort Bliss and gave it to the Soviets because he had no approved feed material. For his handlers at the Army, the biggest concern was that Ralph had shown a tendency in Korea, in the incident with Bruce McCain, to "spill his guts when he had too much to drink."[2]

Louis Martel was sent to see McCain after that incident and have a talk with him. "I talked to the guy and I think I got the message across that he could never discuss what Ralph told him again," Martel says.[3] John Schaffstall remembers that Martel really frightened McCain.

What the Army feared was that Ralph had occasionally had too much to drink when he was with the Soviets, and may have given up details of the Army's counterintelligence operation itself. "Ralph really didn't have access to a lot of secrets unless they were passed to him by us. But where he could do the damage was in how we operated. He had been our star double so long and he knew so much," Martel said.

Of all the things on Ralph's list that should have set off alarm bells, but did not, was his mention of a "guilty feeling" while waiting for radio contact. According to Martel, it was not an area that was deeply explored. Had it been, it might have given the Army clues into a whole other side to Ralph's activities.

On March 30, 1976, Carlos Zapata called the director of security at Fort Bliss, Lt. Col. Robert L. Davenport, to request that Ralph be released from his temporary duty at White Sands. On March 31, Colonel Davenport made the appropriate arrangements for Ralph to return to Fort Bliss. During that same week, Bill Vaughn at Fort Bliss called Colonel Webster, Ralph's boss at White Sands, and requested leave for Ralph for one week. Colonel Webster said, "Okay. I can live with that."

On April 1, 1976, Ralph submitted his paperwork for his leave from April 4 through April 10. It indicated that he was going to spend a week with his father in Pennsylvania. That same day, Ralph took his daughter, Karin, with him to the hospital at Fort Bliss for his final retirement physical. His examination showed he was in good health. He stole a copy of his physical from the hospital. When they got back to the house, Ralph went into the garage, removed the carpet from the floor of the trunk of the new Trans Am, placed the copy of his physical on the trunk floor, and then reglued the carpeting. This may have been an indication that Ralph believed things were turning against him and he wanted some independent corroboration of his good health and sanity before he went to Fort Meade.

Before Ralph left for Washington, he told his commanding officer Colonel Webster and his colleagues at White Sands that he would be back on April 7 to handle a routine assignment.[4] He also told Ilse he would return around April 7. At 1:00 P.M., Sunday, April 4, 1976, Ilse and Ralph left for the airport. He told her he had to go to Washington to meet with the KGB. It was an important meeting. He told her nothing about the upcoming polygraph exam.

Just after they left the house, according to Ilse, two men in white shirts and black ties, driving a red pickup truck with an Army sticker, pulled out from a side street just a few blocks from the house, and followed them to the last turn into the airport. When they made a left turn, the red pickup went straight and a man in a white pickup truck pulled out. Ilse recognized him. He had been at the house the day before, talking to Ralph. On the left side of the street, two men were sitting in a green car when Ralph pulled up in front of the airport. Later, Ilse would recognize the green car as the same one used by Joe Prasek.

When Ralph got out of the car, he said to Ilse, "Good-bye. I'll see you Wednesday or Thursday. I'll call you." Ralph picked up his ticket at the airport. He flew from El Paso on American Airlines to Balti-more-Washington Friendship Airport. The round-trip ticket indicated a return to El Paso on April 7, 1976.

After Ralph arrived at the airport in Baltimore, he took a taxi from the airport to the Howard Johnson's Motor Lodge near the airport, about thirty minutes from Fort Meade, Maryland. He registered at 10:35 P.M. After he had unpacked, he called John Schaffstall at home in Virginia to tell him that he had arrived safely and was staying in room 620. As in San Francisco, they made arrangements to meet for breakfast at the motel restaurant the next morning.[5]

Army Intelligence did not bring Ralph into Fort Meade for the polygraph, because they still considered him a viable agent with his cover intact. If they could work out his difficulties with the lie-detector test, the operation would continue until his retirement. There were concerns that Fort Meade had been penetrated by the Soviets. If he was seen at the fort, the GRAPHIC IMAGE/LANDWARD HO operation would be over.[6]

At 8:30 A.M. on April 5, 1976, Ralph met Schaffstall for breakfast at Howard Johnson's. Ralph was in good spirits and appeared very con-fident. Over coffee, Ralph told Schaffstall that he had no problem areas left, and he was ready to pass the test. Schaffstall took Ralph up to room 404, which the Army had rented for the polygraph testing. Odell King was waiting for them. As in San Francisco, King had prepared three types of questions: first, administrative questions or irrelevant questions (for example, "Is today April 5, 1976?"); second, control questions, dealing with Ralph's background, used only for overall evaluation of each test; and, third, relevant questions dealing with Ralph's work with the Russians. Schaffstall left King and Ralph alone, and after the usual preliminary questions and instructions, King started again to test Ralph. The morning session was uneventful. They broke for lunch and then continued.

Again, when questions about his meetings with the Soviets were asked, Ralph displayed significant emotional reactions. At the end of six hours and twenty minutes of testing, King "mildly" confronted Ralph with his responses to these questions. Ralph became anxious. He tensed up in the chair, and King could see the strain in his face. Ralph provided little information to clear up these issues.[7]

At around 4:00 P.M., John Schaffstall returned to the Howard John-son's Motor Lodge and discovered that Ralph was still having prob-lems. As King left the room, he indicated to Ralph that he would be back. King then returned to Fort Meade to brief his superiors. Well into the night, Schaffstall and Ralph went over every single meeting Ralph had had with the Russians to try to figure out what the problem might be. Schaffstall remembers that he told Ralph "not to worry about anything. Whatever it was, we could work it out so that there was no problem. And I said, 'We can usually turn everything around where it will benefit both yourself and Army Intelligence.' And Ralph said, 'I don't know what it could be.' "

It was during the course of these discussions that Ralph admitted he had told a fellow Army officer, Bruce McCain, of his intelligence affiliation, indicating to McCain that he worked for the DIA and that he was a "national asset." But he denied that he had told the Russians he worked for Army Intelligence, or that he had passed the names of his intelligence contacts to the Soviets. Then Ralph dropped a bombshell. He said in passing that he had reviewed his notes before coming to Maryland, and those notes confirmed he had not passed on information regarding his intelligence contacts to the Soviets. Trying to project calmness while he tried to control his shock and dismay, Schaffstall asked Ralph about his notes. Matter-of-factly, Ralph responded that he kept diary-like notes in a well-concealed location at his home. Keeping notes on the operation was strictly forbidden, but Ralph displayed no remorse or apprehension. He told Schaffstall that he and Joe Prasek had often joked about their writing a book together about the operation. Ralph thought that at times Prasek was serious, but he assured Schaffstall that he never was. Ralph kept assuring Schaffstall that he had done nothing to damage the operation.

At this same time, the Special Operations Detachment at Fort Meade was in a state of near panic. Could one of their most trusted agents be working for the other side? What was Sigler keeping from them? Jones and Grimes felt that John Schaffstall was too close to Sigler for him to admit to Schaffstall that he had done something wrong. They decided that Sigler might feel more comfortable confiding his transgressions to a stranger than to a friend. Everyone involved knew that there was no way to clear up Sigler's deception on the polygraph test unless he told someone what was bothering him.

When Schaffstall left Ralph at the Howard Johnson's that evening, he did not know that at Fort Meade, that same afternoon, Noel Jones and Donald Grimes had decided to take him off the case. Schaffstall would never see Ralph again. He would have to rely on daily briefings to find out what was happening on the case. He remembers what Noel Jones told him when he got back to Fort Meade: "And then Noel came in and he said . . . and I agreed with him—maybe Ralph didn't want to tell me anything because . . . Ralph might have had some sense of loyalty to me and he was saying, 'Gee, I've messed this guy up not telling him everything. I'm not going to talk to him. I won't tell him.' "

Louis R. Martel was assigned to be Ralph's new project officer. Martel had worked with Schaffstall and was familiar with the GRAPHIC IMAGE operation, but he did not know Ralph as well as Schaffstall did.

He had met Ralph only once, in 1974 in El Paso, just after his trip to Vienna to meet with the Soviets. "Lou was . . . a good guy. Everybody liked Lou. In fact, he drank with everybody," John Schaffstall recalls.[8]

That night at the Howard Johnson's, Ralph called Ilse to tell her he had arrived safely. Ilse asked him how he was doing. "I'm fine," Ralph replied. Ilse wanted to know where he was. "I'm in a motel room, watching TV," Ralph said. He said he would be home Wednesday or Thursday.

On the morning of April 6, 1976, Noel Jones took Lou Martel over to the Howard Johnson's to meet Ralph Sigler. Ralph was surprised to see them, since he was expecting Schaffstall. "How come John is not here?" Ralph asked. Jones explained that for now Ralph would not be seeing John, but that he would be seeing Lou instead. Ralph did not seem either pleased or disappointed by the change of personnel.[9] They began discussing the polygraph tests, and Ralph again insisted that he did not know why he was having problems with the exams. For about an hour the three men talked. Martel and Jones emphasized that Ralph should not worry about anything he might tell them. The Army had no intention of prosecuting him for any actions he might have taken, or of punishing him in any way. They encouraged him to tell them anything that was bothering him. Ralph denied that he had done anything wrong. Then Jones asked Martel to leave the two of them alone. Martel left the motel and drove around the area for a while.[10]

Noel Jones thought it was time to have a heart-to-heart talk with Ralph. For three hours he tried to help Ralph figure out what was causing his polygraph problems. Jones told Ralph that everyone at Army Intelligence believed he could not have done any irreparable harm to the operation. If it would make Ralph more comfortable, Jones said he would get Ralph a letter of immunity from prosecution. Ralph said he did not think he needed any such immunity.[11]

Throughout this meeting, Ralph professed an inability to understand why he was unable to pass the polygraph examination, and said repeatedly, "I don't know what to tell you." At several points, just when Jones was about to give up, Ralph would seem quite introspective. Each time, Jones believed that he was considering making a confession. But each time Ralph would become more and more frustrated and would again express his bafflement over what might be causing the problem. He appeared to be uncertain whether he should reveal any information to Jones or not.[12]

Lou Martel returned from his drive to the motel. He called the room they had reserved for the polygraph, and talked to Noel Jones. Jones told Martel that he was getting nowhere, that Ralph was still sticking to his story. Jones said he did not see any reason to continue at that time, since they were not getting anywhere. He told Martel that he was going to tell Ralph he was leaving and that they would see him the following day. Martel hung up the phone and went to the car to wait for Jones.[13]

When Jones finally came, he was excited. He said he thought that he had the key to this whole situation. When he had told Ralph, "Okay, this is it for today, I'll see you tomorrow," Ralph had dropped another bombshell.[14] He had told Jones that he had had meetings with the FBI or CIA about his work with the Russians that he had not told the Army about.[15] He seemed relieved to have confessed. He said that perhaps that was the reason he had failed the polygraphs. Jones agreed with Ralph, and said he thought his actions would not be held against him. Ralph appreciated Jones's reassurance. Jones remembers leaving Ralph's room "absolutely fuming. The FBI had done this to us before. You would call those guys on it, and they just were not capable of telling you the truth."[16] When Jones left Ralph, he indicated to him that Martel would be over the next day to see him, and that there probably would be another polygraph test.[17]

That evening, between 10:00 and 11:00 P.M., Ralph called Ilse to tell her he would not be home on Wednesday. "Something came up," he told her. He said he would call her later and tell her when he was coming home.[18]

At around 10:30 A.M. on April 7, 1976, Lou Martel went to the Howard Johnson's to see if he could get more details from Ralph about his earlier confession. He brought with him some office notes about the operation to help jog Ralph's memory. Again, nothing. Martel kept telling Ralph that it didn't make any difference, the operation would continue. All the Army wanted was to find out what was bothering him.[19]

By this time, Martel was convinced "Ralph was playing both sides against the middle . . . I thought he was working for the Russians, stringing us along and doing the same to them. . . . It's a real temptation for agents to say the Russians are demanding this, this, and this. Then he goes back to them and says, 'I might be able to get you this and this and this, but the price has got to go up.'. . . That's what I thought he had done."

Four hours later, Martel told Ralph that Odell King would be over in the morning to administer the polygraph test. In response to this news, Ralph made another confession about his work. He told Martel that because of increasing pressure from the Soviets in recent years for more and better information, he had decided on his own to tell them whatever they asked that he knew. He said that he had done this because he felt that if he did not, the Soviets would lose interest in him and the operation would end.[20] Martel replied that it was fine, the Army could live with that. He said, "We will be home free. This will resolve all our problems." Before he left to return to Fort Meade to report in, he told Ralph, "Please don't overindulge in alcoholic beverages, and don't take any medicine unless absolutely necessary, or any stimulants, anything of that nature. And please attempt to get a good night's sleep." [21]

At the afternoon debriefing, Noel Jones, John Schaffstall, Lou Martel, Odell King, and Donald Grimes wanted nothing more than to clean up Ralph's polygraph once and for all. They did not like the idea of Ralph having notes at his home. It was decided that these notes might contain some information that would be of value in resolving the situation. They decided to send John Schaffstall to El Paso to pick up Ralph's operational notes, since he knew Mrs. Sigler.[22] Martel said that Odell King had cautioned that there was little point in doing any more polygraph tests, because Ralph had been through so many that the responses were becoming meaningless. Grimes and Jones overruled King.

At 8:30 A.M. on April 8, 1976, John Schaffstall boarded a plane at Dulles International Airport for El Paso. While Schaffstall was still in the air, Odell King arrived at the Howard Johnson's to perform the next polygraph examination. Ralph was beginning to know King quite well. King explained that he was there mainly to verify on the polygraph the information Ralph had provided to Noel Jones and Lou Martel about his work with the FBI or CIA and his disclosures to the Soviets, to make certain that these revelations were the cause of Ralph's questionable responses. Ralph gave King substantially the same information that he had given Jones and Martel, but he began to change his story. King and Ralph worked on some questions to clear up some of these issues on the polygraph.[23]

Odell King asked Ralph a series of baseline questions and then studied the charts. He was unable to determine the number of the question Ralph had lied on, and he told Ralph that this might indicate that he was not testable that day. Ralph agreed, explaining that he had had very little sleep the night before and was very tired. He *looked* tired. He said he wanted to go home. King told Ralph to take a lunch break, relax, and have a bite to eat. When he came back to the polygraph suite, King would administer another test to see if Ralph was relaxed enough to undergo a polygraph exam. Ralph said, "Okay," and left the suite.[24]

King wanted to attend to some personal business during lunch, so he drove back to Fort Meade. Forty-five minutes later he returned to the Howard Johnson's, where Ralph was anxiously waiting for him downstairs. Ralph said he wanted to talk to King some more about the questions they had discussed. When they got back to the room, Ralph began to deny his earlier admissions. He said he was no longer certain that the account he had previously given was true. He said he knew that some remarks he had made were jocular in nature, but he could no longer be sure that the account he had previously given was accurate. Stunned, King asked him why he felt that way. Ralph replied that he must have convinced himself that it had happened in the way he had described, but now he was not really sure.[25]

King knew they could not continue. There was no real reason to attempt further polygraph testing on Ralph's recent disclosures, because he could not answer an unqualified "yes" or "no" regarding the actual occurrence. So King ended the session.[26]

Disappointed, King called Martel at his office at Fort Meade, told him things were not going well, and asked him to come over to the motel. He did not want to get into much detail on the phone. When Martel arrived, Odell explained that there was no way he could administer the test because Ralph claimed to have gotten only two hours' sleep and was too tired. If Ralph was not physiologically prepared to take the test, it would be invalid.

Lou Martel was getting angry; he knew Ralph was deliberately skewing the tests by his actions. When King said Ralph was now denying that the events he had admitted to earlier had even occurred, Martel walked over to Ralph and said, "Ralph, in a matter of less than two days you've made these admissions, and now you want to take it all back. What the hell's going on?" But Ralph had no answer. He was not rational. King left Martel and Ralph alone in the suite, and returned to his office at Fort Meade.[27]

For a while, Martel tried to talk to Ralph about why he now wanted to recant his story. Finally, Martel thought, "Well, we're not getting anywhere here now. He's tired. He's run down," so he said, "Okay, Ralph, let's go down to the bar and have a beer and relax and just forget about this crap for a little while." Ralph was relieved, and agreed immediately. They went downstairs and sat at the bar. They were the only customers in the lounge. They had a beer and talked in general about automobiles and various things. Ralph told Martel about buying his daughter a car, and they discussed the pros and cons of buying a new car. Martel had just bought a new Chrysler Cordoba, and Ralph wanted to know how he liked it.[28]

Martel left Ralph alone at the bar for a few minutes and went to the phone to call Noel Jones. He told Jones in general terms that Ralph could not be "fluttered" successfully because of his fatigue. Jones reminded Martel that Schaffstall was in El Paso, and told him to ask Ralph to give his permission for Schaffstall to retrieve the notes concealed in his house. Martel put down the phone and went back to the bar to ask Ralph, who said, "Hey, yes, those notes might help jog my memory." To Martel, Ralph seemed to cheer up. He returned to the phone to tell Jones that Ralph said he would go back to the room, call his wife in El Paso, and tell her that Schaffstall would be coming to their home to retrieve some papers, and that she should assist him.[29]

In El Paso, Ilse Sigler was at work. As Martel and Ralph left the bar, Ralph said ironically, "Boy, you're lucky that you're dealing with a guy with a good memory. It's not every guy who knows his wife's work telephone number. But," he continued, "I remember it, so I can . . . call her."

"Fine," Martel replied.

As they got off the elevator and walked toward the room, Ralph commented blandly, "Well, you know, if you're going to use these notes against me, maybe I should have her destroy them."

Martel could not tell whether Ralph was serious or just joking around, but felt that he was just throwing the comment out to get a reaction.

Inside the room, Martel explained, "Ralph, we don't want the notes for any other purpose but at this time to help you. And they are not going to be used against you. We want to review them."

Ralph apologized for keeping the notes in the first place. Martel continually reassured him that the Army merely wanted the notes to help clear all this up. Ralph said, "Okay. Fine," and at around 3:30 P.M. he placed the call to his wife at the El Paso dress store where she worked. When Ilse got on the line, Ralph said in a joking manner, "This is your loving husband." Never before had he said that to Ilse. Today, Ilse thinks Ralph was trying to send her some kind of warning.[30]

During their telephone conversation, Ilse heard a funny noise in the background that sounded like a military radio transmission. Ralph sounded as if he had had a few drinks. Ralph told Ilse that Schaffstall was coming by the house. "Do you remember John—the one who came to see you . . . at the house at Fairfax and [then] Kenworthy?" he asked. He said Schaffstall would be coming by that evening to pick up some material he had in the house that he had forgotten.

"Where are the papers?" Ilse asked him.

"In the stereo. John will know," Ralph explained. "He will pick them up at six."

Ralph hung up, turned toward Martel, and told him where the notes were hidden. He said, "The stuff that you're interested in is in the Grundig, the stereo . . . just take it apart . . . and you'll find it." He explained that Schaffstall would have to take the back off the stereo to get the notes. He insisted that Schaffstall not go to the house until his daughter had left for school. Karin was taking some evening courses at Texas Tech and she left around 6:00 P.M. Martel told Ralph that he would make sure Schaffstall got the message.[31]

Then Martel asked Ralph why he had kept the notes in the first place. Ralph answered that he had used the notes to refresh his memory for the debriefings. Then, half joking and half sincere, he admitted that he had thought about writing a book, but he really was not serious about it. Martel told Ralph that he would be back the following day and that they would talk some more then. Maybe, if they just talked, they could get more information, and then possibly another polygraph could be scheduled, for a later date.[32]

John Schaffstall arrived in El Paso at around 1:15 P.M. Shortly after he checked into the La Quinta hotel, he called Noel Jones. Jones told Schaffstall that Ralph had called his wife to make arrangements for him to pick up the notes at the house. Jones instructed him not to go to the house until after Ralph's daughter left for school at 6:00 P.M.

Between 2:00 P.M. and 3:00 P.M. in El Paso, Schaffstall phoned Ilse Sigler at work. She had already heard from Ralph, and was prepared for the call. Schaffstall said he would like to come out to the house and pick up the items Ralph had left. Ilse agreed. She said, "I will be working until six and I will be home after six-thirty." She knew she had to close the store and then stop by the grocery store on her way home from work.[33]

Schaffstall went to the house early and waited in a small brown rental car parked down the street until he saw Karin leave for school. Honoring Ralph's request, he wanted to make certain that he saw her leave before he went to the house. When Ilse got home, she noticed Schaffstall sitting in his car, waiting for her to arrive. She rushed over to the stereo to see if she could find the papers, but she found nothing.

About five minutes later, Schaffstall walked up to the house. He and Ilse exchanged pleasantries as he walked into the house.

"How are you?" Ilse said.

"Long time no see," replied John.

Ilse said, "Sit down, John. Please sit down." She thought they were going to talk for a few minutes, but he did not sit down.

He indicated that he was there on business and said, "You know why I am here."[34]

Ilse then took Schaffstall back to the spare bedroom where Ralph kept all of his things. She helped him move the stereo away from the wall, and he noticed that the back was screwed on. He asked Ilse if she had a screwdriver. She left, and returned with two screwdrivers, a Phillips and a regular. After John had unscrewed the back, he looked inside. He was surprised to see that there was more inside than just a few operational notes. In the speaker wells were a gray metal box, ten by seven by four and a half inches, with a little metal handle; a large, white, plastic three-ring notebook; a U.S. government manila envelope containing handwritten notes and two black and red notebooks labeled in gold-colored letters "Journal" and "Record"; and another manila envelope, with more notes and sketches. The metal box was locked. Ilse said Schaffstall looked for the keys and found them—two keys. "Here are the keys," she remembers him saying as he dangled them in front of her. "Ralph was a little sneaky. Sometimes too sneaky," she recalls Schaffstall saying. In a later interview, John Schaffstall insisted there were no keys, and that he had to pry open the box.[35]

Schaffstall gathered up all of the material and headed for the front door. He was very nervous. In the hallway, he dropped some of the papers. Ilse asked him if he would like a paper bag to help carry everything. He said, "Yes. I would appreciate it." She brought him a bag. He put the notebook, the envelopes, and the box in the bag and started to leave. On his way out, he commented to Ilse, "It was nice seeing you again. We will have to talk soon. *Very soon*." He returned to the hotel and called Joe Prasek to come over and review the materials with him.[36]

At around eight o'clock that night, Joe Prasek arrived at Schaffstall's La Quinta hotel room. Upon opening the gray metal box, they found used train tickets; maps of Mexico and Zurich; photographs of Vienna that Ralph had taken during his operation there; ten passports with different names; the Soviet code pads Ralph used for his messages; a little blank address book and photographs of Ralph with three or four different men at some beach. To John, the beach looked as though it was in Mexico—it was a tropical beach. The men had on bathing suits and were carrying towels. John wondered about the photographs. Why would he keep them in a box? What did the pictures mean? Other than Ralph, he did not recognize any of the men. One thing they did *not* find in the box were the Canadian identification cards the Russians had given Ralph. They thought Ralph would have hidden them in the box too.

Prasek took a secret writing pad that the Soviets had given Ralph, unexposed microfilm that the Soviets had provided for intelligence photography, and the written radio transmission schedules and codes that the Soviets used to communicate with Ralph. Prasek expressed surprise that Ralph was having difficulty with the polygraph tests. "Well, he [Prasek] thought that they were just reading the test improperly," Schaffstall remembers.[37]

The next morning, Schaffstall flew back to Washington with the notebooks and the gray metal box. Waiting for him at Washington National Airport was Richard J. McGhee, a courier from Army Intelligence, who picked up the materials and took them back to Fort Meade.[38]

April 9, 1976, was a beautiful spring day in Washington. That morning, Lou Martel went to his boss, Noel Jones, and suggested, "Hey, look, why don't I take him out today and we have a few beers? We'll go have a few drinks." Throughout the polygraph ordeal, Ralph had begged first Schaffstall and then Martel, "You guys, you've got to help me. . . . There's something—there's something. I don't know what it is. You've got to help me get it out. Now let's talk. Help me get it out, whatever is bothering me." So Martel decided, "Well, maybe he will loosen up if he has a few drinks in a friendly atmosphere. Maybe the alcohol will be the crutch he needs to bring this out. Maybe he just doesn't want to say it while completely sober or in complete control of his faculties, but if he has a few drinks in him, then he can, in his own mind, rationalize it—'I didn't tell him that while I was in complete control of my faculties.' "[39]

Looking back, Schaffstall now thinks this approach was hopeless. "Ralph had been with Soviets who tried to get him drunk and everything else, and they never got anything away from him . . . he didn't fall into that type of trap. I don't think he would have gotten drunk with Martel. I think Martel would have gotten drunk before Ralph got drunk."

But Noel Jones told Martel to go ahead and try it. They had tried almost everything else. What was there to lose? So Martel drove over to the Howard Johnson's and asked Ralph if he would like to go out drinking. Martel said, "It might be better for you, and something might come of it. You need some time, anyway."

"Okay, I'll go with you," Ralph replied.

So they started out to visit the bars in the area and have a few beers. Initially, Martel tried to keep the conversation completely away from intelligence matters. He talked in general terms about world affairs. But after a couple of sips of beer, Ralph turned to him in desperation and said, "Gee, you've got to help me remember things. I don't know why I'm reacting to this poly."

"Hey, neither do I," Martel responded. "We've been over it. There's basically nothing left to explore, Ralph. We've explored about every avenue. But if you want me to, we'll talk some more about it."[40]

"Well, it might. Maybe it will help," Ralph replied. ·

He and Martel went back over a few of the things they had talked about during the week. Then Martel said, "I know that you've been asked this before, but I'm going to throw it out again. . . . [Portions of this conversation were withheld by the government on grounds of national security.] Now I think that's where we're having problems here."

Ralph turned to Martel and said, "That's it. You hit the nail on the head."

Surprised, Martel thought, "After all this time we [have] been together [and now he's saying] that's it."

"Let's get out of here. This isn't a good place to talk about this," Martel told Ralph. They finished their beer, went to the car, and started driving around the area.[41]

Ralph had told Martel he had given the Soviets unauthorized information. Some of the information included the names of the men he worked with in Army Intelligence. "He says that all he did was mention names," John Schaffstall said. Later, in an interview, John Schaffstall said he did not believe Ralph. "My gut tells me that he told the Soviets a lot about us. . . . I think he got in a bind and he gave them a list of intelligence officers that he knew on the post or he knew around. Maybe he traded me and Zapata." [42]

During the drive, Ralph continued to talk about the operation. He admitted to doing certain things to "improve the operation" and for his own ego. Growing more and more encouraged, both Ralph and Martel finally convinced each other that Ralph's latest confession was the key to unlocking the mysterious deceptions on Ralph's polygraph examinations. Ralph felt that with this admission out in the open, the Army could go on with the polygraphs. To celebrate, Martel took Ralph to the Timbuktu cocktail lounge, where they had a few more beers. "He was in a more outward mood. He was damned near jovial," Martel remembers. Ralph flirted with the waitresses and he and Martel talked. Ralph started up a conversation with two men at the next table who were getting drunk while waiting for their plane to Cleveland.[43]

Martel left Ralph with the two men, laughing, smoking, and joking, and went to the phone to call Noel Jones. Excited, he told Jones that he thought he had the answer to the whole thing. Ralph had finally divulged what was bothering him. He advised headquarters that he and Ralph were going to have a few more beers, then he would drop Ralph off at the motel and return to Fort Meade. Jones said, "Fine, go ahead." [44]

After a few more beers, the two men at the next table had to leave for the airport. Shortly after they had left, Martel said, "Well, Ralph, I'm going to take you back now." Ralph was intoxicated, but not staggering. He was in control of himself, but one could tell he had had a few beers. On the drive back to the motel, Martel realized that he had not taken any notes of their conversation. How could he? He was either drinking at a bar or driving the car. And he had had a few drinks himself. What Ralph had told him seemed a little vague in his mind, and he knew he would have to talk to Ralph the next day to get down on paper exactly what he had divulged.[45]

Even though the following day was a Saturday, Martel told Ralph that he would probably see him in the morning. "Do you mind if I call my wife tonight?" Ralph asked.

"Hey, you're free to call anybody you want," Martel responded. "No, I don't mind; go ahead, call your wife."

Ralph was in a good mood. They said good night. Martel left Ralph at the rear entrance of the Howard Johnson's and returned to Fort Meade.[46]

That evening in El Paso, Colonel Webster called Ralph's home to see why he was not back at work. He asked Ilse if she had heard from Ralph, and if she knew when he would be home. She said she had spoken to her husband and she expected him back that weekend. Colonel Webster asked her to have Ralph call him when he returned.[47]

April 10, 1976, was another beautiful day. That morning, Schaffstall, Jones, and Martel reviewed the notes and other material Schaffstall had retrieved from the Sigler house. All three were surprised by the depth of detail of the notes, which were the equivalent of a complete history of Ralph's intelligence activities and contained specific information on the names of American and Soviet intelligence personnel with whom he had dealt, the dates and places of his contacts with intelligence personnel, and information passed by Ralph to the Soviets at these meetings.

In his haste to get to the motel that morning, Lou Martel only had a few minutes to look through the notebooks. He saw nothing that Ralph had not already admitted to. Outside of violating operational rules by keeping the diaries, Martel saw no big breakthrough in what Schaffstall had brought back from El Paso. Instead he focused on Ralph's admissions from the previous day. His plan was to hand Ralph a blank ledger book and have him write down everything he could remember. Noel Jones decided to go with Martel to the Howard Johnson's. Martel picked up a blank ledger and they drove to the motel.[48]

Before Jones and Martel arrived, Ralph went to the front desk and checked out of Howard Johnson's. He used his MasterCard to pay the bill, which came to $132.22 for the week. Ralph knew that using his MasterCard was against Army procedures. He was instructed to use cash always. "The rules were pay cash. Never pay with your credit card," John Schaffstall said. "But he had enough money to pay in cash. And he knew he was going to see us again, and if he needed anything, all he had to do was ask for money."[49]

At around 10:00 A.M., Jones and Martel went to the coffee shop at the Howard Johnson's and had a cup of coffee while Ralph finished his breakfast. They left the coffee shop, and as they walked around, Martel gave Ralph the ledger and told him to write down everything he had told him the previous day, and anything else that he could remember. He should take the weekend and do it thoroughly. They would pick up the ledger on Monday. Ralph agreed, and commented that it would give him something to do. Martel asked in passing if he had called his wife the night before. Ralph said, "No. I decided not to." Even though Ralph had used his MasterCard, he told them that he had paid his bill at the motel and needed some cash. Martel gave him twenty dollars of his own money to "tide him over." He reminded Ralph that if anything came up over the weekend, he should call Schaffstall at home, and John would relay any messages. To Jones and Martel, Ralph did not seem unduly concerned about what was going on, but he did appear to be repentant about the disclosures he had made throughout the week. They said good-bye, and Jones and Martel returned to Fort Meade.[50]

At 10:57 A.M., Ralph re-registered at the Howard Johnson's. The carelessness of allowing Sigler to hang around the Howard Johnson's for a week under his own name and then to re-register was described by intelligence experts interviewed for this book as an unforgivable security breach. It is also curious that in a similar fashion, Ralph had checked out early from the Vagabond Hotel in San Francisco.

That evening Ralph placed a call to his wife. When Ilse answered, Ralph said he had tried to call earlier, but had not gotten an answer. Ilse explained that she had been out with Karin and they had just returned. She asked him how he was, and Ralph replied, "Fine."

But he did not sound fine to Ilse. He sounded tired. His pronunciation did not sound right. He seemed to be watching what he was saying. Ilse told Ralph about Colonel Webster's call the night before, and suggested that he make sure there were no problems with his leave. She asked if he had gotten the materials he had asked for, the ones Schaffstall had picked up. Ralph replied, "Yes, the papers got to me. How long did John stay?"

"Just for around ten or fifteen minutes," Ilse replied. Since it was Saturday, she asked, "Are you calling me tomorrow?" because Ralph always called home on Sundays when he was out of town.

"It depends on the way I feel," Ralph answered strangely. Then he asked, "By the way, will you be home Monday?" He wanted to make sure that she was, as usual, not working at the store on Monday.

"Yes," she assured him, but, explaining that she had had to move a doctor's appointment to Monday morning, she said, "I will be home after ten."[51]

Ralph did not mention a letter he wrote to Ilse, which was dated April 10 and was on Howard Johnson's stationery. He could have written it to her after their Saturday phone conversation. But he did tell her about it in their Monday conversation, and he was very interested Saturday in whether Ilse would be home for his call on Monday.

For the rest of the weekend, no one from Army Intelligence saw Ralph Sigler. On Sunday afternoon, April 11, Ralph called John Schaffstall at his home in Virginia and told him he was running low on money and needed to have his leave extended. Ralph told Schaffstall that his wife had told him that Colonel Webster at White Sands had called to inquire why he was not back at work. Schaffstall advised Ralph that he would get him some money, and he would have Carlos Zapata call Colonel Webster and straighten out any problems. He asked how things were going. Ralph replied that things seemed to be going okay. The conversation was brief. To Schaffstall, Ralph did not sound upset or depressed.[52]

On Monday morning, April 12, 1976, Lou Martel met with Noel Jones and Colonel Grimes at Army Intelligence at Fort Meade. They decided that for security reasons Ralph had been at the Howard Johnson's long enough. For over a week, Ralph had been drinking at the bar and eating at the restaurant. They did not want anyone to wonder why Sigler had been hanging around the motel all this time. They decided to move Ralph from the Howard Johnson's to the Holiday Inn down the street.[53]

Later that morning, Lou Martel went to the Howard Johnson's, and Ralph gave him the ledger. Martel said to Ralph, "Well, we're going to go to the Holiday Inn on Route 1. We'll check out of here." He explained that they wanted to move him for security reasons. Ralph was glad to get some new surroundings. He had been at the same motel for over a week, and indicated that he would enjoy a change in scenery. Martel gave Ralph some cash and waited in the car for him to check out so he could drive Ralph over to the Holiday Inn.[54] Instead of using the cash, which was standard procedure, Ralph again put the motel bill on his MasterCard. Later, Martel and Schaffstall would find Ralph's actions very strange, since they both had given Ralph plenty of cash to cover his expenses.[55]

Ralph came out of the motel and got into the government car Martel was waiting in. They drove to the other motel. Again, Martel waited in the car while Ralph checked into the Holiday Inn. When he registered, Ralph indicated on the form that he would be there three days, and would be checking out on Wednesday, April 14. Ralph came back out to the car and told Martel he would be in room 326. Martel replied, "Fine. I have to go back now to Fort Meade. Why don't you go . . . to your room, hang up your clothes . . . and I will be back to talk to you later." Martel then drove back to Fort Meade with the ledger.[56]

When Martel got back to the office later that morning, he, Jones, and others had a meeting to go over the ledger. They decided that Martel should go back to the Holiday Inn and go over the ledger with Ralph, point by point. They wanted to see if he had any additions to what he had written, or if he wanted to give further, verbal explanations.

Martel said that he told the others in the meeting that the polygraph questions were "too vague. . . . Let's give Ralph a solid question that he has to give a yes or no answer to. . . . My feeling was that what [we] needed to do was ask him if the Russians had given him a telephone number to call in San Francisco."

Noel Jones decided that Peter Conway, another member of the Gold Team, would go with Lou Martel. Jones thought that while Martel was reading the ledger and Ralph was answering questions, Conway might pick up expressions or comments that Martel might miss.[57]

Schaffstall did not like Pete Conway very much. "I wouldn't ask him to do my operation. . . . I didn't like his attitude. Sort of standoffish. Abrupt. Sometimes he'd joke about everything and other times he wouldn't say anything. . . . I don't think he was compatible with the group that we had. He was different."[58] Other Army Intelligence operatives remember Conway as a "loner."

Pete Conway and Lou Martel drove to the Holiday Inn and went through the ledger with Ralph, page by page, taping the session. Neither the ledger itself nor Ralph's remarks that afternoon disclosed anything of significance beyond what Martel remembered Ralph telling him on the previous Friday. When Martel finished, Ralph seemed to be in a good mood. Martel never asked Ralph about the notes Schaffstall had retrieved from his house, or the contents of the gray metal box. To the Army, these materials were a disappointment. They did not contain anything that would give them a clue about what was bothering Ralph.

Martel told Ralph that the next day, Tuesday, April 13, there would be another polygraph examination and that he felt very confident now that they had cleared everything up. Ralph agreed. He said, "I'm going to pass now. There's not going to be any problems. No more problems."

Martel responded that he hoped there wouldn't be, and that he felt very good about it. As they shook hands, Ralph said, "I think we've got it now."

Martel replied, "Yes . . . we're on the right track now." For the fourth time since he had been seeing Ralph over the past week, Martel repeated, "Ralph, please don't drink tonight, and try to get a good night's sleep. I feel very confident that we've got it made now, and you should be able to sleep well now. You've divulged everything. And be ready for the poly. . . . Please don't go out drinking."[59]

Martel and Conway left Ralph in the room. They decided to have a drink, so they went downstairs and sat in a booth in the cocktail lounge and ordered drinks. As the waitress removed the drinks from her tray and put them on the table, Ralph walked into the bar. He saw them in the booth, but paid no attention to them. He walked up to the bar, sat on a stool, and ordered a beer. Stunned, Martel and Conway gulped down their drinks, left some money on the table, got up, and left Ralph sitting at the bar. Neither man stopped to admonish Ralph for his behavior, or tried to encourage him to quit drinking and return to his room.[60]

That afternoon, Ralph called Ilse at home. He asked about her blood pressure. Ilse told him the reading was down from the last time. Then he changed the subject. "There is a letter coming for you," he told her in a long, drawn-out voice.

Ilse asked him to talk louder. He sounded depressed.

"I will speak up. I have gotten in trouble, but it is not us. It is them. They don't want to do that anymore," Ralph explained.

All Ilse could say was, "Oh."

Ralph continued, "If the test turns out good, they will let me go home tomorrow."

Ilse asked, "Will you be home for Easter?"

But Ralph replied despondently, "I don't know. Be a good girl. I will call you. How is Nicky [their dog]?" "He is fine," Ilse responded.[61] She was now very worried.

The first thing Tuesday morning, members of the Gold Team, along with Noel Jones and Donald Grimes, met with Odell King to discuss Ralph's upcoming polygraph. They decided which areas were to be covered in the polygraph that day. Martel's question about the San Francisco phone number from the Russians was included, as well as some more specific questions about contacts with the Soviets.

Throughout the past week, Ralph had admitted to unreported contacts with the Soviets, failure to report Soviet tasking, passing unauthorized information to the Soviets, false reporting of money paid him by the Soviets, and reporting untruthfully about a member of the U.S. Army whom he had recommended to the Soviets as a recruitment target.[62]

That morning, the letter Ralph had mentioned to his wife the night before was mailed. (It has an April 13, 1976, A.M. postmark.)

Since King was not quite sure where the Holiday Inn was, Martel said, "Okay, I'll run out with you. You follow me out." Before they left, Martel called Ralph to make sure he was there. Martel drove his car, and King went in his.

As King was setting up his equipment, Martel talked to Ralph and said, "Now, is there anything that you thought of overnight? Have you had a good night's sleep?"

"Yes, everything's fine," Ralph replied.

"Didn't get drunk last night, did you?" Martel continued.

"No."

"Okay, good," Martel said, and wished Ralph the best of luck.[63]

Martel only stayed for around fifteen minutes. Ralph appeared to be in a very good mood. Throughout his conversation with Ralph, Odell King reinforced Martel's encouragement. "Well, from what I've learned, we have a pretty good chance of resolving this," King said.

Martel said, "Good-bye, Ralph. I'm leaving you in the capable hands of Mr. King."

Martel walked out the door at around 11:00 A.M. on Tuesday, April 13, got in his car, and drove back to Fort Meade. He never saw Ralph Sigler alive again.[64]

Sigler: The Last Polygraph

Poor Ralph. He got the short end of everything.

John Schaffstall

FOR OVER THREE HOURS on Tuesday, April 13, 1976, Ralph Sigler underwent his final polygraph examination with Odell King at a separate room rented for the test at the Holiday Inn in Jessup, Maryland. After the usual formalities—"Have you eaten?" "How much sleep have you received?" "Have you taken any drugs or alcohol?"—and the completion of the appropriate consent forms, Odell attached the instruments to Ralph's body and began the test.

Again, when the questions began to center on the operation and Ralph's previous disclosures, emotional responses indicating deception were recorded on the polygraph charts. " 'Have you had any contacts with any foreign intelligence that you haven't told us about?' 'Is there anything that you haven't told us about?' 'Have you ever told the Soviets [something you should not]?' He was showing deception there. But he could show deception on all those questions. . . . Once

you show deception on one, you are going to do it on the rest of them,"
John Schaffstall later explained.

King asked Ralph Lou Martel's question. "Did the Soviets give you
a phone number to call in San Francisco?" Ralph said no. The polygraph needle jumped again.

Ralph did not seem surprised when King told him that the results
were not altogether favorable to him. As Ralph looked at the polygraph
charts, he remained calm. He agreed with King that emotional responses were indicated on the charts, but said that he felt better about
this particular test than he had about previous ones.

King gave him a chance to explain the significance of his responses,
but Ralph said he could not. Although King never directly accused
him of lying, he beseeched Ralph to provide some explanation for his
reactions, or he would have to conclude that Ralph had not been
completely truthful. Ralph asked if the Army was planning to use a
truth serum on him. King replied that he knew of no such plan.[1]

King called Lou Martel at Fort Meade to tell him that Ralph was
still failing his polygraph. After a short discussion at Fort Meade, Noel
Jones called King back and told him to pack up his equipment and
return to the base. Shortly after 2:00 P.M., as King was leaving the
motel room, Ralph asked him to get him a six-pack of beer. King
replied that he was sorry, but he did not have time. He suggested that
Ralph go down to the bar in the motel if he wanted a beer. Ralph said
he did not feel like going down and drinking at the bar. Besides, the
bar was expensive, and he could not take the bottles or cans from the
bar to his room. King assured Ralph that he would tell Lou Martel
about his request when he got back to Fort Meade, and he was sure
that Martel would bring him some beer if that was possible. At 2:45
P.M., King left Ralph alone in the room, never to see him again.[2]

Ralph wrote in his pocket diary on April 13:

> *No go again today, why?*
> *I guess I'm afraid*
> *Sell my guns*
> call home *and ask about*
> *hi-blood pressure*
> *My surgical records*
> *in car.*

In the back of his diary he wrote:

> *Remember to change cars*
> *with Karin. The old*
> *one will do for*

me. She needs
something flashy. Poor
kid. I'm too overbearing.
My papers belong to my
daughter. She should know
what her father was
John
I want to be cremated

When Odell King arrived back at Fort Meade, Jones, Schaffstall, Martel, and he had another meeting. The men who had recruited Ralph ten years ago, the men now in charge—all their careers were in jeopardy. If they could not find out what was wrong, Ralph Sigler would become a giant black mark on their records. "He kept saying he didn't know why. He didn't know why. But he would cooperate. He would cooperate. But he didn't know why and all that. And he gave us all these things. Every day he would add a little bit more. And . . . at that point we'd have to say, 'This could go on forever,' " John Schaffstall remembers.

Desperate to find out what Ralph was withholding from them, they decided that the next day, April 14, they would bring Ralph to Fort Meade and begin a hostile interrogation. The interrogations would take place within the prepared interrogation rooms at the Special Operations Detachment. No one would give Ralph any advance warning. They would just pick him up at eight-thirty the next morning and take him to Fort Meade. It was time to get tough. "Well, it had just reached that point. I had to have something," Colonel Grimes admits. Tomorrow they were going to rough Ralph up a little bit, and they knew just the man who could handle the job: Donnel J. Drake.[3]

Donnel Drake is an intimidating man. He is over six feet tall, and has a dark complexion and a big handlebar mustache. Drake had a reputation throughout the intelligence community as a tough interrogator. His commanding voice alone would scare a strong opponent. A cigar always hung from the side of his mouth. His nickname was "the Duke." He was the best in the Army at his job. "The purpose of bringing Don Drake in is that Drake is a stranger. Drake is overpowering, and if Ralph was just purposely hiding something, he might be intimidated to bring it up," John Schaffstall explains. "And he [Drake] would intimidate you to pieces."

Donnel Drake had first met Ralph in 1966, when he came to the Washington area from El Paso for training with Army Intelligence and the FBI. He had seen Ralph again in 1969 or 1970, when he was doing fixed-point surveillance in Mexico for one of Ralph's meetings with the Soviets. The last time he had seen Ralph was in the debriefing after

Ralph's trip to Vienna. Drake still remembers what happened: "Sigler had come back. We were down there debriefing, and I was in the motel room when Prasek came in . . . like a whirlwind, and I looked at John and John looked at me and when he [Prasek] came in, he wanted to let us know that, by God, he was running that outfit. He came in all decked out in cowboy boots. He come in there like a tornado. And he wanted to know everything that was going on." In Drake's opinion, this kind of conduct raised serious questions about how well the security of the operation was being maintained.

Drake was on vacation from the Special Operations Detachment from April 1 through April 15, 1976. On April 13, his boss, Noel Jones, called him at his home in Arlington, Virginia. Jones told him that Ralph had been on the polygraph and it did not look good. He asked Drake if he would mind ending his leave a couple of days early and coming up to Fort Meade the next day to start a hostile interrogation of Sigler. Drake agreed. Since he was single, Drake decided later that afternoon to drive up to Fort Meade and either spend the night in the BOQ or get a motel room so that he would be ready to start very early the next morning.[4]

Drake arrived at Fort Meade around 6:00 P.M. Noel Jones gave Drake the details of Sigler's latest polygraph failure, and told him the indications were that Ralph had been telling the Soviets a little more than he should have, and that there was misappropriated money involved. Ralph had indicated that he had not reported to his agent-handler all of the money he received.[5]

At roughly this same time, 6:30 P.M. in Washington, 4:30 P.M. in El Paso, Karin Sigler answered the phone at her home. Her father was on the line. He asked her how she was doing, and said he was having some trouble with some people, but expected to be home by the eighteenth. Then he started sounding strange, and asked Karin what she was going to do with her future. When Karin asked him what was wrong, Ralph replied, "Well, I'm . . . " and the phone went dead.[6]

Karin, very upset, then called her mother at work and said, "Mother, Daddy called. He asked me in a funny way . . . he wants to know what I want to do later in life." Karin explained that her father had started to tell her something and then the phone had gone dead.

Ilse did not react to Karin's anxiety. One of the other salesclerks at the store had not shown up for work that day, and Ilse was alone on the floor with a customer. "Mom, don't you care?" Karin asked.

Ilse said, "I will call you back in a minute. I have a customer."[7]

A few minutes later, the phone at the dress store rang again. The cashier said to Ilse, "There's a phone call for you from your husband. It sounds like his breathing is heavy." At first, Ilse thought perhaps her husband was back in town. "What is wrong?" she asked him.

Ralph told her to take the phone call in the back of the store, on the extension, and hang up the other phone.

"Can you call me back after six, when I get home?" Ilse wondered. "No!" Ralph replied. His voice was very thick, as if he was about to vomit. She could hear his heavy breathing. There was a great deal of noise on the line. "Okay, I take the phone in back," Ilse said.

"Make sure the cashier doesn't listen in," Ralph told her, still breathing very heavily and deeply.

Ilse went to the back and picked up the extension, and Ralph said, "There is a letter coming for you."

Ilse asked again, "What is wrong?"

"Just *listen* to me," Ralph demanded. "I want you to get a respectable lawyer. Maybe your boss can recommend one for you. And sue the U.S. Army. I am dying. I never lied."

Ilse could tell that Ralph had broken down. It sounded as if he was crying. She wanted to say something, but the phone went dead. In a panic, Ilse shouted into the phone, but there was no reply.

She started to cry. She knew she had to get someone to relieve her on the sales floor. The cashier asked her what was wrong. Ilse told her. The cashier said Ralph had sounded different. Sobbing, Ilse replied, "I just want to go home." Finally someone came to relieve her, and Ilse went home.

Ilse had to talk to Karin. "Sit down," she told her pretty, seventeen-year-old daughter. In the spotlessly clean living room, with its massive German furniture, she said frantically to Karin, *"They're killing your father."* Karin got very upset. Then Ilse let it rush out. "He was an agent," she explained, but she did not tell her he was a double agent. She told Karin that her father worked for the CIA and Army Intelligence.

At first Karin did not believe her mother, because her father had never said anything about it. But the more she listened to her mother, the more hysterical she became. Why had no one told her before? Ilse tried to calm her down. They argued and they waited. They were both very upset. "Can't you do something?" Karin sobbed. But Ilse knew she had to wait for Carlos Zapata to call her. She was always told she would be contacted by Zapata if anything went wrong. She was not to contact him.

Ilse and Karin waited for an hour, but Zapata never called. Finally, Karin said to her mother, "If you don't do something, I will." She begged her mother to call Zapata. Ilse dialed Carlos's number, but there was no answer.[8] Karin kept saying, "Go call somebody or I will." At around 6:00 P.M., El Paso time, frantic, Ilse decided to call Colonel Webster at White Sands, since he had checked the week before on Ralph's whereabouts. Maybe he knew where Ralph was. Ilse told Webster that she had spoken to her husband and that he sounded upset and worried. She said she was afraid for his life. Webster did not know how to react to this conversation. Trying to calm Ilse down, he said, "Mrs. Sigler, please believe me, I do not know where your husband is. I didn't send him away. I will contact someone at Fort Bliss who perhaps can give you more information than I can provide." Ilse then went through the Army chain of command at Fort Bliss in what she remembers as an exercise in frustration and futility.

Colonel Webster put Ilse in touch with Bill Vaughn, who was handling Ralph's leave at Fort Bliss.[9] She told Vaughn that all she wanted was a telephone number where she could reach Ralph, and that if Vaughn could not do that, she wanted the telephone number of the Commanding General. If she could not get that, she said, she would call the Pentagon. Vaughn explained that Ralph was fine, that his leave had been extended to April 18, that he was probably at his father's home now (Sigler's cover story always was that he was visiting his father in Pennsylvania), and that they should try to call him there. "There's no need to, I know he's not there," Ilse replied. She knew immediately that Vaughn did not know anything.[10]

Vaughn offered to come to the house, but Ilse refused the offer. All she knew was that her husband was in trouble and the Army was somehow responsible. She did not want anyone from the Army coming to her house. Vaughn gave Ilse his superior officer's name and number to call, and tried to convince Karin, who was on the extension, that her father was fine. But Karin could not be consoled. She told him that her mother was going to call the FBI.[11]

Ilse called the number Vaughn had given her, but the colonel provided no information or comfort. She hung up the phone and called information for the FBI's telephone number. She thought Ralph's name might ring a bell with the FBI, since he worked for them as well as the Army. She hoped they would notify Carlos Zapata. The agent on duty at the FBI's El Paso field office explained to Mrs. Sigler that he could not take a missing-person or kidnapping report on military personnel. She would have to call the military authorities. Ilse then asked Karin to call General Le Van, the commanding general at Fort Bliss. She was too nervous to place the call herself. The woman who answered the phone at the general's home took Ilse's name and number, since the general was not home. Finally, Ilse called the military police and filed a missing-person report.

Then Karin and Ilse waited. Their emotions were churning. Ilse's phone rang. The man on the other end asked her what was the trouble. She assumed this was the general returning her call,[12] and told him her husband had called and told her he was dying. "I think he is kidnapped," Ilse said. "Can you help me?"

"I cannot help you tonight," he said. "Maybe I can do something for you in the morning." [13]

By now, Ilse knew in her heart that Ralph was dead. But she did not know that her calls of desperation were reaching Fort Meade.

While all this was going on, Carlos Zapata received word from Fort Bliss that Mrs. Sigler was very upset. He tried to call Noel Jones at Fort Meade to find out what was going on. Since Jones was not home, he called Lou Martel, who lived on the base. Martel told him, "Well, fine. I'll get hold of . . . [Noel] Jones and we'll get hold of Sigler and have him call his wife." [14]

Martel reached Noel Jones at the officer's club at Fort Meade. He told Jones that Mrs. Sigler was phoning all over El Paso, saying her husband had been kidnapped. Jones called Carlos Zapata back to get some more details and to give him Ralph's motel phone number and room number, to give to Mrs. Sigler.[15] Jones then tried to call Ralph at the motel, but did not get an answer.

Not ten minutes after Ilse finished speaking with the general, Carlos Zapata called. She picked up the phone in the den, and Karin listened in on the extension in her bedroom. "Good evening ma'am. This is Carlos. I heard you were concerned about your husband. There is nothing to worry about. He is fine."

But Ilse did not believe him. "What have you done to him?" she shouted angrily.

"I spoke to him this afternoon. Maybe he will be coming home soon. Maybe he is drinking in the bar," Carlos explained.

Karin was getting nearly hysterical, and spoke abusively to Zapata.

Ilse snapped, "Now listen! He called me. He is dying. I want to know where he is."

Carlos then said, "He's in the Holiday Inn near Fort Meade." He gave Ilse the telephone number for the Holiday Inn.

Karin reiterated her mother's concerns. Carlos answered, "There is nothing to be frustrated about. If there had been anything wrong, I live just one mile from you. I would have come to see you." [16]

Zapata talked again to Noel Jones and told him about his telephone conversation with Karin and Ilse Sigler. Zapata also called Joe Prasek at the FBI to tell him what was going on. After his conversation with Zapata, Noel Jones became concerned. At 10:20 P.M., he told Lou Martel and Donnel Drake to go over to the motel and tell Ralph to call his wife, calm her down, and assure her that he was not in any danger. Before leaving for the motel, Martel tried to reach Ralph by phone and to have him paged. He thought Ralph had gotten drunk and had passed out in his motel room, so he let the phone ring. The desk clerk picked up the phone and said, "There is evidently no one there," and cut Martel off. At 10:25 P.M., Lou Martel and Donnel Drake got into Drake's car and drove over to the motel. They arrived at 10:45 P.M.[17]

Before entering the motel, they searched the parking lot to see if there were any diplomatic license plates or suspicious-looking vehicles. This was standard procedure; every time they went to the motel, they would look for any indications of Soviets or Soviet surrogates in the area. Meanwhile, Ilse was calling the motel, frantically trying to reach her husband.[18]

When Ilse got the desk clerk, she asked to speak to Ralph Sigler. He connected her to the room. The phone rang and rang, but was never answered, and the clerk never came back on the line. Ilse called back and asked the desk clerk if he would go and check the room. She said, "The name is Sigler. His name is Mr. Sigler and he is dying. If you could go and check the room."

The desk clerk replied, "Lady, there is nobody listed under that name. I never saw the man." (Because of Ilse's strong German accent, the desk clerk thought she had said "Segal," not "Sigler.")

Frustrated, Ilse pleaded, "Could you go and knock on the room?"

"That is against hotel regulations," the clerk responded, "but I will connect you."

Again the phone rang and rang. There was no answer. Again the clerk never came back on the line. Finally, Ilse hung up and waited. After hours of struggling with giant bureaucracies, Ilse gave up. She was exhausted. When the ten-o'clock news came on the television, she turned up the volume. She thought there might be a story about Ralph, but nothing was mentioned. She took the phone to the bedroom, plugged it into the jack by her bed, and waited all night to hear something about her husband.[19]

Sitting in the car at the motel, Martel and Drake decided that Drake should go into the motel bar and look for Ralph. Drake looked around the bar. There were only about fifteen or twenty people inside, but he did not see Ralph. A few minutes later, Drake came back to the car and asked Martel whether Ralph's facial features had changed, since he had not seen him "eyeball to eyeball" in years. Martel indicated that he did not think Ralph had changed that much over the years. Martel told Drake to wait in the car. He said, "I'll go in there and see if I can find him." Drake waited in the car for over an hour.[20]

Martel looked in the bar, and then went to the house phone and called Ralph's room. He thought that if Ralph was passed out, the ringing would eventually awaken him. So he let the phone ring for what seemed like a long time. Then Martel got concerned. If Ralph was not in the bar or in his room, where else could he be? He had to talk to Ralph. He thought maybe Ralph had gotten fed up and decided to leave. He decided he had better check Ralph's room to see if he had removed his clothes and other belongings. "I guess I thought he had skipped out, that he [had] had enough," Martel says.[21]

Martel went to the desk clerk, William Henry Chapman, and made up a story to get him to open the room. The story Martel told was that a friend of his, who had a heart condition, was staying in room 326. He told the clerk that his friend was a heavy drinker and didn't have a car, and that his wife was worried. He asked Chapman if he would let him into the room to see if he could rouse him. Chapman got his passkey and a screwdriver, in case the chain was on the door, and went with Martel to the room. They pounded on the door, calling Ralph's name. The clerk looked through the peephole in the door as he tried to unlock it. He said, "There's a light on in there. There must be somebody in there." Chapman then discovered that the door's inside dead-bolt lock had been activated. He said, "I've got to get a different key for that."

Martel waited in the hall by the door as Chapman went to get a special key to unlock the double lock. After the clerk returned and opened the door, they saw Ralph lying facedown on the green shag-carpeted floor, with his feet facing the door. Entering ahead of Martel, the clerk said, "You're right, he's passed out." Martel looked down at Ralph. He noticed stripped lamp wires wrapped around each of Ralph's arms just below the elbow. Over Ralph's shoulder he saw blood coming from Ralph's head. "Passed out, *hell,* he's dead. Get an ambulance. Get a doctor."

The minute the words had left Martel's mouth, Chapman turned around and ran back to the front desk to call the police. He was afraid to use the phone in Ralph's room because he might have trouble getting through the motel's switchboard. Martel noticed that the wires were still burning into Ralph's arms. The plug in the wall receptacle was still conducting electricity. He kicked the plug out of the receptacle with his foot. At approximately 11:00 P.M., Martel went to the phone by the bed and called Noel Jones. He said, "You're not going to believe this, but GRAPHIC IMAGE is dead." Martel had not touched the body, but he could tell Ralph was not breathing.

Shocked, Jones replied, "What did you say?"

"I'm not kidding you," Martel continued, "it looks to me like the man's dead, and you'd better get over here and you'd better get hold of some people."

"All right," Jones said. He told Martel to stay in the room and that he would be right over. Chapman tried to call the room to let Martel know that an ambulance was on the way, but the line was busy.[22]

Martel looked around the room. Everything was very, very neat. There were no empty beer or liquor bottles. There was no indication that there had been any scuffles or altercations. Ralph's wallet, change, eyeglasses, watch, and money clip were neatly placed on the desk. And then Martel noticed a note lying there. He picked it up. In Ralph's handwriting, on Holiday Inn stationery, it read:

> *I don't know what I'm guilty of*
> *Then why the positive responses*
> *Acting*
> *4) Lying?*
> *5) Don't know the difference?*
> *6) Too bad!*
> *I've given up all hope*
> *I wish I knew, I wish I knew.*
> *I tried too hard.*
> *I'm dead*
> *Call home 915-751-8171*
> *notify John 677-5801/5800*

Instantly, a number of thoughts rushed through Martel's head. The telephone number at the end of the note was John Schaffstall's office number; if someone else got the note, they could easily trace the phone number. He did not know who would be coming in the room next, and he thought he should keep Ralph's affiliation with Army Intelligence a secret until his superiors arrived. He put the note in his back pocket. Then he heard footsteps. The door was still ajar. He looked out the door and saw a Maryland state trooper run right by. He said, "Hey, right here." [23]

Two uniformed state troopers entered the room. Martel identified himself as a friend of the deceased. Trooper William Nelson walked in first, bent down, and felt for a pulse in the neck and under the arm. Ralph was dead. The other state trooper said, "Would you please leave the room?" Waiting in the hallway right outside the room, Martel saw a man arrive on the scene who was subsequently identified to him as State Trooper Roger Cassell. He entered the room and looked around. The door leading to the adjoining room, number 324, was locked with a slide bolt. The light switch just past this doorway was on. Cassell plugged the lamp on the desk into the electrical outlet under the desk to see if it still worked. There was a closed gray suitcase on the bed closest to the door. On top of the suitcase were two neckties. The television, on its swivel pedestal stand, was facing the windows and a seating area where normally two yellow plastic chairs were placed on either side of a square pedestal table and lamp. But one of the chairs had been moved.

Several pieces of clothing were hanging in the small closet. There was a shaving kit on the counter by the sink in the bathroom. A plastic ice bucket was on the counter, half full of water. Beside the bucket was a Holiday Inn drinking cup. The shower and bathtub area was dry. The lamp between the two beds was on. But six feet of the lamp's cord had been removed, and the bare ends of the wires had been stuck back into the outlet, causing the light to be on. The six feet of wire cut from the lamp had been split in two, and each of the two wires had been stripped of insulation and wrapped tightly around Ralph's arms. The bright yellow, green, and white flower-print drapes were closed. Next to the inside door leading to room 324, two chairs were stacked on top of each other. Around the back of the top, smaller desk chair, was Ralph's belt, but it was not buckled. Ralph wore a white T-shirt, brown and white striped pants, black military-type socks, and white boxer shorts.[24]

At Fort Meade, Noel Jones called Colonel Grimes to tell him what had happened, and that he was going over to the Holiday Inn. Grimes, who had farther to drive, said he would meet him there. Jones then left for the motel.

A short time later, Cassell came out and talked to Martel. Using his military ID for identification, Martel answered Cassell's questions as if he were just a friend of the deceased. Then a man who identified himself as Charles William Garrett showed up with a forensic kit of some kind. Apparently he had learned of an emergency through monitoring the police calls. The police let him examine the body. He said the man appeared to be dead, and no medical attention would revive him. When Cassell indicated that he was going down to report the death by radio, Martel decided to identify himself fully and ask him not to broadcast Sigler's identity over the radio. He told him that his boss would be there soon. "I knew the Russians really monitored the radio traffic, and we didn't want them to get a hint as to what was going on," Martel said.[25]

All this time, Donnel Drake had remained in the car, waiting for Martel to return. "I noticed the Maryland state trooper drive up, but we were parked at an angle where I didn't have a clear view of what was going on."[26]

At around 11:30 P.M., Noel Jones arrived at the room. The area was crowded with police, rescue personnel, and local authorities. Martel introduced Jones to State Trooper Cassell. Jones identified himself as a member of U.S. Army Intelligence, and advised Cassell that Sigler was also associated with U.S. Army Intelligence and that he was in the Fort Meade vicinity in connection with his intelligence mission. The police let Jones look briefly around the room and then asked Jones and Martel to leave the room so they could photograph it. Suddenly Martel remembered, "Oh, hell, Don is down in the car. I'd better go down and get him." He went down to tell Drake what was going on. The police photographer photographed the room.[27]

Dr. T. F. Herbert, a Maryland State Medical Examiner, arrived on the scene and pronounced Ralph Sigler dead at 12:10 A.M., April 14, 1976. When he moved the head, blood came from the nose. Ralph had a Holiday Inn paper cup crushed in his right hand.[28] The fronts of his T-shirt and pants were wet. There was nothing in the pockets of his trousers.[29]

Martel walked out to the car and said to Drake, "Say, we've got a problem upstairs." He explained what had happened. Drake jumped out of the car and they went back upstairs. As they were walking down the hallway, Jones came out and said, "We'd like both of you to wait downstairs." He told them that he had spoken to Colonel Grimes, who was on his way over. They went back downstairs to wait for Colonel Grimes to arrive.[30]

As they were standing in front of the motel's main entrance, Martel pulled the note he had taken from Ralph's room out of his back pocket and showed it to Drake. Shocked, Drake said, "Lou, that's evidence. You should never have taken that." They decided to wait in the lobby for Colonel Grimes. At about that time, Noel Jones walked over. As Martel was telling Jones about the note, they saw Colonel Grimes walking in from the parking lot. Jones started to brief Grimes on what had happened as they headed upstairs to Ralph's room. Jones told Drake and Martel to wait in the lobby until they were called. Martel went to the bar to get a Scotch and soda; he thought it would help settle his nerves. About twenty or thirty minutes later, Jones came back downstairs. Grimes had instructed him to call Eugene Peterson at home and to tell him, in a cryptic way, what had happened. Jones said, "Guess what happened?" Peterson replied, "Tell me." Peterson did not suggest that the Army personnel who were present take any specific action, but stated only that if possible he would prefer that FBI involvement not be mentioned on the scene.[31]

Jones then phoned John Schaffstall and Carlos Zapata in a conference call, and informed them of the events. "Well, it was in the early-morning hours, because I was in bed," Schaffstall remembers. "He said, 'The Image is dead. He killed himself.' . . . Well, that's the shocker. When everybody you talked to before, they all say, 'No. Nothing was wrong. Nothing was wrong.' And I talked to him [Ralph] before and he was worried, as anybody normally would be, but not upset. And then to get a phone call that said, 'He killed himself.' It never set right."

Jones suggested that Zapata might be the appropriate person to notify Mrs. Sigler, but it was decided that it would be best if Fort Bliss handled it, since they had a standard procedure for such a notification. Jones told Zapata, however, that he would have to visit Mrs. Sigler the next day and offer his condolences. After talking to Jones, Zapata notified the proper authorities at Fort Bliss.

When Jones had made his phone calls, the three men went back upstairs. Colonel Grimes met them in the hallway. Martel showed him the note he had taken from Ralph's room, and said, "Look, I've got this note, and I know it's got to go to the police, but I wanted you to see it and it's got John's work telephone number on it."

"Well," Grimes replied, "we'll give it to the police right now," and he took the note, turned around, and walked back to the room with Martel.[32] They showed a police officer the note. The officer copied down the contents, but did not ask for the note. Then Grimes returned to Fort Meade. At his office, he called the Army medical authorities at Fort Meade to pick up Sigler's body.[33]

To this day, Donnel Drake remembers what he saw when he entered Ralph's motel room. There was a very small foyer with an alcove to hang up clothing on the left, and the door to the adjoining room on the right. Upon entering the bedroom, one saw a window at the far end of the room. The bathroom was on the left. As one walked toward the bedroom window, the credenza that served as a baggage table and writing table was on the right and the two double beds were on the left. Ralph was lying in the narrow walkway between the bed and the writing table, facedown, with his feet toward the door and his head toward the window.[34]

At the motel, the last remaining police official began an inventory of Ralph's room. Always alert, Noel Jones offered to help. He was worried they might find some operational materials. Since it was in the middle of the night, the exhausted police officer accepted Jones's offer. Jones got Martel and Drake and ordered them to make a complete inventory of the room. The police officer introduced himself to Drake and Martel, and they all started logging Ralph's personal effects.

At 2:00 A.M., SP4 Frank G. Black, an ambulance driver from Fort Meade's Kimbrough Army Hospital and FC John C. O'Connor, a ward orderly, arrived to pick up the body. They removed the body, placing it facedown on the stretcher with the lamp wires still attached, just as they had found him. They placed the cord on Ralph's back. When they picked up the body, there was very little blood on the T-shirt Ralph was wearing. However, when they removed the body from the ambulance and placed it in the morgue at Kimbrough Army Hospital at approximately 3:00 A.M., the T-shirt was soaked with blood and there was excess pulmonary edema fluid on the litter, which had to be cleaned off. Sigler's body was placed in the morgue, facedown. It stayed in that position until it was delivered to the Armed Forces

Institute of Pathology at Walter Reed Army Hospital on April 15, for autopsy.[35]

Back at the Holiday Inn, the remaining state trooper was exhausted. He asked to be provided with a copy of the inventory when it was finished, and left.[36] The minute the trooper walked out of the door, Jones, Drake, and Martel started turning over the mattresses, looking through the bedclothes. They were making a detailed and desperate search for any operational information or notes that would indicate once and for all what Ralph had been keeping from them these past few weeks. But they found nothing. They then gathered up all relevant materials from the room.[37]

After leaving the room, Martel went to the motel clerk and told him that he would return the next day to settle the bill. Martel, Jones, and Drake returned to Fort Meade. "In talking that particular night . . . the opinion was, 'Hell, we'll never know just really what happened,' " Donnel Drake remembers. "We'll never know . . . what [Sigler] really told [the Russians]." Grimes went home to get some rest. He would have a busy day ahead of him. Jones, Martel, and Drake secured Ralph's belongings in Jones's office and left. Jones dropped Martel off at the BOQ and then took Drake to get his car at the motel parking lot. Drake got a room at the Red Carpet Inn, where he could get some sleep before their 9:00 A.M. conference. In the meantime, reports were being forwarded from Fort Meade to Fort Bliss to provide information upon which to notify the next of kin of the death.[38]

The next morning, Karin left for school. At around 8:30 A.M., three men arrived from Fort Bliss—Colonel Loeuffler, Captain Cardwell, and Chaplain Miller—to inform Ilse of her husband's death. The men walked into the house and, for a minute, awkwardly stood like statues, not saying anything. One of them finally broke the silence and said they had some bad news for Mrs. Sigler. Inviting them into the living room, Ilse said, "What you want to tell me, my husband is dead? I know he is dead. He called me and told me he is dying." Colonel Loeuffler said, "Mrs. Sigler, you'd better sit down." So Ilse sat down and he sat down next to her and said, "Yes, your husband is dead."

Sitting across from Ilse on the couch, Captain Cardwell opened a folder and read: "Your husband committed suicide this morning in a hotel room in Maryland, at the Holiday Inn in Jessup. They had to break in the hotel room." Without hesitating, Ilse snapped, "I don't believe it is suicide." She told Cardwell that Ralph had told her on the phone that he was dying and that "it was the U.S. Army and to sue them and that is what I have to do. That was his last request."[39]

Chaplain Miller stood silent in the living room doorway.

"Sue the U.S. Army?" Captain Cardwell said. "Why would he say that? The Russians would have set that up. That would have been a gimmick, wouldn't that have been?"

As if to break Cardwell's speculation, Colonel Loeuffler stood up and asked if he could help Ilse notify Ralph's father. Ilse said yes, and gave him the phone number. Then Loeuffler said, "If you need help—anything—somebody to stay with you—"

Ilse said she did not want a chaplain who came to her house and lied about her husband's death, saying it was suicide, staying to comfort her. Fearful of her hostility, the three men left as quickly as possible.[40]

As the group left, they passed Carlos Zapata and Lt. Col. Robert Davenport, the head of security at Fort Bliss, heading into the house. Zapata was wearing sunglasses. "I'm sorry, ma'am," Zapata said upon entering the house. Sitting down in the living room, Carlos restated the same story about Ralph committing suicide.

"I don't believe that," Ilse shot back.

Colonel Davenport then tried to explain that they had security problems at Fort Bliss and that Ralph had been trying to help straighten them out.

Turning to Zapata, Ilse asked, "Where were you when this happened?"

He said he was out of town and had just returned.[41]

Karin came home from school. When she entered the room, Ilse had to explain why Zapata and Colonel Davenport were there. She told Karin that her father was dead. Then the phone began to ring. Ilse left the room to answer the phone, and Karin sat down on the couch. While Ilse was talking on the phone, she heard Karin scream, "Don't you talk about my Daddy that way! My father was no drinker. You had better leave the house, and stop talking about my father like this."

Ilse hung up the phone and rushed back into the room. "What is going on?" she asked.

Karin answered, "He is accusing Daddy of having drinking problems."

Ilse told Karin to leave the room.[42]

The entire episode was getting stranger and stranger to Ilse. It was Carlos Zapata who had called her the night before and assured her that there was nothing wrong with Ralph—that he had spoken to Ralph that afternoon. Ilse reminded Carlos that he was the one who was supposed to notify her if anything ever went wrong with the operation. She sat down, and Zapata said, "I know you and Ralph had problems."

Ilse snapped, "What problems?"

Carlos said Ralph had told him he had problems with his marriage and with his daughter.

"I didn't give him problems. It's *you* who give *us* the problems," Ilse rejoined.

"I know Ralph loved you very much and he loved Karin very much," Carlos continued. "Was he drinking lately? Did he have mental problems?"

Incredulous, Ilse said, "You should know him. He worked with you for eleven years." She had never trusted Carlos, even though Ralph had trusted him.

Just before he left, Carlos said, "I always will remember your name —Ilse."

After Zapata and Davenport had left, Ilse told Karin that Zapata was her father's contact man in the Army. Karin began to hate him for implying her father was a drunk.[43]

Both Karin and Ilse sensed that the government was going to stick to the suicide theory, a theory neither of them could accept. Both knew now that Ralph had been in some kind of trouble. But the authorities seemed to be ignoring any possibility of foul play. And both Karin and Ilse resisted the suggestion that Sigler had drinking or mental problems. In fact, according to Schaffstall, Ralph did not have any mental or drinking problems. "He liked his beer. And he liked to be with the guys and enjoyed telling us what happened. I mean, that was fun for him. . . . He didn't have a drinking problem. . . . No. I never saw him drink liquor."

Back in Washington, Colonel Grimes and Noel Jones spent the day briefing top Army brass from the Pentagon and FBI officials, including Eugene Peterson, at FBI Headquarters on what had happened to GRAPHIC IMAGE.[44] For Grimes, Jones, Martel, and Schaffstall, a decision had to be made on how to deal with the Russians. "We had to decide if we wanted them to think GRAPHIC IMAGE was still alive. We even discussed using a double. . . . One idea was to send another agent to the upcoming meeting with the Russians, and have him explain that the Image was dead, but that he had been recruited by Ralph for the KGB," Martel said.

At around 4:20 P.M. in El Paso, the Survivors Assistance Officer, Maj. Richard Roy Ring, came to see Mrs. Sigler. He had been warned by Colonel Davenport that she was very upset. He had also been told by his superior officer that Ralph had worked with another government agency and that if that fact ever came up, he should report it to Colonel Davenport immediately. Major Ring introduced himself, sat down in the living room, and started to discuss the basic Army survivors' information. Ilse realized quickly that Ring did not know anything about the true nature of Ralph's work or the circumstances of his death. She started to relate, very belligerently, the details of the events surrounding her husband's death. Ring listened to the horrifyingly fascinating story. But she did not tell Ring that Ralph was an intelligence agent.[45]

When Ilse had finished, Major Ring questioned her on such details as where Ralph would be buried. Ilse knew Ralph had wanted to be cremated, but under the circumstances she was hesitant to do that. She wanted to see the body. Filling out the forms, Major Ring asked Ilse her full name and Ralph's name, and then he wrote the word *Suicide* on one of the forms and asked her to sign it. "I don't sign nothing whatsoever, not one paper," Ilse replied; she would not sign any paper that said Ralph's death had been suicide. Ilse thought that if Ralph had wanted to commit suicide, he would have shot himself.

"Okay, we'll leave that part out," Ring said, and suggested that Ralph's death may have been an accident.

Ilse replied, "That is what the Army wants to say."[46]

Late in the day, Ilse called her father-in-law and sister-in-law, only to discover that the Army had not notified Ralph's family. It is clear that the Army mishandled Mrs. Sigler from the moment she got the first disturbing call from Ralph. But what is also clear is that in her stress, Ilse became increasingly difficult for Army officials to deal with. During such a stressful and emotional time, it was hard for anyone to look good.

On April 15, an autopsy was performed on Ralph at the Armed Forces Institute of Pathology at Walter Reed Army Hospital by Lt. Col. Robert W. Hertzog. Dr. Hertzog was trained by Russell Fisher, the Maryland State Medical Examiner who handled the Paisley case. His examination of Sigler's remains revealed burn marks on both arms, chest, and right hand, and an abrasion on the forehead. Hertzog found the alcohol present in Ralph's blood to be three times the concentration required for him to be legally drunk. The higher percentage of alcohol in his stomach indicated the alcohol had been consumed shortly before death.

That same day, Major Ring advised Mrs. Sigler that she would receive two telegrams, one from Fort Meade and one from the Secretary of the Army. At Fort Bliss, John Schaffstall had arrived from Fort Meade to brief Carlos Zapata, Joe Prasek, and Colonel Davenport on the circumstances of Sigler's death. They decided that Colonel Davenport and Zapata then could explain to Ilse what had happened to Ralph, and offer to bring her and Karin to Washington when they were emotionally ready for a more detailed briefing.[47]

At the Sigler house, Karin called the Maryland State Police to find out the circumstances of her father's death. She was told that she would have to contact the Army for that information. She got very upset and told the state trooper that it was the military who had killed her father.[48]

The next morning Mrs. Sigler received two telegrams from the Army. Then the doorbell rang again. It was Carlos Zapata and Colonel Davenport, who had called earlier to ask if they could stop by. Ilse told them to come in right away because Karin was out with Major Ring. They went into the living room, and Zapata sat next to Ilse. He told her that he was honored to have been asked by her to escort the body back to El Paso. Ilse replied that she had changed her mind and now wanted to just let the Army ship the body back. Ilse was very hostile. She told Zapata that he knew what had happened to her husband and that there was no sense in asking her any questions, because he already knew the answers.

But there was no chance for Carlos to ask any questions, since Ilse's anger continued unabated. She told them about the telegrams. Ilse opened the envelopes. One was from the base commander at Fort Meade and the other was from a captain. Ilse said, "Captain? How come it says Assistant to the Secretary? I thought every man who dies in active duty . . . it was supposed to come from the Secretary of the Army." Turning to Zapata, Ilse said triumphantly, "It says Ralph was electrocuted. It doesn't say suicide. It just says electrocuted." Immediately, Zapata asked to read the telegrams. When she gave them to him, he pulled away from her.[49]

But Ilse would not relent. Her heavy German accent got thicker as she became more upset. The Army had told her for years that if anything ever happened to Ralph, she and Karin would be taken care of. Defiantly, she asked, "Can you tell me what's going on . . . who killed him? He was killed from his own people. I am telling you he worked for Washington and I am going to do something. I am going to go up there and I am going to do something."[50]

Colonel Davenport remarked that there had been an investigation by the Maryland State Police and by MPs from Fort Meade, and that Ralph had been found alone in the motel room. There was no evidence of foul play. Ilse said she believed there had been someone in the room with her husband when she talked to him on the telephone. She said there had been a crackling sound on the line, and it had sounded as though people were in the room with him. She asked Zapata why he had not told her where Ralph was. Zapata replied that he had thought she knew, since Ralph had not been told to keep his whereabouts secret from her.[51]

Ilse continued, "I am going to go straight to Washington. I want to know what really happened."

Carlos replied, "We are going to bring you and your daughter up there. We will even pay for your fare. Ralph always told me to be careful about the house, to make sure nobody breaks in. We will put somebody in to watch your house.''

Ilse then wanted to know where the FBI had been. She said only she, Zapata, and the FBI knew anything about Ralph's work. Zapata explained that Ralph had worked for the Army, and that the FBI had only monitored the operation. Ilse wanted to know when Ralph's body would be shipped, since his relatives were postponing their trip until they received word on the shipment of the body. Their strained conversation continued until Karin and Major Ring returned. Then Zapata and Davenport quickly left. They did not come back to the house to see Ilse again.[52]

On April 16, the Maryland State Police called Ilse to interview her about her husband's death. She advised them of her telephone conversations with Ralph over the past week, and told them what had occurred the night Ralph died. She asked if there was an article in the paper. The state trooper said, "No. I can't tell you anything about your husband's case.'' He indicated that the investigation had been turned over to the Army. Ilse was now worried that she would never know the truth. The very people that Ralph, in their last conversation, had told her to sue were now in charge of investigating the case.[53]

Also on April 16, the body was picked up from Walter Reed and returned to the hospital at Fort Meade. That same day the remains were picked up by a mortuary in Baltimore, Maryland, that did work for the Army.[54] The Army paid the $423 undertaker's bill and brought clothing to the funeral home. The embalmer clothed the body, an Army officer inspected it, and the funeral home sent it by air freight to El Paso on April 18.[55]

Meanwhile, Ilse waited for the letter Ralph had mentioned in his phone conversations. She did not tell anyone about it except Karin. She said to Karin, "Don't mention the letter. Don't mention anything,'' because she thought her house and telephone were bugged. In addition, she called a local hospital to see if a second autopsy could be performed. The hospital said it could do another autopsy. It would cost $400, but the body had to have a death certificate. Ilse could not get a death certificate from either the Army or the Maryland State Police.[56]

On Saturday, April 17, Ralph's letter arrived. It was truly a letter from the grave. Ilse noticed that there were two postmarks on the envelope. One was dated April 13, Jessup, Maryland, and the other, on the back of the envelope, was strangely dated April 15, P.M., Seattle, Washington. Also on the back was the word *Personal*. The letter, on Howard Johnson's stationery, said:

10 April 76

Dear Ilse:

Should anything happen to me, suicide, death, or accident sue the U.S. Army for being the cause, naming specifically the following as defendants.

Maj. Gen C. J. Le Van
Maj. Gen. Aarons
Col. Grines [sic]
Maj. Noel Jones
CW4 John Schaafstahl [sic]
CW4 Carlos Zapata
Special Agent Francis Paocek [sic] (FBI).
in addition request all papers picked up by John Schaafstal [sic] on 9 April 76 be returned to you immediately.

Love.
Ralph

over

P.S. get a respectable lawyer, your boss should be able to recommend a good one.

R.

PPS If nothing happens and I return give this back to me

R.

533-7451 [Under the postscript, this telephone number was written upside down; it was Joe Prasek's number.]

Following the letter's instructions, Mrs. Sigler immediately called John Schaffstall's home in Falls Church, Virginia, to ask him to return the gray metal box. Mrs. Schaffstall answered the phone and Ilse, after identifying herself, said, "I want to speak to John."

Mrs. Schaffstall replied, "He is in El Paso. In fact, he's flying out this afternoon." Mrs. Schaffstall explained that her husband had a noon flight and would be back in the Washington area at 5:00 P.M. Hoping to catch Schaffstall before he left El Paso, Ilse then called the FBI and asked to speak with Joe Prasek. When told that he wasn't in, she said, "This is an emergency. This is about the Sigler case and he should contact me."

Ten minutes later, Joe Prasek called. He said he would be right over. He and Special Agent Murphy came to the house and showed Ilse their identification. They went to the living room to sit down. Special Agent Murphy asked if he could take Karin out for a hamburger. Mrs. Sigler agreed and they left.[57]

Ilse immediately asked, "Do you know Joe Prasek?" because the agent's identification gave his name as Francis Prasek, not Joe or Joseph. The tall, nice-looking FBI man said he was Joe Prasek. "So that's you," Ilse remarked. After ten years she had finally met Joe Prasek, face to face.

Prasek immediately started looking around the house, lifting everything in sight, searching for electronic eavesdropping devices. He then made a thorough search of the entire house, going into the garage, the backyard, the bedrooms, everywhere—including the back of the stereo. He found Ralph's gun and said, "This is Ralph's gun and it's still loaded."

"Yeah, it's still loaded," Ilse replied. Ralph had kept a gun in the stereo and one in the nightstand. Prasek also found a tape recording, which Ilse gave to him.[58]

When Joe had finished searching the house, he and Ilse went back to the living room to talk. Prasek told Ilse that Ralph had been picked by a computer in 1966, since his background fit their profile for an agent. He then asked, "Do you know if he worked for both sides?"

Ilse panicked. All she could remember was the secrecy that Ralph had drummed into her. She did not know what to say to Prasek. She had been very careful not to tell anyone that Ralph was a double agent. She had just met Prasek for the first time; should she trust him or not? Ilse said, "Oh, no, no, no." Immediately she realized she had made a mistake. Prasek stopped discussing Ralph's work with her.[59]

Then Ilse showed Prasek the letter from her husband. "I want you to get Schaffstall," she told him. "Schaffstall is the crook with the box. Can you arrest him or get the box?" she asked.

"No," Ilse remembers Prasek saying. Ralph had told Ilse that he and Prasek were writing a book together. She told this to Prasek. According to Ilse, he said, "Yes, that is true."[60]

They were interrupted by a call from the Maryland State Police. When Ilse returned to the living room, she recalls Prasek saying, "Ralph worked for us for eleven years, and I know Ralph better than anyone else. So if the Army gives you trouble, you come to the FBI." Then he left.[61]

After John Schaffstall had arrived at Dulles Airport from his trip to El Paso, his wife told him about Ilse Sigler's call. Schaffstall notified Noel Jones at Fort Meade and then returned Ilse's call. John expressed his sympathy when Ilse answered the phone, but Ilse asked him to hold for a minute so that she could make sure Karin was not on another extension. Ilse then said she wanted the box and two keys that Schaffstall had taken from the house returned to her immediately. She told Schaffstall she was holding him responsible for returning the box. Schaffstall said he had taken no keys. Ilse insisted he had, and said she wanted her things back now. Schaffstall said they were safe at Fort Meade and he would see what he could do.[62]

To this day, Ralph's letter and suicide note still puzzle John Schaffstall and his boss, Donald Grimes. "Well, he says this 'suicide, death or accident.' . . . Most people would say 'in case I die or have an accident.' . . . But to write the suicide and then everybody says it was a suicide, you wonder if somebody had him write this. Because he spells the names wrong on a lot of them. My name is spelled wrong, and I know he'd know how to spell that. And he spelled Grimes with an *n* instead of an *m*. And he called Joe Francis Prasek. But he always called him Joe. . . . And he said something about, 'Notify John.' Of course, at that point I always said, 'Well, I wonder why he's suing me and then also wants her to notify me.' I never could figure out that bit. He tells her to sue me, and then after all this, he writes about his problems, 'I'm dying,' and it says, 'Notify John.' Why? And why didn't they notify me?" John Schaffstall wonders.

Donald Grimes agrees. "Why would he accuse the Army of doing him in when he knew damn well we didn't do him in?"

And Schaffstall cannot understand why Ralph would tell Ilse to have the gray metal box returned. The only contents of the box that Schaffstall could not identify were the pictures of Ralph and the other men in their bathing suits at a tropical beach. Schaffstall also noted that Ralph had spelled his name wrong two different ways in the letter.

On Sunday, April 18, Ralph's father, his sister, Anne Ancas, and her son flew to El Paso from Pennsylvania. Anne's daughter, Ralph's niece, was married to an attorney in Philadelphia, Thomas W. Jennings. Ilse called and asked him to help her find out what had happened to her husband.

On the evening of April 19, Major Ring came to the Sigler house. He told Mrs. Sigler, her sister-in-law, and her nephew that Ralph's body was being shipped to El Paso that night. Ilse asked him how Ralph looked. "Okay," Ring replied, "except he has bruises on his forehead from falling on the hard wooden floor."

Moises Salazar of the Mission Funeral Home in El Paso picked up the body at the El Paso airport around 3:00 A.M. and took it to the funeral home, where he placed it in the garage and went home to bed.[63]

At 7:30 A.M. on April 20, Salazar opened the casket and saw that its lid had been pressing down on Sigler's face, and that the cosmetics had rubbed off the forehead. At around 7:45, Major Ring arrived at the funeral home with the military decorations to pin on the body. Salazar repaired the makeup as best he could, although a bluish tinge still showed.[64]

On the same day, for two hours in the afternoon, Karin and Ilse Sigler went to the funeral home for a private family viewing of the body. Ralph's father and sister, his nephew, and Gary Mears, then Karin's boyfriend, were also there. The casket was in the chapel. The top half was open and the bottom half closed. Ralph's hands were crossed over his waist. Karin and Ilse asked if they could be alone, so the others left the chapel. They then began to inspect the body very closely.

Ilse was shocked when she saw the body. At first she did not even think it was him. It appeared to her that her husband had been badly beaten, possibly tortured, even though the heavy mortuary makeup somewhat covered the bruises. She noticed a false eyelash on his right eye, and a cut on the right side of his face. His eyes looked as if he had been beaten. There was a deep hole in his forehead. His nose looked as if it had been broken. Ilse could not bear to look anymore; she was too upset and nervous to continue. She left Karin and her boyfriend with the body. Karin had studied biology and would know what to look for, Ilse thought.

Karin found blood in the mouth and on the back of the head. The teeth in Ralph's lower jaw had been knocked out. His partial upper plate was missing. She removed the white gloves and pushed up the sleeves. His arms were scarred. There were dozens of needle marks all over the arms and legs. Karin inspected the body as closely as possible within the limitations of the coffin. She then straightened the clothing to make it look undisturbed. She asked Salazar about the gloves, and he explained that there was damage to the hands that he could not quite cover with mortuary makeup.

From 5:00 P.M. to 7:00 P.M. an open viewing was scheduled, but after seeing the body, Ilse changed her mind and wanted the casket closed. Before the rosary was said, Major Ring went to the airport to pick up Bruce McCain, whom he had notified earlier of Ralph's death. Bruce and Ralph had become very close during the year Ralph had spent in Korea. McCain said they had a father-and-son relationship. McCain told Ring that, based on his close association with Ralph, he was of the opinion that Ralph "was not of the nature to commit suicide." When Ring asked him if Ralph had a drinking problem, McCain explained that Ralph did drink, "but he did not have a drinking problem." [65]

When it was time for the rosary, no one was there but Ilse, Karin, and Anne Ancas. Anne said, "Didn't you have any friends?"

Ilse replied, "Well, yes." But nobody was there. Later, a neighbor told Ilse the time of the rosary was listed incorrectly in the newspaper. Ilse had not thought to check. [66]

During the rosary, the phone rang at the funeral home, and Salazar answered it. A reporter with the *El Paso Times* asked Salazar about Ralph Sigler. A "source"—described by the reporter as a man with a Mexican accent—had told the paper to watch the death notices, that a soldier was going to be buried and the Army was not revealing the true nature of his death. The funeral director put Major Ring on the phone.

First the reporter asked to speak to a family member. Ring said that they were unavailable because of the rosary, and that he was the Survivors Assistance Officer. The reporter then explained that the newspaper wanted to do a story on Ralph besides the paid obituary. Ring was "flabbergasted."

"Why do you want to do this?" he asked.

"Well, because of the nature of the obituary, that he had died out of town and it seemed that there were certain facts left out of the obituary," the reporter replied.

Ring answered, "I cannot make this decision. I would want to talk first of all with my superiors, because this is a new job for me as SAO, and I don't want to infringe upon the privacy of the family." [67]

Ilse says that when she walked out of the chapel after the rosary, Major Ring told her, "I am very embarrassed. There's a phone call from our paper for you." Mrs. Sigler picked up the phone. There was a woman on the line who said the newspaper had received a call from someone who said that the U.S. Army was not telling the truth about the death of a local serviceman. The woman asked if she could come to the Siglers' home and get a statement, but Mrs. Sigler refused. She was still trying to cooperate with the Army. [68]

After the rosary, Salazar took Major Ring aside and asked him what he should do with a pair of slacks and a bloodstained T-shirt that he had in a plastic bag. They had been in the coffin when it arrived. Surprised by the amount of blood on the T-shirt, Major Ring told him to hold on to them; the Army might need them later, and he did not think it was appropriate to give them to the family at this point. Apparently these were the clothes Ralph was wearing on the night he died. After the funeral home was closed for the evening, Salazar used soap to remove the wedding band from the body's finger. [69]

A few days before he was scheduled to meet again with the Russians, Ralph Sigler was buried on April 21, 1976, in the Fort Bliss National Cemetery. His grave—number 3750, Section I—is toward the rear of the small cemetery. Originally the plan was to have Ralph's body cremated, but Ilse decided against cremation, since at a later date she might wish to have the body exhumed and another autopsy performed. In addition, Ralph's sister asked that he not be cremated since he was Catholic. There was a large crowd at the funeral, but no high-ranking Army or FBI officials. [70]

Ilse Sigler would not rest until she found out what had happened to her husband. She was determined to take whatever actions were necessary to get to the truth.

Sigler: Ilse's Quest

They beat the living shit out of the guy. . . . The Russians are famous
for using that [electricity]. . . . I think they gave him too much.

Harry Thompson

AT ABOUT THE same time Ralph Sigler died, a down-on-his-luck private investigator with the Arrow Detective Agency in Upper Marlboro, Maryland, went to El Paso on a totally unrelated case. Since
Texas does not honor out-of-state detective licenses, this private investigator, Harry Thompson, contacted a local private eye named
Fred Duvall to see if he could work under Fred's Texas license.[1]
Duvall is a thin man of medium height, with sun-baked skin, who
chain-smokes, wears glasses, and is unmistakably a Texan, with his
jeans and cowboy boots. He had never met Harry before. But Harry
seemed like an honest, hard-working detective. Thompson was half a
head taller and fifty pounds heavier than Duvall. Neither man was
flashy, young, or handsome, as detectives are usually portrayed on
television. Thompson was dogged, very low-key, and thoroughly
professional. "So we had maybe an hour meeting and he impressed

me to be an honest, straightforward, no-b.s. guy, and I said, 'Yeah, okay, Harry,' " Fred Duvall remembers.[2]

Fred felt sorry for Harry because of his financial difficulties. But it was not just sympathy for Harry's money problems that caught Fred's attention. What motivated him to help Harry Thompson was the case Harry was investigating in El Paso. Duvall says Harry told him that he was investigating another Texas private detective—Duvall's longtime competitor, the famous J. J. Armes. Armes, the Melvin Belli of detectives, was both flamboyant and controversial. He had lost both hands, yet was still able to indulge in almost every activity and to do it with a flare for publicity.

And according to Duvall, there was a personal rivalry between him and Armes. "I grew up with him. I knew him when he had hands," Duvall said.

Fred told Harry he could work under his Texas license under certain conditions: "I said, 'Well, if you'll let me tell you a little bit about the guy you're investigating so you don't get yourself hurt, and if you'll listen to me, then, yeah, we can do it. But you're not going to be under my license and go out there and think you're Rockford . . . and get the blank beat out of me, because . . . I'm going to be wholly responsible for you under my license.' "

Fred Duvall said Harry Thompson was a good detective, but he lacked certain skills when it came to surveillance.

Harry did not last long on the case. "And J. J. Armes can scare you. . . . So he worked on it maybe two days and Armes scared the hell out of him . . . and Harry called me and said, 'Okay, I'm leaving. I'm through with this investigation,' " Fred remembers. Fred kept Harry's card and filed it away, just in case he ever needed help with a case in the Maryland area.

In searching the house for clues to her husband's death, Mrs. Sigler started going through Ralph's office in the spare room and the books in the bookcase. When she opened an Army retirement handbook, the pictures of Ralph and Brezhnev and other U.S. and Soviet intelligence officials fell to the floor. She was afraid that if the Russians knew she had them, she and Karin would be in danger. She quickly put the pictures in an envelope, intending to turn them over to the Army. She had no intention, however, of giving the Army the operational notes she found hidden throughout the house—maps of drop sites, calendars, details of meetings and tapes. She always carried them with her in her purse, so that no one else would find them. Fearing her own government, she also carried with her Ralph's medical records, which she found hidden under the trunk carpet of his car.

Among the items Ilse found during her searches, items she later found missing, were the medal Ralph received from the CIA and a complete set of blueprints for the Vagabond Hotel in San Francisco. Schaffstall feels that these provide a further indication that Ralph was involved in some major FBI operation at the Vagabond. In Ralph's pocket diary he wrote "phone oper." Perhaps this note indicates that the FBI was going to monitor calls Ralph was making to or from the Vagabond.

On April 25, 1976, Mrs. Sigler's attorney, Tom Jennings, and his wife, Barbara (Ralph's niece), went to Fort Meade for a briefing by Colonel Grimes on the GRAPHIC IMAGE operation. But first they stopped by the Maryland State Police to meet with Lieutenant W. E. Brooks for an update on their investigation. State Police Officer Cassell, who investigated the case, also attended the discussions. The police advised Jennings of the following:

> Upon arriving at the Holiday Inn he [Cassell] discovered the body of Ralph Sigler lying facedown in a pool of blood. Attached to both arms were bare copper wires that he [Ralph] had stripped from the lamps in the room.[3] In turn, the copper wires were attached to a wall outlet that was operated by a light switch. Immediately adjacent to the light switch [were] two chairs piled on top of one another with a belt on the top chair. Apparently Sigler had attempted to strap himself into the second chair, but the belt was not large enough. When that did not work he sat on the chair and threw the switch. His body must have then been thrown off of the chair and onto the floor immediately alongside of the switch.
>
> The floor itself is covered with a cheap shag rug, which in turn covers a hard concrete floor. When the body struck the floor face down, there was damage done to the nose and temple. Thus the blood that was under the head came from the nose. Additionally, with the electricity flowing through the body and the face on the floor, the blood apparently burned the forehead and right side of his face. Both arms were severely burned and the photographs of the body indicate the wire was still attached to at least the one arm with the other wires immediately adjacent to the arm. When the body was found the upper torso was still warm, while the lower torso was cold and rigor mortis had set in. It is theorized that the electricity flowing through the upper torso kept it warm. It should be noted that it takes approximately two hours after death for rigor mortis to set in.[4]

Curiously, the state police told Jennings that "Sigler had moved to the Holiday Inn at approximately 9:20 A.M. on the morning of his death." That is how they explained Mrs. Sigler's futile efforts to call her husband the night he died. Lieutenant Brooks then told Barbara and Tom Jennings that Trooper Cassell would take them over to Fort

Meade. Brooks warned them that they would be "shocked" at what the Army had to say. "It was something out of a James Bond movie."[5]

Colonel Grimes greeted the Jenningses in the parking lot in front of the Army Intelligence offices. As they walked to Grimes's office, he said he wanted "to completely level" with them. After going through a series of locked doors, computerized combination buttons, telephone checks, and other security measures, they entered Grimes's third-floor office. Grimes began to tell a tale that was far more fascinating than any fictionalized spy story.

According to Jennings, Grimes said that Ralph was not really an electronics repairman, but a double agent for U.S. Army Intelligence, and had for the past ten years "been selling information to the Russians throughout the world regarding radar and missiles systems under the supervision and control of Army Intelligence. In return for this information, he had been paid a substantial amount of money that had, of course, been turned over to the U.S. Treasury. Additionally, Sigler's mother, who was still in Czechoslovakia, was 'taken care of' with a home, medicine, money, and other 'goodies.' "[6]

"Grimes emphasized that Sigler had been an extremely effective and capable agent. He pointed out, for example, that as a result of Sigler's activities, the Army was now aware of fourteen highly placed KGB agents whom they previously had not identified. Additionally, Grimes simply stated that Sigler had done a 'damn good job' for both the Army and his country, and that they were extremely proud of him." Grimes told the Jenningses that Ralph had Soviet contacts around the world and "he was scheduled to meet one of the agents on April 24. Additionally, he had been receiving radio instructions from the Russians . . . at home and that a communication—that the Army [would] now monitor—[was] expected on April 28."[7]

The colonel went on to recount the history of the ten-year GRAPHIC IMAGE operation, from its early days in Mexico to the failed polygraphs in San Francisco and outside of Fort Meade. He explained that the Army felt that Ralph's death was tragic for two reasons: first, they had lost a valuable agent, and, second, the information he gave the Russians had died with him. The Army was now faced with "the impossible task" of reconstructing the last two years of the operation to try to determine what Sigler had told the Soviets.

There were several reasons to keep the circumstances surrounding Ralph's death quiet, Grimes stressed. First, if the Russians still thought Ralph worked only for them, they would continue to give his mother "special attention." Second, if the Russians believed Ralph had died as a "good Russian spy," there was a better than "fifty-fifty chance" that the Russians would support Ilse and Karin for the rest of their lives. They would do this through a bank account of unknown origin in Ilse's name, and replenish it periodically. Grimes said that the Army would not object to Ilse taking the money. Third, if the Russians found out that Ralph was really a double agent, they might want to determine the extent of Ilse's knowledge of the operation. Grimes emphasized, however, that he did not think either Ilse or Ralph's mother was in danger.[8]

He advised that Ilse would be entitled to all the benefits of a widow whose husband had died in the line of duty, and in addition, she should be paid at least part of the money Ralph had gotten from the Russians over the years. Grimes stated that Sigler had accumulated a "substantial amount of money from Russia during the past ten years" and that the Treasury should give this to Mrs. Sigler since Ralph had "earned it." He said that throughout the operation, Ralph had been on an unlimited expense account, had received annual bonuses, and had been otherwise taken care of through promotions, assignments, and new cars. He noted that two years earlier Ralph had been recognized for his outstanding work by the highest-ranking officer in charge of intelligence in the Army—General Le Van. Le Van had congratulated Ralph and expressed the Army's appreciation for the work he was doing.

When Ralph died, the Army offered to explain the circumstances of his death to his wife. Ilse said she wanted to hear this from no one of lower rank than Le Van. Grimes advised Jennings that a meeting had been arranged for Mrs. Sigler and her daughter at the Pentagon on Saturday, May 1, 1976, and that Carlos Zapata would make all the necessary arrangements. When Jennings got back to his office in Philadelphia, he called Ilse to tell her the news.[9]

On Thursday, April 29, 1976, Ilse Sigler flew to Washington. The Army had provided her with two tickets so that Karin could accompany her, but she did not want to leave the house unoccupied. "Someone might break in," Ilse told Karin. "Make sure nobody comes in the house." Besides, Karin was still too upset about her father's death to attend a Pentagon meeting. Ilse told the Army that Karin was not feeling well. She thought they might be trying to get both her and Karin out of town so they could search the house themselves. And Ilse did not want anyone to get Ralph's medical records.

On Saturday, May 1, 1976, Ilse Sigler entered a corridor in the Pentagon where all the portraits of the Presidents hang, and signed the guest register. She was then escorted into a big office and served coffee from a silver service and fine china. But she was too nervous to drink coffee and make small talk. A few minutes later, a general in full uniform walked in and greeted Ilse. She looked at his name tag. It said AARON. Ilse was shocked. H. R. Aaron was the name of one of the people Ralph had told her to sue in his letter. From the start, Ilse knew that she could not trust General Aaron. In her opinion, "the minute I met with him, I know they didn't tell me the truth." [10]

Also at the meeting were Colonel Grimes, General Tenhet, Colonel John L. Heiss, and Tom Jennings, Mrs. Sigler's lawyer. General Aaron talked briefly about the origins of the operation and the sensitivity of their discussions. He told Ilse that she should protect the sensitive information as Ralph had, and that disclosure could affect Ralph's mother in Czechoslovakia. Aaron confirmed that Ralph was a double agent, and talked about other aspects of the operation. Ilse remembers Aaron saying that Ralph had been very helpful in a New York espionage case. He also said Ralph had admitted having a Soviet contact with a 202 area code (Washington, D.C.), but had refused to give them the number. (This was in addition to the San Francisco number Sigler had already told the Army about.) [11] General Aaron said that Ralph was supposed to get in contact with this person if he ever got into trouble and needed help in an emergency. He asked Ilse to give the Army a list of Ralph's telephone numbers.

Mrs. Sigler advised the general that two years ago she had been followed in El Paso. The Army agreed to check on these allegations. General Aaron then talked about Ralph's polygraph examinations in San Francisco and outside Fort Meade, during which he had admitted keeping notes at his home. Ilse explained that Ralph had told her he kept his own set of records in case something happened and he needed to defend himself. She showed him the April telephone bill. Aaron said, "Do you keep records of his telephone bills?"

"This one, yes," Ilse replied.

When he examined the bill, he saw the incoming call from San Francisco and asked about it. Ilse explained that that call was from the time Ralph had to go to the hotel in San Francisco to meet with the KGB. [12] She had no idea that the Army had never scheduled such a meeting, and she was unaware that Army Intelligence suspected that the FBI had been using Ralph independently from the Army.

Ilse then retold the events of Ralph's last week—his telephone calls and John Schaffstall's visit. She had numerous questions that Aaron's aides wrote down and promised they would try to answer. One question she asked was why Ralph was so worried that the FBI had been "cheating him on the money" he was receiving from the Soviets. Mrs. Sigler and her lawyer requested a full Army investigation of Ralph's death. "I am an American, have been patriotic, and deserve an explanation," Mrs. Sigler said to General Aaron. "I want all the names on the letter investigated, and that means you, too." She said everyone closely associated with the operation should submit to polygraph tests just like the ones they had made Ralph take.

General Tenhet said, "If we investigated the people involved, would you accept our investigation?'' ''Yes,'' Mrs. Sigler replied, ''I am loyal.'' She repeated that she wanted a thorough investigation and wanted to resolve the FBI money discrepancy. She described in detail how the FBI, for security reasons, had picked her husband up immediately upon his return from his meetings with the Soviets, thereby eliminating the possibility of any money discrepancies.

General Tenhet asked about the progress of Mrs. Sigler's survivor benefits. Ilse and her attorney brought him up to date on the status of that paperwork. She gave the Army a list of questions she had prepared for the meeting. She also gave them a note from Ralph that she found at home, addressed to John Schaffstall in care of the Outrigger East Hotel, Honolulu, Hawaii.[13]

General Aaron emphasized that they would need Ilse's continued cooperation during the investigation, including any notes or other materials found in her house in the future. Ilse then gave the general the sealed envelope containing the photographs of her husband with Brezhnev and high-ranking CIA and KGB officials. ''I gave those pictures to Aaron. I was scared they would kill me. I was dumb. I give them the original pictures. I brought them along. I was dealing with the government. I thought, 'Maybe now he's [General Aaron] nice to me and tells me [what happened to Ralph].'' But in reviewing what happened at the meeting, she now feels ''I was wrong to go up there.'' Within five minutes after looking at the photographs, Aaron left the room. He said, ''Well, we have to go through his [Ralph's] medical records and see if he had any mental problems.''[14]

Ilse knew Ralph was smart enough to have suspected that if anything happened to him, the Army would use his medical records to discredit him. She protected the medical files Ralph had hidden in Karin's car. These records showed he was in good health and had no history or signs of mental or drinking problems.

Ilse asked General Tenhet, ''Can I go to the hotel—the Holiday Inn —can I go?''

He consented, but her lawyer, Jennings, said, ''Come on. Go back home.''

Ilse replied, ''No. I'd like to see that hotel and I want to go to the police station.'' So she asked if she could take a taxi. The general offered to provide someone to take her there. Jennings said he felt confident that after Ilse met with the state police, she would be convinced, as he was, that her husband's death was a suicide.

The Army picked Ilse up at her motel and took her to the Holiday Inn and the Maryland State Police. When she got to police headquarters, she met with Lieutenant Brooks, who told her that the Army had asked him not to notify her of Ralph's death until after April 24, the date of his next scheduled meeting with the Soviets.[15] Ilse asked to see the police photographs. Brooks told her how terrible the pictures were and suggested that she might not be able to tolerate seeing them. "Listen. I saw during the war people getting killed with bombs. This cannot shock me more," Ilse said. When Brooks showed Ilse the pictures, her reaction was, "He's lying too clean. Gee, you see his arms? He is lying too clean." According to the placement of the chairs in the picture, Ralph would have had to do a complete flip in midair and land perfectly, with his arms straight. "Oh, well," Mrs. Sigler continued, "he didn't die this way. He lays too clean."

Mrs. Sigler then asked why no liquor bottles were found in Ralph's room when he was supposed to be so drunk. The state police replied that Ralph had gotten drunk at the Howard Johnson's and walked the several miles to the Holiday Inn. Unfortunately, the police could not name a single witness who either saw Ralph drinking at the Howard Johnson's or saw him walking to the Holiday Inn.

According to Tom Jennings, General Aaron offered Mrs. Sigler a huge settlement after Ralph's death. He agreed to pay her the $400,000 Ralph had received from the Soviets over the years, as well as additional sums for Karin's education and other expenses. As Mrs. Sigler's lawyer, Jennings encouraged her to accept the Army's offer. But Ilse refused. She wanted to know what had happened to her husband. She would not take what she saw as a bribe for abandoning her pursuit of the truth. John Schaffstall explains the Army's position: "We knew how much Ralph had made over the years. And we had that much money available to give her. We didn't want it. You know, there was no need for us to keep the money. The operation was over. And so we told her how much money was given and she said no." [16]

The suggestion Colonel Grimes made to Tom Jennings—that the Russians might open a bank account for Ilse—worried her. According to Ilse, several months after Ralph's death, the bank where Ilse had an account, the Northgate Bank, advised her that Ralph had an account at one of their branches. Since Ilse always did business with a different branch, she went to check. "Would you believe they couldn't find the account?" Ilse says. What really frightened her, though, was Grimes's remark that the KGB might secretly approach her. "What would I do if I [was] approached? What would I do? They would say, 'She is one.' . . . So I could trust nobody. Honestly . . . I couldn't make one move, either left or right, because if I would have talked to them [the KGB], I would have been the KGB, too. See, I had nobody."

There was only one time when Ilse actually thought the Russians tried to contact her. During the first few weeks after Ralph's burial, she went to the cemetery every day. After several months she started going once a week, on Sundays. One Sunday that fall, she was followed to the cemetery by a man driving a Cadillac. He parked his car and watched her as she walked to the grave. She looked up and saw another car, with two men in the front seat and two women in the back, driving down a side road. The man who was in the Cadillac got out of his car and started walking toward her. He was wearing blue jeans. She bent down to water the flowers on the grave. When she stood up, the man was standing right next to her. She was frightened. He came up very close to her and asked, "Is this your husband?"

Ilse replied, "Yes."

"How did he die?" the stranger asked.

"In an accident," Ilse said nervously.

"Lift up the flowers," he instructed.

Ilse was ready to get the flowers, and he said again, "Pick up the flowers."

She was afraid he was going to stab her. She said, "Oh, I already gave the flowers water."

She was frightened, but she looked closely at the man so she could recognize him later. He returned to his car and drove away. Ilse noticed that his car had license plates from Juarez, Mexico. The other car, with the four people in it, followed him out of the cemetery.[17]

On May 7, 1976, the directive ordering an inquiry into the death of CW3 Ralph Joseph Sigler was signed. Col. Carey G. Tomlinson of the Inspector General's office was assigned to conduct the investigation. But when he got to El Paso to interview Ralph's colleagues, he did not get much encouragement for the Army's suicide theory.

When Tomlinson interviewed Major Ring about the events following Sigler's death, Ring volunteered that Maj. John Ellis, Ralph's immediate supervisor at White Sands, had told him the following: "Major Ellis's opinion from working and knowing Mr. Sigler [was] that it was not suicide. He says [Sigler's] attitude when he left here was excellent. He was getting ready to retire. He had a job lined up with MICOM [a defense contractor] as a tech rep of some sort . . . and had things pretty well lined out. He was well liked by his people, a good supervisor. [Ellis] could not believe it was suicide."[18]

When Ilse returned to El Paso from Washington, she was more convinced than ever that her husband had not committed suicide. But she would wait to see what the Army investigation turned up. A reporter for the *El Paso Times* came to her house and asked about her husband's death, but she refused to cooperate. Although she did not trust the people from the Army and was growing more and more frustrated in her dealings with them, she hoped they would eventually tell her the truth about her husband's death.

Several times after Ralph's death, Mrs. Sigler was awakened at night by the sound of her front gate opening and closing. Once she saw a man leaving. One midnight, shortly before May 13, she heard her French poodle, Nicky, barking furiously. She got up to check on the dog and saw Nicky running to the door of the furnace room and barking. It was hot that evening, and Ilse had the air conditioner running on high. Then she smelled something. She opened the furnace closet door and saw that her furnace was on fire, burning and smoking. A valve on the furnace had been blocked. Ilse screamed, "Karin, get out! Get out!" She ran to the kitchen and got wet clothes from the washing machine and went back to the furnace to try to put the fire out. She kept screaming, "Karin, get out!" as she tried to extinguish the fire.[19]

Then Ilse went back to the kitchen, called the emergency number to summon the fire department. The house was filled with smoke, so Karin and her mother waited in the front yard in their robes until the fire department came and put out the fire. The firemen were puzzled and could not account for the cause of the fire. Not long after the fire, Ilse came home from work one afternoon and found her dog Nicky dead. Someone had poisoned it.[20]

After Karin graduated from high school that spring, the FBI offered her a job. "When she got out of high school, she got this letter from the FBI. When she graduated, they called her up and the lady said if she wants to work, they know she likes fancy cars, she likes sporty cars. And [Karin] said, 'I would be crazy to work for them,' " Ilse Sigler remembers. But Ilse encouraged her daughter to take the job long enough to find out what had happened to her father. But Karin wanted no part of the FBI.

On May 13, 1976, Lieutenant Colonel Tomlinson came to the house accompanied by a woman officer to interview Ilse for the Army investigation. Karin was getting ready to leave for school. He took out a tape recorder and asked to tape their interview. Mrs. Sigler refused, saying she did not want it taped unless there were two tape recorders, and one copy of the tape was left with her. Colonel Tomlinson got angry. "He was pretty snotty to me," Mrs. Sigler remembers. "He had that woman there, and I know had I been alone he would have said all kinds of different things." As Tomlinson remembers it, just after they sat down in the living room, Ilse began a "tirade against the Army" that lasted for over two hours.

By this time, Ilse was emotionally exhausted. Going through the circumstances of Ralph's life and death constantly with the Army made her even more agitated and nervous. Tomlinson tried to interview Mrs. Sigler one more time before he left El Paso, but found, once again, that she was too abusive and her answers too disjointed to be helpful to his investigation.

Tomlinson interviewed people at Fort Bliss, White Sands, the funeral home, the shopping center, and the police department in El Paso, to try to determine the veracity of many of Ilse Sigler's allegations. Back in Washington, he interviewed Ralph's colleagues and superiors at Fort Meade, as well as the ambulance driver, the Holiday Inn clerk, the mortician, and the pathologist to ascertain the circumstances surrounding Ralph's death. Then he wrote the official Inspector General's Report of Inquiry.

In a letter dated June 22 and mailed to Mrs. Sigler in El Paso, the Department of the Army outlined their conclusions of their investigations into the death of Ralph Joseph Sigler. The letter included the opinions of a psychiatrist who had never met Ralph:

> As you were advised, death cases with unusual circumstances are reviewed by the medical authorities in the Office of the Surgeon General. It was their opinion that your husband was not mentally responsible at the time of the act which caused his death. To arrive at this finding, not mentally responsible, the medical examiners reviewed all available reports, including the Autopsy Report and material written by your husband shortly before his death. Further, a discussion was held with a representative of your husband's supervisory agency. It appeared that your husband was acutely and severely depressed and considered suicide for some hours before his death, probably a few days. The self-destruction is considered to have been a symptom and product of the depressive illness. The acute depressive illness is considered to have constituted mental unsoundness with loss of ability to adhere to usual standards of behavior.

The official conclusion of the Inspector General's Report of Inquiry, dated June 11, 1976, stated that "Ralph Joseph Sigler died, a suicide, from self-electrocution." The report also said:

> In just about every statement taken, those persons in contact with Mrs. Sigler have indicated that she dealt with them in a brusque, demanding manner, expressing her desire to sue the Army and all individuals concerned unless she was given a satisfactory explanation to the questions she had posed. Mrs. Sigler complained about the delays in receiving such documents as the autopsy, death certificate, police report and personal effects as well as processing the body for return to El Paso for services. Mrs. Sigler alleged that the Army intended to keep the body until the 26th of April.

The report found that "Military Intelligence personnel are in no way responsible for Sigler's death" and the motive for Ralph's suicide was that rather than admit he had furnished unauthorized information to the Soviets, he killed himself. One of the report's recommendations

was to advise Mrs. Sigler that Ralph's activities "would have to surface . . . in the event of a civil suit."

Mrs. Sigler was devastated. Instead of answering her questions
about her husband's death, the Army's investigation was a complete
whitewash to clear it of any responsibility. It implied that Ralph was
disloyal, mentally incompetent, and a drunk. It even criticized her own
behavior and mental soundness. "I trusted them, you know, until I
received a report saying he had mental and drinking problems," Ilse
remembers. "You know I cooperated with the government for six
months. They said, 'Do not make a statement. Do not talk.' We tried
that because I thought that they would tell me. They didn't."

The Maryland State Police report of its investigation confirmed the
Army's findings. It determined that Ralph Sigler, between the hours of
6:00 and 11:30 P.M., attached a wire he had removed from a lamp cord
to his arms, seated himself in two chairs (one stacked on top of another), poured water on the contact points, and turned on the wall
switch with his elbow, electrocuting himself. That report ignored the
medical examiner's findings, which concluded that Ralph had so much
liquor in his system that he probably could not even have stacked the
chair on the credenza, much less carried out an elaborately contrived
suicide.

Mrs. Sigler's first attorney, Tom Jennings, believed the Army and
the state police.[21] An Army Information Memorandum confirmed Jennings's assistance to these agencies:

> Family of CW3 Sigler has engaged a lawyer, Thomas W. Jennings,
> located in Philadelphia, PA, to represent them. U.S. Army Intelli-
> gence representatives have cooperated with Mr. Jennings in provid-
> ing information about Sigler's association with Army Intelligence,
> and with details of his death. Similarly, Mr. Jennings has assisted in
> easing any misgivings by family that foul play might have been in-
> volved in Sigler's suicide.

Despite the Army's thinly veiled threats that publicity from a court
case might ruin her husband's reputation and jeopardize his mother in
Czechoslovakia, Mrs. Sigler felt that she had no choice but to hire
another lawyer and sue the Army. It was, after all, her husband's final
request. She went to two lawyers who refused to take the case. One
of them said, "The minute I take your case, I'll be investigated. The
IRS will check me out."

All alone and desperate for help, Mrs. Sigler went through the Yellow Pages and found D&N Investigations. That's how she found Fred
Duvall, an El Paso private investigator, and asked him to help her with

Ralph Sigler *(holding cigarette)* with Army buddies in Germany.

(COURTESY OF MRS. ILSE SIGLER)

The Sigler home in El Paso, Texas. (JOSEPH TRENTO)

Ralph Sigler, during the years he served as a double agent for the Army and the FBI.

(U.S. ARMY PHOTO)

Donald B. Grimes. (JOSEPH TRENTO)

John Schaffstall. (JOSEPH TRENTO)

Photographs taken by Ralph Sigler of two of
his drop sites in Mexico.

(COURTESY OF MRS. ILSE SIGLER)

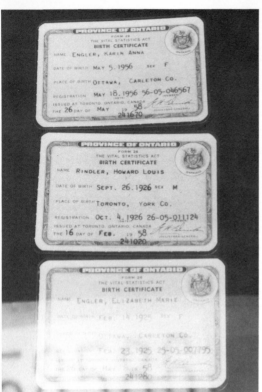

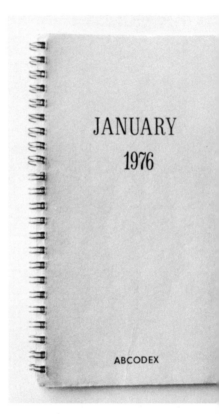

Left: The KGB forged these Canadian identification cards and gave them to Sigler. (JOSEPH TRENTO)

Above: Ralph Sigler's diary for the month of January 1976, one of many that he kept full of detailed notes on his activities.

(PHOTO BY JOSEPH TRENTO
COURTESY OF MRS. ILSE SIGLER)

Left: A page from Ralph Sigler's notebook reflecting the San Francisco meeting with the Soviets about which the Army knew nothing.

(PHOTO BY JOSEPH TRENTO
COURTESY OF MRS. ILSE SIGLER)

The black briefcase in which Mrs. Sigler found the pictures of her husband with Brezhnev and others. Sigler did his codework and much of his intelligence activity in this room. (JOSEPH TRENTO)

The tape recorder Sigler secretly used to record coded radio messages from the Soviets. The tapes still contain the messages. (JOSEPH TRENTO)

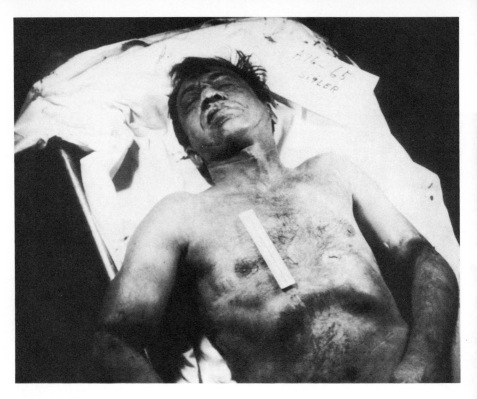

Ralph Sigler after his death *(note damage to his face).* (MARYLAND STATE POLICE PHOTO)

Close-up of wires wrapped around one of Sigler's arms. (MARYLAND STATE POLICE PHOTO)

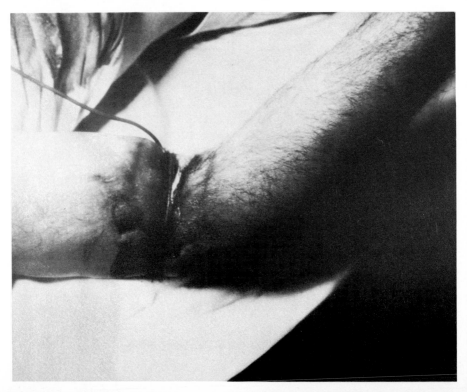

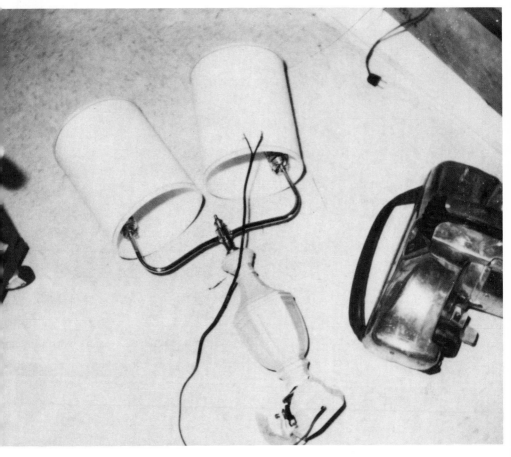

The lamp from which, according to the Maryland State Police, the wires were stripped and then used to electrocute Sigler.

Fred Duvall, Mrs. Sigler's El Paso–based investigator. (JOSEPH TRENTO)

the case. "Well, she didn't have anyone to trust, you see," Duvall explained. "Of course, anybody calls me, I'll go see them. . . . Why not. That's the business. . . ."

Duvall knew they would need some help with the case at the death scene. He looked through his records, and there was Harry Thompson's card. Since Upper Marlboro was not far from Fort Meade and the Holiday Inn where Ralph died, Duvall suggested Mrs. Sigler also hire Harry to investigate that end of the case.

Among the first things Duvall did was to contact an El Paso pathologist to try to determine how many documented suicides there were by self-electrocution. The pathologist assigned a researcher on his staff to the project, and the researcher discovered that out of hundreds of incidents, there had never been a documented self-electrocution suicide. Duvall said that in his opinion, anyone in the intelligence business, like Ralph, would never shoot himself, much less electrocute himself: "They don't blow their head off with a gun, they take a pill or they do the carbon monoxide trick. Something that's not going to hurt them [i.e., cause pain]. . . . And especially when you have worked . . . for a government agency that you have anything that you want at your disposal. . . . And besides that, you're not even sure that 110 [volts] is going to be that effective. It doesn't say that it's going to kill you. A lot of guys live through it." [22]

The pathologist advised Duvall that when one is electrocuted, the heart receives electrical interference that causes the valves to shut. "In other words," Duvall says, "his point to me was that when you're electrocuted the only blood is seepage from your mouth. There is no other blood." But Mrs. Sigler gave Duvall Ralph's blood-soaked T-shirt and boxer shorts. And Harry Thompson had a square of the cheap, green shag carpet from the Holiday Inn where Ralph died, that was soaked in blood. The motel could not get the bloodstains out, so they cut that portion of the carpet out and replaced it. "Well, that whole electrocution theory [went] down the drain once we established with the other pictures that I think the Jessup highway patrol took of him laying there with his shorts and the T-shirt on. And I've since talked to many doctors and that's right. He would not bleed." [23]

To Duvall, the T-shirt and the boxer shorts were very intriguing. He hired a chemist to run a blood test. The chemist said there were two different kinds of type-O blood on the T-shirt. One was the same type as Ralph's. Duvall said that the chemist also found "that the boxer shorts, when folded in the military manner, the bloodstains on the bottom matched the bloodstains on the top. In other words, the shorts with the blood were used to clean up blood, they were not on the person." There were no bloodstains on the inside of the trousers the police said were found on Ralph. An examination of the socks Ralph was wearing showed no sign of small holes or exits made by electrical energy.

Duvall thought he had better protect the T-shirt and boxer shorts, so he went to a local bank and put them in a safety deposit box. "And this is after I realized that I had some company with me all the time," he says. "I had somebody following me all the time." When he drove to Mrs. Sigler's house, he noticed a man was following him in an old, beat-up car. Duvall still remembers what he looked like. "He had kind of a light brown, almost reddish hair, big-shouldered, so he was probably going to top out over six foot. Big hands. I could tell on the steering wheel. And just the regular CIA or FBI look. You know, the sunglasses were just like the Air Force issue. The regular routine that anybody can spot."

Duvall did not let the man following him frighten him. "But what was fun was them following me and then I'd turn around and follow them. They would all of a sudden look in the rearview mirror and there I was." Duvall took down the numbers of the car's license plate and went to the Texas motor vehicle bureau to check on the registration. "But they weren't even registered," Duvall remembers.

Besides someone following him, there were other strange incidents that bothered Duvall. When he tried to get the missing-person report Mrs. Sigler had made to Fort Bliss the night Ralph died, he found that there was no record of it. One morning Duvall went to his office. He was not feeling well, so he did not put on a pot of coffee or light a cigarette as he usually does. Then he suddenly realized that his office was filled with natural gas. "There wasn't any reason for it to be full of natural gas, but there was natural gas in there," Duvall says. "So I called the gas company, fire department, and everybody else and got them out there. . . . There was a big regulator out beside our office that evidently, mysteriously stuck, and for some reason it caused gas to go into our office."

After his third meeting with Mrs. Sigler, they decided that the only safe place for them to meet was at the cemetery at Fort Bliss. Fred explains: "That's the only place that we could go and talk safely because I knew her house was bugged. I checked it. It was bugged. I had a friend at the phone company that continually, I mean, if not almost daily, weekly, would check her line and it was always bugged. So we would meet in the cemetery . . . in different areas and talk. I could look at the front gate and there's a car parked with two dudes sitting there."

Duvall also discovered that Mrs. Sigler's mail was being opened. He could see that letters that were not in window envelopes had been opened and resealed. Mrs. Sigler says her mailman told her, years later, that her mail was still being opened.

But the self-electrocution theory was not the only part of the Sigler death that was not supported by the facts. Duvall says the entire assertion that no one else could have entered or left the motel room was a myth: "What was really a big fallacy was . . . their big statement . . . [that they] based everything on—he was locked in the room with the night latch on and it was impossible for anybody to exit that room. . . . Wrong. . . . All Holiday Inns are built the same and they use basically the same type of doors and all it takes is an electric magnet to take that night latch."

Duvall claims that either the FBI or CIA went to great lengths to follow him while he was on the case. That December, the forensic expert he was working with asked him to go with him to Tegucigalpa, Honduras, on another case, to interpret for him because he did not speak Spanish well. When they got to Tegucigalpa, a man Duvall recognized from the federal courthouse in El Paso mysteriously appeared everywhere they went: "In the restaurant in the hotel. Every place we went, he was with us. Every place. . . . And we're in the restaurant . . . and I even said hello to him. He wouldn't say hello. We're three gringos in a foreign [country] and he doesn't say hello."

One day his friend realized that his passport was about to expire, so they went to the embassy. Duvall was sitting there waiting for his friend when the man walked into the embassy, took his automatic pistol out from underneath his shirt, and routinely handed it to the Marine on guard. "So I have no doubt from that point on that he was either CIA or FBI," Fred remarked.

Duvall told Ilse to go through all of the books in the house to see if Ralph had hidden any messages. She did, and she started finding little things, such as maps to two drop sites. The first drop site was eight miles from Ralph's house, in northeast El Paso, on the right-hand side of the road to White Sands, near the power plant. Ralph wrote:

> One meter above second wooden power pole. Buried under 8 inches of earth. The spot will be marked with a 4 inch diameter stone with an X mark on the under side. A container for equipment will be constructed from $18 \times 8 \times 2$ inch concrete bricks (6). The bricks will provide a storage area of 16 inches in length $\times 12$ inches wide $\times 8$ inches deep. All will be buried 6 to 8 inches underground.

Fred thought about driving out to check the site, but was afraid that the rock might be booby-trapped and it would blow up when he lifted it. He thought to himself, "I'm not going to go messing around with this."

That summer, Duvall also went to the *El Paso Times* to ask why they had contacted Mrs. Sigler earlier. Ilse had changed her mind about not cooperating with the press. Now she was going to make her story public. The paper assigned reporter John Starke to the story. Starke published a long series that echoed Mrs. Sigler's view that the Army had somehow been responsible for Ralph's murder.

Duvall's analysis of the clothes that Ralph was supposed to have been wearing the night he died coincided with information Harry Thompson was getting in Maryland, and the pair of Ralph's trousers that were missing. Tom O'Brien, a bellboy at the Holiday Inn, told Thompson that he had seen Polaroid negatives of Ralph Sigler in the nude, lying on the floor. O'Brien said that while cleaning up in back of the motel, he found, out by the trashcan, negatives pulled off Polaroid pictures, which he picked up and looked at. The police were still in the room, doing their investigation. The body had been removed. One negative was a picture of Ralph Sigler lying nude on the floor. The other was a picture of a car with the car doors open and the trunk lid up and a person sitting on the passenger side of the car. O'Brien took them to the innkeeper, but he said they were of no value and put them in the trash.[24]

O'Brien also told Thompson that when he was sent to the room the next day to clean up the carpet, he found there was so much blood in it that he could not get the stain out, so he had to cut out that section of the carpet and replace it.

When Thompson went to the motel room, he took the small desk chair and stacked it on top of the other chair. It fit, but Thompson could not figure out why Ralph would bother stacking the chairs, since this did not get him closer to the plug or the light switch. The Maryland State Police said Ralph had put a chair on top of the luggage holder attached to the desk. But that would have made it impossible for him to reach the switch with his arm or elbow. The night clerk, William Henry Chapman, confirmed that only one chair was on the credenza or luggage holder when he entered the room, and the luggage holder was "pulled a little bit closer to the door." Later the police claimed the chairs were stacked on the floor at the end of the luggage rack, facing the door, not on the rack. They had pictures to that effect.[25]

The lamp from which Ralph had cut the cord was in the Holiday Inn's storage room when Harry Thompson first went to investigate. The nine-foot cord had been cut to three feet, and the end of the wire had been rolled or braided like that of a wire that was to be spliced to another wire. Harry had an electronics expert test the light switch. "I had an expert test the amount of juice that came from that light switch, and it was not enough to knock him down either. It would make your hair stand up. It's not going to kill you. [The expert] said, 'I am not going to stand there for ten or fifteen minutes, but I will hold it and show you that it will not kill you.' " Then Thompson showed the expert pictures of Ralph's body. "I showed this same man this picture here. He said there is no way 115 [volts] is going to char your hand up like that."

According to the police report, the fifteen-amp circuit breakers at the motel were not thrown the night Ralph died, and the guests staying on the same floor as Ralph heard nothing unusual and noticed no dimming of the electricity.

Harry Thompson thought the entire crime scene was suspicious. "A man that is contemplating suicide that wears glasses all the time, had taken his glasses off, neatly folded them up, taken his change out of his pockets, and neatly put it on the counter. He was supposed to be in a drunken stupor, yet the beds were made, not a wrinkle in them. Suitcase laying there neatly, yet he is in a drunken stupor. And wiring himself up like this and he is an electronics expert. He knew all he had to do was to take a hot wire and drop it in the bathtub and stand in the tub in water without going through this elaborate means of electrocuting himself." Harry said that, based on the autopsy and the amount of alcohol in Ralph's system, he did not believe that Ralph could have fallen out of the chairs, turned around almost in midair, landed cleanly, and not knocked over the chairs. Louis Martel, who discovered the body, agrees: "It was lying there very neatly and that was puzzling." [26]

Although the autopsy report said the alcohol in Sigler's blood was three times the level it takes to be legally drunk, there were no liquor bottles found in the room. If Ralph committed suicide in the room, where were the beer cans or liquor bottles? Thompson concluded that Ralph was killed in another room and brought to room 326. He knew it was very doubtful that a man with that much alcohol in his system, especially a man known to have a low tolerance for alcohol, could have made such intricate preparations to kill himself (as described by the Army and the police), or walked the several miles from the Howard Johnson's back to the Holiday Inn (as the Maryland State Police claimed he did).

Dr. Hertzog, who performed the autopsy, agreed that the alcohol in Ralph's blood did raise suspicion. Hertzog told Mrs. Sigler that Ralph never could have committed suicide the way the police and the Army described. There was too much liquor in his system for him even to crawl into bed, much less stack two chairs, wrap electrical wires around his arms, and flip the switch: "His motor function was so impaired he could not carry out the scheme the police describe to kill himself. In my view, his death was not self-inflicted." [27]

Autopsy pictures show that Ralph was severely beaten before the electrocution. When John Schaffstall saw the pictures, he said, "I wouldn't have recognized Ralph." He had been beaten almost beyond recognition; his face looked like that of a battered, losing prizefighter. The facial damage, Hertzog said, came not from the fall from the chair to the carpeted floor, but from acts of "much greater force. He didn't fall that far, and he looked like a man who was beaten." [28]

But it was Dr. Hertzog's concerns about the security of Ralph's room that kept him from ruling the death a suicide. The night clerk, William Henry Chapman, showed Thompson how the dead bolt could be partially closed with the room key from the outside to make it appear that the door had been bolted from the inside. In addition, he said that usually when someone bolts himself in for the night, he also latches the night chain on the door for added security. The night Chapman entered the room, the night chain was not on the door. And Ralph's room key was never found in his effects. [29]

"I cautiously made no conclusion as to whether [the electrocution] was self-inflicted," Hertzog said. Because of the "question of the security of the room" and the high blood alcohol content, "I cannot exclude the possibility, quite frankly, [that] someone put him in this position. . . . But the high levels raised a question whether someone had gotten Sigler drunk and then wired him." [30]

Harry Thompson confirmed that he, too, was followed when he started investigating the case. Like Fred Duvall, he took down the license-plate number of the car that was tailing him. "And I took the tag numbers and gave them to a police friend of mine to run, and they came back with 'no tag issued yet on those numbers.' "

In the original police reports, there was no mention of the adjoining room. When Thompson tried to contact the man who was supposed to be in the room adjoining Ralph's, he could not find him. There was no listing under either his name or the insurance company where he supposedly worked. When Harry tried to get details of Ralph's stay at the Howard Johnson's, he was told their files had been destroyed.

Additionally, Thompson was advised that there was no way Ralph could have broken his nose or gashed his forehead from falling on the floor. The innkeeper told him that children had fallen off the room beds with no injuries because of the carpeting and padding.

The night clerk confirmed to Thompson that the circuit breaker had not been tripped the night Ralph died, and that the lamp between the two double beds—the same light from which Ralph supposedly stripped the cord—was in an upright position and was on. Thompson checked the windows in the room and felt that no one could have entered or left through the windows without a ladder or a rope, since the room was on the third floor. But he wondered how Lou Martel knew, without touching him, Ralph was dead, when he and Chapman entered the room that night. According to Thompson, the light in the room would have been too dim to tell for certain.

Thompson was curious as to why Chapman left the room after he discovered the body and went downstairs to use the phone, instead of using the phone in the room. Chapman said that Martel had told him to go downstairs. Martel said he had wanted Chapman out of the room so he could call Noel Jones. Thompson then questioned whether someone could have been hiding in the bathroom. "I asked him if he could tell the bathroom light was on in room 326. He said, 'Now that you brought it up, the light was off. The door was closed with about a two-to-four-inch opening.' "

Thompson then interviewed the maid who had been on duty the day Sigler died. She said he had seemed very nervous that day. At 8:00 A.M. on the day Sigler died he had asked her to make up his bed and straighten up his room because he was expecting someone important. She told Thompson that Ralph had said something to the effect that a man—he used the word "he" or "Mr."—was to meet him. While she was making up the room, Ralph walked in and she asked him to wait outside the room while she cleaned, because of a motel rule that male guests cannot be in a room with female maids. He went outside and paced up and down the hallway. He was a very worried man. When she was through, he went into the room and put the Do Not Disturb sign on the door.

Later, around 11:30—she remembered the time because Ralph had asked her what time it was—she saw him again. He had taken the sign off his door. Every time the elevator would stop on the third floor, Ralph would look out into the hallway, as if looking for someone. She asked him if he was going to stay over, and he said he was, and that he had informed the desk clerk of that. He seemed very upset, and had trouble getting a Coke from the machine. She told him to try the machine on the second floor, which he did.

The maid's husband worked as a maintenance man at the motel. When the husband saw his wife and Ralph talking, he asked her if Ralph was giving her any trouble. She told him about Ralph's behavior, and so he, too, watched Ralph and thought he seemed upset about this person who was coming to see him.

When the maid went to clean up the room, she saw no liquor bottles or glasses. But when they opened the room a few days after Ralph's death so she could clean it, she found extra coffee cups, extra Holiday Inn cups, a Coke bottle, a Sprite can, and a ginger ale can in the room. Also, some paper was under the bed with some notes on it, which she put in the trash with the rest of the trash in the can in the room. Thompson could not understand why the state police had not protected the scene of the crime or made any efforts at a real investigation. Chapman said that anyone could have changed the death scene "because there were so many people in there."[31]

The state police never interviewed the maid or the bellboy, Tom O'Brien. As in the Paisley case, the Maryland State Police only added to the mystery. They let the Army Intelligence agents take the inventory of the room and all of Ralph's belongings back to Fort Meade with them. "They more or less stood back and let them run the show," Thompson lamented. "They automatically determined it was a suicide when they walked in the room."

Then the maid told Harry Thompson a story that shocked him. She said that the day after Ralph died, April 14, a man and a woman checked into room number 310. The man looked like a double of Ralph Sigler, glasses and all. It made her "hair stand on end." They stayed in the room all day, or at least she never saw them leave. "If it wasn't his twin, it was his ghost," the maid told the *El Paso Times* in a later interview. Thompson said, "When she opened the door to go in to do some cleaning, they asked her to come back later. She said it scared her at first because it looked exactly like the man she had seen that had died."

Louis Martel said there were discussions of continuing the GRAPHIC IMAGE operation. This might explain why the Army did not want Ralph's body released until after Ralph's next scheduled meeting with the Russians. Martel says that as far as he knows, nothing came of the discussions. "But some pretty wild theories and ideas were thrown out," Martel said.

At first Thompson and Duvall worked together. But soon Thompson started reporting directly to Mrs. Sigler. After months of investigating, Harry Thompson concluded that the KGB had "eliminated" Ralph.

Duvall recommended that Ilse hire a local attorney in El Paso named Gibson, who was a criminal lawyer. But Gibson referred her to another El Paso lawyer, Sidney J. Diamond. Duvall wrote to Diamond on September 13, 1976, shortly after Diamond had accepted the case: "We have been involved in an investigation pertaining to the death of Ralph Sigler. Although we have but a minimal amount of time involved, I am led to place trust and belief in Mrs. Sigler's explanation of what happened to her husband."

From the start, Diamond and Duvall were at odds. "Sid didn't want me to do anything except what he told me to do. And I said, 'Well, that's really not going to work too good.' . . . I've never had an attorney tell me, 'You're only going to do what I tell you.' " Diamond did not want Duvall contacting anyone in the Army or the FBI. Diamond had excellent contacts in the El Paso office of the FBI, and believed he could better handle contacts with the Bureau.

Diamond, like Duvall, had some unusual things happen to him after he took the Sigler case. His house was broken into twice. The first time, a neighbor spotted a man trying to break in the front door. A mad chase ensued. The second time, the burglar tried the back door, but Sid thinks his Alaskan husky scared him away. And "one or more people broke into the office a couple of times," Diamond revealed. "The files were gone through. I am not sure what they were looking for. Whatever it is, they didn't find it." [32]

Mrs. Sigler credits Diamond with gathering important information on the case through the Freedom of Information Act. There is one picture Diamond obtained that he will never forget. "I think the thing that was irrefutable was Sigler shaking hands with Colby and getting the medal—the famous medal pictures. They [the Army] denied it even existed. The picture just showed up on FOIA."

A former Army Intelligence man who knew Sigler told Diamond there was "no way" Sigler would have killed himself. This same man said that torture and electrocution by wiring a victim the way Sigler was wired is practiced by "certain powers"—a reference to the Soviets, Diamond explained. [33]

On September 30, 1977, John Starke, the reporter from the *El Paso Times*, called the Pentagon for comment on his story about Ralph Sigler. The *Washington Post* also sent a reporter to El Paso to do a story. And if the media coverage was not bad enough, in a letter dated October 5, 1976, the Senate Intelligence Committee Chairman, Senator Daniel K. Inouye (D.-Hawaii), asked the Army for "a full report on the details of the death of Army Warrant Officer Ralph Sigler."

It was the Army's worst nightmare come true. For the first time in the history of Army Intelligence, they had to go before a congressional intelligence committee and account for their actions. In addition, they had to brief the Armed Services committees. John Schaffstall understood the repercussions. "The main thing is that if the Soviets did this [killed Ralph] for any reason, it would be to embarrass the Army . . . which they did. . . . The impact would be whether you'd ever run another operation because of the Senate. . . . It made us go to the oversight committee . . . which they didn't before that."

After the inquiry by the Army failed to satisfy Mrs. Sigler, and the press and Congress began to listen to her and investigate, certain officials, to salvage their own careers and reputations, began to try to discredit Ralph Sigler. They exaggerated the amount of unauthorized information Ralph had passed on to the Russians, and said that when they caught him, Sigler committed suicide. They tried to characterize Ralph as a depressed drunk. Some even implied that he was a traitor. But the same man leading the campaign to disparage Ralph's work had also recommended Ralph for the Legion of Merit, one of the Army's most prestigious medals.[34] Noel Jones says flatly, "Ralph Sigler was not working for the Russians."

On February 18, 1977, Ilse Sigler complied with her husband's final request. She filed a lawsuit in the U.S. District Court in El Paso against the men listed in Ralph's letter: H. R. Aaron, C. J. Le Van, Donald Grimes, Noel Jones, Carlos Zapata, Joe Prasek, and John Schaffstall, as well as Louis Martel and Carey Tomlinson, who conducted the "special inquiry" for the Army.

The $22.5-million lawsuit charged "that the defendants, individually and acting in combination, conspiracy and in concert of action, either murdered Ralph J. Sigler or placed him in a position of extreme danger and failed to protect him and that such failure on the part of the defendants resulted in the death of Ralph J. Sigler in violation of the Fifth Amendment." The suit also alleged that the defendants, in violation of the Fourth Amendment, "unlawfully seized papers, personal property and memorabilia of Mrs. Sigler and [were] unlawfully holding" them.[35]

The next five years would prove to be a grueling, unending nightmare for both Mrs. Sigler and the defendants. John Schaffstall said it hurt his and his colleagues' careers. "When I retired, I went over to the Treasury Department. And I had a real good reception there until I had to be honest and I told them that I was being sued and it might come out in the newspapers and all that and I [didn't] know how [they would] feel about that. 'Don't worry about that.' . . . And then they sort of said I wasn't eligible for employment afterwards. There was a lot of employment . . . we didn't get because [of the court case]."

U.S. District Court Judge William S. Sessions was assigned the case. "The judge in El Paso was good and he was fair. . . . He made them do all the depositions in six months," Mrs. Sigler said. Her lawyer, Sid Diamond, agreed: "I think Judge Sessions is a very conservative judge. But once you show him the fact and the law, he has no trouble at all doing the right thing. Protecting the establishment is not his nature."

Most of the defendants filed a request for representation to the Justice Department. After a review of the case, the Justice Department determined that it would be a conflict of interest to represent the defendants and authorized private counsel to be retained at government expense. Attorney Charles N. Brower, with the Washington, D.C., firm of White & Case, refused to take the case partly because of difficulty in receiving payment from the Justice Department for a similar case it had handled earlier.[36] Then defendants Aaron, Grimes, Martel, Jones, and Schaffstall had some luck. James F. Neal, a highly regarded trial lawyer in Washington, accepted the case.

In early 1978 the depositions of the defendants were scheduled. "Two days before the deposition was taken of Zapata, R. John Seibert [an attorney in the Civil Division of the Justice Department] showed up and offered to settle the case. The FBI must have contacted him," Mrs. Sigler speculates. Seibert had not consulted with some of the defendants or their lawyers before he flew to El Paso to meet with Sid Diamond and Ilse and Karin Sigler. Even Mrs. Sigler was not prepared for the offer. "First they said the Army would clear Ralph's name," Mrs. Sigler remembers. Her attorney, Sid Diamond, phoned her and said the government would produce some additional information on how Ralph died. The government also offered Mrs. Sigler approximately $250,000 to settle the case. Diamond advised her to accept it.[37]

"I don't want money. I want the truth," Ilse replied. "If they don't tell me what really happened, I don't want it." Mrs. Sigler insisted that her husband had been murdered. The Army and the individual defendants in the suit said that as long as she used the word "murder," they would not settle. Mrs. Sigler responded, "I still use it because he did not commit suicide." "The Army will see you in court," was the reply from the attorneys of the defendants.

In a letter to Judge Sessions, dated March 6, 1978, Seibert asserted the interest of the United States in the case and made a motion that the Justice Department participate at the depositions. But before the depositions were taken, on June 29, 1978, the case was transferred from Texas to the U.S. District Court in Baltimore, Maryland. Judge Edward S. Northrop was assigned the case. The defense attorneys were ecstatic. They told the defendants that Judge Northrop had been in naval intelligence during World War II, and they felt that he would be "sensitive to the imperatives of an intelligence mission."

Mrs. Sigler discharged Sid Diamond, and started looking for an attorney in Maryland. Harry Thompson recommended James E. Kenkel. Kenkel was a lawyer in suburban Washington who had a general practice and seemed honest and fair to Mrs. Sigler: "In the first contract he just charged the costs. In the second part he was a little bit higher."

The defense attorneys were right about Judge Northrop. He granted the defense's request to stay discovery until after their initial motion to dismiss was resolved. The request was based on the assertion that the *Feres* doctrine of intraservice immunity required complete dismissal of both of Mrs. Sigler's complaints. The doctrine of military immunity, as defined by the Supreme Court in *Feres* v. *United States,* did not allow suits for damages for "injuries incurred incident to service." On January 7, 1980, Judge Northrop dismissed all claims against Joe Prasek, the only defendant not in the military. "Yeah. I don't know how he [Prasek] got off that. I can't figure it," John Schaffstall said.

On Sunday, October 12, 1980, the CBS television show "60 Minutes'' did a segment on Ralph Sigler. Newsman Dan Rather reported the piece.[38] But Mrs. Sigler's court case was not progressing as favorably as the publicity. By the end of October 1980, the court had dismissed all of the original claims—assault, murder, false imprisonment and other charges. The only remaining issues were a number of claims filed by Kenkel regarding entry into the Sigler household to retrieve Ralph Sigler's materials, and the Siglers' rights to these materials. With the most serious charges now dismissed, the defense attorneys pressed for another settlement. Fearful that Mrs. Sigler's luck might improve, the lawyers were anxious to avoid further litigation.

On January 30, 1981, one of the defense attorneys invited Mrs. Sigler's attorney to coffee. Mrs. Sigler's lawyer indicated that he had grown disenchanted with Mrs. Sigler and was ready to settle the case. The defense attorney thought they could settle the case for not more than $70,000, possibly less, but Mrs. Sigler would still insist on a statement in defense of her husband.

During the fall of 1981, the Army offered Mrs. Sigler $25,000 ''to dispose of this matter.'' Mrs. Sigler's lawyer countered with a demand for $43,000. A tentative trial date was set for April 19, 1982. In the meantime, the Army used national security considerations to stymie Mrs. Sigler's legal discovery process. In January 1982, the final details of the settlement were ironed out. The Army would give Mrs. Sigler a letter that was basically a rewrite of Ralph's Legion of Merit citation, and a monetary settlement of $43,000. The money amounted to less than what Mrs. Sigler had already spent trying to find out what had happened to her husband.

On March 25, 1982, Judge Northrop issued an order dismissing the court cases with prejudice. Mrs. Sigler's settlement was for $42,608.90. After deducting legal fees and other expenses, Mrs. Sigler got a check for $28,400, which she divided with her daughter. Ilse Sigler said that by 1982, she had spent over $50,000 of her own money on attorneys and private investigators. For months she had literally lived on bread and water because she could not afford food. She had spent all of Ralph's life insurance and other benefits to pursue the court case. She did not make enough money from Ralph's pension and her job at the dress store to continue the case without taking out a second mortgage on the house. Ilse Sigler never wanted to settle the case, but she could not afford to continue. The Army had worn her down.

It did not cost the defendants a nickel. Their expenses were paid for by the American taxpayers. After five years of heartache and financial hardship, Mrs. Sigler never got the answers she sought so desperately and with such conviction to the still open questions of how and why Ralph Sigler died.

Sigler Epilogue: The Illegal

I really don't think the Army knows what happened. . . . We never
heard from the Bureau. When things go bad, the Bureau takes a run.

John Schaffstall

As ONE OF the FBI's top counterintelligence officers, Eugene Peterson
was short of staff, overworked, and often little recognized. He had
hundreds of cases and could concentrate only briefly on problem
areas. There was no time to spend worrying about what *might* happen
or go wrong on different operations. "I had four hundred other cases
besides that [Sigler]. At least maybe fifty of them were equally as
important . . . " Eugene Peterson remembers. "The volume was so
tremendous that all you could do is read something and read it once
and you either say, 'Okay,'—you'd sign off and throw [it] to the files,
or you'd say, 'Okay, go do this.' I had a girl steno, full time—only guy
that did. And just for that purpose, 'cause I could move paper. . . .
No moss grew on it."

When Peterson took charge in early 1976, the files on Ralph Sigler
and Nick Shadrin were among those in a locked filing cabinet that had

been rolled into his office. But these two operations were successful. To his knowledge, no real problems existed that needed attention, so he left them locked away in files, unread for months. "I don't think I spun the dial on those cabinets for at least six months because I had another hot case," Peterson admits.

The KGB, on the other hand, had unlimited resources and received the highest praise and recognition of any agency in Soviet government. Its job, after all, was to protect and defend the Communist Party and the State. They had the time, the money, and the ability to follow every operation carefully, like a chess game, maneuvering one pawn against another, anticipating their opponent's response.

Among the most respected and revered officers in the KGB were the men and women trained to enter the United States illegally and infiltrate American society—living in communities throughout the United States under false identities, pretending to be average American citizens, usually very conservative politically and very anticommunist. These Soviet agents were and are still known as "illegals."

There is only one real purpose for a modern illegal—"wet affairs." They are sent to assist and supervise assassination and sabotage. They must maintain two distinct lifestyles. In one they must appear to be normal American workers with families who get up every morning and go to jobs just like everyone else. In the other, they must maintain a secret network of communications with KGB headquarters to receive instruction for clandestine assignments from their real bosses.

As John Barron first reported in his book *KGB Today: The Hidden Hand,* in 1955 the KGB recruited a young Czechoslovakian, Ludek Zemenek, to become an illegal.[1] There was no way to know that twenty years later Ludek's life would cross with that of another Czech who was growing up at the same time in the United States—Ralph Sigler. Like Ralph, Ludek was raised during the Depression, and both Ludek and Ralph were no strangers to hard work. Both had domineering fathers who had pushed them to complete their assignments. But when they were both reaching manhood, the similarities ended. Ralph rebelled, dropped out of school, left home, and joined the Army. Ludek, on the other hand, became a dedicated communist after the Russians "liberated" Czechoslovakia from the Germans. Ludek studied Marxist-Leninist philosophy dutifully in school. At seventeen he became a member of the Communist Party and graduated from college in Prague among the top in his class. After a short stint in the military, Ludek was chosen by the Russians to undergo training by the KGB in clandestine tradecraft, preparing him for life as an illegal.

The KGB created a "legend" or cover story for Ludek Zemenek. He became Rudolph Herrmann, an identity taken from a German who had died in the Soviet Union in 1943, and had no close relatives. Rudi, as Ludek was now known, found a job in a small auto-parts store in a town outside of Frankfurt. He and his wife successfully lived as Germans in West Germany for several years. Then, in late February 1961, Rudi was instructed to visit Canada and the United States as a tourist, to see if he could live there. Herrmann traveled through Canada and to Detroit and New York, and advised the KGB that he felt he could live and work effectively in these countries.

Rudi and his wife applied for immigrant visas, moved to Toronto, and opened a delicatessen. From Canada it would be easy to immigrate to the United States. Just as they had been good, loyal, hardworking West Germans, they now became patriotic Canadians. Eventually, Rudi sold the delicatessen and started a commercial and advertising filmmaking business. In February 1967, Rudi became a Canadian citizen. Ten days later the KGB instructed him to obtain a visa and move to the United States.

When Rudi received his American visa in 1968, he moved, under KGB orders, to Hartsdale, New York, about fifteen miles north of New York City. Soon Rudi established a business in which he made training and sales films for IBM and other prestigious clients. On the side, he carried out KGB orders. In March 1969, he mailed a letter to Cape Canaveral, threatening to sabotage the next manned lunar launch. He was instructed to spy on a Soviet defector, believed to be Yuri Nosenko, in Arlington, Virginia, just outside of Washington, D.C. Herrmann had been in contact with Nick Shadrin.

But, more important, Rudolph Herrmann was ordered to service drop sites near U.S. military bases. Herrmann knew through his intelligence tradecraft training that these drop sites were needed because the KGB had infiltrated the military bases, and their operatives could only communicate in this manner.

In mid-1975, Herrmann was told by the KGB to establish two "long-term" drop sites in an area outside El Paso, Texas. These drop sites should be suitable for continuous use and for containment of materials for some time before retrieval. It was obvious to Herrmann that the Russians had an agent in the military in El Paso, because the location they had picked was near the White Sands Missile Range and Fort Bliss. In September, Rudi drove around El Paso for hours, looking for any signs of surveillance before he headed toward the desert. He even doubled back once, looking for pursuing cars. He thought he heard the sound of helicopters overhead, but reckoned that such flights would not be unusual around military installations.

Picking a spot underneath a gas pipeline, Rudi felt that this location would be good for hiding a container for several years. In a cemetery a few miles away, he selected for the second site the tombstone of a child who had died at the age of three. He paused and wondered what would be brought to this child's grave, and what the man who brought it would be like. Before he left El Paso, he made a telephone call.

On May 4, 1977, the FBI, who had been following Rudolph Herrmann, finally confronted him in New York. The Bureau offered Rudi and his family either prison or safe asylum in the United States with new identities in a new location, if he would work with them against the KGB. Herrmann said he would cooperate with the FBI, but he had conditions. "I will not kill anybody," Herrmann said. "The KGB kills people; we don't," one of the FBI agents responded.

During the interrogation of Herrmann, it became obvious that the FBI knew of his drop sites outside of El Paso. Herrmann was certain the FBI had picked up his activities at least by early 1975, and possibly earlier. And he felt that only someone servicing those drops could have revealed his identity to the FBI.[2] Noel Jones says that Herrmann was picked up not by clever FBI counterintelligence work, but by a surveillance camera at a drop site just across the northern Alabama border in Tennessee. Jones said that drop was used by an Army double agent stationed at the Redstone Arsenal in nearby Huntsville.

When Herrmann could not remember the complete telephone number he had called in El Paso, the Bureau administered sodium pentothal. A former high-ranking FBI official confirmed that Rudolph Herrmann was working with Ralph Sigler. Just like Ralph, Rudi met with the same KGB officials in Mexico City, at Chapultepec Park, and in Vienna and other Eastern European and Soviet cities. The travel documents the Soviets gave Ralph were Canadian ID cards, not passports, which were normally used. Ralph's ID card was from Toronto, Canada, where Herrmann lived for several years. General Aaron told Mrs. Sigler and her attorney that Ralph had been helpful in solving a New York espionage case. Herrmann was operating out of New York at the time, and was under FBI surveillance. And Herrmann serviced two drop sites in El Paso. In Ralph's belongings were maps of the same two drop sites. One described a location for long-term use near a power plant and another near a grave marker, very similar to Herrmann's description.

From the beginning to the end of the Sigler double-agent operation, the FBI and the Army fought over control of the case. "That was an argument that we had with the Bureau for years and years and years. If we initiate an operation, we should run it. Pure and simple. They can tag along if they want to," Colonel Donald Grimes explains. But the Bureau saw it the other way. "You go back to traditions that were existing at the time the thing was instituted. The theory was that it was FBI with support from the military. And that's the way it had to be," insists Eugene Peterson. Grimes and Peterson did not get along. "My relationship with Peterson was always a little strained. . . . I didn't trust him. He didn't trust me," Grimes admits.

After Ralph's death, the animosity between the FBI and the Army grew. "He committed suicide. It was an Army problem. They had responsibility for his personal security and obviously they didn't take care of it," Peterson said. The Army asked to see the Canadian ID cards the Russians had given Ralph. The FBI claimed to have them, but refused to let the Army see them. "Prasek and [the FBI] had those [Canadian ID cards]. That's where the odd stuff comes in. There were things that they got that they wouldn't even let us look at afterward," John Schaffstall said.

But Prasek and the FBI did not have the cards. Several years after Ralph's death, Ilse decided to replace the carpet in her living room. When the carpet installers moved a huge wooden breakfront, the cards fell to the floor. Ralph had hidden the cards, and Ilse still has them today.

To this day, members of Army Intelligence—John Schaffstall, Donnel Drake, Donald Grimes, Lou Martel, Noel Jones—wonder what caused Ralph to flunk his polygraph exams. The Army says it had no motive to kill Ralph since it was trying to find out what he had done. And Schaffstall believes that there was no motive for a suicide. "That's why I couldn't believe that he'd kill himself either, because he knew that whatever he did, we could fix it up. He'd always be with us. And it wasn't because he was retiring that he was going to go. We already had him the job. . . . He knew that he had everything."

Schaffstall also believes that Ralph had no reason to distrust the Army. "We were never dishonest with him. Everything we had ever told him, the Army, we always kept our promises. We told him when he'd [get] promoted. We would help on that. We did everything. And we always were truthful to him. He never had cause to say, 'These guys are lying to me,' or 'They [do] not really care for me, they care for themselves only.' So when we assured him that nothing was going to [happen to] him . . . he had to know."

The Army insists that Ralph knew that no matter what he told the Russians, the worst that would happen would be the termination of the operation. "Rest assured that he knew or he was told many, many times that it didn't matter what the hell he said or what he did as long as we knew what it was," Schaffstall states emphatically.

When asked if he thought Ralph had been turned and was really working for the Russians, Grimes replied, "No, I didn't. I think that it would have been more reaction to the questions he was asked. . . . And that's what bamboozled me. I didn't think he was working for the bad guys, but he must have been working for somebody. . . . And the Bureau was the most likely. . . . Sometimes I thought that he might be working on the side for the Bureau."

Noel Jones agrees, "Ralph Sigler never worked for the Russians."

John Schaffstall never thought to question the Bureau. "But we tested Ralph in various ways against any [unauthorized] Soviet contact . . . that he might do. But we never came up with anything. But we never checked the FBI. That's my fault . . . because . . . I wouldn't meet him unless I told the FBI, and I would say to myself, 'They've got to be helping us or cooperating. They're getting the take.' . . . Maybe this is naïve here."

In the history of U.S. counterintelligence, Ralph Sigler will be remembered as the first FBI and Army offensive counterintelligence agent successfully "dangled" in front of the Soviets. "The Sigler case started out as the primary, or first, CI effort to run dangles . . . against the opposition to see how they would respond," Peterson says. "This was our maiden effort."

Ralph was a novelty at first to the Bureau. "So that was the initial thing. We're going to pick him, a good guy, and then we're going to throw him at [the Soviets] and see how they run him. And if it turns . . . into a viable operation for the Army, fine. You want to throw them some stuff that may or may not be true, fine. . . . So then that little thing kicks off and it was good. So then you have success. You say, 'Hey, you'll never guess what happened down at the ranch this past week.' Now we want to run another. And the thing evolved," Peterson explains.

The FBI's objectives—to understand the strengths and workings of the KGB in Mexico and their impact on the United States—were attained. Other branches of the military who had earlier shunned the Bureau's overtures were eager, after Ralph's success, to begin their own operations, particularly the Air Force. "But then, when they saw how good it was, they'd go hog wild around the world. They were running these damn things . . . and we said, 'Jesus, it's overexposure,' " Peterson says.

The Bureau began many similar double-agent operations, and in time, FBI headquarters lost interest in Ralph Sigler. "But after a while, what we were getting was not commensurate with what we were giving," Peterson says. The Army was providing him materials to turn over to the Russians, and the Bureau did not seem to be getting much in return, as far as their objectives were concerned. Yet they refused to relinquish control of the operation. "He [Eugene Peterson] didn't object too much to anything, but he wanted definite control. They had to have the control. And they were always fighting that it would be the Bureau's case," John Schaffstall recalls.

Peterson's opinion is that the real problem arose over the FBI field agent on the case. With FBI Headquarters too busy on other matters to pay much attention to their El Paso operation, Joe Prasek and the others received little supervision. "[Prasek] went out with Ralph when we were not there. Just called Ralph up and [said], 'Let's go get a beer.' . . . I still think that [Ralph] accepted some kind of outside assignment from the Bureau. We played it straight with him," Grimes states. Grimes believes that Prasek and Ralph were working together without telling the Army. "I figured that the FBI was somehow tasking him to do things that we didn't know about."

Prasek, through his lawyer, denied any violation of FBI procedures and refused to be interviewed for this book because he said it would put him in the position of violating his secrecy agreement with the FBI. Prasek's position, that he cannot comment because of his secrecy agreement with the FBI, tends to make him a convenient target for whatever failures his superiors in the FBI were responsible for in the Sigler case.

Grimes complained to FBI Headquarters about Joe Prasek, but they already knew they had a problem.[3] According to Eugene Peterson and William Branigan, Prasek's superiors in FBI Headquarters, Prasek, in his debriefing reports, gave FBI Headquarters an account that differed from what the Army was telling them about the Sigler operation. He did not address what were, in the opinion of his supervisors, obvious questions on his reports.

At first, Peterson says, he was so busy he did not follow up the complaints.[4] When he finally tried to correct the problem, he ran into roadblocks. "I wrote [Prasek] a few nasty ones [memos] and said, 'Hey . . . you've got to clarify this.' Then, of course, he cries the blues. He goes to his SAC [Special Agent in Charge] and says, 'I'm the foremost authority on these things on the border and here this jerk up there is screaming,' and the SAC would call the Assistant Director and complain about headquarters interference."

After Ralph died, Joe Prasek went to the Sigler house without notifying the Army. He searched the house without permission from FBI Headquarters, according to his supervisors. "But it was in the aftermath . . . that may have been when Prasek started getting out of hand," Peterson recalls.

"I knew the FBI went in and searched the house. . . . I don't know why he was in there without us knowing it in the first place. I don't know why Joe went in there," John Schaffstall states.

"Yeah. And I went to Gene [Peterson] and . . . I said, 'What the hell is going on?' Well, he doesn't know. 'I'll check it,' " Colonel Grimes remembers.

In Peterson's opinion, Prasek "envisioned himself as the oracle and the head expert and he would not listen to anybody else. He could do no wrong. You couldn't tell him anything.'' John Schaffstall says, "He used to say he worked a lot of agents. And I said one time, 'Why are you in El Paso? It's not known as a hotbed of espionage down there.' ''

Grimes felt there was a strong possibility that Ralph had gotten the burst transmitter from the Soviets and was servicing an illegal like Rudolph Herrmann: "It didn't seem to me at the time that they [the Soviets] were particularly interested in anything that Ralph had or could give them. . . . Maybe they just did want him to [service an illegal]. . . . Ralph was at a point with them that he could get documents [for them]. But if they could use him as service to an illegal, he would have been a lot better off. Plus he played the role so well that I'm sure they didn't have any questions about him.''

Years later, when the documents Ilse Sigler found hidden in her home after her husband's death were shown to John Schaffstall, he did not recognize many of them. He said, "It was like Ralph was leading a second life as a spy for the FBI. . . . Despite all the interrogations and all the polygraphs, he protected this information from us. He didn't tell us.'' [5]

According to Noel Jones, Ralph protected that information and risked being labeled as disloyal by his old Army friends because the FBI had convinced him he had a higher mission—a mission to service a true Soviet illegal.

As Schaffstall was looking through Ralph's secret operational notes, he came upon a small scrap of paper. He looked at it for a few minutes and said: "Ralph, you little rascal. . . . He did get the burst transmitter from the Russians. That's what this is, the operational instructions for the transmitter.''

APS ' APPOSTRIFY
UML ¨ UMLOT
. PERIOD
, COMMA
—DASH
FI FIGURES (20)
No/
D/W Division of Words
RPT
1 Slash
Last Square empty
1st and last group will be
without meaning and numbers will
be equal first and last group in title.

For Noel Jones, the news that the meetings in San Francisco were in Sigler's operational notes "means that he had to have been there for the FBI."[6]

What Ralph was being asked to do by the KGB was probably just what Grimes, Schaffstall, and Jones suspect—the servicing of Rudolph Herrmann. That is why the KGB gave Sigler the burst transmitter, and that is why Prasek searched Ilse's home after Ralph's death. Since the Army did not know about the Herrmann operation or the burst transmitter, the FBI had to recover it and any operational notes.

The remarkable story of how GRAPHIC IMAGE ended up dead is contained in a postmortem on the Sigler case that is in the FBI's secret, 3,000-page Sigler file. According to FBI sources, in that postmortem is the admission that Ralph Sigler was being used to support the Herrmann operation. As the Shadrin story showed, the Bureau would do just about anything to get an illegal. With the Sigler case, they proved that. Because the FBI did not tell the Army how they were really using Sigler, and because he was sworn to secrecy by the FBI, Ralph Sigler was murdered.

We believe Ralph Sigler was murdered not by the Army or the FBI, but by the KGB.

The KGB realized Ralph knew enough about Herrmann to expose the illegal. They knew he had been in telephone contact with Herrmann. There was no way they were going to risk losing someone the FBI believes was their top illegal resident in America by having Sigler face a hostile interrogation and be "sweated" for his deepest secret—his assistance to Herrmann. The KGB had been fooled by Ralph for ten years. They were not going to be made fools of any longer.

For ten days, Ralph had successfully avoided telling the Army the FBI's secrets. He flunked the polygraphs one after another. But we think that because he promised the FBI he would not tell the Army about their secret operation, he refused to tell the Army anything. Sigler behaved as if he was supremely confident the FBI would bail him out when things got serious. Being under suspicion, the FBI probably told him, would only increase his credibility with the Russians.

What the FBI did not know was that Army Intelligence at Fort Meade was penetrated. The Soviets had a source in Fort Meade. The KGB only ordered an assassination of Sigler when they got information from inside the Special Operations Detachment that Jones and Grimes had decided to bring in Donnel Drake to "sweat" Ralph in a hostile interrogation, that Ralph was being brought into Fort Meade and would no longer be accessible to the outside.

Sometime after Odell King finished his last unsuccessful polygraph, the KGB killer called on Ralph. He could have been a guest in the motel. We believe there is a chance Ralph may have been lured to a meeting. Since Louis Martel noted no smell of burnt flesh in Ralph's room, and since there were no blown circuits or even dimmed lights noted by other guests, Ralph was probably not electrocuted in that room. The KGB killer—or killers—may have tortured Sigler at another location and forced him to make the phone calls to his daughter and wife and write the letter to Ilse, instructing her to sue the Army. It would explain the liquor found in his system but not in the motel room, and the evidence of beatings on his face, injuries the medical examiner decided were far too extensive to come from a fall onto a heavily padded shag carpet.

This theory would explain the confusion over his missing pair of trousers. It would explain the Polaroid negatives showing Ralph in the nude that were discovered in the trash. These pictures may have been the evidence the killer needed to show his bosses that Sigler had indeed been executed. Then there is Sigler's "letter from the grave," with its bizarre Seattle postmark and misspellings of names Ralph had spelled correctly for years. Even today, John Schaffstall wonders if it was some sort of last coded message Ralph was trying to send.

Eugene Peterson was right. The Army was responsible for Ralph's security. But as Donnel Drake and Lou Martel described it, security consisted of no more than looking around the motel parking lot for foreign or diplomatic license plates. The Army did not worry about security. They did not think Ralph was in danger. The fact is that Ralph Sigler was left alone in the Howard Johnson's and the Holiday Inn most of the time. He traveled under his own name, paid his motel bill with a credit card—against orders—and took phone calls under his own name. Had he been under KGB observation, he was a very easy target.

How could this have happened? Who was the mole in Army Intelligence? When asked that question, former top FBI official James Nolan said, "I am going to send you a novel to read." He said the novel was by a former aide to Attorney General Edward Levi, and that it explained the Sigler case. *Convergence,* by Jack Fuller, did not sell very many copies.[7] It also is not about the Ralph Sigler case. Nolan, we thought, must be trying to add to the confusion. John Schaffstall read the book. He confirmed that it did not contain any operational information about Ralph. But then Noel Jones was told about it. Jones explained that the novel is the thinly disguised story of Richard A. Smith, who worked for Jones at Fort Meade during the years of the Sigler operation. Yes, Smith was in the Fort Meade office the week GRAPHIC IMAGE died.

According to Noel Jones, his relationship with Smith began in 1974 in Tokyo, when the young Army enlisted man asked Jones if he might consider giving him a job some day in Special Operations so that he "could play with the big boys." Richard A. Smith was a smart young go-getter who Jones thought had the education and language skills that he wanted to get in his unit. In the early 1970s, when Smith came to Fort Meade, he had already done an earlier tour at the CIA as a low-level employee. Smith worked his own cases and, like all the other case officers, pitched in on GRAPHIC IMAGE from time to time.[8] Louis Martel says, "That's the way it was. It was a small operation and we all helped each other out. No effort was made to keep secrets from people working in the unit. GRAPHIC IMAGE was the shining star of all the cases in our office. It was the first one."[9]

Smith complained to Noel Jones that he could not support his young family on a sergeant's pay, so Jones, as he put it, "stuck my neck out for the guy and got him converted over to civil service as a GS-9."[10] Jones, Martel, and Schaffstall all acknowledge that Smith had access to Sigler's activities the week he was polygraphed and was found dead.

Smith never was a suspect in the Sigler case. No one had ever considered it unusual that Ralph was killed within hours of the decision to do a hostile interrogation inside Fort Meade. Only someone working inside Army Intelligence—in that office—could have known about that decision.

Four years after Ralph died, Noel Jones sent Smith to run the Special Operations Detachment's San Francisco office. Jones said, "I again stuck my neck out for the bastard, because I put him over a lot of senior people for that assignment." Smith asked Jones to give him another man to assist him, and Jones, hopeful of running some operations against the Soviets, complied.

In 1980, after six months in the San Francisco job, Smith suddenly quit. Jones was furious. He flew to San Francisco and gave Smith thirty minutes to clear out of the office. "I was so mad I couldn't be in the office, so I went downstairs and had a cup of coffee," Jones says.

Louis Martel replaced Smith in San Francisco. When going through the files one day, he found a letter from Smith to his wife that Smith had never mailed. Martel remembers the letter saying, "I am going on a dangerous operation. If I do not return, I love you, but I have got to tell you, we are more in debt than you could have imagined." Martel checked. Smith had not been sent on any dangerous mission. At Fort Meade, Martel discussed the letter with his colleagues and most of them "pooh-poohed it because 'Craig' [Smith's nickname] had an overactive imagination." According to Martel, what was never checked was Smith's leave travel. Had they checked, they would have discovered frequent trips to Japan. To make matters worse, the letter was never made part of the official record. Instead it was destroyed.

The next time Noel Jones heard about Richard A. "Craig" Smith was in 1983, when the FBI detained Jones as a suspected accessory to Smith in the unauthorized release of classified documents.[11] At the time, Jones was still in charge of the counterintelligence unit at Fort Meade. When it was learned that Jones had warned the Bureau about Smith some time earlier, the charges against Jones were dropped.

Smith, then forty-two, was arrested for disclosing classified information to the Soviets. He was charged with releasing six names of Army double agents to the KGB during visits to Tokyo. The indictment said that Smith had passed the names to Victor Okunev in the Soviet Commercial Compound in Tokyo.

After several years of procedural delays, Smith successfully defended the charges by saying that he had been working for the CIA and had released the names under their instructions. A CIA employee named Charles Richardson, who supervised Smith's bizarre activities, was fired from the Agency for "poor judgment."

Schaffstall and Martel think it is possible that Smith may have been either leaking through the CIA or directly to the Russians long before 1980.[12] For Schaffstall, the theory that the KGB killed Ralph Sigler is the first explanation of a series of events in his life that makes any sense. "I knew Ralph for many years. And the things that I know he did—the man had a lot of courage. . . . If he had wanted to kill himself, he would have gone like that [Schaffstall points his hand at his head like someone using a gun.] Not electrocution. . . . Ralph was his own person. That's another reason that suicide, to me, was not in Ralph's nature. . . . Ralph had no reason to kill himself."

Schaffstall handled some fairly big cases during his career in Army Intelligence. Ulysses Harris and Leonard Safford were two of the cases that he worked on with Jim Wooten, Nick Shadrin's FBI control agent. "Yeah, and I always thought I did real well until [Ralph's death] . . . and now I always feel like I'm an outsider." Not long after Schaffstall returned from his trip to El Paso to brief Carlos Zapata and Joe Prasek about Ralph's death, Army Intelligence at Fort Meade cut him out of the investigation. "I felt ostracized," he says. As it had done with Mrs. Sigler, the Army tried to convince him that Ralph had committed suicide. "I don't think he would kill himself. I never did."

In May 1976, one month after Ralph's death, John Schaffstall retired. After Ralph died, Joe Prasek was transferred from the El Paso FBI Field Office to Phoenix, and then retired. He has consistently refused to speak about the Sigler matter. Colonel Grimes, who at the time of Ralph's death was overweight, had high blood pressure and smoked "like a furnace," had a stroke, and retired. Lou Martel is retired and living in Florida. Donnel Drake is retired in Las Vegas. Noel Jones wrote a 600-page analysis of the Sigler case, which the Army refused to accept. "They didn't want to hear anything about this case when I tried to tell them. We could learn from it. . . . I was treated like the drunk at the party," he said. Jones retired in 1988. Carlos Zapata closed up the Army Intelligence office in El Paso and retired from the Army in 1978.

Today, Ilse Sigler still lives in the same house in El Paso that she and Ralph built twenty-two years ago. She has not made many changes to the house over the past thirteen years since her husband's death. She still has Ralph's radio, and the tapes with the coded messages he received over the years. A picture of Ralph is kept on a table in the living room, with his medals draped over it. She says she never moved from El Paso because she did not want the Army to think it had defeated her. Of all of her experiences—growing up during World War II in Stuttgart, the Berlin Crisis, the double-agent operation—none has been as harrowing as trying to find out the truth about what happened to her husband.

The court case, the costs, the private investigators have only added to the mystery and to her frustration. Because of the letter from Ralph, she has focused most of her energies on the Army. But the Army does not hold the secret to what happened to Ralph early one evening in a motel room in Maryland. There is one agency that to this day still refuses to cooperate. In 1987, Ilse and Carlos had a conversation at the Kmart not far from their homes in El Paso. Carlos told her, "The FBI really knows what happened to your husband. And it's in the files."

Mrs. Sigler replied, "I hope Judge Sessions gets the job. I maybe succeed then." A month later, Judge Sessions was appointed FBI Director.

After Ralph died, the FBI did not want to be associated with the case, and for good reason—guilty knowledge. "They didn't want anything to do with it. . . . They didn't want anything to point [in] their direction at all," Grimes confirms. The Bureau was never questioned by the private investigators, the Maryland State Police, the Army investigators, the reporters, the congressional oversight committees, or the court. Today the FBI is still stonewalling all requests for information about the Sigler case.

The FBI may have had an even more important reason for not wanting anything to do with the Sigler case. There are those in Army Intelligence who are convinced that the arrest of Richard Craig Smith was an attempt to divert attention from something more devastating to U.S. Intelligence—a Soviet penetration of FBI Headquarters. The penetration was discovered in 1983 through a Soviet KGB officer, recruited by Army Intelligence, who warned his Army handlers that sensitive operational information was leaking to the Soviets from the FBI.

The example this KGB source gave the Army was that an American Army officer working as a double agent, much like Sigler, for the Army and *known* to be a double agent by the KGB, was going to be assigned to accompany all shipments for the construction of the ill-fated new American Embassy building in Moscow. His job was to let the United States know where the Russians would plant their inevitable listening devices. The KGB source warned the Army that their double agent would be killed if he were sent to Moscow.

Only a handful of FBI and Army counterintelligence officials were aware of this mission, yet it had leaked back to Moscow Center less than three weeks after it was planned in a secure FBI office. In late 1983 President Ronald Reagan personally authorized the Department of the Army to investigate the FBI to determine if the FBI had been penetrated by the KGB. The Army's Moscow Embassy operation was canceled. (In 1988, President Reagan ordered the new U.S. Embassy in Moscow to be torn down because of fatal security compromises in its construction.)

The Army's investigation of the FBI resulted in top FBI counterintelligence officials undergoing polygraph examinations. As in most leak investigations, the source was never successfully traced. The FBI was then allowed to clean its own house. Their own internal probe resulted in the arrest of William Miller, a Los Angeles FBI agent. But at least one former Army Intelligence official feels that Miller, like Smith, was merely a smoke screen. He said bluntly, "The Soviets had a man inside the FBI, and he still may be there."

For Ilse Sigler, the visits to Fort Bliss National Cemetery continue. So do, according to her, the mail-opening and the surveillance. She sits in El Paso knowing that her husband was a hero. She walked away from hundreds of thousands of dollars to prove that. She thinks about what Ralph said when she asked him years ago why he became a double agent. His answer was, "Because I want to do something good for my country."

Epilogue

❦

If I were asked to single out one specific group of men, one type, one category, as being the most suspicious, unbelieving, unreasonable, petty, inhuman, sadistic, double-crossing set of bastards in any language, I would say without any hesitation—the people who run counter-espionage departments.

Eric Ambler, *Light of Day*

FOR THOSE WHO have read these three stories thinking our intelligence services must have learned something from these experiences, there is the recent story of Igor Orlov's widow.[1]

Eleonore Orlov was straightening up her picture-framing shop in Alexandria on January 6, 1988. She was still recovering from the emotional stress of having lost many personal possessions in a fire some months before. The last thing on her mind that Saturday afternoon was the nightmare of the mid-1960s, when her husband was under investigation for being the Soviet agent SASHA.

Eleonore Orlov, a tiny, gentle woman, surrounded by the beautifully framed Austrian prints in her shop, remembers how embittered Igor had become. In the years following the FBI probe he refused to leave the shop. He didn't really have to; the family quarters were upstairs. The FBI never had the evidence to arrest him, let alone take him to court. When cancer invaded his body and took his life on May 1, 1982, his widow thought the nightmare was over.

That same Saturday afternoon there was a knock at the door. The young woman at the door introduced herself as Stephanie P. Gleason, "Special Agent FBI." With her was Charles K. Sciarini, also an FBI agent from the Washington Field Office. They were there, Gleason told Mrs. Orlov, "to search your house." [2] Special Agent Gleason told her the FBI had come into important and convincing information that Igor Orlov was a KGB agent and that he had recruited both of her sons —George and Robert—to work for the KGB. At precisely the same time, FBI agents in Chicago were approaching George Orlov, and in Boston they were approaching his brother Robert, who was on a family outing with his children.

None of the agents had warrants, and as it turned out, none seemed to have read the tens of thousands of pages in the FBI files on Igor Orlov and his family. What triggered this bizarre raid were the statements of the defector who went home, Yuri Yurchenko—the same defector who told the CIA that Nick Shadrin was accidentally killed by the KGB in Vienna in 1975.

Mrs. Orlov was frightened. The agents told her that they suspected that hundreds of thousands of dollars in cash, as well as other illicit materials, were hidden on her property. Agents Gleason and Sciarini said that they wanted Mrs. Orlov's permission to dig up her backyard. She told them that the only thing buried in the backyard was her dead cat.

Mrs. Orlov went along with this outrage because, she says, Agents Gleason and Sciarini strongly suggested that if she did not, her son George's security clearance would be lifted. So the agents searched her house and questioned her. They dug up her backyard, but found nothing. The nightmare that had dominated her husband's life now was following her. Mrs. Orlov's shop does not make a great deal of money. After all, how many pictures can one little old lady living alone frame in one day? Special Agent Gleason confiscated her thirty years of business records. Now, one by one, the FBI is investigating the picture-framing clients of the Orlovs to determine whether they are Soviet agents.

The FBI may not be the crack counterespionage organization we all think it is. It seems that investigating a case in such a way that it does not harm the innocent is something not taught at Quantico these days.

One wonders how dozens of FBI agents, far more experienced than Ms. Gleason and Mr. Sciarini, will feel when they learn they are being looked into because they had their pictures framed at Gallery Orlov. One can only imagine the reaction of the ultimate security man, Bruce

Solie, getting a call from Special Agent Gleason and being asked about why he dropped off a picture to be framed at the gallery just a few days before he left on the last Shadrin mission to Vienna in December 1975. But then, Special Agent Gleason has probably never heard of Bruce Solie or the KITTY HAWK operation.

Agents Sciarini and Gleason also confiscated Mrs. Orlov's dead husband's English lessons. Yes, the very same lessons that were arranged by the CIA. They thought that George and Robert's boyhood belongings—batteries, letters, nails, a school yearbook—might be the evidence they needed to crack their big espionage case.

Robert Orlov, astounded by the FBI's intrusion in his life, told the agents who approached him that Saturday afternoon that if they wanted to see him, they could make an appointment. In Chicago, George Orlov, knowing full well what the FBI could do to his career, was skeptical enough to force the agents there to do something shockingly unprofessional. To convince Orlov how serious they were, they asked him to come down to their office. There, Agent Vincente Rosado handed Orlov a three-page transcript of a portion of the Yurchenko debriefing. They then played a tape of the actual debriefing to reinforce what Orlov was reading.

"Yurchenko identified my father as a KGB agent. He said Igor Orlov is an agent, lives in Arlington, has two children who went to school in Boston, and that he recruited both of them. One travels a lot. One lives in Boston. One lives in Chicago. The one in Chicago went to San Diego, San Francisco, and named all the cities I had been to. He said one or more of us had been recruited and we were both working for the KGB," George Orlov said.[3]

George Orlov said that he took a polygraph exam because he felt "it was the only way I could clear myself." His father had taken half a dozen and never managed to clear himself. It turned out that the Bureau had been following and monitoring the Orlovs since 1985, when Yurchenko first made the allegations. The Orlovs' mail is opened by the FBI, and their telephones are tapped, all because a defector who suffers serious credibility problems carries back the message that Igor Orlov recruited his sons. Like KITTY HAWK, whose words two decades earlier caused the Bureau to waste manpower and take resources away from the immediate threat of Soviet agents literally looting this country of our technological secrets, Yurchenko in 1985 captivated the CIA and FBI with his revelations. But if you ask any senior FBI official who has reviewed the KITTY HAWK operation if he thinks KITTY HAWK was real, not one will say yes.

Four years into the second SASHA probe, according to Special Agent Rosado in Chicago, the Bureau has not even bothered to talk to the original FBI agents on the case, or the counterintelligence people at the CIA.[4] The KGB must be amazed at how little we learn from our past experiences, how easy we are to manipulate.

George Orlov's own words best describe what it is like to be under suspicion for something that you do not understand and cannot convince the FBI you did not do: "They have been following me for a number of years now, to my in-laws' house in Princeton. They follow me when I go running, when I go bike riding. I went running at the Institute for Advanced Studies at Princeton. They have a beautiful soft running trail there. They had a couple of agents follow me there. After I ran through, there were some little red and blue nylon strings tied to fenceposts, which are supposedly signs of dead-drop points, they said to me. I said, 'What?' I said, 'You guys are on drugs.' "

At home in Chicago, the FBI followed George during his daily runs and "they said they found a white chalk mark on a bridge after I crossed it. . . . They had it analyzed. They said they found it to be soapstone and they asked me if I knew what soapstone is. I said, 'Yeah, it's surveyor's chalk.' They said, 'Yeah, the same kind you use down where you work.' They said I drove too fast, an indication I was trying to lose tails and stuff.

"One reason they thought I was a KGB agent is that after I had gone running one time in Washington . . . I was standing on the third floor of my mother's house and looked down at the same time a Soviet KGB agent was looking up at me. I didn't know he was there, but apparently that is a sign of . . . recognition, they told me." After George Orlov passed his polygraph exam, an embarrassed Vince Rosado took him out to dinner.

Mrs. Orlov, a woman used to being worked over by authorities, submitted to a polygraph examination in May of 1988 in a suite the FBI rented at the Morrison House Hotel in Alexandria, Virginia. She said she agreed to take the exam on the condition that the FBI would ask all its questions and this would be the last one. The FBI agreed. Mrs. Orlov took the test and passed. After the authors contacted the FBI about their investigations, Mrs. Orlov received a call from Special Agent Gleason requesting that Mrs. Orlov submit to another test. It seems the FBI remembered a few questions they forgot to ask her earlier. This time Mrs. Orlov refused.

All Mrs. Orlov wants is for her sons to be left alone. Her husband wanted his ashes sent to Russia to be spread among the birch trees of his native land. But his widow is afraid to ask the Soviet Embassy to carry out his wishes. She thinks the FBI might misinterpret it. The ashes of SASHA still sit on the mantel of the beautiful little gallery in Alexandria, Virginia.

Notes on Sources and Interviews

❦

Chapter One / The First Death

1. The other stations were in London, Paris, Rome, Cairo, Lisbon, and Shanghai.
2. Narodnyi Kommissariat Vnutrennikh Del (NKVD)—The People's Commissariat for Internal Affairs—the forerunner to the KGB.
3. An American whom Sir Anthony Blunt, a Soviet spy in British intelligence, recruited to work for the Soviets while they were both at Cambridge University in the 1930s. See Peter Wright and Paul Greengrass, *Spycatcher* (New York: Viking Penguin, 1987), p. 213. Further documentation can be found in Straight's own book and in *Mask of Treachery* by John Costello (New York: Morrow, 1988).

Chapter Two / Paisley: The Replacement?

1. Interview with Donald Burton on October 14, 1987.
2. The details and color of John Paisley's early life are based upon interviews with his sister, Katherine Lenahan; her husband, Pat; his younger brother, Dale Paisley; and his sister-in-law, Mary. The interviews were conducted on August 10 and 11, 1987.
3. Interview with Dale Paisley and Katherine Lenahan, August 11, 1987.
4. Interview with Mary Paisley, August 11, 1987.
5. Interview with Katherine Lenahan, August 11, 1987.
6. Ibid.
7. Ibid.
8. John Paisley's Coast Guard and Merchant Marine records were obtained under a Freedom of Information request through the United States Coast Guard. These documents include "tickets" for his Merchant Marine voyages, and verify his early employment history.
9. From Paisley's Atomic Energy Commission background forms, filled out by Paisley in 1961 and certified by the CIA after an FBI investigation ordered by J. Edgar Hoover. This background check gave Paisley the "Q" clearance for atomic secrets.
10. John Paisley's FBI file, obtained under the Freedom of Information Act.
11. John Paisley's application for a "Q" or atomic security clearance made in 1961.
12. Deposition of Maryann Paisley, November 5, 1980 (*Maryann Paisley v. The Travelers Insurance Company*).

13. Interview with Mary Paisley, August 11, 1987.

14. Interview with Katherine Lenahan, August 11, 1987.

15. During his University of Chicago days, Paisley worked for the Lickenback Steamship Company in Brooklyn, New York, the Olsen Steamship Company in San Francisco, and the Keystone Shipping Company in Philadelphia, according to CIA security records.

16. Deposition of Maryann Paisley, November 5, 1980 *(Maryann Paisley* v. *The Travelers Insurance Company).*

17. Ibid.

18. Ibid.

19. Interviews with Mr. and Mrs. Leonard Masters, November 1987 and 1988.

20. See William R. Corson and Robert T. Crowley, *The New KGB: Engine of Soviet Power* (New York: Morrow, 1985), for a history of the Comintern or Third Communist International.

21. Interview with Robert T. Crowley, July 1, 1988.

22. Interview with Katherine Lenahan, August 11, 1987.

23. Ibid.

24. Ibid.

25. Interview with William Tidwell, October 5, 1988.

26. Office of Security memo on Paisley, dated November 22, 1978, released under the Freedom of Information Act.

27. Interview with Clarence Baier, July 7, 1988.

28. Interview with Henry Knoche, February 18, 1988.

29. Interview with Gladys Fishel, November 3, 1987.

30. Interview with Katherine Lenahan, August 11, 1987.

31. John Paisley's CIA biographical profile, released under a lawsuit filed by Maryann Paisley. Paisley's CIA serial number was 14496.

32. Paisley's CIA file reveals numerous letters of appreciation for his efforts in these areas by COCOM/CHINCOM, the two international organizations that police exports.

33. CIA document, "Standard Assessment of Paisley," dated May 14, 1957, obtained under the Freedom of Information Act.

34. J. Edgar Hoover FBI memorandum, dated August 8, 1961, obtained under the Freedom of Information Act.

35. Interview with Katherine Lenahan, August 11, 1987.

36. Ibid.

37. Interview with Peter and Ellie Sivess, January 19, 1988. Sivess probably processed more defectors than anyone else in the CIA.

38. Interviews with Paisley's colleagues Victor Marchetti, Clarence Baier, Donald Burton, and Peter Sivess.

39. Interview with Betty Myers, August 20, 1987, Cumberland, Maryland.

40. The will was made on February 17, 1968. After Paisley's death, it was probated on July 5, 1979. His total estate was inventoried at $36,806.86. This did not include stock he had in Pace Technologies, a computer concern run by a longtime CIA friend, Eugene Leggett.

41. Interview with Betty Myers, August 20, 1987.

42. Interview with Henry "Hank" Knoche, February 13, 1988.

43. Deposition of Maryann Paisley, November 5, 1980 *(Maryann Paisley* v. *The Travelers Insurance Company).*

44. Interview with Lt. Gen. Samuel V. Wilson, June 14, 1988. Edward Proctor did not respond to the authors' requests for an interview.

45. Interviews with Victor Marchetti, February 17, 1988, and with Clarence Baier, March 3, 1988.

Chapter Three / Paisley: The Plumbers

1. Interview with Phil Waggener, July 22, 1988.
2. Deposition of Maryann Paisley, November 5, 1980 *(Maryann Paisley* v. *The Travelers Insurance Company).*
3. Ibid.
4. Angleton made these comments in the aftermath of Paisley's 1978 disappearance.
5. The Imperial Defence College still accepts CIA staff today. While the course work varies from year to year, it has remained approximately the same as it was when Paisley attended.
6. Interview with Edward Paisley, October 30, 1987.
7. The existence of the box was discovered when one of the authors of the present work, Joe Trento, then a reporter for the *Wilmington News Journal,* learned that Paisley had given the box number at Greenham Common to the alumni office at the University of Chicago.
8. Interview with Edward Paisley, October 30, 1987.
9. None of Paisley's colleagues, and nothing in his files released under the Freedom of Information Act, explain either why he would be as pressed in London as Maryann describes, or why he would have a need for the post-office box.
10. Interview with Dale and Mary Paisley and Patrick and Katherine Lenahan, August 11, 1987.
11. Edward Paisley is convinced that his father was approached by the Soviets during this time, and that he was instructed by the CIA to play along with the approach. That might be an explanation for the events in London, but it is an explanation that Paisley's CIA superiors say is simply not true.
12. Interview with Bruce Clarke by author Joe Trento, November 1978. Interview with Hank Knoche, February 13, 1988.
13. First reported on ABC's "World News Tonight," on March 5, 1979.
14. Interview with Edward Paisley, October 30, 1987.
15. A big, rawboned man with bright red hair who stood taller than President Johnson was put in charge of CHAOS. Richard Ober was carried on the National Security Council staff as an aide. This position gave him instant access to the President and the White House staff so that he could keep them apprised of CHAOS's progress in linking the KGB to the antiwar movement. Since very few, if any, real links between the communists and the American anti–Vietnam War movement were found in the three years the program operated during the Johnson administration, one might assume that Ober would be among the first to be shipped back to Langley, and the operation shut down when Nixon took office. But just the opposite occurred. Ober quickly gained direct access to Nixon; his position was enhanced, not downgraded. As one former military man assigned to the Nixon White House put it, "When Haldeman and Ehrlichman came in, this guy spoke their language and appeared to help them get through the barriers that were up at CIA." It was from the CHAOS files that Nixon compiled his enemy list. After only five months in office, the new administration began a program of wiretaps on White House aides and reporters whom they deemed untrustworthy. These wiretaps followed news reports that were leaked to the media detailing the Nixon admin-

istration's secret bombing of Cambodia. By 1971, rumors were flying within the CIA that some sort of massive domestic surveillance program was under way and that the intelligence services were somehow involved. In fact, CHAOS was suspected of being merely an appendage of James Jesus Angleton's counterintelligence shop. It wasn't. Richard Helms, who spent much of his later career trying to talk two presidents out of making the CIA continue to break the laws against domestic spying, allowed CHAOS to continue because he thought he had no choice. He was under orders from the President. Angleton, of course, was given copies of everything relating to CI from the CHAOS program.

16. Young had first met Henry Kissinger in the Rockefeller campaign of 1968. After Nixon was elected, Young volunteered his services and was made a lawyer on the NSC staff. Young went to work for Kissinger with high hopes in 1969. According to others who were NSC aides at the time, Young picked out Kissinger's clothes while Young's wife handled Kissinger's laundry. John Lockwood, a friend of Kissinger's, suggested that Young would make a good appointment secretary for the new national security adviser. But Young, according to Kissinger, did not get along with Alexander Haig, nor did he work out as Kissinger's appointment secretary. Kissinger sent him off to work "on files" in the White House Situation Room. Was Young really "downgraded," as Kissinger claimed, or did he remain a mysterious force on Kissinger's staff? Pulitzer Prize–winning reporter Seymour Hersh points out in the *The Price of Power*, his book about Kissinger, that Young continued to be invited to the most sensitive meetings in the Nixon administration after his transfer to work on declassifying files. An example Hersh uses is that Young attended a session with top Atomic Energy Commission officials on the subject of a security clearance for a company in Pennsylvania that was suspected of diverting two hundred pounds of highly enriched uranium to Israel.

17. This entire history is detailed in a FBI Washington Field Office memorandum based on an interview with David Young on July 3, 1972. This interview was part of the early FBI probe into Watergate that seems to have missed the point.

18. Specifically, the administration made a major effort to leak embarrassing information about the Kennedy administration on the Bay of Pigs, the Cuban Missile Crisis, and the fall of the Diem government in South Vietnam. All this was aimed at neutralizing the man Nixon was convinced was his chief political rival—Senator Edward M. Kennedy. Though Kennedy's presidential ambitions had already been destroyed by his involvement in the Chappaquiddick automobile accident—costing the life of a young volunteer for his late brother Robert—Nixon was still obsessed with the Kennedys. Colson and Young began to ferret out all the information they could that showed bad judgment by the Kennedys and their appointees. Various government agencies, including the State Department and the CIA, were ordered to turn over such material. But the CIA frustrated the Nixon administration's efforts to get the documents they wanted. The Agency would give the White House only what it specifically asked for. Unless they knew what to ask for, the kind of damaging documentation Colson believed existed could not be obtained. Colson ordered Howard Hunt to examine documents, including the Pentagon Papers, to find material that could harm the reputation of the Kennedys. At the same time, Young and Colson began personally interviewing people involved in the policies in the hopes that they would be willing to cast a negative light on what went on. Hunt interviewed old colleagues at the CIA who were involved in Saigon with the overthrow of Diem. While Young was working

with the CIA to release files embarrassing to the Kennedys, efforts were implemented to tighten up the release of any materials that reflected negatively on Nixon from his vice-presidential days during the Eisenhower administration.

19. Interview with William Branigan, the former FBI counterintelligence head.

20. This information comes from three former subordinates of James J. Angleton. Clare Edward Petty, in an interview on July 21, 1988, said that he had a recollection of "someone being sent over on the leak problem at the White House. . . . Helms would have absolutely turned to Angleton on this sort of security question. That's how he always dealt with these things."

21. CIA memorandum dated September 30, 1971. Also a series of memoranda from Peter Earnest of the Office of Legislative Counsel of the CIA to Robert Gambino, the Director of Security at CIA, dealing with Paisley's connections to the Plumbers.

22. White House memorandum dated August 20, 1971, for John Erlichman from Egil Krogh and David Young.

23. Interview with Donald Burton, October 14, 1987.

24. Bob Woodward and Carl Bernstein, *The Final Days* (New York: Simon and Schuster, 1974), p. 24.

25. Interview with Robert Maheu, February 1988.

26. Interview with William Colby, June 6, 1988.

27. A number of veteran CIA and FBI men believe that it had the unmistakable touch of the FBI's onetime premier black-bag artist. This man, who has been in continuing legal trouble in recent years, refused through his lawyer to answer any questions about Romaine Street or the possibility that he was recruited for the Plumbers and worked with Paisley.

28. Interview with Dale and Mary Paisley, August 11, 1987.

29. The voucher was released in part under the Freedom of Information Act and lists a variety of Paisley's travel destinations for 1972 and 1973.

30. Interview with Katherine Lenahan, August 11, 1987.

31. The Washington, Virginia, records office contains land records and corporate resolutions laying out the deal for the lodge. The records clerk said no investigators had ever asked to see the file, previous to the author's visit.

32. The first detailed account of the Koecher story appeared in *Washingtonian* magazine in an article by Rudy Maxa and Phil Stanford in February 1987.

33. According to numerous CIA employees in positions to know.

34. Details of the case are based on court records (At Law No. 38430) filed in Fairfax, Virginia.

35. Interview with Donald Burton, October 14, 1987.

36. Interview with Carl Bernstein, December 12, 1987.

37. Interview with Bob Woodward, February 11, 1988.

38. Coauthor Joseph Trento was the *Wilmington News-Journal* reporter who had the meeting with Tim Robinson. Shortly after this conversation, Robinson left on a fellowship to Yale Law School and became the editor of the *National Law Journal*.

Chapter Four / Paisley: Mole

1. Interview with Clare Petty, July 21, 1988.

2. Peter Wright, *Spycatcher* (New York: Viking Penguin, 1987), p. 303.

3. Interview with James Jesus Angleton, June 1977, at the Army Navy Club, Washington, D.C.

4. Two books on the subject of SASHA and the subsequent investigations are David Martin's *Wilderness of Mirrors* (New York: Harper & Row, 1980) and Henry Hurt's *Shadrin: The Spy Who Never Came Back* (New York: Reader's Digest Press/McGraw-Hill, 1981).

5. Interview with Mrs. Eleonore Orlov, July 10, 1988, Alexandria, Virginia.

6. Lt. Col. Alexander Sogolov is dead, so it was not possible to get his version of events. Nicholas Kozlov has said he cannot comment on these matters because he still works for the United States government.

7. According to his wife, Eleonore, Igor Orlov had selected Alexander as a first name for his cover identity and had acquired the nickname because "Sasha" is the diminutive of "Alexander" in Russian. Agents generally have "cover" or "work" names under which to operate.

8. Interview with Clare Edward Petty, July 22, 1988.

9. Interview with Lt. Gen. Samuel V. Wilson, June 14, 1988.

10. Interview with Robert T. Crowley, July 7, 1988.

11. Interview with George Kisevalter, July 13, 1988.

12. Ibid.

13. Interview with Clare Edward Petty, April 5, 1988.

14. Interview with William E. Colby, June 6, 1988.

15. For a detailed version of Nosenko's defection see Edward Jay Epstein, *Legend: The Secret World of Lee Harvey Oswald* (New York: Reader's Digest Press/McGraw-Hill, 1978).

16. What he did not take into account was the possibility that Hunt may have filtered the report down to a one-line representation that Angleton did not take seriously. Both Hunt and Angleton are dead, so we have only Petty's version of events.

17. For the best account of the bungling of the Kim Philby affair, see Peter Wright, *Spycatcher* (New York: Viking Penguin, 1987).

18. When contacted by the authors, Raymond Rocca declined to be interviewed.

19. Kollek would later become the legendary mayor of Jerusalem.

20. See *Spycatcher* for a history of VENONA.

21. See David Martin, *Wilderness of Mirrors* (New York: Harper & Row, 1980), for an overview of how William King Harvey closed in on Philby.

22. According to William Colby, although Angleton was asked to resign in December 1974, he did not vacate his second-floor CIA office until the following October. Leonard McCoy said his former boss, George Kalaris, who replaced Angleton as counterintelligence chief, finally had to ask Angleton to give up the office.

Chapter Five / Paisley: The Jabbermole?

1. Interview with David S. Sullivan, July 1, 1988.

2. Interview with David S. Sullivan, June 23, 1988.

3. Ibid.

4. Interviews with Norman Wilson and Gordon Thomas, April 25, 1988.

5. From ABC's "World News Tonight," March 5, 1979.

6. Interview with Clarence Baier, March 3, 1988.

7. Thomas Powers, *The Man Who Kept the Secrets: Richard Helms and the CIA* (New York: Knopf, 1979).

8. Deposition of Maryann Paisley, November 5 and December 4, 1980 *(Maryann Paisley v. The Travelers Insurance Company).*

9. Maryann Paisley made this claim to Joseph Trento in several interviews in 1978–79 and in her deposition in 1980 *(Maryann Paisley v. The Travelers Insurance Company).*

10. Interview with Leonard McCoy, March 11, 1988.

11. Interview with William E. Colby, June 6, 1988.

12. Deposition of Maryann Paisley, November 5 and December 4, 1980 *(Maryann Paisley v. The Travelers Insurance Company).*

13. Interview with Norman Wilson, April 25, 1988.

14. Interview with Clarence Baier, March 3, 1988.

15. This account comes from the court records of the accident available in the Fairfax, Virginia, Courthouse. (Law numbers 325748 and 34684.)

16. Court records from Paisley's sentencing, on file in the Fairfax County, Virginia, Courthouse.

17. Interview with Hank Knoche, February 13, 1988.

18. Interview with David S. Sullivan, June 23, 1988.

19. Interview with Lt. Gen. Samuel V. Wilson, June 14, 1988.

20. Interview with Dale Paisley, August 11, 1987.

21. Interview with Richard and Mary Jo Bennett, October 18, 1987, aboard their houseboat, *The Last Gasp.*

22. Interview with Lt. General Samuel V. Wilson, June 14, 1988.

23. Interview with Hank Knoche, February 13, 1988.

24. Interview with Barbara Wilson, April 25, 1988.

25. Interview with Gladys Fishel.

26. U.S. Congress, Senate Select Committee on Intelligence, *Report of the Subcommittee on Collection, Production and Quality* 16 February 1978.

27. Harvard professor Richard E. Pipes chaired one of the B Teams and confirmed that Paisley "was our conduit to the CIA."

28. Interview with David S. Sullivan, July 1, 1988.

29. David Binder, in an interview for the *Wilmington News-Journal,* conducted by Joseph Trento, June 24, 1979.

30. Deposition of Michael Yohn, September 25, 1980 *(Maryann Paisley v. The Travelers Insurance Company).*

31. Deposition of Gretchen Yohn, October 1, 1980 *(Maryann Paisley v. The Travelers Insurance Company).*

32. Deposition of Maryann Paisley, November 5 and December 4, 1980 *(Maryann Paisley v. The Travelers Insurance Company).*

33. Seymour Weiss in an interview for the *Wilmington News-Journal,* June 23, 1979.

34. Both the Vogt and Graham quotes are from a June 27, 1979, *Wilmington News-Journal* article.

35. Yohn stated in his 1980 deposition in the *Maryann Paisley v. The Travelers Insurance Company* lawsuit that he had made the arrangements to introduce Myers to Binder for Binder's June 11, 1979, *Look* article. Binder told Joseph Trento on June 24, 1979, that the reason he could reveal Paisley as his source was that Betty Myers had convinced him that Paisley had committed suicide. Yohn arranged for Betty Myers to supply David Binder with tape recordings that Betty had made of Paisley reflecting on his dissatisfaction with life.

36. National Foreign Assessment Center document number 271, dated December 28, 1976, addressed to Mr. John Rizzo of the CIA and signed by John A. Paisley.

37. See Shadrin section, pages 151–265.

Chapter Six / Paisley: The Investigator

1. Interview with David S. Sullivan, July 1, 1988.
2. Interview with Leonard V. McCoy, July 1, 1988.
3. Interview with David S. Sullivan, July 1, 1988.
4. Interviews with David Sullivan, June and July 1988.
5. Interview with Phil Waggener, July 22, 1988.
6. CIA memorandum dated July 26, 1978, obtained under the Freedom of Information Act.
7. Interview with Mary Paisley and Katherine Lenahan, August 11, 1987.
8. Interview with Mary Paisley, August 11, 1987.
9. Interview with Katherine Lenahan, August 11, 1987.
10. Interview with Dr. K. Wayne Smith, June 20, 1988.
11. Deposition of Maryann Paisley, November 5 and December 4, 1980 *(Maryann Paisley* v. *The Travelers Insurance Company).*
12. Deposition of Kay Fulford, September 16, 1980 *(Maryann Paisley* v. *CIA).*
13. Deposition of Maryann Paisley, November 5 and December 4, 1980 *(Maryann Paisley* v. *The Travelers Insurance Company).*
14. Soviet defector Yuri Nosenko was living in North Carolina at the time.
15. According to numerous Paisley friends and associates, including Norman and Barbara Wilson in an interview with the authors on April 25, 1988. Similar sentiments were reported to the Maryland State Police by the Wilsons and others.
16. Deposition of Maryann Paisley, November 5 and December 4, 1980 *(Maryann Paisley* v. *The Travelers Insurance Company).*
17. Admiral Stansfield Turner refused to be interviewed for this book, and instead corresponded with the authors. His letters are quoted where appropriate.
18. Robert Gambino declined to be interviewed for this book.
19. Interview with David S. Sullivan, July 1, 1988.

Chapter Seven / Paisley: The Bay

1. When asked, in a 1979 interview with Joseph Trento, this reporter denied being an FBI informant, but FBI documents clearly identify him as their source. George Beveridge, who was at that time the *Washington Star*'s assistant managing editor and ombudsman, told Trento he had no idea to whom the FBI was referring in the documents, but that this particular employee was the only reporter on the newspaper working on the Paisley case.
2. This section is based on documents obtained in a Freedom of Information request of FBI files on Paisley. The first of the FBI memos confirming the calls to the *Washington Star* was dated September 21, 1978. Ironically, the FBI memo stated that that was the day Paisley disappeared. In fact he disappeared on Sunday, September 24, 1978.
3. Deposition of Maryann Paisley, November 4 and December 5, 1980 *(Maryann Paisley* v. *The Travelers Insurance Company).*
4. Ibid.
5. Thomas, in the authors' interview with him on April 25, 1988, opened the conversation by asking, "You know this place was known as Spooks' Cove, don't you?"
6. From a Maryland State Police report of an interview with Gordon Thomas and his son Richard, conducted October 10, 1978. Author's interview with Colonel Thomas, April 25, 1978.

7. Interview with Gordon Thomas, April 25, 1988.

8. Interview with Michael Yohn in 1979.

9. Deposition of Michael Yohn, September 25, 1980 *(Maryann Paisley* v. *The Travelers Insurance Company).*

10. According to Yohn and his wife in separate depositions, the couple separated a month after Paisley's disappearance. *(Maryann Paisley* v. *The Travelers Insurance Company).*

11. Maryland State Police interview with Mrs. Gretchen Yohn, October 16, 1978.

12. From an interview with the Maryland State Police, October 3, 1978.

13. Maryland State Police interview with Schellhas, October 12, 1978.

14. Deposition of Ray Westcott, December 19, 1980 *(Maryann Paisley* v. *The Travelers Insurance Company).*

15. Maryland State Police report, based on interviews with the owner of Chaw Rippon's Crabhouse and other boaters on October 13, 1978.

16. Deposition of Barbara Wilson *(Maryann Paisley* v. *The Travelers Insurance Company).*

17. Joseph Trento, "The Spy Who Never Was," *Penthouse,* March 1979.

18. Maryland State Police report (CIR-J-8308252) based on an interview with Robert McKay on October 6, 1978.

19. The woman asked that her privacy be protected. She explained that she was simply walking her dog when she saw *Brillig* run aground.

20. K. Wayne Smith's responsibilities for Coopers were enormous. Each office was set up as almost a separate organization. His position, that of a managing partner, was like being the CEO for that office. According to a March 2, 1979, memorandum from the FBI to the Senate Select Committee on Intelligence, Smith had met Paisley earlier, when he was working for the government on defense and intelligence matters. He had read many of Paisley's intelligence assessments and had been impressed with Paisley's mind and his ability to write. Both Paisley and Smith still served in an advisory capacity for the CIA; both men served on the Military Economic Advisory Panel (MEAP); and both worked as consultants for the CIA.

21. Maryland State Police report, dated October 10, 1978.

22. Sword's own official Maryland Park Service Report (IR-45-78-268) and testimony given on September 16, 1981 *(Maryann Paisley* v. *The Travelers Insurance Company).*

23. Maryland State Police report submitted by Corporal John L. Murphy on October 20, 1978.

22. Sword's own official Maryland Park Service Report (IR-45-78-268) and testimony given on September 16, 1981 *(Maryann Paisley* v. *The Travelers Insurance Company).*

23. Maryland State Police report submitted by Corporal John L. Murphy on October 20, 1978.

24. Natural Resource Police reports dated September 25, 1978. The report also has the notation scrawled across it, "Don't give out."

25. Interview with Yeoman Maxton and his Coast Guard colleagues on October 5, 1978, and official Coast Guard documents obtained under the Freedom of Information Act.

26. Based on a 1978 interview with Joseph Haraburda and Archie Alston. When contacted, Alston said he had no idea who Paisley was.

27. These events were confirmed in a September 28, 1978, memorandum from the CIA's Director of Security, Robert W. Gambino, to then FBI Director William Webster.

28. Interview with Betty Myers, August 20, 1987.
29. Interview with Philip A. Waggener, July 22, 1988.
30. Interview with James Maxton, October 5, 1978.
31. Central Intelligence Agency memorandum written by Security Director Robert W. Gambino on November 22, 1978.
32. The memorandum was sent to the FBI on September 28, 1978, and gave the FBI only a paragraph sketch of Paisley's background with the CIA. The rest of the memo sketched out the circumstances surrounding Paisley's disappearance.
33. Paisley was called out of retirement to see if a team of outside experts would reach similar or different conclusions about Soviet strategic strength if they had access to the same information as the CIA's internal experts. What the outside experts agreed on was that the CIA was seriously underestimating Soviet strategic strength. See Chapter 5.
34. Maryann interviewed and chatted with the dying Clara Paisley into a tape recorder.
35. FBI memorandum released under the Freedom of Information Act in 1980.
36. Memorandum written by CIA Director of Security Robert W. Gambino.
37. Rupach's testimony, given on September 16, 1980 *(Maryann Paisley* v. *The Travelers Insurance Company).*
38. "Nightcrawler" targets would have been low-level Commerce Department employees for economic intelligence, or, for counterintelligence, perhaps a clerk-typist working in the FBI's Washington Field Office. Then, of course, there are the more obvious targets, such as aides in the White House, the State Department, or the Pentagon, as well as the huge pool of retired and fired intelligence officials in the Washington, D.C., area.
39. From Courtland Jones, William Lander, William Branigan, all former top FBI counterintelligence officials.

Chapter Eight / Paisley: Death on the Bay?

1. May 3, 1980, interview with the informant.
2. The February 5, 1978, memorandum accompanied the copies of the files that were sent to the attention of William O. Cregar, Deputy Assistant Director of the FBI's Intelligence Division.
3. CIA travel vouchers released under the Freedom of Information Act.
4. Deposition of Michael Yohn, September 25, 1980 *(Maryann Paisley* v. *The Travelers Insurance Company).*
5. The body was floating off the shore of the Patuxent River Naval Weapons Testing Center.
6. Corporal John Murphy's investigation report, dated October 3, 1978, made available by the Maryland State Police.
7. Interview with Harry Lee Langley, Sr., June 27, 1978.
8. Interview with Dr. George Weems, June 27, 1979.
9. Edward Paisley was surprised to hear that Norman Wilson had found a 9mm bullet on *Brillig.* Paisley said that he had thoroughly searched *Brillig* when she was sailed back to Lusby, and had found no bullet.
10. Maryland State Police report dated October 10, 1978.
11. The official autopsy (#78-1628) of John Arthur Paisley.
12. Both the FBI and the CIA claimed they had no fingerprints on file for Paisley. The FBI said all such prints were destroyed years before in an effort

to protect employee privacy, and the CIA said it did not take fingerprints of employees.

13. Joseph Trento reported and wrote the original breaking stories on the Paisley case for the *Wilmington News-Journal.*

14. Deposition of Raymond Westcott, December 19, 1980 *(Maryann Paisley* v. *The Travelers Insurance Company).*

15. Interview with Katherine Lenahan for the *Wilmington News-Journal,* June 28, 1979.

16. CIA Office of Security memorandum dated November 22, 1978.

17. Ibid.

18. Based on an interview with Dr. Russell Fisher, November 26, 1978. Also confirmed in the autopsy file.

19. Joseph Trento, "The Spy Who Never Was," *Penthouse,* March 1979.

20. Maryland State Medical Examiner's file on John Arthur Paisley.

21. In an interview with a former Senate investigator on the Paisley case, the investigator said the hands were sent to the FBI for fingerprinting, and he saw the hands at the FBI with a copy of the fingerprints, although the Maryland State Medical Examiner's records do not show that the FBI ever received the hands. The investigator also said the fingerprints were not given to the Senate committee handling the investigation. In addition, requests for the fingerprint files on John Paisley under the Freedom of Information Act have been ignored by the FBI.

22. Interview with Dr. Russell Fisher, November 17, 1978.

23. The reporters were Joseph Trento and Richard Sandza, then with the *Wilmington News-Journal.*

24. Depositions of Maryann Paisley, November 5 and December 4, 1980, and of Norman Lewis Wilson, October 2, 1980 *(Maryann Paisley* v. *The Travelers Insurance Company).*

25. For an account of the incident, see Judy Chavez, *Defector's Mistress* (New York: Dell, 1979).

26. Shevchenko refused to be interviewed about the matter.

27. According to Bob Porterfield, the general manager of the Colonial Funeral Home, Falls Church, Virginia, the Paisley case file contains a signed statement by Maryann Paisley saying that she had identified her husband's body as required by Maryland law. Since Mrs. Paisley declined to be interviewed for this book, the authors could not get an explanation of why she told reporters and said in a deposition that she never saw the body recovered from the Bay and then signed the statement. Funeral director Ernie Meyers says he cannot remember if Mrs. Paisley actually came in to look at the corpse. But Porterfield says "the signed statement is in the file."

28. CIA memorandum from Herbert E. Hetu to Admiral Stansfield Turner, dated January 31, 1979.

29. The CIA made Joseph Trento the subject of a full-scale Office of Security investigation. The reason given for the investigation was that he had learned details of Turner's secret travel schedule. In fact, as documents revealed, he was targeted because he seemed to have sources inside the CIA. Trento had originally shown up in CIA files as an old associate of Jack Anderson in the January 1972 leaks investigation that Paisley was conducting for David Young, one of the Watergate "Plumbers." A CIA memo dated one month before Paisley's disappearance revealed the results of a preliminary leak investigation of Trento. That investigation continued throughout the Paisley investigation. CIA documents reveal that the probe into Trento went on

until the early 1980s. While Gambino had time and staff to investigate a reporter who wrote embarrassing stories, he did not apparently consider it necessary to investigate David Sullivan's accusations that Paisley was a mole. The above conclusions are based on CIA memoranda dated January 17, 1972, and August 21, 1978, obtained under the Freedom of Information Act.

30. Deposition of Maryann Paisley, November 5 and December 4, 1980 *(Maryann Paisley* v. *The Travelers Insurance Company).*

31. Ibid.

32. Ibid.

33. Fensterwald ran an organization called the Committee to Investigate Assassinations.

34. When Joseph Trento first broached the idea of Paisley's involvement in Watergate to Mrs. Paisley, she bristled. When Trento asked Mrs. Paisley if she would answer some questions in writing, she agreed to meet with him. When he asked her about Paisley's involvement in sex clubs and the possibility that he had leaked classified material, she cut off further contact with him. Trento interviewed Mrs. Paisley several times on the phone in October and November of 1978. He met with Mrs. Paisley and Bernard Fensterwald, Jr., for lunch in Washington in early 1979.

35. Letter from Mrs. Maryann Paisley to Admiral Stansfield Turner, dated January 16, 1979.

36. *Wilmington News-Journal,* November 18, 1979.

37. Interview with Dr. K. Wayne Smith, June 20, 1988.

38. Maryland State Police report dated October 18, 1978.

39. The National Diving Center receipt is included in the official Maryland State Police report.

40. Deposition of Maryann Paisley, November 5 and December 4, 1980 *(Maryann Paisley* v. *The Travelers Insurance Company).*

41. *Wilmington News-Journal,* January 23, 1980.

42. *Wilmington News-Journal,* May 20, 1979. Perhaps the most useful information divulged in the lawsuit was the story of Maryann Paisley herself. Because she has run hot and cold on reporters and eventually tired of the entire subject, she had consistently refused consent to a comprehensive interview about her life. Under oath, at the prodding of lawyers, Mrs. Paisley revealed the most intimate details of her life with her husband. When an attorney asked her if she believed at the time of his disappearance that John still worked for the CIA, she answered that she believed he did.

43. *Wilmington News-Journal,* April 25, 1980.

44. Deposition of Maryann Paisley, November 5 and December 4, 1980 *(Maryann Paisley* v. *The Travelers Insurance Company).*

45. Deposition of Maryann Paisley, November 5 and December 4, 1980 *(Maryann Paisley* v. *The Travelers Insurance Company).*

46. Interview with Barbara Wilson, April 25, 1988.

Chapter Nine / Shadrin: The Escape

1. The *New York Times,* June 26, 1959.

2. Henry Hurt, *The Spy Who Never Came Back* (New York: McGraw-Hill/Reader's Digest Press, 1981).

3. From a series of interviews during 1987 and 1988 with Mrs. Ewa Shadrin and her lawyer, Richard Copaken.

4. Ewa Gora was born in Gdynia, Poland, on July 18, 1937. Her father was Zygmunt Gora and her mother was Jadwiga Gora, née Lenardt. Her Polish

education was seven years of public school, four years of high school, and five years at the Gdynia Academy of Medicine, which she completed in May 1959. She visited Belgrade for five weeks in preparation for her dental studies. She also traveled in Czechoslovakia and Hungary.

5. Hurt, *The Spy Who Never Came Back*, p. 30.

6. Interview with Mrs. Ewa Shadrin, February 24, 1988.

7. Interviews with Ewa Shadrin, 1987 and 1988.

8. Gdynia was chosen for the turnover of the ships to the Indonesians rather than Gdansk (formerly Danzig), which is some thirty-five kilometers to the east, because it was more secure from the Soviets' point of view. Gdansk still harbored some pockets of the resistance that had erupted three years earlier out of sympathy with the Poznan rioters. The KGB believed, quite wrongly, that the Western intelligence agencies were operating in and around the city. For these and other reasons, the Soviets were extremely leery of letting any of their naval personnel come into contact with the Poles in Gdynia.

9. Hurt, *The Spy Who Never Came Back*, p. 32.

10. Interviews with Ewa Shadrin in 1987 and 1988.

11. The first leg of Artamonov's projected course from the Gdynia anchorage required him to pass around the eastern tip of the Hel Peninsula, which juts out into, and protects, the waters of the Zatoka Pucka. The distance of this leg of the voyage was approximately ten nautical miles, and Artamonov estimated an elapsed time of two hours, at an average speed of five knots. The pace selected by Artamonov for this leg of the voyage was leisurely because it would still be light and he wanted to give the appearance to anyone who might be observing their progress that its purpose was in fact a night-fishing expedition. Once they had cleared the tip of the Hel Peninsula, the launch would pass into the open seas of the Gulf of Danzig and the Baltic Sea. From this point to the proposed landfall of Öland Island, the approximate distance was 105 nautical miles. Artamonov believed he could make approximately seven knots on this leg of the voyage. Overall, Artamonov calculated that the voyage would take fifteen to sixteen hours. This was based on the expected tidal conditions and currents. Counting backwards in order to gain the maximum cover of darkness in the open sea area, Artamonov calculated that the best time for departure was approximately 2000 hours or 8:00 P.M. In June, in those latitudes, the days are long and the nights are short. Artamonov was more concerned about his being sighted by a "bystander" kind of vessel in the Baltic than by a naval vessel per se. Contrary to some published reports, Artamonov was not concerned about being detected by Soviet or Polish radar. This was never a realistic danger to the mission. There was no radar worthy of the name available to the Poles or the Soviets in 1959 in that area, and such radar as existed was totally incapable of picking up a twenty-two-foot "spit kit" kind of launch.

12. *Farjestaden*, translated into English, means "Ferrytown." It is located at the narrowest point between Öland Island and the Swedish mainland. At the western end of this crossing lies the town of Kalmar, a city of approximately thirty thousand. At the time of Artamonov's defection, the ferry was the only way to get from the mainland to Öland Island. Today, Farjestaden is served by a concrete bridge linking Kalmar and the Swedish mainland with Öland Island. Öland is a favorite summer resort of the Swedes and other Scandinavians.

13. It was known to the people of Farjestaden as the "Finnish ferry" because it was owned by a family of Finns.

14. It is of some passing interest that the Soviets in Sweden circulated a

"disinformation" story alleging that Artamonov had defected because the Soviet government had denied him permission to get a divorce and that he was so physically taken with Ewa that he had lost his socialist sense of reality.

15. The headquarters was a nine-story modern building then located at 62 *Banergatan* in downtown Stockholm. Swedish Naval Intelligence was located on the seventh and eighth floors of the headquarters building. There were electronically secure facilities on these floors, and Artamonov was shuttled from one to the other to meet with different experts in the Swedish Navy.

16. Interview with Ewa Shadrin, October 1987.

17. Based on official naval records of the incident.

18. The fact that Garbler was a "squid" (a former member of the U.S. Navy) might have had something to do with Caputo's attitude, but more likely it was based on Caputo's extensive combat experience. Also, it should be recognized that in those days and in the existing political climate, cooperation between the CIA and the military attachés was uneasy at best. Too often, if the military attachés shared information they had acquired with the CIA station, it was not reciprocated. Also, in 1959, many ambassadors were kept in the dark concerning the identity of the CIA station chief in their embassy. JFK tried to change this by presidential edict after he took office, but this action did not change the CIA's attitude that "I've got a secret and it's all mine."

19. Interview with Paul Garbler, April 1988.

20. Ibid.

21. Edward D. Goloway, who replaced Paul Garbler as the CIA station chief in Stockholm in the summer of 1959, also had a naval background. He was a bull of a man, but gentle in his appproach to Ewa. Goloway was a graduate of the U.S. Naval Academy in the class of 1946 (President Carter and Stansfield Turner's class). He remained on active service until 1953, at which time he resigned his regular commission as a lieutenant commander and entered the U.S. Naval Reserve, from which he retired with the rank of captain in 1978. His career in the CIA was similar to those of many who served abroad under State Department cover.

22. Under the provisions of the intelligence liaison agreement between the United States and Sweden, the information provided to the Swedes by Artamonov would eventually be provided to the U.S. Naval Attaché for information and transmission to the Office of Naval Intelligence in Washington, D.C., where it would subsequently be disseminated to other interested agencies in the intelligence community. The CIA was not about to wait for Colonel Caputo and his colleagues to process this information.

23. An NIP message from the field is guaranteed to get the attention of headquarters personnel. The reason is obvious: the individual so named may be able to shed light on the very critical question, "Are hostilities imminent?" No matter the "potential" of an NIP case, there are procedures to be followed to prevent disinformation from entering the intelligence system. If these procedures are not followed, there is no telling where the mischief will lead. In the Artamonov case, the NIP procedures were violated from the very beginning, and the results were totally predictable.

24. Interview with Leonard V. McCoy, July 27, 1988. John M. "Jack" Maury was a former Marine Reserve officer who was assigned as the Assistant Naval Attaché in Moscow at the time of Hitler's invasion of Russia in June 1941. He stayed on to help out with the lend-lease program and, because of his Russian language ability, was regarded in the CIA as an expert on Soviet matters.

25. Interview with Leonard V. McCoy, January 21, 1988.

26. Sven Olof Joachim Palme was born to upper-class parents, Gunnar Palme and Elizabeth von Knieriem Palme, in Stockholm on January 30, 1927. After graduating from Sigtuna Humanistisa Laroverk, an elite prep school outside Stockholm, he did his compulsory military service. In the years following World War II, he traveled widely throughout the world and studied politics and economics in the United States, at Kenyon College in Gambier, Ohio. After acquiring his B.A. degree at Kenyon in 1948, he hitchhiked around the United States, deliberately roughing it, for several months. Upon his return to Sweden, Palme entered Stockholm University's law school and received his law degree in 1951. In 1954, Palme began his long association with Prime Minister Tage Erlander, as a secretary and speechwriter, and in 1955 he became a member of the Board of the National Social Democratic Youth League. In 1956 he was elected to his first eight-year term in the upper house of the Riksdag, the Swedish parliament. In 1960 he served in the Swedish Agency for International Assistance. Palme joined the cabinet of Prime Minister Erlander, without portfolio, in 1963, and two years later he became Minister of Communications. In 1967, Palme relinquished the communications portfolio to become Minister of Education and Religious Affairs. Erlander announced his retirement in September 1969. Palme, Erlander's choice as his successor, was unanimously elected prime minister at a Social Democratic Party convention on October 1 and sworn in by King Gustav VI on October 14. Palme remained in this office until the night of February 26, 1986, when he was assassinated while walking home with his wife from a movie. To date, Palme's killer has not been found and no motive has been established. Palme was an early and frequent critic of the U.S. involvement in Vietnam. He was also a critic of Soviet actions, but remained an "active" neutralist throughout his long public-service career.

27. Allegations and rumors persist to the present that Olof Palme was on the CIA's payroll and that he had been recruited while at Kenyon College. There is no way to confirm or reject these rumors; the Dulles message does suggest some kind of personal relationship. Also, there are instances of other senior CIA officials claiming long-standing personal associations with Palme. In addition, the fact that the Aliens Commission did speed up the processing of Artamonov and Ewa is evidence of something more than Palme acting as a friend of the court.

28. As part of this process, they were brought to the embassy under strict security provisions to fill out the visa request. Preparation of the actual request was handled by Sara L. Andren, a second secretary in the consular section, who had considerable intelligence experience during World War II and was very experienced with the procedure for handling "special visa requests." The most important was the identification of the request with a specially coded CIA number out of its stock of one hundred no-questions-asked visa applications. The placing of this number on the request guaranteed special handling in State Department channels and rapid dissemination of the details to appropriate officials in the CIA.

Chapter Ten / Shadrin: Westport

1. Although Frankfurt was no longer in the mainstream of the U.S.-USSR intelligence war, the East German intelligence service, SSD (Staatsicherheitsdienst), was extremely active in the Frankfurt area. The SSD, under the inspired leadership of Markus Johannes, a protégé of Gen. Aleksandr

Semenovich Panyushkin, the head of the KGB's First Chief Directorate, had made fools of the CIA in Germany many times.

2. "Big George" Carroll, as he was known to his friends and enemies, was one of the unpublicized true professionals in the CIA. Unable to convince Director Dulles that the CIA had lost its way, at least in Europe, Carroll left the CIA, but not government service. In his last assignment, before retirement in 1969, he served as National Security Adviser to then Vice-President Hubert Humphrey. In passing, it can be said that Big George did his best at all times. He won a few and lost a few. His last loss was his inability to convince Humphrey in the summer of 1968 that the Vietnam War, like the Cold War that had preceded it, was unwinnable because we did not know how to fight it. After leaving government service, George Carroll served as the president of Berea College in Kentucky, where he characteristically did his best to inculcate the students with the desire to do *their* best, no matter what.

3. The CIA's Frankfurt Base in 1959, at the time of the Artamonov defection, was a shadow of its former self. The flow of defectors from East Germany and the rest of the Soviet Bloc had been reduced to a trickle, thereby eliminating much of the justification for keeping the base.

4. A "safe house" is, as the term implies, a place where a witness, defector, or agent is kept temporarily during the course of an operation. It may be used as a refuge, or a place to carry out an additional briefing or debriefing. In Berlin, during the heady days of the Berlin Tunnel, the CIA maintained in excess of forty safe houses. As a result, at a time when housing was still at a premium in postwar Berlin, the CIA was the biggest single landlord in the divided city. Because each of the safe houses required "house sitters" and security lookouts, a large number of personnel were assigned to keep up and maintain the network of safe houses. At the time of the Artamonov defection, there were approximately twenty-five safe houses in Frankfurt. These ranged from rather austere flats to expansive mansions.

5. The Westport complex's official title was the Defector Reception Center. It was a sprawling facility of office buildings, secure interrogation sites, living quarters for some hundred to eight hundred base personnel, and transient facilities for the defectors passing through Germany on their way to ultimate destinations in the United States, Israel, and elsewhere. In the period 1945–55 the U.S. Army of Occupation headquarters was located at Frankfurt. In those days, in many ways, Frankfurt was a "heavenly" duty station because almost anything could be acquired by bartering with cigarettes. Some allied military personnel were also seconded to the DRC and interrogation operation. From 1955 on, as the U.S. Army headquarters was phased out and moved to Heidelberg, the CIA took over most of the operational control of the Westport defector operation and its facilities.

6. Although most of Frankfurt was leveled by Allied bombing in World War II, when the city was liberated by U.S. Army forces, the eleven-story I. G. Farben building was found to be unscathed. As a result, it was commandeered to become the U.S. Army of Occupation's Headquarters. It was a very pleasant building, and successive Army generals came to appreciate the thoughtfulness of the leaders of I. G. Farben in providing them with such a fine headquarters. At the time of the Artamonov defection in 1959, the generals had gone and the CIA station and some elements of U.S. government agencies were housed in the spacious and palatial building. Big George's office was located on the top floor, from which he could look out at the German "miracle" in the form of a rebuilt city. In later years he wondered to friends about who had really won the war.

7. David E. Murphy was born on June 23, 1921. He graduated with a B.A. from Cortland State Teachers' College in 1942. After service in the Army during World War II, Murphy entered the CIA and began to climb the promotional ladder in its clandestine services. At the time of the Artamonov defection, Murphy was the chief of the Berlin Base, having relieved the legendary William K. Harvey some months earlier. Murphy has never been far from the bureaucratic action. As the head of the Soviet Branch at the time of the Nosenko defection, he became embroiled in the dispute over Nosenko's bona fides. Murphy and the man who was at that time the head of the Plans Directorate, Richard Helms, were convinced that Nosenko was not telling the truth, although whether he himself thought his story was true was a different matter. Because Nosenko claimed that the KGB had nothing to do with the assassination of John Kennedy, the bona fides of his defector status created a disagreement within the CIA that exists to this very day. Murphy was also identified as a Soviet agent by James Angleton, who reported his suspicions to the head of French intelligence. At the time, Murphy was the CIA's station chief in Paris. All in all, David Murphy has had a controversial career in the CIA. (See John Ranelagh, *The Agency: The Rise and Decline of the CIA* [New York: Simon and Schuster, 1986].)

George Kisevalter was born of Russian parents in Kiev, Russia. He came to the United States at an early age with his parents before the Bolshevik Revolution in 1917. His father operated a large-caliber shell factory for the Russian Imperial government. He was trained and educated as an engineer and graduated with a degree in engineering from NYU in 1931. In 1933 he worked for the WPA and developed the tiger cages for the Bronx Zoo. He began his military career with the Army Corps of Engineers. During World War II and the immediate occupation of Germany, he served in Army Intelligence, rising to the rank of colonel. After the CIA was established in 1947, Kisevalter shifted to it and became one of the best defector and agent handlers in the CIA's tumultuous history. Kisevalter is a superb linguist and, in the opinion of unbiased observers, probably the preeminent authority in the U.S. intelligence community concerning defector psychology. Besides Kisevalter's involvement with the Artamonov defection, he was also directly involved in the Popov, Oleg Penkovsky, and Yuri Nosenko cases. In each of these cases Kisevalter, the genuine expert, was shunted aside or cut out of the handling and decision phases of these cases by the overzealous amateurs who looked upon the defectors as their ticket to the CIA's executive suite.

8. By allowing Kisevalter to question Artamonov, Frankfurt Base possibly exposed the United States' most important agent handler directly to the Soviets, if Carroll's concerns about East German and Soviet intelligence penetrations were justified.

9. Interview with George Kisevalter, April 19, 1988.

10. Based on a series of interviews with Peter Kapusta in the spring of 1988.

11. Vetting of a source or a defector, that is, the establishment of whether the individual is bona fide, is the most essential phase of the intelligence process in dealing with intelligence information acquired from a defector. Failure to determine, insofar as possible, that a source/defector is reliable creates false conclusions and the acceptance of flawed premises in the conduct and planning of positive intelligence operations. Also, it is important not to elevate the defector's experience to such a level that he is used to verify or establish the accuracy of information about which he knows very little. For example, very few members of the KGB have much of an overview about its operations, owing to the compartmentalization of those operations. To be

successful, vetting must be kept separate from the collection of information; that is, those who pass on the bona fides of a source should not be the same persons who have recruited that source. The bias of the recruiter is a major threat to any objective consideration of the worth of a source by persons who are operating under the imperative of producing more and more information, regardless of its value.

12. The repressive nature of sex "education" and Communist Party–approved sexual practices in the Soviet Union made it difficult for defectors to answer "lifestyle" questions truthfully concerning their sexual preferences and practices. For example, oral or anal sex was and is almost as serious a crime in the Soviet Union as "capitalist tendencies," "bonapartism," etc. When these kinds of sexually "delicate" questions were asked of Soviet defectors, the needle quite often went off the paper. In Artamonov's case, although he displayed some areas of deception in the lifestyle questions, these were of less concern than the inconsistencies in his personally provided biographical background. Some in the CIA argued that Artamonov's polygraph troubles could be explained, but there was no questioning his knowledge of the Soviet Navy. According to Leonard McCoy, the decision was made to accept him despite his polygraph results, because of the valuable information he provided.

13. Interview with Ewa Shadrin, June 1988.

14. Ibid.

15. Interview with Thomas Dwyer, January 19, 1988.

16. Ibid.

17. Tad Szulc, "The Shadrin Affair: A Double Agent Double-crossed," *The New York Times Magazine,* May 8, 1978.

Alexander Sergeyevich Pushkin, *The Queen of Spades and Other Stories* (New York: Penguin Books, 1983).

18. Peter Sivess is the CIA's legendary defector handler. He has seen them all, and is a shrewd judge of a defector's character, or lack thereof. Sivess, a 1936 graduate of Lehigh University, had a career as a major-league pitcher with the Philadelphia Phillies before World War II. During the war, Sivess had an interesting career in the world of U.S. Naval Intelligence, and in its aftermath came into direct contact with the Soviets in connection with their acquisition of U.S. merchant vessels and former German Navy ships. Consequently, Sivess had more than a passing understanding of the Soviet Navy. Born of Russian parents, he is fluent in Russian.

19. Interview with Peter and Ellie Sivess, January 19, 1988.

20. In 1947, when the National Security Act was passed and the CIA was established under its authority, the Director of Central Intelligence was given the further authority to "sponsor" for citizenship 250 aliens per year. This authority is contained in sections 313(a) and 313(c) of the Immigration and Nationality Act; these sections are known as the "CIA Sections." This sponsorship capability was specifically authorized to give the DCI the discretionary authority to enable the CIA's field personnel to promise potential defectors American citizenship in connection with their defection. This authority was meant to be a "recruiting" tool for the CIA. The number of aliens who were given "automatic citizenship" never reached the level of 250 per year, and at present the authority stands at 125. The process was supposed to work this way: In return for the defector's cooperation in naming names, helping to uncover penetration agents, and providing insight into what the United States believed or thought it believed about the enemy, the defector might, if he was valuable enough, be promised the reward of citizenship and/or other emolu-

ments. However, over time the CIA has reneged on promises that were made to defectors, and as a consequence, the stream of defectors with important information has all but dried up. The exception to this situation can be found in the case of some defectors who know their own real worth and have extracted, in addition to citizenship, annual honoraria or "retainers" well into six figures.

21. William R. Corson is one of the authors of this book.

22. Vice Adm. Rufus Lackland Taylor, U.S. Navy, was one of the giants of American intelligence. He was equally at home in the world of communications intelligence as in that of clandestine operations. A 1933 graduate of the U.S. Naval Academy, Admiral Taylor was a superb Japanese linguist, a scholar, and an inspirational leader. He was an accomplished, hands-on intelligence officer in all facets of the business. His later career placed him at the heart and in command of the most sensitive intelligence operations ever carried out by the United States. He served as the Director of Naval Intelligence from 1963 to 1966. He was promoted to vice admiral and was made Deputy Director of the Defense Intelligence Agency in June 1966. On September 20, 1966, a scant three months later, President Johnson appointed him Deputy Director of Central Intelligence. Admiral Taylor served as the DDCI (responsible for the day-to-day operations of the CIA) until February 1, 1969, when he resigned from that position and retired from the U.S. Navy.

23. Shadrin, Ph.D. dissertation, pp. 675–76: "Starting in 1958 an arms deal with Indonesia was closed, and the first groups of Indonesian naval officers and crews started to be trained by the Soviet Navy in Poland. During the next five years, one *Sverdlov*-class cruiser *(Ordzhonikidze)*, seven *Skory*-class destroyers, twelve W-class submarines, seven *Riga*-class destroyer escorts, about two dozen torpedo boats, a number of minesweepers, *Komar*-class missile boats, and auxiliary ships were transferred to the Indonesian Navy. Neither were the majority of transferred ships suitable for the environment and operational requirements, nor was the Indonesian Navy ready [for them] or capable of operating them properly. Moreover, it is doubtful that the Indonesians needed such a collection of naval armament. The Soviet Navy at least was honest in the deal involving the cruiser, trying to persuade the Indonesians that they did not need it. *As for the rest of the ships transferred, the majority of them were obsolescent and the Soviet Navy was glad to get rid of them, not a difficult task in the case of such an eager "buyer" as Sukarno was."* (Emphasis added.)

24. Corson complained to Taylor about how useless Artamonov had been. At that point, Taylor handed Corson a debriefing report from Artamonov. The report, derived from an interview with Artamonov, was a personal profile of an obscure Soviet naval officer who was a "running mate" of Artamonov's, by the name of Vladimir Nikolayevich Chernavin. Both Artamonov and Chernavin were the same age, had reached Captain Third Rank on the same promotion list, and had come into the Soviet Navy's officers corps by way of attendance at the Nakhimnov school system. Chernavin's name meant little to the author; however, as Captain Taylor said in farewell, "If Chernavin turns out to be the top sea dog in the Soviet Navy, we'll finally know just how worthwhile a find young Artamonov has been."

Chapter Eleven / Shadrin: The Trusted Adviser

1. In the early 1950s, the buildings in which Shadrin worked had been the site of some of the most secret activities carried out by ONI. With the opening

in the mid-1950s of additional new facilities at the Naval Security Group Head-quarters, located at Massachusetts and Nebraska avenues, this work was transferred from the Naval Observatory facilities. Although Shadrin's actual workspace at the Naval Observatory was austere by today's standards, it was a pleasant place to work.

2. At the time, Rufus Taylor was Assistant Director of Naval Intelligence.

3. Shadrin's contract as a special consultant provided that he be compensated at the equivalent of a GS-11, Step 5. This amounted to approximately $9,000 per annum in 1960. The GS-11 status, roughly equivalent to the military rank of lieutenant commander, enabled Admiral Taylor to use Shadrin as a foil, or cat's paw, in some of the internecine battles in Naval Intelligence as well as in the community at large. Shadrin was identified as a former Soviet naval officer with unique qualifications in naval science, tactics, marine engineering, and ordnance both conventional and nuclear.

Nick and Ewa Shadrin purchased their modest Arlington house with a payment for his services from the CIA. They were no longer protected by security personnel. Outside of their new names, the couple lived like any suburban working couple. Shadrin's $9,000 salary barely covered Ewa's dental-school expenses and the costs of setting up housekeeping.

4. Interview with Jerry Edwards, February 2, 1988. Edwards, a former naval officer himself, was one of the most competent Russian linguists in ONI. His gentle demeanor and friendship with Shadrin were important to Shadrin's adaptation to the ONI bureaucracy.

5. Interview with Thomas Dwyer, January 19, 1988.

6. U.S. Congress, House, *Testimony of Captain Nikolay Fedorovich Artamonov (Former Soviet Naval Officer),* Hearing Before the Committee on Un-American Activities, 86th Congress, 2nd sess., September 14, 1960 (Washington: U.S. Government Printing Office, 1960).

The committee members present included William M. Tuck of Virginia and August E. Johansen of Michigan. Also present were Frank S. Tavenner, Jr., the HUAC staff director; Alfred M. Nittle, counsel; and Donald T. Appell. Mr. Alexis Schidlovsky of the Library of Congress was sworn in to serve as the interpreter or clarifier of Shadrin's remarks when he had to switch from English to Russian.

7. "Legend" is intelligence jargon for a cover story or false biography.

8. Artamonov testimony, HUAC, as above, p. 1911.

When Nittle tried to pin Shadrin down on how he had gained access to war plans, to nuclear attack scenarios, which had been restricted to those of flag rank and above, he fudged the issue by producing a journal, available to high-ranking officers, which discussed the subject of surprise attack. The journal *Voyennaya Myal (Military Thought),* although supposedly restricted to officers of high rank, was and is not an operational document. Instead, it is a professional military journal not completely unlike our own, which deals with matters of strategy and tactics in terms of physical feasibility rather than political desirability.

9. The *New York Times,* September 15, 1960.

10. Artamonov testimony, HUAC, as above, p. 1911.

11. Ibid., p. 1920.

12. Foreign Broadcast Information Service (FBIS) summary 26, September 1960.

13. From a copy of Nick Shadrin's resumé provided by Ewa Shadrin. Also their marriage license, as well as other open sources.

14. Henry Hurt, *Shadrin: The Spy Who Never Came Back* (New York: McGraw-Hill/Reader's Digest Press, 1981), p. 33.

15. Interview with Captain Albert Graham, March 21, 1988.

16. See Elena Skrkilabina, *Siege and Survival: The Odyssey of a Leningrader*, translated, edited, and with an afterword by Norman Luxembourg. (Carbondale, Ill.: Southern Illinois University Press, 1971), pp. 52–59.

World War, 1939–1945-Soviet Union Personal Narratives, Russian. Leningrad-Siege, 1941–1944-Personal Narratives, Russian. Both published by Soviet State Press. Also Leon Goure, *The Siege of Leningrad* (Stanford: Stanford University Press, 1962).

17. Artamonov testimony, HUAC, p. 1909.

18. Ibid., p. 1908.

19. Ibid., pp. 1908–9.

20. Shadrin resumé, see note 13, above.

21. Interview with Frank Steinert, March 23, 1988.

22. Artamonov testimony, HUAC, p. 1908.

23. Hurt, *Shadrin,* p. 32.

24. Colonel Artamonov had a reasonably successful military career. He was awarded the Hero of the Soviet Union medal on October 17, 1943, for fording the Dnieper, an Order of Lenin, and two Orders of the Red Banner. At the time of his death, which occurred suddenly on July 9, 1944, he was the commander of the 25th Guards Nezhin Mechanized Brigade, 7th Guards Nezhin Mechanized Corps, 60th Army on the Central Front. Although Shadrin never officially acknowledged his father's true identity, he did, in social conversations with Walter Onosco and another CIA official, refer to the above, and claimed that his father was a "guards general." *In vino veritas,* perhaps, or at the very least the statement is a bit of an exaggeration.

25. Nicolas Ikonnikov, *La Noblesse de Russie, duxieme edition,* "Les Artamonov," (Paris, Maret, 1970), pp. 293–298.

26. Interviews with Ewa Shadrin, 1988.

27. Ibid.

28. These tidbits of unofficial biographical information are vacuumed up by the Soviets for possible use at a later date and in other surroundings. For example, a former colleague in the Marine Corps who shifted over to the CIA after the Vietnam War was posted abroad under State Department cover. While in his assignment he was approached at a social occasion by a Soviet, who was known to him to be KGB. The KGB officer very politely inquired about his health and how he was enjoying the pleasures of Country "X." This kind of chitchat is the staple diet at diplomatic functions around the world. What made this conversation noteworthy was that the Soviet indicated that my colleague had been a former Marine. This was no big secret, and my colleague nodded in assent. The Soviet pointed to my colleague's wife and said, "She is certainly an attractive woman." This was acknowledged as well. Then the Soviet said, "Your wife certainly doesn't look like a former Marine." To which the colleague replied, "She isn't a former Marine." The Soviet then said, "Oh, I didn't mean your present lady, I meant your former wife." The point of this conversation was that the Soviet was letting my colleague know that the KGB knew that his former wife had been a Marine. These kinds of exchanges are not exercises in political one-upmanship; rather, they are designed by the Soviets to test, prod, and take the measure of U.S. intelligence personnel no matter where they are stationed, and to do this they are provided with everything that can be found out about American personnel. (Note by author William R. Corson.)

29. Shadrin received his degree in June 1964. The subject of his research was a treatment of certain problems in the U.S. maritime industry. It is a first-class piece of work. It also reflects the state-of-the-art thinking about containerization that was being developed in the Soviet Union in connection with their own maritime fleet.

30. Interview with Tom Koines, March 12, 1988.

31. Interview with William and Mary Louise Howe, January 12, 1988.

32. The bill read as follows:

Be it enacted by the Senate and House of Representatives of the U.S.A. in Congress assembled, that Nikolai Artamonov, lawfully admitted for permanent residence in the U.S. on August 22, 1959, shall be held to be included in the class of applicants for naturalization exempted from the provisions of section 313(a) of the Immigration and Nationality Act, as such class is specified in section 313(c) of the said Act. April 30 (legislative day, March 30), 1964. (Report No. 1571) Passed the Senate September 24, 1964.

S.2789 also included a "Statement of Facts" in support of the bill, which says in part:

The beneficiary of the bill is a thirty-six-year-old native of the USSR who now claims to be stateless. He presently resides in Arlington, Virginia, and has been employed since June 1, 1960, by the U.S. Navy Department in Washington as a consultant. He and his wife were paroled into the U.S. on August 22, 1959, and their status was subsequently adjusted to that of lawful permanent residence as of that date.

33. As the new Cold War began to heat up, Shadrin's call to arms and alarms fell on receptive ears. For example, after he delivered a lecture to the staff and students at the Naval War College on March 19, 1965, the President of the Naval War College, Vice Adm. C. L. Melson, wrote a letter to Admiral Taylor, then Director of Naval Intelligence, in which he said:

Once again, the students and staff officers of the College found Mr. Shadrin's lecture and answers to questions of the highest possible interest and of great relevance to their course work here. His lecture was received with enthusiasm, and a barrage of questions continued through the luncheon in his honor and the afternoon post-lecture conference, right up to his evening departure. Obviously, as you remarked in your kind letter of 9 March, Mr. Shadrin's presentation is unique and, I believe, not likely to suffer in its intrinsic value with the passage of time. It certainly affords incomparable insights into the many persisting attitudes and problems of Soviet naval personnel, and of the Army and Party members who dominate the military picture.

34. This added an important string to Shadrin's bow. It enabled him, in connection with his translation duties, to put the approved spin on Soviet technical articles that had become a high-priority collection target of the Navy and the rest of the intelligence community. In commenting on Shadrin's performance, Comdr. Bland W. Drew, Assistant Officer in Charge of the Naval Scientific and Technical Intelligence Center, said, in a "to whom it may concern" letter on February 7, 1966:

Mr. Shadrin performed excellent to outstanding services for the technical and scientific personnel of this activity, especially in areas associated with marine engineering, ordnance, and translation services of technical articles printed in the Russian language. Mr. Shadrin has a remarkable background in technical, engineering and scientific areas pertaining to the USSR and provided much valuable information, analysis and interpretation to all units of this activity during the period of his contract. Mr. Shadrin is a reliable and sincere person, and gets along with all with whom he comes in contact. His services for STIC left nothing to be desired.

35. FURTSEVA, Yekaterina Alekseevna, Government and Party official; USSR Min. of Culture s. 1960; member, CC CPSU, s. 1956; member, CP, s. 1930; b. 1910 Vyshniy Volochek, now Kalinin Oblast, educ.: 1935 grad. Higher Acad. Course of Civil Air Fleet, Leningrad; 1942 grad. Moscow Inst of Fine Chemical Technology; 1948 grad. Corresp. Dept., Higher Party School, CC, All Union CP(b); pos.: after graduating from factory and plant school worked as weaver at "Bol'shevichka" Plant; s. 1930 Secretary Korenevo Rayon Komsomol Committee, Kursk Oblast, then Secretary Feodosyia City Committee and later dept. head, Crimean Oblast Committee, All Union Komsomol; 1935–36 Asst Head, Pol. Dept, Aeroflot Aviation Technicum; 1936–37 instructor, CC, All Union Komsomol; 1937–42 member, Party Bureau, then Secretary Party Organ, Moscow Institute of Fine Chemical Technology; 1942–50 Secretary, Second Secretary, then First Secretary, Moscow Frunze Rayon Committee, All-Union CP(b); 1950–54 Second Secretary, Moscow City CPSU Committee; 1954–57 First Secretary, Moscow City CPSU Committee; 1956–60 Secretary CC, CPSU; Career: 1952–1956 candidate member, CC, CPSU; 1956–57 candidate Presidium Member, CC, CPSU; 1957–61 Presidium Member, CC, CPSU; s. 1924 worked for Komsomol; Deputy, USSR Supreme Soviet of 1950, 1954, 1958 and 1960 convocation; Deputy and Presidium member, RSFSR Supreme Soviet of 1955 and 1959 convocation; 1954 member, USSR Party and government delegation to Peking for 5th anniversary celebration of Chinese People's Republic; 1955 member, USSR Supreme Soviet delegation to Yugoslavia; 1956 headed USSR Supreme Soviet delegation to England; 1960 member Soviet government delegation to India and Austria; 1961 visited France, Denmark and Britain; 1964 visited Denmark and Italy; 1965 visited Poland, Rumania, England and France; 1966 visited Bulgaria, Japan and headed Soviet delegation to Mongolia. *Awards:* two Orders of Lenin; Order of Red Banner of Labor; Badge of Honor; medals: 4 USSR, Moskva, ul. Kuybysheva 10 Ministerstvo kul'tury SSSR. *Died: 25 October 1974.*

FIRYUBIN, Nikolai Pavlovich, Dipl. with rank of Amb. Extraordinary and Plenip.; USSR Dep. Min. of For. Affairs s. 1957; Secr. Gen., Pol. Advisory Comt., Participating Members of Warsaw Pact, s. 1966; member CP, s. 1929; b. 1908; *Educ.:* 1935 grad. Ordzhonikidze Aviation Inst., Moscow; *Pos.:* 1935–38 eng. posts in aviation ind.; 1938–53 exec. Party and govm. posts; 1940–43 Secr., Moscow Oblast CPSU Comt.; s. 1946 Secr., Moscow City CPSU Comt.; s. 1953 dipl. posts; 1953–55 counselor, USSR Embassy in Czechoslovakia, then USSR Amb. to Czechoslovakia; 1955–57 USSR Amb. to Yugoslavia; *Career* Dept. USSR Supr. Sov. of 1946 convoc.; 1956–66 cand. member, CC, CPSU; 1955 attended Warsaw Conference of European States; 1956 signed Sov.-Yugoslav agreement on cooperation in peaceful uses of atomic energy; 1956 signed agreement on trade and credits with Yugoslavia; 1956 accompanied Khrushchev on trips to Yugoslavia and attended talks between Khrushchev, Tito and Erno Gero; 1957 attended talks between CC, CPSU, and CC, Union of Yugoslav Communists, headed by Khrushchev and Tito; 1958 accompanied Voroshilov to Afghanistan; 1959 headed Sov. deleg.

at 15th session of UN Econ. Commission for Asia and the Far East in Australia; 1959 member, USSR Party and govm. deleg. to Albania, headed by Khrushchev; 1959 headed Sov. deleg. at 20th session of UN Econ. and Soc. Counc. in Geneva; 1959 member USSR Party and govm. deleg. to Poland, headed by Khrushchev; 1960 headed Sov. deleg. at 15th Session of UN Econ. Commission for Europe in Geneva; 1960 handed note of protest to Iranian govm. for permitting American mil. aircraft to use Iranian air space; 1960 signed Sov.-Polish frontier agreement; 1961–62 headed Sov. deleg. at 16th and 17th sessions of UN Econ. Commission for Europe in Geneva; 1963 signed Sov.-Hungarian convention on dual nationality; 1965 member, So. Party-Govm. deleg. to Hungary; headed Sov. deleg. to 20th session of UN Econ. Commission for Europe; visited Pakistan and Ceylon; 1966 visited India, Ceylon, Nepal and Cambodia. *Awards:* Order of Lenin, 1967; Order of Red Banner of Labor; Order of Yugoslav Banner; A. USSRm Moskva, Smolenskaya-Sennaya pl. 32–34, Ministerstvo inostrannykh del SSR. *Died: 12 February 1983.*

Source: Edward L. Crowley, Andrew I. Lebed, and Dr. Heinrich E. Schulz, eds., *Prominent Personalities in the USSR* (Metuchen, New Jersey: Scarecrow Press, 1968).

36. KOZLOV, Frol Romanovich (1908–1965) Russian govt and Party official; metallurgical eng; CP member from 1926; b. 18 August 1908 in vil Loshchininom Ryazan' Oblast; educ: 1928–31 studied at Communist higher educ establishment, then at Workers' Fac, Leningrad Mining Inst; 1936 grad Leningrad Polytech Inst; *Career:* 1923–26 worker; then asst shop foreman at Red Textile Worker Plant in Kasimov; 1926–28 secr, Komsomol Comt at this factory; then head, Econ Dept, Kasimov Uyezd Komsomol Comt; 1936–39 eng and head of the blooming mill at a metallurgical plant in Izhevsk; 1939–40 Party CC organizer and secr of the Party Comt at this plant; 1940–41 secr, Izhevsk City CPSU(B) Comt; 1941–44 coordinated arms production and deliveries to the front; 1944–47 worked for CC, CPSU(B); 1947–49 second secr, Kuybyshev Oblast CPSU(B) Comt; 1949 worked for CC, CPSU(B); then Party organizer for CC, CPSU at the Kirov Plant in Leningrad; 1949–52 secr, 1952–53 second secr, 1953–57 first secr, Leningrad Oblast CPSU Comt; 1956–57 and 1958 member, Bureau for the RSFSR, CC, CPSU; from 1952 member, CC, CPSU; Feb–June 1957 cand member, June 1957–64 member Presidium, CC, CPSU; from 1962 member, Presidium, USSR Supreme Soviet; 1957–58 chm, RSFSR Council of Min; 1958–60 firs dep chm, USSR Council of Min; 1960–64 secr, CC, CPSU; dep, USSR Supr Sov of 1950, 1954, 1958 and 1962 convocations; dep RSFSR Supr Sov of 1955 and 1959 convocations. *Awards:* Hero of Socialist Labor (1961); three Orders of Lenin; two orders of the Red Banner of Labor; Order of the Fatherland War, 2nd Class; Order of the Red Star; medals. *Died 30 January 1965.*

37. The account of this conversation came from a reliable Soviet source who asked that his identity be protected.

Chapter Twelve / Shadrin: KITTY HAWK

1. Interview with Courtland Jones, April 14, 1988.
2. Interview with Sam Papich, February 19, 1988.
3. According to many of Turner's colleagues, the inability of the FBI to locate files on the early history of Lee Harvey Oswald in the days following President Kennedy's assassination caused outsiders to think the Bureau had engaged in a cover-up. Turner was the fall guy and was sent down from a fast-

track job in headquarters to the Washington Field Office, where, as fate would have it, he would end up back in the middle of the Oswald case.

4. Interview with William Lander, February 27, 1988.

5. Julia Helms is deceased.

6. Helms did not respond to requests from the authors for an interview.

7. Interview with William Branigan, January 27, 1988.

8. Interview with Courtland Jones, April 14, 1988.

9. Elbert "Bert" Turner now practices law in Solomons, Maryland. He forcefully declined the authors' request for an interview.

10. Interview with Bruce Solie, January 28, 1988.

11. Interview with William Branigan, January 27, 1988; interview with Courtland Jones, April 14, 1988; interview with William Lander, February 27, 1988.

12. According to Richard Copaken, who became Mrs. Shadrin's lawyer after her husband's disappearance, James Angleton told him the reason he did not allow the case to go to the Soviet Division was to send the KGB a message that everyone who came over was under heavy suspicion.

13. Gus Hathaway still works for the CIA. As of this writing, he is head of counterintelligence, James Angleton's old job. He did not respond to the authors' requests for an interview.

14. According to a meeting between Angleton and Mrs. Shadrin's lawyer, Richard Copaken, in 1977.

15. Interview with former FBI official James E. Nolan, Jr., March 7, 1988.

16. Interview with Eugene C. Peterson, former Section Chief of Counterintelligence for the FBI, July 28, 1988. Peterson was William Branigan's assistant at the time of the KITTY HAWK approach in June 1966.

17. Interview with Eugene Peterson, July 28, 1988.

18. Interview with William Lander, February 27, 1988. Lander had read the complete FBI file on Shadrin.

19. Ibid.

20. Ibid.

21. According to Courtland Jones, the only evidence the Bureau had previous to the information from KITTY HAWK that Igor Orlov had gone to the Soviet Embassy came from a surveillance team that had been watching Orlov. That team took no photographs that day. Instead they relied upon the constant photographic coverage of Soviet Embassy visitors by *other* FBI agents.

22. Today the renovated building is a tourist center in downtown Washington, featuring shops, restaurants and food stands. At the time Shadrin worked downtown, it was a depressing area, devoid of anything of much interest.

23. See chapter 4.

24. Interview with Eugene Peterson, May 31 and July 28, 1988.

25. Interview with Peter Sivess, January 19, 1988.

26. Interview with Lt. Gen. Samuel V. Wilson, June 14, 1988.

27. From the classified records of the President's Foreign Intelligence Advisory Board investigation in the Shadrin matter in 1978–79.

28. During this time, John Paisley was the number-two man in the Office of Strategic Research.

29. John T. Funkhouser will only confirm for the record that he thought "Nick Shadrin was a fine gentleman" and refuses to discuss the KITTY HAWK operation or John Paisley in any detail.

30. Interview with James Wooten, March 23, 1988.

31. Interview with Peter Kapusta, March 1988.

32. From the files of Richard Copaken.

33. Ibid.

34. Interview with Richard and Maria Oden, February 10, 1988.

35. Interview with John Novak, March 29, 1988.

36. Strangely, none of the investigating bodies—the FBI, the CIA, Congress, or the President's Foreign Intelligence Advisory Board—ever questioned the emigrés and defectors Shadrin worked with. If they had, they might have gotten a very different view of the FBI's double agent. Sadly for the defectors and emigrés, the Shadrin episode kept them from getting security clearances and better jobs. All of them are still paying for their involuntary association with Shadrin.

37. Interview with Maria Oden, February 10, 1988.

38. Interview with Yanka Urynowicz, February 24, 1988.

39. Interview with Richard Oden, February 10, 1988.

40. Bernard I. Weltman was an Annapolis graduate in the class of 1956. Exercising one of the options available to him, he entered the U.S. Air Force. After flight training and service in the operating forces, he gravitated into intelligence. In this capacity he ended up as the commanding officer of the Air Force's defector translation activities in Syracuse, New York. After DIA came into being in 1961, the Syracuse operation was closed down and its defector personnel were transferred to the Post Office operation. After an intervening tour with the Air Force staff, Weltman took over the Post Office operation shortly before Shadrin came on board in early 1966.

41. From an interview with James Wooten, March 23, 1988, and from a series of interviews with Frank Steinert during 1988.

42. Nick took his general examinations in July 1969, and failed political theory the first time. In February 1970 he passed the course work. His dissertation, "The Development of Soviet Maritime Power," was "in preparation" from September 1964 to 1970. He was examined on it on July 11, 1972, and his degree was conferred in September.

43. Interview with William Lander, February 27, 1988.

Chapter Thirteen / Shadrin: Tightrope

1. Sokolov arrived in the United States in 1966 as a second secretary. Among his assignments was to work and recruit on Capitol Hill. Sokolov moved up in the KGB/Foreign Service. When he left Washington in the fall of 1987 he had been promoted to a minister consular/major general in the KGB. He remained in Moscow for a little more than six months. He speaks perfect English. At present, Oleg Sokolov is the Soviet ambassador in the Philippines, and has taken full control of the NPA communist insurgency there.

2. The tradecraft included dead drops on utility poles, secret writing, and meetings outside the normal allowed radius of Soviet officials in the Washington area. The FBI's William Lander said the "Soviets made contact about as complicated as possible for Shadrin. . . . Shadrin, who was a very bright man, had trouble getting all the instructions straight."

3. Interview with Ewa Shadrin, 1988.

4. Interview with James E. Nolan, Jr., March 7, 1988.

5. Shadrin had traveled with Ewa to Europe and the Caribbean, but his FBI handlers say these earlier trips involved no operational activities.

6. The Shadrin meeting was not the only attempt by the CIA and RCMP to entrap Bennett.

7. Interviews with Leonard V. McCoy, 1987 and 1988. Also included in his book review for the Agency of Peter Wright's book, *Spycatcher*.

8. The CIA acquired a burst transmitter in Germany in 1966. That was how the Bureau eventually learned that the device sent to Shadrin was an older model.

9. The *Washington Post*, October 26, 1974.

10. During the Olympic Games, as the world watched on TV, two Israelis were killed resisting the attack on their facilities, and nine others were taken hostage. All the hostages, five terrorists, and a West German policeman died in a gun battle with German police several hours later. After the Shadrins returned from the trip, Nick indicated to friends that something like the Olympic massacre would never take place in the Soviet Union.

11. Interviews with Branigan, Wooten, and other officials involved in the Shadrin operation.

12. Interview with Eugene Peterson, May 31, 1988.

13. Interviews with Ewa Shadrin, 1988.

14. John Barron's *KGB Today: The Hidden Hand* (New York: Berkley Books, 1987) relates the history of the Herrmann case. Among the details Barron reports is how the couple was backed up with an elaborate KGB-prepared legend. They married in 1957 and settled in West Germany. In 1960, under orders from Moscow Center, the Herrmanns and their son were ordered to establish life in Toronto, Canada. After a successful stay in Canada, the couple and two children were ordered by the Center to go to the United States. (See chapter 22.)

15. See Clyde W. Burleson, *The Jennifer Project* (London: Sphere Books, 1979).

16. Tom Dwyer confirmed his role in Glomar, and that Shadrin visited him in Hawaii during this period, but stated that he knew nothing of Shadrin's involvement in the operation and had been careful not to mention it to him.

17. Interview with Lt. Gen. Samuel V. Wilson, June 14, 1988.

18. Interview with Richard Oden, February 10, 1988.

19. William E. Colby, *30 Ans de CIA* (Paris: Presses de la Renaissance, 1978), pp. 331–35. In the French version of William Colby's autobiography, published before it had been screened by the CIA, Colby stated that the *Glomar Explorer* had failed to retrieve nuclear missiles, steering and transmission devices, and codes. A year after the *Glomar Explorer* operation, the story was floated in Washington circles, and on Capitol Hill, that the reason the United States didn't go back for a second attempt to get the other half of the submarine was that the operation had been "blown" in the press. Whatever the reason, the secrets contained in the other half of the submarine were left for the fishes.

20. Interview with William Branigan, January 27, 1988.

21. Interview with Frank Steinert, March 23, 1988.

22. The Shadrins' house is not very far from where John Paisley kept his sailboat.

23. Interview with Stanley and Janka Urynowicz, February 24, 1988.

24. Interview with Peter Sivess, January 19, 1988.

25. George Kalaris declined to be interviewed for this book.

26. Interview with William Lander, February 27, 1988.

27. Interviews with James Wooten, William Branigan, and Ewa Shadrin.

28. Interviews with Leonard V. McCoy, 1987 and 1988.

29. Interview with Bruce Solie, January 28, 1988.

30. Interview with James Wooten, March 23, 1988.

31. Interview with William Branigan, January 27, 1988.

32. Philip Agee, *Inside the Company: CIA Diary* (New York: Stonehill, 1975).

33. Interview with Eugene Peterson, June 1988.

Chapter Fourteen / Shadrin: Going Home

1. Interview with Bruce Solie, January 28, 1988.

2. Interview with James Jesus Angleton, June 1977.

3. The background on George Weisz comes from more than one hundred interviews with colleagues, family, and friends, and from his personal papers made available by his widow, Etta Jo Weisz.

4. Interview with Lt. Gen. Samuel V. Wilson, June 14, 1988.

5. Men like Paul Bellin, who gave Artamonov his polygraph exams at the Westport Defection Center, advised Weisz that there were problems with Shadrin. Weisz confided his theory that Shadrin was "sent" to Dr. Robert Kupperman. The authors interviewed Dr. Kupperman, a friend of both Shadrin and Weisz, on January 22, 1988.

6. According to Maryland State Police reports, which contain interviews with the secretary concerning the apparent suicide of George Weisz.

7. Interviews with Stanley Jeffers, spring and summer 1988.

8. Interview with sources on the Vienna State Police, May 1988.

9. Interviews with Ewa Shadrin, 1987 and 1988.

10. This information comes from Shadrin's FBI handlers and still-classified reports from the Shadrin debriefing done by Cynthia Hausmann that evening.

11. Interviews with Ewa Shadrin, 1987 and 1988.

12. Interview with Bruce Solie, January 28, 1988.

13. The physical description of Ms. Hausmann comes from Mrs. Shadrin, her lawyer Richard Copaken, and colleagues at the CIA and officials of the FBI who met her. Cynthia Hausmann did not respond to repeated requests for an interview. She is now married to the former head of the Romanian intelligence service, a defector whom she handled while still in the CIA and who presently is living somewhere in the United States.

14. According to Austrian authorities.

15. From the classified files of the President's Foreign Intelligence Advisory Board.

16. These paragraphs, unless otherwise noted, are the views of the Vienna authorities after their investigation of the case. Many of the facts have been confirmed by James Wooten and other FBI officials.

17. Interview with James Wooten, Nick Shadrin's FBI case officer.

18. Interview with Burton V. Weides, March 10, 1988.

19. The Viennese officials, who agreed only to open their files and speak if their identities were protected, provided this information as their theory on what transpired.

20. These details generally coincide with what is in the CIA and FBI classified files on the remainder of the first meeting with Oleg Kozlov.

21. From Cynthia Hausmann's still-classified report of the first meeting.

22. According to a version of the debriefing given to Ewa Shadrin's lawyer, Richard Copaken, by the late George Weisz in March 1977.

23. The tortes at the Imperial omit the jam filling and are drier in taste and texture.

24. Interviews with Ewa Shadrin, 1987 and 1988.

25. This is confirmed by information George Weisz provided Richard Co-paken, Mrs. Shadrin's lawyer, several months after Nick's disappearance.

26. From the Vienna police report of what Shadrin was wearing the evening he disappeared.

27. According to the Vienna police report on Shadrin's disappearance.

28. According to Viennese intelligence sources.

29. Ibid.

30. Interview with Leonard V. McCoy, August 4, 1988.

31. Interviews with Stanley Jeffers, spring and summer of 1988.

32. This maid at the Bristol was interviewed twice by Austrian police. Both times she conveyed the same story about seeing a man in front of the third-floor elevator landing at the Bristol, dressed exactly as Shadrin was dressed when he disappeared. The police speculated in the report that Shadrin may have chanced a return because he had forgotten to take his supply of hyper-tension medication that might not be available during his return trip to the Soviet Union, and also he wanted his reading glasses. After swearing in police statements to her sighting, she denied them in 1980 to author Henry Hurt, who interviewed her for his book on Shadrin.

33. According to the Vienna police report.

34. According to Austrian Interior Ministry files.

35. Interview with Bruce Solie, January 28, 1988.

Chapter Fifteen / Shadrin Epilogue: The Theory of the Admirals' Plot

1. Maintaining one's personal power as the Soviet leader has been likened to the trick of sitting on a three-legged stool. In this metaphor, the three legs represent the Communist Party and its bureaucracy, the Soviet military, and the KGB. Each of these legs is important, and during Khrushchev's regime it was very important for him to maintain effective control over the armed forces and the KGB through the Communist Party *apparat*. It required a careful balancing act, especially in view of the alliance that had been forged between the army and the KGB during the Hungarian uprising.

2. Vice Admiral V. D. Yakovlev, *Sovetskiy Voenno-Morskoy Flot (The Soviet Navy)*, (Moscow: 1969).

3. See William R. Corson and Robert T. Crowley, *The New KGB: Engine of Soviet Power* (New York: Morrow, 1985), pp. 265–70.

4. See Chester L. Cooper, *The Lion's Last Roar: Suez, 1956* (New York: Harper & Row, 1978).

As Chester Cooper notes, "It [the Suez crisis] marked a turning point in the post–World War II configuration of power in Europe and the Middle East. 'Suez' cleared the way for a strong Soviet presence in the Middle East and thus changed the strategic balance there. It produced a major shift in Britain's perception of its international role. In part, as a consequence of these devel-opments, America began to play a dominant role in the Arab-Israeli struggle and in Middle Eastern affairs generally."

5. Nicholas George Shadrin, *Development of Soviet Maritime Power*, Ph.D. dissertation abstract, George Washington University, Washington, D.C., 1972. Although no source citation or date is given for Admiral Gorshkov's statement, it is not inconsistent with his other public statements and writings.

6. Corson and Crowley, *The New KGB*, pp. 31–80.

7. Arthur Koestler, Ignazio Silone, Richard Wright, Andre Gide, Louis Fischer, and Stephen Spender, *The God That Failed: A Confession*, edited by Richard Crossman (New York: Harper & Brothers, 1949).

Each of these apostates has his own tale to tell; however, Koestler speaks to the issue that seems to characterize the defector's changed mental outlook, or the one that must be adopted by the "trust operative": he must convince his new mentors of his changed heart by disavowing

the fallacy of the unshaken foundations, the belief that a State-capitalist economy must of necessity lead to a Socialist regime. I shall not repeat the argument: I have only mentioned this epilogue to my Party days, my clinging to the last shred of the torn illusion, because it was typical of the intellectual cowardice which still prevails on the Left. The addiction to the Soviet myth is as tenacious and difficult to cure as any other addiction. After the Lost Weekend in Utopia the temptation is strong to have just one last drop, even if watered down and sold under a different label. And there is always a supply of new labels on the Comminform's black market in ideals. They deal in slogans as bootleggers deal in faked spirits; and the more innocent the customer, the more easily he becomes a victim of the ideological hooch sold under the trade-mark of Peace, Democracy, Progress or what you will.

8. Corson and Crowley, *The New KGB*, pp. 191–92.

9. Yakovlev was the youngest of the three, having been born in either late January or early February 1930. He was well connected politically by being the second and only surviving son of Admiral Yakovlev. Yuri, like the other two, was a graduate of the Soviet Naval Academy. After his graduation with distinction in 1952, for which he was commissioned as a lieutenant, junior grade, rather than as an ensign, he served as a line officer with the Baltic Fleet. In 1955, Yakovlev attended the Soviet equivalent of our Naval War College. Upon his graduation in 1956, he was promoted to the grade of lieutenant commander and assigned to the personal staff of Admiral Grishanov, who, at the time, was the chief of the Political Directorate of the Baltic Fleet. In January 1958, Yakovlev was assigned as the "navigator" on the "destroyer" then commanded by Nikolay Artamonov. This assignment was consistent with Artamonov's "command," which consisted of two destroyers that were destined to be turned over to the Indonesian Navy as part of the Soviet Navy's "fire sale" of old and useless vessels. In this assignment the two DDs, for lack of a more appropriate designation, sailed the short distance from Leningrad to Gdynia and the turnover "training" of the Indonesian officers and men was commenced. Although Yuri Yakovlev's title was that of navigator, his real chore in connection with the turnover of the Soviet ships to the Indonesians was to coordinate the "scrubbing down" of the Indonesian officers and men in search of potential converts into the service of the GRU. Subsequent U.S. intelligence operations in Indonesia indicated that Yakovlev and his minions did a fair job of recruiting Indonesians to the Soviet side, if not its point of view. Yakovlev obviously did not get the assignment to be sent to the West; however, he did enter the Soviet Military Diplomatic Academy at the end of 1959 and is presumed to have graduated therefrom in early 1965. Since then, Yakovlev has become a "nonperson" as far as the Western intelligence organizations know. What else is known is that Yakovlev, a tall, slightly blond, well-appearing man, had a flair for languages and was a dedicated communist. It is suspected by some persons in the intelligence trade that Yuri Yakovlev was picked up by the KGB and subsequently assigned to serve as an illegal. Yakovlev's facility in English was so good that it is not out of the question to suppose that today he may be one of the Soviet spies among us, operating undetected and providing his KGB masters with all manner of secrets.

The second man out in the Soviet admirals' search for an agent to send to the United States was Lev A. Vtorygin. He was the oldest of the three, having been born on January 13, 1926, in Uritsk. Vtorygin was tall and had a fair complexion and sandy blond hair. He enlisted in the Soviet Navy in August 1943 and was appointed to the Nakhimov Naval Cadet School the following year, after which he entered the Soviet Naval Academy. Upon graduation from the academy in 1949, he was assigned for operational training on one of the Soviet "never sails" destroyers assigned to the Baltic Fleet. Besides the credential that his father, a naval officer, had been killed in World War II, his mother, who had been trained as a biologist, held a high position in the security arm of the KGB. These credentials guaranteed Lev a position on the *nomenklatura;* they were augmented, however, by his marriage in May 1950 to Eugenia Vasilevsna Arkhipovich, whose father was a very high-ranking officer in the KGB. Eugenia was born on March 23, 1928, in Baku. The Vtorygins had one daughter, Elena, who was born on June 27, 1950. Lev's family connections helped his assignment to the Military Diplomatic Academy in January 1951. He graduated from the academy in June 1956 and was certified to be fluent in Portuguese, Spanish, and English. These certifications indicated a fairly wide range of potential GRU assignments for Vtorygin. His wife and child may have militated against Lev's being chosen as the sent agent, but he, along with his wife and child, was given an important role in the operation once Artamonov had made it to the United States and made the first penetration of the U.S. Navy. In this connection, Lev, along with his wife and daughter, had been posted to Buenos Aires as the Soviet assistant naval attaché in February 1959. This assignment was abruptly terminated in January 1960, when he was transferred to Washington, D.C., and became the Soviet assistant naval attaché under the senior naval attaché, Rear Admiral Boris Dmitriyevich Yashin. Lev prospered as Artamonov did. He was promoted to captain, second rank, in August 1964. He completed his tour in Washington on August 2, 1965. In the early 1970s he was assigned to New Delhi as a member of a Soviet "naval assistance mission." Reports available to the authors indicate that Vtorygin was under KGB/GRU "discipline" (effective control) while in India, rather than under Soviet naval authorities in charge of the mission. At present, according to U.S. intelligence sources, he is stationed in Moscow, with the equivalent rank of commodore, in charge of the British Desk for the GRU. Vtorygin was, and is, a very effective member of Soviet military intelligence.

10. The most explicit statement of the criteria for a sent agent is set forth in *Voennye kontrrazvedchiki: Osobym otdelam VChK KGB 60 let.* redaktsionnaia kollegia: G. K. Tsinev, N. A. Dushin et al., Sost. Iurii Viktorovictch Selivanov (Moscow: Veonizdat, 1978), 422 str. Translation: *Military Counterintelligence Agents: Special Department VChK KGB 60 years,* editorial group: G. K. Tsinev, editor in chief; N. A. Dushin, assistant editor; I. V. Selivanov, researcher/compiler (Moscow: Veonizdat, 1978), 422 pages.

11. In a related sense, the former Director of the FBI, J. Edgar Hoover, mentioned to author William Corson that the maximum time for an FBI agent who has been sent to infiltrate organized crime, is five years. In Hoover's view, the human pressures become intolerable after five years.

12. Captain Artamonov had to command a ship chasing an early-model nuclear attack submarine to prove himself before he was selected.

13. See Peter Wright, *Spycatcher* (New York: Viking, 1987), pp. 72–75, for an interesting account of this affair.

14. For those who might harbor the belief that the admirals' vision of a

blue-water navy, and their decision to send an agent to the United States to hasten the process, was a pie-in-the-sky hallucination, it should be remembered that the fleet that Admiral Gorshkov took over in 1956 grew dramatically in the next twenty years. This is the legacy of Gorshkov, and much of its accomplishment is due to the sent-agent mission successfully carried out by Nikolay Fedorovich Artamonov.

15. Interview on April 14, 1988, with Courtland Jones, former senior FBI counterintelligence officer: "The average noncounterintelligence devotee cannot understand the value of personality information, physical descriptions, who is sleeping with whom, who lives where, who goes to what church, who works where, etc. . . . A good counterintelligence operation gathers all this extraneous—if you wish to call it [that]—background information. And it is invaluable in the long run."

16. The records of Ewa Shadrin's lawyer, Richard Copaken, reveal an interview with Robert Barry of the State Department's Soviet Desk, telling him about the discovery of the phony IAEA passport in 1976. The details of the Artamonov visit can be found in the Austrian State Police report dated February 13, 1976.

Unfortunately, American intelligence was so sloppy in Austria in 1958 that the simple immigration record that might have flagged a false defection a year later was never turned up by the CIA's Vienna station.

17. According to Tom Dwyer, Vtorygin had a reputation as the best marksman in the Soviet Navy.

18. Interview with Robert Kupperman, January 22, 1988.

19. Interview with Nikki Weisz, February 1, 1988.

20. From a series of extensive interviews with Richard Copaken. Copaken opened up his files and contributed enormous amounts of time to the authors.

21. Frank Meehan declined to be interviewed for the book.

22. *Novodevichy* means "Young Maidens" in English. The buildings adjoining the cemetery in Tsarist days were a monastery. Since the Bolshevik Revolution in 1917, these buildings have been converted to a girls' school, hence the name Young Maidens.

Chapter Sixteen / Sigler: The Search for GRAPHIC IMAGE

1. From a series of interviews with William Branigan and Eugene C. Peterson, both former Directors of Counterintelligence at the FBI, and Col. Donald Grimes, formerly with Army counterintelligence.

2. Interviews with Ilse Sigler, 1982 and June 1987; *El Paso Times,* October 17, 1976.

3. *El Paso Times,* October 17, 1976; interview with Ilse Sigler; Ralph Sigler's Army personnel records. Ralph Sigler's father is dead. His sister, Anne, declined to be interviewed for the book.

4. During the summer of 1944, Ralph had gotten a job at the National Carbon Company in Cleveland, Ohio. When he returned home to West Wyoming, Pennsylvania, that fall for high school, his father's latest girlfriend was abusive to him. Desperate to get away, he took $205 from this "housekeeper" and tried to run away. He wanted to go to Texas, but only made it as far as Columbus, Ohio, and was arrested by the Ohio State Police on September 19, 1944. His father's girlfriend had issued a complaint. Ralph was charged with larceny and incorrigibility, and sent to the Kis Lyn Industrial School in Luzerne County, Pennsylvania, for a month. On October 20, he was released in his father's custody.

5. Interviews with Ilse Sigler between 1979 and 1988.

6. Interviews with Ilse Sigler, June 1987.

7. Interview with Eugene Peterson, May 31, 1988.

8. According to Radigan's superiors in the FBI.

9. Interview with Donald Grimes, March 25, 1988.

10. Interviews with John Schaffstall in January, March, and April 1988. The authors wrote to Joe Prasek, repeating the opinions and judgments of some of his colleagues. We received only the following reply from his lawyer in Baltimore, Maryland, Alan I. Baron, dated May 10, 1988:

> As you are undoubtedly aware, Mr. Prasek took an oath of secrecy when he retired, which precludes him from replying to your letters in the manner you seek. We are putting you on notice, however, that in the event that the falsehoods in your letter are published, you and your publisher run the risk of incurring substantial liability for injuring a man who has served his country with valor and honor.

11. Interviews with John Schaffstall, January, March, and April 1988.

Chapter Seventeen / Sigler: The Operation

1. Interviews with John Schaffstall, January 12, 1988, and March 21, 1988.

2. This material is based on articles by Joseph Trento for the *Wilmington News-Journal* and by Robert Lindsay for the *New York Times*.

3. Interview with John Schaffstall, March 21, 1988.

4. According to the May 16, 1988, issue of *Newsweek,* the Soviets' use of ceramic armor on their tanks was more successful than the U.S. Army knew. The Army underestimated the Soviets' engineering abilities starting in the mid-1970s. "Today, it turns out, their latest tanks (with ceramic armor) can probably destroy our tanks, while most of our tanks and antitank weapons pose little threat to them."

5. Interviews with John Schaffstall.

6. Interview with John Schaffstall, March 21, 1988.

7. Ibid.

8. Eugene Peterson advised that this procedure was an expensive waste of time, and the Bureau eventually quit tracing the money.

9. Interview with John Schaffstall, January 20, 1988.

10. Interviews with John Schaffstall.

11. Ibid.

12. Interview with John Schaffstall, March 21, 1988.

13. Ibid.

14. Ibid.

15. Ibid.

16. Interview with Col. Donald B. Grimes, March 25, 1987.

17. Interview with John Schaffstall, March 21, 1988.

18. Interviews with John Schaffstall, January 20 and March 21, 1988.

19. Interview with Col. Donald B. Grimes, March 25, 1988.

20. Interview with John Schaffstall, March 21, 1988.

21. Interviews with Ilse Sigler, 1982 and June 1987.

22. Interviews with Ilse Sigler, 1982 and June 1988.

23. Interviews with Ilse Sigler, 1982 and June 1987.

24. Interviews with Ilse Sigler, 1987 and 1988.

25. Interview with Col. Donald B. Grimes, March 25, 1988.

26. Interview with John Schaffstall, January 20 and March 21, 1988.

27. According to Eugene Peterson, William Branigan, and others interviewed by the authors.
28. Interviews with Ilse Sigler, 1982 and July 1987.
29. Interview with John Schaffstall, January 20, 1988.
30. Interview with Eugene Peterson, May 31, 1988.
31. Interview with Noel E. Jones, August 5, 1988.
32. Interview with John Schaffstall, March 21, 1988.
33. Ibid.
34. Ibid.
35. Ibid.
36. Interviews with John Schaffstall, January 20 and March 21, 1988.
37. Interview with Donnel Drake, August 5, 1988.
38. Department of the Army materials released under the Freedom of Information Act. Mrs. Sigler says that she received postcards and letters from Ralph in Tokyo during this time.

Chapter Eighteen / Sigler: LANDWARD HO

1. Interview with John Schaffstall, April 26, 1988, and with Col. Donald B. Grimes, March 25, 1988.
2. Interview with John Schaffstall, March 21, 1988.
3. Ralph Sigler's handwritten notes.
4. Interviews with John Schaffstall and Ilse Sigler; interview with FBI source.
5. John Schaffstall's June 1, 1976, memorandum for the record.
6. Interviews with Ilse Sigler; John Schaffstall's June 1, 1976, memorandum for the record.
7. Interview with John Schaffstall, January 20, 1988.
8. Interview with John Schaffstall, March 21, 1988.
9. See the Shadrin section.
10. Department of the Army records, released under the Freedom of Information Act.
11. Interview with John Schaffstall, August 5, 1988.
12. Interview with Col. Donald B. Grimes, March 25, 1988.
13. Interviews with John Schaffstall, January 12 and January 20, 1988.
14. Ibid.
15. Interview with John Schaffstall, April 26, 1988.
16. Interviews with John Schaffstall, March 21 and April 26, 1988.
17. Interviews with Ilse Sigler, 1982 and June 1987.
18. In another press interview, Mrs. Sigler said the call came from Joe Prasek.
19. Interview with John Schaffstall, March 21, 1988.
20. Interviews with John Schaffstall, January 20 and March 21, 1988.
21. Interviews with John Schaffstall, January, March, April, and August 1988; John Schaffstall's testimony to the Inspector General's Report of Inquiry; interview with Ilse Sigler; Ralph Sigler's March calendar.
22. Interview with John Schaffstall, January 20, 1988.
23. Interview with John Schaffstall, March 21, 1988.
24. Interviews with John Schaffstall, January, March, and April 1988; interview with Col. Donald B. Grimes, March 25, 1988; materials released from Department of the Army under the Freedom of Information Act; John Schaffstall's April 21, 1976, memorandum for the record.

25. Odell King's testimony for the Inspector General's Report in Inquiry; John Schaffstall's April 21, 1976, memo to file.

26. Interviews with John Schaffstall, January, March, and April 1988; John Schaffstall's April 21, 1976, memorandum for the record.

27. Department of the Army documents.

28. Interviews with John Schaffstall, January 20, March 21, and April 1988; Ralph Sigler's March pocket diary; interviews with Ilse Sigler.

29. According to Sigler's notes, dinner cost him nine dollars and he took two more taxis, which totaled eighteen dollars. Penciled in the back of his pocket diary is the notation "Oakland—MacArthur & Broadway." John Schaffstall called him at 2:00 P.M. He then made a note for a drink called a "wet dream," which consisted of coffee, Irish whiskey, and three different liqueurs. On March 24, breakfast and lunch cost Ralph $6.50. He went to the lobby of the Ramada Inn at 570 Bay Street at 9:00 A.M. and took along his SF-171 (his government employment application). He had a $4.50 snack.

30. Depositions in Ilse Sigler's suit against the Army; John Schaffstall's interview for the Inspector General's inquiry.

31. Interview with John Schaffstall, March 21, 1988.

32. Ibid.

33. Ibid.

34. John Schaffstall's answers to interrogatories in *Sigler* v. *U.S. Army*.

35. Depositions of Odell King, John Schaffstall, and Noel Jones in Ilse Sigler's suit; Odell King's IG Report of Inquiry statement; interview with John Schaffstall on March 21, 1988; John Schaffstall's April 21, 1976, memorandum for the record.

36. Depositions from Ilse Sigler's suit against the Army.

37. Interview with John Schaffstall, March 21, 1988.

38. Odell King's answers to interrogatories; John Schaffstall's April 21, 1976, memorandum for the record.

Dilantin is categorized as an anticonvulsant prescription drug used primarily in the treatment of epilepsy or to control possible seizures during neurosurgery. Since Ralph did not have epilepsy and had not had neurosurgery, it is curious why he would say he had taken this medication. Possibly, Odell King remembered the wrong name. But another consideration is whether Ralph was trying to send King a message, since Dilantin would obviously have an effect on the polygraph test.

39. John Schaffstall's April 21, 1976, memorandum for the record.

40. Deposition of Odell King.

41. Interview with John Schaffstall, March 21, 1988.

42. Ibid.

43. Interview with John Schaffstall, January 20, 1988; John Schaffstall's April 21, 1976, memorandum for the record.

44. Depositions of Odell King and John Schaffstall; testimony of Odell King and John Schaffstall for the Inspector General's Report of Inquiry.

45. Interview with John Schaffstall, March 21, 1988.

46. Ibid.; John Schaffstall's April 21, 1976, memorandum for the record.

47. Depositions of Odell King, Noel Jones, and John Schaffstall; John Schaffstall's memorandum for the record, dated April 21, 1976. (In John Schaffstall's statement for the Inspector General's inquiry, however, he says that Noel Jones met with Ralph the evening of March 26, but in his response to interrogatories, he says it was the afternoon of March 27.)

48. Depositions of Noel Jones and John Schaffstall. In Schaffstall's testi-

mony for the Inspector General's Report of Inquiry, he says the meeting between Noel Jones and Ralph took place the evening of March 26.

49. Depositions of Noel Jones and John Schaffstall; John Schaffstall's April 21, 1976, memorandum for the record.

50. Interview with Ilse Sigler; Army papers released under the Freedom of Information Act. Ralph Sigler's pocket diary for the month of March.

51. Depositions of John Schaffstall and Odell King; testimony of John Schaffstall and Odell King for the Inspector General's Report of Inquiry. In his Report of Inquiry statement, Odell King says that Ralph told him on March 27, not March 26, that he had taken two Dilantin tablets the night before, and had only gotten two hours of sleep. For these reasons, King said his tests on March 27 were inconclusive. In his deposition he says these events happened on March 26.

52. Interview with John Schaffstall, March 21, 1988.

53. Odell King's testimony for the Inspector General's Report of Inquiry.

54. Interviews with John Schaffstall during 1988; Schaffstall's deposition and his testimony for the Inspector General's Report of Inquiry; John Schaffstall's April 21, 1976, memorandum for the record.

Chapter Nineteen / Sigler: The Last Assignment

1. Ralph Sigler's March 1976 pocket diary; Odell King, John Schaffstall, and Noel Jones's responses to interrogatories.

2. Interview with John Schaffstall, August 5, 1988.

3. Interview with Louis Martel, August 5, 1988.

4. Inspector General's Report of Inquiry.

5. Interview with Ilse Sigler, June 13, 1987; copy of Ralph Sigler's airplane ticket; copy of Ralph Sigler's Howard Johnson's bill; interview with John Schaffstall.

6. Telephone interview with Donnel Drake.

7. Odell King's answers to interrogatories.

8. Interviews with John Schaffstall; deposition of Louis Martel in Ilse Sigler's suit against the Army.

9. Deposition of Louis Martel in Ilse Sigler's suit against the Army.

10. Depositions of Louis Martel and Noel Jones.

11. Deposition of Noel Jones.

12. Depositions of Louis Martel and Noel Jones.

13. Deposition of Louis Martel.

14. Deposition of Noel Jones.

15. Odell King's testimony to the Inspector General's Report of Inquiry.

16. Interview with Noel Jones, August 5, 1988.

17. Depositions of Noel Jones and Louis Martel.

18. Interview with Ilse Sigler, June 13, 1987.

19. Deposition of Louis Martel.

20. Odell King's testimony in the Inspector General's Report of Inquiry; General Aaron's "talking points" for his May 1976 meeting with Mrs. Sigler.

21. Deposition of Louis Martel.

22. Ibid.

23. Odell King's testimony for the Inspector General's Report of Inquiry; John Schaffstall's April 20, 1976, memorandum for the record.

24. Odell King's testimony for the Inspector General's Report of Inquiry.

25. Ibid.

26. Ibid.

27. Ibid.; deposition of Louis Martel.

28. Deposition of Louis Martel.

29. Ibid.

30. Ibid.; interviews with Ilse Sigler; Ilse Sigler's May 13 interview for the Inspector General's Report of Inquiry.

31. Deposition of Louis Martel; interview with Ilse Sigler, June 13, 1987; interview with John Schaffstall, March 21, 1988.

32. Deposition of Louis Martel.

33. Interview with John Schaffstall; interview with Ilse Sigler, June 13, 1988; John Schaffstall's testimony for the Inspector General's Report of Inquiry.

34. Interview with John Schaffstall; interview with Ilse Sigler, June 13, 1988.

35. John Schaffstall's testimony for the Inspector General's Report of Inquiry; interview with Ilse Sigler, June 13, 1987; interviews with John Schaffstall; John Schaffstall's memorandum for the record.

36. John Schaffstall's testimony for the Inspector General's Report of Inquiry; interview with Ilse Sigler, June 13, 1987.

37. According to the Army, the following is an inventory of papers and effects recovered from Ralph's residence and retained by the Secretary of the Army:

1. 1 tan calendar/notebook, 1970
2. 2 pages typewritten notes
3. 1 black and white photograph
4. 1 color picture postcard
5. 4 color photographs, with negatives
6. 14 maps
7. 3 3 × 5 cards
8. 7 handwritten sheets
9. 1 packet, 39 pages, operational notes
10. 16 pages document listings
11. 8 pages notes in document protectors
12. 1 black/red book "Record," 5" × 8", 160 pages
13. 1 black/red book "Journal," 5" × 8", 160 pages
14. 1 sheet graph paper, 4" × 5"
15. 1 photocopy, 8½" × 6¼"
16. 3 photocopies, 8" × 10"
17. 2 sheets note paper
18. 8 sheets graph paper, 8½" × 11"
19. 9 Xerox copies
20. 86 [or 36] pages of handwritten notes, in document protectors

38. John Schaffstall's testimony for the Inspector General's Report of Inquiry; interview with Ilse Sigler, 1982.

39. Deposition of Louis Martel.

40. Ibid.

41. Ibid.

42. Interviews with John Schaffstall, January 12 and March 21, 1988.

43. Deposition of Louis Martel; Inspector General's Report of Inquiry.

44. Deposition of Louis Martel.

45. Ibid.

46. Ibid.

47. Colonel Webster's testimony to the Inspector General's Report of Inquiry.

48. Deposition of Louis Martel; Inspector General's Report of Inquiry.

49. Interview with John Schaffstall; Ralph Sigler's bill from Howard Johnson's; Maryland State Police report.

50. Deposition of Louis Martel; Noel Jones's response to interrogatories and the Inspector General's Report of Inquiry.

51. Interviews with Ilse Sigler, 1982 and June 1987.
52. John Schaffstall's response to interrogatories; Ralph Sigler's Holiday Inn bill showing phone calls.
53. Deposition of Louis Martel.
54. Ibid.
55. Copy of Ralph Sigler's motel bill and MasterCard receipt.
56. Deposition of Louis Martel.
57. Ibid.
58. Interviews with John Schaffstall. Colonel Grimes confirms Schaffstall's views on Conway. Conway declined to be interviewed for this book.
59. Deposition of Louis Martel; interview with John Schaffstall by phone, January 12, 1988.
60. Deposition of Louis Martel.
61. Interviews with Ilse Sigler, 1982 and June 1987.
62. Information Memorandum of General Harold R. Aaron.
63. Deposition of Louis Martel.
64. Ibid.

Chapter Twenty / Sigler: The Last Polygraph

1. Odell King's testimony for the Inspector General's Report of Inquiry, and his answers to court interrogatories and the Inspector General's Report itself.
2. Odell King's testimony for the Inspector General's Report of Inquiry; the Inspector General's Report of Inquiry.
3. Interviews with Donnel Drake and Colonel Grimes. Odell King's testimony for the Inspector General's Report of Inquiry; the Inspector General's Report of Inquiry.
4. Donnel Drake's testimony for the Inspector General's Report of Inquiry.
5. Telephone interview with Donnel Drake.
6. Article by John Stark, *El Paso Times*, October 20, 1976.
7. Interview with Ilse Sigler, 1982; the Inspector General's Report of Inquiry.
8. Interviews with Ilse Sigler, 1982 and June 1987.
9. Interview with Ilse Sigler, June 13, 1987; Colonel Webster's testimony for the Inspector General's Report of Inquiry.
10. Bill Vaughn's testimony for the Inspector General's Report of Inquiry; interviews with Ilse Sigler.
11. Interviews with Ilse Sigler, 1982 and June 1987; Bill Vaughn's testimony for the Inspector General's Report of Inquiry.
12. Ilse Sigler assumed she was talking to General Le Van, that he was returning her earlier call. But others, including General Lunn's wife, said that Ilse spoke to General Lunn, not Le Van, that evening.
13. Interviews with Ilse Sigler.
14. Deposition of Louis Martel; Inspector General's Report of Inquiry; Donnel Drake's testimony for the Inspector General's Report of Inquiry.
15. According to the Inspector General's Report of Inquiry, Jones told Zapata that Sigler was in Room 136 of the Holiday Inn.
16. Interviews with Ilse Sigler, 1982 and June 1987.
17. Noel Jones's response to interrogatories; Inspector General's Report of Inquiry; deposition of Louis Martel; Donnel Drake's testimony for the Inspector General's Report of Inquiry.

18. Donnel Drake's testimony for the Inspector General's Report of Inquiry.

19. Interviews with Ilse Sigler, 1982 and June 1987.

20. Inspector General's Report of Inquiry; Donnel Drake's testimony for the Inspector General's Report of Inquiry; deposition of Louis Martel.

21. Interview with Louis Martel, August 5, 1988.

22. Deposition of Louis Martel; Maryland State Police report.

23. Inspector General's Report of Inquiry; deposition of Louis Martel.

24. Ibid.; Maryland State Police report.

25. Interview with Louis Martel, August 5, 1988.

26. Interview with Donnel J. Drake, August 5, 1988.

27. Inspector General's Report of Inquiry; deposition of Louis Martel; Donnel Drake's testimony for the Inspector General's Report of Inquiry; Noel Jones's answers to interrogatories.

28. The Maryland State Police report says that a cup was found in Sigler's left hand, but the autopsy pictures show the cup in his right hand.

29. Maryland State Police report.

30. Donnel Drake's testimony for the Inspector General's Report of Inquiry.

31. Inspector General's Report of Inquiry; Noel Jones's responses to interrogatories; Donnel Drake's testimony for the Inspector General's Report of Inquiry; deposition of Louis Martel.

32. Inspector General's Report of Inquiry; deposition of Louis Martel; Donnel Drake's testimony for the Inspector General's Report of Inquiry; Noel Jones's responses to interrogatories.

33. Donnel Drake's testimony for the Inspector General's Report of Inquiry.

34. Interview with Donnel Drake; Drake's testimony for the Inspector General's Report of Inquiry.

35. Inspector General's Report of Inquiry; SP4 Frank C. Black's statement to the Inspector General's Report of Inquiry.

36. Inspector General's Report of Inquiry; deposition of Louis Martel; Donnel Drake's testimony for the Inspector General's Report of Inquiry. Noel Jones's responses to interrogatories. The following is the inventory of Sigler's belongings found in the motel room, as taken by Martel and Drake:

Movie Camera Nizo Special 136 8mm
Camera case black
Tudor Rolex watch—silver colored
Prescription sunglasses w/case & prescription
Shaving brush
Colgate toothpaste
8x4 deodorant stick
Score hair groomer
Pro toothbrush in toothbrush case
Desitin skin care hand lotion
Bossa Nova deodorant stick
Bright Side Shampoo
8:15 after-shave lotion

Schick injector blades
Pro bar comb
Schick injector razor
Johnson waxed dental floss
One broken septic stick [styptic pencil]
One nail clipper*
One Q-tip
One green shaving bag
One gray Samsonite silhouette suitcase
One blue striped suit (AQ custom tailors)
$282.46 in cash
One pair black shoes (military)

* Items held by Maryland State Police

One pair glasses (bifocals—civilian frame)
One pair black socks w/ red stripe
One pair blue socks
Two undershorts white (boxer)
Two T-shirts white
One pair green socks
One pullover shirt white (Ceceba) long sleeves
One solid white handkerchief
One patterned handkerchief
One brown belt size 34–36
Portion of matchbook cover
One DA Form 31
One black comb
One white ball-point pen (Bk Accountant)
One pair glasses w/ case (military frame)
One partial pack Certs (two left in pack)
One pocket knife (Old Timer brand)*
One engraved money clip*
One airline ticket
One black wallet
One DD Form 2A
Master Charge card†
Texaco charge card
JC Penney charge card
Two ten-cent U.S. postal service stamps wrapped in wax paper
Certificate of registration for Braun Nizo movie camera*

Certificate of registration for Olympus Pen F 35mm camera and Yashica Electro 8, 8mm movie camera dated 2-10-74
One piece of notepaper with name and address of LTC Webster & "Smithy"
One plastic picture holder insert for wallet
One Cross pen and pencil set—silver colored
One pocket calendar Sunland Park Race Track
Veterans Administration ID card
Avis credit card
Texas drivers license†
National Car Rental credit card
Social Security card
Northgate National Bank ID card
Two photographs of Karin
Fort Bliss, Texas, Special Services Library ID Card*
Fort Bliss, Texas, Race & Gun Club Membership card
Medical Health Card, White Sands Missile Range, New Mexico
Military drivers license*
Receipt for insured mail #872964 dated 10 March 1976 sent from: White Sands Missile Range to: Benton Harbor, Michigan 49022 Postage $1.28, Insurance $.30

37. Inspector General's Report of Inquiry; Noel Jones's response to interrogatories; Donnel Drake's testimony for the Inspector General's Report of Inquiry; deposition of Louis Martel.

38. Inspector General's Report of Inquiry; Donnel Drake's testimony for the Inspector General's Report of Inquiry; deposition of Louis Martel.

39. Interviews with Ilse Sigler, 1982 and June 1987; Inspector General's Report of Inquiry.

40. Ibid.

41. Interviews with Ilse Sigler, 1982 and June 1987.

42. Ibid.

43. Ibid.

44. Inspector General's Report of Inquiry.

45. Major Ring's testimony for the Inspector General's Report of Inquiry; interviews with Ilse Sigler.

46. Ibid.

* Items held by Maryland State Police
† Mrs. Sigler never received Ralph's drivers license, his Master Charge, his gun, or a missing pair of trousers.

47. John Schaffstall's April 22, 1976, memorandum for the record.

48. Maryland State Police report.

49. Interviews with Ilse Sigler; John Schaffstall's April 22, 1976, memorandum for the record.

50. Interviews with Ilse Sigler, 1982 and June 1987.

51. John Schaffstall's April 22, 1976, memorandum for the record.

52. Interviews with Ilse Sigler; John Schaffstall's April 22, 1976, memorandum for the record.

53. Interviews with Ilse Sigler, June 1987.

54. The embalming was done by Purnell Oden. Oden stated to the Army that since there had been a complete autopsy, he was working on a hollowed-out shell. He performed a six-point injection of embalming fluid and waxed the forehead because there were "burns" on it. Since the body was to be transported a long distance, he used extra-strength embalming fluid. He performed a standard closure on the mouth, sealing it with sealer and threading a suture string through the lower lip muscle, through one side of the nostril (from inside the mouth), out the other side of the nostril, and through the upper lip muscle. He then tied a square knot, closing the mouth. He filled the arms with wax to fill where the wires were. This conflicts with Karin and Ilse Sigler's observations of the body.

55. Inspector General's Report of Inquiry; Harry Thompson's investigative reports; interview with Harry Thompson.

56. Inspector General's Report of Inquiry; interviews with Ilse Sigler and Mrs. Sigler's private investigator, Fred Duvall, who confirms finding an electronic eavesdropping device in Mrs. Sigler's house.

57. Interviews with Ilse Sigler, June 1987.

58. Ibid.

59. Ibid.

60. The authors' attempts to get former FBI agent Joseph Prasek to agree to an interview were fruitless. Instead, Prasek engaged a lawyer, who wrote the authors saying his client was unable to be interviewed because of an FBI oath he took promising never to reveal details of his work. The letter included a general denial that Prasek did anything unprofessional regarding the Sigler case.

61. Interviews with Ilse Sigler, June 1987.

62. John Schaffstall's memo to file, dated April 22, 1976.

63. Interviews with Ilse Sigler, 1982 and June 1987; Moises Salazar's testimony for the Inspector General's Report of Inquiry; Inspector General's Report of Inquiry.

64. Inspector General's Report of Inquiry. Moises Salazar's testimony for the Inspector General's Report of Inquiry. Salazar placed white gloves on the hands to cover a cut between the thumb and forefinger on one of the hands, and discoloration of the fingernails. He had to close the mouth, since the lips were parted approximately an eighth of an inch. The body's eyes were discolored and sunken. Mrs. Sigler complained to Salazar of two errors on the obituary notice provided the papers. She said her husband was a CW3 rather than a CW, and that the date of death was wrong. She wanted the changes made and the corrections initialed. The funeral director submitted the changes for the afternoon papers. He could tell that Mrs. Sigler was overly demanding and frustrated, but there was no way for him to know why.

65. Maj. Richard Roy Ring's testimony for the Inspector General's Report of Inquiry.

66. Interviews with Ilse Sigler, June 1987.

67. Maj. Richard Roy Ring's testimony for the Inspector General's Report of Inquiry.

68. Interviews with Ilse Sigler, June 1987; Maj. Richard Roy Ring's testimony for the Inspector General's Report of Inquiry.

69. Testimony of Moises Salazar and Maj. Richard Roy Ring for the Inspector General's Report of Inquiry.

70. Fort Bliss National Cemetery records; interviews with Ilse Sigler, June 1987.

Chapter Twenty-one / Sigler: Ilse's Quest

1. Harry Thompson is dead, but Joseph Trento conducted a taped interview with him several years before his death.

2. Interview with Fred Duvall, June 12, 1987.

3. The single-based lamp with two separate units, both with shades and individual switches, stood on a shelf built into the wall between the twin double beds. Part of the wire to this lamp had been cut off and stripped. The portion of the cord still connected to the lamp had one end stuck in the electrical socket just by its bare ends.

4. Tom Jennings's memo to file, April 27, 1976.

5. Ibid.

6. Ibid.

7. Ibid.

8. Ibid.

9. Ibid.

10. General Aaron is dead. In his court deposition on the case, he denied any wrongdoing in the Sigler matter.

11. According to John Schaffstall, "This is nonsense. Ralph never refused to give us anything. He may not have told us things—but he would not admit to it and then not give it to us. That just never happened."

12. Interview with Ilse Sigler, June 1987; Colonel Heiss's Army memo on the meeting with Mrs. Sigler.

13. Ibid.; John Schaffstall said the Hawaii address on the note was merely a contact point for Ralph to write Schaffstall when he was leaving Korea: "An old Army agent was running that hotel, and would then call me to let me know GRAPHIC IMAGE had sent the message that he was coming home."

14. Ibid.

15. Interview with Ilse Sigler. Brooks said to the *El Paso Times* in an article dated October 23, 1976, in reference to the Army's having asked him not to notify Mrs. Sigler until after April 24, "It was nothing aimed at covering up or anything else. It had to do with the national security of this country and I am not going to say any more." According to a *Prince George's (Maryland) Journal* newspaper article of February 10, 1977, "sources familiar with the case confirmed military intelligence officers expected Sigler to meet with a new Russian contact in Mexico. As a result, Army officers asked State Police to withhold information about his death until the new contact was identified."

16. Interviews with John Schaffstall, Tom Jennings, and Ilse Sigler.

17. Interview with Ilse Sigler, June 1987.

18. Major Ring's testimony for the Inspector General's Report of Inquiry.

19. Interviews with Ilse Sigler, June 1987.

20. Interviews with Ilse Sigler, June 1987. In a telephone interview with Fred Duvall in June 1988, he confirmed that the fire had suspicious origins. In

the June 1987 interview, Duvall said he thought the dog was killed by someone who wanted to search the house and did not want the dog barking.

21. Jennings declined to cooperate with the authors of the book.

22. Interview with Fred Duvall, June 12, 1987.

23. Interview with Fred Duvall, June 12, 1987. Donnel Drake, in his interview, also remembered that Ralph was in his boxer shorts when he went to the room.

24. Interview with Harry Thompson, 1982.

25. Interview with Harry Thompson; Harry Thompson's investigation report; Chapman's interview with Dan Rather for the "60 Minutes" television show.

26. Interview with Louis Martel, August 5, 1988.

27. Autopsy report; Maryland State Police report; interview with Dr. Robert W. Hertzog, 1982.

28. Interview with John Schaffstall, March 21, 1988; interview with Dr. Robert W. Hertzog, 1982.

29. Interview with Harry Thompson; interviews by Dan Rather of Dr. Robert W. Hertzog, William Henry Chapman, and Harry Thompson for the "60 Minutes" television show.

30. Kay Miller, article for the *Prince George's Journal*, February 19, 1977.

31. Harry Thompson's investigation report; interview with Harry Thompson; Chapman's interview with Dan Rather on the "60 Minutes" television show.

32. Interview with Sid Diamond, June 11, 1987.

33. Phil McCombs, article in the *Washington Post*, February 8, 1977.

34. The citation reads:

Chief Warrant Officer (CW3) Ralph J. Sigler, United States Army, distinguished himself during the period 9 December 1966 to 13 April 1976 by voluntarily rendering his services on behalf of the U.S. Government in a sensitive capacity for the U.S. Army. Working long and arduous hours without open recognition of his efforts, Mr. Sigler repeatedly proved his dedication to the security of the Armed Forces of the United States. Through his direct efforts, valuable information of vital interest to national security was provided to the intelligence community of the United States Government. Mr. Sigler's distinguished performance of duty during this period reflects great credit upon himself and is in keeping with the finest traditions of the military service.

35. Court complaint. *Ilse Sigler and Karin Sigler* v. *United States Army et al.*

36. Correspondence between Brower and General Aaron.

37. Mrs. Sigler and Sid Diamond remember that the offer from the Army was around $250,000 to $300,000. The terms of the initial offer, according to court correspondence, were as follows:

1. A payment of $130,000 would be made by the Army, of which $100,000 would go to the Siglers and $30,000 would be paid to Sid Diamond.
2. Certain nonclassified items taken from the Sigler home would be returned to Mrs. Sigler.
3. The Army would make the following statements:

   a. Mr. Sigler had never provided unauthorized information to the Russians.

   b. Mr. Sigler was never known to have had any drinking or mental problems.

   c. The Army had never ques- ment would be taken off the
      tioned his loyalty. death certificate.
   d. Mr. Sigler had died in the line e. Carlos Zapata would apolo-
      of duty, and the suicide judg- gize to the Siglers.

38. Kenkel declined to go on camera for the television show. Mrs. Sigler said she asked him to go on but he declined because he did not want to publicize the case. "Everybody went on . . . but not him," Mrs. Sigler said.

Chapter Twenty-two / Sigler Epilogue: The Illegal

1. John Barron, *KGB Today: The Hidden Hand* (New York: Reader's Digest Press, 1983).
2. Some of the Rudolph Herrmann information was taken from John Barron's book, *KGB Today: The Hidden Hand*. The FBI denied our request to interview Herrmann about his drop sites in El Paso and his ties to Ralph Sigler. In a letter dated June 16, 1988, the FBI said, "Colonel Herrmann was contacted on your behalf and he was apprised of your proposal and the topics in which you are interested. After thoughtful deliberation, however, he indicated that he could not accede to your request."
3. Interviews with Eugene Peterson.
4. Ibid.
5. Interview with John Schaffstall, August 5, 1988.
6. Interview with Noel E. Jones, August 5, 1988.
7. Jack Fuller, *Convergence* (New York: Doubleday, 1982). Fuller is now an editor with the *Chicago Tribune*. When asked, he said that in writing the novel, he had in mind no specific cases he had run across as Levi's assistant.
8. Interview with Noel Jones, August 5, 1988.
9. Interview with Louis Martel, August 5, 1988.
10. Interview with Noel Jones, August 5, 1988.
11. Interview with Philip A. Parker, August 9, 1988. Former FBI official Parker confirms that the unauthorized destruction of the letter was part of the subsequent investigation into the Smith case.
12. Smith's lawyer, A. Brent Carruth, did not respond to repeated telephone calls asking for an interview with his client.

Epilogue

1. See chapter 4.
2. Gleason, reached at her FBI office and asked about the investigation, said she was not permitted to talk about the case.
3. Interview with George Orlov and Special Agent Vincente Rosado.
4. Telephone interview with Special Agent Vincente Rosado, August 5, 1988.

Index